The Encyclopedia of Ancient Egyptian Architecture

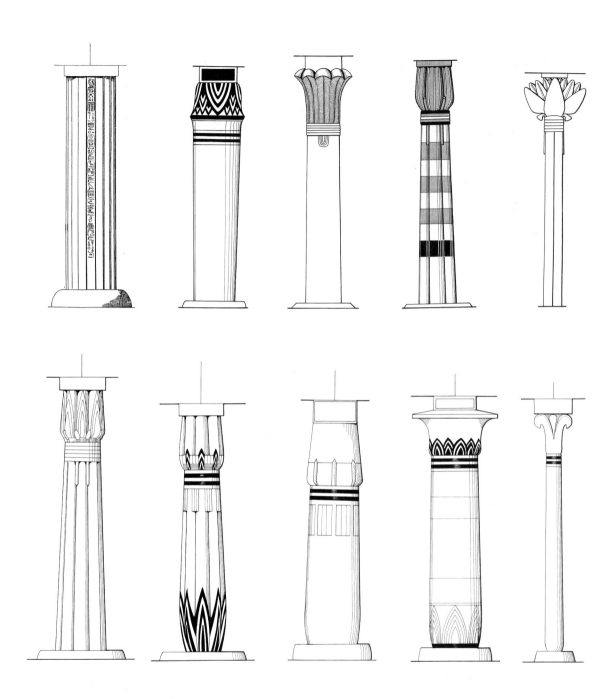

Examples of columns, from top left to bottom right: fluted (fasculated); tent-pole-shaped; palmiform; lotiform bundle, closed capital with four stems; lotiform bundle, open capital (not preserved); lotiform bundle, closed capital with eight stems; papyriform with closed capital and eight stems; papyriform bundle with closed capital and turned shaft; papyriform bundle with bell-shaped open capital and turned shaft; liliform (not preserved).

The Encyclopedia of
Ancient Egyptian Architecture

Dieter Arnold

Translated by Sabine H. Gardiner and Helen Strudwick
Edited by Nigel and Helen Strudwick

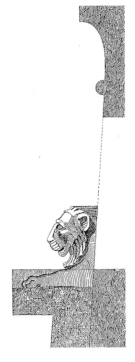

Princeton University Press

Copyright © English language edition I.B. Tauris & Co Ltd, 2003
6 Salem Road, London W2 4BU
175 Fifth Avenue, New York NY 10010
www.ibtauris.com

Published in North America by Princeton University Press
41 William Street, Princeton, New Jersey 08540
www.pupress.princeton.edu

First published in German in 1994 as *Lexicon der ägyptischen Baukunst* by
Artemis & Winkler Verlag. Copyright © Artemis & Winkler Verlag, 1994, 1997

The translation of this book has been supported by Inter Nationes, Bonn.

ISBN 0-691-11488-9

A full CIP record for this book is available from the British Library

Library of Congress Control Number: 2002112371

Designed and typeset in Minion Condensed by Dexter Haven Associates, London
Printed and bound in Great Britain by the Bath Press, CPI Group UK

Contents

Editors' Note

Dieter Arnold is responsible for almost all of the most up-to-date writing on ancient Egyptian building techniques. His *Building in Egypt* was written in English, but until now his other important contribution for the general reader, the *Lexikon der ägyptischen Baukunst*, has been available only in German.

For this translation, Dr Arnold has revised his original text, and added a number of new entries. He has also provided many new diagrams, plans and photographs. The style of this book has been changed a little from the original, which was composed in a more compact and abbreviated form than we considered appropriate for the general English reader, and the translation reflects this. It is also essential that a book for the general reader in English should include a selection of references for further reading which reflect what is easily accessible to that reader. Hence, the references have been supplemented with popular but reliable works in English wherever possible.

The initial translation was undertaken by Sabine Gardiner, and then edited by ourselves. We are most grateful to I.B.Tauris for taking on the task of producing an English edition of this book. We thank Jonathan McDonnell for suggesting that we undertake the work, and all members of his staff for seeing the book through the long stages of the road to publication.

Nigel and Helen Strudwick

A

Abacus

A square cover-plate connecting the **capital** with the **architrave**, which in Egyptian architecture is found on polygonal **columns** and **pillars** with floral capitals. The visible side was frequently inscribed with a horizontal cartouche. In late temples dedicated to female deities (**Philae**), the abacus is often worked into a **Hathor**-headed capital or decorated with a Bes figure. Rounded abaci are found only at **Tanis** on palm columns re-used from the Old Kingdom.

Bibliography: Prisse d'Avennes, *Histoire*, Plate 47.

Papyrus column of Amenhotep III with abacus and architrave

Abahuda (Abu Hoda)

A rock-cut temple built by Horemheb, at Gebel Adda slightly south of **Abu Simbel** and on the opposite bank of the Nile. It is dedicated to Amun-Re, Thoth and local gods and has an entrance hall with four papyrus **columns**, a raised sanctuary and two side-chambers.

Bibliography: Jaroslav Č erný and Elmar Edel, *Abou-Oda* (Cairo 1963); Silvio Curto, *Nubien* (Munich 1966) 333–340; W. Helck, Abu 'Oda, in: Helck, *LÄ* I 23–24.

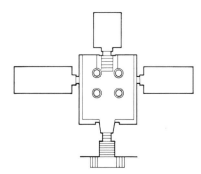

Plan of the rock temple of Horemheb at Abahuda

Abgig (Begig)

A cult courtyard containing a **granite stela** of Senwosret I, lying 3 km south-west of **Medinet el-Faiyum**. It was a 12.9 m high, tapering, rectangular stela, with a rounded top crowned with a figure (of a falcon?). Remains of decoration indicate that it was dedicated to Month-Re/Amun-Re and Ptah/Re-Horakhty, and to other gods. It is the only surviving remains of the pillared cult place of a kind probably widely distributed in Egypt. It now stands in a square in Medinet el-Faiyum.

Bibliography: *Description* IV, Plate 71; *LD* II, Plate 119; M. Chaaban, Rapport sur une mission à l'obélisque d'Abguig (Fayoum), in: *ASAE* 26 (1926) 105–108.

Reconstruction of the pillar-like stela at Abgig (Begig)

Abu Ghalib

The remains of a fairly small **town** on the south-west edge of the Delta which originated in the 12th Dynasty. Several **houses** were excavated in 1934–37.

Bibliography: H. Larsen, Vorbericht über die schwedischen Grabungen in Abu Ghâlib, in: *MDAIK* 6 (1935) 41–87 and 10 (1941) 1–59.

Abu Ghurob, *see* Niuserre, Abusir

Abu Roash, *see also* Djedefre

An important **mastaba** field of the Thinite Period and the Old Kingdom, 9 km north of **Giza**. It encompasses the pyramid of **Djedefre** standing on a rocky plateau and a large brick-built structure in the cultivation nearby (perhaps a pyramid of the 3rd Dynasty).

Abu Simbel

The scale and quality of execution of the two temples at Abu Simbel demonstrate that they were the climax of Ramesses II's programme of temple construction in Nubia, completed in the 34th year of his reign. The larger temple is dedicated to the state gods Amun-Re (in the south) and Horus of Mehu (in the north), and also to Ptah and, in particular, to the deified Ramesses. The seated figures, 22 m high, cut out of a deep recess in the rock façade, correspond to the **colossal statues** of this king at the **Ramesseum** and at his capital city in the Delta, **Per-Ramesses**. These statues were conceived of as 'living' beings and had their own names. The sloping front of the rock represents a **pylon** or temple façade. There is a noticeable emphasis on the solar cult in the frieze of solar apes on the upper edge of the façade, in the separate **sun temple** north of the main temple, and in the complete illumination of the cult images twice a year at sunrise on 20 February and 20 October. The figure of the sun god, stepping out of the temple façade, is a representation of the king as the incarnation of the sun. The attributes of the figure, the sun disc (= Re), the *user*-sign (carried in his right hand) and the Ma'at figure (in his left hand) are to be read as User-ma'at-Re, the throne name of Ramesses II. The interior of the temple is 60 m deep and contains all the necessary inner accommodation, from the hall of appearances to side-chambers and store rooms. The painted relief decoration is completely preserved, most impressively in the **hypostyle hall**, which has two rows of **statue pillars**.

The smaller temple is dedicated both to Hathor of Abshek and to Queen Nefertari as the deified Isis-Hathor. Here too, colossal figures of the king and queen emerge from the sloping rock façade, which is conceived as the front of a pylon. The ceiling of the hall immediately inside

the rock is supported on six **Hathor**-headed pillars. The rooms beyond are unfinished. In 1964–68, both temples were cut out of the rock and rebuilt on a higher site behind.

Bibliography: Johann Ludwig Burckhardt, *Travels in Nubia* (London 1819); see most recently *Reisen in Nubien* (Tübingen 1981) 1071–1014; Gau, *Antiquités*, Plates 54–61; Georg Gerster, Saving the ancient temples at Abu Simbel, in: *National Geographic Magazine* 129 (1966) 694–742; William MacQuitty, *Abu Simbel* (London 1965); Christiane Desroches-Noblecourt and Ch. Kuentz, *Le petit temple d'Abou Simbel*, 2 Vols (Cairo, 1968); Christiane Desroches-Noblecourt and Georg Gerster, Le monde sauve Abou Simbel (Vienna-Berlin 1968); *The Salvage of Abu Simbel Temples. Concluding Report* (Stockholm 1976); S. Donadoni, H. El-Achiri and Ch. Leblanc, *Grand temple d'Abou Simbel* (Cairo 1975); E. Otto, Abu Simbel, in: Helck, *LÄ* I 25–27; Jean Jacquet, Quelques remarques sur le grand temple d'Abou-Simbel, in: *Cahiers d'histoire égyptienne* 10 (Cairo 1966) 194–209; E. Otto, Abusimbel, in: Helck, *LÄ* I 26–27; Hein, *Ramessidische Bautätigkeit* 31–36; F.-X. Héry and T. Enel, *Abou Simbel et les temples de Nubie* (Aix-en-Provence 1994).

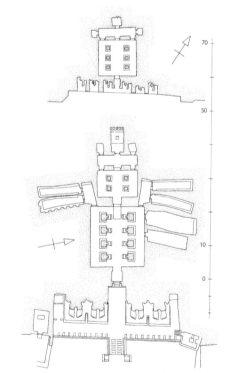

Plan of the large and small temples of Ramesses II at Abu Simbel

Abusir

Royal necropolis of the 5th Dynasty, between **Giza** and **Saqqara**, with examples of **pyramid temples**. The pyramid complexes of **Sahure**, **Neferirkare**, **Niuserre**, **Neferefre** and one other still unidentified ruler of the 5th

Dynasty are here, together with relatively few tombs of their royal households. Most prominent among them are the **pyramid** complex of Queen **Khentkawes** and the **mastaba** of **Ptahshepses**. The **sun temples** of **Userkaf** and **Niuserre**, slightly to the north (at Abu Ghurob) count as part of Abusir. To the south-west, in the desert, is a necropolis of large shaft tombs of the 30th Dynasty, including that of **Wedjahorresnet**.

Bibliography: J. de Morgan, *Carte de la nécropole memphite* (Cairo 1897); Miroslav Verner, *Forgotten Pharaohs, Lost Pyramids, Abusir* (Prague 1994); Edwards, *Pyramids*, 174–184; Lehner, *Complete Pyramids*, 142–153; M. Verner, The tomb of Iufaa at Abusir, in: *Egyptian Archaeology* 14 (1999) 39–40; J. Krejčí, The origins and development of the royal necropolis at Abusir during the Old Kingdom, in: Bárta, *Abusir 2000* 467–484.

Abydos

One of the principal sites of Egypt, containing many of the most important tombs, temples and town remains of the period from the 1st Dynasty to the New Kingdom. At least 12 royal cult complexes are attested to either archaeologically or from other sources, dating from the 12th to the 26th Dynasty ('**houses of millions of years**', places where the king was re-united with Osiris).

Bibliography (general): Eberhard Otto, *Osiris und Amun* (Munich 1966); B. Kemp, Abydos, in: Helck, *LÄ* I 28–41.

1. Tombs of the kings and funerary enclosures

The cemetery of the kings of the 1st and 2nd Dynasties is at Umm el-Ga'ab, in the desert to the west of the temple of **Sety I**. Various researchers have questioned whether the royal tombs at Abydos are 'real', seeing them merely as **cenotaphs** of the kings who were actually buried at **Saqqara**.

The development of the tombs at Abydos proceeded at a different pace to those at **Saqqara**, their use starting and finishing earlier than at the latter site. Current research by the German Archaeological Institute at Cairo has revealed the oldest burials, dating to Dynasty 0 and the period of the unification, those of Iry-Hor, Ka, Narmer and Hor Aha. From the reign of King Djer onwards, **funerary enclosures**, lying to the north-east, can be ascribed to each tomb. The tombs consist of pits sunk 2.5 m down into the floor of the desert and lined with **bricks** or, later, **limestone** blocks, being open above. Within the pits were the actual burial chambers, which were protected by buttress-like spurs and constructed of beams and **mats**. These spurs in the tomb of Djet are **niched**. The ceiling of beams was overlaid with a covering of sand, which protruded slightly or not at all above the level of the desert. According to Dreyer, the layout of the chambers reflects the arrangement of the royal **palace**, confirming the function of the tombs as

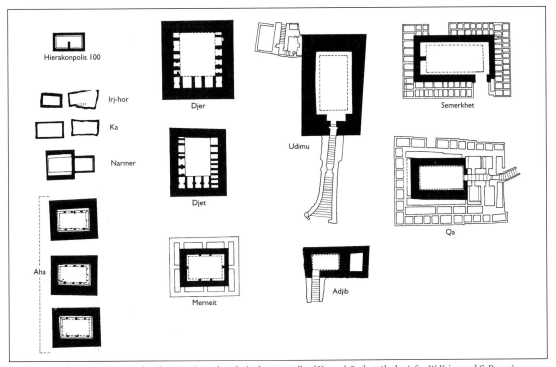

Development of the Pre-dynastic and Early Dynastic royal tombs in the necropolis of Umm el-Qaab at Abydos (after W. Kaiser and G. Dreyer)

palaces of eternity. Whether there was a superstructure over this is debated, but it is quite possible that the royal **stelae** (such as those of Aha and Djer, Djet and Meryneith) stood on the sand filling. In the tomb of Wadj, and possibly also in the tombs of Aha (B 15) and Dewen, it is possible that a small tumulus, hidden within the burial pit, was constructed over the pit itself and contained within a brick wall. From the middle of the 1st Dynasty onwards, the pits were sunk to a greater depth, being accessible by a stairway. The tombs were surrounded by a row of subsidiary burials, which are thought to be an Upper Egyptian feature. Their low, **mastaba**-like superstructures have a slightly **vaulted** roof, on which there may have been a stela bearing the name of the tomb owner. This development ceased around the middle of the 2nd Dynasty.

Royal tombs and funerary enclosures of the Early Dynastic Period at Abydos (figures in brackets represent the number of secondary burials; the numbering follows Petrie)

	Tombs	Funerary enclosures
Dynasty 0		
Scorpion		
Ka	B 7–9, 1–2	–
Narmer	B 17–18	–
1st Dynasty		
Hor Aha	B 10–15–19	–
Djer	O (326)	A (269)
Djet	Z (174)	B (154)
Meryneith	Y (41)	–
Den	T (121)	C (?) (80)
Adjib	X (63)	D (?)
Semerkhet	U (69)	D (?)
Qa'a	Q (26)	Deir Sitt Damiana
2nd Dynasty		
Peribsen	P	'Middle Fort'
Khasekhemwy	V	Shunet el-Zebib

Bibliography: E. Amélineau, *Les nouvelles fouilles d'Abydos*, 3 Vols (Paris 1899–04); W.M.F. Petrie, *The Royal Tombs of the First Dynasty*, 2 Vols (London 1900–01); B.J. Kemp, Abydos and the Royal Tombs of the First Dynasty, in: *JEA* 52 (1966) 13–22; B.J. Kemp, The Egyptian 1st Dynasty royal cemetery, in: *Antiquity* 41 (1967) 22–32; W. Kaiser, Zu den königlichen Talbezirken der 1. und 2. Dynastie in Abydos und zur Baugeschichte des Djoser-Grabmals, in: *MDAIK* 25 (1969) 1–21; J.-Ph. Lauer, Le développement des complexes funéraires royaux en Égypte, in: *BIFAO* 79 (1979) 355–394; D. O'Connor, New Funerary Enclosures (Talbezirke) of the Early Dynastic Period at Abydos, in: *JARCE* 26 (1989) 51–86; G. Dreyer, in: *MDAIK* 47 (1991) 93–104; R. Mainz, Sandtumulus oder Ziegelplatte?, in: *Discussions in Egyptology* 26 (1993) 25–46; G. Dreyer, Recent Discoveries at Abydos Cemetery U, in: *The Nile Delta in Transition: 4th.–3rd. Millennium B.C.* (Tel Aviv 1992) 293–299; Excavation Reports of the DAI by W. Kaiser and G. Dreyer in *MDAIK* 35 (1979) 155–163; 38 (1982) 211–269; 46 (1990) 53–90; 47 (1991) 93–104; 49 (1993) 23–62; 54 (1998) 77–175; 56 (2000) 43–129; Günter Dreyer, *Umm el-Qaab I* (Mainz 1998).

2. Cenotaphs

Several kings constructed an **Osiris tomb** at Abydos, either following the tradition of earlier royal tombs, or in order to participate in the resurrection of Osiris by means of a false burial. Two examples have been found to date:

a) King Senwosret III erected a monumental cult complex in the desert, with a **brick** enclosure below the desert escarpment, surrounding a gigantic subterranean **rock tomb**. Its structure is in the form of four successive funerary complexes. The first tomb finishes at the lowest level, with one central and two side-chambers. Above it is a second tomb, with a system of shafts similar to the shafts near the entrance of the **kings' tombs** in the Valley of the Kings. This is followed by the 'true' tomb, which contained the **granite** sarcophagus and canopic chest, and from there a winding passage led to the actual Osiris tomb, which was never finished. The most important corridors and chambers are faced with **limestone** and **quartzite**. At the edge of the desert is a royal statue temple, surrounded by accommodation for priests, which was part of this complex. This temple is one of the earliest examples of a type which became common in the New Kingdom, consisting of a colonnaded courtyard, **hypostyle hall**, offering chamber and triple sanctuary (**multiple shrine**).

b) The **cenotaph** of Ahmose is in the form of a **pyramid**-like cult structure on the edge of the cultivation, with a memorial chapel to Queen Tetisheri, some priests' houses and an Osiris tomb in the desert. An S-shaped winding passage leads past a pillared hall, containing three rows of six pillars, to the actual burial chamber, which remains in an unfinished state.

To the north of the temple of Ramesses II, there is an extensive necropolis of the 12th Dynasty, containing private cenotaphs. The structures consist of an **enclosure** around a vaulted chapel, made of bricks and painted white, and in some cases surrounded by a small garden.

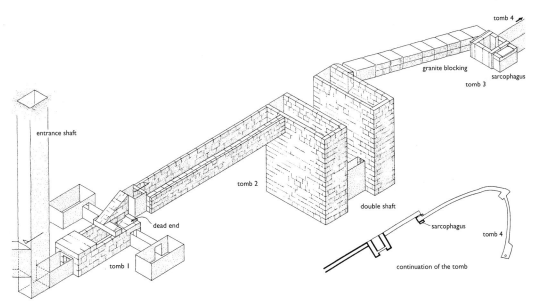

Isometric projection of the inner chambers of the Osiris tomb of Senwosret III at Abydos

Bibliography: E.R. Ayrton et al., *Abydos III 1904* (London 1904); William K. Simpson, *The Terrace of the Great God at Abydos: The Offering Chapels of Dynasties 12 and 13* (New Haven and Philadelphia 1974); D. O'Connor, The 'Cenotaphs' of the Middle Kingdom at Abydos, in: *Mélanges Gamal Eddin Mokhtar* (Cairo 1985) 161–177; J. Wegner, South Abydos: Burial Place of the Third Senwosret?, in: *Kemet* 6 (1995) 59–71; J. Wegner, Excavations at the Town of Enduring-are-the-Places-Khakaure-Maa-Kheru-in-Abydos, in: *JARCE* 35 (1998) 1–44; S. Harvey, Monuments of Ahmose at Abydos, in: *Egyptian Archaeology* 4 (1994) 3–5.

3. Temple of **Sety I** at Abydos
4. Temple of **Ramesses II** at Abydos

5. Town
Within the enclosure of Kom el-Sultan are the remains of a **town**, which dates from Naqada III onwards, as well as the scant remains of a temple to Osiris-Khentyimentyu.

Bibliography: William Flinders Petrie, *Abydos I 1902* (London 1902) and *II 1903* (London 1903); B.J. Kemp, The Osiris Temple at Abydos, in: *MDAIK* 23 (1968) 138–155; B.J. Kemp, The Early Development of Towns in Egypt, in: *Antiquity* 51 (1977) 185–200; M.D. Adams, Community and Social Organization in Early Historic Egypt, in: *NARCE* 158/159 (1992) 1–9.

Addorsed chapel, addorsed temple (chapelle adossée)
This is a cult structure built on the outside of a temple and attached to the rear wall, which enabled the deity in the sanctuary inside to be addressed by people standing outside the temple. The image of the deity displayed on the outside wall is frequently made prominent by a **metal overlay**, and is sometimes also protected by a **kiosk**-like annexe or a small temple. Rear chapels are found attached to most of the main temples at **Karnak** (**Amun**, **Mut**, **Khonsu**, **Month**), at **Deir el-Medina**, **Deir el-Shelwit**, the temple of **Shanhur**, the Isis temple of **Dendera** (with a cult niche), **Kalabsha**, **Dakka** (with a cult niche) and **Tanis**.

Against the rear of the Amun temple at Karnak is a Re-Horakhty temple, and against the Mut temple a sanctuary of Maat. The temple of **Ptah** at Memphis and the Re-Horakhty temple at **Heliopolis** had two cult axes facing each other.

Bibliography: Ludwig Borchardt, *Allerhand Kleinigkeiten* (Leipzig 1933) 8–9; F. Laroche and C. Traunecker, La chapelle adossée au temple de Khonsou, in: *Karnak* 6 (1980) 167–196; W. Guglielmi, Die Funktion von Tempeleingang und Gegentempel als Gebetsort, in: Kurth, *Tempeltagung* 55–68.

Ain Amur
The ruins of a Roman temple between the oases of **Dakhla** and **El-Kharga**. It is surrounded by a **brick** wall and consists of two badly damaged antechambers, a stone transverse hall and three **naoi**.

Bibliography: H.E. Winlock, *Ed Dakhleh Oasis* (New York 1936); A. Fakhry, in: *ASAE* 40 (1941) 761–768.

Ain Asil, *see also* Balat

A fortified **town** covering an area of 330,000 sq m.

Bibliography: Excavation Reports by L. Giddy in: *BIFAO* 79 (1979) 31–33; 80 (1980) 257–262; 81 (1981) 189–205; 83 (1983); 84 (1984); 87 (1987); G. Soukiassian, in: *BIFAO* 90 (1990) 347–358; Georges Soukiassian, A Governor's palace at 'Ayn Asil, Dakhla Oasis, in: *Egyptian Archaeology* 11 (1997) 15–17.

Ain Birbiya (Dakhla Oasis)

The site, in the Dakhla Oasis, of a well-preserved Roman temple, possibly of Augustus, which is dedicated to Amunnakht (similar to Horus) and Hathor. Excavations and restoration have been underway since 1995.

Bibliography: A.J. Mills, The Dakhleh Oasis Project: Report on the 1990-1991 Field Season, in: *JSSEA* 20 (1990) 14–16.

Ain el-Muftella, *see also* Bahariya Oasis

A major site of the Late and Roman Periods near El-Qasr in the Bahariya Oasis with substantial remains of a temple built in the reign of Amasis (26th Dynasty) by the governors Djed-Khonsu-ef-ankh and Sheben-Khonsu. Excavations by Zahi Hawass in 1977 showed that the four separate cult chapels, recorded by Ahmed Fakhry in 1942, are actually part of one larger building. The temple contained an early example of a **pronaos**. The temple walls are decorated with interesting processions of gods.

Bibliography: Ahmed Fakhry, *Bahria Oasis I* (Cairo 1942) 150–171; Zahi Hawass, *Valley of the Golden Mummies* (New York 2000) 192–195.

Akhmenu

A structure erected by Thutmosis III at the eastern end of the **Amun** precinct at **Karnak**. It has an unusual plan and was probably built against an older building now lost, so that it lies across the axis of the old temple and could only be entered from the south-east corner of the temple of Senwosret I. Its names, 'Exalted is the Memorial (of Thutmosis III)' and **'house of millions of years'**, indicate that the building was dedicated above all to the cult of the king as a manifestation of Amun-Re. The Akhmenu, together with the temple of **Thutmosis III** at Deir el-Bahari and his temple next to the **Ramesseum**, may have formed a cultic unit. All three, in their own way, served the cult of the deified king. The principal sanctuaries of Amun and the deified king are located in the centre of the east wall. The Akhmenu has cultic buildings similar to those of the 'houses of millions of years' on the West Bank at **Thebes**, with a solar cult area on the roof, a Sokar sanctuary and a chapel for the royal ancestors. The festival hall is of particular architectural interest; it consists of a raised central space with two rows of ten **columns** in the form of tent posts, surrounded on all sides by lower side-aisles with pillars. The basilica-like central space stands like a festival tent within a pillared courtyard. Another hall, known as the 'botanical garden', due to its wall decoration which shows exotic animals and plants, is linked to the central sanctuary by a **'window of appearances'** and has particularly beautiful papyrus bundle columns. Behind this is an **altar** court, with two rows of four small statue niches and a larger central one.

Bibliography: Paul Barguet, *Le temple d'Amon-Re à Karnak* (Cairo 1962) 157–217; J. Lauffray, Le sécteur nord-est du temple jubilaire de Thoutmosis III à Karnak, in: *Kêmi* 19 (1969) 179–218; Nathalie Beaux, Le cabinet de curiosités de Thoutmosis III, *Orientalia Lovaniensia Analecta* 36 (Louvain 1990) 7–37; Nathalie Beaux, L'architecture des niches du sanctuaire d'Amon dans le temple de l'Akh-menou à Karnak, in: *Karnak* 9 (1993) 101–107.

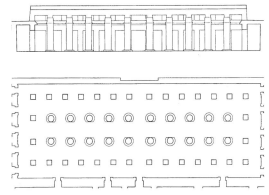

Plan and section of the hypostyle hall of the Akhmenu temple of Thutmosis III at Karnak (after G. Haeny)

Akhmim (Panopolis, Chemmis)

An important ancient city in Middle Egypt, with the remains of temples and necropoleis (at **Hawawish** and **Salamuni**). The temple of Min and Triphis was still in a good state of repair in the Middle Ages. Because of its size, stonework and beautiful decoration, it was regarded as equivalent to one of the Seven Wonders of the World. Descriptions indicate that the building must have resembled the temple of **Edfu**, with **pylons**, **pronaos** and temple building. The pronaos was 86 m wide and 30 m deep, and it had 40 columns, 21 m in height, which were probably arranged in four rows of ten, making it close to the size of the great **hypostyle hall** at **Karnak**. Herodotus mentions two **colossal statues**. The temple was demolished in 1350 AD and used as building material. A monumental gate structure, with colossal statues of Ramesses II and his daughter Merytamun, has been undergoing excavation since 1981.

Bibliography: Herodotus, *History* Book II 91; S. Sauneron, *Le temple d'Akhmim décrit par Ibn Jobair*, in: *BIFAO* 51 (1952) 123–135; J. Karig, Achmim, in: *LÄ* I 54–55; Klaus-Peter Kuhlmann, *Materialien zur Archäologie und Geschichte des Raumes von Achmim*, Sonderschrift 11 des Deutschen Archäologischen Instituts Kairo (Mainz 1983); N. Kanawati, *Akhmim in the Old Kingdom*, The Australian Centre for Egyptology Studies 2 (1992).

Akhtihotep, *see* Ptahhotep

Akoris, chapel of

A **barque station,** begun by Psammuthis, on the bank of the Nile in front of the temple of **Amun** at **Karnak,** was completed by Akoris. This unusual building served as a resting place and turning point for the barque of Amun before it was loaded on board a boat, and also on its return to the temple. The building had a timber roof, and consisted of an antechamber, surrounded by six columns, and a rear portion surrounded by a wall. The two half-columns attached to the **antae** of the rear hall, in the form of plant-bundle **columns**, are of particular interest, although their capitals are unfortunately missing.

Bibliography: Jean Lauffray, *La chapelle d'Achôris à Karnak. I – Les fouilles, l'architecture, le mobilier et l'anastylose* (Paris 1995).

Aksha (Serra West)

The remains of a temple of Ramesses II, 330 km south of **Aswan,** consisting of a **pylon,** forecourt surrounded by a pillared colonnade on three sides, and a **hypostyle hall** or offering chamber with three parallel sanctuaries for the deified king, Amun and Re. It is now in the museum of Khartoum.

Bibliography: J. Vercoutter and A. Rosenwasser, Preliminary Report of the Excavations at Aksha, in: *Kush* 10 (1962) 109–114; 11 (1963) 131–134; 12 (1964) 96–99; E. Otto, Akscha, in: *LÄ* I 118; Hein, *Ramessidische Bautätigkeit* 38–40.

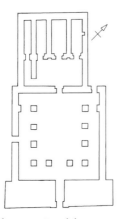

Plan of the temple of Ramesses II at Aksha

Alabaster (calcite)

Calcite (travertine) was acquired from the quarries at Wadi Gerawi (near Helwan) and between Minya and **Asyut** (particularly at **Hatnub** near **Amarna**). Due to its colour and consistency, it was regarded as particularly pure and so was used for chapels (such as the chapel of Amenhotep I and the **barque station** by the **sacred lake** at **Karnak**), **paving** in temples (e.g. **Khafre** and **Unas**), sarcophagi (such as those of Hetepheres and **Sety I**), **altars** (e.g. **Niuserre**) and, above all, for sculptures.

Bibliography: Nicholson, *Materials* 21–22, 59–60; W. Helck, Alabaster, in: Helck, *LÄ* I 129–130; J.A. Harrel, Misuse of the term 'alabaster' in Egyptology, in: *GM* 119 (1990) 37–42; De Putter, *Pierres* 43–46; Klemm, *Steine* 199–223.

Alexander the Great, tomb of

On his deathbed, Alexander the Great expressed the wish that he be buried in the **Ammoneion** at **Siwa** (Diodoros XVIII, 3, 5). When Perdikkas attempted to move the body, which had been embalmed in Babylon, to Aigai in Macedonia, Ptolemy I Soter had the funeral car (which had been constructed over a two-year period) intercepted in Syria. Alexander's body was buried first at **Memphis**, before later (possibly in the reign of Ptolemy II Philadelphos) being moved to **Alexandria**, where it was laid to rest in a golden sarcophagus in a funerary monument. Ptolemy IV Philopator erected a magnificent new communal tomb (the Soma or Sema) for Alexander and the Ptolemaic royal family, with underground vaults and a superstructure in the form of a pyramid. Ptolemy X substituted an alabaster sarcophagus for the golden one. Alexander's mummy was visited by Julius Caesar, Augustus and other Roman emperors. After the tomb's destruction in 273 AD (Aurelian), an important cult of Alexander is known to have continued in existence until 323 AD. According to Strabo, the Sema lay in the palace area close to the sea, and it is thought that the tomb may lie in the area of the Nabi Daniel mosque in the Kom el-Demas, at the west end of the Kom el-Dikka. However, the excavations of Breccia, Adriani and the Polish mission have not found any trace of it. Other traditions suggest the church of St Mark or the mosque of Attarin, where the sarcophagus of Nectanebo II (now in the British Museum), thought originally to be that of Alexander, was used, until approximately 1799, as a bath.

Bibliography: E.D. Clarke, *The Tomb of Alexander the Great* (Cambridge 1805); H. Thiersch, Die alexandrinische Königsnekropole, in: *Jahrbuch des Deutschen Arch. Inst.* 25 (1911) 55–97; P.M. Fraser, *Ptolemaic Alexandria* (1972) Vol. I 15–38. Jean-Yves Empereur, *Alexandria Rediscovered* (London 1998) 145–153.

Alexandria

Sea port founded by Alexander the Great, in 332–31 BC, near Rhakotis on the Mediterranean, further developed by Ptolemy I and Ptolemy II. It was the capital city of the Ptolemies and became a cosmopolitan city of the Hellenistic and Roman Era. According to the plan of the architects Deinocrates of Rhodes and Cleomenes of Naukratis, it was built to a regular layout, surrounded by city walls of approximately 2.2 x 5 km. The most important monuments are the royal palace in the centre, near the sea, the library of Ptolemy II in the Museion, the 120 m high lighthouse, built by Sostratos of Knidos for Ptolemy I on the Pharos peninsula (now known as Qait Bey), and the funerary complex of Soma or Sema with the tombs of Alexander and the Ptolemies (**kings' tombs**). Of particular significance was the **Serapeum** of Ptolemy III at Rhakotis, covering 70 x 160 m, built by the architect Parmeniskos, which stood at the south-west edge of the city but is now unfortunately destroyed. The beautiful Caesareum of Cleopatra VII and Augustus, a building at the eastern harbour, dedicated to the imperial cult, containing the two 'Cleopatra's needles' (**obelisks**) has also been destroyed. A Roman temple to Isis, at Ras el-Soda, is better preserved. There are many re-used blocks from pharaonic buildings, particularly from **Heliopolis**.

There are important necropoleis, varying in date from Ptolemaic to Roman times, at Anfukhi, Kom el-Shukafa, Wardian/Mex in the western part of the city, and at Hadra, Khatby, Sidi Gabr, Ibrahimiah and Mustafa Kamil in the eastern part. The tomb complexes are sunk into the rock, following on from the native Egyptian funerary **palaces** of the Late Period. They are decorated in a style which is a mixture of Hellenistic and Egyptian elements. The tombs consist of peristyle-like **sun courts**, with **altars** and benches carved out of the rock. The 'multi-storey' catacombs at Kom el-Shukafa, dating from the 2nd century AD, are in a mixed Egypto-Roman style.

The ancient city has largely been built over and has disappeared. Important late Roman remains have been excavated in the city centre (Kom el-Dikka), consisting of a theatre, baths and living areas; they have been preserved in a protected monuments zone.

An underwater excavation, headed by Jean-Yves Empereur, around Qait Bey has revealed c. 3000 ancient **sphinxes**, **obelisks**, statues and blocks, perhaps fallen from the Pharos lighthouse in 1303 AD. A second group of divers is currently exploring the remains of the Ptolemaic palaces in the east harbour.

Bibliography (select): for older bibliography on Alexandria see Ida A. Pratt, *Ancient Egypt*, 1st Ed. (New York 1925) 115–118, 2nd Ed. (New York 1942) 91–92; *PM* IV 2–6; F. Noack, Neue Untersuchungen in Alexandrien, *AM 1900* 215–279; Ernst Sieglin, *Ausgrabungen in Alexandria*, 2 Vols. (Leipzig 1908–1924); Hermann Thiersch, *Pharos, Antike, Islam und Occident. Ein Beitrag zur Architekturgeschichte* (Leipzig-Berlin 1909); Hermann Thiersch, Die alexandrinische Königsnekropole, in: *Jahrbuch des Deutschen Archäologischen Instituts* 25 (1911) 55–97; Evaristo Breccia, *Alexandrea ad Aegyptum* (Bergamo 1914); Achille Adriani, *Repertorio d'arte dell'Egitto greco-romano*, 2 Vols (Palermo 1961); E.M. Forster, *Alexandria. A History and a Guide* (New York 1961); André Bernard, *Alexandrie la Grande* (Paris 1966); Kazimierz Michalowski, *Alexandria* (Vienna-Munich 1970); P.M. Fraser, *Ptolemaic Alexandria*, 3 Vols (Oxford 1972); Norbert Hinske, Ed., *Alexandrien. Kulturbegegnungen dreier Jahrtausende im Schmelztiegel einer mediterranen Großstadt* (Mainz 1981); K. Parlasca, esch-Schugafa (Alexandria), in: Helck, *LÄ* V 739–741; Patrizio Pensabene, Lastre di chiusura di loculi con naiskoi egizi e stele funerarie con ritratto del museo di Alessandria, in: *Alessandria e il mondo ellenistico-romano*, Vol. 4 (Rome 1983) 91–119; Reports of the Polish Mission, in: *ET* 11 (1979), 13 (1983), 14 (1990), 16 (1992); Birger A. Pearson, The New Alexandria Library, in: *Biblical Archaeologist* 56 (1993) 221; Barbara Tkaizow, *The Topography of Ancient Alexandria (An Archaeological Map)* (Warsaw 1993); Günther Grimm and Michael Pfrommer, *Alexandria. Die erste Königsstadt der hellenistischen Welt* (Mainz 1998); *La gloire d'Alexandrie*, exhibition catalogue, Petit Palais (Paris 1998); Jean-Yves Empereur, *Alexandria Rediscovered* (London 1998).

Altar

Among the numerous different forms of altar in ancient Egypt, the most important in architectural terms are the high, generally accessible altars for offerings which stood in the open air. In most cases a ramp leads up to a platform, finished with a **cavetto cornice**, on top of which

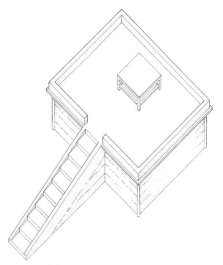

Reconstruction of the solar altar in the Hatshepsut temple at Deir el-Bahari

stood an altar or a base for an altar protected from view by a **screen wall**; examples may be found at **Edfu, Kom Ombo, Medamud** and the **Ramesseum**. In solar cult contexts (**Amarna, sun temples** and 'house of millions of years'), the altar faced east so that the cult rituals were directed towards the rising sun. At **Amarna**, the main altars of the Aten cult stand in a **hypaetral** holy of holies, or occasionally in the passageway between the towers of a **pylon**. Another unusual feature at **Amarna** is the series of vast altars in the desert, one 40 x 40 m in area, which have ramps leading up on to them on four sides, and the numerous small solar altars which fill the courtyards of the temples. The **alabaster** altar in the sun temple of **Niuserre**, which faces the four points of the compass, is unique. The altar in the solar sanctuary at **Abu Simbel** is provided with two **obelisks** and solar baboons.

Bibliography: Jéquier, *Manuel* 337–341; Peet, *City of Akhenaten* II 101–102; R. Stadelmann, Altar, in: Helck, *LÄ* I 145–149.

Amara West (Amarah)

The ruins of a fortified **town** on an island in the Nile, 145 km south of Wadi Halfa, including the remains of the palace of the governor and a temple to Amun built by Sety I and Ramesses II. The partially destroyed temple is relatively important and has a colonnaded court, a **hypostyle hall**, with four rows of three columns, and three parallel sanctuaries. The first building was a small structure of **brick** which was later rebuilt in **stone** and decorated with reliefs. 11 km further south, on the island of Sai, is a **fortress** of the 18th Dynasty with a temple to Amun.

Bibliography: Hein, *Ramessidische Bautätigkeit* 51–60; Patricia Spencer, *Amara West I. The Architectural Report* (London 1997) 27–51.

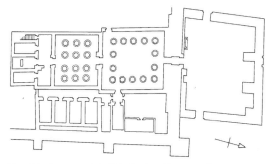

Plan of the Amun temple built by Sety I and Ramesses II at Amara West

Amarna (Tell el-Amarna)

A site of immense archaeological importance, founded in year 5 of the reign of Akhenaten, on the East Bank of the Nile opposite Mallawi. It was abandoned under Tutankhamun and subsequently fell into ruin. It covers an area of approximately 800–1200 x 7000 m, and follows a linear organisation, with loosely arranged areas of sacred buildings, administrative districts and residential buildings on both sides of a central street.

1. Sanctuaries (**Aten temples**)

When the city was founded, temporary Aten cult areas were provided in the form of brick **altars** in the open air. These developed gradually into stone temples, but this process was not complete by the time of the death of Akhenaten. The stone structures were completely dismantled under Ramesses II for re-use in building projects at **Hermopolis**. Only the foundation trenches and remains of the **brick** structures are still visible. Representations of the temples in **rock tombs** have been essential for reconstructing them. The manner in which the temples functioned and their associated rooms are still largely unknown.

a) The largest temple, measuring 290 x 760 m, is the Per-Aten, which lay to the east of the royal processional road. Inside, only two buildings, which stood on the central axis, 350 m apart, were completed. That at the

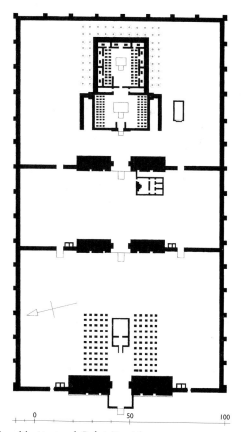

Plan of the Aten temple Pa-hut-Aten at Amarna

rear, the main temple (known as the Sanctuary), was originally a high altar approached by an avenue of **sphinxes**, flanked by a garden of trees. This was later developed into a form of **terraced temple**. The front was formed of an open terrace on which were eight rows of twelve altars. Behind this, on a higher terrace, was an altar court, surrounded by chapels, with a **gateway** of unusual construction. The Sanctuary contained a large number of statues and statue groups of the king and queen, and it was the principal cult focus of the temple complex, perhaps to be identified with the 'shadow of Re' depicted in the tomb of Huy (at Amarna).

The avenue of sphinxes and the garden were later built over with the Gem-pa-Aten temple, a structure measuring 32 x 210 m, divided into sections by six pairs of **pylons**. Behind the first pylon was a festival hall, the Per-hayi. Instead of having a raised central nave, the central passage was not roofed. The sections following consisted of open courtyards containing small altars. The rear portion of the fifth section was covered with a pillared **canopy**. In the last two sections, chapel-like cult areas flanked the walls. There were monumental altars in the centre of the sixth and seventh sections. Within the temple enclosure, on both sides of the temple at the front, were several hundred altars, wine stores, a slaughter-house and a *benben* **stone** set on a podium. There were probably extensive gardens here also.

b) Further south along the Royal Road lay the slightly smaller Pa-hut-Aten, measuring 108 x 191 m. Its **enclosure wall** had projecting rectangular towers reminiscent of a **'house of millions of years'**. The complex was divided into three courtyards by three pairs of pylons. The first had a passageway 8.8 m wide, which was blocked by a stepped construction, like a podium, on top of which would have been an altar. In the first court, the main altar was surrounded by 108 small altars. The actual sanctuary was in the third court, which had some similarities to the sanctuary of the Per-Aten. It is likely that, like the latter, it was divided into two and furnished with a large number of altars. The front part of the building is flanked by walls. Before the construction of this building, a large high altar, measuring 9.35 x 14.4 m, stood in the area of the first court.

c) At the southern end of Amarna, there were two garden sanctuaries, known as the Maru-en-pa-Aten (**Maru temple**). The larger of these was partly occupied by a **sacred lake**, measuring 60 x 120 m, and gardens, and it was termed the 'sun shade' of Nefertiti. In the north-east corner there was a unique construction, consisting of a pillared courtyard with 11 T-shaped ponds. The bottom and sides of the basins were painted

with plants. In front of this 'greenhouse' were flower beds and small islands, surrounded by canals, on which were three temples. The whole complex was a miniature representation of the cosmos for the celebration of the birth of the Aten, with representations of the 11 stretches of water that the sun god had to cross during his nightly journey, and with the 12th round basin forming the point of climax where the island sanctuary emerged out of the water like the **primeval mound**. Another interpretation sees this as a representation of the seasonal cycle consisting of 11 months, with the 12th month as a cult festival at the time of the start of the inundation.

d) A further sanctuary, surrounded by gardens and service buildings, lies at Kom Nana to the south.

2. Palaces

a) The 'official' **palace** on the edge of the cultivation, only half-preserved, was probably a *sed*-festival complex. The northern part contains a huge 'coronation hall' with 544 pillars (or perhaps altars). The walls were decorated with faience tiles. The main building in the centre of a massive courtyard measures 100 x 170 m and has a pillared portico in the middle flanked by royal **statue pillars**. The interior is laid out in three symmetrical parts consisting of numerous **pillared halls** interconnected by ramps.

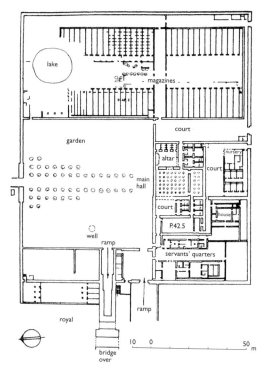

Plan of Akhenaten's palace in the central area of Amarna (after A. Badawy)

The so-called 'harim', which lay along the Royal Road, was made up of long series of rooms, pillared halls and courtyards, some with pools of water, and a sunken garden in the northern part. Interpretation of this complex is difficult.

b) The building thought to be the king's living quarters lay on the opposite side of the Royal Road to a), being accessible via a **bridge**. The building was surrounded by an enclosure, 123 x 140 m in size, and was laid out in a U-shape around a garden, with the actual residence at the rear, and servants' quarters and store rooms forming the side-wings. The royal residence was in the form of an enlarged type of the normal villa found at Amarna; it was rather modest and consisted of a dwelling area, a court and store rooms.

c) The North Palace, measuring 112 x 142 m, was another cult palace serving an unknown purpose; it is horseshoe-shaped, built round a pool of water and has a throne room at the end of its central axis. To the side of the pool are buildings for rearing animals. The walls, ceilings and floors were decorated with scenes from nature, and there was a frieze of grapes made of fired clay.

d) The meagre remains of the 'North Riverside Palace' lie at the very northern end, surrounded by a turreted wall; this may have been the 'this life' palace of the king.

3. Settlements

Residential areas have been found in four sites: a northern settlement, a northern suburb, the centre and a southern suburb. The **houses** of the upper classes are particularly prominent, in the form of villas lying along the main streets of the southern part of the city. They consist of large enclosures containing courtyards, gardens, stabling, workshops, a well, store houses, servant accommodation, a garden shrine and, most important, the main house. This was usually only one storey high but with a roof terrace. In the centre, projecting above the level of the roof, was a pillared hall. The inner part of the house contained the owner's bedroom and bathroom. Such houses were often lavishly decorated.

Good examples of smaller houses are found in the 'workmen's village', 70 x 70 m in size, which lies in the desert. It was divided by five narrow streets into six strips, each containing twelve separate houses.

4. Tombs

On the eastern edge of the bay of Amarna are 43 only partially complete tombs of the courtiers of Akhenaten. In contrast to the great variety of the preceding tombs at **Thebes**, these are reduced to three main types: a) a simple

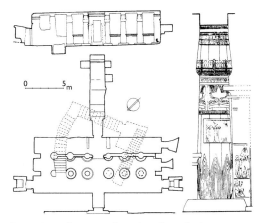

Plan, section and papyrus column from the tomb of Tutu at Amarna (after A. Badawy)

T-shaped plan, b) a rock-cut chamber with a recess for a colossal image of the deceased and c) one or two pillared halls with a statue niche. The tombs of Meryre I and Meryre II (Nos 4 and 2), Panehsy (No. 6), Tutu (No. 8) and Ay (No. 25) are architecturally significant, consisting of pillared halls with two to four papyrus **columns**, carved out of the rock in elaborate forms and painted. The antechamber of the tomb of Ay was intended to have three rows of eight columns, and that of Tutu would have contained two rows of six columns, with the rearmost columns joined by **screen walls**. The burial chambers lay 20–25 m below, following the traditions of the Theban tombs of the time of Amenhotep III. Their spiral descending passageways may have been intended to reflect the cyclical progress of the sun.

The royal tomb is located 6 km east of the town in a desert valley. Its plan diverges from that of the previous royal tombs by the replacement of the L-shaped arrangement of rooms and corridors by a straight axial alignment, probably to conform to the ideology of the course of the sun's disc. This innovation continued in use in the royal tombs of the 19th and 20th Dynasties.

Bibliography (select): W.M. Flinders Petrie, *Tell el Amarna* (London 1894); Norman de Garis Davies, *The Rock Tombs of El Amarna*, 6 Vols (London 1903–1908); Paul Timme, *Tell el-Amarna vor der Deutschen Ausgrabung* (Leipzig 1917); F.G. Newton, Excavations at El-'Amarnah, 1923–24, in: *JEA* 10 (1924) 289–305; T. Whittemore, The Excavations at El-'Amarnah, *JEA* 12 (1926) 3–12; H. Frankfort, Preliminary Report on the Excavations at Tell el-'Amarnah, 1926–7, *JEA* 13 (1927) 209–218; Peet, *City of Akhenaten* I-III; Badawy, *Architecture* II 76–126; R. Stadelmann, swt-Rc als Kultstätte des Sonnengottes im Neuen Reich, in: *MDAIK* 25 (1969) 159–178; B.J. Kemp, Tell el-Amarna, in: Helck, *LÄ* VI 309–319; B. Kemp, The City of el-Amarna as a Source for the Study of Urban Society in Ancient Egypt, in: *World*

Archaeology 9 (1977/78) 123–139; Borchardt, *Tell el-Amarna* (Berlin 1980); A. Badawy, Le symbolisme de l'architecture à Amarna, in: *L'Égyptologie en 1979* (Paris 1982) 187–194; B.J. Kemp, Report on the Tell el-Amarna Expedition, 1977-82, in: *ASAE* 70 (1984/85) 83–97; B.J. Kemp, *Amarna Reports* I–VI (London 1984–1994); D.B. Redford, *Akhenaten. The Heretic King* (Princeton 1984); G.T. Martin, *The Royal Tomb at el-Amarna*, 2 Vols (London 1974, 1984); E.L. Meyers, Component Design as a Narrative Device in Amarna Tomb Art, in: *Studies in the History of Art*, Vol. 16 (Washington 1985) 35–51; B.J. Kemp, The Amarna Workmen's Village, in: *JEA* 73 (1987) 21–50; Cyril Aldred, *Akhenaten, King of Egypt* (London 1988); B.J. Kemp, *Ancient Egypt: Anatomy of a Civilization* (London-New York 1989, reprinted 1993) 261–317; B.J. Kemp and S. Garfi, *A Survey of the Ancient City of El-Amarna* (London 1993).

Ambulatory temple

A type of temple or chapel common in Egyptian architecture from the Middle Kingdom onwards: not identical but similar to Greek peripteral temples, surrounded on three or four sides by a corridor lined with **pillars** or **columns**. In a wider context it includes structures whose centre does not consist of a solid structure, serving instead as a temporary resting place for barques etc. (**kiosk**). The following types can be distinguished in their form and function:

a) Temples whose outer walls, which are only visible at the corners, are interrupted by rows of columns with **screen walls**, and whose **pillared halls** surround a solid inner temple building. The outer walls have a slight **batter**. These are predominantly **birth houses** and barque shrines, above all of the Ptolemaic period.

b) Temples surrounded on three or four sides, including the corners, by a corridor lined with pillars or columns, surrounding a solid inner temple building. The outer walls are vertical. The earliest example is found in the temple of **Mentuhotep** at Deir el-Bahari; otherwise, this type is typical of the Thutmoside period (**Buhen**, **El-Amada**, Satet temple at **Elephantine**).

c) Free-standing kiosks surrounded on all four sides, including the corners, by rows of columns. There is no central structure. Kiosks were popular in the Ethiopian period.

d) Chapels with a surrounding pillared corridor served as *sed*-festival chapels and **barque stations**. This was the only type of ambulatory temple which stood on a podium. Their outer walls are vertical. The earliest example is the **Chapelle Blanche** (Fig.); later examples first appear in the 18th Dynasty.

Bibliography: Borchardt, *Tempel mit Umgang*; H. Steckeweh, Oberägyptische Architektur zu Beginn des Mittleren und des Neuen Reiches, in: *VI. Internationaler Kongreß für Archäologie 1939* (Berlin 1940); Arnold, *Temples* 285–288; G. Haeny, Peripteraltempel in Ägypten, in: M. Bietak, Ed., *Archaische Griechische Tempel und Ägypten* (Vienna 2001) 89–106.

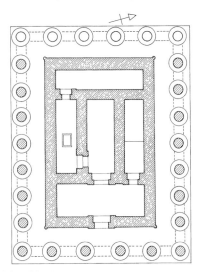

Restored plan of the Thutmoside ambulatory temple of Horus at Buhen (see also Buhen, for façade)

Amenemhat I, pyramid of

An incomplete tomb of Amenemhat I lies in a remote wadi behind the **Ramesseum** at Thebes, but the temple complex which had been planned following the traditions of the temple of **Mentuhotep** did not progress beyond the initial stages. After the removal of the court to **El-Lisht**, the pyramid 'The Places of Amenemhat Appear' was built following Memphite traditions but using strange elements which may have originated in Thebes. The complex contains blocks from the pyramid temples of **Khufu**, **Khafre**, **Userkaf**, **Unas** and **Pepy II**. The pyramid measures 84 x 84 m and was perhaps 59 m high. The sloping entrance corridor, which is still blocked, led into a small burial chamber with a shaft, possibly for canopics, which disappears down into the groundwater. Standing in front of the eastern protecting wall of the pyramid, on a lower level, is a temple of unknown date, measuring 21 x 32 m. Its foundations contain blocks from a temple jointly built by Amenemhat I and Senwosret I. To the east are the remains of a ramp and a small **valley temple**.

Bibliography: J.-E. Gautier and G. Jéquier, *Fouilles de Licht* (Cairo 1902); excavation reports in *BMMA* 2 (Apr 1907) 61–63; 2 (July 1907) 113–117; 3 (May 1908) 83–84; 3 (Oct 1908) 184–188; 9 (Oct 1914) 207–222; 16 (Nov 1921) 5–19; 17 (Dec 1922) 4–18; Dorothea Arnold, Amenemhat I and the Early Twelfth Dynasty at Thebes, in: *BMMA* 26 (1991) 16–21.

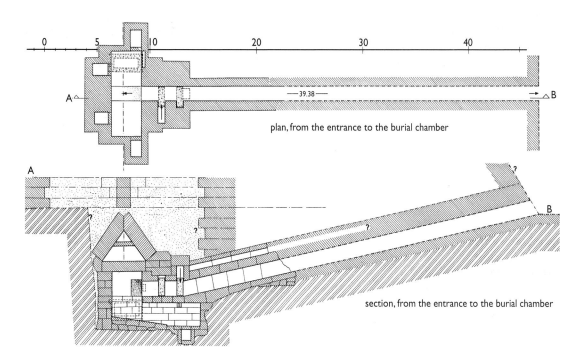

Plan and section of the inner chambers of the pyramid of Amenemhat II at Dahshur

Amenemhat II, pyramid of

The pyramid complex 'Amenemhat is Provided for', measuring approximately 93 x 225 m, is at **Dahshur**. The pyramid itself, 84 m high, possibly called 'Amenemhat is Prepared' consisted of a stone core supported by radial walls, but it has been completely destroyed. The entrance corridor, faced with stone, was protected from the weight above by weight-relieving slabs. Two **granite sliding blocks** sealed the entrance to the small burial chamber. The sarcophagus was made of slabs of **quartzite** and set into the ground. The complicated construction of the relieving slabs over this chamber's flat ceiling is unique. From this chamber, a sloping corridor in the reverse direction led to some sort of possible subsidiary tomb. The buildings of the pyramid complex and the temple, flanked by two massive entrance bastions, have been completely destroyed.

Bibliography: De Morgan, *Dahchour 1894–95.*

Amenemhat III, pyramid at Dahshur

Amenemhat III began construction on his pyramid complex at Dahshur early in his reign. The pyramid, measuring 105 x 105 m and 75 m high, consists of a **brick** core with a **limestone** casing. Inside is a complicated system of corridors and chambers. In addition to the burial chamber, the king was provided with 15 antechambers and a *ka*-tomb. The **vaulted** burial chamber contained a beautiful **granite** sarcophagus with **palace façade** decoration. To the west was a side-entrance into the complex of chambers belonging to two queens, who were also provided with antechambers and a *ka*-tomb each. The pyramid was enclosed within a wall which was **niched** on the front and had a smooth interior. There was also a causeway and a **valley temple**, as well as pits for boat burials in the south. No remains of the **cult temple** have survived. An inscribed **pyramidion** of black **basalt** belonging to the pyramid (now in the Egyptian Museum, Cairo) was found in the debris of the **pyramid temple**. To the south of the **causeway** were the remains of a brick building similar to a **palace**. To the north of the pyramid was the virtually intact but relatively poor burial of King Awibre Hor of the early 13th Dynasty. The rooms within the pyramid were so badly damaged as a result of subsidence during construction that attempts to support the structure proved futile; work on the complex was abandoned and a new pyramid was erected at Hawara (**Amenemhat III**).

Bibliography: De Morgan, *Dahchour 1894* 86–117; De Morgan, *Dahchour 1894–95* 98–109; Arnold, *Amenemhet III.*

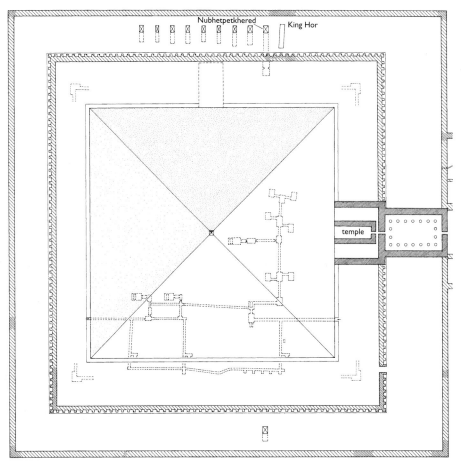

Plan of the pyramid precinct of Amenemhat III at Dahshur

Amenemhat III, pyramid at Hawara

The pyramid complex built by Amenemhat III at the entrance to the Faiyum as a replacement for the damaged pyramid at **Dahshur** was probably called 'Amenemhat Lives'. The complex was described by Herodotus, Strabo and Diodoros and compared with the 'labyrinth' at Knossos on account of its size and complexity. The 158 x 385 m precinct is orientated north–south and so badly damaged that, even using old travellers' descriptions, it cannot be reconstructed. It is possibly based on an Early Dynastic **divine fortress**, and has numerous chapels, reminiscent of the buildings of the precinct of **Djoser**, which represented the gods of each nome in Egypt as well as emphasising the royal statue cult. The **brick** pyramid, 102 x 102 m in size and 58 m high, was cased in **limestone**. Technical improvements were incorporated in order to prevent the catastrophe which had befallen the preceding structure: the king's chamber was carved out of a monolithic block

of **quartzite**, weighing more than 100 tonnes; the ceiling was built using horizontal slabs of quartzite, with a weight-relieving vault of limestone beams, weighing 55 tonnes, and a 7 m high brick **vault** which rested on the surrounding rock rather than on the chamber itself. The quartzite sarcophagus, which now lies submerged under subsoil water, was **niched**.

Nearby was the pyramid burial of Princess Neferuptah, now completely dismantled, and the court necropolis.

Bibliography: Herodotus, *History* II 148–49; *LD* I 47, Text II 11–28; W.M.F. Petrie, *Hawara, Biahmu and Arsinoe* (London 1889); W.M.F. Petrie, *Kahun, Gurob and Hawara* (London 1890); W.M.F. Petrie, *The Labyrinth, Gerzeh and Mazghuna* (London 1912) 28ff.; N. Farag and Z. Iskander, *The Discovery of Neferwptah* (Cairo 1971); A.B. Lloyd, The Egyptian Labyrinth, in: *JEA* 56 (1970) 81–100; K. Michalowsky, The Labyrinth Enigma: archaeological suggestions, in: *JEA* 54 (1968) 219–222; L. Habachi, Hawara, in: Helck, *LÄ* II 1072–1074; D. Arnold, Labyrinth, in: Helck, *LÄ* III 905–907.

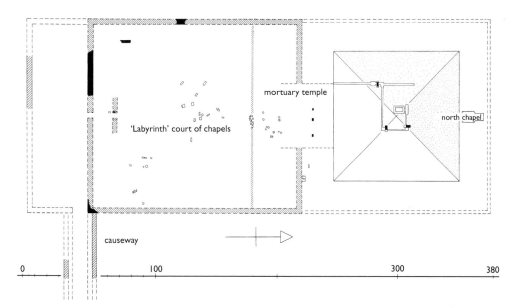

Plan of the pyramid precinct of Amenemhat III at Hawara, with the 'Labyrinth'

Amenemhat Surer, tomb of

A large Theban tomb (TT 48) dating from the transitional period between Amenhotep III and Akhenaten. Unfinished, it is the largest example of the monumental excesses of the private tombs of this period. With its length of 63 m and its four consecutive halls of columns, it is only exceeded in size by the temple of **Abu Simbel**. An additional room, inserted between the normal longitudinal room (containing a colonnade of two rows of ten columns) and the cult chamber, is particularly remarkable for its four rows of six tent-pole **columns** (only otherwise found in the **Akhmenu**).

Bibliography: Ludwig Borchardt, *Allerhand Kleinigkeiten* (Leipzig 1933) 23–24, Bl. 10; Torgny Säve-Söderbergh, *Four Eighteenth Dynasty Tombs* (Oxford, 1957) 33–49.

Amenemopet, tomb of

The Theban tomb of Amenemopet (TT 41) dates from the early 19th Dynasty and has an architecturally beautiful superstructure. The forecourt, which is sunk into the rock, has two lateral **pillared halls**, that on the south side decorated with **statue pillars**. Beyond are a transverse hall with four pillars, a deep passage and a statue cult chamber.

Bibliography: Jan Assmann, *Das Grab des Amenemope TT41*, 2 Vols (Mainz 1991).

Amenhotep III, mortuary temple (Thebes)

The **'house of millions of years'** of Amenhotep III, of which only a small amount of debris is now visible, lies on the West Bank at Thebes. This was originally the largest temple ever erected in Egypt. It was surrounded by an **enclosure wall** measuring 700 x 550 m, 8.5 m thick. The southern part was occupied by the temple complex, which was divided by four **brick pylons** into four courtyards and the main building of the temple. The two **colossi of Memnon** stood in front of the first pylon, and there were two further colossi in front of the second. An avenue of **sphinxes** led from the third pylon to the fourth **gateway**, which stood in front of the magnificent colonnaded court, measuring 85 x 86 m, surrounded on all four sides by columned halls containing three or four rows of papyrus **columns**, 14.20 m high (the height of those at the Luxor temple is 11.55 m). Between the columns of the front rows on the east and west sides of the courtyard stood statues of the king, 8 m high; those in the northern half were of **quartzite**, in the southern **granite**. All that is left of the main temple building beyond are the remains of the **hypostyle hall** which followed the courtyard. It is safe to assume that, besides the cult of the king, there were separate cult axes for the cult of Amun-Re in the southern half and that of Ptah-Sokar-Osiris in the northern half. The gigantic proportions of the temple were matched by the liberal provision of statues and **stelae**. Among the countless sculptural remains are hundreds of statues of Sekhmet, alabaster **sphinxes** with crocodile tails, **sandstone** sphinxes with Anubis heads and a life-size **alabaster** statue of a hippopotamus. Also within the enclosure wall were additional brick buildings, gardens and lakes, as well as a temple to Sokar. The temple had poor foundations and was probably destroyed by an earthquake early in the reign of Merenptah (c. 1220 BC). It has been levelled partly as a result of **stone quarrying**, and partly by the inundation of the Nile.

Blocks from the temple have been re-used in the temple of **Merenptah**, in **Medinet Habu** and in the temple of **Khonsu** at **Karnak**.

Bibliography: Strabo, *Geographica* 17/1/46; *Description* II, Plates 20–22; Gerhard Haeny, *Untersuchungen im Totentempel Amenophis' III*, BeiträgeBf 11 (Wiesbaden 1981); *L'Égypte restituée* 163–165; Betsy Bryan, *The Statue Program for the Mortuary Temple of Amenhotep III*; Quirke, *Temple*, 57–81; Susanne Bickel, *Tore und andere wiederverwendete Bauteile Amenophis' III. Untersuchungen im Totentempel des Merenptah in Theben*, Vol. 3, BeiträgeBf 16 (Stuttgart 1997).

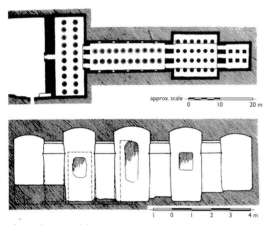

approx. scale
0   10   20 m

Plan and section of the tomb of Amenemhat Surer (TT 48) at Thebes (after L. Borchardt)

Amenhotep (son of Hapu), temple of
A particularly large private mortuary temple of this famous civil officer of Amenhotep III, who (in company with Imhotep) was worshipped up to the Roman period as a god of learning. The 45 x 110 m **brick** structure bore the hallmarks of a '**house of millions of years**'. The layout of the first court is particularly interesting, with a very deep pool, 25 x 26 m in size, fed by subsoil water, its four sides planted with 20 trees in pits. At the rear of this court is the front of the temple, decorated with a pillared portico. Amenhotep's tomb is likely to be somewhere in the hills further to the west.

Bibliography: C. Robichon and A. Varille, *Le temple du scribe royal Amenhotep fils de Hapou* (Cairo 1936).

Ammoneion (Siwa Oasis)
Famous oracular temple of Amun at Aghurmi, 500 km west of the Nile valley and 300 km south of the Mediterranean coast. The present building, founded by Amasis (Ahmose II), probably dates from c. 570 BC. Despite its basically Egyptian features, some construction techniques, vertical walls, the absence of rounded corner posts, and the like, suggest that Greek artisans from Cyrenaica were involved in its construction. Like all oasis temples, the plan of the main temple building, measuring 15 x 51.6 m, is remarkably elongated. An open forecourt at the front is entered from a **pronaos**. Votive offerings from grateful oracle recipients, mentioned in literary texts, are likely to have been placed in both court and **pronaos**. Behind was an inner chamber with two pillars and the sanctuary, joined along their western elevation by the hall, where oracles may have been proclaimed. The oracle was consulted in 331 BC by Alexander the Great. Next to the temple, to the west, lie the remains of the **palace** buildings of the ruler of the oasis, with the women's quarters housing the queen and the harem in the north-eastern corner, and the priests' accommodation and barracks in front of them to the south-east.

Situated slightly to the south are the remains of the temple of Umm Ubayda, with a pillared pronaos and several adjoining rooms beyond. The two temples are likely to have been connected by a processional way, suggesting the existence of a cultic link between them.

Bibliography: A. Fakhry, Recent Excavations at the Temple of the Oracle at Siwa Oasis, in: *Festschrift Ricke* 17–33; A. Fakhry, *The Oases of Egypt I. Siwa Oasis* (Cairo 1973); Klaus P. Kuhlmann, *Das Ammoneion* (Mainz 1988). Reconstruction: *L'Égypte restituée* II 155–156; Klaus P. Kuhlmann, The Preservation of the Temple of the Oracle, in: *ASAE* 75 (1999–2000) 63–89.

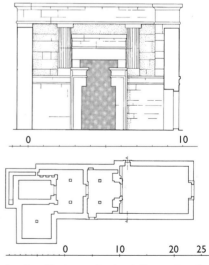

Plan and section of the Ammoneion, founded by Amasis, at Siwa Oasis

Amun precinct (Karnak)

The Amun precinct of Ipet-sut at Karnak was, in size (530 x 510 x 510 x 700 m = 123 hectares) and accumulation of outstanding monuments, Egypt's most important and splendid sanctuary. It was connected by processional ways with the **Mut** precinct, the **Luxor** temple, 2.5 km away, and the bank of the Nile, from where Amun would set off to visit the temples of the kings on the West Bank (for plan, see **Karnak**). The main construction periods were:

1. Middle Kingdom

This period has the oldest architectural remains: the first large **limestone** temple, built in the reign of Senwosret I, was surrounded by a **brick enclosure wall**. In front of this 37.4 x 39.6 m structure stood engaged **statue pillars**. The front half of the temple, probably consisting of a sacred garden, was surrounded by **pillared halls**. In the rear half were three cult chambers, one behind the other, the last one furnished with the **alabaster** plinth for the shrine of the cult image. The brick enclosure wall surrounded several other, smaller **barque stations** (**Chapelle Blanche**).

2. Early 18th Dynasty

The precinct was enlarged to become a sanctuary of supra-regional importance, particularly in the reign of Amenhotep I. In the reign of Thutmosis I, the temple was surrounded by an enveloping stone **enclosure wall** connecting with the fourth and fifth **pylons** newly erected at the front. Between these pylons is the pillared court 'Wadjet'. In front of the fourth pylon there was originally a festival court of Thutmosis II with an east pylon (later removed in the reign of Amenhotep III), a secondary pylon to the south and pairs of **obelisks** erected by Thutmosis I, II and III; at the front lay the quay installation. In the reigns of Hatshepsut and Thutmosis III the temple was enlarged by a **brick** enclosure wall fortified with towers, and at the same period the **sacred lake** was either constructed or enlarged. In front of Senwosret I's structure stood a great fore-temple with a new barque sanctuary (**Chapelle Rouge**). Standing in front of the barque shrine are the two **heraldic pillars** of Upper and Lower Egypt. Hatshepsut set up two obelisks, 30.34 m high, between the fourth and fifth pylons, which were later hidden from view by walls erected by Thutmosis III. A new pylon (the sixth) was erected between the barque shrine and the fifth pylon. Two new large pylons were erected on the southern axis (leading towards the **Mut** precinct), the eighth, built by Hatshepsut, with four **colossal statues**, and the seventh, built by Thutmosis III, with two seated colossal statues

and a pair of obelisks. East of Senwosret I's temple, on the remains of an earlier building possibly of Thutmosis I, Thutmosis III built the **Akhmenu**; a small temple to Ptah, outside the old enclosure wall, to the north, was also built by him; and to the east of this wall he erected a solar sanctuary with a single central obelisk (33 m high, now in front of the Lateran in Rome). Six barque stations were erected along the processional way leading to Luxor.

3. Amenhotep III

The temple axis was extended to the west and south: the third pylon was added, with eight approximately 40 m high **flagpoles**, replacing the older pylon of Thutmosis II. Blocks of stone from many earlier small chapels and monuments in this area, dating from the 12th and early 18th Dynasties, were incorporated into the foundations of this structure. The southern axis concluded with the 10th pylon, 35 m high, and two **quartzite** colossi of the king. The processional ways connecting the complex with the temple of Mut and the Luxor temple were probably rebuilt and furnished with 60 **sphinxes**. Construction work in front of the Amun temple meant that the tree-lined harbour basin at the front was continually being pushed further west, until it ended up in front of the **podium,** which still stands today, connected to the first pylon by an avenue of sphinxes.

4. Post-Amarna

Following the interruption caused by the Amarna period, a new phase of construction work began in the reigns of Tutankhamun and Horemheb, with the addition of the ninth pylon along the southern axis, and the 35 m high, 98 m wide second pylon in the west, using material derived from the demolished **Aten** precinct (*talatat*). Between the second and third pylons the **hypostyle hall** was erected during the reigns of Horemheb, Sety I and Ramesses II. In the reign of Ramesses III, a larger barque station was added in front of the second pylon and, in the south-west corner of the precinct of Amun, a new temple to **Khonsu** was built.

5. Third Intermediate and Late Periods

Under Sheshonq I, the area in front of the second pylon was closed off to form a colonnaded court with its main entrance on the west side and secondary entrances on the north- and south-facing sides (the 'Bubastite Portal'). In the reign of Taharqa, a monumental pillared **kiosk** (**Taharqa**, colonnade of) was erected in this courtyard, and also roofed colonnades in front of three other pylons: at the **Month** precinct to the north, at a solar sanctuary of Ramesses II to the east and at the temple of **Khonsu**.

The reign of Nectanebo I, when the present enclosure wall, 21 m high, was constructed with monumental gateways in the northern area leading to the precinct of **Month** and in front of the temple of **Khonsu** (Bab el-Amara). The barque turning station of **Akoris** dates to the 29th Dynasty. The enclosure was completed under the rule of Ptolemies III and IV. The main entrance was through the first pylon, 100 m in width, which never reached its intended height of 34 m. The final important cult building at Karnak was the **Opet** temple built in the Ptolemaic period.

Bibliography (select): Auguste Mariette-Bey, *Karnak, Étude topographique et archéologique* (Leipzig 1875); L. Borchardt, Zur Baugeschichte des Amontempels, in: *Untersuchungen zur Geschichte und Altertumskunde Ägyptens* 5 (1905); Georges Legrain, *Les temples de Karnak* (Brussels 1929); Paul Barguet, La structure du temple Ipet-Sout d'Amon à Karnak du Moyen Empire à Aménophis II, in: *BIFAO* 52 (1953) 145–155; Paul Barguet, *Le temple d'Amon-Re à Karnak. Essai d'exegèse* (Cairo 1962); *Karnak* I–VIII; J. Lauffray, *Karnak d'Égypt. Domaine du divin* (Paris 1979); R.A. Schwaller de Lubicz, G. Miré and V. Miré, *Les Temples de Karnak*, 2 Vols (Paris 1982); Claude Traunecker and Jean-Claude Golvin, *Karnak. Résurrection d'un site* (Paris 1984); Karnak en Égypte, in: *Dossiers histoire et archéologie* 61 (1982); J. Lauffray, *Karnak d'Égypte* (Paris 1987); Golvin, *Karnak* (Paris 1987); *L'Égypte restituée* 81–120; Franz-Jürgen Schmitz, *Amenophis I, HÄB* 6 (Hildesheim 1978); F. Le Saout et al., Le moyen empire à Karnak: Varia I, in: *Karnak* VIII 293–323; J.-C. Golvin and El-Sayed Hegazy, Essai de l'explication de la forme et des caractéristiques générales des grandes enceintes de Karnak, in: *Karnak* IX 145–160; L. Gaboldé, La 'cour de fêtes' de Thoutmosis II à Karnak, in: *Karnak* IX 1–100. General: *Karnak* I–IX; N. and H. Strudwick, *Thebes in Egypt* (London 1999) 44–66.

Anathyrosis

A method of fitting masonry to achieve perfect joints, used by Greek masons. Only the outer, visible edges of blocks were carefully dressed, along the contact bands, while the centres of the blocks were left rough and slightly recessed. A similar method was used in Egypt from the Old Kingdom onwards. Tool marks show that the front edges of adjoining **casing** blocks were sawn with a short copper **saw** or a sheet of metal. From the New Kingdom onwards, the rear edges of blocks were treated in the same way.

Bibliography: H.E. Winlock, *The Temple of Hibis in El Khârgeh Oasis* (New York 1941), Plates 15, 16, 24, 48; Lauer, *Histoire monumentale* 253; D. Arnold, *Der Tempel des Königs Mentuhotep von Deir el-Bahari* (Mainz 1974) 41; Jean Jacquet, *Le trésor de Thoutmosis Ier* (Cairo 1983) 124, Fig. 25; Arnold, *Building* 43, 45, 123, 267.

Aniba

The Egyptian administrative centre of Lower **Nubia** with a **fortress** on the West Bank of the Nile between Amada and Qasr Ibrim. The fortress, measuring 87 x 138 m, was erected in the Middle Kingdom over an earlier structure of the Old Kingdom. It was enlarged in the New Kingdom, becoming a fortress **town** covering an area of 200 x 400 m (80,000 sq m). Inside are the remains of a Thutmoside temple to Horus built over an earlier Middle Kingdom structure.

Tombs belonging to the Egyptian colony of the Middle Kingdom consist of a **vaulted** cult chapel with the actual burial below it. In the Ramesside period, this became a combination of a pyramid and a cult chapel, fronted by a forecourt with a **pylon**, and the burial not far underground.

Bibliography: Georg Steindorff, *Aniba*, 3 Vols (Glückstadt 1935, 1937); T. Säve-Söderbergh, Aniba, in: *LÄ* I 272–278; Hein, *Ramessidische Bautätigkeit* 27–29.

Ankhhaf, tomb of

The large stone **mastaba** G 7510 of Prince Ankhhaf (brother of Khufu) at **Giza**, 51.8 x 100 m in size, with a massive core containing a cult chapel and *serdab*, and fronted along the southern end of the east side by a **brick** offering chapel. The tomb contained the delicately modelled and painted bust of Ankhhaf, now in the Museum of Fine Arts, Boston, 27.442.

Bibliography: D. Dunham, in: *Bull. of the Mus. of Fine Arts Boston* 37 (1939) Fig. p. 43; Reisner, *Giza* I, Fig. 8.

Ankhhor, tomb of

An important Theban tomb in the Assasif (TT 414), belonging to the Late Period (c. 590 BC). Its superstructure is divided into three parts. The subterranean rooms are arranged in the sequence open courtyard, **pillared hall**, cult chamber and burial apartments. The tomb has benefited from particularly thorough archaeological research and restoration.

Bibliography: Manfred Bietak and Elfriede Reisner-Haslauer, *Das Grab des Anch-Hor*, 2 Vols (Vienna 1978, 1982).

Anta, *see also* pilaster

A **pillar**-like fronting piece on a wall, frequently found in Egyptian architecture:

a) Where the front of a temple is open, then ends of the walls are formed into antae. In the temple at **Deir el-Medina** they are formed into three-sided **Hathor** pillars. In **pronaoi** and **birth houses**, double antae formed at the corners due to the opening up of all four walls have all the characteristics of the walls themselves (sloping exterior, vertical interior surfaces and decorated like the rest of the wall).

b) Antae or **pilasters** may support the **architrave** as the final element in a row of **columns**, for example at the junction with the sloping face of a **pylon** or the front of a temple (as at **Medinet Habu** and the **birth house** at **Dendera**). Depending on the slope of the adjoining wall, they widen towards the top, to the width of the architrave. The **cavetto cornice** on the top is separated from the architrave by a small **abacus** (as in tombs at **Amarna**).

c) A form particular to Egypt is found at the temple of **Medinet Madi** and the two main temples at **Amarna** (Per-Aten and Pa-hut-Aten), in the form of two extended side-walls whose purpose is unknown.

The corner pillars of **barque stations** are not true antae: they only continue the row of pillars along one side and, like them, have a shaft and their own **capital**.

Bibliography: Prisse d'Avennes, *Histoire,* Plates 36–37; Davies, *El Amarna* VI, Plates 11–12; Jéquier, *Manuel,* 102–106.

Anta extending the architrave above a row of columns up to the sloping front of a pylon

Antaeopolis (Qaw el-Kebir)

The ruins of a formerly grand **limestone** temple of Ptolemy IV and Arsinoe, dedicated to Anty, measuring 45 x 60 m, lie within a large **brick** enclosure on the edge of the river, 45 km south of **Asyut**. Structures which have survived are the 4 m high **granite naos** from the sanctuary and the later **pronaos** of the temple, which consisted of three rows of six **columns** with palm capitals, together with their **architraves** and beams from the ceiling. Above the 18.6 m high façade was a dedicatory inscription in Greek of Ptolemy VI and Cleopatra. The temple was washed away between 1813 and 1821 by Nile floods, which in 1798 had already approached to within 15 m of it. The remaining stones were removed by Ibrahim Pasha for re-use in a palace at Asyut.

On the eastern edge of the desert near Qaw el-Kebir are the ruins of a brick temple (measuring 16.8 x 28 m) of the early New Kingdom, covering the remains of a brick temple, 20 m in length, of the First Intermediate Period, with an **altar** court and two sanctuary chambers beyond it.

Bibliography: *Description* IV 89, Plates 38–42; J. Gardner Wilkinson, *Topography of Thebes and General View of Egypt* (London 1835) 391.

Antinopolis (Antinoe)

The ruin of a Roman city near Sheikh Abada, opposite Ashmunein, founded by Hadrian in memory of Antinous, who drowned there. Considerable remains of parts of the city wall, including columned streets, a triumphal gateway, two temples, a theatre and a hippodrome to the east in the desert, were found by the Napoleonic Expedition. Almost nothing remains now. The meagre remains of a temple of Ramesses II with a columned courtyard, a **hypostyle hall** and a sanctuary survive to the west of the city.

Bibliography: *Description* IV, Plates 53–61; S. Donadoni, Antinooupolis, in: Helck, *LÄ* I 323–325; *Missione Archeologica in Egitto dell' Università di Roma, Antinoe (1965–1968)* (Rome 1974).

Ruins of a Roman portico at Antinopolis (after *Description* IV, Plate 55)

Anubieion (Saqqara)

An important Graeco-Roman temple precinct of Anubis, situated on the edge of the desert escarpment at **Saqqara** (north of the **Bubasteion**). It is enclosed by a **brick** wall measuring 250 x 250 m, which is crossed by the **causeway** of the **Serapeum,** with a great number of cult buildings on either side. In the south-west is an elevated platform occupied by the remains of the temple to Anubis. There are also some interesting subterranean structures consisting of chambers whose walls were decorated with figures of Bes modelled in clay. Other notable features are a dog cemetery, some administrative buildings and dwelling **houses**.

Bibliography: Auguste Mariette, *Le Serapéum de Memphis* (Paris 1882); H.S. Smith and D.G. Jeffreys, The Anubieion, North Saqqara, in: *JEA* 64 (1968) 10–21; 65 (1979) 17–29; 66 (1980) 17–27; 67 (1981) 21–23; D.G. Jeffreys and H.S. Smith, *The Anubieion at Saqqara. I. The Settlement and the Temple Precinct* (London 1990).

Apries, palace of

The vast **fortress palace** of Apries, measuring 110 x 136 m, is situated in the north-west corner of the city walls at **Memphis**. It follows the form of late fortress palaces in being on a platform, 13 m high, above a substructure built using **cellular construction**. It was paved with **limestone**, on top of which stood the actual structure, most of which is now lost. The entrance **gateway** was decorated with reliefs, based on Old Kingdom models, followed by an entrance hall, 8 x 35 m, with a double row of seven columns. These structures led into a central hall measuring 32 x 35 m, whose ceiling was supported on four rows of four palm **columns**, 13 m high. An open, pillared court to the north contained columns 15 m high.

Bibliography: W.M. Flinders Petrie, *The Palace of Apries (Memphis II)* (London 1909); B. Kemp, The Palace of Apries at Memphis, in: *MDAIK* 33 (1977) 101–108; W. Kaiser, Die dekorierte Torfassade des spätzeitlichen Palastbezirkes von Memphis, in: *MDAIK* 43 (1986) 123–144.

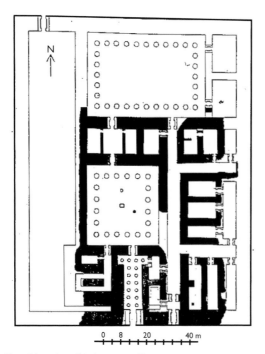

Plan of the palace of Apries at Memphis

Architect

Egyptian architects did not sign their buildings, so their activities can only be identified from their titles such as 'Royal Master Builder', 'Chief Royal Master of Building Works', 'Overseer of Constructions' and from their biographies, which recount their achievements. Several texts from the Old Kingdom appear to confirm that these 'masters', like the master builders in medieval building projects, were responsible for the technical execution and are identical with the architects who created the designs. Famous names among them were Imhotep (precinct of **Djoser**), **Nefermaat** and **Hemiunu** (responsible for the pyramids from Sneferu to (possibly) **Khufu**); five generations of the family of Senedjemib Inti (Mehi, Khnumenti, Nekhebu and Impy, after Inti himself) constructed pyramids from **Djedkare** to **Pepy II**; other architects included **Ineni** (responsible for obelisks and the tomb of Thutmosis I), **Senenmut** (who may have built the temple of **Hatshepsut**), Hepusoneb (architect of the tomb of Hatshepsut), **Amenhotep**, son of Hapu (responsible for the **colossi of Memnon**, and building works at **Karnak**), Amenemone (architect of the **Ramesseum**) and Hatey (who built the **hypostyle hall** at Karnak).

Bibliography: G.A. Reisner, in: *ASAE* 13 (1913) 248–249; Junker, *Giza* I 149–153; F.W. von Bissing, Baumeister und Bauten aus dem Beginn des Neuen Reiches, in: *Studi in memoria di Ippolito Rosellini* (Pisa 1949) 127–234; H. Kees, Eine Familie königlicher Maurermeister aus dem Anfang der 6. Dynastie, in: *WZKM* 54 (1957) 91–100; W. Helck, Bauleiter, in: Helck, *LÄ* I 654–655; Rosemarie Drenkhahn, *Die Handwerker und ihre Tätigkeiten im alten Ägypten*, Ägyptolog. Abh. 31 (Wiesbaden 1976) 89–94; R. Stadelmann, Die hntjw-s, der Königsbezirk s n pr'3 und die Namen der Grabanlagen der Frühzeit, in: *BIFAO* 81 Suppl (1981) 158; N. Strudwick, *The Administration of Egypt in the Old Kingdom* (London 1985) 217–250.

Architectural ceramics (inlaid tiles)

Made of bluish green or brightly coloured faience, and varying from simple tiles to figured motifs, ceramics were of great decorative value in architecture. In tombs, from as early as the 1st Dynasty royal tombs at **Abydos**, green tiles are used to imitate wall hangings of **matting**. The faience tiles that cover complete walls in the 'blue chambers' of the main tomb and the South Tomb at the precinct of **Djoser** are particularly beautiful. They were meant to represent a **palace** of the afterlife made of reed matting and were fixed using a complicated system.

In New Kingdom temples and palaces (for example at **Amarna**, **Malqata**, **Medinet Habu**, **Merenptah**, **Qantir** and **Tell el-Yahudiya**) wood and stone elements, such as door frames, **columns**, **cavetto cornices** and throne pedestals, were decorated with brightly coloured inlays set into a cell-like series of recesses in the surface. There was occasionally a pattern of inlaid rectangles within the decorative bands on **bases** in New Kingdom temples.

Bibliography: W.M. Flinders Petrie, *Tell el Amarna* (London 1894) 9–10; Richard Borrmann, Die Keramik in der Baukunst, in: *Handbuch der Architektur* 14 (Stuttgart 1897); Cecil M. Firth and J.E. Quibell, *The Step Pyramid* (Cairo 1935), Frontispiece, Plates 13–17, 38–45; William C. Hayes, *Glazed Tiles from a Palace of Ramesses II at Kantir* (New York 1937); J.-Ph. Lauer, Restauration et transfer au Musée Égyptien d'un panneau orné de faiences bleues, in: *ASAE* 38 (1938) 551–565; Hölscher, *Medinet Habu* IV 38–46; Lauer, *Histoire monumentale* 76–82; Lucas, *AEMI* 156–164; F.D. Friedman, Gifts of the Nile, Exhibition Catalogue (Cleveland 1998) 180–181, 188–190, 194–197, Plates 72–73, 80, 86–88, 92–93. Also useful: Susan Tunick, *Terracotta Skyline: New York's Architectural Ornament* (New York 1997).

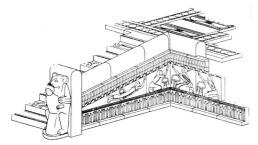

Reconstruction of a throne base of Ramesses II at Qantir, decorated with faience tiles (after W.C. Hayes)

Architectural decoration

Decorations on Egyptian cult buildings were not intended as ornaments, their purpose being to indicate function (**symbolism**): **niching** in **mastabas**, papyrus bundles, **statue pillars**, **water spouts** in the shape of lion protomes, statue groups showing the king slaying his enemies (?) on the **High Gate** of **Medinet Habu**, the meandering snake's body on the **balustrades** of the ramps of the temple of **Hatshepsut**, the frieze of baboons above the great temple of **Abu Simbel**, **friezes of uraei**, heraldic plants and walls inlaid with green faience tiles in the precinct of **Djoser** (**architectural ceramics**), **cavetto cornices** and torus mouldings on temples from the 3rd Dynasty onwards). The different forms of **column** also frequently bear some meaning. Purely structural decoration as such exists at best in the **metal overlays** on doors and **obelisks** or in the cloisonné faience inlays on doors and columns of **palaces** and **temples** of the Ramesside period. Fully or three-quarter engaged sculpture, similar to the figures on Greek temple pediments, such as acroteria and so on, are unknown in Egyptian architecture.

Bibliography: U. Hölscher, Gessodekorationen, Intarsien und Kachelbekleidungen in Medinet Habu, in: *ZÄS* 76 (1940) 41–45; U. Hölscher, *Medinet Habu* IV, Figs. 51–54; Arnold, Bauschmuck, in: Helck, *LÄ* I 663–664.

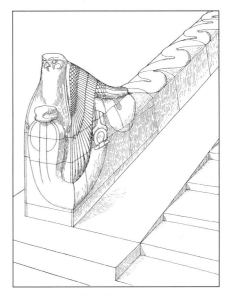

Apotropaic snake and falcon decoration on the upper ramp of the Hatshepsut temple at Deir el-Bahari (after L.F. Hall)

Architectural depictions

Representations of buildings are numerous (as in hieroglyphs or standardised images), including true architectural depictions of sanctuaries and dwelling houses found on the walls of **temples** and **tombs** (for example at **Amarna** and at **Thebes**), as well as in workmen's drawings with measurements found on papyri and ostraka. Following the principles of all Egyptian art, plans and elements of the side-view (such as gates, **columns** and **stairs**) were combined, all appearing as if flattened out and standing upright. The resulting irregularities can often only be understood if the plan of the building concerned is known.

Bibliography: Heinrich Schäfer, *Von ägyptischer Kunst* (Leipzig 1930) 128–139; Badawy, *Dessin architecturale*; Alexandre Badawy, Architekturdarstellung, in: Helck, *LÄ* I 399–420.

Architectural symbolism, *see* symbolism

Architrave

Architraves are used to join together groups of **columns** and **pillars**, and to support the roof of a building. They are usually connected to each other using dowels (**cramps**) or to the **abacus** of the column beneath by tenons. Where there was a change of direction, or where three architraves met on top of a single column, interesting angles had to be used. In order to simplify work, large architraves were sometimes made of two parallel beams. Beams were also sometimes placed on top of each other, but this was structurally less sound. In order to reduce their weight, the architraves in the pyramids of **Senwosret III** and **Amenemhat III** at Dahshur were hollowed out. The length of architraves, and their loading tolerance, depended on their material. As in structures with a flat roof (**ceiling construction**), the width of axes spanned by architraves was limited to 7 m and the space between the columns was restricted to 4–5 m. The sides and undersides of architraves were often decorated with bands of texts.

Bibliography: Jéquier, *Manuel* 277–287; Clark, *AEM* 151–154; Arnold, Architrav, in: Helck, *LÄ* I 420–422; J. Karkowski, The Arrangement of the Architraves in the Hatshepsut's Temple at Deir el Bahari, in: *ET* 13 (1983) 139–153.

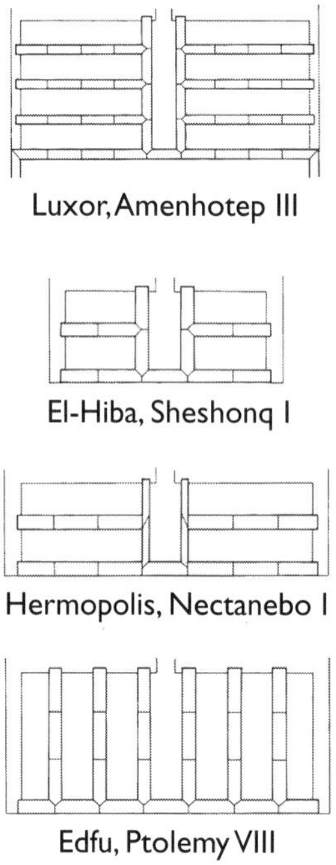
Luxor, Amenhotep III
El-Hiba, Sheshonq I
Hermopolis, Nectanebo I
Edfu, Ptolemy VIII

Development of orientation of architraves in pronaoi

Argo, *see* Tabo

Armant

An area of ruins at Hermonthis, a short way to the south of Thebes, containing the ruins of several cult buildings. Parts of a **pylon** of Thutmosis III, 47 m wide, have been excavated. These are part of the main temple of Month-Re and his companion Rait-tawy, which faces south-east, and they contain a depiction of goods brought back from Africa, as well as mentioning the killing of a rhinoceros. Behind the pylon was the courtyard of the temple whose foundations were found to contain numerous re-used older blocks of stone. 82 m behind the front of the temple lie some **granite** blocks from the temple's core, which was built in the reign of Senwosret III. There was perhaps also a new building of the late Ptolemaic period with a monumental hall of columns added by Hadrian. North-west of the temple lies a **sacred lake**, and the south-west facing late Ptolemaic **birth house,** which was decorated by Cleopatra VII and Caesarion and dedicated to Rait-tawy and her son Harpre. A central building, including the sanctuary, originally surrounded on all sides by **pillared halls**, was later extended to a length of 46 m and raised in height to 16.35 m by the addition of two **kiosks** of pillars rising in steps at the front. In 1861–62 these buildings were removed for the construction of a sugar factory.

Bibliography: *Description* I, Plates 91–93; Sir Robert Mond, *Temples of Armant, Text and Plates* (London 1940); *L'Égypte restituée* 143–144; A. Eggebrecht, Armant, in: *LÄ* I 435–441; Dieter Arnold, Zum Geburtshaus von Armant, in: *Stationen*, Beiträge zur Kulturgeschichte Ägyptens (Mainz 1998) 427–432.

Askut

A large (77 x 87 m) **fortress** of the Middle Kingdom on an island in the Nile at the Second Cataract. Due to the rocky terrain of the island its plan is rather irregular. The walls are 5.3 m thick with bastions protruding like spurs. A vast gatehouse in front protects a temple and storage rooms at the harbour. Inside the fortress are the commander's house, barracks and huge magazines.

Bibliography: Badawy, *Architecture* II 219–222; Alexander Badawy, Archaeological problems relating to the Egyptian fortress at Askut, in: *JARCE* 5 (1966) 23–27; H. Guksch, Askut, in: Helck, *LÄ* I 473; S.T. Smith, Askut and the role of the Second Cataract Forts, in: *JARCE* 28 (1991) 107–132.

Aswan, necropolis of Qubbet el-Hawa

Opposite Aswan, on the hill known as Qubbet el-Hawa, are the **rock tombs** of the ruling class of the first nome of Upper Egypt. The most interesting in terms of their architectural significance are the 17 Old Kingdom monuments, including the double tomb of Sabni and Mehu (Nos 25, 26), provided with monumental rock stairs leading up from the river bank and **obelisk**-like **stelae** at the entrance. Within the rock are two transverse halls, partitioned by two rows of pillars or three rows of columns lying across the axis of the tomb. Stairs in the west wall lead to a chapel-like niche containing the main **false door**.

Among the tombs of the 12th Dynasty are the splendid complexes of Sarenput I and II and Heqaib (Nos 30–32). These have stairways leading up to them from the Nile and a courtyard cut into the **sandstone**, with a portico at the rear. Inside the rock is a pillared hall and a pillared cult chamber, separated by a long corridor, in which, in the case of Sarenput II, are two groups of niches with mummiform statues cut in the wall. The rising floor level and the gradually reducing level of the ceiling reflect the light into the statue niche of the cult chamber.

Bibliography: Hans-Wolfgang Müller, *Die Felsengräber der Fürsten von Elephantine aus der Zeit des Mittleren Reiches* (Glückstadt 1940); L. Habachi, Assuan, in: Helck, *LÄ* I 495–496; K. Lange and M. Hirmer, *Egypt* (New York 1961), Plates 99–101.

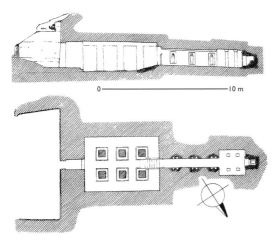

Plan and section of the tomb of Sarenput II, necropolis of Qubbet el-Hawa, Aswan (after H.-W. Müller)

Aswan, temple

An almost completely preserved temple to Isis built by Ptolemy III, which lies buried in debris on the southern fringe of the present city. It contains an offering chamber with two pillars, and three parallel sanctuaries. A small temple of Domitian and Nerva, with a four-pillared **pronaos**, probably dedicated to Khnum, Satis and Anuket, has disappeared completely under a rubbish dump.

Bibliography: A. Mariette, *Monuments divers*, Plate 22; Edda Bresciani, *Il tempio tolemaico di Isi* (Pisa 1978); H. Jaritz, Untersuchungen zum 'Tempel des Domitian' in Assuan, in: *MDAIK* 31 (1975) 237–257.

Asyut

One of the largest and most important, yet least adequately explored, necropoleis of **rock tombs** of the First Intermediate Period and the Middle Kingdom in Middle Egypt. The first and only time a structural examination was carried out at the site was by the Napoleonic Expedition. There are two particularly important groups of tombs:

a) Nos 3–5, the tombs of the provincial rulers of the First Intermediate Period, which are distinguished by their vast rock halls, up to 18 x 30 m. Like the tombs of **Beni Hasan** of a similar date, they were divided into front and rear sections by rows of pillars.

b) The tombs of the provincial rulers of the 12th Dynasty, Hapdjefai I and III, which are laid out like **rock temples**, up to more than 50 m in length. As with the tombs of the nomarchs at **Qaw el-Kebir**, these **temple tombs** consisted of a forecourt with a portico of columns or pillars, an antechamber (possibly with pillars), a longitudinal hall 7 m high (perhaps corresponding to the **Per-weru**), a rock chamber (without supports, at least 16.6 x 20.9 m in size) and a room for funerary offerings with three statue chapels. The elaborately twisting complexes of chambers below remain almost completely unexplored, while these once lavishly decorated tombs are now almost completely ruined. The **valley temples** and **causeways** survive only in inscriptions. All that remains of the Wepwawet temple of the ancient city, attested from the First Intermediate Period onwards, are a few stone blocks of Akhenaten and Ramesses II.

Bibliography: *Description* IV, Plates 43–49, Vol. 4 (Paris 1822) 133ff.; S. Gabra, Un temple d'Aménophis IV à Assiout, in: *CdE* 6 (1931) 237–243; W.St. Smith, *MDAIK* 15 (1957) 221ff.; H. Beinlich, Assiut, in: Helck, *LÄ* I 489–495.

Aten precinct (Karnak)

Before the move to Amarna in year 6 of his reign, Amenhotep IV began work at the temple of Aten at **Karnak**. Using the new name of Akhenaten, he erected the Gem-pa-Aten sanctuary as well as a residential **palace** to the east of the **Amun** precinct. The east-facing complex, measuring 130 x 200 (?) m, consisted of a court, probably divided by cross-walls and surrounded by halls with 5 m high **statue pillars**, which represented the king as a type of primordial hermaphrodite creator god. Inscriptions record the existence of other cult areas dedicated to the Aten: Rudj-menu en Aten, Teni-menu and also the **benben** house, the last of which stood possibly further to the east at the centre of the court (still unexcavated at present). The *benben* house probably contained a number of pillars, 9.5 m high, depicting Queen Nefertiti below the rays of the Aten. The architectural context of this colonnade remains unknown because the Aten precinct was demolished by Horemheb and his successors, in whose own buildings tens of thousands of re-used *talatat* blocks have been found.

Bibliography: D.B. Redford, Reconstructing the temples of a heretical Pharaoh, in: *Archaeology* 28 (1975) 16–22; Ray W. Smith and Donald B. Redford, *The Akhenaten Temple Project* I (Warminster 1976), II (Toronto 1988); D.B. Redford, Report of the First Seasons of Excavation in East Karnak, 1975–76, in: *JARCE* 14 (1977) 9–32; D.B. Redford, Interim Report on the Excavations of East-Karnak, 1977–78, in: *JARCE* 18 (1981) 11–41; D.B. Redford, Interim Report on the Excavations of East-Karnak, 1981–1982 Seasons, in: *JSSEA* 13 (1983) 203–224; D.B. Redford, *Akhenaten, The Heretic King* (Princeton 1984) 86–136; *L'Égypte restituée* 121–124; J.-L. Chappaz, Un nouvel assemblage de talâtât: une paroi du rwd-mnw d'Aton, in: *Karnak* VIII 81–119 (with further references).

Aten, temples

The temples to the Aten, erected by Akhenaten at **Karnak** (**Aten** precinct), **Amarna** and possibly **Heliopolis**, were originally built of **brick** and later gradually replaced by stone structures (*talatat*). Construction work ceased on the death of Akhenaten, and the Aten temples were without exception demolished in the reigns of Horemheb to Ramesses II. Their shape, however, can be determined on the evidence of foundation trenches, depictions in the tombs at Amarna and the evidence of the *talatat*. While **enclosure walls** and **pylons** with **flagpoles** make them seem externally similar to conventional temples, there are significant differences:

a) The towers of the **pylons** are separate buildings, intended to be gateways of the sun, and are not joined by a doorway structure.

b) Interior rooms stand open to the sky, like courtyards; the centre of colonnaded courts was also unroofed and there were gaps in the lintels. All of these were intended to prevent interruption to the path of the sun's rays.

c) The rear parts of temples contained a **hypaetral** sanctuary, surrounded by chapels, with an accessible monumental **altar** in the centre. The front courtyards were filled with numerous smaller altars.

d) The decorative programme was completely restructured as a result of the theological changes of the period.

Bibliography: Badawy, *Architecture* II 200–214; J. Assmann, Atonheiligtümer, in: Helck, *LÄ* I 541–549.

Athribis (Tell-Atrib)

An important *kom* (mound of ruins; 700 x 900 m) in the southern corner of the Delta, with the sanctuary of Khentekhtai. Streets dating from Roman times intersect each other at a central crossing point. The site is occupied by many individual monuments, removed from their place of origin (**naoi**, sculptures, collections of silver). A former **brick** pyramid has disappeared, but there are remnants of a temple of Amasis (area 20 x 50 m), some Roman structures and components of other buildings.

Bibliography: A. Rowe, Short report on excavations…at Athribis, in: *ASAE* 38 (1938) 523–532; K. Michalowski, Les fouilles polonaises à Tell Atrib, in: *ASAE* 57 (1962) 49–77; B. Ruscczyc, Le temple d'Amasis à Tell-Atrib, in: *Études et Travaux* 9 (1976) 117–127; P. Vernus, Athribis, in: Helck, *LÄ* I 519–524; L. Habachi, Athribis in the XXVIth Dynasty, in: *BIFAO* 82 (1982) 213–235; K. Myslewiec, Polish archaeological activities at Tell Atrib in 1985, in: *The Archaeology of the Nile Delta* (Amsterdam 1988) 177–189; K. Myslewiec, Excavations at Tell Atrib in 1985, in: *Études et Travaux* 16 (1992) 383–391.

Athribis (Wannina)

A temple precinct of the lion goddess Triphis, to the south of Sohag. A processional way leads to the remains of a monumental **gateway** of Ptolemy VIII Euergetes II; the meagre remains of the main temple, built by Ptolemy VIII, are set against the slope of the hill behind it. Next to this stands the older **granite** temple of Apries. The **birth house** built by Ptolemy XII Auletes lies across the axis of the precinct; the building, measuring 45 x 75 m, with a **pronaos** containing two rows of six pillars, has remained well-preserved by the sand. The rear section was possibly surrounded by a **pillared hall** or it may have stood in the middle of an open colonnaded court. On the side of the hill is a Graeco-Roman **rock temple** to Asklepios with a forecourt, two rock-cut chambers and a cult niche. There are some particularly interesting half-**columns** with palm **capitals** along its façade.

Bibliography: William Flinders Petrie, *Athribis* (London 1908); Borchardt, *Tempel mit Umgang*; R. el-Farag et al., Recent archaeological explorations at Athribis (Hwt Rpjj.t), in: *MDAIK* 41 (1985) 1–8.

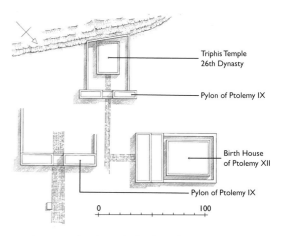

Temple precinct of Triphis at Athribis, dating from the Ptolemaic period

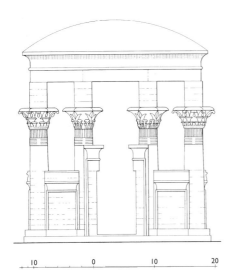

Kiosk of Augustus at Philae

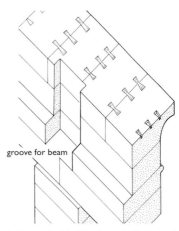

groove for beam

Cramp slots in the cornice blocks and grooves for beams in the upper courses of the kiosk of Augustus at Philae

Bibliography: *Description* I, Plates 26–28; Borchardt, *Tempel mit Umgang* 13–14, sheets 5–6.

Augustus, kiosk of (Philae)

The largest free-standing **kiosk** in Egypt (ground area 15.4 x 20.7 m, height 15.45 m) with four by five **composite columns** with unfinished tympana (possibly to be decorated with sistra or Bes figures). Due to its wide span of more than 10 m, the kiosk was provided with a **roof** consisting of two thin skins of timber. The building served as a **barque station** for Isis and the gods of Philae. The kiosk was probably built under Augustus, but the decoration, begun in the reign of Trajan, remained unfinished.

Avenue of sphinxes, *see* sphinxes, avenue of

Ayuala

Some blocks from a temple **gateway**, dating to early in the Roman Imperial age, were transported in 1911 from Ayuala (Lower **Nubia**) to **Elephantine**. The site of the temple to which they belonged has never been found.

Bibliography: H. Jaritz and E. Laskowska-Kusztal, Das Eingangstor zu einem Mandulisheiligtum in Ajuala/Unternubien, in: *MDAIK* 46 (1990) 157–184.

B

Baefba (Babaef, Khnumbaef), tomb of

One of the most important and best-preserved mastabas in the western cemetery at **Giza** (G 5230), 12.78 x 41.25 m in size, dating to the reign of Shepseskaf. The core and outer casing are built of monumental blocks of stone. In front, on the eastern side, is a courtyard with two *serdab* (Fig.) houses.

Bibliography: *LD* I 24; Junker, *Giza* VII 151–155; Reisner, *Giza* I 248–250; D. Arnold, Old Kingdom statues in their architectural setting, in: *Egyptian Art in the Age of the Pyramids,* exhibition catalogue (New York 1999) 47, Fig. 25.

Bahariya Oasis

An oasis 180 km west of the Nile valley which, on the evidence of rock drawings, was inhabited from prehistoric times. The oasis contains many remains of settlements and ruins of smallish temples dating from the 26th Dynasty up to the Roman period, which are under examination: **Ain el-Muftella**, El-Ayun, El-Bawiti (temple of Amasis), El-Qasr (temple of Apries), Qasr el-Megysbeh (temple of Alexander the Great). The important **rock tombs** of the 26th Dynasty necropolis at El-Bawati are richly decorated; their central rooms have rock pillars and columns. In 1996, at the southern end of the oasis, a Ptolemaic-Roman cemetery was found containing several communal tombs with a great number of mummies, some buried in well-preserved gilded coffins.

Bibliography: Ahmed Fakhry, Bahria and Farafra Oasis, in: *ASAE* 38 (1938) 397–434; 39 (1939) 627–642; 40 (1941) 823–836; Ahmed Fakhry, *Bahria Oasis,* 2 Vols (Cairo 1942, 1950); Ahmed Fakhry, *Oases of Egypt. II. Bahriyah and Farafra Oases* (Cairo 1974); Zahi Hawass, *Valley of the Golden Mummies* (New York 2000).

Bakenrenef, tomb of

Monumental **rock tomb** of one of the viziers of Psamtek I in the eastern desert escarpment at **Saqqara**. On the entrance level is a hall with four columns, a deep hall with eight pillars and a cult complex, similar to an **Osiris tomb**, completely surrounded by a corridor. The burial accommodation occupies two subterranean levels. This and the tomb of **Tjary** at **Giza** are good examples of rock tombs of the Late Period in Lower Egypt.

Bibliography: *LD* I 40; S. El-Naggar, Étude préliminaire du plan du tombeau du Bocchoris, in: *Egitto e Vicino Oriental* (1978) 41–56; Edda Bresciani et al., *Saqqara IV. La Tomba di Bakenrenef* (L.24) (Pisa 1988).

Balat

A settlement and necropolis of the Old Kingdom in Dakhla Oasis. The settlement (at **Ain Asil**) is 3 km east of Balat and, alongside **Elephantine** and **Hierakonpolis**, represents the best-preserved ruin of an Old Kingdom **town**. The rectangular area (measuring 110 x 230 m) is enclosed by a wall and there is a fortress-like structure adjacent to it in the south. There are important remains of **houses**, ceramic workshops and so on.

The necropolis (Qila' el-Dabba) is 2 km to the west and contains four large **brick mastabas** belonging to the late 6th Dynasty rulers of the oasis. They consist of a large brick enclosure surrounding a courtyard and a mastaba with a **niched** facade. Inside the mastabas are **multiple shrines**. The burial chambers have barrel **vaults** of brick.

Bibliography: Settlement: excavation reports by L.L. Giddy in *BIFAO* 79 (1979) 21–39; 80 (1980) 257–269; 81 (1981) 189–205, 93 (1993) 391–402; 97 (1997) 19–34. Necropolis: excavation reports by A. Minault-Gout, G. Castel and M. Valloggia in *BIFAO* 78 (1978) 35–80, 80 (1980) 271–286; 93 (1993) 391–402; 95 (1995) 297–328; Michel Valloggia, *Balat. I. Le mastaba de Medou-nefer* (Cairo 1986); Anne Minault-Gout, *Balat. II. Le mastaba d'Ima-Pepi* (Cairo 1992); M. Zimmermann, Bemerkungen zu den Befestigungen des Alten Reiches in Ayn Asil und in Elephantine, in: *MDAIK* 54 (1998) 341–359.

Baldachin, *see* canopy

Ballas (Deir el-Ballas)

The remains of a royal settlement with two **palaces** of the early 18th Dynasty on the West Bank of the Nile between Qena and Luxor. Standing inside a 156 x 303 m enclosure and forming the nucleus of that settlement is the North Palace with a central residential tower, built on several storeys, surrounded by **pillared halls**. The South Palace (measuring 45 x 100 m) is outside the enclosure to the south on a desert elevation. It has a pillared court at a lower level facing the valley, from where a wide **brick** stairway (**stairs**) led up to the actual living quarters, now lost. A few fragments of figured wall paintings have survived. Numerous domestic structures of the period are located between the two palaces.

Bibliography: W. Stevenson Smith, *The Art and Architecture of Ancient Egypt* (London 1958) 156–159; A. Eggebrecht, Deir el-Ballas, in: Helck, *LÄ* I 1025–1027; Peter Lacovara, The Hearst excavations at Deir el-Ballas: the eighteenth dynasty town, in: *Essays in Honor of Dows Dunham* (Boston 1981); Peter Lacovara, *Deir el-Ballas. Preliminary Report on the Deir el-Ballas Expedition, 1980–1986* (Winona Lake, Indiana 1990); Peter Lacovara, Deir el-Ballas and New Kingdom royal cities, in: *House and Palace* 139–147; P. Lacovara, *The New Kingdom Royal City* (New York 1997) 81–87.

Balustrade

Stone walls flanking **stairways**, ramps and high **altars**, also found as inter-columnar screens in pillared chapels. A balustrade at the temple of **Hatshepsut** is in the shape of a serpent crowned with a falcon (a combination of Wadjet and Horus). Balustrades occur particularly frequently in buildings of the Amarna period, profusely decorated in relief.

Bibliography: I. Shaw, Balustrades, stairs and altars in the cult of the Aten at El-Amarna, in: *JEA* 80 (1994) 109–127. For Hatshepsut, see H.E. Winlock, *Excavations at Deir el Bahari* (New York 1942) 220.

Barque chamber

An elongated rectangular shrine, room or hall, lying in front of the **naos** on the processional axis of a temple. As shown in the decorative programme of depictions of the divine barque, the chamber usually contained a stone base on which the barque was placed. For unknown reasons, the barque chamber was sometimes divided in two. It usually opened directly into the offering chamber.

It was originally a wooden structure (**canopy**), which was recreated in stone in larger temples and, unlike the monolithic **naos**, was constructed out of masonry (for example the **Chapelle Rouge**, the barque chambers of Philip Arrhidaeus at **Karnak**, of Alexander the Great at **Luxor**, in the temple of **Sety I** at Abydos, at **Edfu** and at **Dendera**). In Ptolemaic temples, barque chambers were free-standing, surrounded by a U-shaped corridor. Larger temples have more than one barque chamber.

Bibliography: D. Arnold, Barkenraum, in: Helck, *LÄ* I 625–626; Mahmud Abd El-Raziq, *Die Darstellungen und Texte des Sanktuares Alexanders des Großen im Tempel von Luxor* (Mainz 1984); G. Legrain, Le logement et transport des barques sacrées et des statues des dieux dans quelques temples égyptiens, in: *BIFAO* 13 (1917) 1–76; Sylvie Cauville, *Edfou* (Cairo 1984) 32–39; Sylvie Cauville, *Dendera* (Cairo 1990) 44–47; Sylvie Cauville, La chapelle de la barque à Dendera, in: *BIFAO* 93 (1993) 79–172.

Barque station, way station

A resting place for the god's barque during processions either inside or outside the temple enclosure walls. In theory, it sufficed to be a **canopy** or tent-like shelter, but these structures were usually enlarged into a small stone **kiosk**. The first way station on the route of the divine barque is usually the **hypostyle hall** of the temple, which was hence known as the hall of appearances (of the cult image). The raised central nave in particular could serve as a columned **kiosk** set within a hall composed of halls of lower columns (examples: the hypostyle hall at **Karnak** and the West Hall of the **Ptah** temple at Memphis).

The second barque station often takes the form of a **kiosk** within the courtyard of the temple. In contrast to the barque station in the hall of appearances, these subsequent barque stations were, according to Egyptian beliefs, set in a potentially hostile environment and hence the inter-columnar spaces were filled with walls. The next barque station is again a kiosk, which, particularly in the Ethiopian period, was erected in front of the **pylon** with its rear wall leaning against the pylon's façade (*hayit*). The outer columns are either joined by half-height screens with passageways only on the axes, as for example at the Hibis temple (**El-Kharga**), or they consist of parallel rows of columns, open at the front and sides to form no more than a shady roof for cult activities. There are several examples of these entrance porches at Karnak and **Luxor**.

Further barque stations were built at greater distances from the temple, for example on a river bank (as at **Philae**). These more distant barque stations frequently took the form of **ambulatory temples**. The barque would be borne into the building up a ramp at the front and set down on a platform in a shrine surrounded by pillars. Barque stations had a particularly important role in the barque processions of the New Kingdom. The most elaborate form of the barque station is probably the **Maru temple**.

Bibliography: Borchardt, *Tempel mit Umgang* 56–105; Henri Chevrier, *Le temple reposoir de Ramsès III à Karnak* (Cairo 1933); Herbert Ricke, Das Kamutef-Heiligtum Hatschepsuts und Thutmoses' III, in: *Karnak* (Cairo 1954) 18–41; A.M. Badawy, The approach to the Egyptian temple, in: *ZÄS* 102 (1975) 79–90; R. Stadelmann, Stationsheiligtum, in: Helck, *LÄ* V 1258–1260; L. Bell, The New Kingdom 'divine' temple: the example of Luxor, in: Shafer, Ed., *Temples of Ancient Egypt* (Ithaca 1997) 157-178.

Basalt

A very hard blackish brown volcanic rock, used in Egyptian architecture, especially during the Old Kingdom. Its specific gravity is 2.9–3.0. It was used almost exclusively in **paving** in the **pyramid temples** of **Khufu**, **Sahure**, **Niuserre** (see also **orthostats**) and **Userkaf**, and in the temple of **Tanis**. It was occasionally used for sarcophagi and **naoi**. An ancient mine is at Gebel el-Qatrani in the Faiyum.

Bibliography: Nicholson, *Materials* 23-24; De Putter, *Pierres* 51–54; Klemm, *Steine* 413–422.

Base, *see also* column base, plinth

The bases of **columns** and **pillars** are circular, often in the shape of a cushion, or else flat with bevelled or vertical side-edges and with bevelled upper edges. **Obelisks** stand on tall rectangular **granite** bases. **Colossal statues** also sometimes sat on a separately worked base. The bases of **statue pillars** are usually part of the whole structure.

Bath

The existence of baths in the Old Kingdom is only attested to from inscriptions, but there are model baths in tombs from as early as the 2nd Dynasty (for example the tomb of Ruaben at **Saqqara**). Several cult baths have been found in the so-called 'palace' in the precinct of **Djoser**. From the Middle Kingdom, the bath becomes a regular feature in larger **houses**, while from the New

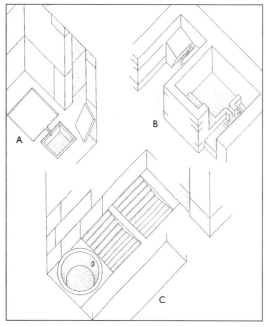

Egyptian baths. A: priestly bath in the pyramid temple of Senwosret I at El-Lisht; B: toilet and bath in a house at Amarna; C: priestly bath in the 'palace' of the Djoser precinct at Saqqara

Kingdom onwards bathrooms have been shown to have existed in houses and palaces. They often have a stone floor and (not always) a drain to the outside or to a cesspit, with walls clad in stone to half their height. They were usually separated from the toilet by a **screen wall**. Baths (*per-duat*) in the shape of rectangular basins with a drain to a cesspit allowed priests to cleanse themselves before entering the rooms of a temple. Numerous bath complexes of a Graeco-Roman type, fed by water lifting devices and tanks, have survived in the ruins of towns or are attested to in texts (such as at Abu Mena, **Alexandria**, towns of the Faiyum, and **Hermopolis**).

Bibliography: Lauer, *Step Pyramid*, Plate 25; A. el Khashab, Ptolemaic and Roman Baths of Kom el Ahmar, in: *ASAE* 10 Suppl. (Cairo 1949); Ricke, *Wohnhäuser*, Figs 7, 9, 11, 28; W. Decker, Bad, in: Helck, *LÄ* I 598–599; G. Castel, Un grand bain gréco-romain à Karanis, in: *BIFAO* 76 (1976) 231–275; Arnold, *The Pyramid of Senwosret* I 51, Fig. 16; S. Ziegler, Einige Bemerkungen zur Wasserversorgung antiker Badeanlagen in Ägypten, in: *GM* 132 (1993) 75–84.

Batter

The outer walls of Egyptian **stone** and mud **brick** structures are sloped, partly to provide balance, partly to relate back to earlier methods of building and partly to increase the monumental nature of structures. This is most noticeable in **mastaba** and **pyramid** construction. The batter in masonry structures is usually 82°, in queens' and **secondary pyramids** most often 63° and in the case of the pyramids of the kings of the Old Kingdom between 52 and 54°, which decreased gradually during the Middle Kingdom to between 49 and 52°. The angle is defined by the relationship of the horizontal offset to the vertical height per **cubit** (*seqed*). This was probably transferred onto the wall blocks by means of a wooden template. Checking was done by sighting along angled slopes on brick walls temporarily erected at the corners of the building concerned, such as at **Meidum mastaba 17**.

Bibliography: L. Borchardt, Wie wurden die Böschungen der Pyramiden bestimmt? *ZÄS* 31 (1893) 9–17; W.M. Flinders Petrie, *Medum* (London 1892) 12, Plate 8; J.-P. Lauer, *Observations sur les pyramides* (Cairo 1960) 93–97.

Battlements

From ancient Egyptian depictions, the top edge of the walls of **temples** and **fortresses** took the form of battlements from the Middle Kingdom (similarly with Canaanite fortresses). The remains of battlements have survived at **Nubian** fortresses (such as **Dorginarti**). The **High Gate** of **Medinet Habu** has decorative rounded stone battlements; the remains of semi-circular **limestone** battlements, decorated on the front, have been found on the temple of Onias at **Tell el-Yahudiya**. **Model houses** and depictions of private **houses** occasionally show the **roof** with an undulating edge, while **grain stores** had corners which curved upwards, reminiscent of battlements.

Bibliography: W.M. Flinders Petrie, *Hyksos and Israelite Cities* (London 1906) 26, Plate 26; Hölscher, *Mortuary Temple*, Vol. 2, 33 Figs 38–39, Plates 19–20.; Badawy, *Dessin architectural* 143–158; J. Knudstad, Serra East and Dorginarti, in: *Kush* 14 (1966), Plate 24a.

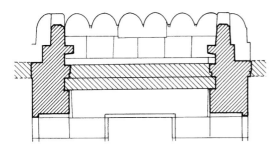

Battlements on top of the High Gate of Ramesses III at Medinet Habu

Behbeit el-Hagar, *see Iseum*

Beit el-Wali

A small **rock temple** near **Kalabsha**, 50 km south of Aswan, dating from the early years of the reign of Ramesses II and dedicated to Amun-Re, Re-Horakhty, the king, Khnum, and Anuket. The temple was fronted by a **pylon**. An entrance hall, corresponding to a courtyard, was set into the rock but, because the rock lacked height, it was given a **brick**-built barrel **vault**, 6 m wide and 7–8 m high, probably constructed of layers of rings supported against the rock wall behind. Behind lay an offering table room with two squat, polygonal **pillars**.

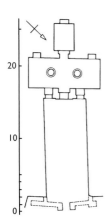

Plan of the rock temple of Beit el-Wali, from the time of Ramesses II

The sanctuary contained three rock-cut cult images, possibly of Amun, Ramesses II and Ptah. The delicacy of the reliefs, as well as the unusual plan of Beit el-Wali, differentiate this structure from the later temples of this king further south. The temple has been moved to the new site of the temple of Kalabsha near Aswan.

Bibliography: Gau, *Antiquités,* Plates 12–16; Prisse d'Avennes, *Histoire*, Plate 42; Günther Roeder, *Der Felsentempel von Bet el-Wali* (Cairo 1938); Herbert Ricke, George R. Hughes und Edward F. Wente, *The Bet el-Wali Temple of Ramesses II* (Chicago 1967); E. Otto, Beit el-Wali, in: Helck, *LÄ* I 686–687; Hein, *Ramessidische Bautätigkeit* 6–9.

Beit Khallaf

Five monumental mud **brick mastabas** of the 3rd Dynasty, north of **Abydos**. Like other **step mastabas** of the period, the core of the colossal mastaba, K1, of the reign of Djoser, area 45 x 85 m, height 8 + x m, is constructed of sloping mantles; it may have protruded above the substructure, which may have been **niched**. A ramp leads from the east to the roof, which was probably vaulted. From here a steep entrance stairway, sealed by blocking stones weighing tonnes, leads down to the burial chambers. The vaulted ceiling over the stairs is constructed of descending barrel vaults leaning against mud brick arches, the oldest known **vaults** in Egypt. The burial chambers are arranged after the manner of a multi-room dwelling **house** or **palace**, and they were filled with

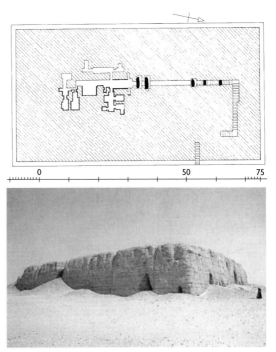

Plan and view of 3rd Dynasty mastaba 1 at Beit Khallaf

huge numbers of clay and stone vessels. Although K1 has been attributed to Horus Netjerykhet (King Djoser), and the smaller mastaba, K2, to Horus Zanakht, it seems more likely that both were private tombs of the period.

Bibliography: John Garstang, *Mahâsna and Bêt Khallâf* (London 1903); P. Kaplony, Beit Challaf, in: Helck, *LÄ* I 686.

Benben stone

A pillar-like monument, having an irregular conical shape, related to the cult of the sun. The original benben stone stood at **Heliopolis**, and it was later also found at other sun cult locations such as **Karnak** and **Amarna**. It is the developmental forerunner of the **obelisk**. No benben stone has been found.

Bibliography: H. Kees, Benben, in: Hans Bonnet, *Reallexikon der ägyptischen Religionsgeschichte* (Berlin 1952) 100–101; E. Otto, Benben und Benben-Haus, in: Helck, *LÄ* I 694–695; J. Baines, Bnbn: mythological and linguistic notes, in: *Orientalia* 39 (1970) 389–404.

Beni Hasan

A famous necropolis of **rock tombs**, 23 km south of Minya. Into the steep limestone cliffs on the East Bank of the Nile were cut 39 tombs of the ruling class of the 16th Upper Egyptian Province, with important wall paintings and architectural features. There are two main groups:

a) An early group, which comprises six tombs with inscriptions from the First Intermediate Period and the 11th Dynasty. The tombs of Baket III (No. 15), Khety (No. 17) and tomb No. 18 are architecturally interesting. Behind a plain façade lies a cult chamber, shaped like a deep rectangular hall, with its rear section separated by four rows of columns standing across the axis, giving the impression of the façade of a house in the middle of a subterranean court.

b) A later group, belonging to the 12th Dynasty, predominantly the tombs of the nomarchs Amenemhat (No. 2) and Khnumhotep III (No. 3). The motif of the

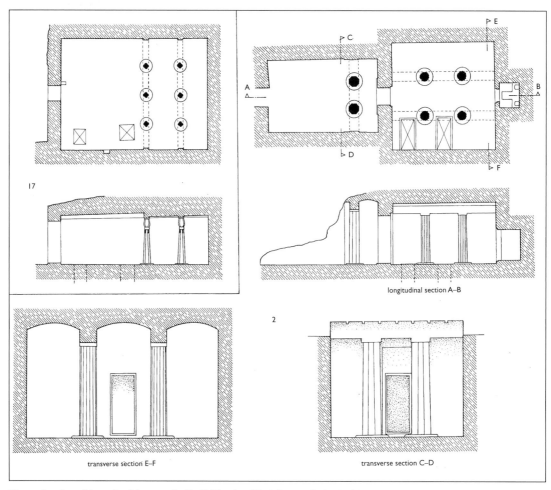

Plans and sections of the tombs of the nomarchs, No. 17 (Khety) and No. 2 (Amenemhat) at Beni Hasan

View into the cult chamber of the tomb of Khety, No. 17 at Beni Hasan

house façade has been moved from inside the hill to the exterior in the form of a portico, with two octagonal or channelled **pillars** (**protodoric columns**). The deep rectangular cult chamber is intended to suggest the interior of a house with a columned hall. The ceiling is formed of three lengthways barrel **vaults** cut into the rock in the direction of the axis and supported on four **channelled columns** decorated with carpet patterns. At the centre of the rear wall is a statue niche. The closed-lotus **columns** in Nos 17 and 18 are an important feature

taken over from residential buildings and translated into stone.

Bibliography: Percy E. Newberry, *Beni Hasan*, 4 Vols (London 1893–1900); F. Junge, Beni Hassan, in: Helck, *LÄ* I 695–698; W. Schenkel, Chnumhotep I.-IV., in: Helck, *LÄ* I 954–956; Abdel Ghaffar Shedid, *Die Felsgräber von Beni Hassan* (Mainz 1994).

Bent Pyramid

The southern, stone pyramid at **Dahshur**, named 'Appearance of Sneferu', was the first planned as a true pyramid. Its construction, which began around the 12–13th year of Sneferu's reign, has a tangled history. It was planned to have an original base length of 157.5 m, an angle of slope around 58–60° and a height of 137.5 m. Damage caused in the course of construction necessitated the addition of a 15.75 m deep stone coating around the lower section of the pyramid (resulting in a new base length of 187 m) while, due to internal damage, the slope at a height of 49 m had to be reduced to 54°31'13" and the overall height was lowered to 104–5 m.

The Bent Pyramid is provided with two complexes of chambers, accessible from the north and the west, which were separately constructed, being planned this way from the start. They were later joined by a roughly cut connecting passage. The northern complex consists of an

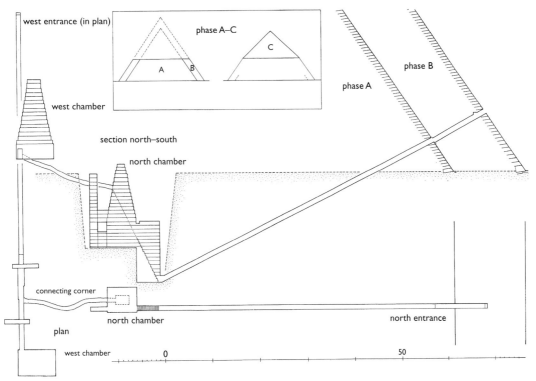

Plan and section of the interior chambers of the Bent Pyramid of Snefru at Dahshur, showing construction phases A–C

antechamber with a **corbelled vault** connecting to the main chamber 6.5 m higher up, which has a corbelled vault 17.5 m high. In its southern wall is a chimney-like **canopic recess** (**corbelled vault**, Fig.). From the western entrance, situated 33 m up, a steep corridor leads straight to a chamber with a corbelled vault 16.5 m high. Due to damage during its construction, its walls had to be reinforced with 16 beams of cedar wood. The **secondary pyramid** to the south, 26 m high, may have been erected to include a chamber, reminiscent of the **South Tomb** at the precinct of **Djoser**. Two **stelae** bearing the name of Sneferu stand on the north side of the secondary pyramid.

In front of the east side of the Bent Pyramid there is a cult area (**pyramid temple**, Fig.) flanked by two inscribed stelae, 9 m high. Halfway between the pyramid and the cultivation, at the bottom of the **causeway**, is a temple, 26.2 x 47.2 m, with six chapels for statues. A **valley temple** could have existed further to the east.

Bibliography: A. Fakhry, The southern pyramid of Snefru, in: *ASAE* 51 (1951) 509–522; H. Mustapha, The surveying of the Bent Pyramid at Dahshur, in: *ASAE* 52 (1952) 595–601; H. Ricke, Baugeschichtlicher Vorbericht über die Kultanlagen der südlichen Pyramide des Snofru in Dahschur, *ASAE* 52 (1952), 603–623; Ahmed Fakhry, *The Monuments of Sneferu at Dahshur*, 3 Vols (Cairo 1959–61); *MRA* III 98–101; R. Stadelmann, *Pyramiden* 87–100; R, Stadelmann, in: *MDAIK* 47 (1991) 380–381; J. Dorner, Form und Ausmaße der Knickpyramide, in: *MDAIK* 42 (1986) 81–92.

Biahmu

A double sanctuary of Amenemhat III, 7 km north of **Medinet el-Faiyum**, with two cult courts surrounded by a sloping stone wall (area 34 x 39 m). In each court was a **quartzite** seated statue of the king, 11 m high, set on a 6.4 m high **base**. The sanctuary appears to have been erected on a dam created by Amenemhat III on the bank of the former Lake Faiyum. The statues did not merely

Reconstruction of the statue temple of Amenemhat III at Biahmu

commemorate the agricultural development of the Faiyum; they were living images of the king and recipients of a cult in which Amenemhat III probably was worshipped as a creator and fertility god.

Bibliography: Herodotos, *History* II 149; W. M. Flinders *Petrie, Hawara, Biahmu and Arsinoe* (London 1889); L. Habachi, The monument of Biahmu, in: *ASAE* 40 (1941) 721–739; A. Eggebrecht, Biahmu, in: Helck, *LÄ* I 782–783.

Birket Habu

The harbour basin and 'pleasure lake' in front of Amenhotep III's **palace** city of **Malqata** (**Thebes**). The creation of the 1 x 2.4 km artificial lake and its opening to the Nile produced 11 million cu m of excavated earth, which was piled in a double chain of hills along its banks.

Bibliography: D. O'Connor, The Univ. Mus. excavations at Malkata. A palace and harbor of Amenhotep III, in: *Newsletter ARCE* 83 (1972) 30; B. Kemp and D. O'Connor, An ancient Nile harbour, in: *Intern. Journ. of Nautical Arch. and Underwater Exploration* 3 (1974) 101–136.

Birth house

A birth house (Coptic, *mammisi*, Eg. *per-meset*) usually consists of a sanctuary with several rooms and a pillared corridor around the four sides (**ambulatory temple**); the spaces between the pillars are protected by intercolumnar walls (**screen wall**). The roof is supported on floral columns. *Mammisi* stand inside a surrounding temple **enclosure wall**, usually at right angles to the processional avenue which leads to the main temple. Birth houses started as way stations or processional stations entered by the procession of gods performing the mysteries attendant on the birth of the divine child. *Mammisi* are also dedicated to the king in his youth, his birth being celebrated as a kind of renewal of the reign. The origin of this type of building probably lies in prehistoric structures, consisting of a protective roof of **timber** and **mats** used in early times over 'summer houses'. *Mammisi* became particularly prominent in Egyptian architecture from the Late Period until Roman times. Precursors in the Ramesside period and earlier phases are suggested by the decorative programmes of older temples, showing the divine marriage, birth and suckling of the young god. Examples exist at **Philae**, **Kom Ombo**, **Edfu**, **El-Kab**, **Armant**, the **Mut** precinct (Karnak), **Dendera** and **Athribis**.

Bibliography: A. Badawy, The architectural symbolism of the mammisi-chapels in Egypt, in: *CdE* 38 (1933) 78–90; Ludwig Borchardt, *Ägyptische Tempel mit Umgang* (Cairo 1938) 3–12; François Daumas, *Les mammisis des temples égyptiens* (Paris 1958); François Daumas, Geburtshaus, in: Helck, *LÄ* II 462–475.

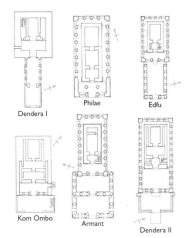

Examples of plans of temple birth houses

Block connection, *see* cramps

Bosses

Bossed stones are blocks whose surface has been left completely or partly unfinished. This feature is not a decorative element in Egyptian architecture, but is instead an indication that the smoothing process has not been completed. Stone buildings in Egypt were erected

Bossed masonry at the first pylon and the barque station of Sety II at Karnak

using blocks transported in bossed condition and only finished at the end of construction by being worked on step by step (for example the **granite** dressing on the pyramid of **Menkaure**, the 'ring bands' on the pyramid at **Meidum**, columns in the first courtyard of **Karnak**, **cavetto cornices** and torus mouldings, winged sun discs, the capitals of some columns at **Philae**, **Deir el-Shelwit**). The method is the cause of the **joints** occurring close to, but not directly in, an inside corner. Less common are the examples of a simple form of edge protection: that is, the blocks already have a smoothed surface but with thickened edges. Graeco-Roman buildings constructed in the Egyptian style adopted the concept of rough surfaces known in Hellenistic architecture as a decorative element, for instance at the south temple of **Karanis**. Other bosses, serving as points for fitting ropes and **levers**, were used for lifting and transporting.

Bibliography: Boak, *Karanis* II, Plates 26–27, 29; Jaritz, *Terrassen*, Plates 2–3, 27, 38; Arnold, *Building* 132–141; Zivie, *Deir Chelouit*, Plates 48–50.

Brick

Egyptian bricks consist of a mixture of brown- or blackish-grey Nile mud, sand, plant fibres or small stones and fragments of brick (adobe). Occasionally yellowish bricks are found with a strong admixture of clay (**tafl**). Bricks were struck using a box-shaped wooden mould (originals have survived), marked with **brick marks** and left to dry in the air. In addition to the normal bricks for walls, there were also special moulded bricks (**bricks, moulded**). The specific gravity of bricks is estimated to be 1250–1650 kg/cu m, the average brick weighing 5 kg.

Fired bricks are rare in pharaonic architecture (**brick construction**). Bricks are usually laid on a base of Nile mud or dry sand. The use of mortar is uncommon.

Bibliography: Spencer, *Brick Architecture* 140–141; J. Krejcí, Eine Lehmziegelwerkstatt aus dem Alten Reich in Abusir, in: *GM* 148 (1995) 63–69; Nicholson and Shaw, *Materials* 78–88; A. Hesse, Essai techno-chronologique sur la dimension des briques de construction, in: J. Vercoutter, *Mirgissa I* (Paris 1970) 102–114.

Brick bonding, *see* brick construction

Brick construction

Building in **brick** developed in pre-historic times in Egypt (Badarian/Amratian) from using mud (*pisé*) for simple constructions.

1. Development
From Naqada I onwards, air-dried bricks were the construction material of Egypt. They were forced out of use in sacred architecture by **stone construction** from the 3rd Dynasty and almost completely from the 12th Dynasty. Fired bricks were rarely used (street paving at **Kahun** and in the 12th Dynasty **fortresses** of **Buhen** and **Shalfak**; a 5 x 30 x 30 cm format was used in **floors**). Fired bricks became more frequent from the 21st Dynasty, but were not commonly used until the second half of the 1st century BC. Brick **walls** were protected against the weather by an application of mud plaster and painted white. Starting in the 1st Dynasty the interior of some walls was packed at regular intervals (every 4–6 courses or groups of courses) with reed **matting**, for example in the **enclosure wall** of **Senwosret II** at Illahun, the Nubian **fortresses** of the 12th Dynasty,

Brick making, as depicted in the tomb of Rekhmire

the temple of **Sety I** at Abydos and at the tomb of **Montuemhat**. This was intended to prevent the bricks from cracking during drying and laying. In order to prevent cracks being produced during settling, individual structural elements (building blocks) were separated by isolation joints.

Monumental brick architecture flourished from the 1st Dynasty onwards, in the form of **palaces**, **divine fortresses** and **funerary enclosures** at **Abydos**, **Hierakonpolis**, **Memphis** and in the Delta, as well as **mastabas** at Naqada, Abydos, **Beit Khallaf** and **Saqqara**. Intricate **niching** and surface articulation became one of the hallmarks of Early Dynastic architecture, differing markedly from the unarticulated wall surfaces of later buildings. Vast brick-built **fortresses** appeared from the 1st Dynasty onwards in Egypt and **Nubia**, most particularly during the Middle Kingdom. Starting in the reign of Senwosret II, the core of **pyramids** was built of bricks. Some **temples** were converted into stone structures, from the Middle Kingdom onwards, but with brick temples continuing alongside them (**pylons**, enclosures and secondary complexes such as magazines). Enclosures, especially in the Late Period, were vast, with walls up to 30 m thick and the side length of surrounding walls exceeding 600 m.

2. Forms
In order to provide stability, brick walls are often slightly sloped (**pylon**) with rounding at the top. The breaking away of corners is prevented by upward-sweeping corner joints, with a **battlement**-like finish. From the 1st Dynasty onwards, arched and barrel **vaults** of considerable size play an important part in non-sacred and tomb structures (**ceiling construction**, **grain stores**). Intricate constructional decoration required **bricks moulded** to the appropriate size and shape.

3. Techniques
Egyptian forms of brick bonding are limited to a few combinations: for the fronts of walls regularly alternating courses of 'headers' and 'stretchers' are dominant. The interior of the wall always consisted of headers. The thickness of walls was reduced by the use of 'herringbone' bonding inside the wall. The bases of walls often rested on a course of brick-on-edge. From the 13th Dynasty onwards horizontal courses in the walls of dwelling **houses** undulated (**wavy walls**), probably in order to prevent the corners of tall buildings from breaking away. This technique became more frequent after the New Kingdom and predominated in the construction of houses in the Ptolemaic period (**Karanis**, **Dima**). Many temple enclosure walls erected in subsequent periods were constructed using the same method. Occasional examples are found of combined stone and brick masonry, such as corners of brick structures reinforced by upright beams of stone, or by quoins, i.e. blocks laid using the stretcher-header system (as in the **pyramid temple** of **Neferirkare**, the **valley temple** of Amenemhat III and at **Karanis**). The brick walls at Nubian fortresses were built on a substructure of stone. Brick-built pyramids and pylons frequently had a stone **casing** (for example, the Ptolemaic pylon at **Medinet Habu** and New Kingdom tombs at **Saqqara**). Large structures were reinforced internally with wooden

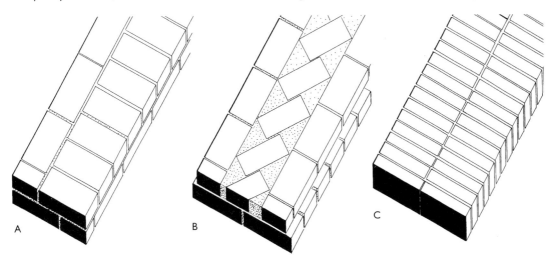

Methods of brick construction. A: alternating headers and stretchers; B: herringbone bonding inside a wall to reduce its thickness; C: brick-on-edge, mainly as part of foundations

beams (**timber construction**) and were also provided with air channels to allow the brickwork to dry. However, bricks in large-scale walls were laid 'dry' on a sand base.

Bibliography: S. Clarke, Ancient Egyptian Frontier Fortresses, in: *JEA* 3 (1916) 176–179; Clark, *AEM* 207–215; Boak, *Karanis* I; Robert Mond, *The Bucheum* III (London 1934), Plates 112–114; Robert Armant, *Temples of Armant* (London 1940), Plates 34–39; Spencer, *Brick Architecture*; Nicholson, *Materials* 88–92.

Brick marks

Bricks were often marked by scratching the wet surface with a finger, usually producing a simple mark (such as fingerprints, lines, circles, crosses and so on). In the **mastaba** of **Nefermaat**, the name of the tomb owner is scratched into the bricks. In large royal constructions, bricks are found with numerous different marks, and thus they must have indicated either the builder or the supplier rather than the owner of the building or the structure itself. Deeper holes on the end of a brick have been interpreted as hand holes.

Bibliography: De Morgan, *Dahchour* I 49, Fig. 110; Dieter Arnold, *The Temple of Mentuhotep at Deir el-Bahari* (New York 1979), Plates 2–3.

Bricks, moulded

Bricks which, for construction or decorative purposes, deviate in shape from the normal format (**bricks, shape of**). They were used in brick structures from the Old Kingdom onwards to produce the corners of buildings in the form of **cavetto cornices,** torus mouldings, panels, profiles and **columns**; also in the construction of **vaults**, where they took the shape of particularly flat or very slightly curved bricks with deep lengthwise grooves for more effective adhesion of the **mortar** (**Balat**, 6th Dynasty: 6.5 x 17 x 30 cm; **Sety I** at Abydos: 7.5 x 22 x 60 cm). In the Old Kingdom special shaped bricks were used at **Giza** for **vaulted** buildings, in which case tooth-like protrusions provided improved stability within the vault structure. Square bricks were occasionally used as **floor** tiles, examples existing in the palace garden at **Medinet Habu** (43 x 43 cm) and at the temple of Sety I at **Abydos** (16 x 44 x 44 cm). Recent excavations at a **fortress** near Tell el-Heir (Qantara) have recovered some cylindrical bricks, perhaps of Persian origin. Sculpted or terracotta brickwork was not used in ancient Egypt, but walls were decorated with faience tiles or inlays (**architectural ceramics**). See also **funerary cones**.

Bibliography: A. Badawy, Brick vaults and domes in the Giza necropolis, in: Abdel-Moneim Abu-Bakr, *Excavations at Giza 1949–1950* (Cairo 1953) 129–143; Spencer, *Brick Architecture* 140–143; Eigner, *Grabbauten* 75–78; F. Kampp, *Die thebanische Nekropole* I (Mainz 1996) 68–69.

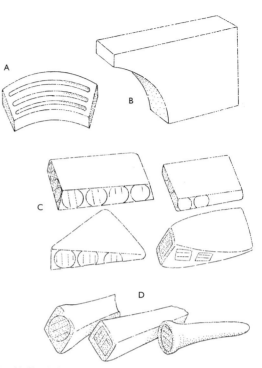

Moulded bricks for different purposes. A: vaulting brick; B: cornice brick; C–D: stamped frieze bricks (see funerary cone), C from corners of buildings

Bricks, shape of

The shape of **bricks** changed considerably in the course of Egyptian history, depending on locality and on the field of application; changes occurred even within the same structure. Size generally is around 10 x 20 x 30 cm (dating structures on the evidence of bricks alone is usually impossible; the suggested relationship between brick size and the size of structures in which they were used has to be questioned):

Structure	Brick size (cm)
Naqada I/II	7.5 x 11.5 x 29
Mastaba of **Menes** at Naqada	7-8 x 12-13 x 25.5–29
Beit Khallaf mastaba	9 x 12.5 x 28
Mastaba 17 at **Meidum**	12.5 x 18.5 x 39.5 and 13 x 22 x 41
Mentuhotep temple, Deir el-Bahari	8–10 x 16–18 x 34–37
Pyramid of **Senwosret II**	19 x 22–25 x 45–49
Pyramid of **Senwosret III**	11.5 x 19.5–21 x 39–42 and 15 x 22 x 43
Fortresses at **Buhen, Semna, Kumma**	8 x 15 x 32

Palace of **Malqata**	10 x 16 x 33
Sety I temple enclosure wall	
at Abydos	14 x 20 x 40
Palace of **Merenptah**	
at Memphis	8 x 19 x 39
Ramesses III temple, **Medinet Habu**	14.5 x 21.5 x 44
Enclosure wall at **Karnak**	12–14 x 17–18.5 x
	36–37
Temple at **Tukh el-Qaramus**	
(reign of Philip Arrhidaeus)	12.5 x 19 x 38
Houses at **Dima**	11 x 14–15.5 x 29–30

Occasionally smaller bricks, better suited to achieving the required effect, were used to create the **niching** of Early Dynastic **mastabas**:

Tomb of **Menes**, Naqada	7 x 9 x 17
Saqqara 3035	5 x 5 x 17
Saqqara 3070	5 x 5 x 10
1st dynasty mastabas,	
south-east of **Giza**	6.5 x 7 x 15

Some square bricks occur in the Middle Kingdom Nubian **fortresses** at **Buhen** and Shafalk (5 x 30 x 30 cm) and in the Saite fortress at Gerar (33 x 33 and 36 x 36 cm).

Bibliography: Spencer, *Brick Architecture* 147–148.

Brick stamps

From the New Kingdom onwards, **bricks** were sometimes stamped with the cartouche of the royal owner of the structure or, more rarely, the name of a private individual. Several examples of the latter are found in the Late Period tombs at **Thebes**. **Funerary cones** found in Theban tombs of the New Kingdom and the Late Period are stamped at the head end.

Bibliography: N. de Garis Davies and M.F.L. Macadam, *A Corpus of Inscribed Egyptian Funerary Cones* (Oxford 1957); Spencer, *Brick Architecture* 144–146, Plates 21–36; Eigner, *Grabbauten* 75–77.

Bridge

Bridges in the sense of crossings over wide expanses of water, such as the Nile, were unknown in ancient Egypt. Tradition relates the existence of some kind of crossing over the Pelusian branch of the Nile at Sile (**canal construction**) in the reign of Sety I. There are several examples of bridge-like structures, 3 m wide, allowing passage under the **causeways** leading to **pyramid temples** for north–south traffic along the desert edge (**Khufu, Khafre, Khentkawes I, Amenemhat II** (?), **Senwosret III, Amenemhat III**). Remains of a bridge have been found at **Amarna**, linking two parts of the palace separated by the Royal Road. Ramps led from both sides onto the bridge, which was 15 m in length and supported on two pillars, 5 m apart. The suggestion that the bridge had a colonnade with a **'window of appearances'** is doubtful. Bridges as crossings over the moats of Nubian **fortresses** are known to have existed.

Bibliography: De Morgan, *Dahchour* II 99–100, Fig. 144; A.H. Gardiner, The ancient military road between Egypt and Palestine, in: *JEA* 6 (1920) 104–106; G. Jéquier, L'avenue de la pyramide de Senousrit III, in: *ASAE* 25 (1929) 60, Fig.1; Peet, *City of Akhenaten* III 86, Plate 2; O.R. Rostem, Bridges in ancient Egypt, in: *ASAE* 48 (1948) 159–166; E. Otto, Brücke, in: Helck, *LÄ* I 871–872.

Bubasteion (Saqqara)

The Graeco-Roman temple precinct of Bastet on the edge of the desert escarpment at **Saqqara** (south of the **Anubieion**). The almost completely unrecorded precinct is surrounded by an **enclosure wall**, measuring 275 x 325 m, with an imposing entrance **gateway** in the south. There are also a cat cemetery and habitation remains.

Bibliography: For an overall plan see D.G. Jeffreys and H.S. Smith, *The Anubieion at Saqqara* I (London 1988), Fig. 1.

Bubastis

A **town** with an important Bastet temple, now in ruins. The principal temple, measuring 50 x 180 m, stands inside a 313 x 400 m wide enclosure. Although little is known of its construction history, some building activity by Khufu, Khafre, Amenemhat I, Senwosret I and Senwosret III is attested by re-used stone blocks. Situated behind a columned **kiosk**, 17 m high, and surrounded on three sides by columned halls, is the 24 x 48 m wide court of Osorkon I with a gate structure of Osorkon II in its rear wall, decorated with an exceptionally complete depiction of a *sed*-festival cycle. The gate forms the entrance to the **hypostyle hall**, consisting of a central hall with unopened papyrus **columns** and lower side-halls with **Hathor**-headed and palm columns. The final section of the structure is the temple house of Nectanebo II. Most of the structure is built of red and black **granite**, with a **cavetto cornice** and a **frieze of uraei** round the top edge.

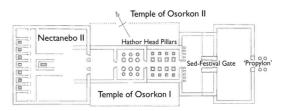

Plan of the Bastet temple at Bubastis

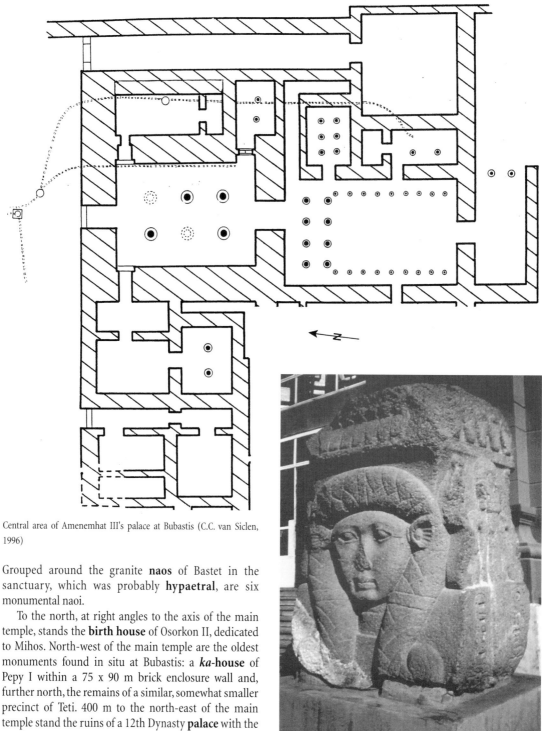

Central area of Amenemhat III's palace at Bubastis (C.C. van Siclen, 1996)

Grouped around the granite **naos** of Bastet in the sanctuary, which was probably **hypaetral**, are six monumental naoi.

To the north, at right angles to the axis of the main temple, stands the **birth house** of Osorkon II, dedicated to Mihos. North-west of the main temple are the oldest monuments found in situ at Bubastis: a *ka*-**house** of Pepy I within a 75 x 90 m brick enclosure wall and, further north, the remains of a similar, somewhat smaller precinct of Teti. 400 m to the north-east of the main temple stand the ruins of a 12th Dynasty **palace** with the remains of a *sed*-festival gate of Amenemhat III.

Bibliography: Herodotus, *History* II 137–138; Edouard Naville, *Bubastis (1887–1889)* (London 1891); Edouard Naville, *The Festival-Hall*;

Hathor capital of Osorkon II from Bubastis, in the Egyptian Museum, Cairo

Labib Habachi, Tell Basta, *ASAE* 22 Suppl. (Cairo 1957); Labib Habachi, Bubastis, in: Helck, *LÄ* I 873–874; S. Farid, Preliminary Report on the Excavations…at Tell Basta, in: *ASAE* 58 (1964) 85–98; Ahmad el-Sawi, *Excavations at Tell Basta* (Prague 1979); C. van Siclen, The city of Basta: an interim report, in: *NARCE* 128 (1984) 28–29; C. van Siclen, The shadow of the door and the jubilee reliefs of Osorkon II from Tell Basta, in: *Varia Aegyptiaca* 7 (1991) 81–87; Charles C. van Siclen, Remarks on the Middle Kingdom palace at Tell Basta, in: Bietak, *House and Palace* 239–246; C. Tietze and M. Omar, Tell Basta: Geschichte einer Grabung, in: *Arcus* 4 (Berlin 1996).

Bucheum

The burial precinct of the sacred Buchis bulls of **Armant**, reminiscent of the **Serapeum**, situated in the fore-desert 5 km south-west of **Malqata**, which was in use from the 30th Dynasty to the Roman Period. The superstructure of the walled temenos has disappeared, but the subterranean corridors have been explored, which contain approximately 33 **vaulted** burial chambers branching off to sides with the stone sarcophagi of the bulls. Situated 300 m to the east is a smaller precinct, the 'Baqariyyah', for the mothers of the Buchis bulls.

Bibliography: Robert Mond, *The Bucheum*, 3 Vols (London 1934).

Buhen

Important remains of a fortified city of the Middle and New Kingdoms on the West Bank of the Nile opposite Wadi Halfa, covering an area of 215 x 460 m. The following remains have been discovered:

a) an outer **enclosure wall** of Senwosret I, 712 m long and 4 m thick, with 32 semi-circular towers, which backs onto the river and has an irregular course;

b) an inner **fortress** of Senwosret I, 150 x 170 m in size, with walls 5 m thick and 11 m high, fortified with rectangular towers and exceptionally strong bastions at the corners. There are two river gates and a monumental entrance gate in the west wall. An outer container wall is fortified at the corners with semi-circular wall

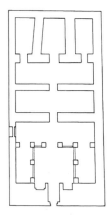

Plan of the Isis temple of Ahmose (North Temple) at Buhen

towers in a cloverleaf arrangement. A commandant's quarters and a temple (?) stood in the north-eastern corner;

c) an outer enclosure wall along all four sides, built before the end of the 12th Dynasty, reinforced with many rectangular towers alternating with larger corner and intermediate bastions. A monumental gate structure stands in the north–south and the west-facing wall, that in the latter reminiscent of a barbican castle with a double outer wall.

Burnt down in the Hyksos period, the fortress was re-erected in the 18th Dynasty.

Standing between the inner fortress (b) and the north-facing wall (c) are the remains of a mud **brick** Isis temple of Ahmose (North Temple), now consisting of only the stone pillar halls around the three sides of the courtyard. Beyond this lie two transverse halls (hall of appearances and offering table hall) and the sanctuary with two flanking rooms.

Situated inside the fortress of the Middle Kingdom (b) is a stone temple of Hatshepsut and Thutmosis III (South Temple), dedicated to Horus of Buhen. Along with

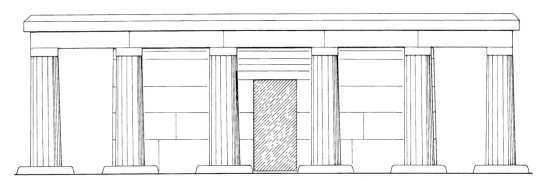

Façade of the Horus temple of Hatshepsut and Thutmosis III (South Temple) at Buhen (after L. Borchardt); see also Ambulatory temple, for plan

Amada, this is a good example of an **ambulatory temple** of the Thutmoside period. Stone blocks removed from it have been found at **Faras**.

Situated along the river bank, a little to the north, are the remains of a walled **town** of the Old Kingdom, area approximately 120 x 950 m. A section of the wall is protected by a fore-wall 65 m away with 18 semicircular wall towers. Buhen stood under floods in 1965. The South Temple has been moved to the museum of Khartoum.

Bibliography: D. Randall-Maciver and C.L. Wooley, *Buhen* (Philadelphia 1911) 84–94; S. Clarke, Ancient Egyptian Frontier Fortresses, in: *JEA* 3 (1916) 161–163; Ricardo Caminos, *The New Kingdom Temples of Buhen*, 2 Vols (London 1974); L. Habachi, *Buhen*, in: Helck, *LÄ* I 880–882; excavation report by W.B. Emery, in: *Kush* 7 (1959) 7–14; 8 (1960) 7–10; 9 (1961) 81–86; 10 (1962) 106–108; 11 (1963) 116–120; W.B. Emery, H.S. Smith and A. Millard, *The Fortress of Buhen, The Archaeological Report* (London 1979); Hein, *Ramessidische Bautätigkeit* 41–47.

Building ramp, *see also* ramp

Many examples of ramps used in construction work are attested, from the pyramids of the 3rd and 4th Dynasties to the temples of the Middle Kingdom: they are illustrated in the tomb of **Rekhmire**. These structures are usually supported on both sides by walls of rock or mud **brick**. The interior of ramps was in many cases strengthened by the insertion of heavy beams, often re-used from ships. These do not form the surface of the ramp, which is provided instead by a layer of **mortar** and chips, as hard as cement, covering the working surface. The average ramp was 10 **cubits** (5.25 m) wide, the angle of slope varying from 10 to 17°. Papyrus Anastasi I describes a theoretical mud brick building ramp, 400 m long and 30 m high.

In quarry areas, there are numerous examples of transportation roads and loading ramps. Generally all that remains of them now are their supporting side-walls of closely packed stone. The longest road known, 10 km long, leads from the **basalt** quarries of Gebel el-Qatrani to Lake Faiyum. A slipway for boats, 77 m long, dating from the Middle Kingdom, has been found at **Mirgissa** in Nubia. This road is strengthened with wood and clay and enabled boats up to 3 m wide to be dragged overland to avoid the dangers of the Second Cataract.

Bibliography: Arnold, *Building* 79–101; Klemm, *Steine*, Figs 180–181, 336, 378, 474.

Building stones, *see also* stone quarry, stone quarrying techniques, stone working

Only a few of the types of stone customarily used in sculpture and the production of stone vessels were employed in Egyptian architecture. The following data are available about the various types of stone used in construction:

Stone type	Specific gravity (kg/cm^2)	Pressure resistance
Compact **limestone**	2.65–2.85	
Porous fossil-rich limestone	1.70–2.60	
Nubian **sandstone**	2.00–2.65	600–1200
Siliceous sandstone (**quartzite**)	2.60–2.80	
Calcite (**alabaster**)	2.70	
Granite (rose granite)	2.60–3.20	1000–2000
Diorite	2.75–2.87	2000
Basalt	2.80–3.30	2500–5000
Dolerite	2.93–3.05	800

Bibliography: Kurt Sethe, *Die Bau- und Denkmalsteine der alten Ägypter und ihre Namen* (Berlin 1933); Jéquier, *Manuel* 26–31; Alfred Lucas, *Ancient Egyptian Materials and Industries* (4th Ed., revised by J.R. Harris, London 1962); Klemm, *Steine*; De Putter, *Pierres*.

Construction ramp for a pylon (?), as depicted in the tomb of Rekhmire

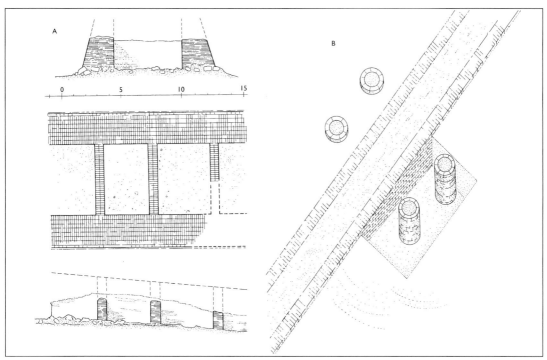

A: demolition ramp of New Kingdom date at Giza; B: building ramp at the pyramid of Senwosret I at El-Lisht, with bases for hoisting devices

Butic

The term applied to a form of buildings developed on the model of the pre-dynastic royal tombs of Lower Egypt and the state sanctuary (the **Per-nu** or Per-neser) at **Buto**. The actual prototypes at Buto have been lost, and so the form is only preserved in the hieroglyph. It is most clearly represented in the royal sarcophagi of the 12th Dynasty. The structure was probably a longish, rectangular building with a vaulted roof and tall corner posts of wood or reed. It

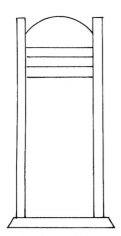

Hieroglyphic representation of the possible Butic shrine

was later translated into **brick** and covered with a long barrel **vault** with high sides at the short ends. It is not likely that the Lower Egyptian **niched** brick structures ('tomb of **Menes**') developed out of that form. Butic chapels appear to have stood in palm groves, which explains why the shape of the palm **column** is interpreted as Butic and why courts and halls furnished with that type of column are regarded as Butic structures.

Bibliography: Müller, *Monumentalarchitektur* 8–10.

Buto

The ancient twin **town** of Dep and Pe in the Delta. At its north-west perimeter are the unique remains of archaic structures, possibly with some cultic significance. Situated between the two mounds of rubble of former settlements are the remains of the temple of Wadjet, attested to from the 12th Dynasty. The outer enclosure (174 x 260 x 234 x 306 m) surrounds the large south-facing temple (31 x 65 m), which is itself contained within two **enclosure walls**, the inner of which is of **limestone** covered with slabs of **quartzite**. According to Herodotus, the antechamber was 17.76 m high. The ceiling was constructed of slabs of quartzite and decorated with stars. Herodotus's statement that the monolithic **naos** was 17.76 m high is probably an exaggeration. The temple was probably of Saite origin (possibly of the reign of Amasis). It was destroyed by the Persians, and rebuilt by the early Ptolemies but it soon fell into ruin again.

Buto has become better known in recent years for its pre-historic remains. Studies and excavations by the German Archaeological Institute, Cairo, have brought to light remains of settlements that flourished from late pre-historic to Byzantine times. Layers dating from the Early Dynastic Period and the Old Kingdom contained several interesting **brick** structures, some apparently decorated with clay cones (**funerary cones**). A connection with Mesopotamia cannot be excluded.

Bibliography: Herodotus, *History* II 155–156; W.M. Flinders Petrie, *Ehnasya 1904* (London 1905) 36–38, Plates 43–44; C.C. Edgar, Notes from the Delta, Buto and Chemmis, in: *ASAE* 11 (1911) 87–90; M.V. Seton-Williams, Reports of the English excavations, in: *JEA* 51 (1965) – 56 (1970); H. Altenmüller, Buto, in: Helck, *LÄ* I 887–889; T. von der Way, Reports of the German excavations, in: *MDAIK* 42 (1986) – 44 (1988); T. von der Way, Excavations at Tell el-Fara'in/Buto in 1987–1989, in: *The Nile Delta in Transition: 4th.–3rd. Millennium B.C.* (Tel Aviv 1992) 1–10; T. von der Way, Early dynastic architecture at Tell el-Fara'ain-Buto, in: Bietak, *House and Palace*, 247–252; T. von der Way, *Tell el-Fara'in. Buto I* (Mainz 1997).

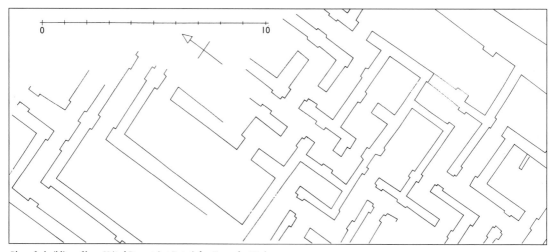

Plan of a building of layer V (3rd Dynasty) at Buto (after T. von der Way)

C

Caisson

An invention of the 12th Dynasty at **El-Lisht** by which deeper pits could be cut into unstable substrata. It consisted of a monolithic **limestone** box, open at the bottom, which was sunk into the ground until it reached bedrock and the ensuing side-walls, which were at risk of collapsing, were stabilised with **brick** walls.

Bibliography: Arnold, *Building* 211–212; D. Arnold, *The Pyramid Complex of Senwosret I* (New York 1992) 33–34, Fig. 10.

'Campbell's tomb'

A monumental Saite **shaft tomb**, north of the causeway of **Khafre** at **Giza**. In the main shaft is a crypt lined with blocks of stone and containing an anthropoid sarcophagus of hard stone. The ceiling is an interesting double **vault**. The main shaft is surrounded on all sides by four rows of four side-shafts, from which loose sand fed into the main shaft to prevent robbing. The complex was not completed. The tomb of **Wedjahorresnet** at **Abusir** is similar.

Bibliography: Vyse, *Operations* II 131–144; Arnold, *Building* 201.

stone vault

sand

Section through the burial chamber of 'Campbell's tomb' at Giza, with its weight-relieving structure and true stone vault

Canal construction

Artificial dams and canals required to control the inundation waters of the Nile and to facilitate boat traffic were created by means of the corvée system. Several such man-made constructions are known from literary sources, but none are as yet attestable in archaeology. In the Old Kingdom, man-made waterways were provided leading to the **pyramid** building sites (subsequently used as approach paths to the **valley temples**). The First Cataract near **Aswan** was made navigable in the 6th Dynasty by the provision of a canal 75 m long.

Three sections of canal attested from written sources and for which there is partial archaeological evidence may have been forerunners of the Suez Canal: a) the fresh water canal from the Pelusian arm of the Nile leading through Wadi Tumilat to the Bitter Lakes; b) the Pelusian branch of the Nile ('East Canal'), which passes **El-Hebua** and feeds into the Mediterranean, which was used as early as the Middle Kingdom to irrigate Northern Sinai and to act as a frontier (Sety I's **bridge**). From the Late Period onwards, perhaps, it was replaced by a canal running further to the east, its course recently verified by aerial photography; and c) an actual shipping route connecting the Bitter Lakes with the Red Sea, which was not started until the reign of Nekho II, who (according to Herodotus) cancelled the project after the loss of 120,000 workmen. It was continued by Darius I, finishing at Suez (three memorial **stelae** have been found north of Suez) and was, according to Herodotus, approximately 384 km long; it was renewed by Ptolemy II to a width of 45 m and a depth of 5 m.

Bibliography: Herodotus, *History* II 158; H. Goedicke, Wadi Tumilat, in: Helck, *LÄ* VI 1124–1126; A. Sneh et al., Evidence for an Ancient Egyptian frontier canal, in: *American Scientist* 63 (1975) 542–548; W. Shea, A date for the recently discovered eastern canal of Egypt, in: *BASOR* 226 (1977) 31–38; Wolfgang Schenkel, *Die Bewässerungs-revolution im Alten Ägypten* (Mainz 1978); Wolfgang Schenkel, Kanal, in: Helck, *LÄ* III 310–312; K.W. Butzer, Kanal, Nil-Rotes Meer, in: Helck, *LÄ* III 312–313; Margaret Cool Root, *The King and Kingship in Achaemenide Art* (Leiden 1979) 61–68; Günther Garbrecht and Horst Jaritz, *Untersuchungen antiker Anlagen zur Wasserspeicherung im Fayum/Ägypten* (Brunswick-Cairo 1990).

Canopic recess, canopic shrine

The earliest known burials of canopics date from the 3rd Dynasty (**Dahshur**, near **Senwosret III**'s pyramid), consisting of sarcophagus-size chests of **alabaster**, sometimes in a specially provided shaft. The first example from a royal context was a stone chest of canopics in a recess of the burial chamber of Hetepheres I at **Giza** (4th Dynasty). The canopic containers of Sneferu and **Khufu** were probably placed in the chimney-like southern recesses of their burial chambers. Canopic recesses have been found in private tombs from the early 4th Dynasty onwards at **Meidum** and Dahshur (northern and southern **mastabas**), and subsequently at Giza and **Abusir** (**Ptahshepses**). Canopic shrines were traditionally placed at the foot-end of the coffin, either at the eastern end of the south wall or at the southern end of that facing east. In later royal tombs of the Old Kingdom, the canopics were set into the floor of the burial chamber (**Khafre, Djedkare Isesi, Merenre**). In the Middle Kingdom, in **queens' tombs** or those of private persons, their location is at the southern end of the east wall. The small purpose-made wall recesses of earlier periods changed in the course of the 12th Dynasty, developing into a chapel at man's height (**Senwosret II** and **III, Amenemhat III** at Dahshur), often no longer in the burial chamber itself but on the east side of an anteroom. After the Middle Kingdom canopic shrines became reduced to canopic chests. The canopic chest of Tutankhamun was enshrined in a magnificent gilded **canopy**.

Bibliography: K. Martin, Kanopen, Kanopenkasten, in: Helck, *LÄ* III 315–320; Arnold, *Amenemhet III* 99–103; Aidan Dodson, *The Canopic Equipment of the Kings of Egypt* (London-New York 1994); Salima Ikram and Aidan Dodson, *The Mummy in Ancient Egypt* (London 1998) 276–292.

Canopy, baldachin

The original form of the **kiosk**, made of wood, in the form of a shady roof on supports lending distinction to the person or deity below it. In royal ceremonial, it represented 'heaven' over the throne and was especially important in coronations or *sed*-festivals with its characteristic double-curved roof. In the **barque chamber** of a temple it took the form of a wooden shrine over the divine barque, but inside a temple it was usually made of stone (i.e. a kiosk). As a secular feature, canopies were found in gardens and on boats. They are also widely found in Western architecture.

Bibliography: A.M. Badawy, The approach to the Egyptian temple, in: *ZÄS* 102 (1975) 79–90; Adolf Reinle, *Zeichensprache der Architektur* (Zürich-Munich 1976) 337–344. D. Arnold, Baldachin, in: Helck, *LÄ* I 607–608; M. Müller, Schrein, in: Helck, *LÄ* V 709–712.

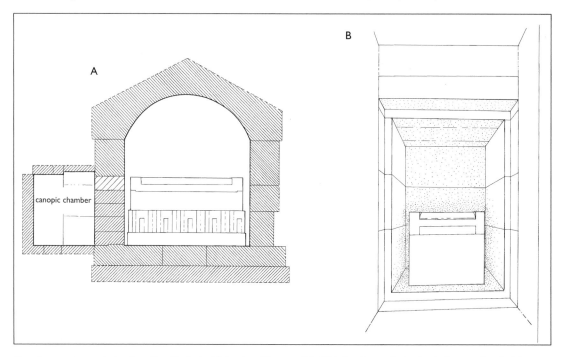

Canopic recess: A: canopic chamber adjacent to the burial chamber of Senwosret III at Dahshur; B: canopic chamber in the queens' tomb of the same pyramid

Capital

A connecting structure between a **column** or **pillar** and the entablature (**abacus**, Fig.), in the form of a floral or other figured ornament. In Egyptian architecture it is part of the shaft of the column and is predominantly floral (**composite capital**), exceptions being the **Hathor** (sistrum) and Bes-shaped capitals.

Bibliography: D. Arnold, Kapitell, in: Helck, *LÄ* III 323–327.

Casing, pyramid casing

The coarse **core masonry** of **pyramids**, **mastabas**, and so on, was clad with carefully cut blocks of Tura **limestone** resting on 'backing stones'. Until the beginning of the 4th Dynasty (**Bent Pyramid**), casing blocks were tilted slightly inwards, but later they were laid horizontally. The height of the individual courses of casing decreases from 1.2–1.5 m near the base to 50–70 cm at the top. Corner blocks were large and particularly carefully cut, and from the 12th Dynasty onwards they were firmly anchored with dowels (**cramps**). The **pyramidion** forms the tip of the casing. Lever holes in the casing blocks shows that they were slid into place sideways, their somewhat sloping outer surface being dressed after a complete course had been laid. Damage caused by settling required extensive repairs using small stones. The suggestion that the casing of pyramids was painted red cannot be proved. Herodotus mentions huge figures on **Amenemhat III**'s pyramid at Hawara. Inscriptions found by the entrance of several Old Kingdom pyramids are reminders of the restoration work undertaken by Khaemwaset in the reign of Ramesses II. The casing of many pyramids had already been removed in the New Kingdom. The robbery of the casing of the pyramids at **Giza** for Islamic building projects in Cairo and in the Delta did not start until the 12th century AD. There are considerable remains of the casing on the pyramids of **Khafre, Menkaure**, on the **Bent Pyramid** and at **Meidum**. For **granite** casing of pyramids, see **pyramid construction**. The rubble core of mastabas was cased with rough blocks, overlaid with the actual casing of block masonry and filled in behind with rubble.

Bibliography: Herodotos, *History* II 148; Reisner, *Giza* I 178–183; Arnold, *Building in Egypt* 164–176.

Causeway

The connection between the **valley temple** on the edge of the cultivation and the **pyramid temple** on the desert plateau. There are no causeways associated with the funerary complexes of the kings of the Early Dynastic Period and they first appear in the east–west orientated pyramid precincts introduced in the reign of Sneferu. They could be quite lengthy, due to the distance which sometimes separated these two structures:

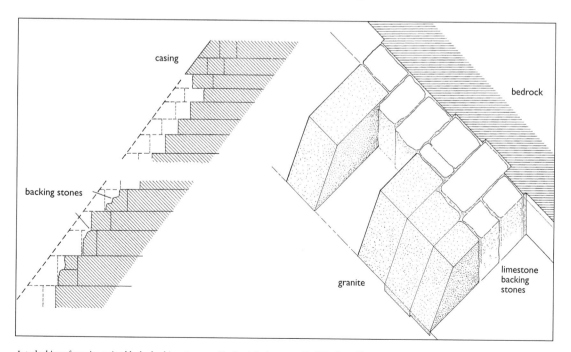

Interlocking of granite casing blocks, backing stones and bedrock in the pyramid of Khafre at Giza

Meidum	241 m
Khufu	616 m
Khafre	494 m
Djedefre	1500 m
Menkaure	600 m
Sahure	235 m
Niuserre	400 m
Unas	666 m
Pepy II	515 m
Amenemhat III (Dahshur)	181 m

Causeways were narrow, roofed corridors built of stone, dimly lit through slits in the ceiling. As they hindered movement, they were often provided with passageways beneath (**bridge**). From the 5th Dynasty onwards, the walls were decorated with reliefs depicting, at the lower end, apotropaic scenes of the triumph of the royal **sphinxes** over the enemy and, further up, tribute bearers as well as scenes from life (**Niuserre, Unas**). The causeway of **Senwosret I** included some royal **statue pillars**. In terms of their significance, causeways were simply elongated inner rooms which connected two spatially separate but functionally closely linked buildings. In the Middle Kingdom, causeways were flanked on both sides by protective **brick** walls. In many cases it is only these walls which survive and they are often mistaken for 'open' causeways. This kind of false causeway is found only at Deir el-Bahari leading to the temples of **Mentuhotep**, **Hatshepsut** and **Thutmosis III**, the latter of which was planted at the lower end with a double line of trees. These were actually processional ways, especially associated with the festivals of Amun. From the 6th Dynasty, imitation causeways were built leading up to the tombs of the provincial rulers of **Aswan** and **Qaw el-Kebir**.

Bibliography: Borchardt, *Ne-user-Re* 42–49; Selim Bey Hassan, Excavations at Saqqara, in: *ASAE* 38 (1938) 519–520; R. Drenkhahn, Aufweg, in: Helck, *LÄ* I 555–556; Oltri Egitto: Nubia, Exhibition Catalogue (Milan 1985), Fig. 17; numerous examples in Mark Lehner, *Complete Pyramids*.

Cavetto cornice, torus moulding

The cavetto is an important structural feature in Egyptian architecture. The torus moulding forms the finishing element along the vertical or horizontal edges of buildings, and the cavetto cornice emerges out of a horizontal torus moulding. The latter first appeared at the **Djoser** precinct, where it was not accompanied by a cavetto cornice. Torus mouldings are usually painted in yellow surrounded by a black band. They developed out of the protective edges on bundles of reed or, perhaps more likely, the corner posts of early structures built of **brick** or wooden **mats**; in later buildings they rest on a square base.

The origin of the cavetto cornice can be traced to palm fronds planted in a row on the tops of walls, customary in Egypt to this day. For this reason, its lower surface is usually decorated with an abstract form of red, blue and green palm fronds and occasionally inlaid with coloured faience tiles (**Malqata, architectural decoration**). Its symbolism is probably related to the *seh-netjer* chapel (**divine booth**). The earliest classic cavetto cornice is the upper finishing element on the **Harmakhis** temple; it then spread rapidly in **pyramid temples**, **mastabas** and sarcophagi of the Old Kingdom, and subsequently also on **pylons**, gates, **pillars** and **screen walls**, with interesting cropped forms appearing in passageways (**Deir el-Medina**, Fig.). Later cavetto cornices and torus mouldings on brick buildings are constructed of **bricks moulded** specially. Cavetto cornices are occasionally crowned with a **frieze of uraei**. Cavetto cornice decoration spread to Palestine and Syria, and as far as Persia and Lower Italy (Doric temples).

Lower end of torus mouldings in the temple of Kom Ombo

Bibliography: W.M. Flinders Petrie, *Egyptian Decorative Art* (London 1895) 97–100; Jéquier, *Manuel* 72–76; Junker, *Giza* XI 101, Fig. 50a; Ricke, *Bemerkungen* I 89–90, 151, A.279; Arnold, Hohlkehle, in: Helck, *LÄ* II 1263–1264; Arnold, Rundstab, in: Helck, *LÄ* V 320–321.

Ceiling construction, *see also* roof, vault

Egyptian architecture has broadly four types of ceiling:

a) Flat ceilings in **stone** buildings (made of **limestone**, **sandstone**, **granite**) were the only form of ceiling until the end of the 3rd Dynasty, and also the preferred form until the latest periods of Egyptian architecture; the burial chamber of the pyramid of **Khufu** has granite beams (2 m thick, with a span of 5.25 m). It was not until the New Kingdom that distances of up to 7 m were spanned using sandstone beams (**hypostyle hall** of **Karnak**: sandstone slabs 1.25 m thick and 9 m long, spanning 6.7 m). In a few cases, the sides of ceiling beams were hollowed out, giving them a cross-section like girders today, in order to reduce their weight (pyramids of **Senwosret III** and **Amenemhat III** at Dahshur). Flat ceilings in **brick** architecture have received little detailed study. They seem mostly to have been a framework of rafters, or the split stems of palm trees, and often they were no more than palm ribs or dense reed matting. This framework was overlaid with reed **mats** covered with a layer of straw mixed with clay. At **Amarna**, rafters of medium size and side-rafters bear ceilings of this kind made of palm ribs and mats. The underside of the ceiling is covered with white **plaster** and frequently painted with a carpet pattern. The ceiling plaster contains fine plant fibre, and the structure of the rafters is usually visible. At **Malqata**, poles with straw mats are fastened to the underside of the rafters and covered with rough-cast **gypsum** decorated with designs, such as carpet patterns or vultures in flight. Ceilings in the 1st Dynasty **mastabas** at **Saqqara** consist of round beams with heavy planks laid side by side, over which was placed reed matting with a thick layer of sand or brick masonry on top. Round ceiling beams are sometimes represented in stone, for example in the entrance hall of the precinct of **Djoser**, in mastabas of the Old Kingdom and in tombs of the reign of **Senwosret III** at **Dahshur** and **Abydos**.

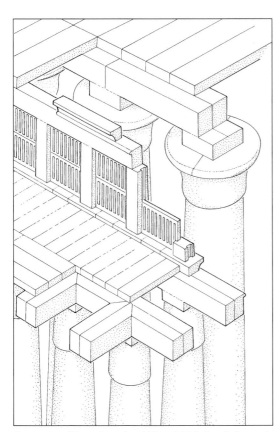

Construction of the roof over the middle and side halls at the hypostyle hall at Karnak

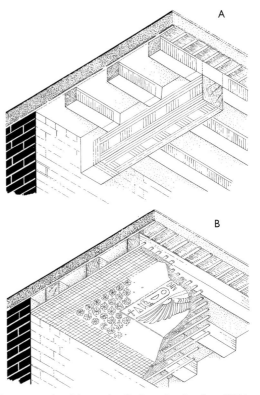

A: reconstruction of decorated roofing beams in private house V.36.6 at Amarna; B: reconstruction of a roofing beam decorated from below with a carpet pattern, from the palace at Malqata

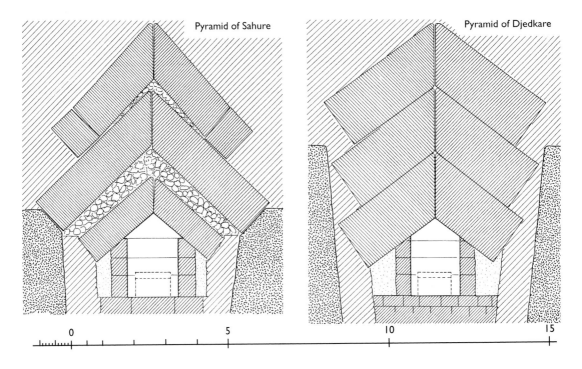

Above: section through the ceiling (with triple relieving slabs) over the burial chambers of Sahure and Djedkare. Below: section through the ceiling of the burial chambers of Shepseskaf, Menkaure and a queen's tomb of Senwosret III at Dahshur

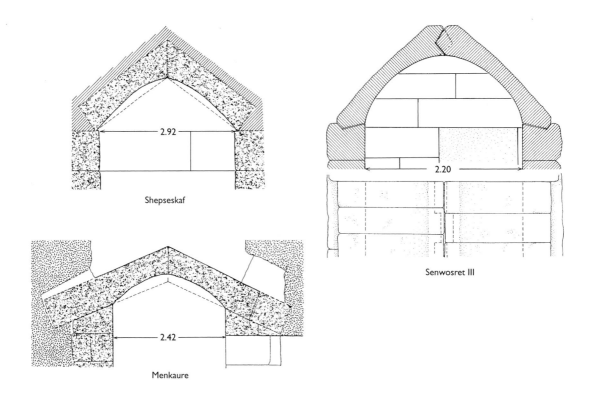

b) *See* **corbelled vault**.

c) Relieving or slab vaults and stone saddle roofs were only used in subterranean structures such as pyramids and tombs, and for the first time in the pyramid of **Khufu**, where the relieving slabs are 7–8 m long, weighing up to 36 tonnes. The burial chambers in the pyramids of the 5–6th Dynasties had gigantic roof structures consisting of relieving slabs (in that of **Niuserre** the slabs weighed 90 tonnes each). Pressure was diverted sideways into the filler masonry and the actual walls of the chamber stood detached in front of the ceiling slabs. The development reached its peak in the pyramids of **Amenemhat II**, **Senwosret III** and **Amenemhat III** at Hawara and their neighbouring tombs. Occasionally, the roofing slabs were designed to interlock at the apex of the roof by a system of complicated **joints**.

d) The first true stone **vaults** were built under Sneferu at **Dahshur**, a practice not revived until the 25th Dynasty. Brick vaults were common from the 3rd Dynasty (**Beit Khallaf**), constructed without centring by laying the first arch against a vertical, supporting wall. Subsequent arches were therefore all inclined.

Vaults are found, usually in the shape of a shallow arch imitated in the rock, in **rock tomb** construction from the Middle Kingdom onwards, and particularly in the New Kingdom under the influence of **temple** sanctuaries and the halls of **palaces**. In the tomb of **Senenmut** (TT 71), the ceiling of the transverse hall takes several forms united by their symbolism: a flat ceiling, a saddle roof, a barrel vault and a **Per-wer**-shaped ceiling.

Bibliography: Choisy, *L'art de bâtir* 66–69; L. Borchardt, Die Entstehung der Teppichbemalung an altägyptischen Decken und Gewölben, in: *Zeitschrift für Bauwesen* 79 (1929) 111–115; Jéquier, *Manuel* 289–295, 303–14; Clark, *AEM* 154–161; Walter B. Emery, *Great Tombs of the First Dynasty* I (Cairo 1949), II (London 1954), III (London 1958); Walter B. Emery, *The Tomb of Hemaka* (Cairo 1938) 4–5; Walter B. Emery, *Archaic Egypt* (London 1961) 184–188; J. Brinks, Gewölbe, in: Helck, *LÄ* II 589–594; Spencer, *Brick Architecture* 123–127; G. Haeny, Decken- und Dachkonstruktion, in: Helck, *LÄ* I 998–1002; Arnold, *Building* 183–201; *Studies on the Palace of Malqata* (University of Waseda 1993), Plates 5–13; Salah El-Naggar, *Les vôutes dans l'architecture de l'Égypte ancienne*, 2 Vols (Cairo 1999).

Cellar

Attested to in many dwelling **houses** (**Kahun, Amarna, Deir el-Medina, Karanis**), cellars are usually small rectangular pits, lined with **brick** and roofed with beams (occasionally with a brick **vault**). For better security, they were often below the bedroom. Some food storage cellars at **El-Lisht** are covered with beehive-shaped brick domes and are accessible via a lockable entrance hole.

Bibliography: Peet, *City of Akhenaten* II, 52, Fig. 6; Borchardt, *Tell el-Amarna,* Figs 6, 25; Arnold, *Pyramid Complex* 50–52, 72.

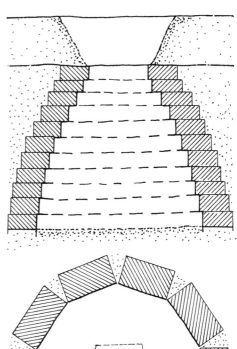

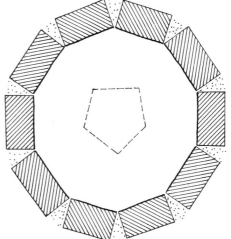

Subterranean, beehive-shaped cellar store room at Amarna

Cellular construction

A technique of constructing **foundations** in **brick** buildings. In order to save on materials and to increase the stability of (in particular) **fortresses** and **palaces**, tall substructures were constructed in the form of a regular grid of brick walls, and the spaces between were filled with sand or rubble. Good examples exist from the New Kingdom onwards (such as at **Ballas, Kom el-Abd, Tell el-Dab'a, Medamud** and **Amarna**) and in late fortresses (for example at **Defenna**); earlier forms are found in **mastabas** of the 1st Dynasty and in brick **pyramids** of the Middle Kingdom. In late complexes (such as the palace of **Apries**, at **Mendes, Defenna** and

Tell el-Maskhuta) the spaces were oval-shaped and had a domed roof (**cupola**). Cellular construction was also used in brick **building ramps**.

Bibliography: Spencer, *Brick Architecture* 79; B.J. Kemp, The Palace of Apries at Memphis, in: *MDAIK* 33 (1977) 104–106; A.J. Spencer, Casemate foundations once again, in: A. Leahy and J. Tait, Eds, *Studies on Ancient Egypt in Honour of H.S. Smith* (London 1999) 295–300.

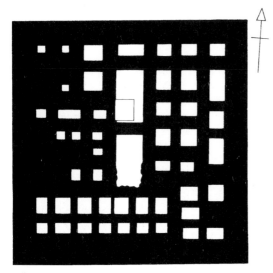

Cellular construction of the foundations of the central fortified tower at Defenna

Cenotaph

Duplicates of **tombs**, or false tombs, were erected either at the burial sites of several kings (**South Tomb** in the **Djoser** precinct, **Mentuhotep**'s temple with the Bab el-Hosan), or as separate structures at **Abydos** (**Osiris tomb**, **Senwosret III**). Private commemorative chapels without a tomb were also set up at Abydos in the Middle Kingdom. These were **brick**-built courtyards with a vaulted single room memorial chapel containing one or more **stelae**. A clear separation between tomb and cenotaph was provided in New Kingdom **kings' tombs** with an upper and a lower tomb, and at **Thebes** several officials of the 18th Dynasty also had two separate tombs (**Senenmut** TT 71 and 353, User-Amun TT 61 and 131, Menkheperreseneb TT 86 and 112, Djehutinefer TT 80 and 104, Nakhtmin TT 87 and Sennefer TT 96). The underlying intention was to unite a lower tomb, acting as the magical, underworld burial place, with the upper tomb, which represented the splendid, living cult place. Private memorial cenotaphs are also found at Gebel el-Silsila. Conflicting interpretations exist concerning the concept of multiple burial places, for example places for statue burials, Osiris tomb, ***ka*-tomb**, the duality of Upper and Lower Egypt, tomb for the placenta of the king or Sokar tomb, as well as the survival of earlier, locally divergent burial practices. Cenotaphs for rulers are also widely found in cultures outside Egypt (medieval England and France had the notions of the 'royal corpse' and the 'body politic').

Bibliography (general): J.-P. Lauer, *Histoire monumentale* 131–142; W.K. Simpson, *The Terrace of the Great God at Abydos: The Offering Chapels of Dynasties 12 and 13* (New Haven und Philadelphia 1974); W.K. Simpson, Kenotaph, in: Helck, *LÄ* III 387–391; H. Altenmüller, Doppelbestattung, in: Helck, *LÄ* I 1128–1130; Edwards, *Pyramids* 52–53; David O'Connor, The 'Cenotaphs' of the Middle Kingdom at Abydos, in: *Mélanges Gamal Eddin Mokhtar* (Cairo 1985) 161–177; Arnold, *Amenemhet III.*, 99–103; Peter F. Dorman, *The Monuments of Senenmut* (London 1988) 141–164; E. Dziobek, in: *MDAIK* 45 (1989) 118 A.34; Peter F. Dorman, *The Two Tombs of Senenmut* (New York 1991) 163; Peter Metcalf and Richard Huntington, *Celebrations of Death* (Cambridge, Mass. 1991); Friedrike Kampp, *Die thebanische Nekropole* I (Mainz 1996) 90–91.

Cestius, pyramid of

The completely preserved pyramid tomb of the praetor and people's tribune Gaius Epulo Cestius near the Porta Ostiensis at Rome, erected between 18 and 12 BC following Cestius's stay in Egypt. The core is of **brick** plastered with cement and coated in **marble**, and it stands on a travertine base of 30 sq m. Its height is given variously as 27, 36.4 and 37 m. Inside, the decorated burial chamber measures 4.10 x 5.95 m. It was later incorporated into the Aurelian city fortifications.

Another, larger pyramid, the 'Meta Romuli', on the bank of the Tiber near the Castel S. Angelo, was destroyed in the 16th century.

Bibliography: Ernest Nash, *Pictorial Dictionary of Ancient Rome* II (Tübingen 1962) 59, 321–323.

Pyramid of Cestius in Rome

Chamber of the Seasons

An Egyptological term for the inner room of the two chambers of the chapel beside the base of the **obelisk** in the **sun temple** of Niuserre. This was not a real cult chamber, but rather an antechamber in the approach to the base of the obelisk. The walls were decorated with depictions of events in nature caused by the sun during the seasons of inundation (Akhet) and harvest (Shemu).

Bibliography: Borchardt, *Re-Heiligtum* 49–50; William Stevenson Smith, *Interconnections in the Ancient Near East* (New Haven-London 1965) Figs 178–179; Elmar Edel and Steffen Wenig, *Die Jahreszeitenreliefs aus dem Sonnenheiligtum des Ne-user-re*, Vol. 1 (Berlin 1974); *Egyptian Art in the Age of the Pyramids*, exhibition catalogue (New York 1999) 356–357.

Channelling, of columns

Vertical grooving (also called fasciculation) on the shafts of **columns**, either intended to represent the texture of the bark of a tree or the marks left by working with an adze, or simply a reflection of the need to make divisions in the surface. First seen in buildings at the **Djoser** precinct, it is found frequently in polygonal **pillars** (**Beni Hasan**, **Semna**, **Beit el-Wali**). Since Champollion such columns have been incorrectly referred to as **protodoric**.

Bibliography: Jéquier, *Manuel* 177–184; Ricke, *Bemerkungen* I 77–84.

Chapelle Blanche

White **limestone barque station** at **Karnak**, erected for the *sed*-festival of Senwosret I, recovered from the foundations of the third **pylon** in 1927–38. The **kiosk** is 6.54 x 6.54 m, with four rows of four pillars, and stands on a 1.18 m high base. The pillars are decorated on

The Chapelle Blanche of Senwosret I, with stepped ramp, now reconstructed at Karnak

every side with magnificent raised relief; the roof, fitted with **water spouts**, is surrounded with a **cavetto cornice**. Ramps lead up to it from the east and the west. In the centre was a **base**, no longer preserved, probably for a statue of the king. This probably represents a symbolic 'petrified' *sed*-festival **kiosk**. The perfection of this small building suggests the existence of earlier models. It has been re-erected in the Open Air Museum at Karnak.

Bibliography: Excavation reports of H. Chevrier in *ASAE* 28 (1928) 115–116; 29 (1929) 135–142; 31 (1931) 91–92; 34 (1934) 172–175; Pierre Lacau and Henri Chevrier, *Une chapelle de Sésostris Ier à Karnak*, 2 Vols (Cairo 1956–65); Ch. Strauß-Seeber, Bildprogramm und Funktion der Weißen Kapelle in Karnak, in: Kurth, *Tempeltagung* 287–318; Andere Monumente Sesostris' I., in: *Karnak*; C. Traunecker, Rapport préliminaire sur la chapelle de Sésostris Ier découverte dans le IXe pylône, in: *Karnak* VII 121–126.

Chapelle Rouge

Monumental two-room barque sanctuary for Amun, which was set up by Hatshepsut in the centre of **Karnak**. It is 15 m long, with a base decorated with **niching**, and is built of black **granite** with red **quartzite** walls. It was broken up by Thutmosis III, and then built into the foundations of the third **pylon** by Amenhotep III. 319 stone blocks have been found bearing an important decorative programme, and the chapel was reconstructed in the Open Air Museum at Karnak in 1999–2000.

Bibliography: Pierre Lacau and Henri Chevrier, *Une chapelle d'Hatshepsout*, 2 Vols (Cairo 1977, 1979); F. Le Saout, Un nouveau bloc de la chapelle rouge, in: *Karnak* VII 71–73.

Circular construction

This architectural form was customary in Egypt only in pre-historic habitation structures (with a domed roof: Merimde-Benisalame, El-Omari, **El-Ma'adi**), and it died out with the introduction of rectangular **brick** buildings. Circular structures survive only in hieroglyphic signs and in the image of the traditional Min sanctuary. This was probably a circular tent with a protruding central support and side-supports. Rounded corners are found in temple T in the precinct of **Djoser** and the '**High Sand**' at **Hierakonpolis** and **Heliopolis**, which may reflect earlier circular structures.

Bibliography: P. Lacau, L'érection du mât devant Amon-Min, in: *CdE* 28 (1953) 13–22; A. Badawy, Min, the cosmic fertility god of Egypt, in: *Mitt. d. Instituts für Orientforschung* 7 (1959) 163–179; I. Munro, *Das Zelt-Heiligtum de Min*, Münchner Ägypt. Studien 41 (Munich 1983); M. Bietak, Rundbauten, in: Helck, *LÄ* V 318–320.

Chisel, *see stone working*

Colossal statue, *see also* statue pillar

Considerably 'larger than life' statues of a king or a god, seated or standing, were frequent in Egyptian architecture from Naqada II (**Koptos**); in some cases their size was dictated by the surrounding building. They were never purely decorative, but in most cases had some special significance and, like all statues, were considered living entities and supplied with offerings. They were primarily intended to indicate that the king broke the bonds of the human dimension, entering the realm of the divine. There was also certainly the intention to impress, to frighten away enemies and to act in a protective function. The height of colossal statues increases from 4.30 m in the Naqada II period (**Koptos**), to 8 m in the Middle Kingdom (**Biahmu, Amenemhat III**'s pyramid at Hawara), and to 20 m in the reigns of Amenhotep III and Ramesses II (**colossi of Memnon, Per-Ramesses, Ramesseum**). There are several different types:

a) Free-standing cult images in a cult building: **Djoser, Userkaf, Biahmu.**

b) Detached colossal statues, seated or standing: **Karnak** (early 18th Dynasty in front of the seventh and eighth **pylons**, Amenhotep III standing in front of the tenth pylon); **Amenhotep III**, mortuary temple; **Ramesseum; Akhmim; Memphis; Per-Ramesses; Abu Simbel**; Amenhotep III and Tiye, originally from **Medinet Habu** (?).

c) Detached colossal statues, standing or seated, inside or in front of colonnades: **Ehnasya el-Medina; Luxor**, Ramesses II.

d) Statues of the king performing a cult act: kneeling figure in the temple of **Hatshepsut.**

e) **Statue pillars** integrated into the architecture: from Senwosret I onwards, seen in his structures at **Karnak** and **Abydos**, and on the causeway of his pyramid at El-Lisht, these statues, closely associated with

Colossal statues of Thutmosis III, Amenhotep I and Amenhotep II in front of the eighth pylon at Karnak

his **sed**-festival, mark the façades and colonnades of '**houses of millions of years**' (Hatshepsut, Aten precinct, **Karnak, Ramesseum, Medinet Habu**).

f) The king as **sphinx**: sphinx at **Giza**, Amenemhat II at **Tanis, Heliopolis.**

Less frequent are non-royal colossal statues: Amun and Amunet (behind the sixth pylon at Karnak); baboon statues of Amenhotep III at **Hermopolis.**

Bibliography: A. Badawy, Egyptian colossal monoliths: why and how were they erected?, in: *Gazette des Beaux Arts* 129 (1987) 97–105; Klemm, *Steine* 94–97; M. Eaton-Krauss, Ramesses-Re who creates the gods, in: *Fragments of a Shattered Visage* (Memphis, Tenn. 1991) 15–23.

Colossi of Memnon

Two seated **quartzite** statues of the king, 40 **cubits** (21 m) in height, wearing a head-cloth and crown, the latter now lost, in front of the 1st **pylon** of **Amenhotep III**'s mortuary temple at **Thebes**. Standing beside the legs of the king are the figures of Queens Tiye and Mutemwiya. Their weight, excluding the separate bases, is estimated at 800 tonnes. According to inscriptions, both statues came from the quartzite quarries at **Gebel el-Ahmar**. Petrographic examination indicates that **Aswan** is more likely. The northern colossus was famous in ancient times for a strange acoustic phenomenon, which ceased after its restoration under Septimus Severus. The statues bear a great number of inscriptions of visitors. They are under imminent threat of collapse.

Bibliography: *Description* II, Plates 20–22; L. Borchardt, Die Aufstellung der Memnonskolosse, in: *ZÄS* 45 (1908–09) 32-34; A. and E. Bernand, *Les inscriptions du Colosse de Memnon* (Cairo 1960); R. Bianchi, Memnonskolosse, in: Helck, *LÄ* IV 23–24; A.H. Gardiner, The Egyptian Memnon, in: *JEA* 47 (1961) 91–99; M. Eaton Kraus and B. Fay, Beobachtungen an den Memnonkolossen, in: *GM* 53 (1981) 25–29; Gerhard Haeny, *Untersuchungen am Totentempel Amenophis' III, BeiträgeBf* 11 (Wiesbaden 1981); H.Bowman et al., The northern colossus of Memnon: new slants, in: *Archaeometry* 26 (1984) 218–219; D.D. Klemm et al., Die pharaonischen Steinbrüche des silifizierten Sandsteins in Ägypten und die Herkunft der Memnon-Kolosse: Heliopolis oder Aswan?, in: *MDAIK* 40 (1984) 291–296.

Column, *see also* pillar

Wooden columns are not unusual in Egyptian temples (for example in the **valley temple** of **Menkaure**, and in the **pyramid temples** of **Neferirkare** and **Neferefre**), although they are much more frequent in dwellings (**Kahun, El-Lisht, Amarna**). In poorer houses they took the form of simple upright posts, but in more lavish buildings they appeared in a wide variety of forms, colourfully painted and decorated with sashes and garlands of plants (known mostly from illustrations).

As in Greek architecture, some forms of wooden column were replicated in stone, and it is for this reason that stone columns still regularly stand on a **column base** and have an **abacus** connecting them with the **architrave** above. Like their wooden prototypes, all stone columns were colourfully painted, usually with representations of plants. These columns would have been too delicate to support anything heavy but rather stood tall and independently. The selection of specific column types certainly has some symbolic connotations (papyrus and lotus = Lower Egypt, lily = Upper Egypt, palm = Buto), but artistic considerations cannot be ruled out.

Half-columns, i.e. engaged columns, are less common in Egyptian architecture (**pilaster**). They mainly served to create the impression of the façade of a building or door decorated with columns. Examples are found at the precinct of **Djoser** (**channelled columns** with a cleat capital), at the Hathor shrine in the temple of **Hatshepsut**, in the **Akhmenu** (façade of the nine-niched sanctuary) and on the front of the **rock temple** of Asklepios at **Athribis** (palm capital). Many smaller examples exist on cult niches and door frames of Late Period tombs in the Assasif at Thebes.

Bibliography (general): Perrot, *L'Égypte* 539–587; Borchardt, *Pflanzensäule*; W.D. Spanton, The water lilies of Ancient Egypt, in: *Ancient Egypt 1917*, 1–20; Jéquier, *Manuel* 167–274; P. Jánosi and D. Arnold, Säule, in: Helck, *LÄ* V 343–348; Dieter Kurth, *Die Dekoration der Säulen im Pronaos des Tempels von Edfu* (Wiesbaden 1983).

The following types of stone column can be distinguished (for illustrations of several types of column, see frontispiece on page ii, opposite title page):

a) It is not clear whether the channelled, engaged columns at the precinct of **Djoser** represent the stems of conifers with the bark removed, with cleat **capitals**, or *Heracleum giganteum*; nor is there a clear connection with later channelled ('**protodoric**') columns or with multi-faced pillars with an abacus. Octagonal forms may be counted as **pillars**, whereas those with 16, 20, 24 and 32 sides are counted as columns (**Buhen**, Fig.). There are many genuinely channelled examples like the shafts of Greek Doric columns. However, the Egyptian examples lack the echinus below the wide capital and do not swell, many of them having a vertical band of inscriptions along the front (entasis). The relationship is also dubious because the Egyptian examples date back to the 3rd–2nd millennia, while the earliest Greek examples date from the 7th century BC. Examples are at the temple of **Mentuhotep**, the tombs at **Beni Hasan**, the 12th Dynasty funerary structures at **El-Lisht** and **Qaw el-Kebir** (Wahka I), the temple of **Hatshepsut**, the temple of **Ptah** at **Karnak**, and the temples at **Buhen**, **Amada**, **Semna** and **Beit el-Wali**.

Bibliography: Jéquier, *Manuel* 177–184; I.E.S. Edwards, Some early dynastic contributions to Egyptian architecture, in: *JEA* 35 (1949) 123–128; Ricke, *Bemerkungen* I 77–82.

b) Tent-pole columns imitate the wooden supports of lightweight tents and structures of reed **matting**. The diameter of the shaft increases steadily from the base upwards; the shaft itself has a ridge in the uppermost fifth, above which is a bell-shaped, rounded top with no capital. This type of column is attested from the Old Kingdom onwards, in the form of wooden examples and depictions. The only stone examples are found in the **Akhmenu** (dating from around 1480 BC), and in one tomb, that of **Amenemhat Surer** (c. 1360 BC). It is not clear whether they have any connection with the similar columns found in Minoan palaces (c. 1600 BC).

Bibliography: Borchardt, *Pflanzensäule* 56–57; Jéquier, *Manuel* 193–196.

c) Palm columns represent a shaft with palm fronds (*Phoenix dactylifera* L.) growing up from the top, which is bound with several circles of cord. A triple loop of cord hangs at the front below the central frond. Old Kingdom columns with circular abaci have been found at **Tanis**; the shape of the **abacus** elsewhere is always square. Distinctly different from both palm and channelled columns are the spur walls found in the entrance colonnade in the precinct of **Djoser**, whose free ends are formed like vertical reed matting, interpreted as a protective edge in the shape of palm ribs. The earliest examples of true free-standing monolithic palm columns of **granite** are in the **pyramid temple** of Djedefre. They are frequently found in the pyramid temples of **Sahure**, **Djedkare** and **Unas** (for their production, see **column manufacture**). Palm columns become frequent again from the 18th Dynasty onwards, being embellished with new elements.

Examples are found at the tomb of Djehutyhotep at **El-Bersha** (12th Dynasty), **Tanis** (usurped from the Middle Kingdom (?), height more than 11 m), **Soleb**, **Sesebi**, **Ehnasya el-Medina**, **Amarna** (tombs), the Hibis temple (**El-Kharga**), **Antaeopolis** and **Philae**. In the palace at **Amarna**, the underside of palm leaves is decorated in the cloisonné technique, with gilded fillets between the inlaid green faience and red paste designs. In Graeco-Roman buildings they are also shown with dates and an obliquely chequered band at the top. Palmettes are frequent in **composite capitals**. Many palm columns of the Old and Middle Kingdoms were re-used in temples in the Delta and in the mosques in Cairo.

Bibliography: W.M. Flinders Petrie, *Tell el Amarna* (London 1894) 9–10, Plate 6; Borchardt, *Pflanzensäule* 44–49; Edouard Naville, *Bubastis* (London 1891) 11–13 (BM) 49; E. Chassinat, A propos d'une tête en grès rouge du roi Didoufré, in: *Monuments Piot* 25 (1921–22) 55; Jéquier, *Manuel* 196–201; Pierre Montet, *Les nouvelles fouilles de Tanis (1929–1932)* (Paris 1933) 63–69, 95–101.

d) Lotus columns with a closed capital represent bundles of four, six, and later also eight closed lotus flowers (*Nymphaea lotus* L., white lotus with rounded petals and buds) tied together at the neck, the drooping stems of some very small florets hanging down on the shaft (**Ptahshepses**, Fig.). Unlike papyrus columns, their shafts are straight all the way down to the ground. This type is frequent in the Old and New Kingdoms and later again in the Late Period. Examples exist in the tomb of **Ptahshepses**, at **Memphis**, at **Beni Hasan**, in the pyramid complex of **Senwosret III**, at the **palace** of **Apries** and in depictions. True open-lotus capitals are attested from depictions dating to the Old to the New Kingdom, but the earliest surviving examples are from the Ptolemaic period as part of composite capitals with numerous petals arranged in several layers.

Blue lotus with pointed petals and buds (*Nymphaea caerulea* L.) is found very occasionally in open-lotus columns (in New Kingdom tombs at **Thebes**); it is also found in a fragment of a column of the temple of Arensnuphis at **Philae**.

Bibliography: Prisse d'Avennes, *Histoire*, Plates 15–20, 24, 26; Jéquier, *Manuel* 201–211; Borchardt, *Pflanzensäule* 3–16.

e) Papyrus columns (*Cyperus papyrus* L.) with a closed capital resemble the lotus columns in having bundles of six to eight plant stems (**abacus**, Fig.; **Soleb**, Fig.). However, they differ from them by the noticeably retracting foot, which is surrounded by up to five pointed leaves. Another feature is bundles of three smaller papyrus plants fitted in between the stems in the capital.

The earliest examples are in the pyramid temple of **Sahure**; later examples occur in the pyramid temples of **Senwosret III** and **Amenemhat III**, at **Bubastis** (now in the Louvre, E 10589), in the **Akhmenu**, in the **Luxor** temple, in the **barque station** of Amenhotep III at **Elephantine**, at **Soleb**, in tombs at **Amarna**, in the 'house of millions of years' of Sety I at Qurna, at **Medamud** and at **Hermopolis**.

Bibliography: Jéquier, *Manuel* 211–220; Borchardt, *Pflanzensäule* 25–34; Edouard Naville, *Bubastis* (London 1891) 11–13, 49 (columns called 'lotus-bud').

f) Papyrus columns with a closed capital and smoothed shaft and capital; despite appearing late (start of the 19th Dynasty) it is one of the most common types of column in Egypt, being distinctive by its squat, plump shaft (**Khonsu**, Fig.). The smooth surfaces bear inscriptions, rows of cartouches and relief scenes. Examples are found in the **'houses of millions of years'** of **Sety I** at **Thebes** and **Abydos**, in the **hypostyle hall** at **Karnak**, at **Medinet Habu**, in the temple of **Ramesses III** at Karnak, and the temple of **Khonsu**.

Bibliography: Jéquier, *Manuel* 227-30; Borchardt, *Pflanzensäule* 35–36.

g) Papyrus columns with open capital (campaniform) and plain shaft exist as lamp stands from the Middle Kingdom, in depictions from the early 18th Dynasty, and in the form of actual columns in buildings from the reign of Thutmosis III onwards (at **Karnak**). The papyrus element is reflected in the shape of the shaft, with a slight hint at the three-cornered section of the stem of the papyrus plant, while the capital is decorated with rows of open papyrus umbels. The type was preferred in free-standing **kiosks** and the central naves of **hypostyle halls** (plants 'opening' along the path of the god). Examples are found in the colonnade of **Luxor** temple, in the hypostyle hall of **Karnak**, at the **Ramesseum**, at **Medinet Habu**, at the temple of **Khonsu**, at **Edfu** and at **Philae**.

Bibliography: Jéquier, *Manuel* 220–227; Borchardt, *Pflanzensäule* 37–43.

h) Lily columns with a red calyx and two or four curled petals are also found (the plant cannot be identified as an iris, and may perhaps be the wild banana: *Musa ensete*, *Ensete ventricosum* or *Kaempferia aethiopica*). It appears as the Upper Egyptian plant in raised relief on one of the **heraldic pillars** of Thutmosis III. It is represented in tombs of the 18th Dynasty as part of composite capitals made of wood (**canopy**, **kiosk**). There may be some connection with the proto-Ionic (Aeolian and Timora) capitals which appeared all over the Near East in the 10th century BC, themselves likely to be connected to the appearance of the true Ionic capital in the 6th century BC. Stone lily capitals do not appear in Egypt until the Ptolemaic period, when the form is either multi-layered or a composite capital. Earlier stone forerunners with only four flower petals are attested to in the Late Period by stonemasons' sketches.

Bibliography: Borchardt, *Pflanzensäule* 18–24; Jéquier, *Manuel* 263–271; D. Arnold, New evidence for liliform capitals in Egypt, in: *Chief of Seers. Egyptian Studies in Memory of Cyril Aldred* (London 1997) 20–28.

i) Cyperus columns. Borchardt identifies the plant in the 'palmette' ornament as *Cyperus alepocuroides* (Rottb.)

True 'cyperus columns' do not exist, but the palmette motif frequently appears in **composite capitals** in combination with papyrus motifs.

Bibliography: L. Borchardt, Die Cyperussäule, in: *ZÄS* 40 (1902) 26–49.

j) **Hathor pillars**
k) **Composite capitals**

Column base, *see also* base, plinth

Column bases can be divided into four broad types, which range from short and wide to tall and narrow: a) flat, with an angled or rounded edge (mainly used in the Old Kingdom and the Middle Kingdom under plant-bundle **columns** and multi-faced pillars), b) tall, rounded off at the top, c) tall, rounded off at the top and bottom like a cushion (especially under smoothed papyrus columns of the Ramesside period, many bearing inscriptions) and d) cylindrical, sometimes with an angled or bevelled edge (especially in Graeco-Roman buildings). Bases are manufactured as part of the **paving** and many are carved as part of paving blocks. The bases of particularly large columns consist of several blocks fitted together. Shafts are in some instances fitted into the base. On some bases there are score marks for fitting the shaft.

Bibliography: Jéquier, *Manuel* 173–174.

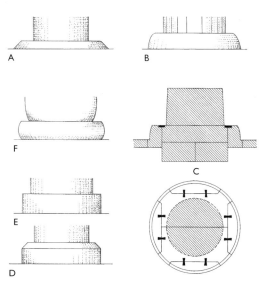

Column base types. A: angled off at the top; B: rounded off at the top (Middle Kingdom to New Kingdom); C: base constructed of blocks dowelled together (temple of Amenhotep III at Soleb); D–E: vertical and tapered bases of composite columns of the Graeco-Roman period; F: cushion-shaped base (Ramesside period)

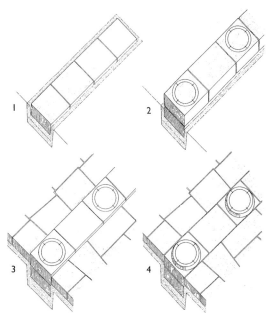

Manufacture of column bases by means of working the rough surface of paving blocks (after J. Jacquet)

Column manufacture

Monolithic stone **columns** were manufactured at **stone quarries** and delivered complete. According to Isler, as with **obelisks**, the outlines were marked horizontally on to the surface of the rock and then hammered out of the rock, with constant monitoring using semi-circular wooden templates. Columns made of **limestone** or **sandstone** were built up out of drums and half-drums (with regularly offset touch **joints**) and joined together with **cramps**. The outer surface was left in a **bossed** state and dressed only after the column had been erected. Markings scored on the **column base** and on the **abacus** provided a basis for

Finishing of columns constructed of rough blocks in the first court at Karnak (after U. Hölscher)

measurements. The manufacture of a palm column made
of wood is illustrated in a Theban tomb.

Bibliography: Theban tomb: *LD* III 26, 1a; Clark, *AEM* 82–83, 141ff.;
R. Engelbach, An experiment on the accuracy of shaping a monolithic
column, in: *ASAE* 28 (1928) 144–152; M. Eisler, The technique of
monolithic carving, in: *MDAIK* 48 (1992) 45–55.

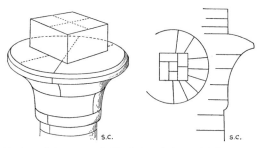

Massive capitals constructed of blocks from the hypostyle hall and kiosk
of Taharqa at Karnak (after S. Clark)

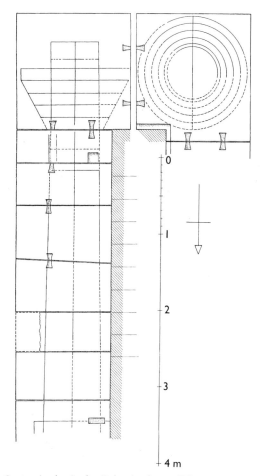

Construction drawing for a Ptolemaic column at Philae

Column, proportions of

The proportions of Egyptian **columns** of the same type
fluctuate, having a height of between five and seven times
their diameter (in contrast to Greek architecture, where
their height is between eight and ten times their
diameter), thus giving the particular **style** of a period.
The columns of the Old Kingdom and those from the
Ptolemaic period onwards are particularly slender,
whereas particularly stocky ones date from the reign of
Ramesses III. The spacing between individual columns
fluctuates between one and two-and-a-half times their
diameter. There is likely to have been some kind of
relationship between the proportions of columns and the
space between them, but the nature of this is difficult to
determine without precise structural measurements. The
following list shows the relationship between maximum
diameter (D) and total height (including **column base**
and **abacus**):

Palm columns
  Sahure, pyramid temple   7 D
  Unas, pyramid temple   8 D
  Amenhotep III, **Soleb**   5 D
  Roman, **Philae**   6 D
  Roman, **Kalabsha**   6 D
Closed-papyrus columns
  Sahure, pyramid temple   6–7 D
  Niuserre, pyramid temple   5.5–6.0 D
  Thutmosis III, **Akhmenu**, Karnak   5.5 or 6 D
  Amenhotep III, **Luxor**   6.8 D
  Amenhotep III, Soleb   5.3 D
Smoothed open-papyrus columns
  Karnak, hypostyle hall   5.2 D
  Ramesseum   5.0 D
  Ramesses III, **Medinet Habu**   4.5 D
Composite columns
  Roman, Medinet Habu   8.0 D
  Roman, **Dendur**   5.2 D

Bibliography: Vitruvius, *Architecture* III, Chapters 2–3; Jéquier,
Manuel 174–175.

Composite capital

The earliest composite capitals, made of wood and
decorated with colourful inlays and sashes, appeared on
canopies and **kiosks**, as depicted in tombs of the New
Kingdom. The **palace** at **Amarna** was furnished with
papyrus **columns** of stone decorated with a wreath of
hanging ducks, closed columns with garlands of lotus
flowers and a **frieze of uraei**, and also an (otherwise
unknown) type of column with vines. Composite capitals

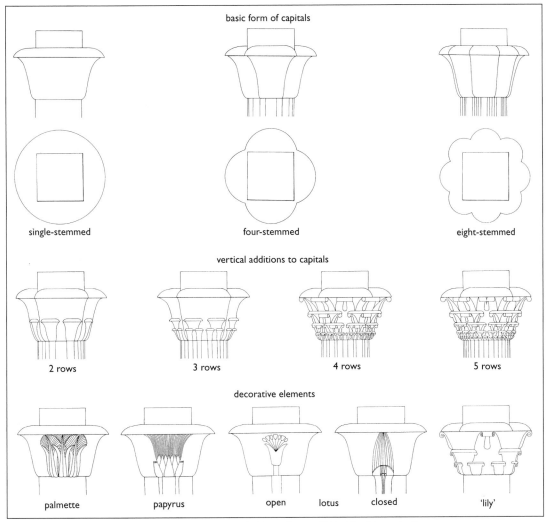

basic form of capitals

single-stemmed   four-stemmed   eight-stemmed

vertical additions to capitals

2 rows   3 rows   4 rows   5 rows

decorative elements

palmette   papyrus   open   lotus   closed   'lily'

Orders of capitals. Upper: the form of basic capital; middle: vertical additions; lower: individual floral decorative elements

were translated into stone from the 26th Dynasty onwards (Hibis temple, **El-Kharga**). Their use flourished in buildings of the Graeco-Roman period (**Deir el-Medina**, Fig.), appearing as palmettes, papyrus umbels, lotus flowers and lilies arranged on a bell-shaped capital core, either singly or in four- to eight-fold sections, arranged layer upon layer, in two to five rows. Spaces were covered in vines, bundles of dates or ears of grain. A few examples bear a wreath of Greek acanthus leaves on the lower part of a composite capital (**Philae**). The lotus capitals and newly created lily capitals are not true composite capitals. In all, G. Jéquier distinguished 27 forms. The composite capitals on columns at **Philae** carry a raised **abacus** shaped like a **Hathor** capital or depicting a Bes figure. Some composite capitals in **Alexandrian** architecture

appear as half-columns (**pilaster**). The lowest part of the column shaft is smoothed, so that the bundled section is visible only at the neck.

Bibliography: Many examples in *Description* I–IV; Prisse d'Avennes, *Histoire*, Plate 17–20, 25, 47, 58–61; Jéquier, *Manuel* 230–274; Borchardt, *Pflanzensäule*; M. Haneborg-Lühr, Les chapiteaux composites étude typologique, stylistique et statistique, in: *Amosiadès: Melanges offerts au professeur Claude Vandersleyen* (Louvain-la-Neuve 1992) 125–152.

Construction damage

Egyptian architecture can provide many examples of construction damage which occurred during building, and necessitated either very costly repairs or the abandonment of the project concerned. Sagging of some masonry during the construction of the **Bent Pyramid** meant that it to be covered with a 15 m deep stone mantle, the western burial chamber had to be propped up with 12 transverse beams and the angle of the slope had to be reduced, giving it its 'bent' shape. Despite all these efforts, the pyramid had to be abandoned. The pyramid of **Pepy II** had to be covered with a stone mantle, 6.5 m thick, to prevent the cracking of the **core masonry**. That of **Amenemhat III** at Dahshur was abandoned due to the sagging of the substratum and the collapse of the interior accommodation. In many pyramids, the **casing** blocks were damaged by the subsidence of the (heavier) centre of the pyramid and the outer surface had to be patched with thousands of stones.

Extensive errors in measurement have been observed in the upper part of the **Khafre** pyramid. The eastern edge of the pyramid of **Sahure** deviated from true by 1.88 m.

Bibliography: Arnold, *Building* 234–243.

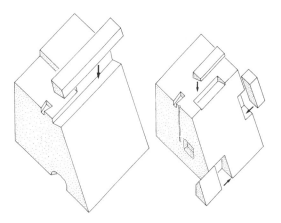

Small pieces of stone used to repair casing blocks on the pyramid of Amenemhat III at Dahshur

Construction plans, *see also* architectural depictions, planning

Although Egyptian draftsmen were capable of producing **architectural depictions**, it is doubtful whether architectural plans in the modern sense existed at all. Approximately 25 drawings have survived, but these are really only rough pocket-sized sketches on ostraka (flakes of **limestone**), occasionally bearing measurements as an aide-mémoire for the workmen. It is more likely that work was carried out on the basis of verbal descriptions (together with measurements) of the type handed down in 'sacred books' in the temple inscriptions of the Ptolemaic period. Such architects' books continued to be used in classical antiquity. The largest surviving architectural plan is a sketch 1.6 m long of an unknown

temple in the **stone quarries** at Sheikh Said. Two carefully drawn and very detailed plans have survived, one of the tomb of Ramesses IV (Papyrus Turin 1885) and the other of and the tomb of Ramesses IX (on an ostrakon now in the Egyptian Museum at Cairo, CG 25184), but these probably served as illustrative plans. Stonemasons drew onto the surface of the stone using a 1:1 scale, as was the case with medieval building practices; examples are the constructional drawings of the profile of a **vault** in the tomb of Ramesses IV in the Valley of the Kings, a column on the **pylon** at **Philae**, or a **cavetto cornice** on one of the walls at the temple of **Edfu**).

Bibliography: L. Borchardt, Altägyptische Werkzeichnungen, in: *ZÄS* 34 (1896) 69–76; N. de Garis Davies, An architectural sketch at Sheikh Said, in: *Ancient Egypt 1917*, 21–25; Clark, *AEM* 46–59; E.A.E. Reymond, *The Mythical Origin of the Egyptian Temple* (Manchester 1969); D. Arnold, Baupläne, in: *LÄ* I 661–663; R. Stadelmann, Baubeschreibung, in: Helck, *LÄ* I 636–37; H.S. Smith and H.M. Stewart, The Gurob Shrine Papyrus, in: *JEA* 70 (1984) 54–64; Arnold, *Building* 7–10, 22, 47. For the development of plans in general: Henry A. Millon, Ed., T*he Renaissance from Brunelleschi to Michelangelo. The Representation of Architecture*, Exhibition Catalogue (Washington 1995).

Control notes

Stone blocks in Egyptian buildings frequently bear inscriptions, marks or symbols, applied during construction either by chiselling or being painted on in black or red to enable construction managers to check the rate of performance or to help craftsmen with orientation in their work:

Sketch plan of a temple found on the wall of a quarry at Sheikh Said (Middle Egypt)

a) Team marks. Like markings used by present-day stone-masons in that they also stand for the group of persons responsible for the production of a stone, these are mainly imitations of hieroglyphs or invented symbols applied by illiterate workmen using coarse tools (such as a pointed hammer or coarse colour brushes). These marks, up to 100 cm, were used until Roman times.

Bibliography: Jaritz, *Terrassen* 85–94, Plates 39–42; V. Dobrev, Les marques sur les pierres de construction de la nécropole de Pépi I, in: *BIFAO* 96 (1996) 103–142.

b) Transportation marks. Written in transit by literate supervisors, these are found on the roughly finished sides of blocks, in most cases appearing as hieratic formulae such as: 'Year 12, Winter month 2, Day 6. Brought from the quarry by workers of the 3rd district of Heliopolis.' Such annotations, including the transport date, give important information concerning the *termini post quem* for the erection of a building. They were used by the construction managers to check performance.

Bibliography relating to a) and b): M. Verner, Zu den 'Baugraffiti mit Datumsangaben' aus dem Alten Reich, in: *Mélanges Gamal Eddin Mokhtar* (Cairo 1985) 339–346; Felix Arnold, *The Control Notes and Team Marks. The South Cemetery of Lisht*, Vol. 3 (New York 1990); Miroslav Verner, *Abusir II. Baugraffiti der Ptahschepses-Mastaba* (Prague 1992); Miroslav Verner, *Abusir III, The Pyramid Complex of Khentkaues* (Prague, 1995) 43–54; Zivie, *Deir Chelouit* 75–81.

c) Positioning marks. In complicated projects, or ones where space was limited, such as burial chambers and their stone roofs, or the golden shrine of Tutankhamun, the parts of the construction were fitted together above ground, as a trial run, then numbered and taken inside in the correct order. A simple system was used consisting of a numbered sequence, detailed indications such as 'second layer, east side, middle', or symbols showing how the blocks fitted together, such as an ankh sign on each side of a joint or where two blocks met at a corner.

Similar in nature are the central crosses or broken lines used to show the precise point of connection between sections of **columns**, **pillars** with their bases, or **architraves** on the **abacus**.

Bibliography: Arnold, *Building* 18–21.

d) Height marks. These were frequently used in the pyramid precincts of the Old Kingdom, to aid measurement, in the form of encircling marks to show the horizontal or vertical orientation lines (construction shaft in the lower pyramid of **Zawyet el-Aryan**). Horizontal lines were often accompanied by directional arrows and notes of distances such as '1 **cubit** above the baseline'. Rather than the bedrock level, the zero level was taken as the intended level of the **paving** (*neferu*); in the case of pyramids this was the courtyard paving.

Bibliography: Arnold, *Building* 17–18.

e) Depth marks. These were applied on wall and rock surfaces while still rough and waiting to be worked. The stonemasons were given directions concerning the depth to which smoothing was to be applied by small rectangles inserted to the required measurement and leaving a black mark. Many unfinished walls are found bearing hundreds of marks arranged in parallel rows. Using a different method, places to be smoothed were made to appear prominent by sliding a piece of red-painted board or the like over the surface to be treated, similar to the colour strips used by dentists in biting tests.

Bibliography: W. Flinders Petrie, *The Labyrinth, Gerzeh and Mazghuneh* (London 1912) 54; Arnold, *Building* 45.

Corbelled vault

Ceiling construction common in Egyptian architecture from the 2nd to 4th Dynasties, in which rows of headers on the long sides of a room project in a step formation, becoming ever closer to each other, until the distance between them is bridged. Stone corbelling exists in burial

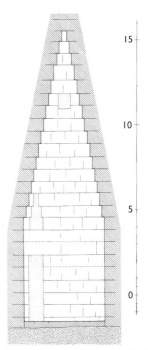

Section through the corbelled vault of the northern burial chamber of the Bent Pyramid; at the top, access to the west chamber system; on the left, the 'chimney'

chambers of tombs of the 4th Dynasty at **Dahshur** and **Meidum**. Other examples are in the **Bent Pyramid** (5.26 x 7.97 m in area, 16.48 m high), the **Red Pyramid** of Sneferu (4.18 x 8.35 m in area, 14.67 m high) and the pyramid of **Khufu** (ascending gallery 46.71 m long, 8.50 m high). False barrel vaults were created in the New Kingdom by carving out the protruding corbelled ledges, thus converting them into vaults (temple of **Hatshepsut** and that of **Sety I** at Abydos). **Brick** corbelled vaults are used in Upper Egyptian tombs from the 2nd Dynasty (necropoleis of Naga el-Deir and El-Amra) and are also widely found in Egypt.

Bibliography: Clark, *AEM* 184–185; Arnold, *Building* 184–188; N. Swelim, A reason for the corbelled roof, in: *JSSEA* 14 (1984) 612.

Core masonry

Transport costs in masonry construction were minimised by restricting the use of valuable materials to the outer casing, the core being built of materials locally available. The use of an outcrop of **limestone** inside a core was rare (examples are at the **valley temple** of **Khafre** and in the **Harmakhis** temple at **Giza**), but some pyramids were erected above a nucleus of rock (**Khufu**, **Khafre**, **Senwosret II**). Interior masonry normally consisted of rough-hewn stone, individual pieces in some cases being huge, although the majority were of moderate size. Wide and irregular gaps were frequently filled in by the insertion of smaller stones and **mortar**; material from earlier structures was often re-used in the cores (**re-use of blocks**), an example being the ninth **pylon** at **Karnak**, which was completely filled with *talatat*.

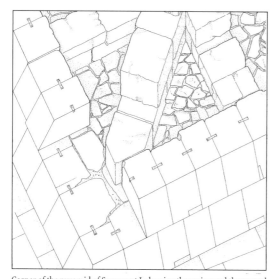

Corner of the pyramid of Senwosret I, showing the casing and the central core with radial supporting walls

The cores of many **mastabas** and **pyramids** were constructed of **brick** covered by a stone **casing**. Interior masonry was in some cases stabilised by interspersing of the fill with walls made of large blocks radiating out from the centre, examples being found at the pyramids of **Senwosret I**, **Amenemhat II** and **Senwosret II**.

Cramps, dowelling (connecting blocks)

Anchors of wood, bronze or stone, inserted between two blocks to prevent the construction elements from slipping. In Egypt they were mainly dovetail cramps, often bearing the cartouche of the monarch responsible for the building. In the Middle and New Kingdoms cramps were predominantly made of wood. They were usually 30–50 cm in length; the longest, measuring 1.5 m, was used at Karnak (Sheshonq I). Bronze cramps are less common (**Khafre**, copper or bronze, weighing 20–25 kg, **Unas**, **Chapelle Rouge**, **Tanis**, **Iseum**). Stone cramps are also rare (**Sety I** at Abydos). **Gypsum** was used to fix the cramps into holes cut into the surface of blocks once they were in place. They were first used in the 4th Dynasty (**valley temple** of **Khafre**). During the Old Kingdom their use was restricted to parts of the structure thought to be vulnerable (**architrave**); their usage became more extensive in the Middle Kingdom, when they were applied

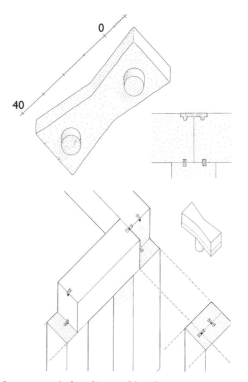

Copper cramps in the architraves of the valley temple of Khafre at Giza

in the overall outer **casing** of the pyramids (**core masonry**, Fig.) and blocks were connected not only in the direction of the wall, but also cross-wise; in some instances several were fitted side by side (**Augustus kiosk**, Fig.). Frequently small pieces of filling stone were fastened in place with cramps and repairs on vertical walls were sometimes held in place by cramps. **Architraves**, **columns** and **pillars** were often secured with vertical cylindrical pins or with hemispherical protuberances on the upper side of the **abacus**.

Bibliography: Clark, *AEM* 112–213; H. Frankfurt, *The Cenotaph of Seti at Abydos* (London 1933), Plate 8 (stone dowel); Jaritz, *Terrassen*, 36–37, Plate 26 (stone dowel); Arnold, *Building* 124–128; Golvin, *Karnak* 113–114.

Crypt

A secret chamber in a temple, accessible only via a hidden entrance in the floor or a wall. While they are rather uncommon in the Middle and New Kingdoms, they are found particularly in late temples. The largest system of crypts is that in the **foundations** and walls of the temple at **Dendera**, where crypts were used for the storage of cult images and the observance of secret rites. Early examples are at **Buhen**, the temple of Ramesses III at **Medinet Habu**, the **pyramid temple** of **Senwosret I**, **Qasr el-Sagha** and **Sesebi**; late crypts are found at **Deir el-Shelwit**, **Dendera**, **Dendur**, **Kalabsha**, **Kom Ombo**, **Month** precinct (Karnak), **Opet** temple and **El-Tod**. Occasionally the crypt is no more than an unused space created by the layout.

Bibliography: Louis A. Christophe, *Karnak-Nord III* (Cairo 1951), Plate 42; Arnold, *Qasr es-Sagha* 12–13; C. Traunecker, Krypta, in: Helck, *LÄ* III 823–830; C. Traunecker, Cryptes décorées, cryptes anépigraphes, in: *Hommages François Daumas* (Montpellier 1986) 571–577; C. Traunecker, *Les cryptes du temple d'Opet Karnak* (Paris 1975); Silvie Cauville, *Le temple de Dendera* (Cairo 1990) 54–59; Zivie, *Deir Chelouit* 34–36.

Cubit

The normal unit of measure used in Egyptian architecture. From the time of the Unification onwards, it is known at first to have measured 51.89–53.18 cm; then, from the Old Kingdom, it measured 52.3–52.5 cm. It was subdivided into seven hand-breadths, each equivalent to 7.5 cm, each consisting of four fingers of 1.875 cm. From the New Kingdom onwards, many cubit rods have survived, mainly as votive offerings or grave goods. Another unit occasionally used was the *nby*, measuring 67–8 cm, and there is a single occurrence of the foot as a unit of measurement in the mastaba of **Ptahshepses**.

Bibliography: Richard Lepsius, *Die alt-aegyptische Elle* (Berlin 1865); H. Carter and A. Gardiner, The tomb of Ramesses IV as compared with the Turin Papyrus, in: *JEA* 4 (1917) 149–158; J. Dorner, Überlegungen zur Fassadengliederung der großen Mastabagräber aus der 1. Dynastie, in: *MDAIK* 47 (1991) 81–92; Arnold, *Building*, 10, 251–252; Elke Roik, *Das Ellenmaß-system im Alten Ägypten* (Hamburg 1993).

Cult pyramid, *ka*-pyramid, satellite pyramid, secondary pyramid, subsidiary pyramid

From the reign of Sneferu, a small secondary pyramid becomes part of the royal pyramid complex. The latest example is that of **Senwosret I**. It stood within the inner **enclosure wall** either on the south side or in front of the south-east corner of the main pyramid. The angle of the slope is always 63°; the length of the base and the height were identical, often being 1/5 of the base length of the main pyramid. The dimensions of the inner rooms were at best adequate for the burial of a statue. No cult places or inscriptions have been found. The function of this kind of structure is not known; did it represent a revival of the **south tomb** of the 3rd Dynasty or was it intended for a *ka*-statue?

Bibliography: Mark Lehner, *The Pyramid Tomb of Hetep-heres and the Satellite Pyramid of Khufu* (Mainz 1985) 74–85; Arnold, *Amenemhet III* 99–103; Jánosi, *Pyramidenanlagen* 280–287.

Cult target

The ultimate cult room of a temple or tomb with an imaginary sphere beyond occupied by the deity or a deceased person. The cult target was indicated by a **false door**, a niche for a statue or simply by a scene depicting the owner of the tomb or temple. The place of offering lay in front of the cult target. The whole scheme of texts and decoration was directed towards the cult target, which either lay on the axis of the temple or tomb or else was reached by an offset axis.

Bibliography: Arnold, *Wandrelief*, 128; Eigner, *Grabbauten* 128–133; Henry G. Fischer, *The Orientation of Hieroglyphs* (New York 1977) 41–47.

Cult temple, statue temple, *see also* pyramid temple

The front section of a **pyramid temple**, usually dedicated to the cult of the statues of the king. At the **Bent Pyramid** of Sneferu, the cult temple stood in the valley, and from **Khufu** onwards the cult temple was situated in front of the east side of the pyramid. At the transition from the 4th to the 5th Dynasty it was combined with the newly added mortuary temple, and it becomes part of the new pyramid temple, which predominates from then on. The cult temple incorporates a **Per-weru** hall, a courtyard with pillars or columns, a transverse corridor and the actual statue chamber with five chapels for the various manifestations of the king as Osiris, or as king with the red or white crown.

Bibliography: Ricke, *Bemerkungen* II 35ff.; Brinks, *Grabanlagen*, 103,107; D. Arnold, Royal cult complexes of the Old and Middle Kingdoms, in: B.E. Shafer, Ed., *Temples of Ancient Egypt* (Ithaca 1997) 31–85.

Cupola

Cupolas made of reeds are represented in early hieroglyphs (such as the reed hut of Min). From the 1st Dynasty onwards, the form was used in circular **grain stores** (diameter in the New Kingdom up to 8 m). In the Old Kingdom **mastabas** it was used as roofing over cult chambers and **serdabs**, or to cap the mouths of shafts (**Abydos**, **Dendera**). One example at **Giza** is constructed of stone. The inside of private **brick pyramids** of the New Kingdom was hollowed out into a cupola shape in order to relieve pressure on the barrel vault which was constructed below (**Thebes**, **Abydos**, **Aniba** and **Soleb**). Domed walling was installed in kilns and in cupola-shaped **cellars** (**Amarna**, the first settlement of the 21st Dynasty at **El-Lisht**). It was also used as a cap over the hollow spaces in the **foundation** blocks of **cellular constructions** at **Defenna**, **Naukratis** and **Memphis**.

Cupolas were constructed of concentric rows of bricks or stones in a corbel construction (**corbelled vault**) or concentric rows of headers angled down towards the centre with their outer edges supported on stones. An isolated case has been observed as a corner spandrel (pendentive or support cupola) in a New Kingdom tomb at Dra Abu el-Naga.

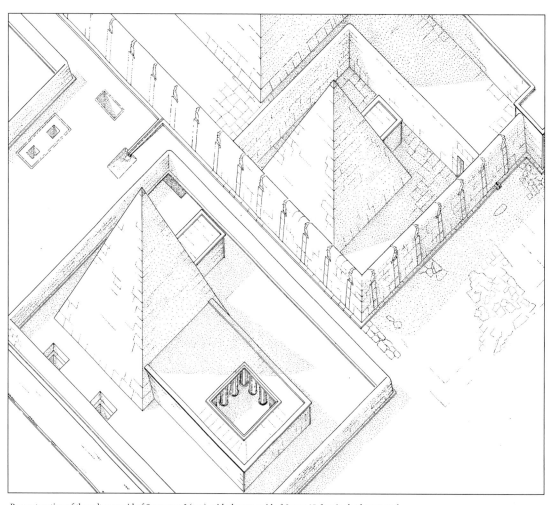

Reconstruction of the cult pyramid of Senwosret I (top), with the pyramid of Queen Neferu in the foreground

Bibliography: Auguste Mariette, *Abydos II* (Paris 1869), Plate 66; John Garstang, *El-Arabah* (London 1901), Plate 36; H. Pieron, Un tombeau égyptienne coupole sur pendentifs, in: *BIFAO* 6 (1908) 173–177; Clark, *AEM* 185–186; Junker, *Giza* III 26–28, V, Fig. 3; A. Badaway, *Brick vaults and domes in the Giza necropolis*, in: Abdel-Moneim Abu-Bakr, *Excavations at Giza 1949–1950* (Cairo 1953); Spencer, *Brick Architecture* 126; Brinks, Kuppel, in: Helck, *LÄ* III 882–884.

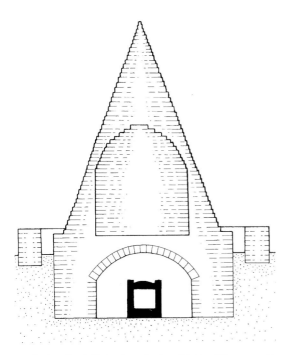

Cupola-shaped corbelled vault made of mud brick within a pyramid over a New Kingdom tomb at Abydos

Curved wall, *see also* wavy wall

Curved walls are attested from the reign of **Sekhemkhet** onwards and were in frequent use in the 11–13th Dynasty. **Brick** walls are often not straight, curving instead in a snakelike (sinoid) fashion and half a brick wide. They were usually used in short-term enclosures surrounding a construction site, incomplete cult buildings or tombs and similar structures. Having greater resistance than straight walls, they were used particularly as sand-breaks. Some pyramids of the 12th and 13th Dynasties were also enclosed by carefully laid **wavy walls**, up to 1.05 m wide (**cenotaph** of Senwosret III at **Abydos**, **Mazghuna**, an unknown king of the 13th Dynasty at **Saqqara**). It may have been for a religious or symbolic reason; G. Jéquier believes this may be a representation of a primitive woven fence.

Bibliography: Jéquier, *Manuel* 64–65; Clark, *AEM* 213; Jean Vercoutter, *Mirgissa I* (Paris 1970) 97–101.

Remains of a curved wall of the pyramid of an unknown king of the 13th Dynasty at Saqqara (after G. Jéquier)

D

Dabenarti (Dabaynarti)

A **fortress**, covering an area of 60 x 230 m, set on an island of the Nile opposite **Mirgissa**, a few kilometres south of Wadi Halfa. Because of its island position, its **enclosure wall** has no strengthening other than its deep, projecting buttress pillars.

Bibliography: S. Clarke, Ancient Egyptian Frontier Fortresses, in: *JEA* 3 (1916) 167; J.W. Ruby, Preliminary Report of the University of California Expedition to Dabnarti, in: *Kush* 12 (1964) 54; Dows Dunham, *Uronarti Shalfak Mirgissa, Second Cataract Forts*, Vol. 2 (Boston 1967) 177.

Dabod

A temple originally 15 km south of Aswan. The single-room chapel dedicated to Amun was erected by Azekheramun, a Meroitic king who reigned in the first half of the 3rd century BC, on top of the remains of a New Kingdom temple at ancient Parembole. The building was built and decorated on a similar design to the somewhat later Meroitic chapel on which the temple of **Dakka** is based. Later, in the reigns of Ptolemy VI Philometor, Ptolemy VIII Euergetes II and Ptolemy XII Auletes, it was extended on all four sides to form a small temple, 12 x 15 m, dedicated to Isis of Philae. Some of its decoration dates to the time of Tiberius. From the quay, a long processional way leads to the stone-built **enclosure wall**, through three stone **pylon gateways** and finally to the temple proper. The **pronaos**, which had four columns with **composite capitals**, collapsed in 1868 and is now lost. Behind was the original sanctuary of Amun, the offering table room and a later sanctuary with several side-rooms and stairs to the roof. Two **granite naoi** of Ptolemy VIII Euergetes II Physkon and Ptolemy XIII still survived in the sanctuary in the 19th century. The temple was dismantled in 1960 and re-erected in the Parque de Rosales in the centre of Madrid in 1972.

Bibliography: Gau, *Antiquités,* Plates 2–6; Günther Roeder, *Debod bis Bab Kalabsche* (Cairo 1911–1912) 1–100; Günther Roeder, Die Kapellen zweier nubischer Fürsten in Debod und Dakke, in: *ZÄS* 63 (1928) 126–141; W. Schenkel, Debod, in: Helck, *LÄ* I 997–998; J.J. Clère, Sur l'existence d'un temple du Nouvel Empire à Dabod, in: *Festschrift Hintze* (Berlin 1977) 107–113.

Dahamsha, *see El-Mahamid Qibly*

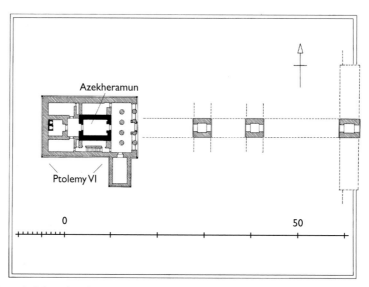

Plan of the Amun temple at Dabod, dating from the Meroitic period

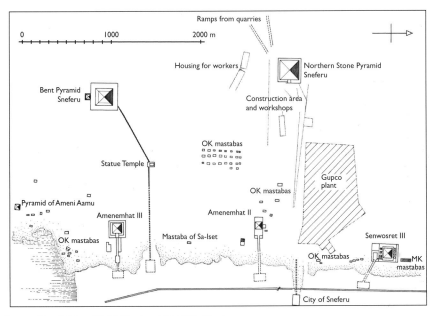

Plan of the royal necropolis at Dahshur. OK, Old Kingdom; MK, Middle Kingdom

Dahshur

One of the most important royal necropoleis of the 4th and 12th Dynasties, 40 km south of Cairo, with the **Bent Pyramid**, the **Red Pyramid** of Sneferu and the mud **brick** pyramids of **Amenemhat II**, **Senwosret III** and **Amenemhat III**. Also at this site are the important, but badly destroyed, **mastabas** of the officials of these kings. The **valley temples**, **pyramid towns** and residences of the early 4th and later 12th Dynasties probably lay in the nearby cultivation.

Bibliography: J. de Morgan, *Carte de la nécropole memphite* (Cairo 1897); D. Wildung, Dahschur, in: Helck, *LÄ* I 984–987; R. Stadelmann and N. Alexanian, Die Friedhöfe des Alten und Mittleren Reiches in Dahschur, in: *MDAIK* 54 (1998) 293–317; N. Alexanian and S.J. Seidlmayer, Die Nekropole von Dahschur, in: Bárta, *Abusir 2000* 283–304; see individually under the names of kings.

Dakka

The site of ancient Pselkhis (56 km south of Aswan) where, in the reign of the Ethiopian King Ergamenes, a one-room shrine to Thoth of Pnubs (Paotnuphis) was set up, replacing a small temple of the 18th Dynasty. It had an unusual north–south orientation. To this Ptolemy IV Philopator added an antechamber and a gate structure. Ptolemy IX Euergetes II subsequently enlarged the temple by adding a **pronaos** with two rows of probably three columns. This structure was further enlarged in the reigns of Augustus and Tiberius by the addition, at the rear, of a second sanctuary as well as inner and outer **enclosure walls** with a large **pylon**. The sanctuary contained a **granite naos**. Gau, in his day, saw considerable remains of brick buildings surviving around the temple (reminiscent of those at the **Ramesseum**). At the time of its removal to **Wadi el-Sabu'a**, between 1961 and 1968, some re-used stone blocks of Thutmosis III, Sety I and Merenptah were discovered, which came either from an earlier structure or from **Kubban**.

Bibliography: Gau, *Antiquités*, Plates 33–36; Günther Roeder, *Der Tempel von Dakke* (Cairo 1930); Günther Roeder, Die Kapellen zweier nubischer Fürsten in Debod und Dakke, in: *ZÄS* 63 (1928) 126–141; E. Bresciani, Dakke, in: Helck, *LÄ* I 988; Hein, *Ramessidische Bautätigkeit* 11–12.

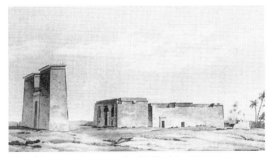

View of the Graeco-Roman temple of Dakka (after F.C. Gau)

Dara

The site, near Manfalut (35 km north of **Asyut**), of the monumental tomb of a ruler called Khui of the First

Intermediate Period, in the form of a mud **brick mastaba**, 136 x 146 m in size, height 18 m, 40 m thick. The exterior is steeply battered and the corners are rounded. The interior is filled with sand. Entering from the north, a corridor with a barrel **vault** leads axially through the masonry, descending by a sloping ramp to the burial chamber walled with **limestone** beams. The side-walls of the corridor are shored up by 11 transverse brick arches. The outer covering of the mastaba (whether level with the ground or mounded) is uncertain.

Bibliography: Ahmed Bey Kamal, Fouilles à Dara, in: *ASAE* 12 (1912) 128–134; R. Weill, Fouilles de Dara, in: *ASAE* 46 (1947) 323–334; Raymond Weill, *Dara* (Cairo 1958); H. Beinlich, Dara, in: Helck, *LÄ* I 990–991.

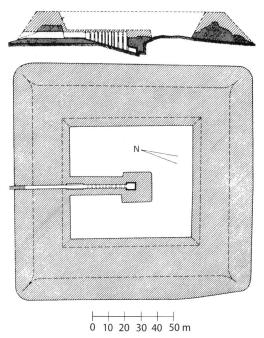

0 10 20 30 40 50 m

Plan and reconstructed section of the tomb at Dara

Defenna (Defenneh, Daphnae)

An important **fortress** and military settlement on the Pelusian branch of the Nile near Lake Manzalah. It was probably founded in the Ramesside period, and later enlarged in the reign of Psamtek I as a garrison for foreign (especially Greek) soldiers. It served as one of the main defence bases on the Sinai border of Egypt against the Babylonians and Persians. The central building, standing inside a rectangular **brick** enclosure of 385 x 640 m, is a fort (43.5 sq m in area) erected on top of a brick base, 10 m high, and built using **cellular construction**. The site has not been properly studied.

Bibliography: W.M. Flinders Petrie, *Nebesheh (Am) and Defenneh (Tahpanhes)* (London 1888) 47–61.

Deir el-Bahari, *see* (temples of) Hatshepsut, Mentuhotep, Thutmosis III

Deir el-Hagar

A temple dedicated to the Theban Triad, on the western edge of **Dakhla Oasis**. It is 7.30 x 16.20 m in size with a central sanctuary and two side-chapels opening onto a shared offering table room, a small **pillared hall** and a **kiosk**-like **pronaos**. The temple has cartouches of Nero, Vespasian, Titus and Domitian. The stone building stands inside an enclosure, 43 x 82 m, which is still preserved and has a monumental **gateway** and a processional way flanked by pillared halls. The restoration of the temple complex by the Canadian mission is exemplary.

Bibliography: H. E. Winlock, Ed., *Dakhleh Oasis, Journal of a Camel Trip Made in 1908* (New York, 1936) 29–33, Plates 17–25; S. Sauneron, *Notes de Voyage* 294–296.

Deir el-Medina

1. The settlement

This settlement lies in a sheltered side-valley of the Theban necropolis and was built for the craftsmen and artists who produced the **kings' tombs**, and their households, from the early 18th Dynasty onwards. Within a narrow, rectangular enclosed area (50 x 132 m; **town**, Fig.), on a slope, are approximately 70 single-storey **houses** (c. 5 x 15 sq m in area) built of rough stone to a regular plan, which testify to the relative prosperity of their inhabitants. The settlement was enlarged several times until it reached its ultimate size. The associated tombs are situated on the slopes of the hill (**town**, Fig.).

Bibliography: Bernard Bruyère, *Rapport sur les fouilles de Deir el Médineh (1922–1930)*, 15 Vols. (Cairo 1924–1953). Settlement: D. Valbelle, Deir el-Medineh, in: Helck, *LÄ* I 1028–1034; D. Valbelle, Le village de Deir el-Médineh, in: *First Intern. Congress* (Cairo 1976) 131–133.

2. Temples

Deir el-Medina is astonishingly rich in sanctuaries: as well as a temple of Amun and a temple of Hathor built by Ramesses II, Sety I built a **brick** temple to Hathor with a number of interesting architectonic peculiarities. It rises in steps, following the terrain, to three high terraces. The temple of Hathor, begun by Ptolemy IV and completed by Ptolemy VI and Ptolemy IX Euergetes II, was the actual 'Deir' el-Medina and still stands inside the original brick enclosure. Within is a small, particularly carefully built and decorated **sandstone** building with a small **pillared**

hall, its taller rear section being hidden behind a **screen wall** and arranged in the form of an offering table room. Stairs lead from there to the roof. Beyond the offering table room lie three sanctuaries.

Set in the rocky path between Deir el-Medina and the Valley of the Queens is a small cult grotto of **Meretseger**.

Bibliography: *Description* II, Plates 34–37; Prisse d'Avennes, *Histoire*, Plate 36; B. Bruyère, *Rapports sur les fouilles de Deir el-Médineh*

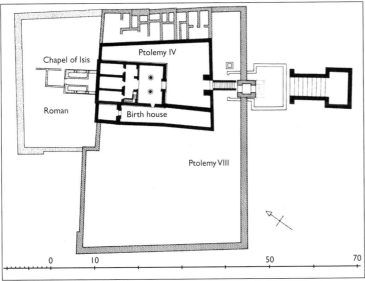

Hathor pillar, composite column and cropped screen wall in the Deir el-Medina temple, with a window and stairway behind

Plan of the Ptolemaic temple precinct at Deir el-Medina

Ptolemaic temple precinct at Deir el-Medina, with brick enclosure wall

(1935-40), Part 2, FIFAO 20 (Cairo 1948) 99–104, Figs 52–55, Plates 3–10; Aufrère, *L'Égypte restituée* 152–155; P. du Bourguet, Le temple d'Hathor à Deir el-Medineh, in: *MIFAO* 92 (Cairo, not yet published).

3. Tombs

The associated necropolis lies on the slope of the hill, with many small, steep **brick pyramids** (75° slope), which stand behind and above the forecourt of the **tombs**. The wealthier tombs possess either a pillared court or a pillared antechamber, exhibiting interesting individual solutions to architectonic problems. Many of the cult rooms and burial chambers are **vaulted** and magnificently painted.

Bibliography: Bernard Bruyère, *Rapport sur les fouilles de Deir el-Médineh (1922–1923)* (Cairo 1924) to *(1934–1935)* (Cairo 1937).

Deir el-Shelwit

A small, well-preserved temple of Isis at the southern end of the Theban necropolis. It has a sanctuary surrounded on all sides by a corridor onto which the side-chapels, the *wabet* and stairs to the roof open. The outside surfaces of the 13 x 16 m temple are dressed with **bosses**. The temple is surrounded by a **enclosure wall**, 58 x 78 m, with a propylon.

Bibliography: D. Wildung, Deir esch-Schelwit, in: Helck, *LÄ* I 1034–1035; Zivie, *Deir Chelouit*, 4 Vols; Aufrère, *L'Égypte restituée* 155.

Deir Rifa (Rifeh)

A Middle Kingdom necropolis of **rock tombs**, 10 km south of **Asyut**. Most interesting from the architectural perspective is the monumental tomb of an unknown person of the 12th Dynasty, fronted by two octagonal pillars, followed by a deep entrance hall and a four-pillared hall, 13.8 x 18.4 m, with a shallow vault and a statue chapel beyond. Other tombs here were either modified or newly built in the New Kingdom. The necropolis has not been adequately studied.

Bibliography: W.M. Flinders Petrie, *Gizeh and Rifeh* (London 1907) 11–12; M. Pillet, Structure et décoration architectonique de la nécropole antique de Deir-Rifeh, in: *Mélanges Maspero* I (Cairo 1934) 61–75; H. Beinlich, Deir Rifeh, in: Helck, *LÄ* I 1034.

Dendera

The ruins of a city, a necropolis and the justly famous temple of Hathor at the bend of the Nile west of Qena. The temple building proper stands inside a **brick** enclosure (10 m thick, area 280 sq m, dating from the reign of Shabaka or possibly Roman), with a propylon at the centre of the north side. The final, completely preserved, temple structure, 35 x 81 m in size, replaces several earlier buildings of the Old, Middle and New Kingdoms and of Nectanebo I, having been erected in 54 BC in the reign of Ptolemy XII Auletes. The structure is an outstanding example of late Ptolemaic temple architecture in Egypt. The famous **pronaos** with its four rows of six **Hathor** columns was erected later, in the reign

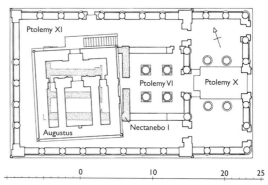

Plan of the birth house of Hathor-Isis at the temple of Hathor, Dendera

Rear of the Hathor temple at Dendera, with the addorsed cult image at its centre

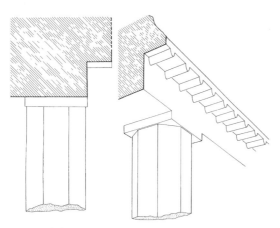

Upper end of pillar and projecting roof-shaped ledge from the 12th Dynasty rock tombs at Deir Rifa

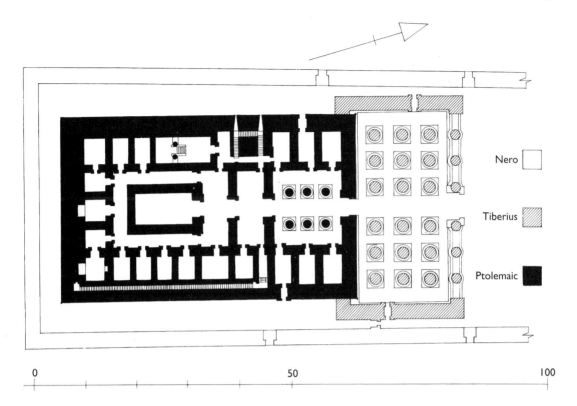

Nero

Tiberius

Ptolemaic

0   50   100

Plan of the temple of Hathor at Dendera, indicating construction periods

of Tiberius, and at the same time the inner stone enclosure was begun, whose front was to have opened on a pillared court with an entrance portal but was never completed. The **birth house** of Nectanebo I, which lay beside the forecourt, was cut through when the foundations of these latter structures were put down. It was replaced in the reign of Augustus (?) with the magnificent new structure directly behind the entrance portal.

Behind the pronaos of the main temple lies the original hall of appearances, with rooms at the side for the storage of cult objects and exits to the sacred wells. The offering table room is followed by the hall of the Divine Ennead, its rear wall occupied by the front of the barque sanctuary (for the barques of Horus of Edfu, Hathor of Dendera, Harsomtus and Isis of Dendera). The barque sanctuary is surrounded by a corridor lined with 11 further sanctuaries for different cults, the principal one lying at the centre of the rear wall (*wabet*, Fig.). Stairs from the offering table room lead to the roof of the temple where there is a well-preserved **roof chapel**. In the north-west and north-east of the roof of the temple there are two places associated with the cult of Osiris (**Osireion**), each consisting of three rooms. The central room of the north-eastern suite of rooms contained the

famous astronomical ceiling, which was removed in 1823 and is now in the Louvre. Within the outer walls of the temple building is a complex of **crypts**, unique in Egyptian architecture, which extend down to the temple **foundations**.

To the west, beside the main temple, stood the *ka*-chapel of Mentuhotep Nebhepetre (now in the Egyptian Museum, Cairo). The **sacred lake**, measuring 23 x 31 m, lies to the south-west. On the southern side of the main temple is the birth house, which was erected by Nectanebo I and dedicated to Harsiese. Ptolemy VI added a **hypostyle hall**, then Ptolemy X surrounded it with columns and finally Augustus gave it a new sanctuary for (Hathor-)Isis (**screen wall**, Fig.).

A processional way, flanked by **pillared halls**, led from a **platform** on the bank of the Nile, past temples of Shay and Thermuthis, to the temple of Hathor. 400 m to the east of the temple stands a sanctuary of Ihy, the son of Hathor and Horus, 135 x 135 sq m, never properly studied. Between them lay the city of Tentyris.

Bibliography: *Description* IV, Plates 2–34; Auguste Edouard Mariette, *Dendérah. Description générale du Grand Temple de cette ville*. Text and plates (Paris-Cairo 1875); G. Daressy, Chapelle de Mentouhotep à Denderah, in: *ASAE* 17 (1917) 226–234; Émile Chassinat, *Le temple de Dendara*, 6 Vols (Cairo 1934–1972); François Daumas, Le sanatorium de Dendara, in: *BIFAO* 56 (1956) 35–57; François Daumas, *Les Mammisis de Dendera* (Cairo 1959); François Daumas, *Dendara et le temple d'Hathor, notice sommaire* (Cairo 1969); François Daumas, Le temple de Dendara, in: *Textes et langages* (Cairo 1972) 267–273; Sylvie Cauville, Les statues cultuelles de Dendera d'après les inscriptions pariétales, in: *BIFAO* 87 (1987) 73–117; Sylvie Caulville and Annie Gasse, Fouilles de Dendara, in: *BIFAO* 88 (1988) 25–32; Sylvie Cauville, *Le temple de Dendera. Guides archéologiques de l'Institut français d'archéologie orientale du Caire* (Cairo 1990); E. Winter, A reconsideration of the newly discovered building inscription on the Temple of Denderah, in: *GM* 108 (1989) 75–85; Aufrère, *L'Égypte restituée* 225–246; S. Cauville, Le temple d'Isis à Dendera, in: *BSFE* 123 (1992) 31–48; S. Cauville, *Le temple de Dendera* (Cairo 1990).

Dendur

An Augustan temple dedicated to Isis of Philae and the local deities Peteisis and Pahor, near ancient Tutzis, 77 km south of Aswan. Facing the Nile is a wide stone-built **platform**, behind which is a portal, which would have been flanked by a **brick** pylon but it was never erected. Beyond the **pylon** and an open court stands the main temple building. The **pronaos** is followed by an ante-chamber for offerings and sanctuary with a flat cult image recess. This small building encompasses the entire cosmos of an Egyptian temple. Since 1980 it has been in the MMA.

Bibliography: Gau, *Antiquités*, Plates 23–26; Prisse d'Avennes, *Histoire*, Plates 10; A.M. Blackman, *The Temple of Dendur* (Cairo 1911); E. Bresciani, Dendur, in: Helck, *LÄ* I 1063–1064; C. Aldred, The Temple of Dendur, *Bulletin of the Museum of Art, New York* 36/1 (1978); Hassan el-Achiri, M. Aly, F.-A. Hamid and Ch. Leblanc, *Le temple de Dandour*, 2 Vols (Cairo 1972, 1979).

View of the Augustan temple of Dendur

Derr

The only rock-cut temple of Ramesses II on the East Bank of the Nile in **Nubia** (156 km south of Aswan), a **'house of millions of years'**, dedicated to the state gods, Amun-Re, Ptah, Ramesses II and, above all, Re-Horakhty. Allowing for the absence of statues in the façade, the 37 m long building resembles the Great Temple of **Abu Simbel** in terms of its plan and decoration. One section of its **pillared hall** is free-standing.

After 1964, sections of the seriously damaged temple were moved to a new site at Amada.

Bibliography: Gau, *Antiquités*, Plates 50–52; A.M. Blackman, *The Temple of Derr* (Cairo 1913); T. Säve-Söderbergh, in: Helck, *LÄ* I 1069–1070; Hein, *Ramessidische Bautätigkeit* 23–25.

Section through the hemispeos of Ramesses II at Derr (after F.C. Gau)

Dima (Dimeh)

The impressive ruins of the city of Soknopaiou Nesos, which cover an area of 350 x 660 m, on the west bank of Lake Faiyum, inhabited from the Ptolemaic period to the time of the Roman empire. Situated at its centre is a temple dedicated to Soknopaios surrounded by a **brick enclosure wall** (85 x 125 m in size, still standing in parts to a height of 10–15 m). A processional way leads to the city gate, cutting axially through the whole site. The temple building is destroyed; a few of the dwelling **houses** were preserved up to the third floor (**windows**, Fig., D).

Bibliography: Arthur E.R. Boak, *Soknopaiou Nesos* (Ann Arbor 1935); D. Hagedorn, Dimeh, in: Helck, *LÄ* I 1094.

Diorite (quartzdiorite)

A dark-grey, medium- to coarse-grained basaltic deep rock, with a specific gravity of 2.75–2.87, used in the manufacture of palettes, mace heads and stone vessels, and occasionally in sculpture and architecture (tomb in the temple of **Mentuhotep** at Deir el-Bahari, **Chapelle Rouge**, temple of **Sety I** at Abydos). It is found near **Aswan**, in the Eastern and Western Desert and at Mount Sinai, and also north-west of **Abu Simbel**.

Bibliography: Lucas, *AEMI* 71, 408–410; Arnold, *Der Tempel des Königs Mentuhotep von Deir el-Bahari* I (Mainz 1974) 48–49; Klemm, *Steine* 339–353; De Putter, *Pierres* 70–76; Nicholson, *Materials* 30–31.

Divine booth

Termed *seh-netjer* in Egyptian, this type of shrine is attested to only in hieroglyphic depictions as a cult structure of reed bundles with a slightly arched roof, thought to have belonged to Anubis. Its shape may have survived in the entrance recesses of Late Period tombs.

Bibliography: Bernhard Grdseloff, *Das ägyptische Reinigungszelt* (Cairo 1941) 39–42.

Divine fortress
A cult precinct of the Early Dynastic Period, called an *ah-netjer*, 'divine palace', which is attested to only in texts. It may be that this is the origin of the **funerary enclosures** of **Abydos** and **Hierakonpolis**, suggesting that it had a **fortress**-like **brick** enclosure with niching), inside which was the house of two tutelary deities of the two lands, Nekhbet and Wadjet (Uto). Behind the main entrance would have lain a small, niched building. This was probably a place of assembly for ritual festivals to be carried out by the Horus king and the divine powers (the Followers of Horus). Its importance lies in that it provided the underlying pattern for subsequent Egyptian architecture (**Djoser** precinct, **funerary enclosure**, **mastaba, niching, palace façade**). The following structures are known from texts:
1. Inebu-hedj, 'The White Castle', reign of King Hor-Aha.
2. Semer-netjeru, 'The Companion of the Gods', reign of King Djer.
3. Isut-netjeru, 'The Seats of the Gods', reign of King Udimu/Den.
4. Qau-netjeru, 'The Mounds of the Gods'.
5. Hut-netjen-netjeru, 'The Divine House of the Gods', reign of King Ninetjer.
6. Qebehu-netjeru, 'The Cool (Places) of the Gods', from the 3rd Dynasty.
7. Neru-tawy, 'Dread of the Two Lands', Djoser.
8. Netjerwy, 'Of the Two Gods', Djoser.

Bibliography: P. Kaplony, Gottespalast und Götterfestungen in der ägyptischen Frühzeit, in: *ZÄS* 88 (1962) 5–16; D. O'Connor, The status of early Egyptian temples: an alternative theory, in: *The Followers of Horus: Studies dedicated to Michael Allan Hoffman* (Oxbow Monograph 1992) 83–98.

Hieroglyphic representation of a divine fortress

Djed pillar
A primeval fetish consisting of a pole with bundles of plants, possibly sheaves, bound to it, which became the symbol of 'permanence'. The erection of the *djed* pillar formed part of the cults of Sokar and Osiris at **Memphis** and Busiris, and also featured in the cult of the king. Although one might expect it, because of the importance of such a symbol, it was never represented in stone. There are, however, examples of **relief pillars** and **pilasters** decorated with *djed* motifs in raised relief.

Bibliography: Jéquier, *Manuel* 158; Amice M. Calverley, *The Temple of King Sety I at Abydos* IV (London-Chicago 1958), Plates 8, 39; H. Altenmüller, Djed-Pfeiler, in: Helck, *LÄ* I 1100-1105.

Djedefre (Redjedef), pyramid of
The tomb precinct 'Star Tent of Djedefre', on a prominent elevation near Abu Rawash, 8 km north-west of **Giza**. The precinct is 217 x 267 m in size and contained a **pyramid** (106 x 106 m) estimated to have been 125 **cubits** (65.5 m) high based on its slope of 51°57'. It was faced with **granite**, of which the lowest layers were laid at a slope of 12° towards the interior. The burial chambers are set deep in the rock. Its construction shaft, 10 x 23 m, was revealed by the activity of stone robbers. The entrance corridor is at a slope of 26 and 28°. A cult complex, east of the pyramid, was paved with **basalt** and has granite columns; it was rapidly completed in **brick**, intended to be only temporary. Many sculptures (**quartzite**) have been found there, including parts of the earliest known royal **sphinx**. There is a secondary pyramid in the south-west corner of the precinct. A **causeway** 1500 m long leads from the **valley temple**, not yet studied, at the mouth of Wadi Qarun to the pyramid plateau. The precinct has been worked on since 1995 by the University of Geneva and the IFAO, Cairo.

Bibliography: *MRA* V; Edwards, *Pyramids* 164; Stadelmann, *Pyramiden* 126–130; Müller, *Monumentalarchitektur* 24–25; M. Valloggia, Fouilles archéologiques à Abou Rawash, in: *Genava* 43 (1995) 65–73 and *Genava* 44 (1996) 51–59.

Djedkare, pyramid of
The funerary complex 'The Pyramid of Isesi is Beautiful' is at South **Saqqara**. The **pyramid** has a base with sides 78.75 m long, a slope of approximately 52° and a height of 41.93 m. The core consisted of six steps. The burial chambers were constructed in a shaft, 9 m deep and open at the top, and have been badly damaged by stone robbery. The sarcophagus chamber is roofed with a triple ceiling of relieving slabs (**ceiling construction**, Fig.). The passage which connects the antechamber and the main room is protected by a weight-relieving arch of

Ruins of the pyramid temple of Djedkare at Saqqara

stone which is an early example of a stone **vault** in Egypt, although it is built into the masonry and not free-standing. From the antechamber leads off a group of three chambers (*serdab*), a feature which recurs in the later pyramids of the Old Kingdom. The complex is completed by a magnificent **pyramid temple**, a feature which was introduced in the reign of Sahure and which consolidated the spatial programme so strongly that (under the influence of the teaching of the **architect**?) all the later pyramids of the Old Kingdom follow this pattern. The pyramid temple is flanked by rectangular bastions similar to those at the pyramids of **Niuserre** and **Amenemhat II**. A **causeway** and a **valley temple** were identified in 1945 but they have not been excavated.

A small pyramid precinct lies to the north-east of the pyramid temple, with a form dissimilar to that of a king or queen; it may have belonged to an unidentified successor of Djedkare. The pyramid measures 42 x 42 m and has a court with 16 papyrus **columns**.

Bibliography: *MRA* VIII 64–116; M. Moursi, Die Ausgrabungen in der Gegend um die Pyramide des Dd-k3-Rc 'Jssj' bei Saqqara, in: *ASAE* 71 (1987) 185–193; Stadelmann, *Pyramiden* 180–184; P. Jánosi, Die Pyramidenanlage der 'anonymen Königin' des Djedkare-Isesi, in: *MDAIK* 45 (1989) 187–202.

Djoser precinct

The mortuary precinct of Djoser at **Saqqara** is built entirely of stone and is one of the world's richest architectural monuments in its use of 'representation'. It was the creation of the **architect** Imhotep, who brought the development of mortuary complexes of the 1st–3rd Dynasty kings to its peak. It is of importance to architectural history because pre-historic forms of construction, made of perishable material, were here translated into stone and have thus been preserved.

The principal element of the precinct is the **niched** wall, 10.50 m high and enclosing an area of 277 x 544 m, with an entrance in the southern end of the east side as well as 14 other, dummy doors. The entranceway leads from behind the gate between a double row of 20 **columns** in the form of bundles of plants, past a representation of a niched entrance palace, to the southern courtyard. This was probably a festival court, and the place where the king's run round the two 'turning markers', by which he took possession of the complex,

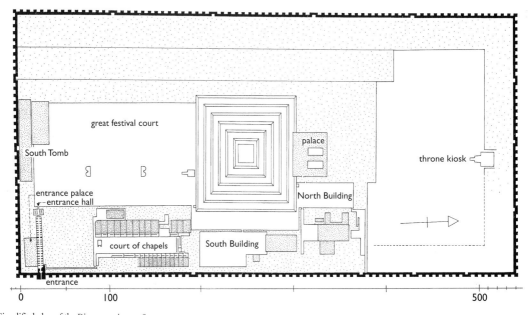

Simplified plan of the Djoser precinct at Saqqara

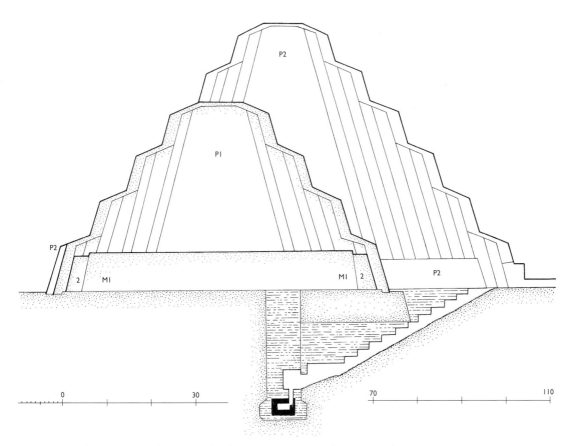

Principal phases of the development of the step mastaba of Djoser at Saqqara (section from east to west)

was carried out. The south face of the courtyard is occupied by the **South Tomb** (Fig.), an east–west orientated **mastaba** with a **vaulted** roof, false burial chamber and an underground copy of a **palace** made of **mats** inlaid with green tiles (**architectural ceramics**). The south-western corner of the courtyard is occupied by a building of unknown purpose, crowned with a **frieze of uraei**. Along the east side is a *sed*-festival structure with the king's throne, surrounded by 25–30 chapels dedicated to the deities of the various parts of the country.

In the centre is the **step mastaba**, 60 m high, containing the North Tomb of the King. The monument was built in stages from an initial square mastaba to a final six-step structure. Probably during this transformation the original underground apartment, representing a royal palace for the afterlife, distinguished by chambers decorated with blue faience tiles, was altered by the addition of a **granite** burial chamber. The South Tomb also received a granite chamber, marking a new phase in the development of royal tomb building. As in the South Tomb, the burial chamber here is surrounded with an intricate system of chambers and corridors, again representing an underground palace. On the north side of the North Tomb is a building like a palace or temple, its purpose unknown, equipped with a purification basin (**bath**). A shrine against the east side contained a statue of the king, now in the Cairo Museum, which was able look up through peepholes to the circumpolar stars. To the east of this are the so-called

Row of chapels in the *sed*-festival court in the Djoser precinct

'Maison du Sud' and 'Maison du Nord', thought to be the state sanctuaries of Upper and Lower Egypt.

The function of many other smaller buildings in the precinct is not known. The northern courtyard, containing a raised **altar** on a platform, is incomplete. The complex may originally have been completely surrounded by vast ditches representing canals.

The original area of the complex was only 240 x 400 m and it may have contained only the South Tomb, the entrance palace, the North Tomb (in the step mastaba), the *sed*-festival chapels and the 'Maison du Nord' and 'Maison du Sud'. It was enlarged in a second construction phase, and the previously independent buildings were enclosed with massive masonry structures. In the south-western section there are rows of subterranean magazines full of offerings, which may originally have been part of the **gallery tomb** of a 2nd Dynasty king. Interpretation is difficult as the complex has no inscriptions apart from six reliefs in the South Tomb. It may perhaps have represented an idealised and stylised royal and divine domain for the exercise of the king's rule after his death. In terms of its prime function, the precinct of Djoser may have united the older tomb concepts of **Abydos** and **Memphis**. The suggestion that the **enclosure wall**, entrance palace, southern courtyard and South Tomb as a whole may be derived from the royal tombs at Abydos with their **funerary enclosures**, and that only the mastaba tomb reflects the concepts of Memphis, is rejected by Stadelmann, who believes that the precinct of Djoser developed out of the (now lost) superstructures of the Memphite **kings' tombs** of the 2nd Dynasty and that they represent the last continuation of the Lower Egyptian **'Butic'** mastaba.

Bibliography: C.M. Firth and J.E. Quibell, *The Step Pyramid*, 2 Vols (Cairo 1935–1936); J.-Ph. Lauer, *La Pyramide à degrés*, 3 Vols (Cairo 1936–1939); J.-Ph. Lauer, *Études complémentaires sur les monuments du roi Zoser à Saqqarah* (Cairo 1948); Lauer, *Histoire monumentale* 65–176; J.-Ph. Lauer, Dix campagnes (1960 à 1970) de travaux d'anastylose, in: *ASAE* 61 (1973) 125–144; W. Kaiser, Zu den königlichen Talbezirken in Abydos und zur Baugeschichte des Djoser-Grabmals, in: *MDAIK* 25 (1969) 1–13; H. Altenmüller, Bemerkungen zur frühen und späten Bauphase des Djoserbezirkes in Saqqara, in: *MDAIK* 28 (1972) 1–12; N. Swelim, The Dry Moat of the Netjerykhet Complex, in: *Pyramid Studies and Other Essays Presented to I.E.S. Edwards* (London 1988) 12–22; J.-Ph. Lauer, Sur certaines modifications et extensions apportées au complexe funéraire de Djoser, in: *Pyramid Studies and Other Essays Presented to I.E.S. Edwards* (London 1988) 5–11; Rainer Stadelmann, Origins and Development of the Funerary Complex of Djoser, in: *Studies Simpson* II 787–800; W. Kaiser, Zu den Granitkammern und ihren Vorgängerbauten unter der Stufenpyramide und im Südgrab von Djoser, in: *MDAIK* 53 (1997) 195–207.

Dolerite

A particularly grainy **basalt**, with a specific gravity of 2.93–3.05, varying from grey to blackish green. It was important in Egyptian construction work for the production of stone hammers ('pounders') used to crush hard stone. These have been found in the **stone quarries** of **Aswan** and **Gebel el-Ahmar** and also at many construction sites from the Old to the New Kingdom. The stone occurs in the Eastern Desert, the Faiyum and at Mount Sinai.

Bibliography: Engelbach, *Obelisk* 12–12; A. Zuber, Techniques du travail des pierres dures dans l'Ancienne Égypte, in: *Techniques et Civilisations* 5 (1956) 161–180, 195–215; Lucas, *AEMI* 61, 410; Arnold, *Building* 262–263; Klemm, *Steine* 421.

Door, *see also* door fastening, door leaf

The door of a stone building ideally consisted of a threshold, door frame (with a door post) and lintel. Where possible, the threshold was a hard stone slab projecting above the level of the floor; less important doors often had no threshold and continuous **paving**. The two door posts stood on the threshold, in most cases projecting forward beyond the surface of the wall, consisting of either built up blocks or monolithic **pillars**. Door posts with a rounded side facing the passageway are an uncommon form (occurring mainly in the reigns of Djoser and Senwosret III). The lintel of smaller **gateways** took the form of a single stone **architrave**, while larger ones consisted of several beams standing upright on end. The door frames in sacred buildings were always crowned with a **cavetto cornice,** which, in the case of large temple gateways, due to its heavy weight above had to be specially secured; the cornice over smaller gateways was in some cases secured to the wall by ropes threaded through bore holes. Between the cavetto cornices above the front and rear of the gateway a bridge was formed above the lintel which, in the case of **pylons**, was used as a crossing between the towers and at **Medinet Habu** for the establishment of a solar cult area. Monumental temple doors are regularly flanked by free-standing pylons. Large passageways (up to 15 m in depth and 7 m wide) have a smaller gateway, open above, either in front or built into the passage, in order to reduce the size of the **door leaves**. An interesting form are the passageways between **screen walls**, found particularly in the Ptolemaic period, which usually have a broken-door lintel (**Deir el-Medina**, Fig.). The side-pillars were fitted with a collared head in order to receive the upper turning spigot on the leaf of the door. Broken-door lintels occurred in the Amarna period in normal doorways, probably to allow sunlight to enter. The ratio of width to height of Egyptian doors is not constant, but depended on the overall system of proportions of the temple in question, fluctuating from 1:2 to 1:3.

Doors had their own decorative programmes (winged sun discs, royal titulary, king purifying). Huge temple gates of the Ramesside and Ptolemaic periods were covered with dozens of scenes. The reveals which were covered by the leaf of the door when open could not bear representations of figures, and so they were decorated instead with a frieze of symbolic signs, and in some cases **metal overlay**.

Secret doors of stone are attested in the shape of wall blocks which could be moved on metal rails, but these were likely to have been a curiosity (**crypt**).

Strong **brick** walls were always fitted with doors which had door frames of stone or at least a threshold of stone. In order to improve the connection between the stonework and the brick wall, the contact parts were left in rough condition. Door frames in **houses** were frequently, and those in tombs occasionally, made of wooden beams, the door posts being pegged to the threshold or just inset into it. Depictions (**false door**) and models suggest that many houses and **palaces** had a

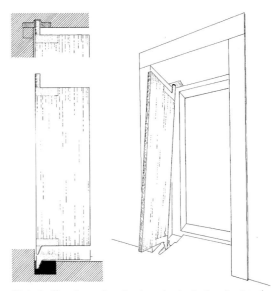

Method of hanging an Egyptian door, showing its insertion into the hinge point via a slot in the floor

supraporte over the lintel consisting of a carved wooden grille (tombs of Huya and Tutu at **Amarna**, palace of Ramesses III at **Medinet Habu**, **window**).

Bibliography: Perrot, *L'Égypte* 608–614; Jéquier, *Manuel* 111–128; Hölscher, *Chefren*, Figs 24, 28–30; Clark, *AEM* 162–169; Koenigsberger, *Tür*; Hölscher, *Medinet Habu* IV 35, Figs 28–30, 42–45; Borchardt, *Tell el-Amarna*, Figs 14–16, 19, 39 and others; Arnold, *Amenemhet III*, Plate 53; P. Behrens, Riegel, in: Helck, *LÄ* V 256–257; H. Brunner, Die Rolle von Tür und Tor im alten Ägypten, in: *Symbolon* N.F. 6 (1982) 37–52; H. Brunner, Tür und Tor, in: Helck, *LÄ* VI 778–787; Thomas Grothoff, *Die Tornamen ägyptischer Tempel* (Aachen 1996).

Door fastening, *see also* door, door leaf

Egyptian **doors** were fastened by means of a bolt. On double doors, the wooden or bronze bolt was mounted on one leaf between two U-shaped staples or loops, and was slid into two other staples on the other leaf. This form was known as a 'blade bolt'. A cross-section of this type of bolt is either round or semi-circular, the centre part typically being thicker. The bolt on a single-leaf door pushed into a hole drilled in the door frame. The cross-section of this type, known as a 'pin bolt', is either circular or rectangular; its front part was sometimes decorated with a recumbent protective lion. Occasionally, for safety reasons, two bolts were combined on the same handle. Thresholds occasionally show drill holes in the centre for vertical bolts. A door fastening allowing secret access from outside exists at the temple of **Qasr el-Sagha**.

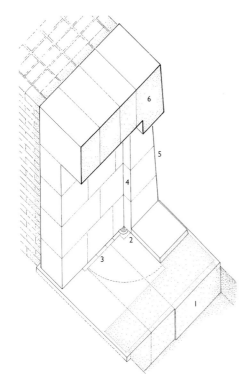

Reconstruction of an Egyptian doorway, viewed from inside. 1: threshold; 2: pivot point; 3: slot for inserting door; 4: door post; 5: door frame; 6: lintel

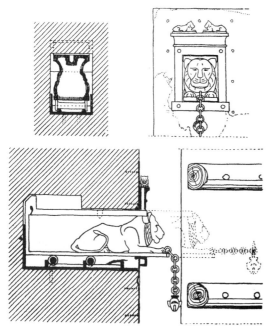

Reconstruction of a door bolt in the form of a lion (after L. Borchardt). Above left, section; above right, view from front; below left, section when closed; below right, section when open

Bibliography: Hölscher, *Chefren* 41–42, Sheet 11; Borchardt, *Ne-user-Re*, Fig. 17; Borchardt, *Sahu-Re*, 56, 59–60; Borchardt, *Re-Heiligtum*, Fig. 7; Koenigsberger, *Tür* 40–63; Ricke, *Userkaf I*, Figs 3–4, 7; Arnold, *Der Tempel Qasr el-Sagha* (Mainz 1979) 13, Fig. 7; E. Graefe, *Die Versiegelung der Naostür*, in: *MDAIK* 27 (1971) 147–155; K. Kuhlmann, *Schloß*, in: Helck, *LÄ* V 658–661.

Door leaf, *see also* door, door fastening

Wooden door leaves have survived from the Old Kingdom onwards, consisting of vertical boards held together by horizontal battens. They were mounted using not hinges but turning pivots, which protruded at the top and bottom of the leaf and rested in a bronze-coated shoe. (Hinges were used very infrequently; examples have been found at **El-Lisht** and in the tomb of Tutankhamun.) The edges or the whole surface of the leaves of important temple **gateways** were also sometimes overlaid with a thin sheet of bronze, even being decorated with electrum, gold and silver (**metal overlay**). Door leaves were mounted with the lower pivot fitted into a socket below (the diameter at the first **pylon** at **Karnak** is 50 cm). This was a hollow either in the threshold in the form of a quarter-circle or in a separate stone (in some cases horseshoe-shaped, consisting of hard stone or metal). The upper pivot turned in a wooden or stone socket in the **architrave**. A leaf would be fitted into a frame already in the wall by running the lower pivot along a groove in the threshold, which was subsequently filled in with wedges of stone. In the Middle Kingdom this gutter ran across the door axis, while in the Old and New Kingdoms it ran along it. In single-leaf doors, the reveal on the side of the wall with the pivot sockets was deepened due to the thickness of the door; in the case of doors with two leaves, the reveals were equally deep. The size of the door leaf of the **High Gate** of **Medinet Habu** was 4 x 6 m, that at the first pylon of Medinet Habu 4 x 11 m, and that at the pylon of **Edfu** 2.93 x 14.35 m. A double door 3.20 m wide is reproduced half-open in stone at the precinct of **Djoser**. The gateways between pylons are often too large to have been closed with wooden leaves, their width therefore having to be reduced by narrower gates fitted into them.

Bibliography: Borchardt, *Ne-user-Re*, Fig. 39; Koenigsberger, *Tür* 13–24; Ricke, *Kamutef*, Fig. 8; J. Jacquet, Remarques sur l'architecture domestique a l'époque méroitique, in: *Festschrift Ricke*, Fig. 30.

Door recess

From the time of Sneferu (lower temple at the **Bent Pyramid**) and **Khufu**, the rear hall of the open pillared courtyard in Old Kingdom **pyramid temples** took the form of a double or triple **pillared hall** immediately in front of the statue shrines of the temple. From the reign of **Sahure** this element was reduced in size, becoming a simple wall recess with stairs inside leading to the five statue shrines situated higher up.

The monumental tombs of the Late Period at **Thebes** have a deep **vaulted** recess in the rear wall of their **sun courts**, the rear wall of which is decorated with reed **matting** to give the appearance of a primeval sanctuary.

Door recess, mastaba of Seshemnefer at Giza (reconstruction by Junker, 1953)

Form and decoration indicate that the door recess was meant to represent a roof of reed matting in front of the inner rooms of the tomb, where the deceased received funerary offerings.

Bibliography: Ricke, *Bemerkungen* II 60–62; Eigner, *Grabbauten* 120–123.

Dorginarti (Dorgaynarti)

A **fortress** of the 18th Dynasty and the 8–5th century BC, which stands on an island in the Nile at the exit of the Second Cataract. It was built to a triangular plan, covering approximately 80 x 194 m, with walls up to 8 m thick.

Bibliography: S. Clarke, Ancient Egyptian Frontier Fortresses, in: *JEA* 3 (1916) 164–165; J. Leclant, in: *Orientalia* 34 (1965) 214; Dows Dunham, *Uronarti Shalfak Mirgissa, Second Cataract Forts*, Vol. 2 (Boston 1967) 177–178; J. Knudstad, Serra East and Dorginarti, in: *Kush* 14 (1966) 178–186; L. A Heidorn, The Saite and Persian Period Forts at Dorginarti, in: *Egypt and Africa* (London 1991) 205–219; Hein, *Ramessidische Bautätigkeit* 48; Lisa A. Heidorn, *The Fortress of Dorginarti and Lower Nubia during the Seventh and Fifth Centuries B.C.* (Chicago 1992).

Double burial. *see* cenotaph, *ka*-tomb

Drainage, *see also* roof drainage, water spouts

Despite scant precipitation, Egyptian buildings are provided with elaborate drainage systems. Water from the sub-soil was directed along sloping levels into stone gutters, where it was channelled into reservoirs or seepage collecting shafts (at the temple of **Niuserre** a round **quartzite** basin beside the **causeway** and round **alabaster** basins in the sun sanctuary, at the temple of **Khentkawes I** a large rectangular basin with stairs). Stone gutters have been found both open or covered with slabs, sometimes running through under a wall. The **mastaba** of Mentuhotep at **El-Lisht** is surrounded on all sides by stone gutters, with an elbow at each corner; gaps were patched with U-shaped pieces coated with **gypsum**.

There are a few rare instances of interlocking clay pipes leading to clay basins (tomb of Djedemankh in **Abusir**, Uronarti). The system of copper pipes in the **pyramid temple** of **Sahure**, which led from the hand-washing basin in the sanctuary all the way through the temple and from there down the length of causeway, is unique. Copper pipes, instead of being connected by soldering, were fastened by being hammered together.

Bibliography: Jéquier, *Manuel* 53–56; Borchardt, *Ne-user-Re* 22, 97, 120; Borchardt, *Sahu-Re* 29, 75–83; Clark, *AEM* 153–161; Selim Hassan, *Excavations at Giza,* Vol. 4 (Cairo 1943) 85–95; Dows Dunham, *Uronarti, Shalfak, Mirgissa* (Boston 1967) 25, Plate 19.

Drilling, *see also* saw, stone working

Drills were used regularly from pre-historic times onwards in the production of stone vessels, and from the 3rd Dynasty onwards in the building industry for cutting holes for pivots and bolts, rope channels, dowel holes for fastening **metal overlays** and the like. Small holes were drilled using a tube, larger ones using a copper tube fastened to a staff which was turned by means of a curved handle or a bow. Machine-like arrangements are conceivable. Abrasives used were dry quartz sand and, for particularly hard stone, perhaps emery or corundum. Some surprisingly deep drill holes are preserved with diameters up to 45 cm. Bore holes as well as cores have been preserved. Series of overlapping bore holes have been found on irregular blocks of **limestone** of the 3rd and 4th Dynasties at the precinct of **Djoser** and **Meidum**; their purpose remains unexplained.

Bibliography: Clark, *AEM* 194, 202–204; Petrie, *Pyramids* 173; D. Stocks, *Sticks and Stones of Egyptian Technology*, in: *Popular Archaeology* April (1986) 24–29; D. Stocks, Ancient Factory Mass-production Techniques, in: *Antiquity* 63 (1989) 526–531; Arnold, *Building*, 265–266.

Drum

A representation in stone of a rolled up reed **mat** curtain, fastened with two cords above the door of a tomb or the opening of a **false door**, particularly found in the Old Kingdom. According to Koenigsberger it represented a cross-beam for the fastening of an upper turning socket. In most cases it consists of a shape like a simple cylinder; drums are represented in the relief niches at the precinct of **Djoser** with detailed designs provided by faience tiles (**architectural decoration**).

Bibliography: Koenigsberger, *Tür* 13, 28–29.

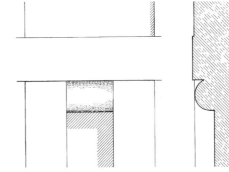

View and section of a stone door drum

Dwelling house, *see* house

E

Edfu

An important settlement, necropolis and, above all, the uniquely well-preserved temple of Horus, 'Throne of Horus'. The present building replaces several earlier structures, of which, in the absence of excavation work, little is known. An exact description exists, however, of the earliest temple. The building erected by Senwosret I is recorded in inscriptions and later structures are known from re-used blocks of the Second Intermediate Period, the New Kingdom and the Late Period found here.

The present building, which was begun on 23 August 237 BC, initially consisted of a **pillared hall**, two transverse halls and a barque sanctuary surrounded by chapels. It was dedicated by Ptolemy VIII Euergetes II on 10 September 142 BC. The **pronaos** in front was built in 140–124 BC, and construction of the colonnaded court and **pylon**, 36 m high, followed in 116–71 BC. The pylon contains an interesting system of stairways and chambers, receiving light through slots in the façade (**pylon**, Fig.). To the east, beside the courtyard, are the remains of

a pylon of the New Kingdom, which faces towards the landing stage on the Nile. The pronaos is 12.5 m high and 34 m wide, with three rows of six **composite-capital pillars**. Built into its **screen wall** there is on the left a chapel for the rites of the 'house of the morning' and on the right a library room. To the side of the **pillared hall** beyond, on the east, opposite the treasury, is a room for the preparation of ointments. Behind this lies the offering table hall with the hall of the Divine Ennead beyond. A door in the east wall of that chamber leads to the *wabet*. A **naos** of Nectanebo II, a relic from an earlier building, is preserved in the principal sanctuary, which stands in isolation. The barque sanctuary is surrounded by nine chapels. The masonry of the **enclosure walls** is thick and contains extensive **crypts**.

In front of the main temple, in the south-west corner, is the Ptolemaic **birth house** of the divine triad of Horus, Hathor and Harsomtus. Opposite it, no longer preserved, was a temple dedicated to the sacred falcon. The course of the outer **brick** enclosure wall has been uncovered only at

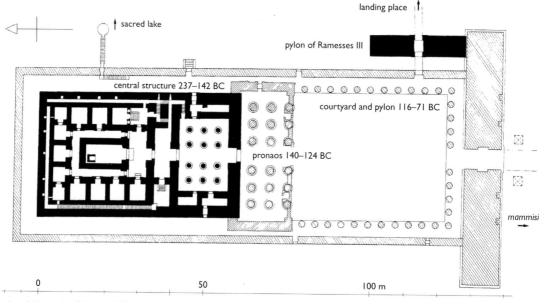

Plan of the temple of Horus at Edfu, showing construction phases

Pylon and courtyard of the temple of Horus at Edfu

the south-west corner. It is known that there existed a **sacred lake**, accommodation for priests and administrative buildings, as well as the grove of the sacred falcon, store rooms for supplies, stables, kitchens etc. To the south-west of the temple is thought to be the Behedet, the necropolis of the primeval gods and the **tomb of Osiris**.

Bibliography: *Description* I Plates 48–65; M. de Rochemonteix and Emile Chassinat, *Le temple d'Edfou*, 14 Vols (Cairo 1897–1934), Vol. I–II revised: Sylvie Cauville and D. Devauchelle, *Le temple d'Edfou I–II* (Cairo 1984–90); Blackman and Fairman, *JEA* 32 (1946) 75–91; M. Alliot, *Le culte d'Horus à Edfou au temps des Ptolémées* (Cairo 1949, 1954); P. Lacau, Notes sur les plans des temples d'Edfou et de Kôm-Ombo, in: *ASAE* 52 (1952) 215–221; H.W. Fairman, *The Triumph of Horus. An Ancient Egyptian Sacred Drama* (London-Berkeley 1974); P. Barguet, La cour du Temple d'Edfou et le Cosmos, in: *Livre du Centenaire* (IFAO 1980) 9–14; Sylvie Cauville, *Edfou. Les guides archéologiques de l'Institut français d'archéologie orientale du Caire* (Cairo 1984); S. Cauville and D. Devauchelle, Les mesures réelles du temple d'Edfou, in: *BIFAO* 84 (1984) 23–34; P. Vernus, Helck, *LÄ* VI, 323–331; Sylvie Cauville, *Essai sur la théologie du temple d'Horus à Edfou* (Cairo 1987); Aufrère, *L'Égypte restituée* 247–255; D. Kurth, Die Reise der Hathor von Dendera nach Edfu, in: Kurth, *Tempeltagung* 211–216; Sylvie Cauville, *Edfou* (Cairo 1984); Arnold, *Temples* 169–171, 200–202, 216–220.

The remains of a small **step mastaba**, still awaiting proper study, are located 5 km to the south-west of Edfu.

Bibliography: Dreyer, *Stufenpyramiden* 45.

Ehnasya el-Medina (Herakleopolis Magna)

An important settlement and cemetery with the temple of Herishef which is attested to from the 1st Dynasty onwards. There are remains of buildings dating from the 12th and 18th Dynasties, which were re-built by Ramesses II, incorporating material from older constructions. The temple forecourt is a noteworthy feature: in front of each column of the side-halls there was a **colossal statue** of Ramesses II, 6–7 m tall. The hall at the back of the courtyard, 50 m wide, has a structure at the rear like a **pronaos** with a double row of eight palm **columns**, each one 5.25 m high, possibly dating back to the Old or Middle Kingdom. Examples of these columns are now in the British Museum, Boston, Manchester, Bolton and Philadelphia. Lying beyond it is a hall with four rows of six **pillars** and the inner chambers of the

Pronaos and courtyard of the temple of Horus at Edfu

temple. The main temple building, excluding the courtyard, measures 22.4 x 42.5 m.

Bibliography: Edouard Naville, *Ahnas el Medineh* (London 1894) 1–14; W. Flinders Petrie, *Ehnasya* 1904 (London 1905); F. Gomaà, Herakleopolis magna, in: Helck, *LÄ* II 1124–1127; Mohamed Gamal el-Din Mokhtar, *Ihnâsya el-Medina*, BdE 40 (Cairo 1983) 75–88; María del Carmen Perez-Die and Pascal Vernus, *Excavaciones en Ehnasya El Medina* (Madrid 1992).

El-Amada

A small temple of Thutmosis III and Amenhotep II, built on the West Bank of the Nile, 200 km south of Aswan, probably on the site of an earlier building of Senwosret III. The temple, measuring 9.7 x 23.6 m, was dedicated to Amun-Re and Re-Horakhty. It was planned to be surrounded on all sides by a colonnade (like the surviving example at **Buhen**), but only the portico at the front, with six **channelled columns**, was completed and connected with a forecourt. The courtyard was modified under Thutmosis IV in to a **pillared hall** containing four rows of three **pillars**. The interior of the temple is carefully decorated and consists of a hall of appearances and an offering table room with two chambers for cult images, which face each other. The façade of the temple was completed under Sety I with a small **pylon**, connecting with the **enclosure wall** of the temple precinct. In the south-west there are the remains of a **barque station**.

In 1964/65, the whole temple was moved on rails to a higher site, on a terrace 2.6 km further west.

Bibliography: Gau, *Antiquités* Plates 48–49; Henri Gauthier, *Le temple d'Amada* (Cairo 1913); Borchardt, *Tempel mit Umgang*, Beiträge zur ägyptischen Bauforschung und Altertumskunde 2 41–44, Plate 13; Christiane Desroches-Noblecourt, Le déplacement du temple d'Amada, in: *Annales de l'Institut technique du bâtiment et des travaux publics* (Paris 1966); M. Aly and M. Dewachter, *Le temple d'Amada* (Cairo 1967); C.C. Van Siclen III, The building history of the Thutmoside temple at Amada and the Jubilees of Thutmosis IV, in: *Varia Aegyptiaca* 3 (1987) 53–66; Hein, *Ramessidische Bautätigkeit* 20–23.

El-Bersha

A necropolis opposite Mallawi at the mouth of Wadi Deir el-Nakhla, with 37 **rock tombs** of the upper class of the 15th Upper Egyptian nome. The 12th Dynasty tomb of the nomarch Djehutyhotep (No. 2) is of architectural importance. Like the later tombs of **Beni Hasan**, it has a portico with two **columns** with palm **capitals**. The deep rectangular cult chamber has a statue niche in the east wall approached by a small stairway and no columns. The depiction in this tomb of the transport of a **colossal statue** has made it famous (**sledge**, Fig.).

Bibliography: Percy. E. Newberry, *El Bersheh*, 2 Vols (London 1892/94); Badawy, *Architecture* II 143–146; F. Junge, El-Berscheh, in: Helck, *LÄ* I 711–715; E. Brovarski et al., *Bersheh Reports* I (Boston 1992).

El-Deir

The ruins of a **brick** temple of the 2nd–3rd centuries AD lying 1.5 km north of the fortification of **El-Deir** (at the southern end of the Kharga Oasis). Its plan is unusually extended, similar to that of the neighbouring temple of **Qasr Dush**. In front of the temple is an antechamber with benches along its sides. The antechamber and the first room, corresponding to a **hypostyle hall**, have a flat roof; the offering table room and the sanctuary, which are the innermost chambers, have **vaulted** ceilings. The temple as a whole is 5.25 m wide and 28 m long.

Bibliography: R. Naumann, Bauwerke der Oase Khargeh, in: *MDAIK* 8 (1939) 15–16.

Elephantine

A large island opposite **Aswan** with significant remains of a trading settlement, whose beginnings go back to prehistoric times and which developed out of a **fortress** of the 1st Dynasty. The **town** and temples have been restored in an exemplary way by the German Archaeological Institute, Cairo.

Bibliography: L. Habachi, Elephantine, in: Helck, *LÄ* I 1217–1225. Detailed excavation reports in *MDAIK* from 26 (1970), particularly

Reconstruction of the façade of the temple of Ehnasya el-Medina (Herakleopolis Magna)

44 (1988) 135–182; Werner Kaiser, *Elephantine: die antike Stadt* (Cairo 1998).

1. Old Kingdom settlement

The earliest parts of the settlement are to be found on the south-eastern corner of the island. It was surrounded by a wall which followed the shape of the terrain and was equipped with rounded towers. To the north, and outside the wall, lies a fortress, 53 x 53 m in area, also with round towers. Both structures were built in the 1st Dynasty.

Bibliography: Martin Ziermann, *Befestigungsanlagen und Stadtentwicklung in der Frühzeit und im frühen Alten Reich* (Mainz 1993); Cornelius von Pilgrim, *Untersuchungen in der Stadt des Mittleren Reiches und der Zweiten Zwischenzeit* (Mainz 1996).

2. Temple of Khnum

Blocks found attest to the existence of an **ambulatory temple** of Hatshepsut and Thutmosis III, to which Amenhotep II added a colonnaded forecourt. The Ramesside kings may have built an additional forecourt with a **pylon**. An important new structure was added under Nectanebo II. This main temple building is almost completely destroyed, with the exception of the king's **granite** portal and a few fragments from the walls and the **foundations** (it can be reconstructed only from the last). The structure was enlarged in the reigns of Ptolemy VI and VIII by the addition of an open **pronaos** with two rows of six **columns**; a granite **gateway** is still standing. A pillared courtyard at the front, planted with trees, and a pylon 48 m wide were added in the Roman period. The total length was 123 m.

Bibliography: Herbert Ricke, *Die Tempel Nektanebos' II. in Elephantine*, BeiträgeBf 6 (Cairo 1960); Peter Grossmann, *Kirche und spätantike Hausanlagen im Chnumtempelhof* (Mainz 1980); Van Siclen III,

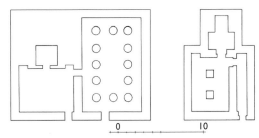

Plans of the Satet temples of Mentuhotep Nebhepetre (left) and of Senwosret I (right), Elephantine

Remarks on the Tuthmoside Temple of Khnum at Elephantine, in: *Varia Aegyptiaca* 6 (1990) 188–194; Jaritz, *Terrassen*; W. Niederberger, Untersuchungen im Bereich des späten Chnumtempels, in: *MDAIK* 46 (1990) 189–193, 51 (1995) 147–164; Ewa Laskowska-Kusztal, Die Dekorfragmente der ptolemäisch-römischen Tempel von Elephantine (Mainz 1996); Hanna Jenni, *Die Dekoration des Chnumtempels auf Elephantine durch Nektanebos' II*, Elephantine, Vol. 17 (Mainz 1998); Walter Niederberger, *Der Chnumtempel Nektanebos' II* (Mainz 1999).

3. Temple of Satis

Beside this, on a level slightly below that of the Khnum temple, lies the temple of Satis, which went through several interesting stages of development. From pre-historic times there had been a simple cult building set amid large **granite** rocks, with a mud **brick** plinth at the front, on which the portable cult image would have rested. It became a small temple in the 6th Dynasty (**temple**, Fig.), then a new building was set up by Mentuhotep Nebhepetre and, later, a **limestone** structure of Senwosret I with fine decoration. Over this Hatshepsut erected a temple with a pillared corridor around it, almost all of which has been reconstructed in recent years using surviving relief blocks

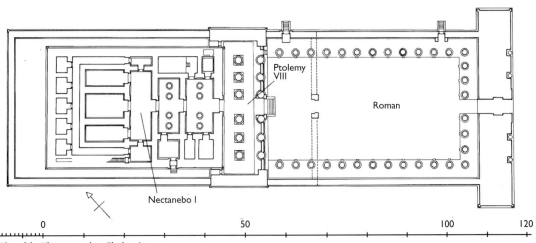

Ptolemy VIII

Roman

Nectanebo I

0   50   100   120

Plan of the Khnum temple at Elephantine

of the Ptolemaic temple which was built over it. Only the traces of the **foundations** remain of the Ptolemaic temple that was built over it, which show that the building was fronted with the traditional open **pronaos**. Next to the temple of Satis, both Mentuhotep Nebhepetre and Senwosret I built a purification chapel made of stone.

Bibliography: Borchardt, *Tempel mit Umgang* 44–47; Günter Dreyer, *Der Tempel der Satet. Die Funde der Frühzeit und des Alten Reiches* (Mainz 1986); W. Kaiser, Zur Rekonstruktion des Satettempels der 12. Dynastie, in: *MDAIK* 44 (1988) 152–157.

4. Step mastaba

In the north-west part of the town was a structure with three steps (**step mastaba**) of the 3rd Dynasty (size 18.46 x 18.46 m, height approximately 12.6 m), of rough blocks of **granite**. A granite cone found nearby bears the name of King Huni.

Bibliography: G. Dreyer, Nordweststadt: Stufenpyramide, in: *MDAIK* 36 (1980) 276–280; Dreyer, *Stufenpyramiden* 43–44.

5. Heqaib shrine

Further to the west, within the town, was the Heqaib shrine, significant in the development of this type of cult structure. It was originally an open cult courtyard with two statue chapels, erected by Sarenput I, a nomarch of the reign of Senwosret I, for his own cult and that of his ancestor Heqaib. A few shrines were added by Sarenput II and some successors of the 12th Dynasty, so that the *ka*-statue house consisted of at least 10 shrines for cult images, with approximately 60 statues, by the end of the Middle Kingdom.

Bibliography: Labib Habachi, *The Sanctuary of Heqaib*, 2 Vols (Mainz 1985); Detlef Franke, *Das Heiligtum des Heqaib auf Elephantine* (Heidelberg 1994).

6. Barque station

Illustrations from the early 19th century indicate the existence of a particularly beautiful, completely preserved **barque station** of Amenhotep III. The **barque chamber** was set on a raised base with a pillared corridor around it and papyrus **columns** at the back and front. It was destroyed sometime before 1837. A similar chapel, possibly of Ramesses II, to the north, has also disappeared.

Bibliography: *Description* I, Plates 34–38; Prisse d'Avennes, *Histoire*, Plate 11; Borchardt, *Tempel mit Umgang* 95–98, 100–101, Sheet 21; M.F. Laming Macadam, Gleanings from the Bankes MSS, in: *JEA* 32 (1946) 59–60.

El-Hebua (Sile)

Now an area of ruins at the former mouth of the Pelusian arm of the Nile to the Mediterranean, this was originally a fortified settlement, 400 x 800 m in area, dating from the Hyksos Period to the end of the New Kingdom (El-Hebua I) maintaining the 'Ways of Horus', having **grain stores**, **houses** and a turreted **brick** wall.

El-Hiba

Ruins of a **fortress** and **town** on the East Bank of the Nile, north-east of Maghagha. There are the remains of a small temple of Amun built by Sheshonq I. Standing inside the **enclosure wall** is a stone-built temple house (17.65 x 35.8 m) with one of the earliest true **pronaoi** (two rows of four papyrus **columns**) and a **pillared hall** (two rows of four pillars), an offering table hall and a **barque chamber** with four side-rooms housing cult images, as well as a **crypt**.

Bibliography: Ahmed Bey Kamal, Description des ruines de Hibe, de son temple et de sa nécropole, in: *ASAE* 2 (1901) 84–91; Hermann Ranke, *Koptische Friedhöfe bei Karâra und der Amontempel Scheschonks I. Bei El Hibe* (Berlin-Leipzig 1926) 58–68; E. Graefe, El-Hibe, in: Helck, *LÄ* II 1180–1181; E. Feucht, Zwei Reliefs Scheschonks I. aus El-Hibeh, in: *SAK* 6 (1978) 69–77.

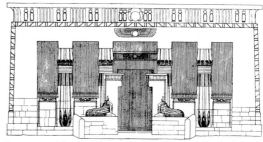

Reconstructed façade of the temple of Sheshonq I at El-Hiba (after H. Ranke)

El-Kab

The **town** of Nekheb, 18 km north of **Edfu**, was an important site from pre-historic times onwards as the

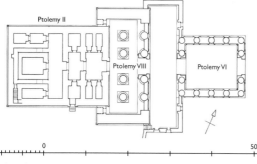

Plan of Ptolemaic Satet temple at Elephantine

seat of the vulture goddess Nekhbet, the mistress of Upper Egypt. It had numerous sanctuaries. In the central area, enclosed by the still extant **brick** wall of the town, stands the precinct of Nekhbet, its 304 x 376 m wide area surrounded by a brick wall. The south-facing principal temple, now totally ruined, was approached by a 600 m long processional way from a **platform** at the edge of the Nile. Remains show the development of the sanctuary, from the 12th Dynasty until Roman times. The last building erected (in the 30th Dynasty) had four **pylons**, and was composed of a **pillared hall** (4 rows of 6 pillars) from the reign of Hakoris, an offering room and a sanctuary of Darius I with several **crypts** and side-rooms. The actual temple building was 54 m long. In the courtyard between the first and second pylons stood a brick **barque station**; the courtyard beyond was occupied by a **birth house** surrounded by a colonnade. Parallel to that complex, along the west side of the temple, stood a 45 m long temple dedicated to Thoth. In 1798 the sanctuaries of the latter and six columns of the **hypostyle hall** of the Nekhbet temple were still preserved up to the **architraves**. 610 m to the north and 56 m west of the town wall are the ruins of two barque stations surrounded by colonnades; the first of these, built by Thutmosis III and resembling the barque station at **Elephantine**, was still completely preserved in 1798; the other one was built in the 30th Dynasty.

Several small temples exist at the mouth of the Wadi Hellal on the road to the gold mines of the Eastern Desert. Standing on the desert edge is a terraced temple dedicated to the goddess Shesmetet (Greek Smithis), which has a wide set of **stairs** leading to a pillared forecourt and a sanctuary carved out of the rock. The complex was erected by Ptolemy VIII Euergetes II and Ptolemy IX Soter II. 70 m to the south-east lie the remains of a small sanctuary of Ramesses II dedicated to Re-Horakhty, Hathor, Amun and Nekhbet.

A small Hathor temple of Thutmosis IV and Amenhotep III exists on a rock plateau further to the east. This building is well-preserved and has four noteworthy **Hathor** pillars. Another structure existing at El-Kab is a Roman fortification (area 50 x 50 m).

Bibliography: *Description* I, Plates 66, 71; J. Capart, *Fouilles de El Kab. Documents* (Brussels 1940); Borchardt, *Tempel mit Umgang* 12–13, 93–95, 102–104; excavation reports, in: *ASAE* 37 (1937) 3–15 and 38 (1938) 623–640; A. Badawy, *Fouilles d'El-Kab* (1945–46); architectural notes, in: *ASAE* 46 (1947) 357–371; Philippe Derchain, *Les monuments religieux à l'entrée de l'ouady Hellal, Elkab I* (Brussels 1971); Frans Depuydt, S. Hendrickx and D. Huyge, *Topographie d'Elkab. 1: Archaeological-topographical surveying of Elkab and surroundings. 2: Inventaire des sites archéologiques* (Brussels 1989); Aufrère, *L'Égypte restituée* 49–52.

El-Kharga, temple of Hibis

A well-preserved temple of Amun of Thebes in the Kharga Oasis built on the edge of a former lake. The building, 27.4 x 62 m in area, was probably erected in the Saite period (Psamtek II?) and decorated in the reign of Darius I

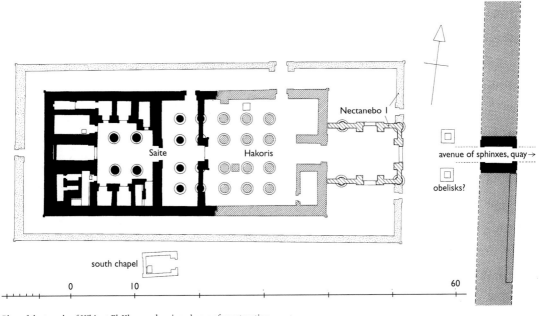

Plan of the temple of Hibis at El-Kharga, showing phases of construction

Reconstruction of the final building phase of the temple of Hibis at El-Kharga (after L.F. Hauser)

and Darius II (?). At the front of the temple is an early form of **pronaos** with four smoothed papyrus **columns** and **screen walls** (as at **El-Hiba**). Beyond the pronaos lie the **hypostyle hall**, an offering table room with a sanctuary, the chapel of the deified king and side-rooms with stairs up to the roof. These lead to an extensive complex of cult rooms on the upper floor. Under Hakoris, 29th Dynasty, instead of the traditional pillared court another hypostyle was built at the front whose front columns open onto a narrow courtyard. The new façade was not finished with a pylon. Nectanebo I and Nectanebo II surrounded the temple with a stone **enclosure wall** which, at the front, enclosed a monumental **kiosk** (Fig.) with eight columns. Because of the excessively wide span of 7.4 m, the kiosk had to be roofed with wooden rafters. The **composite capitals** in the kiosk and hypostyle hall are the earliest known in Egypt. In front of the kiosk are two **obelisks**, and an avenue of **sphinxes** leads up from the quay on the edge of the lake, passing through three enclosure walls with corresponding **gateways**. The temple is in danger of collapsing due to sub-soil water, and preparations have been made to relocate the temple to the site of Bagawât.

Bibliography: H.E. Winlock, *The Temple of Hibis in El Khargeh Oasis* (New York 1941); S. Sauneron, Quelques sanctuaires égyptiens des Oasis de Dakhleh et de Khargeh. Notes de voyage, in: *Cahiers d'Histoire Égyptienne* 7 (1955) 282–284; E. Cruz-Uribe, The Hibis Temple Project 1984–1985 Field Season, Preliminary Report, in: *JARCE* 23 (1986) 157–166; E. Cruz-Uribe, Hibis Temple Project: Preliminary Report, 1985–1986 and Summer 1986 Field Seasons, in: *Varia Aegyptiaca* 3 (1987) 215–230; E. Cruz-Uribe, *Hibis Temple Project I* (San Antonio 1988). Reconstruction: Aufrère, *L'Égypte restituée* II 80.

El-Kula

Remains of a small **step mastaba**, 18.6 x 18.6 m, of the 3rd or early 4th Dynasty, north of **Hierakonpolis**. A small chamber has been found, perhaps a burial chamber.

Bibliography: J. Stiénon, El Kôlah, in: *CdE* 49 (1950) 42–45; Lauer, *Histoire monumentale* I 179, 228–230; *MRA* II 65–67, Plate 11; R. Gundlach, El-Kulah, in: Helck, LÄ III 838–839; Dreyer *Stufenpyramiden* 45–46.

El-Lahun (Illahun), *see* Senwosret II

El-Lahun tomb 621

A royal tomb of the reign of **Senwosret II** at El-Lahun, in the style of the royal tombs of the 5–6th Dynasty; its identity cannot be ascertained. It consists of an antechamber, *serdab*, burial chamber, canopic shrine (**canopic recess**) and a **niched granite** sarcophagus. The tomb was never used and may have been a secondary tomb of Senwosret II.

Bibliography: W.M. Flinders Petrie, *Illahun II* (London 1923) 16–18.

Ellesiya

A site 70 km north of **Abu Simbel** with a small **rock temple** (**hemispeos**) of Thutmosis III dedicated to Amun, the king, Horus and Satis. It consists of a forecourt carved out of the rock, and a rock-cut room with a statue niche. In 1969 it was moved to the Museo Egizio in Turin.

Bibliography: Silvio Curto, *Nubien* (Munich 1966) 263–265; Ch. Desroches-Noblecourt, *Le speos d'el-Lessiya* (Cairo 1968); Hein, *Ramessidische Bautätigkeit* 26–27; R. Gundlach, Der Felstempel Thutmosis' III. bei Ellesiya. Analyse des Dekorationsprogramms, in: Kurth, *Tempeltagung* 69–87.

El-Lisht, *see also* Amenemhat I, Senwosret I

An important royal necropolis of the early 12th Dynasty, in which are found the **pyramids** of **Amenemhat I** and **Senwosret I**, as well as extensive areas covered with private tombs of the Middle Kingdom. Next to the pyramid of Amenemhat I are several large private tomb complexes, one of them bearing the name of the owner (the vizier Inyotef-iqer). Next to the pyramid of Senwosret I are

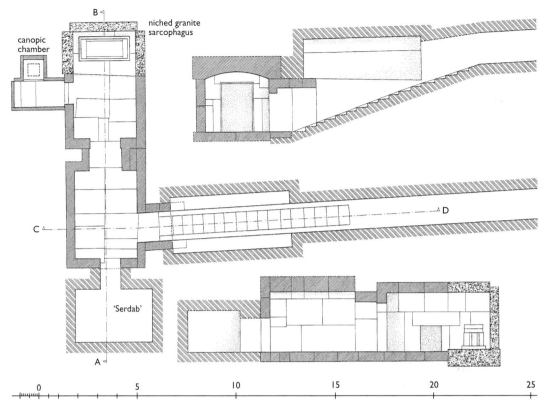

Plan and sections of royal tomb 621 at El-Lahun

remains of the funerary enclosures of high-ranking officials (**Senwosretankh**, Imhotep, **Mentuhotep**) and other tombs without names. The remains of the residential city of Iti-tawy lie abandoned in the area of the towns of El-Lisht and Bamha. The area surrounding the pyramid of Amenemhat I contains considerable remains of settlements of the 13th and 20th–21st Dynasties.

Bibliography: J.E. Gautier and G. Jéquier, *Fouilles de Licht* (Cairo 1902); W.K. Simpson, *Lischt*, in: Helck, *LÄ* III 1057–1061. Settlement: Felix Arnold, Settlement remains in Lisht-North, in: Bietak, *House and Palace* 15–21.

El-Ma'adi

An extensive settlement with several cemeteries, southeast of Cairo, dating from the latest pre-historic phase. There are the remains of some round dwelling **houses** half sunk into the ground. A rough fieldstone building with rounded corners and central supports, the oldest stone building in Egypt, is particularly intriguing.

Bibliography: W. Kaiser, Ma'adi, in: Helck, *LÄ* III 1110; Ibrahim Rizkana and Jürgen Seeher, *Maadi III. The Non-Lithic Small Finds and the Structural Remains of the Predynastic Settlement* (Mainz 1989) 33–60.

El-Mahamid Qibly (Dahamsha)

A sanctuary of Sobek of Sumenu, to the south of **Armant**. It was re-discovered in 1966 during the digging of the Sawahel-Armant Canal on the fringe of the village of Mahamid Qibly. The 18th Dynasty temple is destroyed down to the **foundations**. A statue group, of Amenhotep III with Sobek (now in Luxor Museum), was found in a subterranean (possibly flooded) shaft chamber. A twisting corridor connects this with an antechamber – covered with a slab moved by bronze wheels on rails – perhaps used to keep animals (but unsuitable for crocodiles, which would have needed sunlight).

Bibliography: H.S. Bakry, The discovery of a temple of Sobk in upper Egypt, in: *MDAIK* 27 (1971) 131–146.

El-Maharraqa

An incomplete Roman temple dedicated to Isis and Serapis at Hiera Sykaminos in Lower **Nubia**, 120 km south of Aswan, on the southern border of the Roman empire. The only part completed was a court measuring 13.56 x 15.69 m, surrounded on three sides by **columns**. An architectural curiosity is the winding staircase at a corner of the court leading to the roof (compare winding

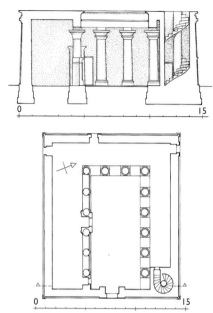

Incomplete Roman temple to Isis and Serapis at El-Maharraqa

stairs in the lost triumphal arch of **Antinopolis**). The building was moved in 1961 by the Egyptian Antiquities Organisation to a place near **Wadi el-Sebu'a**.

Bibliography: Gau, *Antiquités*, Plates 40–41; W. Helck, Hierasykaminos, in: Helck, *LÄ* II 1186–1187.

El-Qal'a

A temple measuring 16 x 24 m, 800 m north of the temple of Min at **Koptos**, dedicated to Isis of Koptos and dating to the time of Augustus. The building is well-preserved and contains all the interior rooms (including the *wabet*) normally present in larger temples, but on the smallest scale. A transverse axis with a wide side-entrance which leads to a secondary sanctuary is an unusual feature.

Bibliography: C. Traunecker, El Qala, in: Helck, *LÄ* V 38–40; Laure Pantalacci and Claude Traunecker, Premières observations sur le temple coptite d'El-Qal'a, in: *ASAE* 70 (1984/85) 133–141; Laure Pantalacci and Claude Traunecker, *Le temple d'El-Qal'a*, Vol. 1 (Cairo 1990); Claude Traunecker, Lessons from the Upper Egyptian temple of el-Qal'a, in: Quirke, *Temple* 168–178; L. Pantalacci and C. Traunecker, Le temple d'El-Qal'a à Coptos, in: *BIFAO* 93 (1993) 379–390.

El-Tarif, *see saff* tomb

El-Tod

The remains of a **town** and a badly damaged temple to Month at Djerty (Tuphium), 20 km south-west of **Luxor**. The oldest object found is a **granite** pillar of Userkaf,

unique evidence of Old Kingdom monumental building activity in Upper Egypt. Blocks bearing the names of Mentuhotep Nebhepetre and Mentuhotep Sankhkare enable one to reconstruct buildings of the 11th Dynasty, which were replaced by a new structure of Senwosret I, of which the foundation base measuring 19 x 26 m and a wall have survived. The 'Treasure of Tod' was discovered in 1936 in the **foundations**, consisting of four bronze chests of Amenemhat II which contained valuables from neighbouring countries to the north-east.

Ptolemy VIII Euergetes II enlarged the Middle Kingdom temple at the front, building the existing façade wall into the newly added structure of a **hypostyle hall** and **pronaos**; work on the decoration continued into the reign of Antonius Pius. In the reign of Ptolemy IV the temple was linked by an avenue of **sphinxes** to a **platform**. Next to the temple is a **sacred lake**, an interesting stone structure, 9 m deep. A **barque station** of Thutmosis III stands to the north of the processional way.

A larger temple of Thutmosis III is believed to lie outside the area of ruins, under the mosque.

Bibliography: F. Bisson de la Roque, *Tôd (1934–1936)*, FIFAO 17 (Cairo 1937); F. Bisson de la Roque, Le lac sacré de Tôd, in: *CdE* 24 (1937) 3–14; D. Arnold, Bemerkungen zu den frühen Tempeln von El-Tôd, in: *MDAIK* 31 (1975) 175–186; D.B. Redford, The Tôd Inscription of Senwosret I, in: *SSEA* Journal 17 (1987) 35–55; J. Vercoutter, Tôd (1946–1949). Rapport succint des fouilles, in: *BIFAO* 50 (1952) 69–87; P. Barguet, Rapport de la saison février-avril 1950, in: *BIFAO* 51 (1952) 80–110; J. Vandier, in: *Textes et langages* III (Cairo 1972) 259–265; Chr. Desroches Noblecourt, Considérations sur l'existence des divers temples de Monthu à travers les âges, dans le site de Tôd, in: *BIFAO* 84 (1984) 81–109; Aufrère, *L'Égypte restituée* 143.

Embalming hall, purification booth

A structure for the cleansing and mummification of the corpse and where the associated rituals were performed. It is depicted in several private tombs of the Old Kingdom (designated as *ibu*). These pictures indicate that the structures, which stood ideally on the West Bank of the Nile, consisted of a **pillared hall** and had protected access because of the secrecy of the rituals. Kings probably had their own complex, possibly the *seh-netjer* (**divine booth**), which was originally a reed hut. Only the embalming hall of the Apis bulls at **Memphis** has ever been found: it is a **brick** building with narrow parallel rooms containing eight stone tables, up to 4 m long, with the foreparts of a lion. (A lion bed is a symbol of resurrection.)

The interpretation of **valley temples** as embalming halls, or as their recreation in stone, is no more convincing than the compromise solution which reconstructs the embalming hall on the roof of the **valley temple**.

Bibliography: Discussion by É. Drioton, in: *ASAE* 40 (1940) 1007–1014; Bernhard Grdseloff, *Das ägyptische Reinigungszelt* (Cairo 1941); Ricke, *Bemerkungen* II 96–98; Selim Hassan, *Excavations at Giza*, Vol. 4 (Cairo 1943) 69–102; J. Dimick, The embalming house of the Apis bulls, in: Rudolf Anthes, *Mit Rahineh* 1955 (Philadelphia 1959) 75–79; D. Arnold, Balsamierungshalle, in: Helck, *LÄ* I 614–615; E. Brovarski, The Doors of Heaven, in: *Orientalia* 46 (1977) 110–113; J.K. Hoffmeier, The possible origins of the tent of purification in the Egyptian funerary cult, in: *SAK* 9 (1981) 167–177; M. and A. Jones, The Apis House Project at Mit Rahinah, in: *JARCE* 19 (1982) 51–58; 20 (1983) 33–45; 22 (1985) 17–28; 24 (1987) 35–46; D. Kurth, *Reinigungszelt*, in: Helck, *LÄ* V 220–222.

Enclosure wall

Towns, **fortresses** and **palaces**, as well as almost all temples and shrines, were surrounded by an enclosure wall. The impressive walls enclosing the precinct of **Amun** at **Karnak** (21 m high, 10–12 m thick) built by Nectanebo I included five large (and five smaller) **gateways**:

First **pylon**: gateway built by Sheshonq, possibly replaced by a gateway of Nectanebo I.

Northern gateway: uninscribed, perhaps 30th Dynasty.

Eastern gate: Nectanebo I (Bab el-Melâkha)

Tenth pylon: begun by Amenhotep III and completed by Horemheb.

Unfinished pylon of Ptolemy III Euergetes at the temple of Khonsu (Bab el-Amara).

The precinct of **Month** has a monumental northern gateway (Bab el-Abd, built by Ptolemy III Euergetes/ Ptolemy IV Philopator), and likewise the precinct of **Mut** (built by Ptolemy II Philadelphus/Ptolemy III Euergetes).

Bibliography: J.-C. Golvin and El-Sayed Hegazy, Essai d'explication de la forme et des caractéristiques générales des grands enceintes de Karnak, in: *Karnak* IX 145–156; J.-C. Golvin and El-Sayed Hegazy, La datation des portes de l'enceinte d'Amon, in preparation.

Entrance chapel, *see north chapel*

Esna

A **town** 58 km south of **Luxor**, formerly known as Latopolis, containing the remains of a large temple of Khnum. The only excavated part of the building is the monumental **pronaos,** which was erected in the Roman period (Claudius to Decius) in front of a Ptolemaic temple building. The façade of the latter protrudes from the rear wall of the pronaos (built by Ptolemy VI Philometor and VIII Euergetes II). The façade of the pronaos is 40 m wide and 17 m high. The ceiling, decorated with astronomical depictions, is supported on four rows of six **columns**, 12 m high, with **composite capitals**. Some blocks of an earlier structure of the 18th Dynasty are preserved. The shrine has cultic connections with smaller neighbouring shrines: a small temple to Isis, built by Ptolemy IX Soter II and Cleopatra Cocce, on the East Bank of the Nile, near El-Hilla (Contralatopolis). It was enlarged in the reigns of Marcus Aurelius and Commodus by the addition of a pronaos measuring 7.4 x 6.3 m. This temple was recorded by the Napoleonic Expedition as still standing, but later fell victim to the construction of an administrative building in 1828. There is another sanctuary, 3.7 km north-west of Esna, at **El-Deir**. The Napoleonic Expedition reported this temple as still standing in parts. It was destroyed in 1843 for the

Front of the Roman period pronaos of the Khnum temple at Esna

Reconstruction of the Roman temple of Isis at El-Hilla (Contralatopolis), near Esna (after *Description* I, Plate 90)

Reconstruction of the small temple of Esna North at El-Deir (after *Description* I, Plate 88)

construction of a factory at Esna. 15 km south of Esna stands the small Roman temple of Anuket at Komir.

Bibliography: *Description* I, Plates 72–83, north Esna Plates 84–88, Contralatopolis Plates 89–90; Serge Sauneron, *Le temple d'Esna*, 7 Vols (Cairo 1959–1982); Serge Sauneron, Le temple d'Esna, in: *Textes et langages* III (Cairo 1972) 249–257; M. Es-Saghir and D. Valbelle, Komir, in: *BIFAO* 83 (1983) 149–170; Aufrère, *L'Égypte restituée* 256–258.

Ezbet Bashindy

The site of a necropolis of the Roman period in **Dakhla Oasis**, occupied by several monumental stone-built tomb structures, erected on a square plan, with **pilastered** external walls. The tomb of Qetinus has six inner chambers with inscriptions and decorations.

Bibliography: Jürgen Osing et al., *Denkmäler der Oase Dachla* (Mainz 1982) 57–69.

Ezbet Rushdi

A site in the region of Avaris where, in 1950/51 and in 1996, the remains of a **brick** temple of the second half of the 12th Dynasty, 31 x 41.5 m in size, were found. The structure underwent several phases of building and enlargement. In its final form it consisted of two large **pylon**-like structures, a forecourt and a transverse hall with two rows of **columns** and three statue shrines,

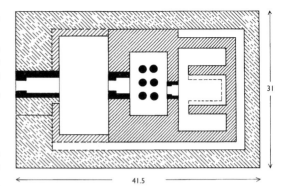

Plan of the Middle Kingdom temple at Ezbet Rushdi

possibly of stone. A strong brick wall surrounding the complex dates from the end of the 12th Dynasty. The plan was probably influenced by nearby temple of Canaanite type at **Tell el-Dab'a**.

Bibliography: Sh. Adam, Report on the Excavations of the Department of Antiquities at Ezbet Rushdi, in: *ASAE* 56 (1959) 207–226; M. Bietak, Kleine ägyptische Tempel und Wohnhäuser des späten Mittleren Reiches, in: *Hommages à Jean Leclant*, BdE 106 (1993) 12–14; D. Eigner, A temple of the Early Middle Kingdom at Tell Ibrahim Awad, in: *The Nile Delta in Transition: 4th.-3rd. Millennium B.C.* (Tel Aviv 1992) 69–77; a monograph on this topic by Peter Jánosi is forthcoming.

F

False door

Throughout Egyptian history, in Egyptian architecture **doors** represented a magic place where the deceased, gods and kings could appear through a sealed passageway, particularly in the **mastabas** of the Old Kingdom (False door Eg. *'arrerut*). From the Middle Kingdom, coinciding with the arrival of new forms of tomb, false doors were superseded by **stelae**. False doors appear in a variety of forms:

a) Occasionally false doors are shown realistically, as a door with every technical detail translated into stone (mastaba of Seshemnefer II at **Giza**). The false doors at the main entrance and in the court of chapels at the precinct of **Djoser** are real doors with huge open wings shaped in stone.

b) The normal false door is a simpler type, forming the door of the house which the mastaba represents, and is thus the starting point of the mortuary cult. The earliest examples consist of simple **door recesses**, or with two steps. From this developed intricately divided slabs of **limestone** or **granite**, with multiple frames, a **drum** and a **cavetto cornice** on top. From the 3rd Dynasty onwards, false doors bear inscriptions and depictions relating to funerary offerings. Occasionally the tomb owner is depicted, in the round, stepping out of the door. Above the lintel a slab was added with a depiction of the offering table (which developed independently in the 2nd Dynasty). From the outset there was a main false door at the southern end and a secondary one at the northern end of the east side of the mastaba, the latter *not* primarily intended for the wife of the deceased. Because at first the king was not thought to live on in the **pyramid**, and **pyramid temples** before the 5th Dynasty were separate from it, up to that time the pyramid did not contain a false door. From the reign of **Shepseskaf**, the southern false door moved into the royal cult complex, and during the course of the 5th Dynasty the northern false door was accommodated in the **north chapel**.

c) The **palace-façade** false door (Ger. *Prunkscheintür*) has its origins in the large **niched** tombs of the 1st Dynasty, which were surrounded on all sides by a large number of palace façades (in most cases having 3 on the short and 9 on the long sides, certain others 4 and 11, and some as many as 7 and 14). From the 3rd Dynasty, at the same time as the amount of niching on the east side of

Double false door with central support in the sanctuary of Re-Horakhty of the temple of Sety I at Abydos (after A.M. Calverley)

Normal false door (left) and palace-façade false door (right) in the tomb of Ptahhotep at Saqqara (after Perrot and Chipiez)

mastabas was reduced, a main and a secondary false door were given more prominence by deepening, and these gradually developed into the funerary offering chapels. The delicate structure of the highly decorated false door, moreover, meant that they needed to be positioned inside the mastaba itself (**Khabausokar**, Fig.). Here they came into competition with the normal false door, were forced out and from the 5th Dynasty moved down into the burial chambers, where they survived, until some time in the 12th Dynasty, in the decoration of the sarcophagus recess (tomb of **Senwosretankh**). Jánosi sees the false door as a representation on the rear wall of the offering chamber of the façade of the royal *seh-netjer* **palace** of the next life.

d) Developing in the 11th Dynasty outside the funerary sphere, especially in the '**houses of millions of years**', is the false door with a central support and two false openings; a supraportal element resembling a wooden lattice perhaps allows entrance to the king's *ba* as it emerges from the fictive palace sanctuary behind. The false door in the reception rooms of palaces and in dwelling **houses** (frequently a stone slab in a **brick** wall) creates the idea of the king's presence 'beyond' while the person in front performs royal functions. These 'doors' in dwelling houses sometimes serve simply as a decorative element (**Amarna**). The false door with a central support in temples apparently developed from these prototypes in domestic building. For that reason, it does not appear in the sphere of the gods but only in connection with the divine aspects of the king, marking the exit from or the entrance to his otherworldly residence.

Bibliography: L. Borchardt, Das Grab des Menes, in: *ZÄS* 36 (1898) 93–102; Junker, *Giza* III, Figs 33–34; Vandier, *Manuel* 389–431; Sylvia Wiebach, *Die ägyptische Scheintür* (Hamburg 1981); J-Ph. Lauer, La signification et le rôle des fausses-portes du palais dans les tombeaux du type de Negadeh, in: *MDAIK* 37 (1981) 281–287; G. Haeny, Zu den Platten mit Opfertischszenen aus Heluan und Gizeh, in:

Realistic false doors in the mastaba of Seshemnefer at Giza (reconstruction by Junker, 1938)

Festschrift Ricke 143–164; G. Haeny, Scheintür, in: Helck, *LÄ* V 563–574; R. Stadelmann, Scheintür oder Stele in Totentempeln des Alten Reiches, in: *MDAIK* 39 (1983) 237–241; P. Jánosi, Die Entwicklung und Deutung des Totenopferraums in den Pyramidentempeln des Alten Reiches, in: Kurth, *Tempeltagung* 143–163; N. Strudwick, *The Administration of Egypt in the Old Kingdom* (London 1985) 9–52; M. Ullmann, Die Mittelstützscheintür im Tempel, in: *Seventh International Congress of Egyptologists, Cambridge 1995* (Leuven 1998) 1177–1189.

Faras

A sprawling area of ruins with the remains of a **town**, situated on the West Bank of the Nile to the north of Wadi Halfa. In the north-west there is a small rectangular **fortress** of the Middle Kingdom (75 x 85 m), a New Kingdom necropolis to the north-east, and to the south-west the so-called Hathor Rock containing the **rock tomb** of Setau and the temple of Hathor. The centre is taken up by a fortified town with the remains of a temple of Tutankhamun, which consists of a courtyard with two porticoes of two rows of seven **columns** each, a hall with four rows of four columns, and the sanctuary area. Several hundred usurped blocks of Thutmosis III have been found, which were probably brought there from the temple at **Buhen** further south; other blocks, bearing cartouches of Ramesses II, probably derive from **Aksha**.

Bibliography: Kazimierz Michalowski, *Faras I Fouilles Polonaises 1961* (Warsaw 1962) 17–73; Kazimierz Michalowski, *Faras II Fouilles Polonaises 1961–1962* (Warsaw 1965) 14–38; Kazimierz Michalowski, in: *Kush* 10 (1962) 220–224; 11 (1963) 236–237; 13 (1965) 179–180; J. Lipińska, Faras, in: Helck, *LÄ* II 114–115; Janusz Karkowski, *Faras V The Pharaonic Inscriptions from Faras* (Warsaw 1981); Hein, *Ramessidische Bautätigkeit* 36–38.

Flagpole

These poles standing in recesses in **pylon** façades have their origin in the ancient standards of deities, planted in the sacred precinct where, as symbols of the deity, they acted as receivers of offerings. Made probably of Cilician fir and Aleppo pine, they were in excess of 30 m high. The tip of the pole was gilded and adorned with coloured pennants; the foot stood on a **granite** base and was held in a copper socket; half-way up, it was held in place with wooden clamps fixed in openings in the pylon. The temple of **Amun** at **Karnak** had 2 x 4 flagpoles; the **Aten temple** at **Amarna** 2 x 5; elsewhere, in most cases the number is only 2 x 1 or 2 x 2. Flagpoles are illustrated in several Egyptian wall paintings.

Bibliography: Hölscher, *Medinet Habu* III 5; Badawy, *Dessin architectural* 181–188; D. Arnold, Flaggenmasten, in: Helck, *LÄ* II 257–258; M. Azim and C. Traunecker, Un mât du IXe pylone au nom d'Horemheb, in: *Karnak* VII 75–92.

Floor

The floors of stone buildings consist of **paving**; in **brick** buildings they consist of a coating of Nile mud or paving made of unbaked or, very occasionally, fired bricks. In **palaces** the floors were beautifully painted (*al secco* on **gypsum** stucco): whether this reflects any Minoan influence (MM III–LM I) remains disputed. Important examples have survived from three palaces of the New Kingdom. The decoration is in most respects arranged as scenes from nature (fish pond, birds in a thicket, leaping calves, plants); it is highly detailed and laid out on a wide central field surrounded by subordinate areas which were more cursorily painted. The palaces are:

a) The palace of Amenhotep III at **Malqata**, consisting of a **pillared hall**, throne hall and audience room. (Found by Robb de P. Tytus in 1902. Fragments are in the Egyptian Museum, Cairo, MMA and Munich.)

b) The Maru-en-pa-Aten at **Amarna**; 11 T-shaped ponds of the 'Water Court'. (Found by Barsanti in 1896 and the Egypt Exploration Society in 1920. Fragments are in the Egyptian Museum, Cairo, MMA and Munich.)

c) The main palace of **Amarna,** in four halls of the 'harim' area. (Found by Flinders Petrie in 1894. The main depiction was destroyed in 1912; a copy and fragments are in the Egyptian Museum, Cairo and MMA.)

A throne podium of Amenhotep III, with painted images of prisoners and bows on the staired ramp (**stairs**), was found in 1974 south of Malqata (Kom el-Samak) by the University of Waseda (Japan) expedition.

Bibliography: W.M. Flinders Petrie, *Tell el Amarna* (London 1894); Robb de P. Tytus, *A Preliminary Report of the Re-excavation of the Palace of Amenhetep III* (New York 1903); Friedrich W. von Bissing, *Der Fußboden aus dem Palaste des Königs Amenophis IV. zu El-Hawata* (Munich 1941); D. Arnold, Fußboden, in: Helck, *LÄ* II 367–368; *Studies on the Palace of Malqata* (Waseda University 1993), Plates 1–2.

Fortress

Egyptian architecture has produced innumerable military structures whose dimensions and technical accomplishment well bear comparison with medieval castles, although their architectonic achievements have yet to be acknowledged in the study of European fortifications.

1. Old and Middle Kingdoms

Hieroglyphs or representations of the names of towns indicate the existence of sites and palaces with surrounding walls and turrets (**divine fortress**) from the period of the Unification onwards. The earliest preserved fortress walls date to the Old Kingdom (**Balat**, **Elephantine**). Then, as later, fortresses had **brick** walls up to 5 m thick, fortified with semi-circular turrets. The two **Nubian** rectangular fortresses of **Aniba** (87 x 138 m) and **Buhen** (150 x 170 m) were equipped, even then, with a keep surrounded by a wall and a dry moat.

In the 12th Dynasty (Senwosret I–III) construction of fortresses blossomed, perhaps based on First Intermediate Period military systems which no longer exist, as well as influenced by the fortified Palestinian cities of the Middle Bronze Age IIA or I (Sharuhen, Tell Beit, Mirsim, Shekhem). The north-eastern Egyptian border was fortified from the Middle Kingdom onwards, although so far no fortress buildings have been found there. Fortified military camps have been found inside Egypt only at Wadi Natrun (Qaret el-Dahr), **Qasr el-Sagha** and in Wadi el-Hudi, south-east of **Aswan**.

A chain of imposing fortresses, known as the Second Cataract Forts, was created in the 12th Dynasty to secure African trade routes in Upper Nubia. Some of these monuments, unique in the history of fortifications, remained standing until 1960, but have since been submerged under the floods of Lake Nasser, in some cases without adequate research or publication. The Cataract Forts set up on the West Bank of the Nile were spaced at distances varying from 3 to 10 km and connected via a chain of watch towers by means of fire signals. Their garrison is estimated to have numbered from 300 to 3000 men. The fortresses contained housing for the troops and their commander, as well as workshops and depots for weaponry and gigantic stores for provisions. Drinking water supplies were ensured by protected stairs to the Nile. The fortresses were always situated right beside the Nile, on level terrain taking the shape of large walled rectangles, and on rocky elevations or islands having a correspondingly irregular plan. The surrounding walls were about 5 m thick, 10–12 m high and fortified with protective walkways and rounded **battlements**. The side facing the enemy dropped vertically, while the inside sloped.

Walls were strengthened with wooden beams inserted at regular intervals along the length and across the width. They had drying drainage channels throughout their length. The exterior of the wall was in most cases of stone or had a stone **casing**. In front was a keep, a wall and semi-circular turrets with multiple arrow slits. Walls were fortified at regular distances with rectangular protruding towers. There were powerful gate structures standing far in front of the wall, with an inner court and a gate chamber. At **Buhen**, the fort was equipped with a removable drawbridge on rollers over the moat. There are frequent instances of spur-like walls, fortified with towers, extending from a surrounding wall, their purpose being to protect harbour installations etc. and to act as breakwaters in the Nile.

(**Ikkur, Kubban, Aniba, Faras, Serra East, Buhen, Khor, Dorginarti, Mirgissa, Dabenarti, Askut, Shalfak, Uronarti, Semna, Kumma** and South Semna)

Nubian fortresses

Fort	Kingdom	Size (m)
Lower **Nubia**		
Ikkur	Old, Middle and New	82 x 110
Kubban	Old, Middle and New	70 x 125
Aniba	Old, Middle and New	87 x 138
Faras	Middle and New	75 x 85
Serra East	Middle	80 x …
Cataract Forts		
Buhen	Old, Middle and New	215 x 460
Khor	Middle and New	250 x 600
Dorginarti	New	80 x 194
Mirgissa	Middle and New	190 x 295
Dabenarti	Middle	60 x 230
Askut	Middle	77 x 87
Shalfak	Middle	47 x 95
Uronarti	Middle and New	57 x 114 x 126 (triangular)
Semna	Middle and New	135 x 135
Kumma	Middle and New	70 x 117

Bibliography: S. Clarke, Ancient Egyptian Frontier Fortresses, in: *JEA* 3 (1916) 155–179; Ludwig Borchardt, *Altägyptische Festungen an der Zweiten Nilschwelle* (Leipzig 1923); A. Fakhry, *Wâdi-El-Natrûn*, in: *ASAE* 40 (1940) 845–848; G.A. Reisner, Ancient Egyptian forts at Semna and Uronarti, in: *Bull. of the Mus. of Fine Arts Boston* 163 (1929) 64–75; Dows Dunham, Ed., The Egyptian forts from Halfa to Semna, in: *Kush* 8 (1960) 11–24; Dows Dunham and Jozef Janssen, *Semna Kumma, Second Cataract Forts*, Vol. I (Boston 1960); Dows Dunham and Jozef Janssen, *Uronarti Shalfak Mirgissa, Second Cataract Forts*, Vol. II (Boston 1967); J. Knudstad, Serra-East and Doginarti, in: *Kush* 14 (1966) 165–186; Badawy, *Architecture*, Vol. 2 198–230, Vol.3 446–474; William Y. Adams, *Nubia Corridor to Africa* (London 1977) 175–192; A. Badawy, Festungsanlage, in: Helck, *LÄ* II 194–203.

2. New Kingdom and later
In the New Kingdom, the **Nubian fortresses** were partly restored and enlarged, and areas of housing were enclosed in surrounding walls (**Aniba, Buhen**). New fortresses (**Dorginarti, Sesebi**) and new fortification elements were infrequent. Dry moats and bastions along the keep were now considered of little use and disappeared. Foreign influence on Egyptian fortress architecture in this period is unlikely because neighbouring countries at that time, in the Late Bronze Age, had no important fortresses. Several are nonetheless shown in Egyptian illustrations of sieges, depicting a military building protruding centrally above a double wall crowned with **battlements**. Egyptian sources and present-day research indicate the existence of many fortified sites along the 'Ways of Horus' (the desert route out of the Nile Delta leading through north-west Sinai towards southern Palestine). Some extensive fortification systems of the New Kingdom and the Late Period exist near **El-Hebua**. At Haruvit (El-Haruba), east of the important administrative centre of Arish, a 50 x 50 m castle of the Ramesside period has been excavated. Its walls, 4 m thick, with massive gates (**High Gate**), enclosed housing quarters and stores surrounding a court. A small Ramesside fort was excavated near Deir el-Balah, south of Gaza. This structure of only 20 sq m, probably several storeys high, had 15 small rooms. Tell

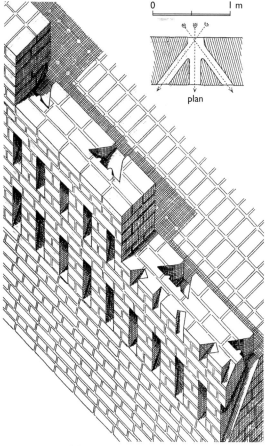

Reconstruction of the system of arrow slits in the Middle Kingdom fortress at Buhen (after W.B. Emery)

Mor on the Mediterranean coast, north-west of Ashdod, was another Ramesside fort, this one 23 sq m. Another fortress is attested to at the Egyptian administrative seat of Jaffa. A tower-like Egyptian fortification existed at Bethshan, the most important Egyptian centre in the north. Further forts lie unexplored in the northern Negev.

The western route, along the Mediterranean coast, was also protected by fortresses in the Ramesside period. This chain of fortifications, still inadequately researched, terminated at Ramesses II's fortress of Umm el-Raham, west of Marsa Matruh.

Following ancient tradition, the temple of Ramesses III at **Medinet Habu** represents a fortress. The main temple was originally surround by a mud brick wall, 136 x 171 m wide, 6 m deep and 15 m high, fortified by 12 corner and wall turrets, subsequently enclosed by a surrounding wall of mud brick 10–11 m thick and 16.43 m high. This wall is **battered** at its foot. Standing in front of this was a keep with a wall 4.4 m high, supporting a defence gallery with rounded battlements. The east- and west-facing walls each had a gate at the centre flanked by towers (**High Gate**). This is an example of a fortified Delta residence of the type later erected by Ramesside and other kings against mass foreign invasions, here intended for use in the next life. **Tel el-Retaba** in Wadi Tumilat is an important heavily fortified settlement of the Ramesside period in northern Egypt, with walls 9 m thick and 375 m long. Egyptian influence caused the governors' residences of the 13–12th centuries BC along the Canaan coast of the Mediterranean (Aphek, Deir el-Balah, Tell el-Farah South, Tell el-Hesi, Tell Sera, Tell Jemmeh, Tell Mor) to become fortified castle dwellings with an inner court and living quarters in the upper storey. After the New Kingdom, there was a considerable increase in the fortification of towns and temples: **El-Hiba**, walls 12.6 m thick, 10 m high; **El-Kab**, walls 5 km long and 12.1 m thick; **Tanis**, walls 800 m long, 18 m thick. Powerful fortresses protected the Sinai route against the Babylonians and Persians (**Defenna, El-Hebua**).

Bibliography: Uvo Hölscher, *Das Hohe Tor von Medinet Habu* (Leipzig 1910); Uvo Hölscher, *Medinet Habu* II 1–10; A. Badawy, *Fouilles d'El Kab (1945-1946)*; Notes architecturales, in: *ASAE* (1947) 357–371; R. Gundlach, Migdol, in: Helck, *LÄ* IV 124–125; Badawy, *Architecture*, Vol. 3 446–474; L. Habachi, The military posts of Ramesses II on the coastal road and the western part of the Delta, in: *BIFAO* 80 (1980) 13–30; E.D. Oren, 'Governors' Residencies' in Canaan under the New Kingdom, in: *JSSEA* 14 (1985) 37–56; E.D. Oren, The 'Ways of Horus' in North Sinai, in: A.F. Rainey, Ed., *Egypt, Israel, Sinai* (Tel Aviv 1987) 69–119; Amnon Ben-Tor, Ed., *The Archaeology of Ancient Israel* (New Haven-London 1991) 221.

The numerous important Roman castles in Egypt (Lower Nubian southern borders, oases of the Western Desert, Eastern Desert route to Mons Claudianus and the Red Sea, Luxor, Babylon/Old Cairo, coastal routes along the Mediterranean Sea and in the North-Western Sinai) cannot be discussed here.

Foundation deposit

From the Old Kingdom to the Ptolemaic period, foundation deposits were placed under the corners or the axis of a building as part of the **foundation ritual** to ensure its protection. These were placed mostly in small pits, but occasionally in spacious walled shafts. Finds include offerings of food and drink (animal bones, ceramics), also building tools, small tablets bearing an inscription of the foundation text sealed in a clay brick, and occasionally scarabs, amulets, linen cloths, bronze figurines, faience pots etc. Rich foundation deposits have been found in the temples of **Mentuhotep** and that of **Hatshepsut** at **Deir el-Bahari**, and also below the pyramids of **Amenemhat I** and **Senwosret I**. Since **rock tombs** have no outside corners, deposits were of necessity placed at some distance in front of the tombs (such as in nine tombs in the Valley of the Kings).

Not all of the many deposits discovered in the neighbourhood of pyramids and tombs were foundation deposits: some were religious objects intended for the benefit of the dead, material polluted by the mummification process or objects that had been used during the funeral.

Bibliography: G.A. Reisner, The Barkal Temples in 1916, in: *JEA* 4 (1917) 213–227; W.C. Hayes, *The Scepter of Egypt* II (New York 1985) 84–88; B. Letellier, Gründungsbeigabe, in: Helck, *LÄ* II 906–912; Nicholas Reeves, *The Complete Valley of the Kings* (London 1996) 28–29, 93–94, 107.

Foundation ritual

This extensive ritual, which arose out of working processes, was performed at the laying of foundation stones for temples and tombs, theoretically by the king together with Seshat, the goddess of measuring. It is frequently portrayed in wall reliefs and is further attested to by the objects left as **foundation deposits**. The sequence of the ritual consisted of a procession to the building site, symbolic pegging out of the areas concerned and **orientation** of the axis (stretching the cord), breaking open of the soil, scattering of foundation sand, making a foundation offering, placing of the foundation deposit, painting of bricks and the laying of the foundation stone.

Bibliography: A.M. Blackman and H.W. Fairman, The consecration of an Egyptian temple according to the use of Edfu, in: *JEA* 32 (1946)

75–91; P. Montet, Le rituel de fondation des temples égyptiens, in: *Kêmi* 17 (1964) 74–100; James Weinstein, *Foundation Deposits in Ancient Egypt*, Dissertation (University of Pennsylvania 1973); Sanaa Abd el-Azim el-Adly, *Das Gründungs- und Weiheritual des ägyptischen Tempels von der frühgeschichtlichen Zeit bis zum Ende des Neuen Reiches*, Dissertation (Tübingen 1981); B. Letellier, Gründungsbeigabe, in: Helck, *LÄ* II 906–912; B. Letellier, Gründungszeremonien, in: Helck, *LÄ* 912–914; K. Zibelius-Chen, Tempelgründung, in: Helck, *LÄ* VI 385–386; M. Isler, The Merkhet, in: *Varia Aegyptiaca* 7 (1991) 53–67.

Foundations

Foundations remained rudimentary up to the 3rd Dynasty, even in the construction of **step mastabas** and stone tomb precincts. The foundations prepared for the **Bent Pyramid** were so inadequate that they caused serious structural damage. Stone buildings in the Old Kingdom were erected on top of three layers of stone: the sub-foundation, foundation and slightly less substantial **paving** slabs. However, **pillars**, including those at **Meidum**, had particularly good foundations, being set either into a rock shaft 1 m deep or in a sand pit lined with stone. Structures erected on rock (pyramid of **Khufu**, or the temple of **Mentuhotep** at Deir el-Bahari) were not specifically provided with foundations. From the 12th Dynasty onwards, foundations were often filled with **re-used blocks**. The foundations of the **hypostyle hall** of **Karnak** were filled with multiple layers of small stones (*talatat*, or even **bricks**), which recede beyond the outer edge of the columns. **Obelisks** were erected on up to six layers of stone beams, 5–6 m long, those in the uppermost layer dowelled together. The actual obelisk base on top of this foundation is a cube made of **granite**. The sub-foundation is in some cases built of bricks, even in the case of stone buildings. Deep underlying masonry and continuous foundation platforms already existed in some places in the Old Kingdom, but they did not become the norm until the Ptolemaic period, when they had a depth of 7–8 m. The foundations of certain large temples accommodate **crypts** (**Dendera**). Some foundation trenches were shored-up with brick walls during construction. Starting from the Old Kingdom the deepest foundation stratum was for preference constructed in sand – occasionally deep piles of sand. The practicality of this (compensation against pressure, isolation) combined with symbolism so that the temple was set up on pure sand, a kind of **primeval mound**. The laying of the foundations of a temple (stretching the cord, hoeing the soil, pouring sand, laying the foundation stone) is part of a **foundation ritual**.

Brick walls invariably stand on a foundation of two or three layers of bricks which protrude slightly at the foot of the wall on both sides. The lowest layer is often a bed of bricks which stand on their long-side edges. Rows of **column bases** within brick buildings frequently stand on a continuous foundation wall. Large walls in cultivated land are set in deep foundation trenches.

Bibliography: Jéquier, *Manuel* 33–38; Clark, *AEM* 62–74; Arnold, Fundament, in: Helck, *LÄ* II 356–359; Arnold, *Building* 109–115.

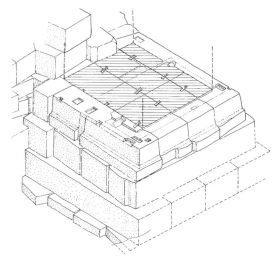

An obelisk base of Amenhotep III in front of the third pylon at Karnak, constructed of stone blocks cramped together

Frieze brick, *see funerary cone*

Frieze of uraei

Lines of rearing cobras spitting poison, which were believed to provide apotropaic protection, are found from the reign of **Djoser** onwards on the façades of stone temples (for example, a monumental frieze of uraei exists on the façade of the main temple building at **Kom Ombo**), and along the top of **screen walls** or **gateways**.

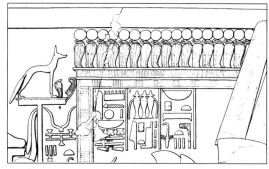

Depiction of a frieze of uraei on the roof of a shrine in the temple of Khonsu at Karnak (after the Oriental Institute)

The frieze appears artistically carved and with inlaid designs on wooden structures such as **canopies**, **kiosks** and shrines. Fragments of a wooden frieze of uraei 30 cm high have been found in the temple of **Sety I** at Abydos.

Bibliography: Jean-Philippe Lauer, *La pyramide à degrés* (Cairo 1936), Plate 54; E.B. Ghazouli, The palace and magazines attached to the temple of Sety I at Abydos, in: *ASAE* 58 (1964) 149, Plate 20.

Funerary cone, *see also* bricks, moulded

Small clay cones (8 cm long) with dish-like bases are known from late pre-historic to Old Kingdom sites at **Buto**, **Balat** and **Elephantine**, and were apparently used as architectural wall decoration. Mesopotamian parallels lends weight to the hypothesis of Mesopotamian influence on early Egyptian architecture.

These early cones may have developed into the much larger funerary cones found at Upper Egyptian tombs from the 11th Dynasty onwards (**bricks, moulded**, Fig., D; **Nebunef**, Fig.) These cones were inserted into the masonry or brickwork on the upper border of the tomb façade, with their bases remaining visible. From the New Kingdom onwards, the base was inscribed with the name and titles of the tomb owner. Cones sometimes assume curious shapes, depending on their position in the architecture; special corner bricks were also made. The longest cones are 52 cm in length.

Bibliography: L. Borchardt et al., Friesziegel in Grabbauten, in: *ZÄS* 70 (1934) 25–35; N. de Garis Davies and M.F.L. Macadam, *A Corpus of Inscribed Egyptian Funerary Cones* (Oxford 1957); A. Eggebrecht, Grabkegel, in: Helck, *LÄ* II 857–859; Lise Manniche, *Lost Tombs* (London- New York 1988); Friederike Kampp, *Die thebanische Nekropole* I (Mainz 1996) 66–68; Thomas von der Way, *Tell el-Fara'in. Buto* I (Mainz 1997) 232–236.

Funerary enclosure

Crowded together in the flat fore-desert of the northern necropolis of **Abydos**, to the west of Kom el-Sultan, are the funerary enclosures of the kings of the 1st and 2nd Dynasties, from King Djer onwards. The earliest buildings were constructed of perishable materials and their locations are only recognisable because of the secondary tombs around them. From the reign of Udimu (or Den), funerary enclosures become more elaborate, in the form of powerful **niched** structures of **brick**. The main entrance was on the particularly elaborate east side, at the southern end. Inside the precincts of Khasekhemwy and Peribsen, free-standing brick buildings have been discovered, behind the main entrance in the south-east corner, which perhaps housed a statue of the king. The discovery announced of a shallow mound in the funerary enclosure of Khasekhemwy

has not been substantiated. The existence of some earlier funerary enclosures, made of perishable materials, cannot be excluded. The funerary enclosures did not serve as tombs, but they had some functional connection with the tombs of the kings at Umm el-Ga'ab, 1.7 km further south. They may be representations of a particular type of structure of the Early Dynastic Period, as a **divine fortress** to be used by the king in the afterlife. Whether these funerary enclosures influenced the development of similar structures at Saqqara, or whether the two are separate branches of the same idea, has not yet been resolved.

At present, the following funerary enclosures are known, or surmised, to have existed (designated A to G, independent of their royal ownership):

Djer: 'A', east of the Peribsen structure, 53.80 x 96.2 m in size, now completely levelled. It is surrounded by 269 tombs of courtiers. The main entrance is at the southern end of the east side, with at least one secondary entrance in the north wall. There is evidence that the façade was niched. Lying outside, to the south-west, are the remains of a niched shrine.

Djet: 'B', east of Peribsen and Djer, a precinct measuring 47.5 x 90 m, surrounded by 154 tombs of courtiers. Not yet excavated.

Merineith: 'C' (according to Petrie, Kemp and O'Connor), to the east of Shunet el-Zebib and the 'West Mastaba', a structure measuring 22.5 x 66.5 m, surrounded by the tombs of courtiers.

Udimu (Den): 'C' (according to W. Kaiser); according to D. O'Connor, a building not yet discovered between A/B and Deir Sitt Damiana.

Semerkhet or a successor: the remains of a massive north wall, immediately east of Shunet el-Zebib. Not excavated.

Anedjib or a predecessor: the 'West Mastaba', a medium-sized brick structure, measuring 28.2 x 66.5 m.

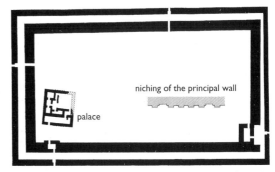

Plan of the funerary enclosure of Khasekhemwy at Abydos (Shunet el-Zebib)

Niched enclosure wall of the funerary enclosure of Khasekhemwy at Abydos

Qa: perhaps 'G', Deir Sitt Damiana, measuring 70 x 100 m; now a village site and not presently investigated.

Peribsen: 'E', the 'Middle Fort' situated north of Khasekhemwy; it measures 50 x 90 + ...m, with its main entrance at the southern end of the east side and at least one secondary entrance in the south wall. Behind the south-eastern entrance is a '**palace**'.

Khasekhemwy: 'F', the Shunet el-Zebib, measuring 65 x 125 m and still standing to a height of 7.5 m. It has a double wall with two main entrances, one at the southern end of the east wall and the other at the eastern end of the

north wall; there are also two smaller **gateways** at west and south. Behind the eastern entrance are a 'palace' and other brick structures. There are also the remains of a mound covered with bricks. From 1991, at the northern end of the north-east side, a fleet of at least 12 wooden boats, 30 m long, has been found.

King Khasekhem probably built another niched funerary enclosure at **Hierakonpolis**, measuring 65.4 x 74.7 m, with a large gateway at the southern end of the east wall. The impressive ruin of the building is still preserved.

Bibliography: B.J. Kemp, Abydos and the Royal Tombs of the First Dynasty, in: *JEA* 52 (1966) 13–22; B.J. Kemp, The Egyptian Ist Dynasty royal cemetery, in: *Antiquity* 41 (1967) 22–32; W. Kaiser, Zu den königlichen Talbezirken in Abydos und zur Baugeschichte des Djoser-Grabmals, in: *MDAIK* 25 (1969) 10–13; W. Kaiser and G. Dreyer, Umm el Qaab. Nachuntersuchungen im frühzeitlichen Königsfriedhof. 2. Vorbericht, in: *MDAIK* 38 (1982) 211–269; W. Helck, Zu den 'Talbezirken' in Abydos, in: *MDAIK* 28 (1972) 95–99; D. O'Connor, New Funerary Enclosures (Talbezirke) of the Early Period at Abydos, in: *JARCE* 26 (1989) 51–86; D. O'Connor, Boat graves and pyramid origins, in: *Expedition* 33 (1991) 5–17.

Funerary palace, *see* divine fortress, funerary enclosure

G

Gallery tomb

The term 'gallery tomb' (as distinct from *saff* **tomb**) is applied to the funerary complexes of the 2nd Dynasty kings at **Saqqara,** which have extensive subterranean galleries where innumerable magazine chambers branch off from a main corridor up to 400 m long. The superstructure above ground probably was an elongated, **niched mastaba.** According to R. Stadelmann every gallery tomb can be expected to have an associated **funerary enclosure** to the west of it, in a manner similar to the **kings' tombs** at **Abydos.** Gallery tombs include:

a) Hetepsekhemwy or Reneb: A 120 m long, 7 m deep gallery directly in front of the **Unas** pyramid. The superstructure has completely disappeared. The associated enclosure, which probably lay to the west of the **Sekhemkhet** precinct, is unresearched.

b) Ninetjer: A gallery tomb outside the south-eastern corner of the **Djoser** precinct. The associated enclosure is believed to be situated in the 'Qisr el-Mudir' (340 x 590 m), west of the Sekhemkhet precinct.

c) Reneb (?): This tomb is attested to by a **stela.** The gallery may have been situated below the western part of the Djoser precinct.

d) Khasekhemwy: This gallery tomb (area 90 x 400 m) may have been below the western half of the Djoser precinct. Some of the subterranean rooms, which have received only scant investigation, remain full of grave goods. Remains of the superstructure may have been integrated in the Djoser precinct. It consisted, possibly, of an elongated mastaba, divided lengthwise into three, the central portion covering the side sections by means of a slightly vaulted roof. The niched eastern side would have been visible from the west side of the courtyard in the Djoser precinct court. The associated enclosure may have lain directly to the west.

Bibliography: Jean-Philippe Lauer, La pyramide à degrés, *Complements* III (Cairo 1939) 53–54, Plate 22; Lauer, *Histoire monumentale* 56–59; R. Stadelmann, Die Königsgräber der 2. Dynastie in Sakkara, in: *Mélanges Gamal Eddin Mokhtar,* (Cairo 1985) 295–307; Stadelmann, *Pyramiden* 31–37.

Gargoyles, *see* water spouts

Gateway, *see also* door, pylon

Strikingly monumental gateways take the form of **pylons,** with the actual structure of the gateway flanked by towers. These structures are usually an integral part of the main temple building; when part of a temple enclosure, on the other hand, gateways are free-standing structures, either the same height as the wall or protruding above it. Examples of all three forms exist within the enclosure of the **Amun** precinct at **Karnak** and other major sanctuaries.

Bibliography: S. Sauneron, *La porte ptolémaique de l'enceinte de Mout à Karnak* (Cairo 1983); Aufrère, *L'Égypte restituée* I (Paris 1991) 38–39, 82–83, 86–87, 99, 116, 142, 154 etc.

Gebel Abu Fedah (Gebel Abu Foda)

The largest of all the Egyptian **limestone** quarries on the East Bank of the Nile, between Manfalut and **Amarna.** Finds there comprise quarry inscriptions and draft sketches of **capitals.**

Bibliography: G. Legrain, Notes archéologiques prises au Gebel Abou Fodah, in: *ASAE* 1(1900) 1–14; R. Gundlach, Gebel Abu-Foda, in: Kelck, *LÄ* II 432; Klemm, *Steine* 130–138.

Gebel Adda, *see* Abahuda (Abu Hoda)

Gebel Barkal

A temple city of Amun at the foot of a distinctive hill, 650 km south of Aswan at the Fourth Cataract. A large number of buildings erected there from the reign of Thutmosis III onwards form the southernmost examples of pure Egyptian temple architecture. The remains were recorded by Reisner, who used the following numbering system:

B.200: **Hemispeos** of Taharqa dedicated to Hathor, Tefnut and Bastet or Isis, with **Hathor** pillars.

B.300: Hemispeos of Taharqa above an earlier Thutmoside structure dedicated to Mut, with an entrance **kiosk,** Bes **pillars** and Hathor columns.

B.500: The central structure, the large Ipet-sut of Amun of Napata, is a 150 m long **sandstone** building, whose origins go back to the reign of Tutankhamun/Horemheb; it was later extended in the reigns of Sety I and Ramesses II. Further restructuring took place under Egyptian rule, followed by repeated Meroitic restorations. An avenue of **sphinxes**, with rams' heads, leads to the first **pylon**, which is 50 m wide, with an entrance kiosk of Amanishakheto (B.551). Beyond this is a spacious court with **pillared halls** along every side, with a **barque station** of the 3rd century BC (B.501) at its centre. Beyond this court the same pylon/court combination is repeated, dating to an earlier construction phase, with a barque kiosk of Tanutamun (B.502) in the centre. This is followed by a third pylon with a pillared hall (two rows of five pillars) and beyond this again lies the original construction, comprising a pylon and a group of sanctuaries arranged at assorted angles, with a **granite altar** of Taharqa.

B.600: Napatan **terrace temple** above an earlier building of the 18th Dynasty – perhaps a *sed*-festival kiosk.

B.700: Building of Atlanersa and Senkamanisken, dedicated to Amun (?), with an entrance kiosk.

B.800: Temple of Kashta or Pi(ankhi) dedicated to the Theban Triad.

B.1800: A Meroitic **ambulatory temple**.

Other structures at this site consisted of Napatan **palaces** and administrative buildings. Many historical inscriptions and sculptures removed from **Soleb** have also been found here. On the West Bank of the Nile are the extensive ruins of the Napatan palace **town** of **Sanam** with a larger temple of Taharqa dedicated to the local form of Amun, 'The Bull of the Land of the Bowmen'.

Bibliography: GA. Reisner, The Barkal temples, in: *JEA* 4 (1917) 213–227; 5 (1918) 99–112; 6 (1920) 247–264; Dows Dunham, *The Barkal Temples* (Boston 1970); T. Kendall, The Napatan palace at Gebel Barkal, in: *Egypt and Africa* (London 1991) 302–313; St. Wenig, Gebel Barkal, in: Helck, *LÄ* II 434–440; Hein, *Ramessidische Bautätigkeit* 65–67; Timothy Kendall, The Gebel Barkal temples, in: *7th Inter. Conference for Nubian Studies* (Geneva 1990).

Gebel el-Ahmar, *see also* quartzite

Quartzite quarries south-east of Abbassiya (Cairo), in use from the Old Kingdom onwards. Rock inscriptions and incomplete sculptures, now largely destroyed by the erection of modern buildings over the site, have been found here.

Bibliography: Clark, *AEM* 30–32; F. Gomaà, Gebel el-Ahmar, in: Helck, *LÄ* II 433–434; D. and R. Klemm, Herkunftsbestimmung ägyptischer Steine, in: *SAK* 7 (1979) 120–121; D. and R. Klemm, Die pharaonischen Steinbrüche des Silifizierten Sandsteins in Ägypten, in: *MDAIK* 40 (1984) 207–220, Klemm, *Steine* 284–289.

Gebel el-Silsila (Silsileh)

A range of **sandstone** hills, 70 km north of Aswan, through which the Nile has cut its course. There are extensive sandstone quarries, especially on the East Bank, mainly of the New Kingdom onwards. Situated on the West Bank are 33 **cenotaphs** (rock chapels) of the 18th Dynasty and the **rock temple** (**speos** of the **rock tomb** type) of Horemheb. The latter has a façade of four pillars, a transverse hall and a sanctuary with seven rock-carved cult images (Amun, Mut, Khonsu, Sobek, Taweret, Thoth and the king). 450 m to the north lie the unexplored remains of another temple of Horemheb, which has a number of **granite** columns.

Bibliography: *LD* I 102, Text IV 84; H.A. Sayce, Excavations at Gebel Silsila, in: *ASAE* 8 (1907) 97–105; Ricardo Caminos and T.G.H. James, *Gebel Es-Silsilah I: The Shrines* (London 1963); R. Caminos, Gebel es-Silsile, in: Helck, *LÄ* II 441–447; R. Klemm, Vom Steinbruch zum Tempel, in: *ZÄS* 115 (1988) 43–45; Klemm, *Steine* 242–266.

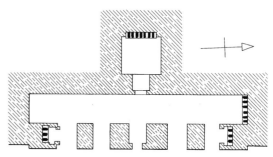

Sketch plan of the hemispeos of Horemheb at Gebel el-Silsila

Gebelein

Remains of an important settlement dating back to prehistoric times, situated on a rocky ridge 28 km south of **Luxor**. There are the remains, in the form of relief fragments, of a totally destroyed temple dedicated to Hathor dating from the 1st Dynasty. Pieces of the outer **limestone casing** bear important reliefs and many royal names from Mentuhotep Nebhepetre to those of the Third Intermediate Period. There are also remains of a fortification of the Third Intermediate Period (stamped bricks of Menkheperre – **brick stamps**), and the pillared tomb of Iti with painting (11th Dynasty; now in Turin).

Bibliography: D. Wildung, Gebelein, in: Helck, *LÄ* II 447–449; *Egyptian Civilization. Religious Beliefs* (Egyptian Museum of Turin 1988) 85–99; L. Morenz, Zur Dekoration der frühzeitlichen Tempel am Beispiel zweier Fragmente des archaischen Tempels von Gebelein, in: Kurth, *Tempeltagung* 217–238.

Gerf Hussein

A **hemispeos** of Ramesses II in Lower **Nubia**, 90 km south of Aswan, erected by Setau, the viceroy of Kush, dedicated to the king, Ptah-Tatenen, Hathor and, most importantly, to Ptah of Memphis.

An avenue of ram-headed **sphinxes** leads from the Nile to the first **pylon** which, like the courtyard beyond, is free-standing. The courtyard is surrounded by an interesting combination of six columns and eight **statue pillars**. The rear section of the building, 43 m in depth, is carved out of the rock, and resembles the great temple of **Abu Simbel**, with a **pillared hall** featuring two rows of three statue pillars and – unusually – four statue recesses, each with divine triads along the long sides. Beyond this lie the hall of the offering table and the **barque chamber** with four cult statues (originally gilded) of Ptah, Ramesses, Ptah-Tatenen and Hathor carved out of the rock. Sections of the temple were cut out of the rock in 1964 and transferred to **Elephantine**; the remainder is lost in Lake Nasser.

Bibliography: Gau, *Antiquités,* Plates 22–28; J. Jacquet, H. El-Achiri, M.A.L. Tanbouli et al., *Gerf Hussein,* 3 Vols (Cairo 1974–75, 1978); D. Wildung, Gerf Hussein, in: Helck, *LÄ* II 534–535; Hein, *Ramessidische Bautätigkeit* 9–11.

Ghurob (Abu Ghurob), *see* Niuserre

Giza (Gizeh)

A necropolis west of Cairo set on a high **limestone** plateau and its south-facing slope, which together with **Saqqara** and **Thebes** is one of the most important necropoleis in Egypt. It has a unique group of early stone constructions: the **pyramid** and cult precincts of **Khufu**, **Khafre**, **Menkaure** and **Khentkawes** I, the great **Sphinx**, the **Harmakhis temple** and hundreds of **mastabas** and **rock tombs** of the 4–6th Dynasties, among them the historically significant complexes of the royal families and the royal households of these kings (**Ankhhaf, Baefba, Giza mastaba 2000, Giza mastaba 2370, Hemiunu, Nensedjerkai, Rawer**). Associated **pyramid towns** and royal residences in the fertile area have disappeared. Only a few monuments of a later period exist here and there ('**Campbell's Tomb', Tjary**). Some large tombs of an early period exist to the south (**Giza, mastabas of the Early Dynastic Period**). Some buildings have suffered damage caused by medieval building activities in Cairo.

Bibliography (refer to individual monuments, as there is no overview): Reisner, *Giza* I; Junker, *Giza* XII 1–27; *PM* III, Part 1, 11–312 (complete bibliography up to 1973); Christiane M. Zivie, *Giza au deuxième millénaire* (Cairo 1976); Christiane M. Zivie, Gisa, in: Helck, *LÄ* II 602–614; M. Lehner, The development of the Giza necropolis: the Khufu Project, in: *MDAIK* 41 (1985) 109–143.

Giza mastaba 2000

The largest stone **mastaba** of the 4th Dynasty at **Giza** (53.2 x 105 m), of anonymous ownership, probably belonging to a prince from the time of Khufu/Khafre. Along the east-facing side stand two cult structures, that to the south having an interior room with a funerary offering chapel added later in front of it. A shaft 40 m deep leads to a 6 x 6 m rock chamber. The superstructure is incomplete.

Bibliography: Reisner, *Giza* 414–416.

Giza mastaba 2370

The 21 x 23 m **mastaba** of Senedjemib/Inti at **Giza** (reign of Unas). The core consists entirely of rooms. There is a **door recess** with a pair of columns, an antechamber and a six-pillared hall, each with a large *serdab* and a cult chamber.

Bibliography: Reisner, *Giza* 264–265.

Giza, mastabas of the Early Dynastic Period (Nazlet El-Batran)

A necropolis on the southern slope of the rocky eminence south of the pyramids (the South Field) with several Early Dynastic Period **mastabas**. Situated in the flat area at the desert edge is a **niched** mud **brick** mastaba of the 1st Dynasty (21 x 48 m) with a timber-lined burial chamber beneath a beamed ceiling and two rows of two magazines. A huge niched mud brick mastaba (area 28 x 54 m) of the 3rd Dynasty ('Covington's Tomb' No. 1) with entrance stairs and a habitation-like burial system similar to **Beit Khallaf** stands on an elevation further to the west.

Bibliography: G. Daressy, Un édifice archaïque à Nezlet Batran, in: *ASAE* 6 (1905) 99–106; M.D. Covington, Mastaba mount excavations, *ASAE* 6 (1905) 193–218; W.M. Flinders Petrie, *Gizeh and Rifeh* (London 1907) 1–9; Karl Kromer, *Nezlet Betran. Eine Mastaba aus dem Alten Reich bei Giseh* (Vienna 1991).

Grain store, silo

Grain stores were very important in the Egyptian economy. They appear in settlements and at temples in three main forms:

a) from the Old Kingdom onwards, as long, **vaulted** chambers in parallel rows, sharing one flat roof which has openings for filling and hatches used for emptying close to the ground (**vault**, Fig.);

b) from the Middle Kingdom, groups of usually three rows of three square interconnected chambers, probably with vaulted roofs, with a working space in front in the **Nubian fortresses** of the 12th Dynasty and at **Kahun**, where their capacity was approximately 300 cu m per house.

c) From the Middle Kingdom onwards are found freestanding, beehive-shaped **cupolas** of **brick**, often built in groups and constructed of concentric rows of brick corbelling. Their brick floors are sunk slightly below ground level. The diameter is usually 2–3 m (at **Amarna** 2.5–8 m, and at **Medinet Habu** up to 8.9 m), and capacity was up to 400 cu m. Openings for filling at the apex, which were capable of being sealed, were accessible via a ladder or stairs.

Bibliography: Borchardt, *Tell el-Amarna*, 334, Fig. 44; B.J. Kemp, Large Middle Kingdom granary buildings, in: *ZÄS* 113 (1986) 120–136; E.M. Husselman, The granaries of Karanis, in: *Trans. of the American Philolog. Soc.* 83 (1952) 56–73; *Le Ramesseum. Les annexes nord-ouest* I (Documentation Center, Cairo 1976).

Granite

A deep-lying granular stone consisting of felspar, quartz, mica, hornblende and pyroxene; specific gravity 2.6–3.2.

The type most used in Egyptian architecture is red 'rose granite' from **Aswan**. A less used darkish grey variant, also from Aswan, is granodiorite or **quartzdiorite**, incorrectly known as **syenite** (Syene = Aswan).

Granite is a hard stone frequently used in Egyptian architecture from the 1st Dynasty onwards, especially in the reigns of Khufu and Menkaure. The main source is in the cataract region of Aswan between the city and Shelal). It was utilised most particularly in the pyramid precincts of the Old Kingdom for outer coverings, corridors and chambers in **pyramids**, **portcullis** structures, sarcophagi, **false doors**, **paving**, thresholds and door frames, **columns**, **architraves**, later continuing to be used for a long time in thresholds, **naoi** and **obelisks** and in **colossal statues**. In the Late Period

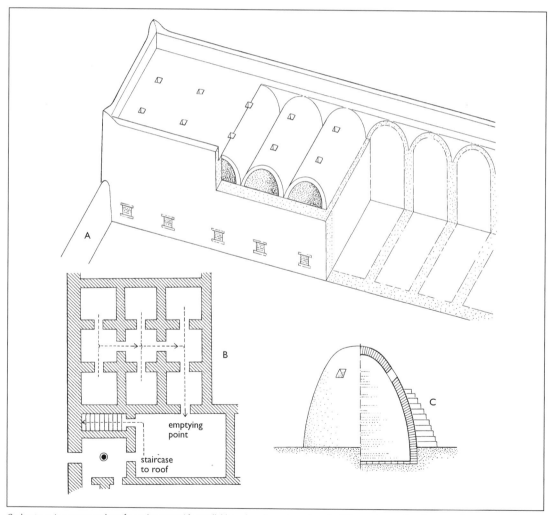

Grain store. A: reconstruction of a grain store with parallel barrel vaults and openings for filling and emptying; B: group of store rooms from an important house at Kahun; C: reconstruction of a silo of the New Kingdom

and the 30th Dynasty granite experienced a renaissance as a construction material (naoi, temple of **Bubastis**, **Iseum**).

Bibliography: Clark, *AEM* 24–30; Lucas, *AEMI* 57–59; W. Helck, in: Helck, *LÄ* II 892–893; Arnold, *Building* 36–40; De Putter, *Pierres* 81–86; Klemm, *Steine*, 305–353.

Gurob

A **town**, **fortress**, **palace** and **temple** precinct and necropolis of the New Kingdom (Thutmosis III–Ramesses III) at the entrance to the Faiyum, which consisted of a square-shaped enclosure (233 x 238 m) with two lengthy parallel buildings, originally thought to be temples, but now believed to be a palace. Sanctuaries can nonetheless be attested to here. Other interior parts of the precincts, including the **foundations**, had already been destroyed at the time of Petrie's excavations in 1889/90 and 1920. The site was the find spot of the wooden head of Queen Tiye and other important objects.

Bibliography: W. Flinders Petrie, *Kahun, Gurob, and Hawara* (London 1890) 32–36; Guy Brunton and Reginald Engelbach, *Gurob* (London 1927) 3–4; D. Arnold, *Gurob*, in: Helck, *LÄ* II 922–923; B.J. Kemp, The Harim-Palace at Medinet el-Ghurab, in: *ZÄS* 105 (1978) 122–133.

Guttering, *see drainage*

Gypsum, gesso

This mineral has been used since pre-historic times (Maadi culture). The Faiyum gypsum bed was already mined in the Early Dynastic Period, but gypsum also appears in many places in crystal form on the desert surface. Gypsum is baked at 150–200°C. Sometimes gypsum was mixed with **lime** to produce a brilliant shade of white.

Some Old Kingdom samples have been found to be particularly pure (99.5%). Gypsum was used for wall and ceiling **plaster** and as a base for paintings in houses, temples and tombs; it also served as a binding medium, repair material and to form a lubricant with which to shift stone blocks.

Bibliography: Lucas, *AEMI* 76–79; C. Traunecker, *Gips*, in: Helck, *LÄ* II 599–660; Arnold, *Building* 292–293.

H

Hakoris chapel

An unusual **barque station** of Hakoris in front of the first **pylon** at **Karnak**. This barque shrine is in the form of a transverse hall open at the front. A **kiosk** of two parallel rows of three papyrus **columns** stands in front of it. Gaps are provided in the intercolumnar **screen walls** north and west in such a way that the barque had to be introduced bow first from the north and taken out sideways from the west.

Bibliography: Jean Lauffray, *La chapelle d'Achôris à Karnak I, des fouilles, l'architecture, le mobilier et l'anastylose* (Paris 1995); Claude Traunecker et al., *La chapelle d'Achôris à Karnak II*, 2 Vols (Paris 1981).

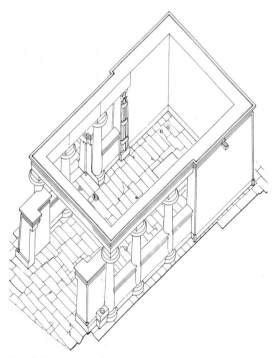

Chapel of Hakoris at Karnak (drawing by R. Mangado/J. Lauffray, 1995)

Hall of Annals

A rectangular hall built by Thutmosis III in front of the hall of barques at **Karnak**, with the two **heraldic pillars** and containing the 'annals' of the king's campaigns and foundations. The building probably had a raised central aisle with basilica-type windows.

Bibliography: L. Borchardt, *Zur Baugeschichte des Amonstempels von Karnak* (Leipzig 1905) 30–32; W. Helck, Annalensaal, in: Helck, *LÄ* I 280–281.

Hall of audiences

The throne room of the king, attested to in inscriptions beginning in the Middle Kingdom, with actual halls of audiences surviving from the 18th Dynasty onwards, for instance in the cult **palaces** at **Amarna** and at **Medinet Habu** and other **'houses of millions of years'** at **Thebes**, at **Malqata** and that of **Merenptah** at Memphis. Working from the evidence of these examples, they seem to have been structures made of **brick**, with four to six columns supporting three lengthwise barrel **vaults**. In the centre of the rear wall stood an elaborately decorated throne dais, with stepped ramps at the front and the sides. The central room of the **houses** of wealthy private individuals was in fact a simplified version of this type of chamber.

Bibliography: R. Stadelmann, Audienzhalle, in: Helck, *LÄ* I 554.

Hall of columns, *see* hypostyle hall

Harmakhis temple (Giza)

Remains of a monumental stone temple east of the great **Sphinx** at **Giza**. This structure, 44.7 x 52.5 m, with an unusual plan, provides important evidence for temple building activities in the Old Kingdom other than **pyramid temples**. The façade, devoid of **niching**, is topped by an early form of **cavetto cornice**. The core of the walls is partly carved out of the native **limestone** and cased with **granite** blocks. Like the **valley temple** of **Khafre** next to it, this temple has two entrances to the interior, which is dominated by a central courtyard with 10 seated **colossal figures** of the king. Chambers with monolithic **granite** pillars open to the east and the west and descend in steps towards the interior (**door recess**), suggesting an east–west orientation of the complex, following the course of the sun. The great Sphinx immediately beyond indicates the association between the sun and the king. The temple may have been erected by **Khufu** or, more likely, by Khafre. It remained incomplete.

Bibliography: Ricke, *Harmachistempel*; J. Assmann, Harmachis, in: Helck, *LÄ* II 992–996.

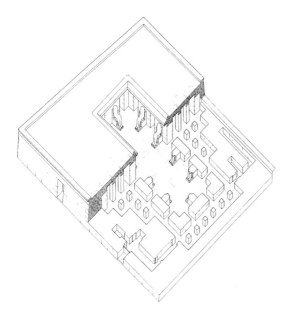

Reconstruction of the Harmakhis temple at Giza

Harwa

A monumental Theban tomb of the Nubian Period (TT 37). The subterranean complex is laid out in the following sequence: **sun court**, entrance recess, two **pillared halls** and a corridor which runs around the whole complex. The tomb, which is 65 x 75 m in area, is incomplete and its superstructure is destroyed.

Bibliography: Eigner, *Grabbauten* 37–40; Tiradritti, Three years of research in the tomb of Harwa, in: *Egyptian Archaeology* 13 (1998) 3–6.

Hathor-headed Capitals of Bubastis

A famous group of six **granite** Hathor **capitals**, generally attributed to the 12th Dynasty. Whereas Naville distinguished a larger and a smaller group, Labib Habachi thought that they were variations of the same group (height 'little above 7 feet' or 2.15 m, according to Naville). From this height it can be estimated that the **columns** may have been 6–8 m high. Their current locations are as follows:

1. Boston 89.555
2. British Museum 1107
3. Louvre E 10590
4. Berlin 10834, usurped by Osorkon I

5. Sydney Nicholson Museum
6. Cairo JE 72134, museum gardens: discovered 1939, height 1.43 m, width 0.97 x 150 m.

Labib Habachi saw at the site (**Bubastis**) pieces of eight more capitals.

Bibliography: Labib Habichi, *Tell Basta* (Cairo 1957), Plates 18–20; E.R. Russman, *Eternal Egypt* (London-New York 2001) 211–214.

Hathor pillar, Hathor column, sistrum column

A type of **pillar** or **column** formed out of the fetish associated with female deities (Hathor, Isis, Bastet), widely used from the Middle Kingdom onwards. The **capital** has the appearance of a sistrum, hence it is sometimes called a 'Hathor-sistrum capital', and is formed with back-to-back Hathor faces on two or four sides, each topped by the sistrum (a divine chapel between two spirals). Occasionally the Hathor motif appears on pillars in partial relief. Hathor pillars are found in the temples of female deities (Hathor, Isis, queen) at, for example, **Bubastis**, **Serabit el-Khadim**, **Hatshepsut** temple etc., and from the Late Period onwards, especially in **birth houses**. Hathor pillars in

Hathor column from the pronaos of the Hathor temple at Dendera (after *Description* IV, Plate 12)

some temples of the Ptolemaic and Roman periods are up to 14 m high and richly decorated (**Dendera, Iseum** – Fig.); they are found in combination with **composite capitals** (**Opet** temple, **kiosk** of Nectanebo at **Philae**).

Bibliography: Jéquier, *Manuel* 184–193; Ricke, *Bemerkungen* I 71–84; Labib Habachi, *Tell Basta* (Cairo 1957), Plates 18–20; H. Bakri, in: *MDAIK* 28 (1972), Plate 22; G. Haeny, Hathor-Kapitell, in: Helck, *LÄ* II 1039–1o41.

Hatnub

Alabaster quarry used from the Old Kingdom to the New Kingdom, situated south-east of **Amarna**. The main quarry P is a pit 55 x 85 m in area, and 16 m in depth. There are remains of workmen's accommodation and a transportation route.

Bibliography: Rudolf Anthes, *Die Felsinschriften von Hatnub* (Leipzig 1928); W.K. Simpson, Hatnub, in: Helck, *LÄ* 1043–1045; I.M.A. Shaw, A survey of Hatnub, in: *Amarna Reports* III (London 1986) 198–212; Klemm, *Steine* 216–219.

Hatshepsut temple (Deir el-Bahari)

The Djeser-djeseru, Hatshepsut's '**house of millions of years**', is one of the most important and idiosyncratic creations of Egyptian temple architecture. Its structure is the result of several changes of plan. It was possibly begun in the reign of Thutmosis II, its form heavily influenced by the temple of **Mentuhotep** (earlier parts are shown in dotted lines on the plan). It acquired its present form in the reign of Hatshepsut, undergoing considerable change in the process; the Hathor sanctuary, for example, was a later addition. Instead of the traditional sequence of first **pylon**, courtyard, second pylon and **pillared hall**, a sequence of two terraces was used here, not fronted by the usual pylons but by open-fronted pillared halls. It differs from the design of the temple of Mentuhotep on which it was based in having the **king's tomb** in a separate location (not far away, within the hill behind the temple, but accessed from the Valley of the Kings). A long **causeway**, 37 m wide, starts at the partially preserved

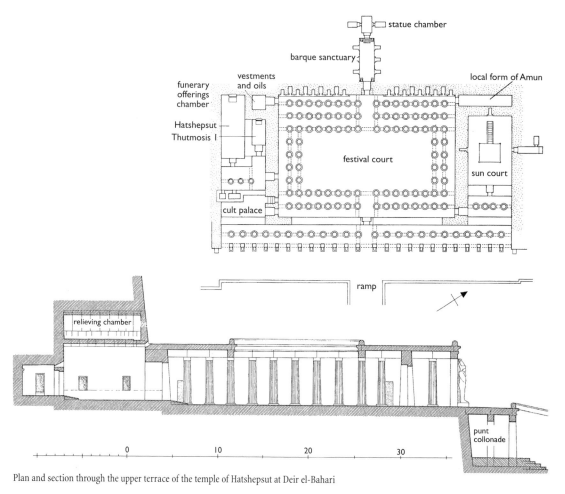

Plan and section through the upper terrace of the temple of Hatshepsut at Deir el-Bahari

valley temple and ascends to the terraced temple situated at the bottom of the cliff face. The upper part of the causeway starts with a pylon and barque station and is fenced in by sphinxes. At the other end it opens out into the spacious forecourt, which was occupied by a temple garden and two T-shaped pools containing papyrus plants. Situated along the front of the lower terrace are two halls whose front pillars are, unusually, rounded at the rear. A ramp at the centre leads to the first terrace, which has a cave-like sanctuary dedicated to Anubis at the north-west corner. The frontage of the upper terrace is again occupied by two pillared halls. The ramp leading there is flanked by side-walls in the shape of serpents crowned with falcons. The upper terrace is taken up by the principal structure, having a monumental pillared frontage of 26 colossal statue pillars of Hatshepsut, with a courtyard behind (*not* a hypostyle) completely surrounded by two rows of 16-sided pillars (three rows on the west-facing side). The rear wall has eight large and ten smaller recesses for royal statues. Situated in the centre, within the rock, are the barque chamber and a room for the cult images of Amun-Re and the queen. South of the pillared hall lie two funerary offering chambers, both with a corbelled vault, for Hatshepsut and her father Thutmosis I, and in front of these a small cult palace. A building connected with the sun cult, containing a well-preserved altar dedicated to Re-Horakhty, lies north of the courtyard; some important relief decoration, showing an expedition to Punt, the journey of the boats conveying the obelisks from Aswan to Thebes, and the birth and coronation of Hatshepsut, are preserved there or have been reconstructed from fragments. The statues and sphinxes of the queen were destroyed in her *damnatio memoriae* in the reign of Thutmosis III; the statue pillars were dismantled and thrown into a nearby stone quarry, where they were found and reconstructed (some at the temple itself, others in the Egyptian Museum in Cairo and others in the MMA).

A separate chapel dedicated to Hatshepsut, in which she is identified with Hathor, is situated to the south of the main temple. It has a pronaos graced with beautiful Hathor columns. Reliefs on the walls show the cult image of the Hathor cow, with which Hatshepsut is united, standing under a canopy on a barque. The pronaos was later enlarged with three additional rows of columns.

The temple is undergoing a major restoration by the Polish Centre of Mediterranean Archaeology, Warsaw University, and the Supreme Council for Antiquities in Egypt.

Bibliography: Edouard Naville, *Deir el-Bahari*, 6 Vols (London 1895–1908); D. Arnold, Deir el-Bahari, in: Helck, *LÄ* I 1017–1022; L. Dabrowsli, The main hypostyle hall of the temple of Hatshepsut at Deir el-Bahari, in: *JEA* 56 (1970) 101–104 (incorrect reconstruction); J. Karkowski, The Arrangement of the Architraves in the Hatshepsut's Temple at Deir el Bahari, in: *ET* 13 (1983) 139–153; Z. Wysocki, The result of research in the Hatshepsut Temple of Deir el-Bahari, in: *MDAIK* 40 (1984) 329–349; 41 (1985) 293–307; 42 (1986) 213–228; 48 (1992) 233–254; *The Temple of Hatshepsut*, pamphlets 1–4 (Warsaw 1979, 1980, 1985, 1991); Aufrère, *L'Égypte restituée* 156–161: F. Pawlicki, Une représentation inconnue de la Fête d l'Hippopotame Blanc dans le Temple de Hatshepsut à Deir el-Bahari, in: *ET* 14 (1990) 15–28; Z. Wysocki, Deir el-Bahari seasons, in: *ET* 14 (1990) 321–347; 16 (1992) 435–485; J. Karkowski, Deir el-Bahari, Temple of Hatshepsut: Egyptological studies 1977-1980, in: *ET* 14 (1990) 349–392.

Hawara, *see* Amenemhat III

Hawawish

The extensive necropolis site of Panopolis, in use from prehistoric times, in the fore-desert and on a high mountain spur north-east of Akhmim. There are rock tombs of the First Intermediate Period and the Middle Kingdom with pillared façades and transverse pillared halls.

Bibliography: Naguib Kanawati, *The Rock Tombs of El Hawawish*, 9 Vols (Warminster 1980–90); Klaus Kuhlmann, *Materialien zur Archäologie und Geschichte des Raumes von Achmim* (Mainz 1983) 52–71.

Heliopolis

An important ancient Egyptian town north-east of Cairo whose architectural remains are still inadequately researched despite their unique importance within the development of Egyptian architecture. The double temple of Re-Horakhty and Atum is surrounded by a brick enclosure wall (c. 900 x 1000 m, 30 m thick). From the west gate in the southern half an avenue of sphinxes c. 500 m long (each limestone sphinx 7 m in length) leads to the west-facing temple of Atum. It is not known whether the Re-Horakhty temple, which faces east, towards the sun, stood back to back with the Atum temple or parallel to it in the northern half of the wide enclosure. The plan of the Re-Horakhty temple (?) of the Late Period is preserved on an inventory (in the Museo Egizio Turin) and shows that in the Late Period the building had three pylons and three courtyards, as well as a temple house, the *benben* house, with its frontage decorated with a pillared hall or four obelisks. This appears to have been a separate building, where the *benben* stone is likely to have stood in an open court as a cult focus. The location of an Aten temple of Akhenaten, known from inscriptions and *talatat*, is not clear.

We do not know whether the Atum temple stood alone or if that of Re-Horakhty also stood on an artificial flat mound, the 'Hoher Sand', examined in 1903–06 by

E. Schiaparelli and in 1911/12 by Flinders Petrie. This mound was 600 sq m in area and surrounded by a **enclosure wall** 65 m thick, which existed, according to Petrie, from the end of the Old Kingdom until the 20th Dynasty. Within the area of the enclosure were found fragments of a chapel of Djoser bearing the earliest depiction of the Divine Ennead of Heliopolis.

As a place of sun worship, Heliopolis was from ancient times a centre of the pillar cult, especially **obelisks**. In its heyday the temple had at least 16 obelisks, the earliest known an obelisk of Teti (6th Dynasty), only 3 m high. On the occasion of his *sed*-festival, Senwosret I erected a new Re-Horakhty temple, also donating a pair of obelisks, 20.41 m high, to the enlarged Atum temple (one of them remains upright, the other collapsed in AD 1161). Before this temple, Thutmosis III erected two obelisks, 21 m high (moved in 13–12 BC to the Caesarium of **Alexandria**, the 'Cleopatra's Needles' now in London and New York).

Two **limestone pylons** with statues and obelisks (known from an ancient architectural model) were erected at the Re-Horakhty temple by Sety I; one of them now stands in the Piazza del Popolo in Rome. The two small obelisks now in the Piazza della Rotunda and at the Villa Celimontana in Rome were set up, along with other monuments, by Ramesses II. The obelisk of Psamtek II now at Montecitorio also came from Heliopolis. A temple inside the northern half of the enclosure was erected by Ramesses IV.

Bibliography: Strabo, *Geographica* XVII, Book 1, 27–28; H. Ricke, Eine Inventartafel aus Heliopolis im Turiner Museum, in: *ZÄS* 71 (1935) 111–133; H. Ricke, Der Hohe Sand in Heliopolis, *ZÄS* 71 (1935) 107–111; L. Habachi, Akhenaten in Heliopolis, in: *Festschrift Ricke* 35–45; Mohamed I. Moursi, *Die Hohenpriester des Sonnengottes von der Frühzeit Ägyptens bis zum Ende des Neuen Reiches,* MÄS 26, (Munich 1972); L. Kákosy, Heliopolis, in: Helck, *LÄ* II 1111–1113; Abdel-Aziz Saleh, *Excavations at Heliopolis*, 2 Vols (Cairo 1981, 1983); A. Roccati, in: *Dal Museo al Museo, Passato e futuro del Museo Egizio di Torino* (Turin 1989) 167; S. Bickel and P. Tallet, La nécropole saïte d'Héliopolis, in: *BIFAO* 97 (1997) 67–86 (with map); D. Jeffreys, Joseph Hekekyan at Heliopolis, in: Anthony Leahy and John Tait, Eds, *Studies on Ancient Egypt in Honour of H.S. Smith* (London 1999) 157–168.

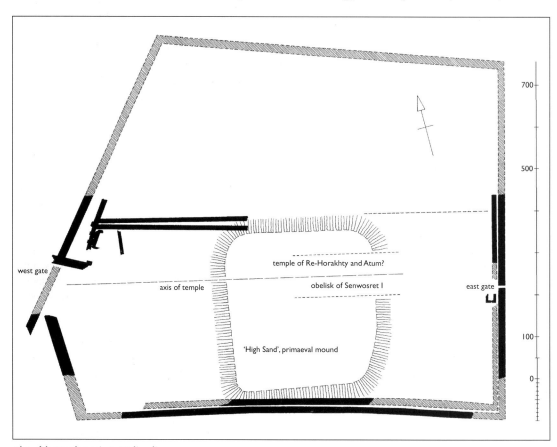

Plan of the temple precinct at Heliopolis

Helwan

A site between **El-Ma'adi** and Helwan with more than 10,000 tombs, comprising the largest Egyptian cemetery of the Early Dynastic Period. There are **mastabas** built of **brick**, some of them plain, others **niched**); they have entrance stairs and a **portcullis**; some have model magazines and boat pits. There are some monumental stepped tombs (probably of the 2nd to 3rd Dynasties) with **limestone orthostats** and paved burial chambers. The interior of stone mastaba 287 H.6 (27 x 56 m in area) contains a stone-lined shaft and a burial chamber with stone-lined walls and rounded beams carved in the stone ceiling.

Bibliography: Zaki Y. Saad, *Royal Excavations at Saqqara and Helwan* (1941–45) (Cairo 1947) 161–252; Zaki Y. Saad, *Royal Excavations at Helwan* (1945–47) (Cairo 1951) 1–84; Zaki Y. Saad, *The Excavations* at *Helwan* (Oklahoma 1969); P. Kaplony, Heluan, in: Helck, *LÄ* II 1115; W. Wood, The archaic stone tombs at Helwan, in: *JEA* 73 (1987) 59–77.

Hemispeos

A **rock temple** whose front portion is free-standing. Examples exist at **Derr**, **Gerf Hussein**, **Gebel Barkal**, **Wadi Miya**, **Wadi el-Sebu'a**.

Hemiunu, tomb of

Hemiunu, the son of **Nefermaat**, was the head of construction (**architect**) at the pyramid of **Khufu** and builder of stone **mastaba** G 4000 (area 26.77 x 53.20 m) at **Giza**. This was originally a smaller structure with two **false doors** (and possibly a **brick** chapel) on the east-facing side. Following enlargement, it had two cult niches at the front, the earlier cult niches being converted into *serdabs* (where the famous statue of Hemiunu in the Pelizaeus Museum, Hildesheim, was found) and a new brick-built mortuary offering chapel was erected in front of the southern niche.

Bibliography: Junker, *Giza* I 132–162; A.O. Bolshakov, Some observations on the early chronology of Meidum, in: *GM* 123 (1991) 11–20.

Heraldic pillar, *see also* column, pillar

Two granite pillars, 6.77 m high, of Thutmosis III in front of the barque sanctuary of the precinct of **Amun** at **Karnak** are decorated in painted three-quarter relief showing the heraldic plants of Lower Egypt, the papyrus, and of Upper Egypt, the 'lily'.

Bibliography: Prisse d'Avennes, *Histoire*, Plate 14; P. Kaplony, Wappenpflanze(n), in: Helck, *LÄ* VI 1146–1152; R.A. Schwaller de Lubicz and G. and V. de Mir, *Les temples de Karnak* (Paris 1982), Plates 131–137.

The two heraldic pillars of Thutmosis III at Karnak

Hermopolis (Hermopolis Magna)

The ruins of the important city of Hermopolis near Ashmunein, with a temple precinct (637 sq m in area) enclosed by walls 15 m deep (30th Dynasty). Situated in the eastern part are sanctuaries of the principal gods, Amun and Thoth. The area enclosed is entered via a gate from the south, followed by a **pylon** of Ramesses II on the processional way leading to the temple. A structure in front of the pylon is furnished with **obelisks**, royal statues, **stelae** and **sphinxes** of Nectanebo I. Further to the north lies the precinct of Thoth. Nothing is known about its front part, which was possibly occupied by a pylon and forecourt. The central area contains a later temple of Thoth (55 x 110 m) of Nectanebo I. Standing at its front is a **pronaos** of Philip Arrhidaeus, 57.75 m wide, consisting of two rows of six **limestone** columns, which is of great importance for the history of construction. This building, preserved at the time of the French expedition with its glorious coloured decoration, was demolished in 1826. Four **colossal statues** of baboons were erected by Amenhotep III.

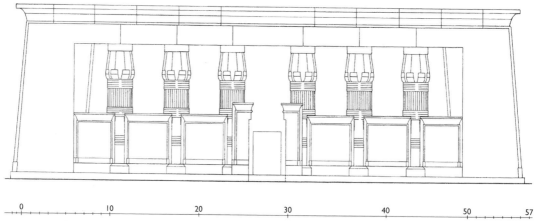

Reconstruction of the pronaos of the Thoth temple of Philip Arrhidaeus at Hermopolis

Lying at right angles to the temple of Thoth are the remains of the east-facing Amun sanctuary of Ramesses II, protected after the manner of a 'house of millions of years' by a turreted fortress wall, the south-east facing corner of the latter possibly occupied by a cult palace. To the south of the Amun temple stands a monumental temple gateway of Amenemhat II, probably the entrance to the original temple dedicated to Thoth and the primeval gods, perhaps situated on the primeval mound attested to in texts as belonging to Hermopolis Magna, but of which no trace has been found to date. A temple dedicated to Ptah (?) of Ramesses II is situated in the southern part of Ashmunein.

More than one thousand decorated blocks (talatat) from Aten temples that had been removed from Amarna were discovered in 1929/30 in the temple precinct, especially in the pylons of Ramesses II, along the processional way and at the Amun temple. On the edge of the desert lie the important necropoleis of Tuna el-Gebel. The site also includes important remains of the Roman city.

Bibliography: Description IV, Plates 50–52; Günther Roeder, Der Urzeit-Bezirk und die Urgottheiten von Hermopolis, in: ZÄS 67 (1931) 82–88; M. Kamal, Excavations … in the so-called 'Agora' of Hermopolis, in: ASAE 46 (1947) 289–295; G. Roeder, Zwei hieroglyphische Inschriften aus Hermopolis, in: ASAE 52 (1952) 315–442; D. Keßler, Hermopolis magna, in: Helck, LÄ II 1137–1147; A.J. Spencer et al., Excavations at El-Ashmunein, 4 Vols (London 1983–91); E. Hornung, Die 'Kammern' des Thot-Heiligtums, in: ZÄS 100 (1974) 33–35. D. Arnold, Zur Rekonstruktion des Pronaos von Hermopolis, in: MDAIK 50 (1994) 13–22.

Hesyre

An important brick mastaba of the late 3rd Dynasty at North Saqqara (22 x 44 m in area). A cult corridor along the eastern side was decorated with unique paintings as well as furnished with 11 elaborate cult niches, their narrow openings faced with wooden panels decorated with delicate carvings. The body of the mastaba was enlarged several times. The history of its construction remains uncertain.

Bibliography: J.E. Quibell, The Tomb of Hesy (Cairo 1913); W. Wood, A reconstruction of the reliefs of Hesy-re, in: JARCE 15 (1978) 9–24.

Hetep, see Ihy and Hetep

Hibis temple, see El-Kharga

Hierakonpolis (Kom el-Ahmar)

The pre-historic capital of Upper Egypt and seat of the Horus falcon (nekhen), closely linked with royalty. The site, rich in remains of particular archaeological significance, fell victim in 1897–99 to untrained excavation work.

The primeval sanctuary of the Horus falcon stood on a sandy mound encased in sandstone. Its enclosure (temple precinct, divine fortress) is 90 x 145 m in area and may date from the early Old Kingdom. Two blocks (now in the Egyptian Museum, Cairo) from a granite gateway of the sanctuary bear the earliest Egyptian temple relief, dating from the rule of King Khasekhemwy. Remains of a 16 x 28 m brick temple have been excavated, consisting of a broad room with five statue shrines arranged in a row. The temple may date from the Old Kingdom and stood on a sacred mound of sand, a 'High Sand' ('Hoher Sand'). A gateway inside the enclosure, part of a palace with niching or divine fortress of the 1st Dynasty, has been damaged by exploratory digging. Outside the enclosure stood the 'fortress' of King Khasekhemwy, a 65 x 75 m niched brick enclosure, of the kind which represents the funerary enclosure of the king found at Abydos. In the necropolis is the earliest tomb (Hierakonpolis No. 100) with painted decoration known in Egypt.

Casing blocks of the 'High Sand' at Hierakonpolis (after S. Clarke)

Bibliography: William M. Flinders Petrie, *Hierakonpolis* I (London 1898); F.W. Green and J.E. Quibell, *Hierakonpolis* II (London 1899); K. Weeks, The early dynastic palace, in: *JARCE* 9 (1971–72) 29–33; J. Crowfoot Payne, The decorated tomb at Hierakonpolis, and B.J. Kemp, photographs of the decorated tomb at Hierakonpolis, in: *JEA* 59 (1973) 31–43; B. Adams, Hierakonpolis, in: Helck, *LÄ* II 1182–1186; Walter A. Fairservis, *The Hierakonpolis Project I, Excavations of the Temple Area on the Kom el Gemuwia* (Poughkeepsie, NY 1983).

High Gate

This description applies to two monumental gate structures in the **enclosure wall** around Ramesses III's temple at **Medinet Habu**. They have a brick core which is encased in sandstone, with two upper floors for habitation (**battlements** – Fig.). The walls are richly decorated with the so-called 'harim scenes'; their total height is 19 m. Whether these gate structures served any military purpose is doubtful; instead they appear to be a copy of the real accommodation towers at the Delta residences adapted for use in the afterlife. Forerunners of this type of gate structure are to be found in the 12th Dynasty Nubian fortresses (**Buhen**). Comparable examples exist in the North (**Tell el-Retaba**) and in some fortress structures in Syro-Palestinian territories.

Bibliography: Uvo Hölscher, *Das Hohe Tor von Medinet Habu* (Leipzig 1910); Hölscher, *Medinet Habu* II, 4–10, Plates 6–26; G.Haeny, Zum Hohen Tor von Medinet Habu, in: *ZÄS* 94 (1967) 71–78; Aharon Kempinski and Ronny Reich, Eds, *The Architecture of Ancient Israel* (New York 1992) 135–136.

Reconstruction of the High Gate of Ramesses III at Medinet Habu (after U. Hölscher)

'Hoher Sand', 'High Sand'

The German name given by Ricke to cult structures consisting of an area of sand heaped up in a rectangle or oval and enclosed by a stone or brick wall like a dam with rounded corners, on which the actual sanctuary stood. It was meant to represent an island emerging from the primeval ocean (**symbolism**). Examples so far excavated are:

	Diameter
Hierakonpolis (early Old Kingdom?)	46 x 46 m
Heliopolis (earlier than Djoser)	600 x 600 m
Tell el-Yahudiya (date?)	450 x 470 m

The phenomenon of temples on a sacred hill has not yet been sufficiently researched for Egypt.

Bibliography: H. Ricke, Der Hohe Sand von Heliopolis, in: *ZÄS* 71 (1935) 107–111.

Horemheb, tomb of

A **temple tomb** at **Saqqara** of General (and later King) Horemheb. The superstructure was completed after two enlargements (possibly in imitation of **pyramid temples**). Divided in two, it consists of a statue temple followed at the back by a mortuary offering temple with a pyramid (**multiple shrine**, Fig., E). The intricate system of burial chambers in five storeys is based on the plan of Theban **kings' tombs**; another element is a hall of four pillars with painted decoration.

Bibliography: Geoffrey Martin, *The Memphite Tomb of Horemheb, Commander-in-Chief of Tut'ankhamun*, Vol. 1 (London 1989).

House

Egypt is extraordinarily rich in domestic buildings of all periods and their study has produced important results in recent years.

The house in pre-historic times was usually a single-room structure, rectangular at Merimde, round at Hammamiya and Omari, oval at Merimde, Omari and **El-Ma'adi**, and in some cases half sunk into the ground, with a courtyard, **grain stores** and hearths. Construction materials were **timber/mats** and Nile mud. From this developed the multiple-room courtyard house of historical times. As is usual around the Mediterranean and in the Near East, and because of climatic conditions, houses of this type had an outwardly defensive **fortress**-like appearance and were orientated towards the inside, being erected around a courtyard or hall. They were built out of mud **bricks** and timber, materials that were climatically advantageous; stone was used only in thresholds, door frames, the bases of **columns, window** grilles and the like. With careful maintenance a house of

this kind would last more than 100 years, or under less advantageous conditions only 30–60 years. The walls of Egyptian houses were usually plastered and often painted white or yellow on the outside, having yellow interior walls, and a black dado area at the base, with a brightly coloured stripe dividing the one from the other and surrounding doors and windows. Ceilings were white; in **palaces** they were decorated. Wall paintings were rare in private houses. Size and expense of construction depended on the social status of the householder. Small houses (30–70 sq m) had a courtyard as a working area and a few multi-purpose rooms. Medium-size houses (70–150 sq m), for minor officials, priests, craftsmen etc, had a central hall and living room for the householder, which were status symbols. The houses of the élite had several halls apparently serving as official or reception rooms. Royal palaces were laid out on the same basis, but on a larger scale. Egyptian civilisation was based on agriculture and the supply of natural products, so Egyptian houses always had some element of the farmhouse about them; even the villas at **Kahun** and **Amarna** resembled the dwellings on country estates.

Old Kingdom remains survive at **Balat, Buto, Hierakonpolis** and 10 complete houses with a area of 150 sq m in the priestly settlement of Queen **Khentkawes I**. A residence of 105 sq m with a garden and pond is mentioned in the biography of Metjen (3rd–4th Dynasty). Some better-preserved remains of the Middle Kingdom display recognisable local characteristics (**Tell el-Dab'a, Kahun, El-Lisht, Dahshur, Elephantine,** Deir el-**Ballas**). Terraced houses, built by the state for workmen and soldiers, are quite common (for example **Qasr el-Sagha**, Nubian fortresses). Their rooms are long and narrow, often having a **vaulted** ceiling. The central feature is an inner courtyard with the other buildings arranged around it. The court contained a pool of water, while its southern side often had a columned portico to keep out the sun. The court was approached from an entrance room with a small chamber on one side, possibly containing a hearth. Leaving the court, one entered the living room of the house, which was in some cases so large that the ceiling had to be supported on columns. Beyond this room lay the private part of the house. The houses of the upper middle class usually contained a bedroom with a bed alcove, a bathroom and attached storage rooms. Larger houses possessed additional suites of rooms for other branches of the family or domestic staff; they also had grain stores. The largest houses at **Kahun**, with more than 70 rooms, had groups of eight or nine huge grain stores. Many houses have **stairs** leading to an roof or to an upper storey.

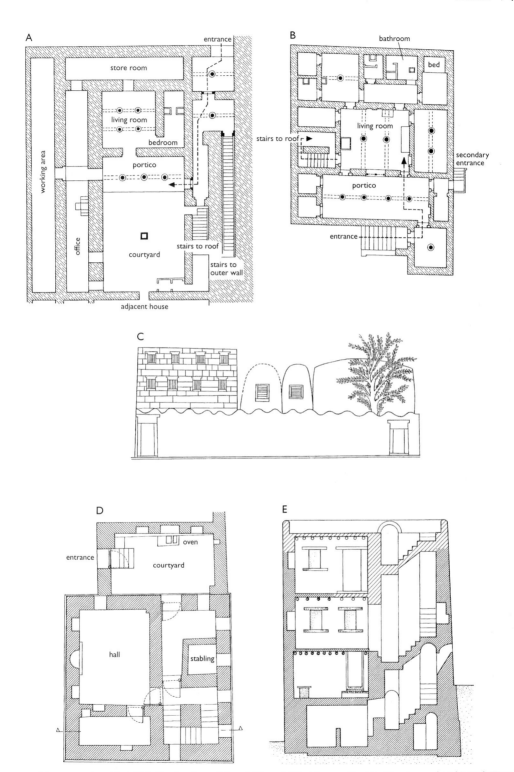

A: House of the commander of the Middle Kingdom fort at Buhen; B: House Q46/1 at Amarna; C: estate of Ineni, scene from his tomb TT 81; D/E: plan and section of house C50/C51 at Karanis

During the New Kingdom a single type of dwelling house, first found in Upper Egypt (Deir el-**Ballas**, **Elephantine**), became widespread throughout the country. The central element is a roofed central room or **pillared hall** protruding above the roofs of the surrounding rooms, with a skylight providing light in the pillared hall. This part is surrounded by private rooms, including a bedroom with a bed alcove, a bath surrounded by stone tiles, a washbasin and the base of a lavatory, in some cases a drain leading out to the street, and a second hall. Houses of the upper classes at Amarna are surrounded by extensive complexes of courtyards and gardens. Like Minoan villas (at Vathypetron, Tylissos) these houses have administrative quarters, with store houses and animal sheds, and facilities for servants and craftsmen. At the craftsmen's village of **Deir el-Medina** a small stairway led from the central road down into the entrance room, which contained a bed-like cult area decorated with religious motifs. Beyond this lay the central room, whose raised roof was supported on a central column. The seat for the house-owner would have stood on a small platform. Beyond this part lay a private room and the kitchen yard with stairs leading to the roof; there was also a storage cellar cut into the rock.

From the New Kingdom onwards, town houses tended to acquire extra storeys, possibly due to lack of space. From illustrations in Theban tombs of the New Kingdom and clay models of the Middle Kingdom at Rifeh (**ka-house**) we can posit the existence of three- or four-storey town houses. The low ground floor contained craftsmen's and agricultural accommodation, while the main part of the house in the upper storeys belonged to the owner of the house. The front part was taken up by servants' accommodation and stairs; at the rear were bedrooms and, on the roof, a shady arbour, storage rooms and the kitchen. Remains of a two-storey house of the New Kingdom are preserved at north **El-Lisht**. Depictions, stone models and preserved buildings from the Ptolemaic period at **Karanis**, **Dima** and **Alexandria** show the existence of three-storey castle-like houses which had an additional vaulted cellar.

The layout of the houses of the gods, the **temples**, was modelled on human dwellings. There are other examples of influence in both directions, such as the development of the type of temple with small double cult-image chambers based on house construction of the 12th Dynasty.

Bibliography (selection): W.M. Flinders Petrie, *Kahun, Gurob and Hawara* (London 1890); W.M. Flinders Petrie, *Illahun, Kahun and Gurob* (London 1891); Fritz Luckhard, *Das Privathaus im ptolemäischen und römischen Ägypten,* Dissertation (Giessen 1914); N. de Garis Davies, The town house in Ancient Egypt, in: *Metropolitan Museum Studies* 1 (1929) 233–255; L. Borchardt, Die Entstehung der Teppichbemalung an altägyptischen Decken und Gewölben, in: *Zeitschrift für Bauwesen* 79 (1929) 111–115; Herbert Ricke, *Der Grundriß des Amarna-Wohnhauses* (Leipzig 1932); Arthur E.R. Boak, *Soknopaiou Nesos* (Ann Arbor 1935); H. Larsen, Vorbericht über die schwedischen Grabungen in Abu Ghalib, in: *MDAIK* 6 (1936) 41–87; 10 (1941) 1–59; Hölscher, *Medinet Habu* IV, V; A. Badawy, Architectural provisions against heat in the Orient, in: *JNES* 17 (1958) 122–128; P. Anus, Un domain thébain d'époque 'amarnienne' sur quelques blocs de remploi trouvés à Karnak, in: *BIFAO* 69 (1971) 69–88; P. Anus, Habitations de prêtres dans le temple d'Amon à Karnak, in: *Karnak* IV (= *Kêmi* 21, 1971) 217–238; J. Brinks, Haus, in: *LÄ* II 1055–1061; D. Arnold, Hausbau, in: Helck, *LÄ* II 1062–1064; Ricke, *Wohnhäuser*; J. Jacquet, Remarques sur l'architecture domestique á l'époque meroitique, in: *Festschrift Ricke* 121–131; Mieczyslaw Rodziewicz, *Alexandria III. Les habitations romaines tardives d'Alexandria* (Warsaw 1984); C. Tietze, Amarna I–II, in: *ZÄS* 112 (1985) 48–84; 113 (1986) 55–78; P.T. Crocker, Status symbols in the architecture of El-'Amarna, in: *JEA* 71 (1985) 52–65; C. Tietze, Amarna, in: *ZÄS* 112 (1985) 48–85; 113 (1986) 55–78; B.J. Kemp, Large Middle Kingdom granary buildings, in: *ZÄS* 113 (1986) 120–136; B.J. Kemp, The Amarna workmen's village, in: *JEA* 73 (1987) 21–50; B.J. Kemp, *Amarna Reports* I–IV (London 1984–87); C. Traunecker, Les maisons du domaine d'Aton à Karnak, in: *Sociétés urbaines en Égypte et au Soudan* (Lille 1988) 73–93; Elke Roik, *Das altägyptische Wohnhaus und seine Darstellung im Flachbild* (Frankfurt 1988); F. Arnold, A study of Egyptian domestic building, in: *Varia Aegyptiaca* 5 (1989) 75–93; M. Bietak, 'Götterwohnung und Menschenwohnung'. Die Entstehung eines Tempeltyps des Mittleren Reiches aus der zeitgenössischen Wohnarchitektur, in: Kurth, *Tempeltagung* 13–22; M. Bietak, An Iron Age four-room house in Ramesside Egypt, in: *Eretz-Israel* 23 (1992) 9–12; A. Endruweit, *Städtischer Wohnbau in Ägypten: Klimagerechte Lehmarchitektur in Amarna* (Berlin 1994); Bietak, *House and Palace*; F. Arnold, Die Priesterhäuser der Chentkaues in Giza, in: *MDAIK* 54 (1998) 1–18; C. Tietze, Amarna. Wohn- und Lebensverhältnisse in einer ägyptischen Stadt, in: Bietak, *Haus und Palast* 231–237. Neighbouring countries: Paulette M.M. Daviau, *Houses and their Furnishings in Bronze Age Palestine* (Sheffield 1993); Kjell Werner, *The Megaron during the Aegean and Anatolian Bronze Age* (Jonsered 1993).

'House of millions of years'

The New Kingdom 'palaces of millions of years' are widely distributed cult buildings of kings. They took over in part the function of the **pyramid temples** of the Old and Middle Kingdoms, in which the continued existence of the king is ensured through his assimilation with the cult of a powerful god, such as Amun, Osiris or Ptah; the mystic union between the two is shown in the cult image and wall reliefs. For this reason, regular barque processions took place in which the cult image of the god concerned was conveyed to the 'house of millions of years', which the king's *ba* could enter via a **false door** in the rear wall of the sanctuary. Thus, the cult of a god, known from experience to have been maintained for a longer period, provided some measure of guarantee for the continuance of the cult of the king associated with it. The two sides of this cultic union required above all a **barque chamber** for the god and an attached cult **palace** for the king. Other associated elements were mortuary cult rooms of the king, as well as sun and Hathor sanctuaries and cult rooms for several other gods. The leitmotif in the decoration of 'houses of millions of years' is the presentation of a palm frond (representing millions of years) by representatives of the gods of Upper and Lower Egypt. The 'houses of millions of years' on the Theban West Bank represent the mortuary temples of the relevant **kings' tombs**. Their earliest forerunner was the temple of **Mentuhotep**; other early forms occurred in the 12th and 13th Dynasties. A 'house of millions of years' is preserved or attestable at **Thebes** for almost every king of the New Kingdom and, outside Thebes, at **Soleb** and **Memphis**, for Amenhotep III; others are those for **Sety I** at Memphis and for **Ramesses II** at Abydos and **Memphis**. The latest examples are those of Osorkon I (at **Memphis**) and Osorkon II (at Leontopolis – **Tell el-Moqdam**).

Bibliography: W.M.Flinders Petrie, *Six Temples at Thebes 1896* (London 1897); Hölscher, *Medinet Habu* I; D. Arnold, Vom Pyramidenbezirk zum 'Haus für Millionen Jahre', in: *MDAIK* 34 (1978) 1–8; R. Stadelmann, Totentempel und Millionenjahrhaus in Theben, in: *MDAIK* 35 (1979) 303–321; R. Stadelmann, Totentempel III, in: Helck, *LÄ* VI 706–711; G. Haeny, La fonction réligieuse des 'Chateaux de Millions d'années', in: *L'Égyptologie en 1979* I (Paris 1982) 111-116; *Thebes. Les temples de millions d'années*, Dossiers Histoire et Archéologie 136 (1989); L.Gabold, Les temples 'mémoriaux' de Thoutmosis II et Toutankhamon, in: *BIFAO* 89 (1989) 127–178; G. Haeny, Zur Funktion der 'Häuser für Millionen Jahre', in: Kurth, *Tempeltagung* 101–106; G. Haeny, New Kingdom mortuary temples and 'mansions of millions of years', in: Byron Shafer, Ed., *Temples of Ancient Egypt* (Cornell 1997) 86–126; Christian Leblanc, Quelques réflexions sur le programme iconographique et la fonction des temples de 'Millions d'années', in: Quirke, *Temple*, 49–56. On Osorkon I, see Kitchen, *The Third Intermediate Period in Egypt (1100–650 BC)* (Warminster 1986) 302ff.

Hypaetral

'Open to the sky'; describes temple sanctuaries without a roof, a form found in Egypt in **Aten temples**, **sun temples** and possibly Late Period temples at **Mendes** and **Bubastis**.

Hypostyle hall

The term 'hypostyle' is generally applied to hall buildings, but in Egypt it is applied particularly to New Kingdom pillared halls with a raised central nave, and above all to the hypostyle hall of **Karnak**, the largest in Egyptian architecture and one of the most extensive pillared halls in the world, covering 5500 sq m. This structure consists of three wide, raised central naves whose ceiling is supported on two rows of six **columns** with open-papyrus **capitals**, 21 m high. The roof of the 14 side-aisles is supported by 122 smooth-sided papyrus columns. The hall receives light from **windows** in the raised walls at a height of 5 m (**ceiling construction**, Fig.). The **architraves**, the longest 7 m long, weigh up to 70 tonnes. Construction is unlikely to have started in the reign of Horemheb, beginning instead in that of Sety I, with completion under Ramesses II. A theory suggesting that the central nave has its origins in the reign of Amenhotep III has been proved to be incorrect. The structure underwent restoration several times in the Pharaonic age.

The hypostyle hall had its antecedents in **houses** and **palace** buildings. The earliest example is the **Mentuhotep** temple with its 8 x 10 octagonal **pillars**, 3 m high, but without a central nave. The original concept of the structure was probably a **kiosk** set inside a festival court with pillared halls, which is why the elements of a raised central hall and the lower pillared courts are always kept separate. Comparable examples are the **Hall of Annals** and the **Akhmenu** of Thutmosis III with two rows of ten columns set inside a surrounding pillared corridor, and there are some monumental structures of Ramesses II (**Ramesseum, Temple of Ptah** at Memphis) and Ramesses III (**Medinet Habu**). In the reign of the lavish master builder Amenhotep III, the transverse hall in Theban private tombs developed into vast pillared halls. Late successors of hypostyle halls are **pronaoi**.

Bibliography: H. Schäfer, Die angebliche Basiliken-Halle des Tempels von Luksor, in: *ZÄS* 61 (1924) 52–57; H. Chevrier, Chronologie des constructions de la salle hypostyle, in: *ASAE* 54 (1956) 35–38; Haeny, *Basilikale Anlagen*; Gerhard Haeny, Hypostyl, in: Helck, *LÄ* III 111–112. For decorative scheme see: P. Gilbert, La conception drammatique de la salle hypostyle de Karnak, in: *Mélanges Mariette*, BdE 32 (Cairo 1961) 71–79; W.Helck, Die Systematik der Ausschmückung der hypostylen Halle van Karnak, in: *MDAIK* 32 (1976) 57–65; V. Rondot and J.C. Colvin, Restaurations antiques à l'entrée de la salle hypostyle de Karnak, in: *MDAIK* 45 (1989) 249–259. Of historic interest: Gabriel Leroux, *Les origines de l'édifice hypostyle en Grèce, en Orient et chez les Romains*, Bibliothèque des écoles françaises d'Athène et de Rome, Fasc. 108 (Paris 1913); Dieter Arnold, Hypostyle halls of the Old and Middle Kingdom, in: *Studies Simpson* I, 39–54.

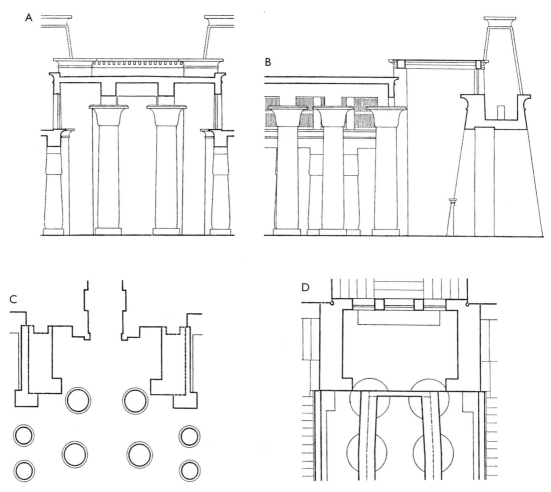

Sections and plan of the hypostyle hall at Karnak (after G. Haeny). A: cross-section; B: longitudinal section of the structure in front of the third pylon; C: plan; D: ceiling plan of the same structure

I

Ibi, tomb of

An important Late Period Theban tomb (c. 630 BC) in the Assasif (TT 36), the superstructure of which follows a very irregular plan due to lack of space. The subterranean complex – **sun court**, **pillared hall** and an intricate complex of burial apartments – is likewise cramped. The tomb has been well examined in archaeological terms, and contains important wall reliefs and inscriptions.

Bibliography: Eigner, *Grabbauten* 51–52; Klaus P. Kuhlmann and Wolfgang Schenkel, *Das Grab des Ibi*, 2 Vols (Mainz 1983); Erhard Graefe, *Das Grab des Ibi* (Brussels 1990).

Ihy and Hetep, tombs of

Two similar stone-built tombs of the 12th Dynasty in close proximity to each other at **Saqqara**, between **Mereruka** and **Kagemni**, consisting of a small forecourt with 3 x 3 pillars, two raised statue chapels, with block statues preserved in situ, and a small mortuary offering room. The structures illustrate the transformation of a **mastaba** to a **temple tomb**.

Bibliography: Cecil M. Firth and Battiscombe Gunn, *Teti Pyramid Cemeteries* I (Cairo 1926) 61–65; R. Freed,Observations on the dating and decoration of the tombs of Ihy and Hetep at Saqqara, in: Bárta, *Abusir 2000* 207–214.

Ikkur (Koshtemma)

A **fortress** on the West Bank of the Nile opposite **Kubban**, 100 km south of Aswan, covering in the Old Kingdom a rectangular area of 50 x 95 m, and provided with a moat and semi-circular turrets. Above it is a newer structure, 82 x 110 m, of the Middle and New Kingdoms with parts of a temple.

Bibliography: G.A. Reisner, *The Archeological Survey of Nubia: Report for 1908–1909*, Vol. 1, 22–25; Vol. 2, Plates 33–36; S. Clark, Ancient Egyptian Frontier Fortresses, in: *JEA* 3 (1916) 160–161.

Illahun, *see* El-Lahun tomb 621, Kahun, Senwosret II

Ineni, tomb of

The Theban **rock tomb** (TT 81) of a royal master builder, of the period Amenhotep I to Thutmosis III, consisting of a pillared front, a passage and a shrine provided with three rock-cut statues. The tomb is adapted from an early 11th Dynasty structure.

Bibliography: Eberhard Dziobek, *Das Grab des Ineni*, Theben Nr. 81 (Mainz 1992).

Inpy, tomb of

The idiosyncratic, architecturally interesting tomb, at **Illahun**, of the architect of Senwosret II. It consists of a **mastaba** top combined with a rock-cut chapel of Upper Egyptian type with a four-pillar façade, behind which lies a cult chapel with three statue shrines. Equally unusual is the burial complex consisting of three rooms as well as, in the forecourt, a shaft, 3 x 8 m wide, the purpose of which is unknown.

Bibliography: W.M. Flinders Petrie et al., *Lahun* II (London 1923) 26–28.

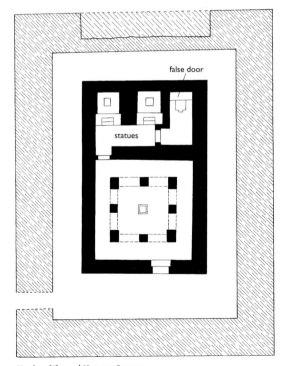

false door

statues

Tombs of Ihy and Hetep at Saqqara

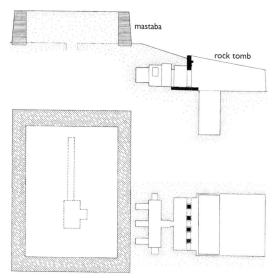

Reconstruction of the combined mastaba and rock tomb of Inpy at El-Lahun (tomb chambers simplified)

Intercolumnium, *see* screen wall

Iseum (Behbeit el-Hagar)

Situated west of Mansura in a **brick** enclosure (area 210 x 362 m, walls 18–20 m thick) is the spectacular mound of blocks from the collapsed Isis temple of Hebet (area 55–80 m). The position of the richly decorated blocks

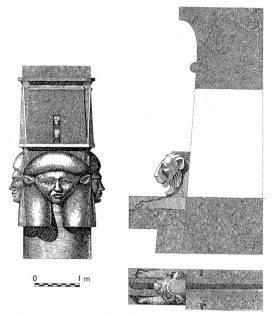

Hathor column, cavetto cornice and water spout of the Iseum at Behbeit el-Hagar (after A. Lézine)

View over the ruins of the collapsed Iseum at Behbeit el-Hagar

on the ground suggests that the building was similar in form to the temple of **Dendera**. The west-orientated front of the temple was probably a pillared court with a **pronaos** beyond, followed by one or more **pillared halls** with **Hathor columns**, 10.15 m high, of Ptolemy II. Situated alongside to the south was an ascent to the roof and, further to the east, the holy-of-holies of Nectanebo II, built of granite. The remaining parts were constructed of rose **granite**, **quartzite** and **basalt**, typical of temples of the 26–30th Dynasties. The earliest cartouches visible are those of Nectanebo I and Nectanebo II in the eastern part of the temple. Further to the west are the cartouches of Ptolemies II and III. The Ptolemaic kings probably found a structure half-completed by Nectanebo II, whose decoration had been interrupted by the final Persian invasion of 343 BC.

Partial reconstruction of the building appears possible.

Bibliography: G. Roeder, Der Isistempel von Behbêt, in: *ZÄS* 46 (1909) 62–73; C.C. Edgar and G. Roeder, Der Isistempel von Behbêt, in: *RT* 35 (1913) 89–116; A. Lézine, État présent du Temple de Bahbeit el Hagar, in: *Kêmi* 10 (1949) 49–57; B.V. Bothmer, Ptolemaic reliefs, in: *Bulletin of the Museum of Fine Arts, Boston* 51 (1953) 1–7; L. Habachi, Behbeit el-Hagar, in: Helck, *LÄ* I 682–683; Christine Favard-Meeks, Un temple d'Isis à réconstruire, in: *Archeologia* 263 (1990) 28–33; Christine Favard-Meeks, *Le temple de Behbeit el-Hagara* (Hamburg 1991).

Ismant el-Kharab (Smint el-Kharb)

An area of ruins (250 x 350 m) in the chief settlement of the **Dakhla Oasis** with the remains of the temple of Tutu and Shait. Its outer walls decorated with **pilasters**, this consists of three rooms. It has three parallel sanctuaries, the side ones and the offering table hall in front with **vaulted** ceilings. The central sanctuary is cased in stone. Beyond lies a small chapel, also dedicated to Tutu.

Bibliography: Herbert W. Winlock, Ed., *Dakhleh Oasis* (New York 1936) 20–21, Plates 11, 13.

J

Joint

Economy in the use of material is often the reason why **masonry** joints lie oblique to verticals or to the course of walls. (This applies mainly in the Old Kingdom and is less frequent in the Middle and New Kingdoms.) However, this was not true polygonal masonry. The use of regular ashlar masonry was rare (**Chapelle Rouge**, *talatat*), becoming commonplace in Graeco-Roman buildings. Bedding joints were usually horizontal, exceptions being those in the inward-sloping **casing** of pyramids of the 3rd Dynasty or in downward-sloping corridors, where joints are correspondingly sloped too. Roofing slabs in sloping corridors occasionally have vertical joints in order to reduce slippage. A striking feature in Egyptian stone buildings of the Old and Middle Kingdoms, but also of later periods, are oblique joints. Often, in the case of larger blocks the joint may be at an angle to the horizontal as well as to the direction of the wall. Such 'trapezoidal' masonry, which must have entailed considerable work for the masons, can only be explained by economy in the use of material.

The joints achieved between casing blocks is often so tight that the course of the joints is not discernible. This was achieved by sawing the facing sides of blocks until they matched exactly. In the process the **saw** sometimes cut into the upper edge of a block directly below, unintentionally causing the position of the upper block to be 'marked'. From as early as the Old Kingdom, in the case of close joints, only a contact band at the front edge of the blocks was smoothed (a form of **anathyrosis**). Where the masonry is irregular, as for example in the cores of pyramids, **mortar** and small stones were used liberally to compensate for the irregularity of gaps.

Lack of time in some of the large building projects of the New Kingdom led to sacrificing the accuracy of joints and the resulting irregularities were disguised with **gypsum**. Close joints were often coated with a lubricant (**mortar**); in Graeco-Roman buildings this was applied to a horizontal contact band that had been roughened. Close joints were filled with mortar which was poured in from above using grooves in the blocks. In some cases the precise layout of joints is likely to have been planned thoroughly in advance. In most cases, joints respected the importance of certain structural elements, for example torus mouldings (**cavetto cornice**), even giving way to decoration, such as the heads of gods and kings. Certain building elements are kept separate by means of vertical joints as a precaution against irregular slippage.

Bibliography: Clark, *AEM* 96–116; Jaritz, *Terrassen* 33–36, Plates 10, 36; Golvin, *Karnak* 108–116; Arnold, *Building* 120–124.

K

Ka-house (*hut-ka*)

A general term for dwellings for the *ka*, for example tombs and especially chapels for *ka*-statues. Many *ka*-houses of kings and private persons of the Old and Middle Kingdoms are preserved, in most cases attached to the temple of a god. Their appearance usually takes the shape of a simple shrine, built of stone or brick (Pepy I and Teti at **Bubastis**, **Mentuhotep** Nebhepetre at **Dendera**, Heqaib at **Elephantine**).

Bibliography: G. Daressy, Chapelle de Mentouhotep III à Dendérah, in: *ASAE* 17 (1917) 226–236; Labib Habachi, *Tell Basta* (Cairo 1957) 11–32; P. Kaplony, Ka-Haus, in: Helck, *LÄ* III 284–287; Labib Habachi, *The Sanctuary of Heqaib*, 2 Vols (Mainz 1985).

Ka-tomb, *see* cult pyramid

Kagemni (Gemnikai)

An important **mastaba** (32.5 x 33.3 m) of the 6th Dynasty at **Saqqara**, north of the **Teti** pyramid. The core is only partially occupied by rooms and includes chambers of great interest constructed in the shape of large boats. Another structure erected in the masonry is a flight of

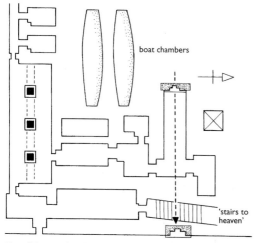

boat chambers

'stairs to heaven'

Plan of the mastaba of Kagemni at Saqqara, with two boat chambers and 'stairs to heaven', and two aligned false doors on the façade and in the cult chamber

symbolic 'Stairs to Heaven'. The western niche of the decorated burial chamber is occupied by a vast sarcophagus.

Bibliography: Friedrich W. von Bissing, *Die Mastaba des Gem-ni-kai* (Berlin 1905); Plan: Cecil M. Firth and Battiscombe Gunn, *Teti Pyramid Cemeteries* (Cairo 1926), Plate 51.

Kahun

Egyptological name applied to a small **town** of workmen and officials called 'Senwosret is Mighty' by the valley temple of the pyramid of **Senwosret II** at **Illahun**. Archaeologically one of the most important settlements in Egypt, in 1888–90 it fell victim to the inadequate excavation methods of Flinders Petrie at that time. This small town (350 x 400 m) was surrounded by a wall and divided into individual quarters by a rectangular system of streets. According to the rank of their inhabitants these plots were occupied by houses of various sizes, from small workers' houses with four rooms (100 sq m) to the eight larger houses for higher officials along the north wall, which had 70 rooms (2400 sq m); they were provided with agricultural facilities such as vast **grain stores** which could have provided for more than 300 persons per household (**house**, Fig., A; **grain store**, Fig., B). One particular administrative property stood on an acropolis-like elevation approached by stairs. Some of the houses were barrel-**vaulted**, while others had a flat roof with the ceilings supported on wooden columns. The walls were covered with plaster and in some cases were decorated with paintings. They had stairs to the roof, grain stores and **cellars**. Streets were provided with gutters. At the south-west corner are remains of a temple, probably the **valley temple** of the pyramid of **Senwosret II**. Among best known artefacts found are the Kahun Papyri; there are also items of Middle Minoan, Cypriot and **Tell el-Yahudiya** ceramics. The population is estimated to have numbered 5000–7000.

Bibliography: W.M. Flinders Petrie, *Kahun, Gurob and Hawara* (London 1890) 21–32; W.M. Flinders Petrie, *Illahun, Kahun and Gurob* (London 1891) 5–15; W.M. Flinders Petrie, *Lahun II* (London 1923) 39–41; Rosalie David, *The Pyramid Builders of Ancient Egypt* (London-Boston-Henley 1986).

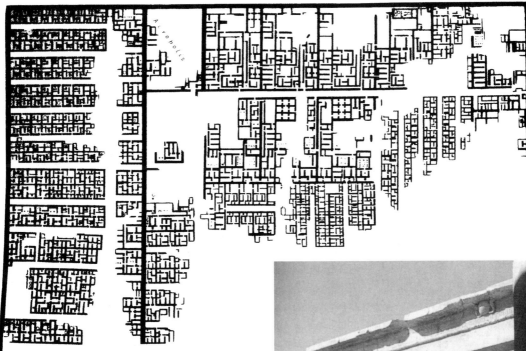

Plan of Kahun, the pyramid temple of Senwosret II (after W.M.F. Petrie)

Kalabsha

An important Augustan temple of Mandulis and Isis of Philae (temple building 77 m long; area of the precinct 66 x 92 m), at Talmis in Lower Nubia, 60 km south of Aswan. It consists of a monumental quay with a **platform**, a brick enclosure 15 m high with a stone **pylon**, a pillared forecourt and a free-standing temple building with an open **pronaos**, which was a later addition. Behind this are a room for guest gods, an offering room and a cult room, a **roof chapel** and **crypts** hidden inside some walls; there is also a small **birth house**. The inscriptions and decoration are incomplete. An investigation of the structures in 1961 revealed the extreme precision of measurements and an expert system of proportions. The slender proportions and wide spacing of the **columns** are evidence of the influence of classical architecture. The temple was moved in 1961–63 to an elevation on the West Bank of the Nile south of Philae; an earlier small structure of Ptolemy IX Soter II, discovered in its foundations during this process, has been reconstructed at **Elephantine**; a **gateway** structure was moved to Berlin in 1973.

Bibliography: Gau, *Antiquités* Plates 17–22; Henri Gauthier, *Le temple de Kalabcha* (Cairo 1911–1914); Hans Stock and Kurt Georg Siegler, *Der größte Tempel Nubiens und das Abenteuer seiner Rettung* (Wiesbaden 1965); Kurt Siegler, *Kalabsha. Architektur und*

View of the pronaos of the temple of Kalabsha

Baugeschichte des Tempels (Mainz 1970); G.R.H. Wright, *Kalabsha: The Preserving of the Temple* (Berlin 1970); Dieter Arnold, *Die Tempel von Kalabscha* (Cairo 1975); E. Henfling, Kalabscha, in: Helck, *LÄ* III 295–296; G.R.H. Wright, *The Ptolemaic Sanctuary of Kalabsha. Its Reconstruction on Elephantine Island* (Mainz 1987).

Kamutef temple (Karnak)

This temple was erected by Thutmosis III and Hatshepsut for Kamutef (a manifestation of Amun) along the processional way which connects the **Amun** and **Mut** precincts. A **pylon** in the brick enclosure walls leads to the avenue of **sphinxes**. The stone temple building, 38.5 x 48.3 m in size, used for the performance of festivals of Min, may have been conceived as an **ambulatory temple**. The rows of nine chapels along the outer walls are an unusual feature. Opposite the temple are the remains of the first **barque station**, with a similar layout to that of the 18th Dynasty temple of **Medinet Habu**.

Bibliography: Ricke, *Kamutef*; G. Haeny, Zum Kamutef, in: *GM* 90 (1986) 33–34.

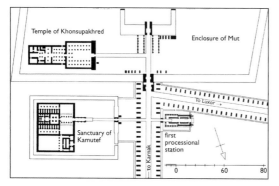

Plan of the temple of Kamutef at Karnak, with the first barque station opposite and the Mut precinct and temple of Khonsupakhred to the south

Kanais, *see* Wadi Miya

Karabasken and Karakhamun, tombs of
Large tombs of the 25th Dynasty in the southern Assasif at **Thebes** (TT 391 and 223). The two unexcavated complexes had temple-like superstructures, 60–80 m long, a **sun court**, entrance recess, **pillared hall** and cult room.

Bibliography: Eigner, *Grabbauten* 40–42.

Karanis (Kom Aushim)
A city, c. 600 x 1000 m in size, on the north-eastern fringe of the Faiyum, settled from the Ptolemaic period onwards until some time in the 5th century AD. The two stone temples of the Roman period, at the north and the south, are well preserved. The north temple (c. 165 AD) has two **pylons** and the main temple building (10.52 x 18.05 m) is of stone, with some **crypts** and **stairs** leading to the roof. The equally well-preserved south temple (second half of the 1st century AD) dedicated to the crocodile gods Pnepheros and Petesuchos, has a podium at its front and its outside walls have **bosses**.

Between 1900 and 1924 the central part of the city was completely removed by diggers for ancient silt (Ar. *sebbakhin*), but a large number of houses on the fringe of the town are preserved in excellent condition up to the third floor, including timber door and window frames, decorated wall recesses and wall paintings. Other surviving features are barracks, **grain stores** and finds of important papyri.

Bibliography: Boak, *Karanis* I–II; E.M. Husselmann, The granaries of Karanis, in: *Trans. of the American Philolog. Soc.* 83 (1952) 56–73; G. Castel, Un grand bain gréco-romain à Karanis, in: *BIFAO* 76 (1976) 231–275; Elinor M. Husselman, *Karanis Excavations of the University of Michigan in Egypt 1928–1935. Topography and Architecture* (Ann Arbor 1979); S. Donadoni, Karanis, in: Helck, *LÄ* III 327–328.

Karnak, *see* Akhmenu, Akoris chapel, Amun precinct, Aten precinct, Khonsu temple, Month precinct, Mut precinct, Opet temple

Kawa
An important cult site on the East Bank of the Nile between the Third and Fourth Cataracts, with temples to Amun from the 18th Dynasty onwards.

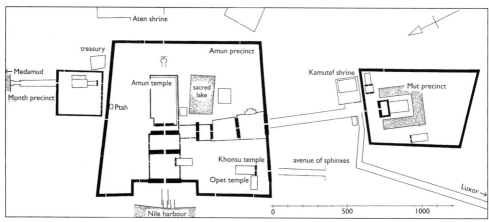

General plan of the monuments at Karnak

Temple A, built by Tutankhamun and usurped by Ramesses II, was enlarged by Taharqa who added a **pylon**, two columned courts and a sanctuary with side-rooms; the decoration tends to be archaistic. The smaller temple, B, is of a later date; it has a Meroitic sanctuary. The temple of Taharqa, temple T, stands inside a large enclosure and has an avenue of ram-headed **sphinxes**, a **pylon**, columned court, **hypostyle hall**, with four rows of four columns, and a house of the god with a sanctuary. Its plan resembles that of the temples of **Sanam** and Argo (**Tabo**).

Bibliography: M.F. Laming-Macadam, *The Temples of Kawa*, 2 Vols (London 1949, 1955); St. Wenig, Kawa, in: Helck, *LÄ* III 378; Hein, *Ramessidische Bautätigkeit* 64.

Khabausokar, tomb of

A double **mastaba** (FS 3073) of Khabausokar and Hathor-nefer-hetep at **Saqqara** which is important for the history of tomb development. It belongs to the late 3rd or early 4th Dynasty, and has two cruciform chapels of the **palace façade** type, the southern one already having a *serdab* (**mastaba**, Fig., D). The façade of the mastaba has painted **niching**.

Bibliography: Reisner, *Development* 267–269, 387–388.

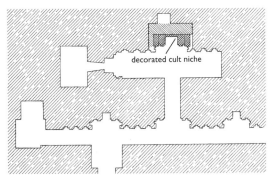

decorated cult niche

Plan of the mastaba of Khabausokar with cruciform cult chamber and a niched façade, which has been transferred to the interior of the tomb

Khafre, pyramid of

The dimensions of the pyramid called 'Great is the Pyramid of Khafre' and its cult buildings (base 215.25 sq m, height 143.50 m, angle of slope 53°10') approach those of the pyramid of **Khufu**. Originally a smaller pyramid was envisaged, and to this earlier project is owed the (now lower) entrance corridor with a 3.12 x 10.41 m chamber cut out of the rock, its gable roof only 2.61 m high. The pyramid was then enlarged with a higher, more southerly central chamber and a new entrance further up in the casing;

the new corridor was connected to the earlier one. The new burial chamber was divided in two, but the separating wall is no longer in place. This double room, 4.99 x 14.15 m, had a ceiling of relieving slabs, 6.83 m high. The bottom two courses of the outer casing are **granite** (**casing**, Fig.) and above this was Tura **limestone**. A considerable portion of the stone casing is preserved at the apex.

In contrast with the simplicity of the chambers inside the pyramid, a monumental **pyramid temple**, 56.2 x 111.2 m, stands in front of the east side of the pyramid. Its front part, as in the valley temple, consists of a combination of a wide and a deep **pillared hall**, both of them probably surrounded on each side with statues of the king. The wide inner courtyard, situated immediately to the west of the deep hall, was surrounded by 12 **colossal statues**. Behind this court lie five huge sanctuaries, corresponding to the later group of five statue chapels, presumably intended for barques and statues of the king. The actual place for presentation of funerary offerings, with a **false door**, as is found in later pyramid temples, is lacking because the cult was not directed to the deceased king, but to the divine aspect of the king in the form of Horus or Re. Situated on the south side are the remains of a secondary pyramid, which once stood 21 m high. A structure of wooden poles was found outside the front, which was probably used to carry a statue to be buried inside the pyramid. The **valley temple**, measuring 45 x 46 m, stands on the desert edge, 494 m further to the south-east. The core of the walls of both of these temples is cut out of the native rock and cased with limestone and granite. The floors are covered with **alabaster** slabs, and the roof beams were supported on monolithic granite pillars (**cramp**, Fig.). Within the eastern façade, 12 m high, are two deep **door recesses** protected by huge sphinxes or lions. The main interior room is a very well-preserved T-shaped pillared hall lined with 23 cult images of the god-king, made of hard stone or alabaster. One of them, depicting the king as a form of Horus, is one of the most important statues from Egypt. The walls of the valley temple, made of polished granite, are not decorated.

Bibliography: Petrie, *Pyramids* 96–109; Hölscher, *Chephren*; A. Hafez Abd el'Al, in: *ASAE* 62 (1977) 103–120; *MRA* V; Edwards, *Pyramids* 154; Edwards, The air-channels of Chephren's pyramid, in: *Studies in Ancient Egypt, the Aegean, and the Sudan: Essays in Honor of Dows Dunham* (Boston 1981) 55–57; M. Lehner and P. Lacovara, An enigmatic object explained, in: *JEA* 71 (1985) 169–174; Stadelmann, *Pyramiden* 130–139; Stadelmann, *Pyramiden von Giza* 176–191; Lehner, *Complete Pyramids* 122–133.

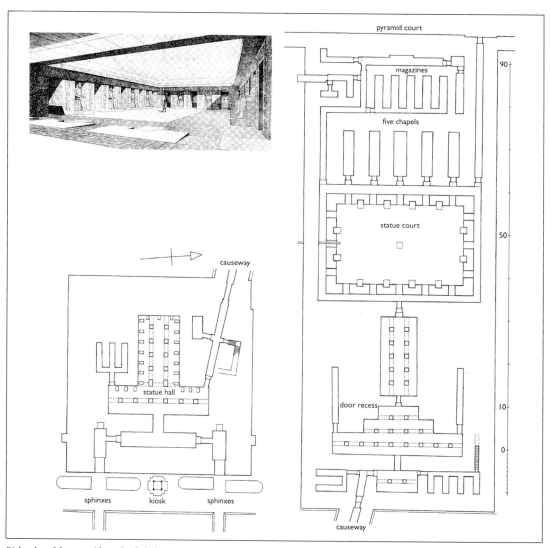

Right: plan of the pyramid temple of Khafre. Upper left: reconstruction of its statue court (after H. Ricke); lower left: plan of the valley temple.

Kheker frieze

The upper decorative element on decorated walls, the *kheker* derives from early wall hangings, and consists of a row of upright bundles and knots of the fringe of a carpet or bundles of reeds. The main variants are: a) pointed at the top and plain inside, and b) with detailed patterning inside (sequence of colours: red, green, blue) and with an open calyx-like top. The earliest examples are found in the precinct of **Djoser** and at **Meidum**. From the New Kingdom, imaginative variants appear (crowned with sun discs etc.).

Bibliography: W.M. Flinders Petrie, *Egyptian Decorative Art* (London 1895) 101–103; E. Mackay, Kheker friezes, in: *Ancient Egypt* (1920) 111–122; M. Kolodko-Dolinska, Studies on the kheker frieze in the temple of Tuthmosis III in Deir el-Bahari, in: *RT* 14 (1990) 29–60.

Khendjer, pyramid of

The pyramid complex of the 13th Dynasty king Khendjer lies at South **Saqqara**. The pyramid had a mud **brick** core, base length 105 **cubits** (55.125 m ?), height 37.35 m, angle of slope 55°. The decorated black **granite pyramidion** has survived. The **quartzite** roof of the sarcophagus, weighing 60 tonnes, was lowered by means of sand channels. Above it was a weight-relieving roof of **limestone** relieving slabs, itself roofed over with a brick **vault** (**mastaba**, Fig.). There is evidence for a small **pyramid temple** to the east and a **north chapel**. The inner enclosure wall was of limestone and **niched**. A smaller queen's pyramid, with two burial chambers, stood at the north-eastern corner.

To the south-west are the remains of another unfinished pyramid precinct of the 13th Dynasty. Only the inner rooms of the pyramid were ever completed. The pyramid itself was planned to be 165 x 165 cubits = 86.625 sq m. These remains represent a masterpiece of late Middle Kingdom building. The 150 tonne quartzite roof of the sarcophagus was intended to be lowered using sand channels; the quartzite ceiling was supported by limestone relieving blocks and a brick **vault**. A smaller tomb, possibly for a queen, leads off from the antechamber. At the entrance two granite pyramidia were found. The construction site is still surrounded by a **curved wall**.

Bibliography: Gustave Jéquier, *Deux pyramides du Moyen Empire* (Cairo 1933); Gustave Jéquier, *Douze ans de fouilles dans la nécropole memphite* (Neuchâtel 1940) 139–155; Stadelmann, *Pyramiden* 249–254.

Core masonry of the tomb of Khentkawes at Giza, sitting on a rock base

Khentkawes I, tomb of

The funerary monument of Queen Khentkawes, the wife of Shepseskaf, mother of Neferirkare and regent, lies at **Giza**. The superstructure of the tomb consists of an almost square rock base cased in **limestone**, 43.70 x 45.80 m in size and 10.50 m high, on top of which stands a structure, 8 m high, in the form of a **mastaba** or a sarcophagus, similar to that of **Shepseskaf**. The cult rooms and the burial chamber are within the rock base and are arranged following the programme of the royal tomb complexes of the 4th Dynasty. The **enclosure wall** has rounded corners. The underlying concept for this unusual structure is not known. A well-preserved priests' settlement is located along the **causeway** and next to the **valley temple**.

Bibliography: Hassan, *Giza* IV; *MRA* VI; Stadelmann, *Pyramiden* 155–158, 174; M. Verner, *Forgotten Pharaohs, Lost Pyramids, Abusir* (Prague 1994) 116–132; F. Arnold, Die Priestersiedlung der Chentkaues in Giza, in: *MDAIK* 54 (1998) 1–18.

Khentkawes II, pyramid of

A small, incomplete pyramid precinct of a second Queen Khentkawes (wife of Neferirkare, mother of Neferefre and of Niuserre), which has been excavated south of the **Neferirkare** pyramid at **Abusir**. The pyramid probably measured 50 sq **cubits**.

Bibliography: M. Verner, in: *BSFE* 91 (1981) 10–12; M. Verner, in: *ZÄS* 107 (1980) 158–164; Miroslav Verner, *Forgotten Pharaohs, Lost Pyramids, Abusir* (Prague 1994) 116–132; M. Verner, *Abusir III, The Pyramid Complex of Khentkaues* (Prague 1995).

Kheruef, tomb of

If it had been completed, the tomb of Kheruef (TT 192), the organiser of the *sed*-festivals of Amenhotep III, would have been the largest of the 18th Dynasty (length 196). It is situated on the valley floor of the Assasif, and is approached via a ramp leading into an open courtyard, 30 x 30 m, with **channelled columns**, 10 x 11/12, on all sides (unfinished). The transverse hall, which normally follows the court, has been enlarged to form a huge **pillared hall** with ten channelled and two rows of ten papyrus **columns**. The corridor has a double row of ten papyrus columns and descends to the cult chapels at the lower level, which are surrounded on three sides by niches for statues. A steep corridor from the pillared hall descends to the rock-cut burial chamber 40 m below ground level, changing direction three times. The tomb is unfinished and severely damaged.

Bibliography: *The Tomb of Kheruef, Theban Tomb 192*, OIP Vol. 102 (Chicago 1980).

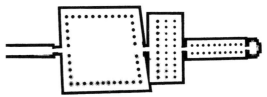

Plan of the Theban tomb of Kheruef, TT 192 (after J. Knudstat)

Khety, tomb of

An important Theban tomb (TT 311) on the north-facing slope of the Assasif, dating from the reign of Mentuhotep Nebhepetre. Standing against the hillside above the steep forecourt is a brick façade, extended to form a **pylon**, 26 m wide and 9 m high, with a deeply echelonned entrance to the tomb. Behind this, a tall corridor, 14 m long and lined with decorated slabs of **limestone**, leads to the cult chamber. From the rear wall a tunnel leads in the opposite direction down to the lower-lying decorated burial chamber, likewise lined with slabs. The sarcophagus is set into the floor. The total depth of the rock chambers is 41 m.

Bibliography: H.E. Winlock, in: *BMMA* 18 II (Dec. 1923) 11–19.

Khnumbaef, *see* Babaef

Khonsu, temple of (Karnak)

This temple dedicated to Khonsu, 'Opposite of the Sun' (i.e. the moon), is closely connected with the cult of the **Opet** temple. This well-preserved building was started in the reign of Ramesses III and completed by Ramesses IV, Ramesses XI and Herihor. There is no evidence for a precursor of this temple, built by Amenhotep III. The **pylon** had four **flagpoles**. Behind was a pillared court with a rear hall at a slightly higher level and a **hypostyle hall**, each of them with a side-entrance. Behind is the self-contained accommodation of the deity: a **barque chamber**, a hall with four **columns** (and fitted with a skylight), a cult image chamber with side-chambers, and **stairs** to the roof. Attached to the back of the temple lies the **addorsed temple** of King Teos. The complex is a good example of the strict sectional planning and architectural style of the late Ramesside period. In front of the pylon is a colonnade of King **Taharqa** with four rows of five columns, from which a wide avenue of **sphinxes** leads in the direction of Luxor. Built into the pylon were numerous blocks originating from the **'houses of millions of years'** in western **Thebes**.

Bibliography: Architecturally unexplored, publication expected: Françoise Laroche-Traunecker, *The Temple of Khonsu*, Vol. 3; Maragioglio, *L'Architecture*; C. Traunecker, *Dossiers d'histoire*,

Pillared court of the Khonsu temple of Ramesses III at Karnak

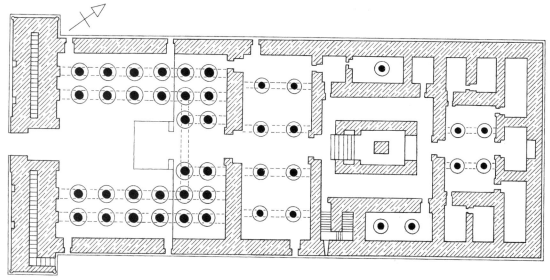

Plan of the Khonsu temple at Karnak

Archeologia 101 (1986) 29–33; Aufrère, *L'Égypte restituée* 110–117; C. Traunecker, La chapelle adossée au temple de Khonsu, in: *Karnak* VI 167–196; F. Laroche-Traunecker, Données nouvelles sur les abords du temple de Khonsou, in: *Karnak* VII 313–337; M. El-Molla et al., L'allée sacrée du temple de Khonsou, in: *Karnak* IX 239–262; The Epigraphic Survey, *The Temple of Khonsu*, Vol 1, *Scenes of King Herihor in the Court* (Chicago 1979).

Khor

The ruins of a large **fortress** dating to the Middle and New Kingdoms, lying on the West Bank of the Nile south of **Buhen**. The **enclosure wall** is c. 250 x 600 m in size and 3.5 m deep, with semi-circular towers. Inside are the remains of some structures.

Bibliography: S. Clark, Ancient Egyptian Frontier Fortresses, in: *JEA* 3 (1916) 162–163; J. Vercoutter, Kor est-il Iken? in: *Kush* 3 (1955) 4–19; H.S. Smith, Kor: Report on the Excavation of the Egypt Exploration Society at Kor, in: *Kush* 14 (1966) 187–221.

Khufu (Cheops), pyramid of

The pyramid of Khufu at **Giza** represents the climax of Egyptian pyramid construction and is regarded as one of the architectural wonders of the world. Its scale, careful workmanship, precision of measurements, mathematical proportions and the difficulties of its construction still puzzle mankind and have unleashed a flood of mostly non-serious 'pyramid literature'. The core of the 'Horizon of Khufu' (area 230.38 sq m, angle of slope 51°50'40", original height 146.59 m, now 138.75 m) consists of local **limestone**. Its outer **casing** is formed of blocks of Tura limestone, whose size diminishes in height towards the top of the pyramid. Only a few blocks remain on the north and west sides following their removal in 1356 by Sultan Hassan. Our understanding of the internal structure is hindered by two unanswered questions: 1) was the provision of three chambers originally intended or is it the result of a change in plans? 2) is the core built in horizontal courses or as sloping mantles after the manner of a **step mastaba**? The entrance lies at the 19th course of the outer casing. A descending corridor leads from there to the deepest chamber, 30 m down inside the rock. Technical problems caused it to be left unfinished, and it was probably replaced by the middle (so-called 'queen's') chamber, 21.71 m above ground level. This chamber is probably better interpreted as a secondary, south or *ka*-tomb of the king. It has an area of 5.23 x

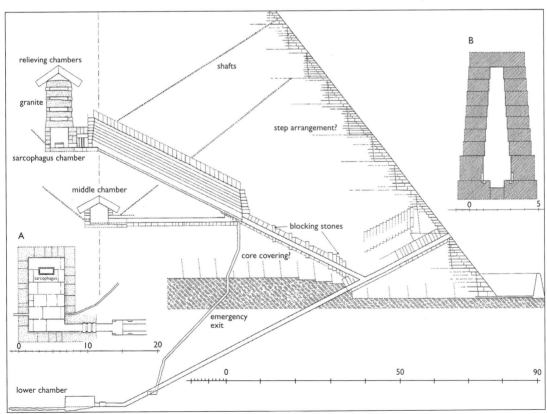

Pyramid of Khufu: section from north to south through the inner chambers, and a section through the ascending gallery

5.76 m and is the first in Egypt known to have a roof of relieving slabs. In its east wall is a recess, 4.725 m high, with a **corbelled vault**, possibly for canopics or a *ka*-statue. The ascending gallery, 46.71 m long and 2.09 m wide, leads to the upper sarcophagus chamber (**portcullis**, Fig.). This stored the 25–26 blocking stones, which were let down into the lower corridor when the pyramid was sealed. For reasons of constructional safety it was roofed by a 8.46 m high corbelled vault, which may itself have been protected above by relieving slabs. Transverse beams, which prevented the blocking stones slipping down prematurely, were secured in small side-niches. The **granite** sarcophagus chamber (5.84 x 10.49 m, height 5.84m) is 43.03 m above ground level. It is roofed with level granite beams, protected by five pressure-relieving chambers; four of these chambers have a flat ceiling of granite beams, while the topmost has a saddle-roof of limestone. From the long side walls of the uppermost and central chambers there are shafts, 20 x 20 cm in section, which lead obliquely upwards through the masonry. Those in the king's chamber lead to the open air, while those from the middle chamber end in the core masonry. A robot sent up the southern shafts of the middle chamber found its way blocked after 65 m by a limestone plug with two embedded copper pegs or pins. These channels have been incorrectly explained as ventilation shafts. They were, rather, intended to allow the royal *ba* to enter and exit. The bottom of the granite sarcophagus, 98.7 x 105.1 x 227.6 cm, is preserved.

In front of the eastern side of the pyramid are the remains of the **pyramid temple** (Fig.), measuring 40.4 x 52.5 m. It has **basalt** paving and there are remains of the bases of the granite pillars which surrounded the court on three sides. A **door recess** at the rear was the entrance to the cult chamber, no longer in existence. In front of the south-east corner (at an angle of slope of 52°) are the remains of a secondary pyramid, only 23 x 23 m in area. Three queens' pyramids (GIa = Hetepheres?, GIb = Meritites, GIc = Henutsen; base length 47.25 m, height 29 m, angle of slope 51 or 52°) are preserved along the east side.

The pyramid of Khufu is surrounded by enormous boat pits: the two on the eastern side had been robbed, while the contents of those on the south side were untouched. From the eastern pit (31.2 m long), a sensationally well-preserved wooden boat, 43.4 m long, was recovered in 1954 and rebuilt in the nearby museum. Directly to the west is another pit, bored into in 1987 to enable explorative photography, which contains another, as yet unexcavated, boat. The remains of a **valley temple** (basalt paving and limestone walls) have been found under the village of Nazlet el-Samman. Excavation has

not yet been possible. The course of the **causeway**, 825 m in length, can be traced on the ground.

Bibliography: Herodotus, *History* II 124–125; Petrie, *Pyramids* 37–95; Ludwig Borchardt, *Längen und Richtungen der vier Grund-kanten der grossen Pyramide bei Gise* (Berlin 1926); Ludwig Borchardt, *Einiges zur dritten Bauperiode der grossen Pyramide bei Gise*, BeiträgeBf 1 (Cairo 1932); J.-Ph. Lauer, Le temple funéraire de Khéops, in: *ASAE* 46 (1947) 245–259; 49 (1949) 111–123; *MRA* IV; George Goyon, La chaussée monumentale et le temple de la vallée de la pyramide de Khéops, in: *BIFAO* 67 (1969) 49–69; George Goyon, *Le secret des bâtisseurs des grandes pyramides Khéops* (Paris 1977); J.-Ph. Lauer, Raison première et utilisation pratique de la 'Grande Galerie' dans la pyramide de Khéops, in: *Festschrift Ricke* 133ff.; J. Brinks, Die Stufenhöhen der Cheops-Pyramide, in: *GM* 48 (1981) 17–23; Mark Lehner, The pyramide tomb of Hetep-heres and the satellite pyramid of Khufu, in: *SDAIK* 19 (1985); Stadelmann, *Pyramiden* 105–125; Stadelmann, *Pyramiden von Giza* 103–174; M. Lehner, The development of the Giza necropolis: The Khufu Project, in: *MDAIK* 41 (1985) 109–143; Zahi Hawass, in: The discovery of the satellite pyramid of Khufu (GI-d), in: *Studies Simpson* I 379–398; Edwards, *Pyramids* 97–119; Lehner, *Complete Pyramids* 108–119.

Kings, tombs of, *see also* Osireion, pyramid, step mastaba

Bibliography (general): D. Arnold and E. Hornung, Königsgrab, in: Helck, *LÄ* III 496–514.

1. Early Period, *see* **Abydos**, **gallery tomb**, **mastaba**, **Saqqara**
2. 3rd Dynasty, *see* **Djoser** precinct, **Sekhemkhet**, **step mastaba**
3. Old Kingdom, *see* **pyramid**, and under name of king
4. Middle Kingdom, *see* **pyramid**, and under name of king

5. New Kingdom

Kings of the 17th Dynasty were buried in Dra Abu el-Naga (in western Thebes), in rock tombs situated beneath pyramids of **brick** and cult chapels. Their location has been lost, although they were discovered and plundered in the 19th century AD.

The essential basic form of the New Kingdom king's tomb does not appear until the reign of Thutmosis I, when the above-ground cult systems (**'house of millions of years'**) became spatially separated from the subterranean burial chambers in the Valley of the Kings. These tombs needed not only to house the burial of the king and the attendant funerary goods, but also to provide wall surfaces to accommodate the books of the royal afterlife, thus fulfilling the symbolic task of showing the king in the barque of the sun on its journey at night through the spheres of the underworld, where the king, now in the form of Osiris, undergoes mystical unification with Re. Instead of a façade, the tomb has underground gates. The principal elements are steep corridors or flights of stairs and **pillared halls**. Until the time of Thutmosis III, these tombs had an oval burial chamber (representing the 12th hour of the night of the Amduat or, perhaps, the underworld as a whole). Up to the Amarna period, tomb entrances were angled like **Osiris tombs**. From the reign of Thutmosis III onwards, the tombs of kings adopted the concept of double tombs (having an upper and a lower funerary area). The entrance corridors passed a well shaft (the 'Cave of Sokar') and ended in the pillared hall which was the tomb of the king, now identified with Osiris as the son of Isis. Steps in the floor of the pillared hall lead to the more elaborate lower sarcophagus chamber, where the Osiris/king becomes united with Re. Side-chambers for funerary equipment become more numerous with time and there is a clear tendency to exceed the dimensions of the predecessor's tomb (wider doors, higher and wider corridors, more pillars).

Beginning in the reign of Horemheb, tombs have a straight axis, while the fundamental idea of the double tomb with a well shaft is retained. The lower sarcophagus hall of Ramesses II has eight pillars, with the sarcophagus sunk in the central nave. From the end of the 19th Dynasty onwards, corridors take the place of entrance stairs and are alternately level and gently sloping. The change in direction of the axis needed in connection with the notion of double tombs was abandoned in the reign of Merenptah, providing a model for all subsequent tombs of kings. Their unfinished, usurped and re-worked condition reflects the situation of royalty in later Ramesside times. The plan had become much simplified: pillars, side-rooms and an upper tomb had disappeared; only the dimensions of corridors and sarcophagi had increased.

An exceptional tomb, KV 5, at present being investigated, has a central hall of 16 pillars from which additional chambers and three corridors branch off with dozens of further small chambers. This is either a multiple burial place for members of Ramesses II's family, or it may be a symbolic structure representing a model of the underworld.

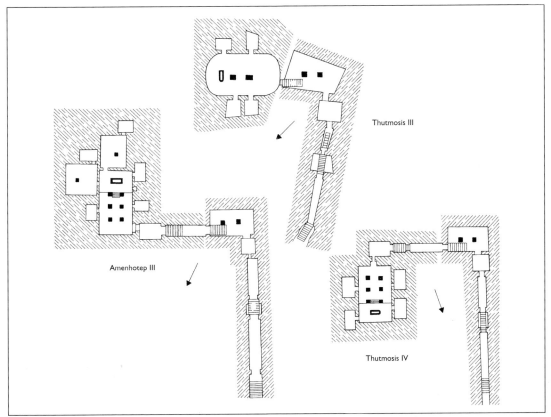

Development of Theban kings' tombs from Thutmosis III to Amenhotep III, showing both 'upper' and 'lower' tombs

Kings' tombs

Main valley

Thutmosis I and Hatshepsut	KV 20
Thutmosis II	KV 42
Thutmosis III	KV 34
Amenhotep II	KV 35
Thutmosis IV	KV 43
Tutankhamun	KV 62
Horemheb	KV 57
Ramesses I	KV 16
Sety I	KV 17
Ramesses II	KV 7
Sons (?) of Ramesses II	KV 5
Merenptah	KV 8
Sety II	KV 15
Amenmesse	KV 10
Siptah	KV 47
Tawosret and Sethnakht	KV 14
Ramesses III	KV 11
Ramesses IV	KV 2
Ramesses V and VI	KV 9
Ramesses VII	KV 1
Ramesses IX	KV 6
Ramesses XI	KV 4

Western valley

Amenhotep III	WV 22
Ay	WV 23

For building techniques, see **rock tomb construction**. See also the royal tomb at **Amarna** (4.).

Bibliography: H.E. Winlock, The tombs of the kings of the Seventeenth Dynasty at Thebes, in: *JEA* 10 (1924) 217–277; Elizabeth Thomas, *The Royal Necropoleis of Thebes* (Princeton 1966); F. Abitz, *Die religiöse Bedeutung der sog. Grabräuberschächte in den ägypt. Königsgrabern der 18. bis 20. Dynastie*, ÄA 26 (Wiesbaden 1974); Elizabeth Thomas, The 'Well' in Kings' Tombs of Bibân el-Moluk, in: *JEA* 64 (1978) 80–83; Erik Hornung, Struktur und Entwicklung der Gräber im Tal der Könige, in: *ZÄS* 105 (1978) 59–66; Erik Hornung, Struktur und Entwicklung der Gräber im Tal der Könige, in: *ZÄS* 105 (1978) 59–66; John Romer, *Valley of the Kings* (New York 1981); Erik Hornung, *Tal der Könige* (Zurich/Munich 1982), new edition: *The Valley of the Kings* (New York 1990) 26–31; H. Altenmüller, Bemerkungen zu den Königsgräbern des Neuen Reiches, in: *SAK* 10 (1983) 25–61; F. Abitz, *König und Gott* (ÄA 40, 1984); A.M. Dodson,

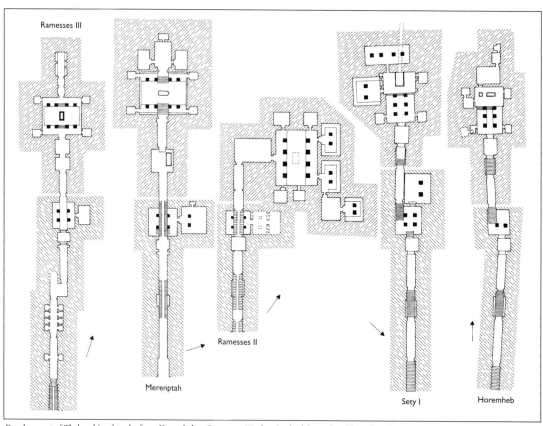

Development of Theban kings' tombs from Horemheb to Ramesses III, showing both 'upper' and 'lower' tombs

The Tombs of the Kings of the early Eighteenth Dynasty at Thebes, in: *ZÄS* 115 (1988) 110–123; W. Helck, Königsgräbertal, in: Helck, *LÄ* III 514–526; F. Abitz, Die Entwicklung der Grabachsen in den Königsgräbern im Tal der Könige, in: *MDAIK* 45 (1989) 1–25; F. Abitz, Baugeschichte und Dekoration des Grabes Ramses' VI., in: *Orbis Biblicus et Orientalis* 89 (Freiburg-Göttingen 1989); C.N. Reeves, *Valley of the Kings: The Decline of a Royal Necropolis* (London-New York 1991); Erik Hornung, *Sety-ein Pharaonengrab* (Basel 1991) 32–43; Erik Hornung, *The Tomb of Pharaoh Seti I/Das Grab Sethos'I.* (Zurich/Munich 1991); C.N. Reeves and Richard H. Wilkinson, *The Complete Valley of the Kings* (London 1997); Schulz, *Egypt* 216–243; Kent Weeks, *The Lost Tomb* (New York 1997); N. and H. Strudwick, *Thebes in Egypt* (London 1999) 92–119.

6. Late Period

Rulers of this period who resided in Lower Egypt had their tombs built in the forecourt of the main temple of their capital city; in most cases these probably consisted of a simple chamber with a small mortuary temple erected above this. In comparison with contemporary private monumental complexes, these were modest tombs and are evidence of the gradually fading concept of Egypt being ruled by a divine king.

a) Situated south of Mitrahina next to a temple precinct (250 m to the west of the colossal statue of Ramesses II) a group of tomb chambers belonging to the royal family of the 22nd Dynasty, including the tomb of

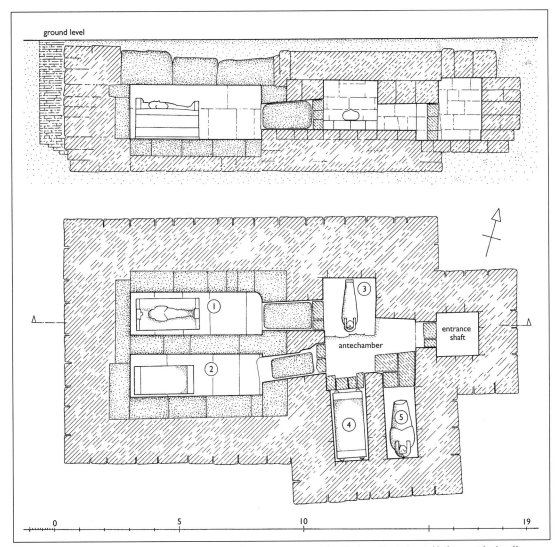

Kings' tomb III at Tanis. 1: Psusennes I; 2: Queen Mutnodjmet (later King Amenemope); 3: Sheshonq II; 4: Prince Ankhefenmut; 5: leader of bowmen, Wendebadjedet

Sheshonq, a son of Osorkon II. The front and inner walls of these rectangular chambers are richly decorated.

b) In 1939 P. Montet discovered, within the Amun temple precinct at **Tanis**, the tombs of kings of the 21st and 22nd Dynasties, some of which were undisturbed. The precinct, which measures 50 x 60 m, contained the tombs of Kings Psusennes I, Amenemope, Osorkon II, Sheshonq III and persons close to them. They consisted of **crypts** entered via an entrance shaft or ramp and with an antechamber and longish tomb chamber. They were potentially threatened by sub-soil water and so were not very deeply sunk below the paving of the court. There are three tomb chambers (with a large number of re-used blocks). Their superstructures, which may have been like those of the tombs of the kings of **Sais**, have completely disappeared. Only 4 out of probably 17 tombs of this kind of the 21st–22nd Dynasties have been found.

c) The burial complex of the 26th Dynasty kings (Apries, Amasis) was, according to an ancient description, situated in the forecourt of the temple of Neith at **Sais**; the tomb of Amasis was, on that evidence, constructed above ground and surmounted by a kiosk with palm columns. The location of the tombs, destroyed by the army of Cambyses, has not yet been discovered. A sarcophagus (?) of Psamtek II has been found at Damanhur.

d) Some indications have been found for the existence of a 29th Dynasty royal necropolis (Nephritis) in the south-eastern corner of the temple precinct of **Mendes**. The tomb chapels were destroyed by the Persians in 343 BC. The 30th Dynasty tombs of Teo and Nectanebo II, which were probably at **Sebennytos**, are lost (the sarcophagus of Nectanebo II was found re-used at Alexandria and is now in the British Museum). The tomb of Nectanebo I is likely to have been somewhere in the Memphite area.

Bibliography: For a): A. Badawy, Das Grab des Kronprinzen Scheschonk, in: *ASAE* 54 (1956) 153–177. For b): Pierre Montet, *La nécropole royale de Tanis*, 3 Vols (I Paris 1947, II Paris 1951, III Paris 1960); R. Stadelmann, Das Grab im Tempelhof, der Typus des Königsgrabes in der Spätzeit, in: *MDAIK* 27 (1971) 111–123; R. Stadelmann, Tempelbestattung, in: Helck, *LÄ* VI 376–377; *Tanis, L'ôr des pharaons*, Exhibition Catalogue (Paris 1987) 200–272; George Goyon, *La découverte des trésors de Tanis* (Ed. Persea 1987). For c): Strabo, *Geographica* XVII 802; Herodotus, *History* II 169–175, III 16. For d): *Description* V, Plate 41; Henri Gauthier, *Le livre des rois d'Égypte* IV (Cairo 1916) 181, 191; Hanna Jenni, *Das Dekorationsprogramm des Sarkophages Nektanebos' II*, Aegyptiaca Helvetica 12 (Geneva 1986); *Bull. Canadian Mediterranean Institute* 13 (1993) 4.

7. Ptolemies

Alexander the Great and the Ptolemies are buried in the Sema (Soma) at the centre of **Alexandria** (tomb of Alexander the Great), a burial complex thought to be situated in a western part of the palace grounds. Set up by Ptolemy I and Ptolemy II for Alexander, it was replaced by Ptolemy IV with the construction of a mausoleum jointly for Alexander and the earlier Ptolemies. The later Ptolemies were buried in individual structures, some of them taking the shape of a pyramid; they were destroyed towards the end of the 3rd century AD.

Bibliography: Strabo, *Geographica* XVII 1,8, 794; Zenobius III 94; H. Thiersch, Die alexandrinsche Königsnekropole, in: *JDAI* 25 (1910) 55–97; P.M. Fraser, *Ptolemaic Alexandria* I (Oxford 1972) 15–17.

Kiosk, *see also* barque station, canopy

A shady covering, like a **canopy**, resting on wooden columns, converted in Egyptian architecture to a structure built of stone. It is found in many places, consisting of a rectangle of columns or pillars (4 x 6, 4 x 8, 6 x 8 and so on), which were linked by a **screen wall**. Some kiosks are open to the sky; others are roofed with timber beams and canvas. Kiosks served to protect cult images and the barques of gods after they had emerged from the temple. For this reason they often stood on a processional route or on a **platform**. Kiosks are attested to from the Middle Kingdom onwards (**Chapelle Blanche**), and were particularly popular in the Ethiopian period: there are several at **Karnak**, **Luxor**, the **Month** precinct at Karnak, **Medinet Habu** (18th Dynasty temple) and at the Hibis temple of **El-Kharga**. Roman examples exist at **Dendera** (**roof chapel**) and **Qertassi** and at **Philae** is the vast kiosk of **Augustus** at **Philae** (15.4 x 20.7 m at the base, 15.45 m high). From the Roman period there is the Meroitic kiosk at Naga, which is modelled on Egyptian kiosks.

Bibliography: Borchardt, *Tempel mit Umgang* 13–20; A.M. Badawy, The approach to the Egyptian temple, in: *ZÄS* 102 (1975); W. Helck, Kiosk, in: Helck, *LÄ* III 441–442.

The kiosk of Nectanebo I in the Hibis temple at El-Kharga

Kom Auskhim, *see* Karanis

Kom el-Abd

Ruins of a brick structure of the 18th Dynasty, 3.5 km south of the palace of **Malqata**, consisting of a 40 x 45 m podium, 3.75 m in height, surrounded by an **enclosure wall** and approached by a ramp. Adjacent are three relatively large and two smaller houses. According to B.J. Kemp this site was used for the erection of tents at a royal hunting camp. The podium might have been employed as a throne **kiosk** similar to that at Kom el-Samak (**Malqata**).

Bibliography: B.J. Kemp, A building of Amenophis III, Kôm el-'Abd, in: *JEA* 63 (1977) 71–82.

Kom el-Ahmar, *see* Hierakonpolis

Kom Ombo

A double temple of Sobek and Horus, built in several phases. The erection of the main part of the temple began in the reign of Ptolemy VI Philometor, and decoration continued into the 2nd and 3rd centuries AD. The temple has two parallel sanctuaries, each with a separate approach. A stone **enclosure wall** (50.9 x 96 m) surrounded both the temple proper and the columned court. The entrance through the stone enclosure, which faces the Nile, was not an actual **pylon** but a double portal. Beyond the court lies the magnificent

pronaos with three rows of five columns, 12 m high. This is followed by a **pillared hall** (with two rows of five columns), three antechambers (among them an offering room and a chamber for guest gods), and the two sanctuaries, surrounded by corridors, with black granite bases for the barques of the gods. There was a New Year's festival court with *wabet* located in the northern half of the temple; this differs from the temples of **Edfu** and **Dendera** because of the temple's location on the East Bank. Many **crypts** are built into the temple walls.

The majority of a once large **birth house** of Ptolemy IX Euergetes II (Physkon), which stood directly in front of the temple, has been swept away by the Nile. The proportions of the temple are extremely accurate and superbly executed in terms of building techniques and sculpting. Earlier structures (12th Dynasty, Amenhotep I, Thutmosides, Ramesses II) are attested to by blocks.

Bibliography: *Description* I, Plates 39-46; Jacques de Morgan et al., Kom Ombos, in: *Catalogue des monuments et inscriptions de l'Egypte antique*, I 2–3 (Vienna 1895-1909); Alexandre Badawi, *Kom-Ombo, Sanctuaires* (Cairo 1952 ?); P. Lacau, Notes sur les plans des temples d'Edfou et de Kôm-Ombo, in: *ASAE* 52 (1952) 221–228; A. Gutub, Kom Ombo, Les textes et leur étude, in: *Textes et langages de l'Égypte pharaonique*, Vol. 3, Hommage à J.-F. Champollion (Cairo 1972) 239–247; A. Gutub, *Textes fondamentaux de la théologie de Kôm Ombo* (Cairo 1972, 1973); Aufrère, *L'Égypte restituée* 259–261; A. Gutub, Kom Ombo, in: Helck, *LÄ* III 675–683.

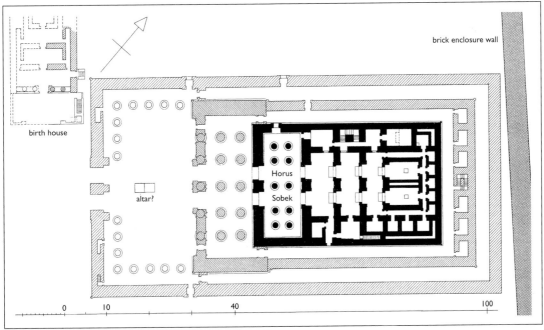

Plan of the temple of Kom Ombo, showing construction periods (see text)

Koptos

Ruins of a formerly important **town**, which was destroyed prior to scientific research at the end of the 19th century with almost nothing saved. A large temple precinct of Min, measuring 235 x 260 m, had an **enclosure wall** 10 m thick with a **gateway**. Two **pylons** used to lead to a triple temple for Hathor/Isis, Min and Horus, built by Ptolemies II–IV. There are remains of some **Hathor columns** 10 m high. Enlargements dating from the Roman period provided three sets of parallel approach stairs (see **Kom Ombo**). Lying below these are some remains of the foundations of an earlier structure of Thutmosis III, measuring 27 x 36 m, with granite pillars and re-used parts of earlier buildings of the Old and Middle Kingdoms. The remains of three unique **colossal statues** of Min, 4.3 m high, indicate the existence of a cult structure from the Naqada II period. The south-west corner of the enclosure is taken up by the remains of a temple, possibly to Geb, with three consecutive gate structures of Caligula and Nectanebo II, accommodating in between the remains of a 'middle temple' of Thutmosis III renewed in the Graeco-Roman period. On the northern border of the area of ruins at Koptos is the small temple of **El-Qal'a**.

Bibliography: Sir Gardner Wilkinson, *Modern Egypt and Thebes* (London 1843) 129–130; W.M. Flinders Petrie, *Koptos* (London 1896); A.J. Reinach, *Rapports sur les Fouilles de Koptos* (Paris 1910); R. Weill, Koptos, in: *ASAE* 11 (1911) 97–141; G.H. Fisher, Koptos, in: Helck, *LÄ* III 737–740; B. Williams, *Narmer and the Coptos Colossi*, in: *JARCE* 25 (1988) 35–59; Claude Traunecker, *Coptos, Hommes et dieux sur le parvis de Geb*, Orientalia Lovaniensia Analecta 43 (Leuven 1992).

Kubban (Quban)

A **fortress** of Senwosret I on the East Bank of the Nile opposite **Dakka**, 110 km south of Aswan, at the entrance to the Wadi Allaqi, where there are gold mines. It had a rectangular **enclosure wall**, measuring approximately 70 x 125 m, fortified by semi-circular turrets, and included a keep with bastions and a gate. It was strengthened in the reign of Senwosret III and renewed under Sety I. There are the remains of an earlier structure of the Old Kingdom, and of several temples, found both inside and outside the walls of the fortress .

Bibliography: Walter B. Emery, *The Excavations and Survey between Wadi es-Sebua and Adindan* (Cairo 1935) 26–33.

Kumma

Rectangular **fortress**, covering approximately 70 x 117 m, dating originally from the 5th Dynasty, constructed on a projecting rock on the East Bank of the Nile opposite **Semna**. The **enclosure wall**, which projects in one place, is 5.5–6 m in thickness, embracing in the north-west corner a small stone-clad temple built of brick, founded by Hatshepsut and Thutmosis III and re-built by Amenhotep II. The sanctuary has two statue chambers and four antechambers. The history of its construction is uncertain. The temple was removed to Khartoum in 1966.

Bibliography: S. Clarke, Ancient Egyptian Frontier Fortresses, in: *JEA* 3 (1916) 172–174; Dows Dunham and Jozef Janssen, *Semna Kumma, Second Cataract Forts*, Vol. 2 (Boston 1960) 113–128; Ricardo A. Caminos, *Semna-Kumma*, 2 Vols (London 1998).

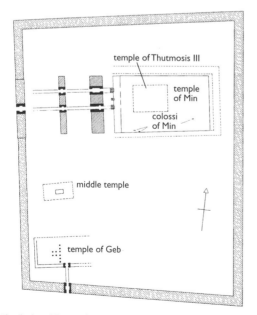

Sketch plan of the temple complex of Min at Koptos

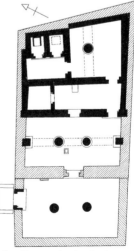

Plan of the temple at Kumma, showing the division between the use of stone and of mud brick

L

Labyrinth, *see* **Amenemhat III**

Laying blocks

Walls were erected on the levelled upper surface of the foundation blocks. **Casing** blocks are frequently found placed in deepened bedding grooves, whereas the **core masonry** rested on the raised **boss** of the **foundations**. Blocks were transported on **sledges** or rollers and levered sideways (not from the front) into position. Holes for **levers** were provided in the surface of the blocks of the lower course and in the block to be moved (on the lever side). The holes were closed with plaster where work was being carried out carefully. Fine gypsum **mortar** was often used as a lubricant. From the 12th Dynasty, and increasingly in the Ptolemaic and Roman periods, strips of stone, 10–30 cm wide and up to 3 m long, were roughened on the surface of a course of blocks for the application of gypsum mortar. In pharaonic buildings, grooves for **gypsum** on touch **joints** were less carefully dealt with. In some cases joints were deliberately held open by the insertion of grids of wood to enable later filling with gypsum. Walls were erected starting from both corners. A thin stone closed any resulting gap, in some cases fitted using a rope which ran through a channel. The use of regular courses of rectangular block masonry (ashlar) was rare in pharaonic Egypt and only developed in the Late Period. New blocks were set into the lower course to a sufficient depth to achieve a continuous level upper edge. Dovetailing of blocks required time-consuming work by a stonemason at the time they were laid. Hence, dowelling (**cramps**) was carried out as needed, and the free end of a touch joint was dressed to fit the next block (**anathyrosis**).

Bibliography: Clark, *AEM* 96–116; Arnold, *Building* 115–120; Golvin, *Karnak* 109–113.

Lever

Levers, along with ropes and rollers, were the basic equipment used by Egyptian workers in lifting, pushing and turning loads (**sliding blocks**, Fig.; **transport**). The use of levers and their size can be recognised from leverage holes: often 20 x 30 cm. The **casing** blocks of pyramids have leverage holes at the lower edge of the side surface, which were filled in with pieces of stone or **mortar** after the blocks had been put into place (**Bent Pyramid, Khufu, Senwosret I**). Depending on requirements, often whole series of levers were deployed on larger blocks, each one operated by several workmen (e.g. in the raising, shifting and overturning of **obelisks**). Levers were suitable for vertical movement, alternately raising and underpinning one end of the load. Modern experiments confirm the capabilities of using levers.

Bibliography: Engelbach, *Obelisks* 24, 37; Reisner, *Mycerinus* 74–75, 272; Pierre Lacau and Henri Chevrier, *Une chapelle d'Hatshepsout* (Cairo 1977) 9; Arnold, *Building* 71–72, 270–271.

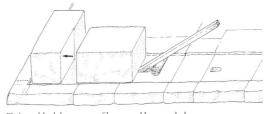

Fitting a block by means of levers and leverage holes

Lime

The use in Egypt of burnt lime is not attested to until the Ptolemaic period; in prior periods its place is usually taken by pure **gypsum**. Latest results reveal that there was earlier use at **Meidum**.

Laying of wall blocks, either in a pre-prepared sunken bed (A) or a subsequent deepening of the ground level at the foot of the wall (B)

Bibliography: Lucas, *Ancient Egyptian Materials and Industries* (London 1962) 74–76; Jean Jacquet, *Le Trésor de Thoutmosis Ier* (Cairo 1994) 125-26; Arnold, *Building* 291–294.

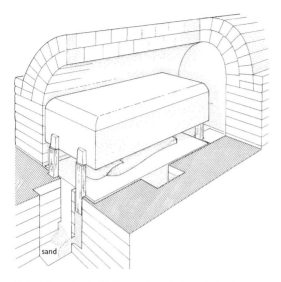

Method of lowering the lid of a sarcophagus in the tomb of Neferibre-Sa-Neith at Saqqara

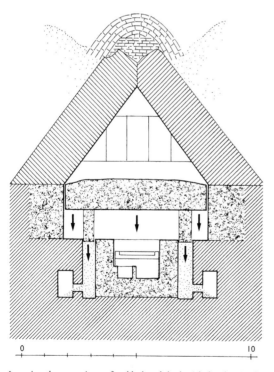

Lowering the quartzite roofing blocks of the burial chamber in the pyramid of Khendjer at Saqqara

Limestone

One of the most commonly used building materials of Egypt, from the 1st Dynasty onwards (tombs at **Helwan**, the precinct of **Djoser**), which became especially prominent in the Old Kingdom in **mastabas** and pyramids. In the Middle Kingdom **sandstone** started to compete with it in construction work, but limestone continued to be used in the **Hatshepsut** temple and Ramesses II's temples at **Abydos**. It was occasionally used in the Ptolemaic period. The two main variants are: 1) porous limestone of an inferior quality, which was used mostly in **foundations** and the **core masonry** of walls, 2) harder and better-quality limestone, mainly used in visible surfaces, casings and similar. The specific gravity of limestone is 1.7–2.6 (porous) and 2.65–2.85 (dense). **Stone quarries** are widespread from Tura and Masara, near Cairo, throughout Middle Egypt down to El-Dibabiyah, near **Mo'alla**.

Bibliography: Clark, *AEM* 12–21; Lucas, *AEMI* 52–55; C. Traunecker, Kalkstein, in: Helck, *LÄ* III 301–303; Arnold, *Building* 27–36; De Putter, *Pierres* 61–69; Klemm, *Steine* 29–197; Nicholson, *Materials* 40–42.

Lowering heavy loads

Sarcophagi and sections of tomb chambers weighing several tonnes were lowered either through sloping corridors or in deep shafts. Rope grooves and drill holes in the lids of sarcophagi, as well as in blocking stones, plus sockets for beams in the side walls of corridors and shafts, show that ropes were used which passed over revolving beams, occasionally involving a change of direction. In the **mastaba** at **Beit Khallaf**, blocking stones of 6–7 tonnes were let down 25 m on ropes. **Paving** slabs were frequently lowered into place using ropes passing through grooves and could be easily lifted again. In the late 12th Dynasty and in the vast tomb shafts of the Late Period the heavy **roof** of the burial chamber was lowered with the help of free-flowing sand, in the following way: while the chamber was still open, the block rested on four posts standing in shafts filled with sand. As the sand was removed, the props would sink into the shafts and the lid would be lowered onto the sarcophagus. One must assume that heavy loads were lowered into shafts by digging away the sand directly below, but there is no evidence for this; however, the **caisson** method is attested to.

Bibliography: Arnold, *Building* 73–79

Luxor, temple of

One of the most important Egyptian **temples**, connected to **Karnak** by a 2.5 km long avenue of **sphinxes** (Fig.) to form an essential component of the Theban cult and temple programme. The temple, erected by Amenhotep III, replaced an earlier structure set up during the Middle Kingdom and modified by Hatshepsut. The front section of the original complex (a **barque station** for the triad of Karnak) consists of a large columned court onto which a **pronaos** opens with 32 particularly beautiful papyrus **columns** (**abacus**, Fig.). Behind lies the **pillared hall**, offering room and the **barque chambers** for Amun, Mut and Khonsu with their side-rooms. The rear part is a cult place for a local Amun, consisting of a transverse pillared hall (compare **Akhmenu**), the Amun sanctuary and many statue chapels. In front of the columned court, forming the closing element of the temple, Tutankhamun constructed what was in effect a gigantic closed **kiosk** in the form of a colonnade consisting of two lines of seven papyrus columns (inside height 21.20 m), lit by two rows of clerestory windows. Ramesses II extended the whole complex to a length of 245 m with the addition of a columned court and a **pylon** with two **obelisks** in front, the western of which was taken to Paris in 1831. In front of the façade of the pylon and in the forecourt are 16 **colossal statues** of Ramesses II. Five more colossi, usurped from Amenhotep III, were added on the occasion of the second *sed*-festival of Ramesses II. In front of the pylon, Shabaka erected a hall with four rows of five columns, as an additional **barque station**.

The temple of Luxor served as an important way station for Amun of Karnak and the rites connected with the renewal of the world observed at the Opet festival, ten-day festivals and the valley festival. The concept of the temple as the location for the annual celebration of the divine birth of the king and the awarding to him of the divine *ka* has recently been discussed. In the Roman period it formed the centre of a fort (**fortress**) with an imperial cult place in the eight-column hall. An ancient

Colonnaded court of the temple of Luxor

burial of 26 royal and divine statues (now in the Luxor Museum) was discovered in 1989 in the court of Amenhotep III.

Bibliography: *Description* III, Plates 6–18; Plate 62; L. Borchardt, Zur Geschichte des Luqsortempels, in: *ZÄS* 34 (1896) 122–138; R.A. Schwaller de Lubicz, *Le temple de l'homme: L'apet du sud à Louxor*, 3 Vols (Paris 1957); Helmut Brunner, *Die südlichen Räume des Tempels von Luxor* (Mainz 1977); P. Barguet, Luxor, in: Helcks, *LÄ* III 1103–1107; L. Bell, Luxor temple and the cult of the royal ka, in: *JNES* 44 (1985) 251–294; M. Azim, Le grand pylone de Louxor: un essai d'analyse architecturale et technique, in: *Mélanges offerts à Jean Vercoutter* (Paris 1985) 19–34. W.J. Murnane, False doors and cult practices inside Luxor Temple, in: *Mélanges Gamal Eddin Mokhtar* (Cairo 1986) 135–148; Égypte, *Louqsor Temple du Ka royal*, Dossiers histoire et archéologie 101 (1986); Afrère, *L'égypte réstituée* 127–141; C. van Siclen, A Kiosk (?) of Shabako at Luxor Temple, *Varia Aegyptiaca* 6 (1990) 177–183; Mohammed El-Saghir, *Das Statuenversteck im Luxortempel*, Antike Welt 22 (Special Issue 1991); Lanny Bell, The New Kingdom 'divine' temple: the example of Luxor, in: Byron Shafer, Ed., *Temples of Ancient Egypt* (Cornell 1997) 127–184; N. and H. Strudwick, Thebes in Egypt (London 1999) 67–71. For obelisk in Paris: Prisse d'Avennes, *Histoire*, Plate 62; Bernadette Menu, *L'obélisque de la Concorde* (Paris 1987).

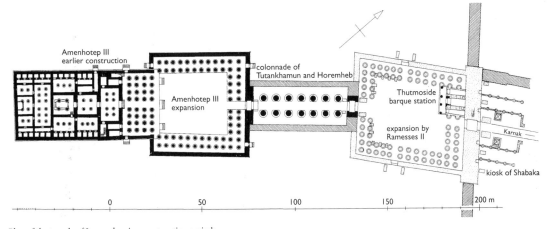
Plan of the temple of Luxor, showing construction periods

M

Malqata

A palace **town** of Amenhotep III on the Theban West Bank, situated next to the vast, c. 200,000 sq m harbour basin (**Birket Habu**) on its eastern side and south of the king's **'house of millions of years'**. Standing at its northern end is a festival hall associated with a **brick**-built temple of Amun. Further to the south are the separate North and Main **Palaces,** and the South Palace, joined to the latter by its eastern wing. The Main Palace, c. 57 x 135 m, has an outside reception courtyard and a throne hall, adjacent to which lies the suite of royal accommodation with a bedroom and bathroom. The centre is taken up by the festival hall, 30 m in length, furnished with two rows of eight carved wooden columns onto which four separate individual apartments open on both sides (probably not 'harims'). The interior was richly decorated: walls and door frames were inlaid with faience and ornamented with golden rosettes, gilded plaster figuring and inlaid wooden **cavetto cornices**. Some of the wall and ceiling paintings are largely capable of reconstruction (egrets in flight framed by rosettes in the bedroom; **ceiling construction**, Fig.). There are many individual dwellings and workmen's settlements (the 'North Village', the 'West Village' enclosed within a wall, and the 'South Village').

After the abandonment of the town in the reign of Horemheb, it was destroyed by rain and fires as well as falling victim to inexpert excavation methods and subsequent vandalism. 2.5 km to the south lies Kom el-Samak, a throne kiosk standing on a high platform and approachable by ramps (**Kom el-Abd**).

Bibliography: Robb de Peyster Tytus, *A Preliminary Report of the Re-excavations of the Palace of Amenhotep III* (New York 1903);

Remains of wall and ceiling paintings in Amenhotep III's bedroom in the palace of Malqata

H.E. Winlock, The work of the Egyptian Expedition, in: *BMMA* 7 (1912) 185–189; H.G. Evelyn-White, The Egyptian Expedition, in: *BMMA* 10 (1915) 253–256; A.Lansing, The Egyptian Expedition, in: *BMMA* 13 (March 1918) 4–18; R. Engelbach, The Great Lake of Amenophis III at Medinet Habu, in: *BIE* 20 (1938) 51–61; B. Kemp and D. O'Connor, An ancient Nile harbour, University Museum excavations at the 'Birket Habu', in: *The Inter. Journ. of Nautical Arch. and Underwater Exploration* 3 (1974) 101–134; D. O'Connor, The University Museum excavations at the palace-city of Malkata, in: *Expedition* 21 (1979) 52–53; D. O'Connor, Malqata, in: Helck, *LÄ* III 1173–1177; Aufrère, *L'Égypte restituée* 150–151; *Malqata-South I Kom el-Samak, Archeological and Architectural Reports* (Waseda University, Tokyo 1983); Shin-ichi Nichimoto, The ceiling paintings of the harem rooms at the palace of Malqata, in: *GM* 127 (1992) 69–80; *Studies on the Palace of Malqata. Investigations at the Palace of Malqata 1985–1988* (Waseda University, Tokyo 1993).

Mammisi, see birth house

Marble

A type of stone which is relatively rare in Egypt and used exclusively for vessels and sculptures, obtained predominantly from Gebel el-Rocham (Eastern Desert).

Bibliography (general): Luciana and Tiziano Mannoni, *Marble. The History of a Culture* (New York-Oxford 1985); R. Gundlach, Marmor, in: Helck, *LÄ* III 1194–1195; De Putter, *Pierres* 108–110; Klemm, *Steine* 427–429; Nicholson, *Materials* 44–45.

Maru temple, see also barque station, Meret

A type of sanctuary mainly known from texts and depictions, surrounded by gardens and situated near a pond or canal. The only examples so far discovered are two building complexes south of **Amarna** (El-Hauwata), possibly to be identified with the Maru-aten known from inscriptions, but their intricate layout remains largely a mystery to us. They are interpreted as miniature representations of the cosmos, reflecting the watercourses which had to be traversed by the sun god on his journey through the night. The Maru temples associated with Ptolemaic temples also have a connection with the cult of the sun.

Bibliography: Peet, *City of Akhenaten* I 109–124; Chassinet, Le mar du Roi Menibré à Edfou, in: *BIFAO* 30 (1930) 299–303; Alliot, *Le Culte d'Horus à Edfou au temps des Ptolémées* (Cairo 1949–54) 575, 581; A. Badawi, Maru-Aten: pleasure resort or temple?, in: *JEA* 42 (1956) 58–64; R. Stadelmann, Swt-R'w als Kultstätte des Sonnengottes im Neuen Reich, in: *MDAIK* 25 (1969) 159–178.

Masonry, see also brick construction, casing, core masonry, pyramid construction

During pharaonic times, stone construction in Egypt was dominated by the archaic practice of piling up huge blocks of masonry which were then, like sculptures, carved into buildings, creating cave-like hollow spaces. From the 30th Dynasty onwards, 'building' in a stricter sense developed, in that carefully prepared blocks of equal size and shape were used, being laid in regular courses of equal heights (isodomic construction). Long experience with building in brick and the occasional appearance of ashlar masonry in pharaonic buildings prove that Egyptian builders were aware of the two different approaches to building in stone; however, in most cases they opted for traditional methods.

The **core masonry** of Egyptian stone structures before the New Kingdom usually consisted of rough blocks of local stone cased within better material. The surface of the wall ideally showed no gaps, and could be decorated or inscribed. The direction of **joints** and surface condition was therefore unimportant.

Egyptian masonry can be divided into types, in the first place according to the internal structure of the masonry, as follows:

1a) Rough stone walls made of irregular stones set into sand and **mortar**, usually with a steep **batter**.

1b) Free-standing vertical walls, using rectangular blocks, only one or two stones thick with headers used as through-stones; often used to separate rooms.

1c) Free-standing walls with an infill, consisting of a rough stone core with an outer **casing**; often noticeably inclined and rounded top stones.

1d) Walls of ashlar masonry several blocks thick, made of large and regularly shaped blocks.

Secondly, support masonry is frequently found, the most common variants being:

2a) Walls of irregular rough stone masonry.

2b) Rough stone masonry walls cased with blocks or slabs.

2c) Rock core walls cased with blocks or slabs.

2d) Walls built of block masonry cased with blocks or slabs.

A third typology based on the structure of the surface is less clear-cut:

3a) Rectangular stonework consisting of stepped courses.

3b) 'Trapezoidal' stonework is not a truly separate type but occurs in a variety of masonry. True polygonal masonry, which is found frequently outside Egypt (in Greek and Inca architecture), is unknown in Egypt.

3c) Masonry consisting of blocks of regular size, laid in courses of equal height with regular changes of joints (isodomic construction), is less common.

3d) A mixture of techniques is frequently found.

3e) Wholly irregular masonry is very uncommon.

3f) A form common in **brick construction**, consisting of regularly alternating layers with headers and stretchers, is rare in stone masonry (see **talatat**).

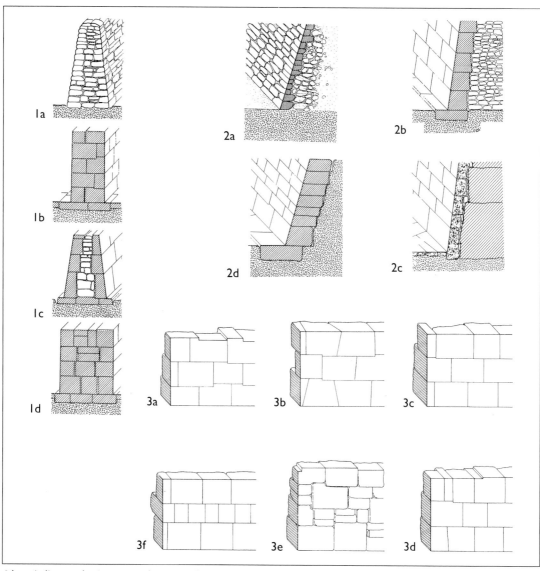

Schematic diagrams showing patterns of masonry. 1: free-standing walls in cross-section; 2: retaining walls with casing blocks; 3: free-standing walls from the front

Bibliography: Clark, *AEM*, 96–116; Arnold, *Building* 148–158; Golvin, *Karnak* 80–83, 111–112.

Mastaba

A free-standing tomb, the superstructure of which resembles a rectangular mass of brick or stone with sloping walls (Ar. *mastaba* = 'bench'), forming a stylised mound of earth as a 'house of the dead'. From the time of the Unification (the earliest examples at Naqada, **Saqqara** and **Tarkhan**) until the end of the Middle Kingdom, the mastaba, together with the **rock tomb,** was the predominant type of tomb in Egypt. With the introduction of the pyramid, mastabas became a purely private form of tomb.

From the beginning there were two variants, which were created and interpreted as a contrasting pair (Upper versus Lower Egyptian, nomadic versus rural, royal versus non-royal ?). The exterior of the first type was smooth, its east-facing side having two initially open cult places (**false door**), embodying the Egyptian concept of the house tomb (*serdab*, Fig.).

The second variant is more striking and is primarily represented by the 1st Dynasty tombs at Naqada (tomb of **Menes**), **Giza**, **Saqqara** and **Tarkhan**. Their size varies (c. 15–25 x 40–60 m) and they are **niched** on all sides with richly colourful paintwork, intended to represent a royal palace or **divine fortress**. They were probably covered with a **vaulted** top with raising side walls. The base is made of **brick** and protrudes at the front; it is surrounded by a brick **enclosure wall** and rows of servants' tombs. The core of the mastaba is divided by cross-walls into up to 50 cells (**cellular construction**); the five central cells below the surface are burial chambers and magazines. They were constructed as open pits and roofed after the burial using heavy beams and then filled in. Built inside some brick mastabas there are shallow (not visible) symbolic mounds. Later, the rooms above ground were also expanded into magazines.

As tombs became increasingly expensive, the superstructure had to be complete prior to the burial, and, from Dewen onwards, this led to the tomb being accessible by a stairway from outside. The type of tomb complex in use until the end of the 1st Dynasty was further developed in the 2nd and 3rd Dynasties, with the subterranean rooms becoming copies of the deceased person's dwelling. Their vast magazines and bath installations reflect all of this life's necessities (**Giza**, **Saqqara**, **Beit Khallaf**, Raqaqna, Naga' el-Deir).

The predominantly niched mastaba of the 1st Dynasty was superseded by a simpler form in the 2nd Dynasty, in which the niching was confined first to the east side and later to the west wall of the corridor, which had by now been placed in front of the façade. The niching was originally in the form of small sections, which soon changed to become projections and recesses decorated with flat grooves.

In the 3rd Dynasty a decisive change in Egyptian religious concepts about death brought about a separation and modification in the construction of private and royal tombs. Moreover, the realisation that accumulations of grave goods would fall victim to robbery brought an elaboration of the ritualistic provision for the dead, with the abandonment of extensive subterranean complexes, which were replaced by burial chambers accessible via a simple vertical shaft in the centre of the mastaba. The principal cult area, which had formerly been open to the air, changed in stages until it became a chapel built into the core of the mastaba or an independent structure in front of the cult place (**Nefermaat and Atet**, Fig.). The development reflected local tradition. It was the also the start of a conflict which continued throughout the Old Kingdom concerning the establishment of cult rooms in

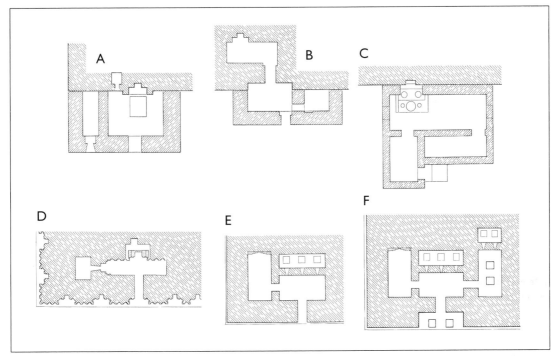

Cult chambers of the Old Kingdom at Giza and Saqqara, located either on the east side of the mastaba or built into the mastaba core. A: Seneb at Giza; B: Giza 7140; C: typical plan for the 4th Dynasty at Giza; D: Khabausokar at Saqqara; E–F: typical plan for the 5th Dynasty at Saqqara

what had been originally conceived as a solid building. Initially, at the change from the 3rd to the 4th Dynasty, cult niches appeared as cruciform chapels, decorated for the first time (for example Akhtihotep, **Khabausokar, Hesyre**, Metjen, **Nefermaat**, anonymous **Saqqara** mastaba No. 3078). The model for the decoration was based on the decorated slab over the false door which developed in the 3rd Dynasty. From the 3rd and early 4th Dynasty onwards, the cult area often continued to be a brick structure in front of the stone mastaba. The earliest stone-built cult chapels were constructed in front of mastabas of the reign of Khufu. The wish to improve one's chances of life after death with the help of a statue led to the construction, within the mastaba, of inaccessible statue chambers (*serdabs*). This concept differed from the statue cult in royal complexes (**cult temple**). 'Late' transitional forms are found in Giza up to the reign of Khufu (**Hemiunu**). In the 4th Dynasty, coinciding with the establishment of cult places for the deceased and the introduction of *serdabs*, came the transition to stone-built mastabas. The earliest monumental examples are **Helwan** 287.H.6 and some mastabas to the east of the pyramid of **Teti** dating from the 2nd–3rd Dynasty. Niching had disappeared or become confined to the **palace-façade** false door in the offering chapel. The **casing** of the outside walls appears mostly rough and stepped. There are noticeable local variations in structure from as early as in the 4th Dynasty (**Giza, Saqqara, Meidum**).

The increasing use of statues in the 4th and 5th Dynasties was accompanied by greater numbers of *serdabs*. Having more rooms inside the mastaba (especially at **Saqqara**) brought about a gradual transformation of the structure of the core, which became similar to that of a dwelling house, with a gate hall, entrance hall, **pillared hall**, pillared court and several cult chambers for the master of the tomb and his family, each with an attendant magazine. The nucleus of some large tombs contained rooms in the shape of boats (**Kagemni, Ptahshepses**) and 'stairways to heaven' built into the masonry, leading to a dead end; their function is unknown (**Kagemni**, Ankhmahor and Neferseshemre, all at Saqqara). Large tombs are found, some with more than 30 rooms, for example **Giza mastaba 2370, Rawer, Ptahshepses, Ty, Mereruka** and **Ptahhotep/Akhtihotep**. Burial places initially consisted of a deep shaft approached from the roof of the mastaba and orientated as far as possible towards the place for offerings. The shaft opens towards the west into an undecorated chamber with a plain sarcophagus, often monumental in scale in the larger tombs, in a recess in the west wall. From the early 6th Dynasty the longish rectangular chamber is entered from the north, the

chamber being almost completely taken up by the sarcophagus. Following the model of the pyramid of **Unas**, the walls are inscribed and decorated with offering lists and scenes of offering.

It is difficult to create a typology of mastabas of the 5th and 6th Dynasties because the number of distinguishing elements is very large, for example numbers of tomb owners, cult requirements, local styles, royal influence, economic considerations and the space available for construction.

Gradually, large tomb 'towns' grew and merged around the pyramids, with tombs lined up in long rows to form 'streets'. Similarly, in the course of the 6th Dynasty, brick enclosures developed around the outside of mastabas; within these walls numerous small tombs with chapels appeared, the whole forming something like a communal tomb.

The construction of mastabas resumed in the 12th Dynasty, the structure generally consisting of a brick core with a casing of stone. Particularly extravagant complexes are elaborately niched (Senwosretankh at **El-Lisht**, Khnumhotep at **Dahshur**), with a false door plus cult niche on the east side or surrounded by bands of inscriptions. Some interesting forms appear to be transitional between the concept of a mastaba and that of temples of the dead (**Ihy and Hetep, Inpy**). Some crypts bear Pyramid Texts in the tradition of pyramids of the Old Kingdom.

Bibliography: Clarence Fisher, *The Minor Cemetery at Giza* (Philadelphia 1924); Reisner, *Development*; George A. Reisner, The history of the Egyptian mastaba, in: *Mélanges Maspero* I, *MIFAO* 66 (Cairo 1935–38) 579–584; Vandier, *Manuel* II 251–294; Junker, *Giza* I 1ff.; A. Badawy, The ideology of the superstructure of the mastaba-tomb in Egypt, in: *JNES* 15 (1956) 180–183; J.-Ph. Lauer, Évolution de la tombe royale égyptienne jusqu'à la pyramide à degrés, in: *MDAIK* 15 (1957) 148–165; J. Brinks, Mastaba, in: Helck, *LÄ* III 1214–1231; D. Dunham, W.K. Simpson and K. Weeks, *Giza Mastabas* I–V (Boston 1974–94); W. Kaiser, Zu Entwicklung und Vorformen der frühzeitlichen Gräber mit reichgegliederter Oberbaufassade, in: *Mélanges Gamal Eddin Mokhtar* (Cairo 1985) 25–38; Müller, *Monumentalarchitektur* 17–21; Nadine Cherpion, *Mastabas et Hypogées d'Ancienne Empire. Le problème de la datation* (Brussels 1989); P. Jánosi, *The Tombs of Officials' in Egyptian Art in the Age of the Pyramids*, Exhibition Catalogue (New York 1999) 27–39; P. Jánosi, Im Schatten der Pyramiden – Die Mastabas in Abusir, in: Bárta, *Abusir 2000* 445–466.

Mastabat el-Fara'un, *see* Shepseskaf

Mat, *see also* woven timber construction

Mats of a network of materials have been used since prehistoric times in the manufacture of huts and enclosures.

Such structures continue to survive in some forms of stone building (**Djoser**) as well as in hieroglyphic representations of early cult structures (**Per-nu, Per-wer**). Fitted in larger buildings, always after five or six layers of bricks, they served to prevent dry cracking. An unusual application was as bundles of loam-coated mats creating the shape of the **cavetto cornice** (Late Period tomb in the lower Assasif).

Bibliography: Badawy, *Dessin architectural* 6–23; Uvo Hölscher, *Das Hohe Tor von Medinet Habu* (Leipzig 1910), Fig. 24; Eigner, *Grabbauten* 79.

Mazghuna

On the edge of the desert south of **Dahshur** there the remains of two pyramids belonging to two unknown rulers of the 13th Dynasty. They have been ascribed to Amenemhat IV and Sobekneferu, but there is no basis for this. Only the subterranean parts of the larger northern pyramid were completed, but even these were not used. The lid of the sarcophagus was intended to be lowered using sand channels. The smaller southern pyramid was intended to measure 100 x 100 **cubits**. It too was unfinished but appears to have been used, as it was enclosed within a **curved wall** and furnished with a temporary cult chapel.

Bibliography: W.M.F. Petrie et al., *The Labyrinth, Gerzeh and Mazghuneh* (London 1912); W.K. Simpson, Masghuna, in: Helck, *LÄ* III 1196; Stadelmann, *Pyramiden* 247–248.

Measuring, *see also* orientation

Numbers and measurements played an outstanding role in the culture of ancient Egypt and belong to its earliest achievements. The **mastaba** of 'Menes' at Naqada was already constructed using the **cubit** as the unit of measurement.

a) Distances were measured using measuring rods of one cubit. There are also some examples that are two cubits in length. The use of measuring cords in the measuring of fields is attested to, but it is doubtful whether this would have been sufficiently accurate for stone construction work. Points of measurement were indicated by crosses scratched on stone slabs. Circular holes chiselled into the bedrock around larger buildings may have served as sockets for wooden marker poles.

b) Determining the **batter** of the exterior sloping walls of mastabas was very important from as early as the 1st Dynasty and later in the construction of the pyramids. From the Rhind Papyrus, a mathematical handbook, as well from checking the dimensions of ancient buildings, it is clear that the angle of slope was defined and constructed by the ratio of the offset distance to the height, known in ancient Egyptian as *seqed* (Fig., C). According to this, an offset distance of 7 palms to a height of 7 palms was equal to an angle of 45°, while the ratio of 5:7 palms gave an angle of 54°. The way the angle was produced in construction is known only from the evidence of one or two cases. The inner, white plastered corners of a wall in the foundation pit of mastaba 17 at **Meidum** were marked with horizontal lines spaced at distances measured in cubits, the inclining angle of the foundation (1:4) displayed as a drawing in that system. How the slope was transferred onto the wall is not known. Similarly, in the case of a much later pyramid of Meroe the outline of the slope of the pyramid was marked onto a wall opposite it. The stepwise receding position of blocks in a secondary pyramid to the **Khufu** pyramid is marked out in lines scratched on at the corners.

c) Levelling was performed with a device known as a 'square level', which continued to be used into the Middle Ages, consisting of right-angled triangle with a plumb line (Fig., B). The results obtained were astonishingly accurate, with an error factor of only +/- 1 cm over a distance of 47 m; the deviation in basal height over the distance of 230 m between the north and south sides of the Khufu pyramid is 2 cm. Several examples have been found of unfinished walls of the Old Kingdom with horizontal height lines at intervals of one cubit each, aiding the upward projection of height lines (Fig., F). To facilitate **orientation**, each line was marked with the number of cubits measured (**control notes**). Height was also indicated by series of limestone slabs (on the causeway and in the forecourt of the **Mentuhotep** temple, and in the corridor of the pyramid of **Senwosret I**).

d) The method of constructing right angles is not known, but it is possible that Pythagoras' theorem ($a^2 + b^2 = c^2$) was known even as early as the time of Djoser. Using this, it would have been easy to construct right-angled triangles in the proportions 3:4:5. An alternative method would have been to use a wooden set-square on a straight line with its outside corner placed at the intersection with the perpendicular. Measuring would be repeated by turning over the set-square, in order to correct earlier inaccuracies (Fig., A). Finally, a perpendicular line could be constructed on a straight line by letting a measured piece of string mark out a curve across it from both ends (Fig., D).

Bibliography: Clark, *AEM* 62–67; W. Schenkel, Meßschnur, in: Helck, *LÄ* IV 115; G. Goyon, Le grand circle d'or du temple d'Osymandas, in: *BIFAO* 76 (1976) 289–300; J.-Ph. Lauer, Le triangle sacré dans les plans des monuments de l'ancien empire, in: *BIFAO* 77 (1977) 55–78; Josef Dorner, *Die Absteckung und astronomische Orientierung ägyptischer*

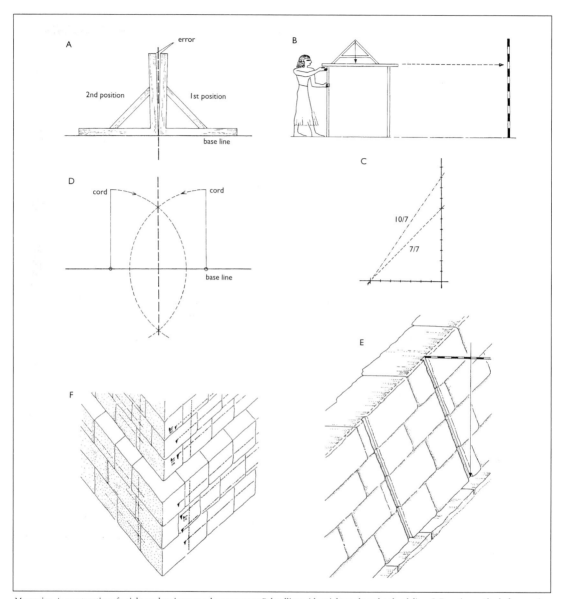

Measuring. A: construction of a right angle using a wooden set square; B: levelling with a right angle and a plumb line; C: Egyptian method of expressing an angle of slope (7 or 10 palms vertical rise by 1 cubit horizontal offset); D: construction of a right angle by drawing arcs; E: determination of the batter of a wall with a measuring rod and plumb line; F: levelling marks with heights above the horizontal on the core masonry of a corner of wall

Pyramiden, Dissertation (Innsbruck 1981); Arnold, *Building* 10–14; M. Isler, The Merkhet, in: *Varia Aegyptiaca* 7 (1991) 53–67; M. Isler, The gnomon in Egyptian antiquity, in: *JARCE* 28 (1991) 155–185.

Medamud

The ruins of the Month temple at Madu, 5 km north-east of Karnak, include extremely important remains of earlier temples which illustrate the development of an Egyptian sanctuary over time. The deepest remains belong to a primitive double shrine dating from either the Old Kingdom or the First Intermediate Period and were surrounded by a trapezoidal brick enclosure with two **pylons**. Two winding corridors inside lead to subterranean chambers, which were indicated on the surface by shallow mounds surrounded by gardens of trees. Replacing this 'primitive temple', Senwosret III erected a building measuring 60 x 100 m, made of brick but with **columns** and **gateways** of **limestone**. It has been possible to erect

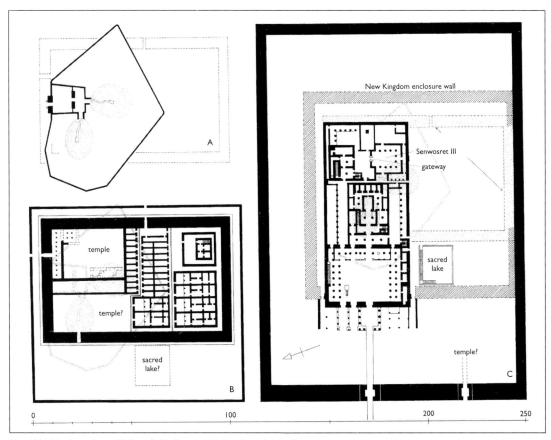

Plan of the Month precinct at Medamud, showing construction phases (see text)

one gateway each at the Egyptian Museum at Cairo and the Open Air Museum at Karnak using re-used blocks surviving from the Middle Kingdom. A wall 5.5 m thick enclosed a cult building with royal **statue pillars**, magazines, six priests' houses, as well as **grain stores**. A new structure was erected in the reign of Thutmosis III above the spot of the western mound and was later replaced in the Ptolemaic period by a building measuring 21 x 32 m. In front of the façade, Ptolemy VIII Euergetes II set up two rows of 11 columns and a forecourt with a monumental double altar and double rows of columns. An avenue of **sphinxes** led from the main gate to a **platform** with two **obelisks**. In the south-west corner there is a well-preserved **sacred lake.** Next to this lie the remains of a destroyed temple of the early Ptolemaic period.

Bibliography: Bisson de la Roque, *Rapport sur les fouilles de Médamoud, 1925–26, 1927–28, 1929–32,* Institut français d'archéologie orientale (Cairo 1926–33); C. Robichon and A. Varille, *Description sommaire de temple primitif de Médamoud* (Cairo 1940); F. Gomaa, Medamud, in: Helck, *LÄ* III 1252–1253; Aufrère, *L' égypte restituée* 146–147.

Medinet el-Faiyum

The site of the temple of Sobek at Crocodilopolis (Arsinoe). This temple is one of the most important, yet least satisfactorily studied, in Egypt. In 1888, the remains of a 250 x 350 m Ptolemaic sanctuary with a granite **gateway** of Amenemhat III was discovered underneath a mound of ruins, 25 m high and spread over an area of 1200 x 1700 m. Lying further south were the shafts of 16 granite papyrus **columns**, 7.2 m high, originally of Amenemhat III but re-inscribed by Ramesses II and Ramesses VI. The site has now been demolished and built over.

Bibliography: Strabo, *Geographica* XVII, Book 1, 38; W.M. Flinders Petrie, *Hawara, Biahmu and Arsinoe* (London 1889) 56–59, Plate 29; L. Habachi, Une 'vaste salle' d'Amenemhat III à Kiman-Farès (Fayoum), in: *ASAE* 37 (1937) 85–95; F. Gomaa, Medinet el-Fajjum, in: Helck, *LÄ* III 1254–1255.

Medinet Habu

1. 18th Dynasty temple

An important religious sanctuary whose focus is the primeval Amun, situated at the southern boundary of the

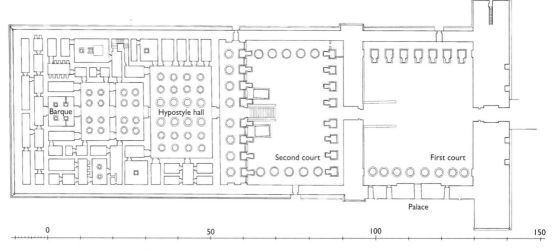

Plan of temple of Ramesses III at Medinet Habu

Theban necropolis. It was believed to be the tomb of the primeval Amun Kematef, where Amun of Karnak regenerated himself once every 10 days. Over a small building of the 11th Dynasty, a six-room temple was constructed, at the front of which stood a barque sanctuary with a colonnade (area 13 x 29 m) of Hatshepsut. During the construction of the large temple of Ramesses III (see 2.), the small temple was enclosed within the surrounding wall. This complex was enlarged in the Nubian period with a corridor consisting of two rows of eight columns and a **pylon** at the front. A further pylon was added under Ptolemy VIII and Ptolemy XI Neos Dionysos and a colonnade erected in front of the Nubian pylon. Construction of a **pronaos**, 42 m wide, with a large forecourt, was begun in the reign of Antonius Pius but was never completed.

Bibliography: Hölscher, *Medinet Habu* II; Stadelmann, *Medinet Habu*, in: Halck, *LÄ* III 1255–1271; Aufrère, *L'Égypte restituée* 183–184.

2. Temple of Ramesses III

The well-preserved '**house of millions of years**' of Ramesses III was originally surrounded by a small enclosure with a stone pylon at the front. It was later enlarged by the addition of an outer **enclosure wall**, 18 m high, measuring 205 x 315 m, which gave the sanctuary a fortress-like appearance. A monumental **platform** on the bank of the canal was followed by the **High Gate**. A **window of appearances** opens onto the first court of the temple from the cult **palace** on the southern side. The main temple building is 150 m long, and its plan is largely a copy of the **Ramesseum**. Two forecourts, decorated with **statue pillars** of the king (**pillar**, Fig.), are followed by a

hypostyle hall, behind which are chambers for guest gods, an offering chamber and the sanctuary for the barque of Amun. Behind this lie some hidden rooms (perhaps for the mysteries of Amun-Re). To the south of the central axis are the treasuries, a place for the cult of Month and the mortuary cult rooms of Ramesses III. which take the form of an Osiris shrine. On the opposite, north side were chapels for the king, Ptah, Amun and other gods, a slaughter court for the cult, a shrine to the cult of the sun with **stairs** to the roof, and a sanctuary for the Divine Ennead. The decoration of this temple is impressive, with important remains of colour. The enclosure wall encompasses store houses, barracks with stables for horses, offices, wells, small ponds and gardens. The temple has been studied in an exemplary fashion and is of great significance for the history of construction.

Bibliography: Hölscher, *Medinet Habu* I, III, V; R. Stadelmann, *Medinet Habu*, in: Helck, *LÄ* III 1255–1271; Aufrère, *L'Égypte restituée* 171–183.

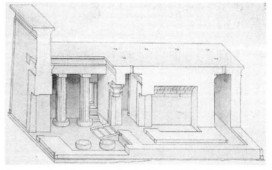

Reconstruction of the tomb chapel of Amenirdis in the forecourt of Ramesses III's temple at Medinet Habu (after U. Hölscher) (see text)

3. Tomb chapels of the 'divine consorts'

In the safety of the forecourt of the temple of Ramesses III stand the tomb chapels of the 'divine consorts' Shepenwepet I, Amenirdis, Nitokris, Shepenwepet II and Ankhnesneferibre (22nd–26th Dynasties). The superstructure is in the form of a temple with a pylon, a small pillared courtyard and a cult chamber set inside a rectangular space; the sarcophagus chambers are set slightly below floor level. The burial chamber of Shepenwepet I (c. 750 BC) and the cult chamber of Amenirdis both have true stone **vaults**. To the west of the temple enclosure are a group of seven private chapels, modified in the 22nd–26th Dynasties to **temple tombs**.

Bibliography: Hölscher, *Medinet Habu* V 17–30; R. Stadelmann, *Das Grab im Tempelhof, der Typus des Königsgrabes in der Spätzeit*, in: *MDAIK* 27 (1971) 111–123.

Columns in the north-west corner of the first court, temple of Ramesses III at Medinet Habu

Medinet Madi

The ruins of an important Ptolemaic **town**, 35 km southwest of **Medinet el-Faiyum**. There is a well-preserved temple dedicated to Ermuthis-Isis (Renenutet, Termuthis) and Sobek of Narmouthis. The core of the temple, which measures 8.5 x 10.7 m, was erected by Amenemhat III and Amenemhat IV and has three parallel shrines for the cult images, which give onto a shared offering chamber (**multiple shrines**, Fig., C). In front there is an antechamber with two papyrus **columns** decorated with flower-bud capitals, and protruding **antae** (**multiple shrine**, Fig., C). In the Ptolemaic period, it was incorporated in a larger complex.

Bibliography: A. Vogliano, Rapporto preliminare della IVa campagna di scavo a Madinet Mâdi, in: *ASAE* 38 (1938) 533–549; Rudolf Naumann, Der tempel des Mittleren Reiches in Medinet Madi, in: *MDAIK* 8 (1939) 185–189; E. Bresciani, Medinet Madi, in: Helck, *LÄ* III 1271–1273; S. Donadini, Le pietre di Madinet Madi, in: *Pyramid Studies and Other Essays Presented to I.E.S. Edwards* (London 1988) 61–67. Reconstruction: Aufrère, *L'Égypte restituée* III 201.

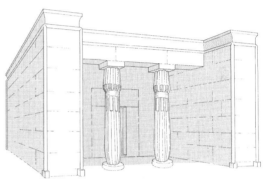

Reconstruction of the Ermuthis-Isis temple of Amenemhat III at Medinet Madi

Meidum

The site of a **step mastaba** and an attendant royal cemetery from the period of the transition from the 3rd to the 4th Dynasties, with examples of early stone constructions of outstanding significance for the history of construction. The initial mastaba had seven steps (E1); before completion this had been enlarged to eight steps (E2), the length at the base being 120.75 m, height 85 m, and angle of slope 75°. The entrance was located 16 m above ground in the centre of the north side, from which a steep corridor led down to a small chamber erected at ground level. The roof of this chamber is the earliest known **corbelled vault**. From year 30 to year 34 of the reign of Sneferu, due to the influence of solar concepts this rectangular royal precinct, with its north–south orientation, was converted to an east-facing complex dominated by step mastaba E2 rebuilt as a true pyramid (E3), with a base length of 144.32 m, angle of slope 51°51' and height of 92 m. A **causeway** led from an as yet undiscovered **valley temple** up to a small cult complex at the foot of pyramid E3, consisting of an offering table

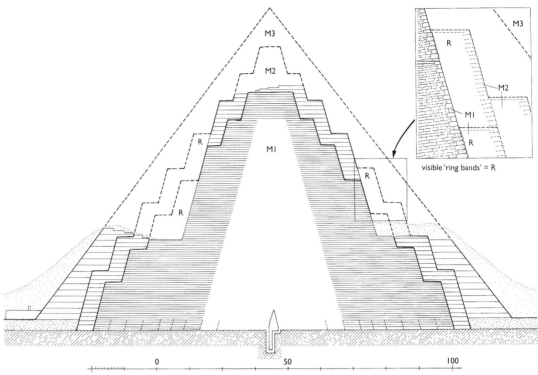

visible 'ring bands' = R

Section through the pyramid of Meidum, showing construction phases M1–M3 and the 'ring bands'

flanked by two **stelae** at the back of a small stone building. To the north and south of the pyramid are remains of two monumental secondary tombs; their purpose is unknown. A re-used block found at the site is decorated with the earliest known *kheker* **frieze**. Important remains of **building ramps** have been discovered at the site. The theory that the outer **casing** may have collapsed during construction has not proved correct.

To the north of the pyramid are some important brick **mastabas** of the 4th Dynasty (**Meidum mastaba 17, Nefermaat and Atet**, and **Rehotep and Nefret**).

Bibliography: W.M. Flinders Petrie, *Medum* (London 1892); W.M. Flinders Petrie, *Medum and Memphis* (London 1910) 1–9; Borchardt, *Entstehung der Pyramide*; Alan Rowe, in: *The Museum Journal* (Museum of Pennsylvania) 22 (1931); *MRA* III; J.-Ph. Lauer, A propos du prétendu désastre de la pyramide de Meidoum, in: *CdE* 51 (1976) 76; D. Wildung, Meidum, in: Helck, *LÄ* IV 9–13; Stadelmann, *Pyramiden* 81–87; Ali El-Khouli et al., *Meidum* (Warminster 1992).

Meidum mastaba 17

An important royal **mastaba** of the early 4th Dynasty at **Meidum**, measuring 52 x 105 m at the base, made of mantles of quarry stones and packed with rubble. Some interesting measuring marks have been discovered. The cult area was unusually wide, measuring 13.5 m across, but

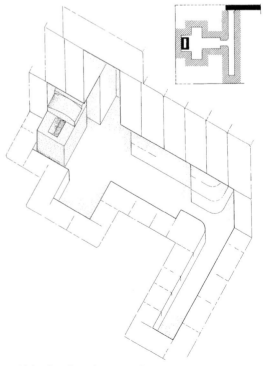

Burial chamber of mastaba 17 at Meidum

it now unfortunately no longer exists. The owner (name unknown) died early and, as the entrance to the burial complex had not been built, his interment in the unfinished burial chamber was effected through the roof. A recess in the magnificent burial chamber (ceiling height 5 m) is occupied by a granite sarcophagus. The door frames in the corridors are rounded; the reason for this is unknown.

Bibliography: W.M. Flinders Petrie, *Medum* (London 1892) 11–14; W.M. Flinders Petrie, *Meidum and Memphis* (London 1910) 13–18.

Meir

A necropolis of **rock tombs** in Middle Egypt. The earliest tomb here dates from the 6th Dynasty and belongs to Niankhpepy Sebekhotep. Later tombs, from the 12th Dynasty, represent a distinctive local style, with the inclusion of a shrine-like structure in front of the statue niche. Prominence is lent to the **cult target** by a raised central aisle through the cult chamber.

Bibliography: Blackman, *The Rock Tombs of Meir*, 6 Vols (London 1914–53); Badaway, *Architecture* II 136–142; D. Kessler, Meir, in: Helck, *LÄ* IV 14–19.

Memnoneion

Gardiner and others assumed that the Greek name Memnon derived from the Egyptian Neb-maat-Re, the prenomen of **Amenhotep III**, and it was therefore given to the pair of **colossal statues** at **Thebes**; and the term Memnoneion was applied to the associated mortuary temple of the king. Haeny argues, however, that Memnoneion was a vulgarisation of *basileion mnemoneion,* 'royal memorial temple', designating all buildings of this type (including the temple of **Sety I** at Abydos). The derivation from the name of the hero Memnon, son of Aurora, may be an ancient misinterpretation. The main classical source is Strabo's *Geography*.

Bibliography: Strabo, *Geographica* VIII, 123; XVII I, 46, 815–816; A.H. Gardiner, *The Egyptian Memnon*, in: *JEA* 47 (1961) 91–99; G. Haeny, L'origine des traditions thébaines concernant Memnon, in: *BIFAO* 64 (1966) 203–212.

Memphis, *see also* Merenptah, Ptah

The largest and most important city in Egypt, traditionally founded by Menes, and capital of the first Lower Egyptian nome. For many years, it was seat of the Egyptian administration and garrisons. It was later supplanted by **Alexandria**. In antiquity it lay on the banks of the Nile, but the course of the river has changed and it is now 4 km away. Apart from some nondescript remains of temples, only a few traces of structures are to be seen in the landscape of *koms* between Badrashein and Mitrahina, which is now largely built over. The Egypt Exploration Society has recently begun systematic exploration of an area measuring 1.375 x 2.5 km. The city was separated into different sections, containing a royal fortification of the Late Period (**palace** of **Apries**) in the north, the **temple of Ptah** in the centre, the palace of **Merenptah** in the south-east and the harbour in the east. The south-west corner of the precinct of Ptah contains a small statue temple of Ramesses II and, further to the east, at the Kom Rabia, there is a temple to Hathor built by the same king. Living areas are attested to but have as yet received little research. There is a close connection with the nearby necropolis (**Saqqara**, **Serapeum**).

Bibliography: W. M. Flinders Petrie et al., *Memphis*, 6 Vols, British School of Archaeology in Egypt, Vols 15, 17–18, 20, 23, 26 (London 1908–13); Rudolf Anthes, *Mit Rahineh* 1955 (Philadelphia 1959); Rudolf Anthes, *Mit Rahineh* 1956 (Philadelphia 1965); C.M. Zivie,

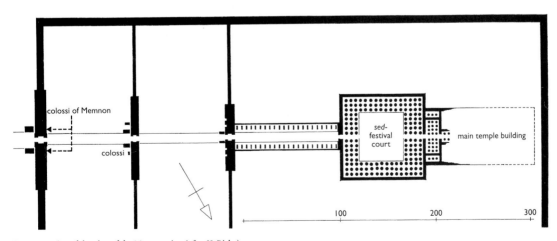

Reconstruction of the plan of the Memnoneion (after H. Ricke)

Memphis, in: Helck, *LÄ* IV 24–41; Dorothy J.Thompson, *Memphis under the Ptolemies* (Princeton 1988). Annual reports of the British excavations, from *JEA* 69 (1983) onwards: K.A. Kitchen, Towards a reconstruction of Ramesside Memphis, in: *Fragments of a Shattered Visage* (Memphis, Tenn. 1991) 87-104; Jaromir Malek, The temples of Memphis, in: Quirke, *Temple* 90–101; D. Jeffreys, House, palace and islands at Memphis, in: Bietak, *Haus und Palast* 287–294; G.T. Martin, Memphis: the status of a residence city in the Eighteenth Dynasty, in: Bárta, *Abusir 2000*, 99–120.

Mendes

An extensive mound covered with ruins marks the ancient double city of Mendes and Thmuis (Timai el-Amdid and Tell el-Rub'a), capital of the 16th Lower Egyptian nome. There are the remains of an Old Kingdom settlement and a necropolis (**mastaba**). The temple precinct of the ram-god Banebdjedet at Tell el-Rub'a, measuring 400 x 700 m, was recorded by the Arab geographer Subh el-A'sha, in the 15th century AD, as intact up to the roof. The main temple building (measuring 70 x 120 m) was orientated north–south with an entrance at the north. One of the four granite **naoi**, 8 m high, dedicated to Re, Geb, Shu and Osiris, has survived and stands in what was probably the **hypaetral** sanctuary of the temple. Foundation pits of the 18th Dynasty and granite blocks bearing the cartouches of Ramesses II and Merenptah hint at the existence of predecessors to Amasis' construction. Some papyrus capitals of red granite and a granite **Hathor** capital (now in the Egyptian Museum in Cairo) belonged to a **birth house** situated to one side. At the south-east corner of the precinct are the

remains of some **kings' tombs** of the 29th Dynasty (Nepherites I), which were destroyed by the Persians. A **sacred lake** lies to the south-east outside the enclosure; there are also some remains of a harbour complex.

Bibliography: *Description* V 29; A. Scharff, Ein Besuch von Mendes, in: *MDAIK* 1 (1930) 130–134; D. Hanssen et al., Mendes 1965 and 1966, in: *ARCE* 6 (1967) 5–51; Herman de Meulenaere and Pierre Mackay, *Mendes II* (Warminster 1976); H. de Meulenaere, Mendes, in: Helck, *LÄ* IV 43–45; R.J. Wenke and D.J. Brewer, The archaic Old Kingdom Delta: the evidence from Mendes and Kom el-Hisn, in: Bietak, *House and Palace*, 265–285; D. Redford, Report on the 9th Season of Excavations at Tell el-Rub'a/Mendes, in: *ASAE* 75 (1999–2000) 17–21.

'Menes', tomb of (Naqada)

Famous **mastaba** near Naqada, measuring 26.5 x 53.4 m, which is probably that of Queen Neithhotep (reign of Horus Aha). The core structure, which probably rose steeply from ground level, had a smooth exterior and contained five rooms. Around this were 16 cells with a **niched** exterior. The niches were constructed on a **cubit** system and made of particularly small **bricks**. This, together with tomb S 3357 of the same period, is the earliest preserved specimen of a niched mastaba. Supposedly developed from the Lower Egyptian (**Butic**) tradition of high officials' free-standing tombs with above-ground funerary chambers, it seems to be rather out-of-place in Upper Egypt.

Bibliography: L. Borchardt, Das Grab des Menes, in: *ZÄS* 36 (1898) 87–105; Spencer, *Brick Architecture* 15–16; W. Helck, Neqada, in: Helck, *LÄ* IV 344–346; W. Helck, Neith-hotep, in: Helck, *LÄ* IV 394–395; W. Kaiser, Zu Entwicklung und Vorformen der frühzeitlichen

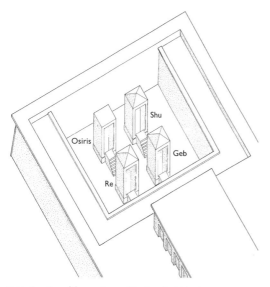

Reconstruction of the sanctuary of the temple at Mendes

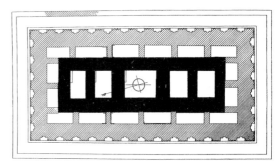

Plan of the 'tomb of Menes' at Naqada (after G.A. Reisner)

Gräber mit reich gegliederter Oberbaufassade, in: *Mélanges Gamal Eddin Mokhtar* II (Cairo 1985) 25–38.

Menkaure (Mykerinos), pyramid of

The pyramid of Menkaure, called 'Divine is the Pyramid of Menkaure', stands at **Giza**. Construction expenditure for this pyramid was considerably less than for its predecessors, the emphasis in this case being on the cult facilities (a tendency also observed in the 5–6th Dynasty). Our understanding of this complex is hindered by the repeated re-designs which took place in the lifetime of the king and the necessarily hasty completion at his death. The length of the sides is 105 m, with the angle of slope 51–52° and height 65–66 m. The nucleus has been shown to have been a stepped structure with an outer **casing** up to the 16th course of **granite** (**bossed** blocks), the upper portion being **limestone**. The construction of the inside chambers has a complicated history: a corridor serving as entrance or construction area which led down to the antechamber was built from above while the erection of the pyramid was in progress; it was later replaced with an entranceway at a lower level. The antechamber itself, 3.83 x 14.20 m and 4.87 m high, with a flat, unlined ceiling, was later enlarged by the addition of a sarcophagus chamber (2.62 x 6.59–6.62 m, height 3.43 m) at a lower level. The latter was faced with granite and roofed with a false granite **vault** of hollowed out relieving slabs (**ceiling construction**, Fig.). From here Howard Vyse removed a **niched** granite sarcophagus (**palace**, Fig., C), lost when the boat carrying it sank on its way from Malta to Cartagena in 1888. From the lower complex, a side-room branches off to one side with six deep recesses in the walls (possibly forerunners of *serdabs*). The later entrance corridor has the first example of a corridor chamber with niching. On the south side of this pyramid are three secondary pyramids, the two to the west being **queens' tombs**, possibly in the shape of stepped structures. The eastern one, a 'true' **cult pyramid** with a burial chamber and a cult building, was larger, with granite casing.

The **pyramid temple** on the east side of the main pyramid is aligned with the pyramid temple of **Khufu**. The nuclear masonry is local limestone, the lower part cased with granite, the top with limestone. On the death of the king, the final part was completed in brick and some **pillared halls** planned to be erected in the courtyard were instead replaced by niched walls. The elongation of the main cult room suggests that it may have been intended to house a barque (possibly reflecting the concept of the king travelling in the barque of the sun). As a precursor to a later change in cultic practices, a mortuary offering chapel with a cruciform cult area was erected against the pyramid in the courtyard. Also, the **valley temple** was only completed in brick. The traditional pillared halls around the courtyard were replaced by walls decorated with niching. The eight chapels on the side by the entrance contained royal statue groups, perhaps representing the eternal unification of the king with the gods of Egypt. Situated along the west side, behind staggered rows of pillars, is the main cult room, its shape again elongated, with a statue group of the king and Queen Khamerernebty.

Bibliography: Petrie, *Pyramids* 104–120; George A. Reisner, *Mycerinus* (Cambridge, Mass. 1931); *MRA* V; W. Wood, A reconstruction of the triads of King Mycerinos, in: *JEA* 60 (1974) 82–93; Edwards, *Pyramids* 147–155; Stadelmann, *Pyramiden* 141–150; Stadelmann, *Pyramiden von Giza* 191–205; Lehner, *Complete Pyramids* 134–137.

Pyramid of Menkaure at Giza, from the east

Mentuhotep, temple of (Deir el-Bahari)
This king's **cult temple**, which lies on the West Bank of the Nile at **Thebes**, is important as evidence of the Upper Egyptian building style and also of the transition from the Old Kingdom **pyramid temple** to the 'houses of millions of years' of the New Kingdom. Like its Old Kingdom predecessors, the Akh-sut, as the complex was called, had a **valley temple** and a **causeway**. The latter is 1200 m in length and 46 m wide, and led to a forecourt with a temple garden and statues of the king. The building was laid out as a **terraced temple**, having an open front with **pillared halls**.

View over the western part of the temple of Mentuhotep at Deir el-Bahari; left foreground, a corner of the central core

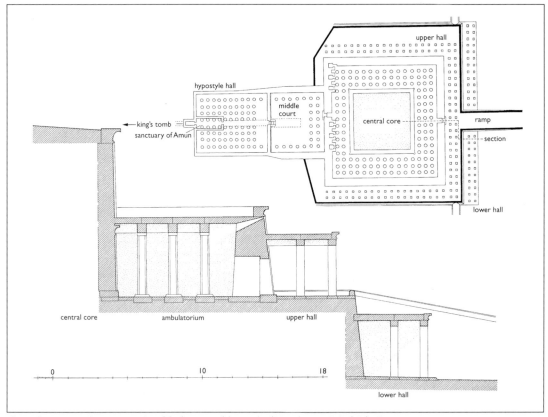

Plan and reconstructed east–west section of the front part of the temple of Mentuhotep at Deir el-Bahari

The plan was divided in two. The front part was dedicated to Month-Re and consisted of a core building, 11 m high, set on a terrace (perhaps conceived as a **primeval mound**). The suggestion that this building was surmounted by a pyramid must be rejected for architectural and other reasons. The core building was completely surrounded by an ambulatory with octagonal sandstone pillars. The rear section of the sanctuary served the cult of the deified king. It was carved into the sheer cliffs, with a courtyard and a pillared hall, containing eight rows of ten pillars, with a statue chapel. Subsequently a sanctuary of Amun was built into it, adding the cult of Amun of Karnak to the original joint cult of Mentuhotep and Month-Re, which changed the complex into a true 'house of millions of years'.

The tomb of the king lies 150 m deep inside the mountain and consists of a **granite** chamber with a shrine-shaped **alabaster** chapel. A deep secondary tomb of the king is situated in the lower courtyard in the 'Bab el-Hosan' in front of the temple; this was where the well-known black seated statue of the king, now in the Egyptian Museum at Cairo, was buried beside

an empty coffin, and was probably an **Osiris tomb** for the king.

Bibliography: Edouard Naville, *The XIth Dynasty Temple at Deir el-Bahari*, 3 Vols (London 1907, 1910, 1913); Dieter Arnold, *Der Tempel des Königs Mentuhotep von Deir el-Bahari*, 3 Vols (Mainz 1974, 1974, 1981); Dieter Arnold, *The Temple of Mentuhotep at Deir el-Bahari*, (New York, 1979); D. Arnold, Deir el-Bahari II, in: Helck, *LÄ* I 1011–1017.

Merenptah, palace of (Memphis)

The important remains of the cult **palace** (Fig., A) of Merenptah at **Memphis** (Kom Qala'a) were excavated between 1914 and 1920, but have been inadequately published. A reception hall situated below a **pylon** was followed by a columned court (27 x 58 m). A colonnade two storeys high beside the entrance may have formed something like a balcony of appearances (**window of appearances**). At the rear of the courtyard there is a hall of appearances with two rows of six columns. Beyond this lay the throne room with a magnificently decorated throne podium, found completely preserved (a model of the room is in the University Museum,

Philadelphia). This is followed by the living quarters, including a bedroom and bathroom. Floors and columns are made of **limestone**. The frame of the 7 m high door, leading to the hall of appearances, as well as its pillars, were inlaid with faience and gold leaf. The plaster on the walls was also richly painted and decorated with inlaid faience and gold.

Bibliography: C.S. Fisher, The Eckley B. Cox Jr. Expedition, in: *The Museum Journal (Philadelphia)* 8 (1917) 211–227; 15 (1924) 92-100; D.G. Jeffreys, J. Malek and H.S. Smith, Memphis 1984, in: *JEA* 72 (1986) 10–13; D. O'Connor, Mirror of the Cosmos: The Palace of Merenptah, in: *Fragments of a Shattered Visage* (Memphis, Tenn. 1993) 167–197.

Merenptah, temple of (Thebes)

The **'house of millions of years'** of Merenptah lies on the West Bank at **Thebes**. In the history of architecture, it is the link between the **Ramesseum** and the temple of Ramesses III at **Medinet Habu**. It consists of two courtyards, two **hypostyle halls**, the holy-of-holies and a sun cult building. The cult **palace** is directly attached to the first courtyard. A large number of beautifully decorated blocks from the temple of Amenhotep III were re-used in the building of this relatively modest complex, including fragments of Anubis **sphinxes**.

Bibliography: William M. Flinders Petrie, *Six Temples at Thebes* (London 1897) 10–13; Horst Jaritz, Der Totentempel des Merenptah in Qurna, in: *MDAIK* 48 (1992) 65–91; Horst Jaritz, The temple palace of Merenptah in his house of a million years at Qurna, in: Bietak, *House and Palace* 99–106; Susanne Bickel, *Untersuchungen im Totentempel des Merenptah in Theben* (Stuttgart 1997).

Merenre, pyramid of

The precinct of the pyramid 'Merenre Appears in Perfection' lies in an inconspicuous wadi at South **Saqqara**. It is badly ruined and has received little scholarly attention. Remains have been found of a mortuary offering room and a rectangular antechamber. Wall reliefs are unfinished. A **north chapel** and a **cult pyramid** are known to have existed. The interior of the pyramid, 90–95 m high, severely damaged by stone quarrying, was restored in 1971–82. The walls are inscribed with Pyramid Texts. A black **basalt** sarcophagus and canopic chest are preserved. The acquisition of the **false door**, offering tables and door frames from the **granite** quarries of **Aswan** is described in the biography of an official named Weni.

Bibliography: Miriam Lichtheim, *Ancient Egyptian Literature* I (Berkeley 1973) 21; Lauer, *Saqqara* 182–184; Lauer, *Mystère* 133–134, Plates pp. 336–337; J. Leclant, in: *Orientalia* 51 (1982) 433–434; Stadelmann, *Pyramiden* 195.

Mereruka, tomb of

The **mastaba**, at **Saqqara**, of the vizier Mereruka, of the 6th Dynasty (Teti), is one of the largest in Egypt, measuring 25 x 42.5 m (915 sq m). Inside are 32 completely decorated rooms for Mereruka (Fig., A), his wife (Fig., B) and his son (Fig., C); they occupy the entire space inside the mastaba core. An interesting feature is the figure of Mereruka stepping forward out of the cult recess in the six-**pillared hall**. A shaft, 16 m deep, leads from one of the two main cult chambers down to the burial chamber, 4.2 x 10 m, which is completely covered with paintings. In its western recess, decorated with **niching**, is the immense sarcophagus (measuring 2 x 3.4 x 4.2 m), equipped with an approach ramp.

Bibliography: Prentice Duell, *The Mastaba of Mereruka*, 2 Vols (Chicago 1938).

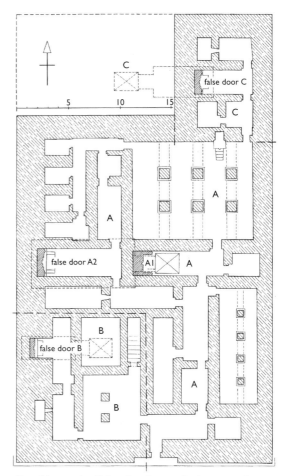

Plan of the mastaba of Mereruka at Saqqara, showing groups of rooms for Mereruka (A), Watkhethor (B) and Meriteti Meri (C), and supposed locations of shafts and burial chambers

Meret

Ten Meret buildings dating from the reigns Sneferu to Pepy II are attested to in inscriptions but not yet in the archaeological record. They may have some connection with **sun temples** or **valley temples** in the ritualistic observance of the sacred marriage of the king, as the incarnation of Re, to Hathor. They may have been the forerunners of the **Maru temples** of the New Kingdom on the edge of the cultivation.

Bibliography: Junker, *Giza* VI 7; Ricke, *Userkaf* I 46–47; S. Allam, *Beiträge zum Hathorkult (bis zum Ende des Mittleren Reiches)*, MÄS 4 (1963) 9; Karola Zibelius, *Ägyptische Siedlungen nach Texten des Alten Reiches* (Wiesbaden 1978) 100–102; W. Barta, Zur Lokalisierung und Bedeutung der mrt-Bauten, in: *ZÄS* 110 (1983) 98–104.

Meretseger, sanctuary of

A small, primeval rock sanctuary of the cobra goddess Meretseger and Ptah lay between Deir el-Medina and Medinet Habu.

Bibliography: B. Bruyère, *Mert Seger à Deir el Médineh* (Cairo 1930)

Metal overlay on stone structures

Overlays of gold, electrum and silver played an important role in the achievement of magic effects (such as deification or immortalisation) in Egyptian temples. No actual overlays have been preserved; the only evidence consists of peg holes.

a) The points of **obelisks** were usually tipped with metal; decoration and hieroglyphs near the top also bore metal overlay in some cases (Senwosret I's Atum temple obelisks at **Heliopolis**, Hatshepsut's and Thutmosis III's obelisks at Karnak).

b) Metal overlays are attested to in several examples of 18th Dynasty columns, on the foot, shaft, capital and abacus.

c) The doorways in some important passageways, in the pyramid temple of **Senwosret III**, the **Ramesseum** and the temple of Ramesses III at **Medinet Habu**, had a metal overlay.

d) The reliefs on some temple walls were overlaid with metal, especially when (as in the case of **addorsed chapels**) they were situated at the centre of a particular cult (**false door** in the central portion of Karnak, the north-facing outside wall of the **hypostyle hall** at Karnak, the rear wall of the temples of **Dendera** and **Edfu**).

Bibliography: Ludwig Borchardt, *Allerhand Kleinigkeiten* (Leipzig 1933) 1–11; P. Lacau, L'or dans l'achitecture égyptienne, in: *ASAE* 53 (1955) 221–250; D. Arnold, Goldverkleidung, in: Helck, *LÄ* II 754–755.

Migdol, *see* Tell el-Kedua

Mirgissa

Iken in Egyptian, an important trade and arms depot on the West Bank of the Nile at the Second Cataract, where Amenemhat II and Senwosret II erected a **fortress**, 100 x 175 m in size. Enlarged in the reign of Senwosret III, it covered an area of 190 x 175 m, surrounded on the three inland-facing sides by a double system of walls fronted with a keep and dry moat. A Hathor sanctuary erected above dates from the 18th Dynasty.

Bibliography: S. Clarke, Ancient Egyptian Frontier Fortresses, in: *JEA* 3 (1916) 165–166; H.G. Lyons, The temple at Mirgisse, in: *JEA* 3 (1916) 182–183; G.A. Reisner, The Egyptian forts from Halfa to Semna, in: *Kush* 8 (1960) 17–24; N.F. Wheeler, Diary of the excavation of Mirgissa fort, in: *Kush* 9 (1961) 87–179; Dows Dunham, *Uronarti Shalfak Mirgissa, Second Cataract Forts*, Vol. 2 (Boston 1967) 141–191; Jean Vercoutter, Excavations at Mirgissa, in: *Kush* 12 (1964) 57–62; 13 (1965) 62–68; Jean Vercoutter, *Mirgissa* I (Paris 1970) 8–13; K. Chen-Zibelius, Mirgissa, in: Helck, *LÄ* IV 144–145; Hein, *Ramessidische Bautätigkeit*, 48–49.

Mo'alla

The site of the **rock tombs** of Ankhtyfy and Sebekhotep of the First Intermediate Period, 30 km south of Luxor. Following Old Kingdom tradition, the tomb of Ankhtyfy consists of a forecourt and a transverse hall, 20 m wide and irregularly shaped, one of the earliest in Egypt, and furnished with approximately 30 **pillars**, varying from four- to eight-sided. The wall paintings are in the style commonly used in the Upper Egyptian nomes and are important for the history of provincial art.

Bibliography: Jacques Vandier, *Mo'alla; la tombe d'Ankhtifi et la tombe de Sébekhotep* (Paris 1950).

Model

Model houses of clay and wood have been found among grave goods dating from pre-historic times to the New Kingdom, most often in the form of **grain stores**, workshops and garden houses intended for use in the next life. An **alabaster** jar stand, probably ornamental, from the **Djoser** precinct takes the form of a tower with battlements with a rope ladder hanging down on one side. A model of the façade of a temple of Sety I at Heliopolis (now in Brooklyn) was probably a votive offering in a temple. The **limestone** model of the subterranean rooms of an unknown king's tomb of the Middle Kingdom (now in a magazine at **Saqqara**) may have been a demonstration sample. Hand-size models of the **capitals** of **columns** and other important architectural elements allowed sculptors of the Ptolemaic period to establish the form and dimensions to be used in particular projects. Stone models of multi-storey town houses, which had an unknown, but probably religious, function, perhaps as votive offerings or lamps, date to the Graeco-Roman period. Models did not have such an important role in Egyptian art and in antiquity generally as in the architecture of later periods. (Models of towns were exhibited in Roman triumphal processions; church models were produced in Italy in the Middle Ages, becoming widespread from the Renaissance onwards.)

Bibliography: R. Engelbach, Four models of Graeco-Roman buildings, in: *ASAE* 31 (1931) 129–131; Jean-Philippe Lauer, *La pyramide à degrés*, Compléments III (Cairo 1939) Fig. 29; C. Desroches-Noblecourt, Un modèl citadine du Novel Empire, in: *RdE* 3 (1930) 17–25; H. Ricke, Ein Hausmodell im Kestnermuseum zu Hannover, in: *ZÄS* 93 (1966) 119–123; A.Badawy, A monumental gateway for a temple of King Seti I, in: *Miscellanea Wilbouriana* 1 (New York 1972); Arnold, *Building* 9–10, Figs 1.6, 47, 55A. 60; Joachim Bretschneider, *Architekturmodelle in Vorderasien und der östlichen Ägäis vom Neolothikum bis in das 1. Jahrtausend, Alter Orient und Altes Testament*, Vol. 229 (Neunkirchen-Vluyne 1991); Modell eines Kultgartens BM 36903: *JEA* 80 (1994), Plate 8. Models in general: Henry A. Millon, Ed., *The Renaissance from Brunelleschi to Michelangelo. The Representation of Architecture*, Exhibition Catalogue (Washington 1995).

Model house

Models of houses are found among grave goods, mainly from the First Intermediate Period and the Middle Kingdom. Three types may be distinguished:

a) Oval or rectangular offering tables, made of clay, having elements of a farmstead with an **enclosure wall** depicted in modelling.

b) Clay offering tables with the rear part modelled in the shape of a tomb chapel or house (**ka**-house).

c) True models, made of wood or, very occasionally, clay, of houses and pavilions which have lost all relation to offering tables or model tombs, and which were included with grave goods together with models of **grain stores** and workshops. A few examples of this type are important for the reconstruction of Egyptian houses thanks to the realistic way their upper storeys and staircases, fresh air shafts, and so on, are shown.

There are also some **limestone** models dating to the Ptolemaic-Roman period, mostly of tower-shaped houses with multiple storeys; their purpose is unknown.

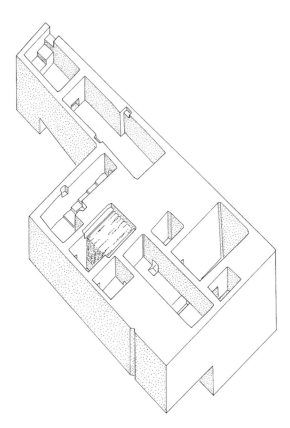

Limestone model of a king's tomb of the late Middle Kingdom, from the valley temple of Amenemhat III at Dahshur

Ceramic model of a house, from Rifa in Cairo

Bibliography: W.M. Flinders Petrie, *Gizeh and Rifeh* (London 1907); Robert Mond, *Cemeteries of Armant* (London 1937) 59, 63, Plate 22; Herbert E. Winlock, *Models of Daily Life in Ancient Egypt* (New York 1955); R. Stadelmann, Hausmodelle, in: Helck, *LÄ* II 1067–1068; A. Niwiński Plateaux d'offrandes et maisons d'âmes, in: *Études et Travaux* 8 (1975) 73–112; A. Niwiński, Seelenhaus, in: Helck, *LÄ* 806–813; M. Stoof, Modelle von Speicherhöfen in Privatgräbern der Ersten Zwischenzeit und des Mittleren Reiches, in: *Hallesche Beiträge zur Orientwissenschaft* 3 (1980) 77–87.

Month precinct (Karnak)

An important sanctuary of the god Month (a deity shown sometimes as falcon-headed and sometimes as a bull), which is situated to the north of the precinct of

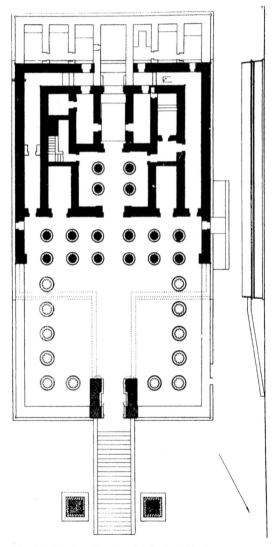

Plan of the Month temple at Karnak (after C. Robichon)

Amun at Karnak. A processional way connected the temple to the main cult centre of Month at **Medamud**, 5 km away. The road included a **platform**, an avenue of **sphinxes** and **barque stations**. The **enclosure wall** of Nectanebo I, measuring 151 x 155 m, had a massive gateway in the north side, the Bab el-'Abd, built by Ptolemy III and Ptolemy IV. The actual Month temple was erected by Amenhotep III to replace a previous structure of the early 18th Dynasty, re-using blocks of the latter. The body of the temple is erected on a platform, 1.15 m in height. The stonework has eroded, with the exception of a few courses of stone. The front part of the building is decorated with two rows of six columns, typical of structures erected by Amenhotep III. The body of the temple consists of a hall with four columns and barque chambers for Month and associated gods. A **crypt** is concealed by a secret **sliding block**. Later in the reign of Amenhotep III, the sanctuary was extended at the rear and a columned court was added at the front, with new **stairs** up to the raised platform, flanked by a pair of **obelisks** . The temple thus covered a total area of 26.25 x 52.50 m (50 x 100 **cubits**). Under Taharqa, a **kiosk** of columns was added in front, and further alterations were carried out in the Ptolemaic period. Against the rear wall of the temple of Month is an **addorsed temple** of the goddess Maat. Standing parallel to the former is the elongated sanctuary of Taharqa, dedicated to Harpre. To the west of the enclosure lies the temple-like treasury building of Thutmosis I, excavated by H. and J. Jacquet.

Bibliography: Clément Robichon and Louis-A. Christophe, *Karnak-Nord, III, 1945–1949*, FIFAO 23 (Cairo 1951) 15–18, Plates 50–52; A. Varille, *Karnak* I, FIFAO 19 (Cairo 1943); Clément Robichon, Paul Barguet and Jean Leclant, *Karnak-Nord IV* (Cairo 1951, 1954); Jean Jacquet, *Karnak-Nord* V (Cairo 1983); Jean Jacquet, *Karnak-Nord V. Le trésor de Thoutmosis Ier* (Cairo 1983); Helen Jacquet-Gordon, *Karnak-Nord VI. Le trésor de Thoutmosis Ier. La décoration* (Cairo 1988); Aufrère, *L'Égypte réstituée* 144–146; H. Sternberg-El-Hotabi, *Der Propylon des Month-Tempels in Karnak-Nord: Zum Dekorationsprinzip des Tores* (Wiesbaden 1993).

Montuemhat, tomb of

The second largest of the great tombs of the Ethiopian period (around 660 BC) in the Assasif at **Thebes** (TT 34). The **pylon**, still visible from afar, is followed by a courtyard measuring 47 x 110 m, which at the back encloses a stylised **primeval mound** and the underground areas, only partially investigated. There are two sun courts laid out in a particularly interesting way (**sun court**, Fig.), the first of which takes the form of a sunken lake surrounded by huge stylised papyrus

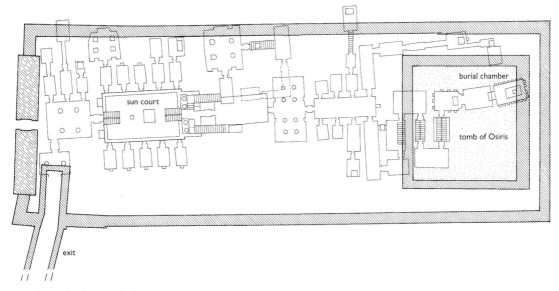

Plan of the tomb of Montuemhat (TT 34) at Thebes

umbels (possibly modelled on the mortuary temple of **Amenophis**, son of Hapu).

There follow innumerable inner rooms, including an intricate burial complex and a sarcophagus chamber, with its sarcophagus set into the floor. Surrounding it are 19 niches containing protective statues of black **granite**.

Bibliography: Jean Leclant, *Montouemhat, quatrième prophète d'Amon* (Cairo 1961); Eigner, *Grabbauten* 44–46, 117; P. Der Manuelian, Two fragments of relief and a new model for the tomb of Montuemhat at Thebes, in: *JEA* 71 (1985) 98–121.

Monumentality

One of the most essential elements of Egyptian architecture, created by colossal scale, mathematical arrangement, geometrical formalism, extensive form, use of hard stone and the sequence in which individual features appear. Monumentality represents the structure's 'patron', whether the king or the State, as guarantor of order and continuity, in opposition to the menace of ruin and chaos. With similar conditions and objectives, therefore, monumental style still appears today.

Bibliography: Ricke, *Bemerkungen* I 14–18.

Mortar, *see also* plaster

Mortar is used in the construction of Egyptian stone buildings for joining stones, as a lubricant and frequently in the repair of damaged stones. Mortar of the pharaonic period consisted exclusively of either clay mixed with pulverised **limestone** and sand, or clay mixed with **gypsum** and sand (used as plaster). Mortar made of burnt **lime** has not been attested to before the Ptolemaic period. When used in brick structures, it could be mixed with pure Nile mud (making a blackish grey mortar), or with sand, pulverised limestone (producing a white mortar), marl clay, *tafl* (yellow) or chaff. Mortar used as plaster contains large quantities of coarse chaff, being finished with a thin layer of fine mortar. Ceiling plaster contains more gypsum or pulverised limestone (true stucco) and fine plant fibre.

Bibliography: A. Lucas and J.R. Harris, *Ancient Egyptian Materials and Industries* (London 1962) 74–76; Arnold, *Building* 291–294; Eigner, *Grabbauten* 79–80; R. Fuchs, Stuck, in: Helck, *LÄ* VI 87–92.

Multiple shrine

A type of structure found regularly in Egyptian architecture from the 1st Dynasty onwards, consisting of three to seven rooms, in front which was a transverse hall. Either all of these rooms were shrines for cult images (as at **Hierakonpolis**, **Medinet Madi** and **Qasr el-Sagha**) or only the outer chambers, which then open onto the central room (as at **Amada**). From the 13th Dynasty, and especially in the New Kingdom and the Late Period, this concept was adopted for the construction of free-standing or underground private tomb chapels. The basic plan of the multiple shrine was occasionally also used in **house** construction. In brick-built structures, either all the rooms, or at least the transverse hall, were roofed with a barrel **vault**.

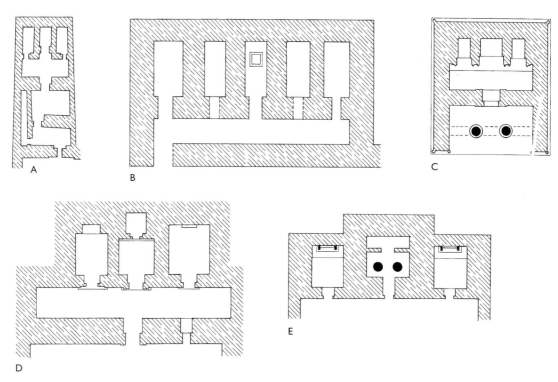

Multiple shrines in temples and tombs. A: 'Khentyimentyu temple' of the 1st dynasty at Abydos; B: temple of Horus of the Old Kingdom (?) at Hierakonpolis; C: temple of Amenemhat III at Medinet Madi; D: tomb of Puyemre (TT 39) at Thebes; E: tomb of Horemheb at Saqqara

Bibliography: Ann H. Bomann, *The Private Chapel in Ancient Egypt* (London and New York 1991); M. Bietak, Kleine ägyptische Tempel und Wohnhäuser des späten Mittleren Reiches, in: *Hommages à Jean Leclant*, BdE 106 (1994), 413–435; G.T. Martin, *The Hidden Tombs of Memphis* (London 1991) 37, 43, 119–20, 153.

Mut precinct (Karnak)

An area, south of the temple of **Amun** at **Karnak**, dedicated to Mut (the consort of Amun), in the form of a vulture or lioness-headed goddess. In the north side of the **enclosure wall**, which measures 250 x 350 m, is the monumental entrance decorated by Ptolemy II and Ptolemy III. The wall encloses at least six sanctuaries. The construction history of the main temple is complex and details are still awaited. A temple is likely to have existed here in the Middle Kingdom, replaced in the 18th Dynasty (possibly by Hatshepsut) with a new structure, and later furnished by Amenhotep III with hundreds of **granite** statues in the form of the lioness-headed Sekhmet. Remains have survived of the alterations to the temple itself during the 25th Dynasty and its renewal in the Ptolemaic period. The **pylon**, like a bulwark, is fronted by a **kiosk** of Taharqa. Situated in the first courtyard is a kiosk

surrounded on three sides by Sekhmet statues; the second courtyard contains a kiosk with **Hathor pillars** and Sekhmet statues. A small **addorsed temple** stands against the back of the main structure. The temple is surrounded on three sides by a horseshoe-shaped **sacred lake**.

On the west bank of the lake are the remains of temple 'C' of Ramesses III. Temple 'A', in the north-east corner, had three small pylons and resembled a **birth house**; it was dedicated to Khonsupakhred (Ramesses II and the 25th Dynasty), and was longer than the main temple.

A large part of the temple of Mut was dismantled in 1840 for the erection of a factory.

Bibliography: J. Benson-Gourlay, *The temple of Mut in Asher* (London 1899); Serge Sauneron et al., *La porte ptolémaique de l'enceinte de Mout à Karnak* (Cairo 1983); M. Pillet, Le temple de Khonsou dans l'enceinte de Mout à Karnak, in: *ASAE* 38 (1938) 469–478; Haeny, *Basilikale Anlagen* 24–26; R. Fazzini, The precinct of Mut during Dynasty XXV and early Dynasty XXVI. A growing picture, in: *JSSEA* 11 (1981) 115–126; R. Fazzini, Excavating the temple of Mut, in: *Archeology* 36 (1983) 16–23; R. Fazzini, Mut Tempel, Karnak, in: Helck, *LÄ* 248–251; R. Fazzini, Precinct of the goddess Mut: South Karnak, in: *Archeological News* 16 (1991) 71ff.; Aufrère, *L'Égypte restituée* 124–127.

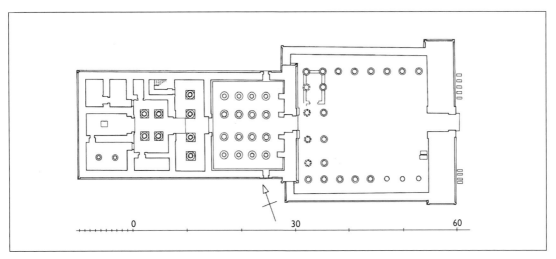

Plan of temple 'A' at Karnak, dedicated to Khonsupakhred (Ramesses II and the 25th Dynasty)

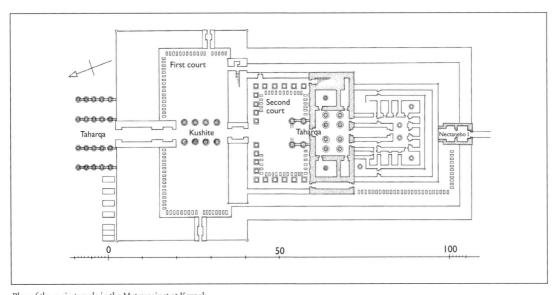

Plan of the main temple in the Mut precinct at Karnak

N

Nadura

Ruins of two small decorated temples in the Kharga Oasis, likely to be outposts of the Amun temple of **El-Kharga**, probably dating to the reign of Antonius Pius.

Bibliography: Reconstruction: Aufrère, *L'Égypte restituée* II 97.

Naos, *see also* kiosk

A free-standing closeable shrine for the accommodation of a cult image. In a tomb or temple, they usually stand in offering chambers, in the sanctuary behind the god's barque, in their own cult image room, or else behind the **barque chamber** against the rear wall of a temple. The ceremonial opening of a naos was subject to specific rituals. The naos in the Early Dynastic Period was made of perishable material (as indicated in hiero-glyphic depictions), appearing in a wealth of different forms (**Per-wer**, **Per-nu**, Min chapel). Some forms are reproduced in stone (such as **granite** and other hard stones). As a 'temple within the temple', the naos is usually an upright rectangular structure on a cube-shaped plinth and crowned with a **frieze of uraei**; its low pyramid-shaped roof represents the **primeval mound** on which the deity emerges from the primeval ocean on the day of creation. Naoi are rich in decoration and texts. At **Gebel el-Silsila** naoi are carved out of the rock, crowned with falcons and a pair of **obelisks**.

Richly detailed depictions of naoi exist in the temple of **Sety I** at Abydos. A sketch for the construction of a naos is preserved on a papyrus in University College London. Some early examples of naoi are: Djoser's at **Heliopolis** (Turin), **Userkaf**'s in his sun temple at Abusir, Pepy I's at **Elephantine** and Senwosret III's at Karnak. Several late examples exist at **Edfu**, **Philae**, **Dabod** and may also be found in the Museums of Cairo, Florence and Marseilles, and in the Louvre. From the Late Period onwards, naoi on a monumental scale are made of hard stone, examples being: the seven naoi in the temple of Bastet at **Bubastis**; the Amasis naos in the temple of Neith at **Sais** (reportedly 21 **cubits** = 10.5 m high); four naoi, 7 m high, in the temple of **Mendes**; and one in the temple of Wadjet at **Buto** (said to be 40 cubits high). The naoi of **Mendes** and **Bubastis** may have stood in unroofed sanctuary courts. Shrines made of wood are also preserved and depicted. In the New Kingdom they were also designed to be nested one inside another.

Bibliography: De Morgan, *Dahchour 1894*, 91, Figs 212–216; Jéquier, *Manuel*, 317–325; Günther Roeder, *Naos*, Catal. gén. des antiquités Égyptiennes du Musée du Caire (Cairo 1914); A.H. Gardiner, A.M. Calverly and M.F. Broome, *The Temple of King Sety I at Abydos*, Vol. III (London-Chicago 1938), Plates 10, 13–14, 16, 33, 41; D. Wildung, Naos, in: Helck, *LÄ* IV 341–342; M. Müller, Schrein, in: Helck, *LÄ* V 709–712.

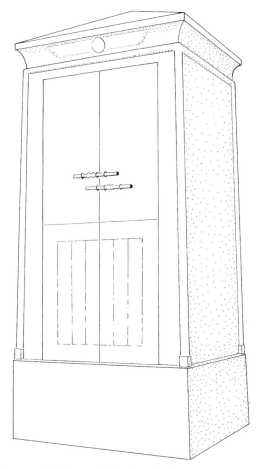

Reconstruction of a naos with closed wooden doors

Naqada, *see* **'Menes', tomb of**

Naukratis (Kom Ga'if)

An offshoot of the town of Milet in the Western Delta, 80 km south-east of Alexandria, founded as a settlement for Greeks at the start of the 26th Dynasty, in the reign of Amasis or earlier. The Kom Ga'if, which was still 400 x 800 m in area in 1885, was only partially examined and is now completely flattened and waterlogged. The main temenos (212 x 250 m) lies in the south. To the north are four temenoi, dedicated to the Dioscuri, Apollo, Hera and Aphrodite, with temples in the Greek style. The Ionic columns of the early Apollo temple date to approximately 566 BC. The site had extensive living quarters.

Bibliography: W.M. Flinders Petrie, *Naukratis I* (London 1886); Ernest A. Gardner, *Naukratis II* (London 1988); William B. Dinsmoor, *The Architecture of Ancient Greece,* 4th Ed. (London etc. 1950) 125–126, 134; William D.E. Coulson and Albert Leonard, *Naukratis* (Cities of the Delta I) (Malibu 1981); H. de Meulenaere, Naukratis, in: Helck, *LÄ* IV 360–361.

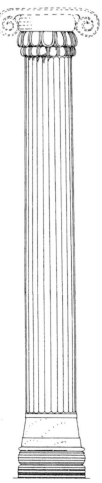

Ionic column from the archaising temple at Naukratis (after W.M.F. Petrie)

Nebwenenef, tomb of

Tomb at Thebes (TT 157) of the high priest of Amun, Nebwenenef, of the reign of Ramesses II. This is an example of the large Theban tombs of the Ramesside period. A forecourt, surrounded by **pillared halls**, is followed by a transverse hall, cut into the rock, 25 m wide, divided by 12 Osiride pillars into two naves. Beyond, a corridor with two rows of 12 pillars leads into the cult chapel with three statue niches. A steep corridor descends from the chapel, changing direction several times, and leads to the sarcophagus chamber with eight pillars and a sarcophagus sunk into the floor. Built on a platform on the side of the hill is an enormous **brick** pyramid.

Bibliography: Unpublished. See: L. Borchardt's reconstruction in *ZÄS* 70 (1934) 29, Fig. 5; C.S. Fisher's description, A group of Theban tombs, in: *University of Pennsylvania, The Museum Journal* 15 (1924) 46–47; L. Bell, The work of the University Museum at Thebes, in: *Expedition* 10 (1968) 38–47; L. Bell, Return to Dra Abu el-Naga, in: *Expedition* 11 (1969) 26–37.

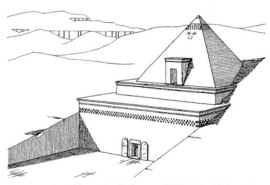

Reconstruction of the tomb of Nebwenenef (TT 157) at Thebes, with a brick pyramid and funerary cones in the façade (after L. Borchardt)

Neferefre, pyramid of

The pyramid of Neferefre (successor of Neferirkare), called 'Divine are the *Ba*'s of Neferefre', is at **Abusir**. It was unfinished on the death of the king, consisting at that time only of the construction shaft with an approach ramp and the lower courses of the pyramid core, and was then completed as a **mastaba**; nonetheless, in front of the east side, there is an important cult building, temporary and made of **brick**, but which contained all the necessary accommodation and – as proved by numerous finds – was in use over a lengthy period. A large slaughterhouse serving cult activities is a particularly interesting feature.

Bibliography: M. Verner, in: *ZÄS* 108 (1981) 77–81; 115 (1988) 77–84; M. Verner, in: *BSFE* 91 (1981) 12–14; M. Verner, in: *MDAIK* 42 (1986) 181–189; M. Verner, *Forgotten Pharaohs, Lost Pyramids, Abusir* (Prague 1994) 133–154.

View over the ruins of the brick pyramid temple of Neferefre at Abusir

Neferirkare, pyramid of

The pyramid of Neferirkare, called 'The *Ba* of Neferirkare', is at **Abusir**. In the absence of excavations and investigation of the structure it is impossible to understand this building. It has a stepped core which was possibly enlarged at a later stage (perhaps from six to eight steps). The actual pyramid was constructed over this, with a side length of 105 m (200 **cubits**) and height 72.8 m. The bottom courses had incomplete **casing** in **granite**, giving a slope of 54°30'. The sarcophagus chamber has a roof of triple relieving slabs of **limestone**. Damage caused by the wrenching away of the facing stones is so severe that it is impossible to excavate the chamber. The axis of the entrance corridor is offset. The only part of the cult complex completed in stone by the time of the king's death were a few rooms of the mortuary temple; the rest was finished in **brick**.

Situated to the south are two boat burials. The **causeway** and **valley temple** were redirected later, in the reign of Niuserre, towards his pyramid precinct.

Bibliography: Borchardt, *Nefer-ir-ke-Re*; *MRA* VII 112–175; Edwards, *Pyramids* 181–183; Stadelmann, *Pyramiden* 171–174; M. Verner, The 'South Boat' of Neferirkare, in: *ZÄS* 107 (1980) 168–169; M. Verner, Remarks on the Pyramid of Neferirkara, in: *MDAIK* 47 (1991) 411–418; M. Verner, *Forgotten Pharaohs, Lost Pyramids, Abusir* (Prague 1994) 76–79.

View of the pyramid of Neferirkare at Abusir

Nefermaat and Atet, tomb of

An early 4th Dynasty brick **mastaba** (M 16) at **Meidum** (measuring 68 x 121 m) with two offering areas. The Fig. shows the development of the cult place. The nucleus consists of layers constructed of Nile mud thickly covered with a mound of pebbles. As yet no burial chambers have been found. The **casing** of the inner chapel (Fig., 1) consists of **limestone** blocks weighing 8–11 tonnes each, decorated with sunk relief filled with an unusual colour paste. The ceiling consists of a single block weighing 33 tonnes. The cult niches were decorated with paintings (including the famous 'Meidum geese'), attesting to the high standard of wall painting reached in the early Old Kingdom. The artist decorated the monumental door frame with inlaid reliefs, a unique artistic experiment, never repeated again: the shapes of the figures were hollowed out and filled with coloured pastes.

Bibliography: W.M. Flinders Petrie, *Medum* (London 1892) 14–15; W.M. Flinders Petrie, *Meydum and Memphis* (London 1910) 18–22;

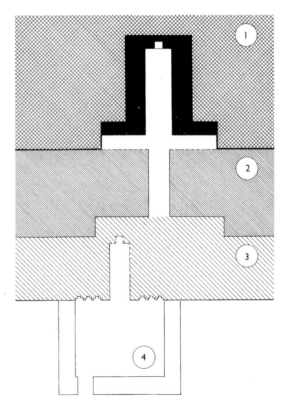

Development of the cult areas of the mastaba of Nefermaat and Atet at Meidum. 1: decorated cult area faced with limestone; 2: conversion into a cruciform chapel; 3: new cult niche surrounded by niched decoration; 4: subsequent addition of stela court

W.S. Smith, *The paintings of the chapel of Atet at Medum*, in: *JEA* 24 (1937) 17–26; A.B. Bolshakov, Some observations on the early chronology of Meidum, in: GM 123 (1991) 11-20.

Nefertari, tomb of, *see also* Abu Simbel

The tomb of Nefertari, the chief wife of Ramesses II (**Abu Simbel**) is No. 66 in the Valley of the Queens (also known as the Biban el-Harim) at **Thebes**. The complex is a compressed version of a **king's tomb**, including a sarcophagus chamber with four pillars and the central floor level sunken for the sarcophagus. The tomb is famous for its spectacular and well-preserved wall paintings which surpass the quality of contemporary wall paintings in the kings' tombs.

Bibliography: Ernesto Schiaparelli, *Relazione sui lavori della Missione Archeologica Italiana in Egitto (Anni 1903–20)*, Vol.1 (Turin 1923); Hedwig Machold, *Nofretari* (publ. G. Thausing und H. Goedecke, Graz 1971); C. Leblanc, Les tombes de la vallée des reines, in: *BIFAO* 89 (1989) 241–247; *In the Tomb of Nefetari. Conservation of the Wall Paintings* (Santa Monica 1992); Fondazione Memmo, The Getty Conservation Institute, *Nefertari luce d'Egitto*, Exhibition Catalogue (Rome 1995). Model in the Museo Egizio, Turin: *Egyptian Civilization. Monumental Art*, The Museum of Turin (Turin 1989), Fig. 76.

Neferuptah, pyramid of

The **brick** pyramid of Neferuptah, the last queen of the 12th Dynasty, stands near Hawara, 2 km to the south-east of the pyramid of her father, **Amenemhat III**. It measures c. 50 x 50 m and has a stone **casing**. There is no approach way: it was erected over the sealed burial chamber containing the sarcophagus. Neferuptah had an earlier burial in the pyramid of Amenemhat III. The burial accommodation, which has not been robbed, has been damaged by sub-soil water.

Bibliography: Nagib Farag and Zaki Iskander, *The Discovery of Neferwptah* (Cairo 1971); E.Martin-Pardey, *Neferuptah*, in: Helck, *LÄ* 381–382.

Nensedjerkai, tomb of

An unusual stone **mastaba** in the shape of a house constructed at **Giza** for a princess of the reign of Khufu. The square mastaba nucleus is fronted to the east by a house-like cult building of stone. Rising beyond a courtyard is a gateway niche with two pillars; this leads into a transverse corridor with two **false doors**. This mastaba is particularly interesting as a **brick** structure translated into stone.

Bibliography: Junker, *Giza* II 97–121.

Nespeqashuty, tomb of

A Late Period Theban tomb (around 680 BC) on the slope of the Assasif (TT 312). The complex, built within a tomb of the 11th Dynasty, differs from contemporary great tombs in the valley in not having a detached tomb temple. Behind the monumental façade is a **vaulted** chamber decorated with beautiful relief slabs and a room with six niches, from which a passage leads down to the burial chamber.

Bibliography: Eigner, *Grabbauten* 50–51.

Niching

From the time of the Unification onwards, the façades of **brick** buildings were elaborately subdivided to produce a

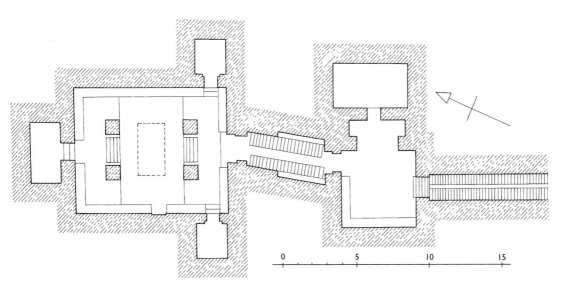

Plan of the tomb of Queen Nefertari in the Valley of the Queens (QV 66)

sequence of regular projections alternating with recesses. Because such niching seems to have appeared without pre-historic precursors, it is assumed that is was influenced by Mesopotamian brick architecture of the Uruk (3400–3200 BC) and Jemdet-Nasr (3200–2900 BC) cultures. However, niching embellished with bundles of papyrus umbels at the tops of the projecting parts suggests a Lower Egyptian origin. As it developed, the symbolism associated with such niches emphasised the connection with the royal palace in the afterlife. There are two main types of niching:

a) Simple niching with projections and recesses like that found in military fortifications, where the projections on the long sides are subdivided with three niches, and the short sides with two niches, while the recesses consist of one main and two flanking side-niches.

b) A more elaborate variant in which the surface of the niches is intricately subdivided (**palace façade**). The panels are decorated with colourful depictions of hanging **mats**. The most ornate examples of such niching occur at the start of the development, becoming increasingly simple with time.

Ornate façades dominate royal structures, but the same structure may bear both kinds of decoration (**Saqqara**, mastaba 3505). Intricate, small niches were occasionally formed out of particularly small bricks (**bricks, moulded**).

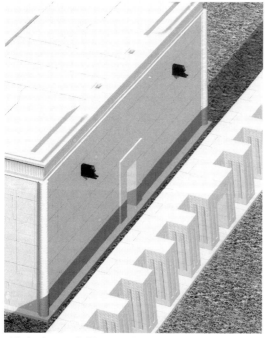
Niched enclosure wall of the pyramid complex of Senwosret III at Dahshur

In the 3rd Dynasty the concept of niching was transferred to **stone constructions** (precinct of **Djoser**, **Sekhemkhet**), but royal tomb precincts from then on were no longer signalled as **palaces**. In the 4th Dynasty niching strayed down into the sarcophagus niches of pyramids and into private burial chambers. Niching resembling the decorated façades is found on both wooden and stone sarcophagi from the 4th Dynasty onwards (**Menkaure**, Khufuankh, **Rawer**). Niche patterns with window slots show that *serdabs* represented palaces in the next life (**mastaba** of Seshemnefer III at **Giza**). Modelled on the tomb precincts of the 3rd Dynasty, the late 12th Dynasty pyramid precincts of **Senwosret II**, **Senwosret III** and **Amenemhat III**, and that of **Khendjer** in the 13th Dynasty all had one or two niched **enclosure walls** of brick or stone. Several examples of private mastabas of the 12th Dynasty had niching to indicate their association with palaces in the next world: **Senwosretankh** at **El-Lisht**, Khnumhotep at **Dahshur**. This archaising trend is followed in Middle Kingdom sarcophagi from the necropoleis of **Dahshur**, **Illahun** and **Hawara**. Usually it was only the plinth or the lower part of the sarcophagus which was decorated in such a way as to suggest a surrounding niched wall.

The use of niching was revived in the New Kingdom, being prominent in the **Hatshepsut** temple, on the plinth of the **Chapelle Rouge**, on the rock façade of several Theban tombs of the 18th Dynasty (User-Amun TT 131, **Ineni** TT 81, **Senenmut** TT 71, **Puyemre** TT39, Nebamun TT 146) and in the burial chamber of the tomb of **Horemheb** at **Saqqara**.

Its final flourishing occurred in the monumental Late Period tombs at **Thebes** (**Pedamenophis**, **Padihorresnet**, **Sheshonq** and **Padineith**), while isolated examples occur as late as the Ptolemaic period. A diluted form of niching is found in some later sarcophagi (those of Ramesses II, of the Apis bulls at the **Serapeum** and of Aspelta). The last niched sarcophagus produced was made in 1882 for Auguste Mariette (at present still in the gardens of the Egyptian Museum at Cairo).

Bibliography: H. Balcz, in: *MDAIK* 1 (1930) 38–92; W. Wolf, in: *ZÄS* 67 (1931) 129–131; Philippe Derchain, *Zwei Kapellen des Ptolemäus' I. Soter in Hildesheim* (Hildesheim 1961); W. Kaiser, *Nischengliederung*, in: Helck, *LÄ* IV 511–513; W. Kaiser, in: *MDAIK* 25 (1969) 4 A.1; G. Haeny, in: Helck, *LÄ* V 568 A.48; Müller, Monumentalarchitektur 7–32; E. Dziobek, in: *MDAIK* 45 (1989) 110–117; J. Dorner, Überlegungen zur Fassadengliederung der großen Mastabagräber aus der 1. Dynastie, in: *MDAIK* 47 (1991) 81–92; A. Krekeler, Nischengegliederte Grabfassaden im nördlichen Teti-Friedhof, in: *MDAIK* 47 (1991) 211–216.

Nilometer

Knowledge of the height of the Nile was enormously important to Egyptian agriculture and from the Early Dynastic Period onwards careful measurements were taken. Staircases or corridors which extend down into the river, marked off with scales for such measurements, first appear in the Late Period. The nilometer at **Elephantine** was particularly important because this was the point in Egypt which the inundation first reached – it is a Roman construction lying to the east of the temple of Satet. Attached to the temple of Khnum (= source deity) is a basin used for measuring the height of the Nile, dating to the reign of Nectanebo II, which has recently been identified with the nilometer described by Strabo. Festivals were held beside such basins at the time of the appearance of the inundation.

Bibliography: Strabo, *Geographica*, XVII.1.48 (C 817); L. Borchardt, *Nilmesser und Nilstandsmarken* (Berlin 1906); H. Jaritz and M. Bietak, Zweierlei Pegelgleichungen zum Messen der Nilfluthöhen im Alten Ägypten, in: *MDAIK* 33 (1977) 47–62; Jaritz, *Terrassen*.

Niuserre, pyramid of

The pyramid 'The Places of Niuserre Remain' at **Abusir** was 50 m high with a base length of 79.80 m and slope of 52°. The nucleus was built in five steps. The inside has been totally destroyed by stone quarrying. The sarcophagus chamber is roofed with three layers of relieving slabs—the blocks weighing up to 90 tonnes each. The customary **pyramid temple** is in two parts because of lack of space. In the centre of the east side there is only the funerary offering room; the commemorative temple with five statue niches was displaced southwards. The north-east and south-east corners of the precinct are developed as massive bastions – their function is not known. The courtyard (with **basalt** paving) was surrounded by corridors with papyrus **columns**. Remains of the **valley temple** and **causeway** have survived, the former, like that of **Sahure**, having two entrances, a main portico in the east and a secondary one to the west. Three shrines inside show clearly that this building was a statue sanctuary.

Bibliography: Borchardt, *Ne-user-Re*; *MRA* 8: Edwards, *Pyramids* 183–184; Stadelmann, *Pyramiden* 175–178.

Niuserre, sun temple of (Abu Ghurob)

The best-preserved **sun temple** of the Old Kingdom, 1 km north-west of the pyramids of **Abusir**. It consists of a **valley temple** (unexplored), a **causeway** 100 m long, and a stone enclosure (83 x 101 m). The cult structure which it encloses was an **obelisk**, possibly 37 m high, built of **limestone** blocks on a base approximately 20 m high accessed via an internal ramp. Attached to the south side is a *sed*-festival chapel and the **Chamber of the Seasons**. To the east of the obelisk is a monumental **altar of alabaster**; the southern courtyard contained slaughtering facilities with gutters and **drainage** pits. To the south, in the desert, is a model of a solar boat in **brick**, 30 m long.

Bibliography: Friedrich W. von Bissing, Ed., *Das Re-Heiligtum des Königs Ne-woser-Re*, 3 Vols (Leipzig 1905, 1923, 1928).

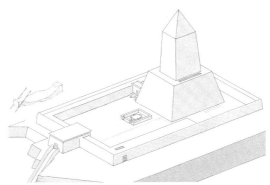

Reconstruction of the sun temple of Niuserre at Abu Gurob

North chapel, entrance chapel

In the course of the 5th Dynasty, single-room chapels developed above the entrance on the north side of the **pyramids** of kings and queens. Measuring approximately 5 x 7 m, they have a **false door** and offering table, and exhibit the type of decorative programme typical of royal offering sites. In the 12th Dynasty the chapel itself remained at the centre of the north side of the pyramid, although the actual entrance was moved elsewhere (**queens' tombs**, Fig.). Queens' pyramids occasionally have a north chapel, but it is rare in private tombs. Any connection with the 'palace' on the north side of the **Djoser** pyramid is unlikely, whereas a link with the secondary cult area on the northern side of private **mastabas** is more plausible. It may be noted at the pyramids of **Djedkare**, **Unas**, **Teti**, **Pepy I**, **Pepy II**, **Senwosret I**, **Senwosret II**, **Senwosret III** and **Amenemhat III** at Hawara.

Bibliography: J.-P. Lauer and J. Leclant, Le temple haut du complexe funéraire du roi Teti (Cairo 1972) 43–44; A. Labrousse, J.-P. Lauer and J. Leclant, Le temple haute du complexe funeraire du roi Ounas (Cairo 1977) 60–61; Jánosi, *Pyramidenanlagen* 275–280; D. Arnold, *The Pyramid of Senwosret I* (New York 1988) 76–83; A. Labrousse, *L'architecture des pyramides à textes* (Cairo 1996) 167–169, Fig. 126.

Nubia

The presence of Egyptian culture in Nubia from the Old Kingdom onwards, in particular the programme of temple and fortress construction of the 12th and 18th Dynasties and in the reign of Ramesses II, left behind an intact cultural and architectural landscape which was unique until the beginning of the 20th century. **Temple, fortress** and **tomb** complexes display forms that are purely Egyptian. From 1892 to 1902 these were periodically flooded as a result of the construction of the first dam at **Aswan** (the height of which was increased in 1907–12 and 1929–34), and were permanently submerged from 1960 in the lake created after construction of the second dam. Between 1960 and 1980 a series of international campaigns were waged to carry out emergency excavations (of only 14 fortresses) and to relocate the c. 20 temples.

Bibliography: Rex Keating, *Nubian Twilight* (London 1962); Rex Keating, *Nubian Rescue* (London-New York 1975); P. Gilbert, L'adaption de l'architecture réligieuse de L'Égypte aux sites de Basse Nubie, in: CdE 35 (1960) 47–64; F. Hinkel, Progress Report on the Dismantling and Removal of Endangered Monuments in Sudanese Nubia, in: *Kush* 13 (1965) 96–101; 15 (1967–68) 1933–1999; William Y. Adams, Nubia, *Corridor to Africa* (London 1977) 163–245; Louis Christophe, *Campagne internationale de l'UNESCO pour la sauvegarde des sites et monuments de Nubie* (UNESCO 1977); Victory in Nubia, *The Unesco Courier* (Feb/Mar 1980); *Oltre l'Egitto: Nubia,* Exhibition Catalogue (Milan 1985); Torgny Säve-Söderbergh, *Temples and Tombs of Ancient Nubia* (London 1987); Irmgard Hein, *Die Ramessidische Bautätigkeit in Nubien,* Göttinger Orientforschungen IV series, Vol. 22 (Wiesbaden 1991); Torgny Säve-Söderbergh, *Victoire en Nubie* (Paris 1992). The lost temples of Nubia: L. Christophe, Sanctuaires Nubiens disparus, in: *CdE* 38 (1963) 17–29.

Nubt

The site of a small **step mastaba** of the 3rd or early 4th Dynasty, near the Upper Egyptian site of Ombos, 35 km north of Luxor, measuring 18 x 18 m (including **casing** of approximately 43 x 43 **cubits**). Like that at **Zawyet el-Mayitin**, it was probably three to four steps high. A small shaft near the centre may have been created by treasure hunters.

Bibliography: Petrie-Quibell, *Naqada and Ballas,* 65, Plate 85; Reisner, *Development* 339; Lauer, *Histoire monumentale* 227–228; Dreyer, *Stufenpyramiden* 46–47.

View of the 3rd Dynasty step pyramid at Nubt (Ombos)

Nuri, see Taharqa

O

Obelisk

A tall, pillar-like stone monument with a pyramid-shaped tip (**pyramidion**), interpreted as an abstract representation of the *benben* **stone** of **Heliopolis** or as a petrified sunbeam. The pyramid-shaped upper end equates to the **primeval mound**, a symbol of eternally repeated creation. Obelisks were erected either singly on a monumental base structure as cult objects in the centre of **sun temples**, or else in pairs in front of a temple or at the entrance of a tomb (the latter in the form of **stelae** with offering tables, for example in the tomb of a queen of **Pepy I** at **Saqqara**). The obelisks in sun temples of the Old Kingdom, massive and stocky in shape, were constructed of blocks (**Niuserre**, height including base c. 57 m). The familiar tall, thin type of New Kingdom obelisk is, however, already attested to in the Old Kingdom, like a tip at **Abusir** and a fragment from the reign of Teti at **Heliopolis**. They bear dedication inscriptions and, in some cases, decoration at the tip. In some examples, the tips were covered with a hammered-on layer of gilded bronze. The earliest completely preserved obelisk still standing is that of Senwosret I at Heliopolis, and the largest known is in front of the Lateran in Rome. Other obelisks still standing at the beginning of the 19th century were one each of Thutmosis I and Hatshepsut at **Karnak**, two of Ramesses II at **Luxor**, one of Thutmosis III at **Alexandria** and one small Ptolemaic obelisk at **Philae**. Descriptions of obelisks more than 100 **cubits** (52.5 m) high existing in antiquity are implausible. Pillar monuments, such as, for example, the stela at **Abgig**, are not true obelisks.

An unfinished obelisk at the **granite** quarries of **Aswan** provides information about its manufacture (**stone quarrying techniques**). It was carved out of the rock by working off the stone percussively with dolerite hammers and hollowed out underneath. Traces of working indicate that around 130 workers were employed simultaneously over a period of approximately one year. An inscription on the obelisk of Hatshepsut at Karnak, 10 m shorter than the Aswan obelisk, relates that it was completed in seven months. It was transported on **sledges,** which were loaded on ships for the downstream journey from Aswan, as illustrated in the temple of **Hatshepsut**. The theory that obelisks were

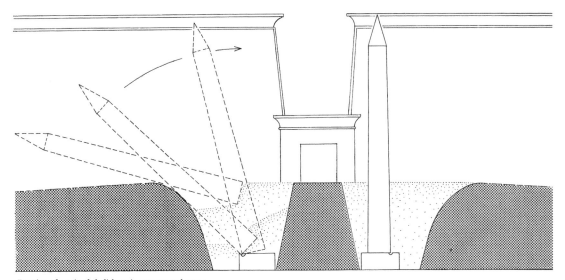

Erection of a pair of obelisks using ramps and ropes

dragged up a high ramp from which they were lowered inside a sand funnel is unproven, although **building ramps**, **levers** and ropes were certainly employed. The bases of some obelisks show transverse grooves where the underside of the obelisk was rotated at erection. Domenico Fontana in 1586 needed 1000 workers and 100 horses to relocate the Vatican obelisk at St. Peter's in Rome (**transport**).

From 10 BC, at least 13, from an originally vast but unknown number of obelisks, were taken to Rome, some probably for the Iseum there, others to be circus turning posts or as sundial pointers. They were re-discovered from the 16th century AD and re-erected in Rome's squares. The only one to survive upright to this day is the Vatican obelisk. One of the obelisks at **Luxor** was taken to Paris between 1831 and 1834. In 1877–78 one of the two 'Cleopatra's Needles' was taken from **Alexandria** to London; the other went to New York in 1881.

Tallest obelisks

Location	Dyn./reign	Ht (m)	Wt (t)
Aswan (unfinished)	18th Dynasty ?	41.75	1168
Lateran	Thutmosis III	32.18	455
Karnak	Hatshepsut	29.56	323
Istanbul	Thutmosis III	28.95	
Vatican, Rome	Thutmosis III	25.37	331
Luxor	Ramesses II	25.00	
Luxor, Paris	Ramesses II	22.55	227
Piazza del Popolo, Rome	Sety I	23.20	235
Mte. Citorio, Rome	Psamtek II	21.79	
Alexandria, New York	Thutmosis III	21.21	193
Alexandria, London	Thutmosis III	20.88	193
Heliopolis	Senwosret I	20.41	121
Karnak	Thutmosis I	19.60	143

Bibliography: Choisy, *L'art de bâtir* 121–127; Engelbach, *Obelisk*; Reginald Engelbach, *The Problem of the Obelisks: From a Study of the Unfinished Obelisk at Aswan* (London 1923): M. Pillet, De l'érection des obélisques, in: *CdE* 6 (1931) 294–305; P. Montet, Les obélisques de Ramsès II, in: *Kêmi* 5 (1935/37) 104–114; J. Leclant and J. Yoyotte, Les obélisques de Tanis, in: *Kêmi* 11 (1950) 73–84; 14 (1957) 43–91; J. Yoyotte, A propos de l'obélisque unique, in: *Kêmi* 14 (1957) 81–91; Eric Iversen, *Obelisks in Exile*, 2 Vols (Copenhagen 1986/72); M. Verner, Discovery of an Obelisk at Abusir, in: *RdE* 28 (1976) 111–118; K. Martin, *Ein Garantsymbol des Lebens* (Hildesheim 1977); Labib Habachi, *The Obelisks of Egypt* (London 1978); K. Martin, Obelisk, in: Helck, *LÄ* IV 542–545; Peter Tompkins, *The Magic of the Obelisks* (New York 1981); Golvin, *Karnak* 127–137; Bernadette Menu, *L'obélisque de la Concorde* (Paris 1987).

Tip of the standing obelisk of Hatshepsut at Karnak

Opet temple (Karnak)

One of the last cult buildings of the Ptolemaic period to be erected at **Karnak**, by Ptolemy VIII Euergetes II. Its cult is closely connected with that of the nearby temple of **Khonsu**, in which Amun-Re dies in the form of Osiris, enters the body of Opet-Nut, and is reborn as Khonsu. The temple harks back to an earlier structure of Amenhotep II. It consists of a **gateway** in a large **enclosure wall**, a **kiosk**, a **pylon** of the Ethiopian period and two courtyards, the first occupied by a further kiosk. This is followed by the main temple building, which is completely preserved and stands on a raised platform, probably representing the **primeval mound**; underground is an **Osiris tomb** and a birth chamber (**crypt**). Interesting features of the temple are some composite **Hathor capitals** and **window** grilles.

Bibliography (no available report on the construction): *Description* III, Plates 58–64; A. Varille, La grande porte du temple d'Apet à Karnak, in: *ASAE* 53 (1955) 79–118; C. De Witt, *Les incriptions du temple d'Opet à Karnak* (Brussels 1958–68); Aufrère, *L'Égypte restituée*, 117–118; M. Azim, A propos du pylone du temple d'Opet à Karnak, in: *Karnak* VIII 51–71.

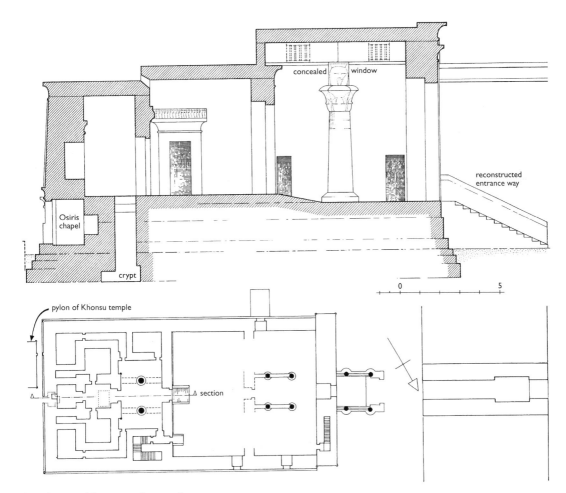

Plan and section of the Opet temple at Karnak

Orientation

Egyptian architecture is part of a comprehensive set of relationships determined by the course of the sun, the flow of the Nile and local geographical and historical conditions. The entrances of **pyramids** are orientated northwards; the sarcophagus in a tomb chamber stands with the head end facing north; wherever possible, **temples** and **tombs** face the Nile (from where processions and bearers of offerings approach), those on the East Bank facing west, and on the West Bank facing east. Where the progress of the Nile or of canals is not exactly south–north, as in the Delta, deviations from this orientation can be as great as 90°. Temple precincts are linked with their own system of processional ways, often following their own conceptual rules, such as the connection from the **Amun** and **Mut** precincts at **Karnak** to **Luxor**). **Birth houses** and **barque stations** often stand at right angles to the main axis.

Compasses being unknown, the axis of buildings was orientated according to the position of the stars or the shadow of the sun on the day of foundation, subterranean systems probably being arranged at right angles. An axis was symbolically determined by the king and Seshat, the goddess of measurement; representations depict the ceremony of 'stretching the rope' between two wooden posts. As in India and China, a gnomon may have been used, the intersections of its shadow with a circle being measured to determine the east–west orientation. Other aids employed would be the Merekhet gnomon and the forked Bayi-palm.

Approximate measurements were usually regarded as sufficient, though in the pyramids of the 4th Dynasty greater care was taken in the accuracy of orientation towards north. Some deviations observed in pyramids/ **mastabas** are:

Pyramid/mastaba	Deviation
Djoser	3° east of north
Meidum	0°24'25" west of north
Bent Pyramid	0°9'12" west of north
Khufu	0°5'30"
Khafre	0°5'26"
Menkaure	0°14'3" east of north
Sahure	1°45' west of north
Neferirkare	0°30' east of north
Senwosret I	1°30' west of north

Bibliography: L. Borchardt, Ein altägyptisches astronomisches Instrument, in: ZÄS 37 (1899) 10–17; 48 (1910) 9–17; Clark, AEM 66–68; Zbyněk Žába, L'orientation astronomique dans l'ancienne Égypte et la précession de l'axe du monde (Prague 1953), discussed by J. Ph. Lauer, BIFAO 60 (1960) 171–183; Zbyněk Žába, Observations sur les pyramides, in: BdE 30 (1960) 99–124; Zbyněk Žába, A propos de l'orientation des grandes pyramides, in: BIE 42/43 (1966) 7–15; G. Goyon, Nouvelles observations rélatives à l'orientation de la pyramide de Khéops, in: RdE (1970) 85–98; G. Vittmann, Orientierung, in: Helck, LÄ IV 607–609; Josef Dorner, Die Absteckung und astronomische Orientierung ägyptischer Pyramiden, Dissertation (Innsbruck 1981); Arnold, Building 15–16; Edwards, Pyramids 97–302; M. Isler, The Merkhet, in: Varia Aegyptiaca 7 (1991) 53–67; D. Magdalen, On the orientation of Old Kingdom royal tombs, in: Bárta, Abusir 2000 491–498; M. Isler, Sticks, Stones and Shadows (forthcoming).

Orthostats

Stone slabs standing on end, used to face the lower part of a wall, best known from their use in Minoan palaces; less frequent in Egypt, one example being the black **basalt** orthostats in the **pyramid temple** of **Sahure**.

Osireion, *see* Osiris tomb

Osiride, *see* pillar

Osiris tomb

The architectural motif of a tomb of Osiris stems from the myth according to which parts of the body of Osiris, scattered over the whole country, lay buried under a mound planted with trees, e.g. at Busiris, **Abydos** and on the Abaton near **Philae**. The only such tomb of Osiris found so far lies in the north-eastern corner of the **Amun** precinct at **Karnak**, based on the building of **Sety I** at Abydos. Kings' tombs were also laid out in the form of a tomb of Osiris: for example, the Bab el-Hosan in the temple of **Mentuhotep**, and the **cenotaphs** of Senwosret III and Ahmose at **Abydos**. Particularly large-scale developments of this motif exist

View over the Osiris tomb of Sety I at Abydos (view corresponds to drawing)

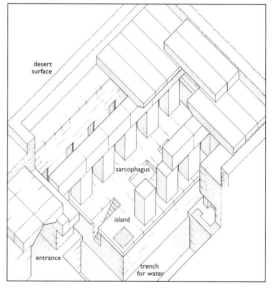

Reconstruction of the Osiris tomb of Sety I at Abydos (view corresponds to photograph)

in the sarcophagus chambers of the New Kingdom kings' tombs, the large Theban tombs of the Late Period and in the **crypts** of the pyramid of **Taharqa** at Nuri. The tomb usually consists of a crypt surrounded by a corridor so that it is separated from the rock, like an island. Standing on this 'island' below a ceiling supported on pillars is the sarcophagus. Several sarcophagi with a lid in the shape of Osiris are preserved; the motif of a funerary mound with a raised surface planted with trees is occasionally found. In the temple of Hathor at **Dendera** an Osiris tomb was constructed at a raised level.

Bibliography: Hermann Junker, Das Götterdekret über das Abaton (Vienna 1913); E. Naville, Le grand réservoir d'Abydos et la tombe d'Osiris, in: ZÄS 52 (1914) 50–55; Eigner, Grabbauten 163–183.

P

Pabasa, tomb of

An important Theban tomb of the Late Period (TT 279, c. 620 BC) in the Assasif at **Thebes**, with interesting wall reliefs. The superstructure has an irregular plan, nonetheless maintaining the traditional three sections. The underground complex consists of an entrance room, **sun court**, **pillared hall** and burial accommodation.

Bibliography: A. Lansing, in: *BMMA* 15, Part II (July 1920) 17–24; Eigner, *Grabbauten* 53; M.A. Nasr, Report on the Restoration of the Tomb of Pabasa (TT 279), in: *MDAIK* 41 (1985) 189–196.

Padihorresnet, tomb of

Monumental Theban tomb (TT 196) of the Late Period (c. 600 BC) in the Assasif at **Thebes**. It has an extensive superstructure with **niching**, separated by **pylons** into three sections. Stairs lead down to the **sun court**, in the central section, which has a **door recess**. Beyond that are two unfinished chambers cut into the rock, with side-chambers, and the descent to the burial complex.

Bibliography: E. Graefe, Fouilles de l'Assasif, in: *CdE* 50, No.99 (1975) 13–64; E. Graefe, Petihorresnet, in: Helck, *LÄ* IV 994–995; Eigner, *Grabbauten* 53–54.

Padineith, tomb of

An important Theban tomb (TT 197) of the Late Period (c. 540 BC) in the Assasif at **Thebes**, consisting of an **niched** superstructure, irregular in plan, and a small **brick** pyramid taking the place of the traditional third courtyard. The underground accommodation is arranged in the order **sun court**, **pillared hall**, cult chamber and burial complex.

Bibliography: Eigner, *Grabbauten* 56–57.

Palace

In accordance with the god-like position of the Egyptian king, the royal palace is a fundamental element of religious constructions, and in the Early Dynastic Period it forms the starting point for Egyptian architecture itself. All but the most meagre remains of palaces of that period are lost (**Hierakonpolis**; the 1st Dynasty palace at **Memphis** is attested to in texts). The only way they can still be envisaged is through their influence on tomb architecture (**mastaba**), their imitation in royal tombs, on sarcophagi and the depiction of Horus resting on top of the **palace façade** (**niching**), bearing the king's name (*serekh*). Palaces probably had a large brick **enclosure wall** and a splendid decorated façade, towers and numerous gates, comparable with later North African brick architecture. Right from the beginning it was closely related to the **divine fortress**, where the divine powers assemble around the Horus king who resides in a palace. A palace of Djedkare-Isesi is mentioned as 116 x 630 m in size, while the furnishings of a palace of Senwosret I are described in the *Story of Sinuhe*. In addition to the residential and governmental palaces, Egyptian religion required cult palaces for the divine aspect of the king. One type of cult palace was connected to '**houses of millions of years**' (**Medinet Habu**, **Ramesseum**, **Merenptah**, **Sety I**), which were constructed from the time of **Hatshepsut** onwards. They are built against the forecourt of the temple, being connected to it by a '**window of appearances**', and provided with a throne hall furnished with a throne dais, as well as living quarters for the king and his entourage. There are some well-preserved remains of a cult palace of **Merenptah** at Memphis. Large parts of the cult palace and the real palace of Amenhotep III, including many cult facilities, have been excavated near **Malqata** and still require further research. We understand little about several cult palaces of Akhenaten at **Amarna**. Typical of these complexes is the large number of **pillared halls** and throne daises in them. Remains of a palace district of the 13th Dynasty have been found at **Tell el-Dab'a** in the Delta and they include a pillared court, a water supply system and a garden. Nearby is a vast Ramesside palace (**Per-Ramesses**, **Tell el-Yahudiya**), where lavish tiled decoration (**building ceramics**) has been found, with workshops.

The actual private accommodation of the king is fairly modest, remains of the Middle and New Kingdoms having at most a slightly more extensive plan and greater lavishness of decoration than private houses of the age (**Amenemhat III** at **Dahshur** and **Bubastis**, Amenhotep III at **Malqata**, Akhenaten at **Amarna**,

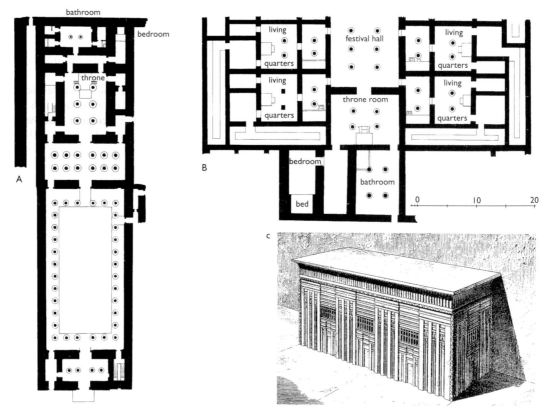

A: plan of the cult palace of Merenptah at Memphis; B: plan of the royal living quarters in the palace of Malqata; C: sarcophagus of Menkaure in the form of a palace of the Early Dynastic Period (after Perrot and Chipiez)

Apries at Memphis). Substructures are preserved of **fortress**-like palaces of the 17th and early 18th Dynasties near **Ballas** and at **Tell el-Dab'a**.

Bibliography: N. de G. Davies, The palace of audience in the palace, in: *ZÄS* 60 (1925) 50–56; Pendlebury, *City of Akhenaten* III 33–105; Hölscher, *Medinet Habu* III 37–59; J. Assmann, Palast oder Tempel, in: *JNES* 31 (1972) 143–155; E. Uphill, The concept of the Egyptian palace as a 'ruling machine', in: P. Ucko, Ed., *Man, Settlement and Urbanism* (London 1972) 721–734; R. Stadelmann, Tempelpalast und Erscheinungsfenster in den Thebanischen Totentempeln, in: *MDAIK* 29 (1973) 221–242; M. Gitton, Le palais de Karnak, in: *BIFAO* 74 (1974) 63–73; B. Kemp, The Palace of Apries at Memphis, in: *MDAIK* 33 (1977) 101–08; B. Kemp, The harim-palace at Medinet el-Ghurab, in: *ZÄS* 105 (1978) 122–133; D. Arnold, Palast, in: Helck, *LÄ* IV 644–646; M. Bietak, Eine Palastanlage aus der Zeit des späten Mittleren Reichs, in: *Anzeiger der phil.-hist. Klasse der Öster. Akad. der Wiss.* 121 (1984) 325–332; M. Bietak, A palace of the early 13th Dynasty at Tell el-Dab'a, in:Bietak, *Haus und Palast*, 73–80; D. O'Connor, City and palace in the New Kingdom Egypt, in: Sociétés urbaines en Égypt et au Sudan (Lille 1989) 73–87; D. O'Connor, Mirror of the Cosmos: the Palace of Merenptah, in: *Fragments of a Shattered Visage* (Memphis, Tenn. 1993) 167–197; Rainer Stadelmann, Temple palace and residential palace, in: *House and Palace* 225–230; D. O'Connor, The city and the world, in: D. O'Connor and E.H. Cline, Eds, *Amenhotep III. Perspectives on his Reign* (Michigan 1998) 125–172; G. Dreyer, *Umm el-Qaab I* (Mainz 1998) 6–7.

Palace façade, *see also* **niching**

A term used to describe a frequent motif in Egyptian art and architecture and one which mainly survived in relation to the king's name (*serekh*). It represents the royal cult **palace** of pre-historic times and the Early Dynastic Period (from Naqada III onwards), having two projecting towers which flank a **gateway** with two or three doors. The front of each tower is divided by three grooves, each of them finishing at the top with the motif of two papyrus plant bundles (possibly representing Lower Egypt) and there is rich decoration in the form of **mats** over the doors. The palace motif is carried over to the **mastabas** of the 1st Dynasty, regarded as mortuary palaces (tomb of **'Menes'**, **Saqqara**), and initially completely surrounded the complexes. From the end of the 1st Dynasty the palace façade motif was reduced to a cult area, and from the 2nd and 3rd Dynasties onwards it was incorporated within the mastaba, in the form of a highly decorated **false door**. From the 4th Dynasty, the palace façade is the principal element in decoration of particularly large sarcophagi and sarcophagus niches, which came to be regarded as mortuary palaces. Striking parallels on scroll seals at Susa and Uruk (IVa–b) may hint at foreign influence.

Bibliography: W. Kaiser, *Palastfassade*, in: Helck, *LÄ* IV 646–647; Winfried Orthmann, Der Alte Orient, in: *Propyläen Kunstgeschichte* (Berlin 1975), Plates 126, 133; Müller, *Monumentalarchitektur* 10–21; H.S. Smith, The making of Egypt, in: *The Followers of Horus. Studies dedicated to Michael Allen Hoffman* (Oxford 1992) 238–241.

Parennefer, tomb of

A Theban tomb of the early reign of Akhenaten (TT 188), which is important architecturally as a precursor of the **rock tombs** at **Amarna**. The inner parts are unfinished and consist of a transverse hall with eight columns.

Bibliography: N. de G. Davies, *Akhenaten at Thebes*, in: *JEA* 9 (1923) 132–152; S. Redford, Two field-seasons in the tomb of Parennefer, No. 188 at Thebes, in: *KMT* 6.1 (Spring 1995), 62–70.

Paving

Stone paving appears as early as the 1st Dynasty royal tombs at **Abydos** in the form of **granite** slabs 2.5 m long and 13 cm thick. In stone buildings either the topmost layer of the **foundations** forms the paving, or else slabs

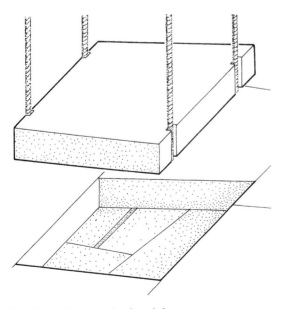

Lowering a paving stone using channels for ropes

of paving are laid on the foundations and pushed against the foot of the wall. The arrangement and shape of the slabs does not follow a specific pattern and was dependent on the available material and the progress of the work. The final stones were lowered into place with the help of ropes passing through notches in the stones. In the Old Kingdom columns were sunk deep into the paving. Paving slabs with integral **column bases** were stronger than surrounding slabs and overlaid so high with **bosses** that the column base and the foot of the wall could be cut out of one and the same block. Paving slabs in the main rooms of the Old Kingdom **pyramid temples** were of **basalt** or **granite,** or very occasionally **alabaster**, but later they were invariably **limestone** or **sandstone**.

Bibliography: Jéquier, *Manuel* 47–52; Arnold, *Building* 141–147.

Pedamenophis, tomb of

The 'mortuary palace' of Pedamenophis (around 670 BC) is the largest Theban tomb (TT 33) of the Late Period. The brick **enclosure wall** (measuring 88 x 110 m) was **niched**. The south-eastern half of the precinct is structured like a **temple**, with three **pylons** and courtyards. The vast underground complex consists of a **sun court** with **pillared halls**, **door recess**, two pillared chambers and a complicated set of burial apartments in the form of an **Osiris tomb** with a corridor, 85 m in length, which completely surrounds the tomb. The **vaulted** sarcophagus chamber is surrounded by 15 recesses in the walls.

Bibliography: Johannes Dümichen, *Der Grabpalast des Petuamenap* (Leipzig 1884); R. Bianchi, Petamenophis, in: Helck, *LÄ* IV 991–992; Eigner, *Grabbauten* 46–48.

Pelusium (Tell el-Farama)

An extensive area of ruins of this once important **town** on the Mediterranean coast of the Sinai. Its monuments are predominantly late Roman in date – thermal baths with a water tower, and a well-preserved theatre. Situated in the centre is a large late Roman fort, 200 x 400 m in area with semi-circular towers. A harbour wall, 300 m long, has been discovered recently.

Bibliography: M.A.El-Maqsoud, Preliminary Report on the Excavations at Tell el-Farama, in: *ASAE* 70 (1984–85) 3–8; H. Jaritz et al., *Pelusium. Prospection archéologique et topographique de la région de Tell el-Kana'is 1993–1994* (Stuttgart 1996).

Pepy I, pyramid of

The pyramid complex of Pepy I, called 'The Completion of Pepy Endures' lies at South **Saqqara**, near the pyramid of **Djedkare**. The centre of the **pyramid** has been so

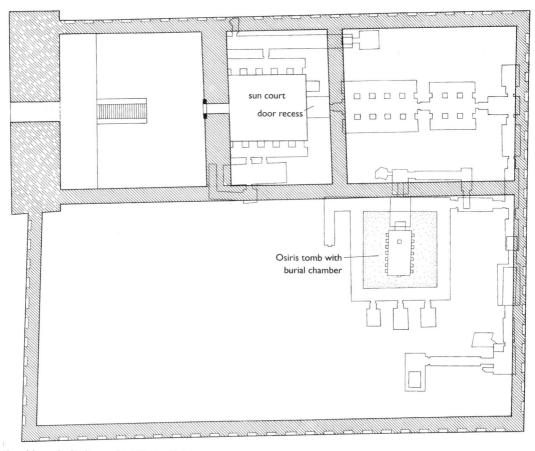

Plan of the tomb of Pedamenophis (TT 33) at Thebes

badly destroyed by stone quarrying that the triple roof of relieving slabs inside is visible on the surface. There are, however, remarkable remains of the core structure. The base of the pyramid is 78.60 m (150 **cubits**) long, and its height is 52.40 m (100 cubits). Its interior follows the traditional layout. Inscribed Pyramid Texts extend along the length of a 'passage chamber' in the corridor at the entrance (in this position since the reign of Sahure). The three-room *serdab*, which had been the norm up to this time, has been simplified down into a single room. The large **pyramid temple**, erected according to the pattern of the 6th Dynasty, was excavated in 1966–88 by a French mission and received exemplary conservation treatment. Excavation of three queens' pyramids on the south side is in progress. No **causeway** or **valley temple** have been found yet; the present-day town of Saqqara has been built over the latter.

Bibliography: J.-Ph. Lauer, in: *CRAIBL* (1970) 491–503; J. Leclant, in: *ASAE* (1982) 55–59; J. Leclant, in: *Orientalia* 51 (1982) 432–433; 52 (1983) 482–483; Stadelmann, *Pyramiden* 193–195; Saqqara aux origines de l'Égypte pharaonique, in: *Les Dossiers d'Archéologie* 146/147 (1990) 52–73; Audran Labrousse, *Regards sur une pyramide* (Paris 1992); Audran Labrousse, *Les pyramides des reines* (Milan 1999); Audran Labrousse, *L'architecture des pyramides à textes* (Cairo 1996), 81, 102, 109–110, 117, 120, 132, 140, 159–160, 162, 173, 175.

View over the pyramid, cult pyramid and pyramid temple of Pepy I at Saqqara

Pepy II, pyramid of

The pyramid complex of Pepy II, 'The Life of (King) Pepy Remains', the last of the Old Kingdom, is situated at the southern end of the necropolis of **Saqqara** immediately next to the Mastabat el-Fara'un (**Shepseskaf**). The length of the base of the **pyramid** was 78.75 m (150 **cubits**), with a slope of 53°13' and a height of 52.50 m (100 cubits). The nucleus of quarried stone was erected in 8–9 steps. Due to damage during construction, the foundations of the pyramid had to be cased in a stone mantle 6.50 m deep. From the passage chamber, the corridor, antechamber and burial chamber are inscribed with Pyramid Texts. Each of the long walls of the sarcophagus chamber, 3.15 x 7.90 m in size, were built from a single piece of stone. Thanks to painstaking recording, it has been possible to restore, in the form of drawings, some of the relief decoration of the **pyramid temple**. The temple follows the layout common in the 6th Dynasty. The north and south-east corners have been enlarged as **pylon**-like bastions. The course of the **causeway**, 520 m long, and the plan of the **valley temple** have been partially reconstructed. The closed façade of the latter was erected behind a terrace, 120 m wide and 20 m high, above the harbour basin, from which it was approached at both ends by ramps. The valley temple contained a **pillared hall**, with two rows of four pillars, probably several statue chambers and 12 large magazines.

Bibliography: Gustave Jéquier, *Le monument funéraire de Pépi II à Saqqarah*, 3 Vols (Cairo 1936, 1938, 1940); Gustave Jéquier, Douze ans de fouilles dans la nécropole memphite (Neuchâtel 1940) 30–131; Edwards, *Pyramids* 194–205; Stadelmann, *Pyramiden* 195–203; A. Labrousse, *L'architecture des pyramides à textes* (Cairo 1996), 134, 141, 159, 161, 174.

Per-nu, *see also* Per-wer

The state shrine of Lower Egypt, formed out of the shrine of the goddess Wadjet and the Per-nezer. No remains exist; our knowledge of its form is based on:

a) the hieroglyph (Fig., A), which shows an upright rectangular chapel with a **vaulted** roof and extended corner posts, and so was probably a structure of wood with a reed roof and **mat** hangings; and

b) the shape of **granite** sarcophagi of the Middle Kingdom with vaulted lids and raised walls, representing a Per-nu made of **brick** with a long barrel roof resting on its side walls. Until the Late Period, the Per-nu generally represented the architecturally symbolic Lower Egyptian counterpart to the **Per-wer** sanctuary. The 'House of the North' in the precinct of **Djoser** may represent the Per-nu.

Bibliography: Henri Frankfort, *Kingship and the Gods* (Chicago 1948) 95–96; Ricke, *Bemerkungen* I 36–38; Jan Assmann, *Das Grab des Basa (Nr.389) in der thebanischen Nekropole* (Mainz 1973) 32–34; D. Arnold, Per-nu, in: Helck, *LÄ* IV 932–933.

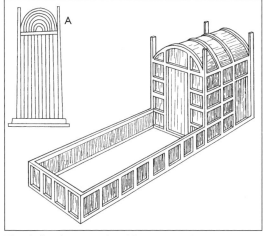

Hieroglyph and reconstruction of the Lower Egyptian Per-nu

Per-Ramesses (Pi-Ramesse, Qantir)

The Delta residence of the Ramesside kings south-west of Qantir on the Pelusian arm of the Nile. It was formerly

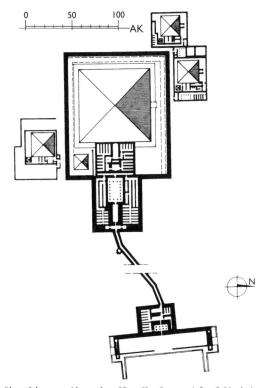

Plan of the pyramid complex of Pepy II at Saqqara (after G. Jéquier)

one of the largest Egyptian **palace** and **temple** complexes (1000 hectares), now completely flattened and partially built over. The palace was founded by Sety I and extended by Ramesses II and his successors. In the 21st Dynasty it was abandoned when the harbour became silted up; the residence moved to **Tanis** and its building materials were transported there and to **Bubastis**.

Several large temples are recorded; the position of the main temple dedicated to Amun-Horakhty-Atum is likely to have been at the centre of the area. In front of the façade were four **colossal statues** of Ramesses II, 21 m high, fragments of which were later used in the temple of Tanis. The temple of Seth in the south was probably identical with the temple of Seth at nearby Avaris (**Tell el-Dab'a**). Situated in the east was an Astarte temple and there was a Wadjet temple in the north. A very impressive festival hall at Per-Ramesses, equipped with **obelisks**, statue groups and columns, 12 m high, was among the buildings erected by Ramesses II for his many *sed*-festivals. There were probably also *sed*-festival complexes of Ramesses III. Tile inlays from the architectural decoration of the palace have been preserved (**building/architectural ceramics**). Military workshops have been found in the area around the palace.

Bibliography: William C. Hayes, *Glazed Tiles from a Palace of Ramesses II at Kantir* (New York 1937); M. Bietak, Ramsesstadt, in: Helck, *LÄ* V 128–146; E.P. Uphill, *The Temples of Per Ramesses* (Warminster 1984); E.B. Pusch, Bericht über die 6. Hauptkampagne in Qantir, in: *GM* 112 (1989) 67–90; E.B. Pusch, Recent work at Northern Piramesse, in: E. Bleiberg and R. Freed, Eds, *Fragments of a Shattered Visage* (Memphis 1991) 199–220; E. Pusch, Towards a map of Piramesse, in: *Egyptian Archaeology* 14 (1999) 13–15.

Per-wer, *see also* Per-nu

The shrine of the ancestral kings and of Nekhbet, Upper Egypt's tutelary goddess, and also the State shrine of Upper Egypt at **Hierakonpolis**. The structure of the complex is preserved in the hieroglyph marked in the figure (A). Originally it may have been a king's tent constructed of reed **matting**, its front adorned with cattle horns and a typical rounded, vault-like roof; the façade had two masts or **flagpoles**. The temenos was surrounded by a low fence. In its architectural symbolism, the Per-wer is the normal Upper Egyptian counterpart to the **Per-nu** sanctuary. The Per-wer type may be represented in the 'House of the South' in the **Djoser** precinct. Such a structure's remains are thought to have been found at Hierakonpolis.

Bibliography: Henri Frankfort, *Kingship and the Gods* (Chicago 1948) 95–96; Ricke, *Bemerkungen* I 27–36; Arnold, Per-wer, in: Helck, *LÄ* IV 934–935; Klaus Peter Kuhlmann, Serif-style architecture and the design of the archaic Egyptian palace, in: Bietak, *House and Palace* 117–137.

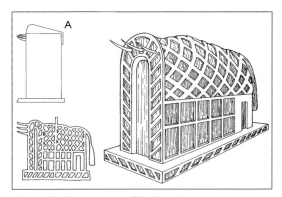

Hieroglyph and reconstruction of the Upper Egyptian Per-wer

Per-weru

The 'House of the Great Ones' refers to the elongated east–west entrance hall of the court of **pyramid temples**. Early forerunners are to be found in the lower temple of the **Bent Pyramid** and the pyramid temples of **Khafre** and **Menkaure**. From the 5th Dynasty, the dimensions became standardised, usually width 5.25 m, length 21 m and height 6.80 m, and roofed with a barrel **vault** of stone, constructed of two semi-arched sections meeting in the middle. The hall received light through window slits in the tympana of the short sides. The structure may have represented a festival tent in the palace courtyard for celebrating various cult festivals; the decorative programme includes, for example, a hippopotamus hunt. Statues of kneeling enemies are also likely to have been displayed here.

Bibliography: Paule Posener-Kriéger, *Les Papyrus d'Abusir* II (Cairo 1976) 496–499; D. Arnold, Rituale und Pyramidentempel, in: *MDAIK* 33 (1977) 6–7; Arnold, *The Pyramid of Senwosret* I, 42–43.

Peripteral temple, *see* ambulatory temple

Petosiris, *see* Tuna el-Gebel

Pharos, *see* Alexandria

Philae

The site of a famous shrine to Isis built on an island (size 140 x 460 m) south of Aswan. From the Old Kingdom to the New Kingdom Egypt's gateway to the south was at **Elephantine**, but from the Ptolemaic period it gravitated to Philae. An **altar** and some relief blocks of Taharqa are evidence of an Amun cult in the 25th Dynasty, while remains of a **kiosk** of Psamtek II and 300 re-used blocks from a temple of Amasis testify to a cult of Isis in the 26th Dynasty. The earliest preserved structure still standing dates from as late as the reign of Nectanebo I, who

The western colonnade in front of the temple of Isis at Philae

Composite pillars, joined by screen walls, of the kiosk of Nectanebo I at Philae (after Prisse d'Avennes, Plate 47)

conceived the overall plan of the complex, beginning with landing stairs at the southern point and a **barque station** on a **platform** high over the Nile. The barque station is an elegant porticus of 14 columns with an interesting combination of **composite** and **Hathor-capital columns**. Two **obelisks** added in the reign of Ptolemy VIII Euergetes II attained special significance due to the double inscriptions in hieroglyphic and Greek on them, used by Champollion in the decipherment of hieroglyphic script. Nectanebo I's plan included a processional way and a large temple with an entrance **pylon**, but only the **gateway** in the first pylon became a reality.

The programme of construction, particularly for the Isis temple with its two 20 and 13 m high pylons, was not taken forward until the reigns of Ptolemy II and Ptolemy III. The lack of available space resulted in an interesting spatial combination of forecourt, **pronaos** and **hypostyle** whose lightness and elegance of proportions is thought to indicate some Hellenistic influence.

Behind the first pylon lies one of the most beautiful and completely preserved **birth houses** in Egypt, dating from the reign of Ptolemy VIII Euergetes II; its triple-room sanctuary has a pronaos with a colonnade which supported a **canopy**-like protective roof over the sanctuary.

Due to the international popularity of the cult of Isis and the site's significance on the Nubian border, further monuments were added in the Roman period: the two long colonnades flanking the processional way and the famous **kiosk** were erected in the reign of Augustus, creating an east–west processional axis to the main temple. A monumental gateway at the north-east with stairs leading up from the Nile was added under the emperor Hadrian. The temples were closely surrounded by **brick** buildings for the accommodation of the cult personnel and pilgrims.

The latest datable hieroglyphic inscription (in Egypt as a whole), from AD 394, and the latest demotic inscription, from AD 452 are found here. After the closure of the temple by Justinian (535–37 AD), Christianity took over, represented by four churches. The monuments remained almost undamaged into the 19th century, but in 1910 Philae was flooded by the old Aswan reservoir. Threatened by the formation of Lake Nasser, the main buildings were removed between 1972 and 1980 to the neighbouring island of Agilkia.

Bibliography (selected): *Description* I, Plates 1–29; Prisse d'Avennes, *Histoire*, Plates 24–25, 27, 47, 58–60; Georges A. Bénédite, Le temple de Philae (Paris 1893–95); L. Borchardt, Der

Augustustempel auf Philae, in: *Jahrbuch des Deutschen Archäologischen Instituts* 18 (Berlin 1903) 73–90; H.B. Lyons, *A Report on the Island and Temples of Philae* (Cairo 1908); E. Winter, Philae, in: *Textes et Langages* (Cairo 1972) 229–237: W. Macquitty, *Island of Isis. Philae, Temple of the Nile* (London 1976); S. Farag et al., Reused blocks from the temple of Amasis at Philae, in: *Oriens Antiquus* 16 (1977) 315–324; S. Farag et al., Reused blocks of Nectanebos I found at Philae island, in: *Oriens Antiquus* 17 (1978) 147–152; Serge Sauneron and Henri Stierlin, *Die letzten Tempel Ägyptens* (Zürich and Freiburg i. Br. 1978) 139–173; A. Giammarusti e Roccati, *File. Storia e vita di un santuario egizio* (Novara, 1980); E. Winter, Philae, in: Helck, *LÄ* IV 1022–1027; G. Haeny, A short architectural history of Philae, in: *BIFAO* 85 (1985) 197–233; Eleni Vassilika, *Ptolemaic Philae,* Orientalia Lovaniensia Analecta 34 (Louvain 1989).

Pilaster, engaged pillar, *see also* anta

An engaged pier topped by a **cavetto cornice**, serving to support the **architrave** which continues beyond a row of **pillars** or **columns** into the wall, for example in the first court of the temple of Ramesses III at **Medinet Habu**, or tomb No. 16 at **Amarna**. Pilasters appear in **brick** structures in burial chambers of the 1st Dynasty (**Abydos, Saqqara, Giza**) as stout buttress-like piers, serving to reduce the span to be covered by beams. The pilasters in the entrance hall of the **Djoser** precinct serve the same purpose.

Bibliography: Jéquier, *Manuel* 161–165.

Pillar, *see also* column, *djed* pillar, heraldic pillar, relief pillar, statue pillar

A vertical support structure, rectangular, square or octagonal in cross-section; some derived forms are polygonal. There are several basic types, which underwent many changes over time:

a) Simple, undecorated square pillars, usually made of **granite** (**pyramid temples** of **Khufu** and **Userkaf, valley temple** of **Khafre, Osireion** of **Sety I** at **Abydos**) or **quartzite** (**Pepy II**), often having vertical areas of inscriptions (Userkaf's at **El-Tod, Mentuhotep** temple) or depictions of plants in raised relief. Examples of the latter are lotus bundles (**Zawyet el-Mayitin**) and the two **heraldic pillars** in the **Amun** precinct at Karnak. A less prominent form in architecture is the *djed* pillar, a derivation of primeval fetishes.

b) Square pillars topped with a **cavetto cornice**, their surfaces decorated with reliefs. This form is less common: an example is seen in the temple of Amenhotep II at **Karnak**, between the ninth and tenth pylons.

c) Square pillars whose surfaces are decorated with symbols of plants, etc., in raised relief (**relief pillar, heraldic pillar**).

d) Octagonal pillars with a **base, abacus** and vertical bands of inscriptions, made of **sandstone** and frequent in the 11th Dynasty (**Beni Hasan, Elephantine, Mentuhotep**). An early form exists in the **pyramid**

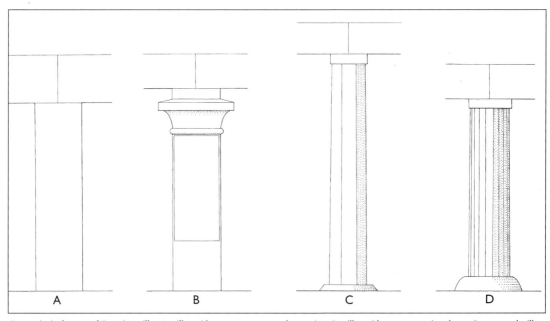

Four principal types of Egyptian pillar. A: pillar with square or rectangular section; B: pillar with cavetto cornice above; C: octagonal pillar; D: polygonal pillar, similar to a column (also channelled)

temple of **Pepy I** and the **mastaba of Ptahhotep and Akhtihotep** at Saqqara (5th/early 6th Dynasty).

e) From the 12th Dynasty onwards, pillars with a polygonal cross-section (16–32 corners, **channelled** column), having a base and abacus (**Amada, Beni Hasan, Buhen, Beit el-Wali, Hatshepsut, Semna**). Smoothed forms (**Sety I** at Abydos) represent a transition to **columns**.

f) From the 12th Dynasty, pillars were often modified to take the form of the **Hathor pillar (Serabit el-Khadim)**. The pillar with an attached statue is a special form (**statue pillar**).

Bibliography: *LD* I 127; Jéquier, *Manuel* 151–165; D. Arnold, Pfeiler, in: Helck, *LÄ* IV 1008–1009; K. Kuhlmann and W. Schenkel, *Das Grab des Ibi. Theben No.36,* (Mainz 1983), Vol. 1, Figs 8, 13; Vol. 2, Plates 33, 91–94; G. Goyon, Un nouveau type de colonne égyptienne dans la pyramide de Pepi I à Saqqarah, in: *SAK* 14 (1987) 99–106.

Royal statue pillar in the festival court of the temple of Ramesses III at Medinet Habu

Pillared hall, *see* hypostyle hall

Piramesse, *see* Per-Ramesses

Pithom (Tell el-Maskhuta)

A **town** and **fortress** in Wadi Tumilat. According to Exodus 1:11 it was built by the oppressed Israelites. Pithom was reinforced by Nekho II in association with his Wadi Tumilat canal project and in order to withstand attacks by Nebuchadnezzar.

Bibliography: Edouard Naville, The Store-City of Pithom and the Route of the Exodus (London 1903); D. Redford, *Pithom,* in: Helck, *LÄ* IV 1054–1058; John S. Holladay, *Tell el-Maskhuta. Cities of the Delta* III (Malibu 1982); P. Paice et al., The Middle Bronze Age/Second Intermediate Period houses at Tell el-Maskhuta, in: Bietak, *Haus und Palast,* 159–173.

Planning, *see also* construction plans

Most Egyptian buildings are the product of innumerable changes of plan conceived while construction was in progress, usually concerning extensions (**Mentuhotep, Hatshepsut, Soleb**). The reason was not so much that the **architects** had no basic concept in mind, but because of the almost limitless possibilities and ever greater demands made by their masters. Planning the layout of a **king's tomb** started immediately on his accession to the throne. In drawing up measurements, both overall and detailed, Egyptian architects preferred to use whole **cubits** (1 cubit = c. 52.5 cm), although fractions (1/2, 1/4 etc. or as expressed in hands or fingers) were unavoidable. It is likely that construction plans were produced using a grid arranged in cubits which would be transferred to the building ground using a 1:1 scale. Similar grid systems were used for the transfer of wall decoration. The meaning of some traditional or otherwise 'sacred' systems of measurement or numbers is not fully understood. The employment of the Pythagorean formula (3:4:5) has been suggested in a few cases (perhaps starting with Djoser). Whether the proportion 5:8 (in the Fibonacci series) was used is uncertain. The calculation of measurements for a complete **pyramid** precinct of the Middle Kingdom appears to have been based on the crossing points of the axes of the pyramid (based on squares of 150, 180 and 220 cubits).

In the Ptolemaic period, planning using a modulus originating in Hellenistic architecture was introduced into Egyptian architecture, measurements then being worked out no longer in cubits but employing a modulus calculated individually for every building as a fraction of a larger measurement. Special numerical ratios have been proposed; however, the bad state of preservation and inexact recording of buildings renders working with such numbers difficult.

Bibliography: J.P. Mayer-Astruc, Trigonométrie pharaonique, in: *CdE* 72 (1961) 321–328; A. Badawy, The harmonic system of architectural design in ancient Egypt, in: *MIO* 8,1 (1963) 1–14; A. Badawy, *Ancient Egyptian architectural design. A study of the harmonic system* (Berkeley 1965); D. Arnold, Grundriß, in: Helck, *LÄ* II 914–915; F.W. Hinkel, Pyramide oder Pyramidenstumpf?, in: *ZÄS* 108 (1981) 105–124; S. Donadoni, Plan, in: Helck, *LÄ* IV 1058–1059; *von Naredi-Rainer, Architektur und Harmonie, Zahl, Maß und Proportion in mittelalterlicher Architektur* (Cologne 1984); Arnold, *Building* 7–22; F.W. Hinkel,The Process of Planning in Meroitic Architecture, in: *Egypt in Africa* (London 1991) 110–233; Karl Georg Siegler, Die Tore von Kalabscha, in: *MDAIK* 25 (1969) 139–153; Karl Georg Siegler, *Kalabscha* (Berlin 1970) passim; W. Meyer-Christian, Der 'Pythagoras' in Ägypten am Beginn des Alten Reiches, in: *MDAIK* 43 (1986) 195–203; G. Robins, Composition and the artist's squared grid, in: *JARCE* 28 (1991) 41–54; H.R. Butler, *Egyptian Pyramid Geometry* (Missisauga 1998).

Plaster, *see also* mortar

A very pliable but quick-setting mixture of **gypsum**, sand and water. It was used in Egyptian architecture from the Old Kingdom onwards for repairing walls and providing a smooth surface as a preparation for painting. It was also occasionally used to repair reliefs or as a binding agent for repair stones and pegs. Ornamental plasterwork, however, does not exist.

Bibliography: A Lucas, Mistakes in chemical matters frequently made in archaeology, in: *JEA* 10 (1924) 128–131; Lucas, *AEMI* 76–79; R. Fuchs, Stuck, in: Helck, *LÄ* VI 87–92.

Platform, podium

When cult images and the barques of gods emerged from a temple they were placed on walled platforms on the bank of the Nile or a canal. The front of the platform protrudes, bastion-like, towards the canal. Side walls are often, though not necessarily, accompanied by stairs down to the water, with the rear (which faced the temple) being left open, for example in front of the first pylon at Karnak (**Amun** precinct), and at **El-Tod**, the temple of Khnum and Satet at **Elephantine**, and at **Dendur**). The wall supporting the terrace on the side facing the river is in some cases concave, probably in order to withstand pressure (as at the temple of Khnum and Satet at **Elephantine**, and at **Philae**, **Dendur** and **Kalabsha**). In later times, these platforms were used for meetings of cult communities. The platform may represent a distant successor of the Old and Middle Kingdom **valley temple**.

Bibliography: J. Lauffray, Abords occidentaux du premier pylône de Karnak. Le dromos, la tribune et les aménagements portuaires, in: *Karnak* IV 77–131; C. Traunecker et al., La tribune du quai de Karnak, in: *Karnak* V 43–76; Jaritz,*Terrassen*; W. Schenkel, Kai-Anlage, in: Helck, *LÄ* III 293–295.

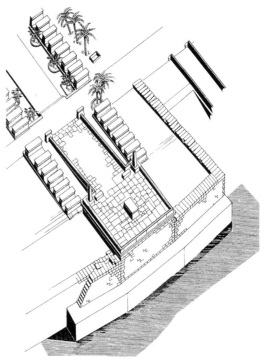

Reconstruction of the podium and avenue of sphinxes before the first pylon at Karnak (after J. Lauffray)

Plinth, *see also* base, column base

A rectangular base for **columns** and **pillars**, not always distinctly separate from other paving slabs, as in the temple of **Mentuhotep**, court of the **pyramid temple** of **Senwosret I**, temple of **Sety I** at Abydos, and temple of **Edfu**. It often has its own foundations and was carved out of a single block together with the column or pillar base.

Podium, *see platform*

Porphyry

Unstratified or igneous rock with dispersed crystals in a homogeneous base matrix, ranging in colour from black to pink to purple. It was used from pre-historic times onwards in the manufacture of stone vessels, mace heads, and so on, but it was not used by sculptors until the Graeco-Roman period. Mining of the 'imperial porphyry' for Roman construction projects began at the start of the 2nd century AD at Gebel Dukhan (Mons Porphyrites on the Red Sea). Pliny's claim that it was used in the manufacture of columns for the Labyrinth (**Amenemhat III**, pyramid at Hawara) appears rather doubtful.

Bibliography: Pliny, *Naturalis Historia* 36, 13 (19); G. Andrew, On the Imperial Porphyry, in: *BIE* 20 (1938) 63–81; Lucas, *AEMI* 416–418, 421–22; B. Bianchi, Porphyr, in: Helck, *LÄ* IV 1071–1073; De Putter, *Pierres* 119-21; Klemm, *Steine* 379–395; Nicholson, *Materials* 48–49.

Portcullis

A device consisting of stone slabs lowered into a tomb corridor to block the entrance, the earliest instances being found in the **mastabas** of the 1st Dynasty at **Saqqara** and **Bet Khallaf**. In the Old Kingdom, from the **Bent Pyramid** onwards, it is found in all **kings' tombs**, where it consists of three slabs close together, which were lowered on rollers (pyramids of **Khufu** and **Menkaure**). From the Middle Kingdom it becomes less frequent, being replaced by **sliding blocks,** which are more difficult to remove. The portcullis in the mastaba of **Senwosretankh** is equipped with barbed hooks to prevent it being pushed back up. Practically every portcullis was either avoided, levered up or tunnelled through by tomb robbers.

Bibliography: Arnold, *Building* 223–228.

Positional marks, *see* control notes

Primeval mound

The concept of a mound, or island of the 'first time', which emerged from the primeval ocean (*nun*) at creation, had a special significance in Egyptian religion and architectural symbolism, conditioned by the phenomenon of the annual retreat of the Nile inundation. It also had a secondary connection to the similarly shaped mound of the **Osiris tomb** (**symbolism**). Shrines of the Early Dynastic Period may also have stood on real or artificial mounds. **Pyramids** too are possibly related to the same concept, as may also be the core structure of the temple of **Mentuhotep**. The **enclosure wall** around the tomb of **Montuemhat** surrounds a primeval mound of 60 x 60 **cubits**. In other tombs of the Late Period, at the centre of the tomb chamber, surrounded by a corridor, a block of stone is marked as the primeval mound (**Harwa**, **Pedamenophis**, **Bakenrenef**). The concept of a mound may have been realised inside the pyramid of **Senwosret II**. The existence of primeval mounds at several towns is known from documents, although not attested to archaeologically (**Heliopolis**, **Memphis**, **Hermopolis**).

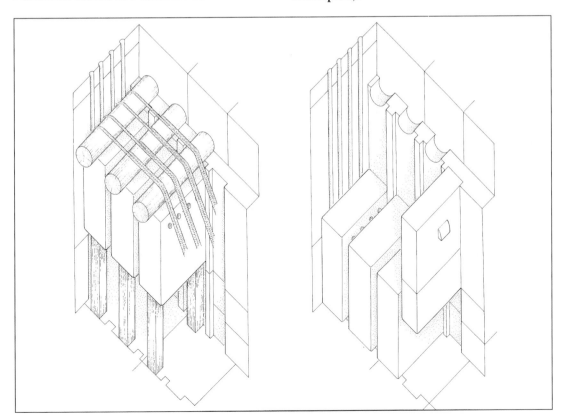

Reconstruction of the portcullis system of the pyramid of Khufu in open and closed positions

Bibliography: Adriaan de Buck, *De Egyptische Voorstellingen betreffende den Oerheuvel* (Leiden 1922); Abdel-Aziz Saleh, The so-called 'primeval hill' and other related elevations in ancient Egyptian mythology, in: *MDAIK* 25 (1969) 110–120; J. Monnet Saleh, Les représentations de temples sur plates-formes à pieux, de la pottery gerzéenne d'Égypte, in: *BIFAO* 83 (1983) 263–296; Eigner, *Grabbauten* 178-80; K. Martin, Urhügel, in: Helck, *LÄ* VI 873–875.

Private tomb, *see also* mastaba, rock tomb

Pronaos

Called *khentis* in Egyptian, a **pillared hall** before the body of a **temple**, either half or completely open at the front. Early forms, from the time of Amenhotep III onwards, develop into a hall at the rear of the columned court (**Luxor**, **Month** precinct, **Soleb**). The earliest true examples occur at the temples of Sety I in **Wadi Miya**, of Ramesses II at **Ehnasya el-Medina** and of Sheshonq at **El-Hiba**. Its peak period of use began in the 30th Dynasty and continued under the Ptolemies and the Romans (see list below). The pronaos is frequently the tallest part of the building and may enclose an existing temple building with a closed front, its roof resting on the latter's **cavetto cornice**. Intercolumnar spaces are half closed by **screen walls** and side walls are closed completely. The central entrance leads through a screen wall with an interrupted **architrave**. Equipped with sumptuous composite columns and a rich decorative programme, the pronaos forms the high point of late Egyptian temple architecture. Acting partly as a **barque station** and partly as a place where the divine images were assembled, it probably took on the function of the earlier hypostyle hall, which had started to decline in use from the Late Period onwards.

Larger pronaoi

	Width (m)	Height (m)	Depth (m)	Columns
Akhmim (Ptolemy IV?)	86.00	c. 26	c. 30	4 x 10
Hermopolis (Philip Arrhidaeus)	57.75	18.375	21.00	2 x 6
Antaeopolis (Ptolemy VI)	45.30	15.25	?	3 x 6
Dendera (Tiberius)	42.60	18.05	26.00	4 x 6
Edfu (Ptolemy VIII)	40.55	15.674	18.705	3 x 6

	Width (m)	Height (m)	Depth (m)	Columns
Kom Ombo (post-Ptolemy VI)	c. 40	c. 14	c. 17	3 x 5
Esna (Claudius)	37.36	14.98	20.2	4 x 6
El-Tod (Ptolemy VII)	24.5	?	9.4	2 x 4
Ehnasya el-Medina (Ramesses II)	22.68	c. 7	c. 6.3	2 x 8
Kalabsha (Augustus)	22.61	12.26	14.95	2 x 4
Hibis temple (Saite)	18.65	7.40	6.38	2 x 4

Bibliography: Good examples in Gustave Jéquier, *Architecture et décoration dans l'ancienne Égypte*, Vol. III (Paris 1924); Dieter Kurth, *Die Dekoration der Säulen des Tempels von Edfu* (Hildesheim 1983); D. Arnold, Zur Rekonstruktion des Pronaos von Hermopolis, in: *MDAIK* 50 (1994) 13–22.

Proportion, *see* planning

Protodoric columns

A misleading term applied to polygonal **channelled** pillars, which are common in Egypt from the 12th Dynasty onwards (**Beni Hasan**); similarities with the Doric order of columns have been wrongly used to demonstrate the dependence of Greek architecture on Egypt.

Bibliography: Perrot, *L'Égypte* 549–551; P. Gilbert, L'architecture dorique et l'Égypte. Impressions d'un Égyptologue en Grèce, in: *Le Flambeau* 37 (Brussels 1954) 699–705; P. Gilbert, Paestum et l'Égypte, in: *Phoibos* 3/4 (Brussels 1948/49, 1949/50).

Ptah, temple of (Karnak)

A small temple precinct north of the temple of Amun (**Amun** precinct). The original small triple-cell structure was dedicated by Thutmosis III, with two polygonal pillars in front and a small forecourt which appears to have been roofed in the Ramesside period. When the large **enclosure wall** of Karnak was built, it cut through the northern part of the precinct. In the reign of Ptolemy III a small **pylon** with rooms for the storage of cult equipment was added in front. Against its façade is a **kiosk** with beautiful **composite capital** columns. In front of the kiosk, on the processional avenue, Shabaka erected his *sed*-festival gate B, as well as gate D. Ptolemy VI Philometor I added gate A and Ptolemy XIII

Neos Dionysos gate C. The stone elements of the complex are still completely preserved.

Bibliography: Georges Legrain, Temple de Ptah ris-anbou-f dans Thebes, in: *ASAE* 3 (1902) 38–66, 97–114; H. Chevrier, Temple de Ptah, in: *ASAE* 53 (1956) 18–19, Plates 9, 11; Haeny, *Basilikale Anlagen* 10–11, 83–84.

Ptah, temple of (Memphis)

One of the earliest and most important shrines in Egypt. In the Ptolemaic period it was surrounded by a trapezoidal **brick** wall measuring 410 x 580 x 480 x 630 m. The area inside was divided in four by the intersection of the axes of the temple, with the main gates facing the four points of the compass. All that is now visible are the remains of the western approach of Ramesses II consisting of a stone **pylon**, 74 m wide, with four **colossal statues** of the king. Many blocks of the Old and Middle Kingdoms were re-used. Behind lies the 'Western Hall', a monumental **hypostyle hall** consisting of four rows of papyrus **columns**, 13 m high, surrounded on all sides by a double row of smaller columns. The hypostyle hall leads to the central part of the temple, starting with an open columned façade. Ramesses II added a forecourt with a pylon to the temple on the north axis and renewed the sanctuary of Ptah. All the great builders, from the Old Kingdom to the Ptolemies, especially Amenhotep III and Ramesses II, sought to immortalise themselves in the main part of the temple by erecting sanctuaries, pillared halls, forecourts, pylons and colossal statues. Remains of a **granite gateway** of Ptolemy IV are all that is left of structures in the eastern wall. At the northern gate are remains of statues and a re-used **architrave** of Amenemhat III. In front of the southern gate there were originally several colossal statues of Ramesses II (one now within a museum on the site, and another in the

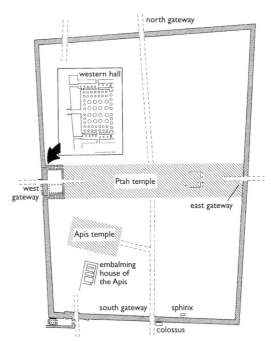

Plan of the Ptah precinct at Memphis

square in front of the station in Cairo). A huge **alabaster sphinx** of the New Kingdom, now in the nearby museum gardens, came from a forecourt situated behind the south gate.

In the south-west corner of the precinct was the temple of Apis, no longer preserved, erected in the 26th Dynasty. Its courtyard, surrounded by halls and **statue pillars**, 6 m high, served as exercise area for the sacred bull. Nearby was the **embalming hall** for the sacred bulls, a simple brick building dating from the reign of Nectanebo II. A processional way, with sphinxes, chapels and other monuments led from there to the catacombs of the **Serapeum**.

Still standing in front of the south wall of the Ptah precinct is a Hathor temple, which is decaying in the sub-soil water.

Bibliography: Herodotus, *History* II, Book 176; Strabo, *Geographica*, Book XVII, 31–32; Rudolf Anthes, *Mit Rahineh 1955* (Philadelphia 1959); Rudolf Anthes, *Mit Rahineh 1956* (Philadelphia 1965); Marion T. Dimick, *Memphis, the City of the White Wall* (Philadelphia 1956); Haeny, *Basilikale Anlagen*, 68–70; H.S. Smith, *A Visit to Ancient Egypt: Life of Memphis and Saqqara 500–30 BC* (London 1974); Abdulla el Sayed Mahmud, *A New Temple for Hathor at Memphis* (Warminster 1978); D.G. Jeffreys, *The Survey of Memphis* I (London 1985); J. Malek, The Monuments recorded by Alice Lieder in the 'Temple of Vulcan' at Memphis in May 1853, in: *JEA* 72 (1986) 101–112; D.G. Jeffreys and J. Malek, *Memphis 1986, 1987*, in: *JEA* 74 (1988) 15–29; L.L. Giddy,

View of the area of the temple of Ptah at Memphis (Western Hall)

D.J. Jeffreys and J. Malek, *Memphis, 1989*, in: *JEA* 76 (1990) 4–11; K.A. Kitchen, Towards a reconstruction of Ramesside Memphis, in: *Fragments of a Shattered Visage* (Memphis, Tenn. 1991) 87–92; L. Giddy, The Ptah Temple Complex, Memphis: 1992 Season, in: *Bulletin of the Australian Centre for Egyptology* 5 (1994) 27–35.

Ptahhotep and Akhtihotep, tomb of

A **mastaba** of the 5th to early 6th Dynasty at **Saqqara**, c. 25 x 26 m in size, famous for its excellent reliefs. It is entered through a **door recess** which leads into an antechamber with a large statue shrine and a *serdab*. Behind this is a **pillared hall** with four octagonal pillars from which the two mortuary offering chapels of Ptahhotep and Akhtihotep are reached (**false door**, Fig.). The large burial area has not been investigated, and no structural investigation of the double mastaba has yet been carried out.

Bibliography: R.F. Paget and A.A. Pirie, *The Tomb of Ptah-hetep* (London 1898); N. de Garis Davies, *The Mastaba of Ptahhetep and Akhethetep*, 2 Vols (London 1900–01); Selim Hassan, *Mastabas of Ny-ankh-Pepy and Others. Excavations at Saqqara, 1937–1938*, Vol. 2 (Cairo 1975) 25–84.

Ptahshepses (Shepsesptah), tomb of

The largest **mastaba** at **Abusir**, measuring 42.24 x 56.24 m, and a first-rank structure of the reign of **Niuserre**. The tomb has a complex plan and a tangled construction history: the earliest part is the north-west corner, which was later extended to the east and south. The magnificent lotus **columns** preserved in the entrance chamber are rare examples of this type. Behind is a statue temple with three statue shrines set at a higher level. The southern section of the complex is occupied by a pillared court of temple-like dimensions, with a **door recess** which leads to the three statue chambers. In the south-west corner is a chamber with a curved side wall for two 23 m long funerary boats. The **canopic recess** in the burial complex is protected by a roof of relieving slabs, 3.3 m high. The plan may have been influenced by the nearby royal **pyramid temple**.

Bibliography: *Preliminary Report on Czechoslovak Excavations in the Mastaba of Ptahshepses at Abusir* (Prague 1976); Miroslav Verner, *Abusir I, The Mastaba of Ptahshepses. The Reliefs* (Prague 1977); Miroslav Verner, *Abusir II, Baugraffiti der Ptahschepses Mastaba* (Prague 1992); M. Verner, *Forgotten Pharaohs, Lost Pyramids, Abusir* (Prague 1994) 173–192; M. Balík and B. Vachala, The scientific restitution of the Ptahshepses' mastaba at Abusir, in: Bárta, *Abusir 2000*, 317–330.

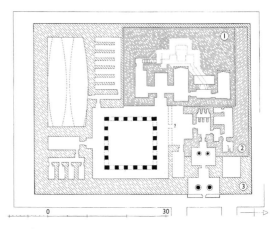

Plan of the mastaba of Ptahshepses, showing construction phases

Puyemre, tomb of

The burial place of Puyemre at Thebes (TT 39), who is believed to have been the builder of the temple of **Hatshepsut**, is one of the most important tombs of the reign of Thutmosis III and is decorated with magnificent reliefs. A forecourt with a portico of columns, two **stelae** and six **false doors** is followed by a magnificently appointed transverse hall within the rock. Opening on the latter are three parallel chapels, each one representing a different type of structure (**multiple shrine**, Fig., D). That to the north has a black-painted door frame and artistically designed skylight; the ceiling inside is vaulted and there is a false door in the rear wall similar to the

Entrance portico of the mastaba of Ptahshepses at Abusir, with closed-capital lotus columns

mortuary offering hall of the **Hatshepsut temple**. The central two-room chapel has a wall niche for a statue group and depictions of false doors on the **vaulted** ceiling. The southern chapel has a vaulted ceiling which slopes similarly to that of the **Per-wer**, with a statue niche in the rear wall.

Bibliography: Norman de Garis Davies, *The Tomb of Puyemrê*, 2 Vols (New York 1923).

Pylon

The Greek word *pylon* means a 'large entrance gateway or gate building'. Pylons formed of twin towers with a sloping outer surface and a **cavetto cornice** are typical in the New Kingdom, prototypes being found in the corner sections of the Old and Middle Kingdom **pyramid temples**. The earliest examples of pylons in front of a courtyard appear in the 11th Dynasty. From the early 18th Dynasty onwards, they form a temple façade and are closely linked to the courtyard beyond. The form changes in the New Kingdom when the pylon is equipped with securing devices for the **flagpoles** which tower over it. The passage through the pylon is closed with heavy wooden doors, in some cases decorated with copper gilding. Motifs illustrating destruction rituals, such as the king receiving the battle sword from a deity or smiting enemies, or the hunting of wild animals, integrate the pylon into the symbolism of achieving and maintaining world order. The pylon may also be construed as the mountains on the horizon between which the sun rises and sets, especially in the temples of the **Aten**.

Narrow, steep staircases ascend to the roof platform, in the New Kingdom leading straight from the narrow side, while at **Edfu** they take a U-shaped course through several storeys provided with **windows** and stair-chambers. The **bridge** across the passage in the **gateway** of the temple of Ramesses III at **Medinet Habu** accommodates a small solar cult area. In front of the pylon there are often **colossal statues** of the king and a pair of **obelisks**.

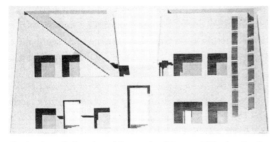

Section through the pylon of the temple of Horus at Edfu, showing the stairway system (after *Description* I, Plate 52)

Sample dimensions of pylons

	Width (m)	Depth (m)	Height (m)
Karnak			
I	122	15	43.5
II	100	13.9	?
III	97	12.6	?
IV	63	10.6	?
VII	63.7	11.0	?
VIII	48.0	9.4	?
IX	65.5	11.0	?
X	66.7	11.7	?
Temple of **Khonsu**	34.5	7.0	18
Sety I, Abydos	60.0	?	?
Edfu	79	11	36
Medinet Habu	65	11	24
Luxor	64.25	8.4	25
Philae	38	6.8	18
Kalabsha	34.27	6.43	16.5

Bibliography: Jéquier, *Manuel* 65–76; T. Dombardt, Der *zweitürige Tempelpylon altägyptischer Baukunst und seine religiöse Symbolik* (New York 1933); U. Hölscher, Der erste Pylon von Karnak. Bautechnische Beobachtungen, in: *MDAIK* 12 (1943) 139–149; H. Sourouzian, L'apparition du pylone, in: *BIFAO* 81 (1981) 141–151; S.B. Shubert, Studies on the Egyptian pylon, in: *JSSEA* 11 (1981) 135–164; B. Jaroš-Deckert, Pylon, in: Helck, *LÄ* IV 1202–1205; M. Azim, La structure des pylones d'Horemheb à Karnak, in: *Karnak* VII 127–166; M. Azim, Le grand pylone de Louqsor, in: *Mélanges Jean Vercoutter* (Paris 1985) 19–34; C. Van Siclen III, A 'new' representation of a pylon from Karnak, in: *Iubilate Conlegae: Studies in Memory of Abd el Aziz Sadek* (San Antonio 1995) 63–80.

Pyramid, see *also* cult pyramid, step mastaba

The influence of the sun cult at the beginning of the 4th Dynasty caused royal mortuary enclosures (**Djoser** precinct) to be replaced with a complex of structures whose chief elements had their origin in **sun temples**: an east–west orientated precinct with a pyramid, representing a solar monument or a **primeval mound**. The **step mastaba** was thereby replaced by the true pyramid, ostensibly the conversion of a natural mound into a crystallised, abstract form. The vast pyramids of the 4th Dynasty which followed demonstrate by their exaggerated monumental proportions their special importance in ensuring the continued existence of the king and the country: their primary purpose was not to serve as a tomb but to be the centre of the nightly transformation of the king, who went to the underworld and was then newly reborn. The inner rooms of the pyramid, usually four in number (passage chamber, antechamber, *serdab* and sarcophagus chamber), had a particular part to play in this cycle. The sarcophagus of hard stone, an innovation of **Khufu**, becomes the place where the king is united with Re-Atum. The antechamber, which can be traced back as far as the **kings' tombs** of the 1st Dynasty, situated as it was between the burial chamber and the corridor, is connected with the ascent of the king to heaven, and is therefore, from **Djoser** onwards, decorated with stars and later inscribed with ascension texts. From the reign of **Menkaure**, a group of chambers developed (named by H. Ricke the *'serdab'*), which from the time of **Sahure** onwards was situated in the east opposite the sarcophagus chamber. In the pyramids of the Middle Kingdom, this appears to have developed into a kind of second tomb for the king. The conceptual change, from the 4th Dynasty, towards an imaginary solar rebirth of the king, coincides with the development of the cultic accommodation on the east of the pyramid, traditionally associated with the rise of the sun, while the introduction at the start of the 5th Dynasty of the **false door** and funerary offerings for the king implied his reduction to the sphere of ordinary human beings. The pyramid was personified as a special power, fused with the king. In the Middle Kingdom the **pyramidion** bears the eyes of the king.

Egyptian kings continued until the end of the 17th Dynasty to be buried in a modest form of pyramid, attached to which, and in some cases erected inside which, were small cult chapels with a **vaulted** ceiling and a small **stela** standing in the background; a small sarcophagus chamber was probably situated below. Remains of such complexes (in **Thebes**) are being excavated by the German Archaeological Institute.

From the start of the New Kingdom, coinciding with the cessation of royal pyramid building, private individuals erected pyramids for themselves, for example at **Abydos**, **Aniba**, **Saqqara**, **Sedeinga**, **Soleb** and, especially **Thebes**. Usually these structures are small **brick** pyramids, sloping steeply at 60–70°, and equipped with a vaulted niche, high up in the east flank over the entrance, for the accommodation of a statue of the tomb owner worshipping the sun. The base of the tomb of Amenuser (TT 131) was **niched**, creating the effect of a pyramid standing in a niched precinct.

The form adopted by the Ethiopian kings of the 25th Dynasty for themselves and their households was a pyramid tomb (necropoleis of El-Kurru and Nuri near Napata, **Taharqa**). These structures, usually only 27–28 m high, with a 68° angle of slope, are steeper than Egyptian pyramids. Their nucleus consists of rubble and gravel

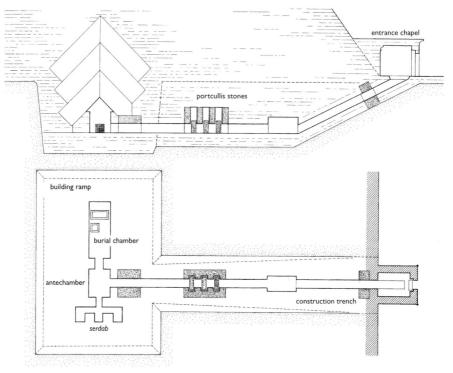

Typical pyramid of the 5–6th Dynasty: north–south section through the inner chambers (built within an open construction trench)

held together by **casing** blocks. Their outer surface was stepped (originally probably covered with plaster) or smoothed, the finished form of corners being cornices or torus moulding (**cavetto cornice**).

Some Egyptian-style pyramids were built outside Egypt in the Roman period, for example in Rome (**Cestius'** pyramid), in North Africa and in Syria, continuing in the 'Egyptian Revival' of the 19th century (for example the earth pyramid of Prince Pückler of Muskow in Silesia).

Pyramid measurements, cubits (metres)

Pyramid	Angle	Base	Height
Meidum M3	51°51'	275 (144.32)	175 (92)
Bent Pyramid (Sneferu)	54°31' (top 44°30')	360 (189)	200 (105)
North **Dahshur** (Sneferu)	45°	420 (220)	200 (105)
Khufu	51°50'40''	440 (230.36)	280 (146.50)
Djedefre	60°	200 (105)	175 (92)
King's tomb, Zawyet el-Aryan	?	210 (110)	?
Khafre	53°10'	410 (215.29)	275 (143.87)
Menkaure	51°	200 (105.5)	125 (65.55)
Userkaf	53°	140 (73.3)	94 (49)
Sahure	50°45'	150 (78.75)	(50)
Neferirkare	54°30'	200 (105)	(72.8)
Niuserre	52°	150 (78.90)	(50)
Neferefre	?	125 (65)	?
Djedkare	52°	150 (78.75)	?
Unas	56°	110 (57.70)	(43)
Teti	?	150 (78.75)	100 (52.5)
Pepy I	?	150 (78.6)	100 (52.4)
Merenre	?	175 (90-95)	?
Pepy II	53°13'	150 (78.75)	100 (52.5)
Amenemhat I	54°	160 (84)	112 (59)
Senwosret I	49°24'	200 (105.23)	116 (61.25)
Amenemhat II	?	160 (84)	?
Senwosret II	42°35'	200 (105.88)	(48.65)
Senwosret III	50°	204 (107.10)	(64.131)
Amenemhat III (Dahshur)	54–56°	200 (105)	143 (75)
Amenemhat III (Hawara)	48–52°	200 (101.75)	(58)
Khendjer	55°	100 (52.5)	(37.35)
Unknown (neighbour of Khendjer)	?	175 (92)	?
N. **Mazghuna**	No figures available		
S. **Mazghuna**	?	100 (52.5)	?

Bibliography (selected): Petrie, *Pyramids*; L. Speleers, La signification des Pyramides, in: *Mélanges Maspero* I/2 (1935–38) 603–621; A. Moret, L'Influence du décor solaire sur la pyramide, in: *Mélanges Maspero* I/2 (1935–38) 623-36; Leslie Grinsell, *Egyptian Pyramids* (Gloucester 1947); Dows Dunham, *The Royal Cemeteries of Kush* I–IV (Boston 1950–57); Wolfgang Helck, Pyramiden, in: *Paulys Realencyclopädie der classischen Altertumswissenschaft* 23 (1959) 2167–2282; Ahmed Fakhry, *The Pyramids* (Chicago-London 1961); *MRA* II–VIII (1963–77); Peter Tompkins, *Secrets of the Great Pyramid* (London 1973); Lauer, *Histoire monumentale*; J.-P. Lauer, *Mystère*; S. Curto, Per la storia della tomba privata a piramide, in: *MDAIK* 37 (1981)107–113; Edwards, *Pyramids*; Brinks, *Grabanlagen*; G. Dreyer and W. Kaiser, Zu den kleinen Stufenpyramiden Ober- und Unterägyptens, in: *MDAIK* 36 (1980) 43–59; F.W. Hinkel, Pyramiden im Sudan, in: *Das Altertum* 26 (1980) 77–88; F.W. Hinkel, Pyramide oder Pyramidenstumpf?, in: *ZÄS* 108 (1981) 105–124; R. Stadelmann and D. Arnold, Pyramiden, in: Helck, *LÄ* IV 1205–1272; K.P. Kuhlmann, Die Pyramide als König?, in: *ASAE* 68 (1982) 223–235; Celeste Rinaldi, *Le Piramidi* (Milan 1983); Stadelmann, *Pyramiden*; E. Dziobek, Eine Grabpyramide des frühen N.R. in Theben, in: *MDAIK* 45 (1989) 109–132; Stadelmann, *Pyramiden von Giza*; D. O'Connor, Boat graves and pyramid origins, in: *Expedition* 33 (1991) 5–17; Lehner, *Complete Pyramids*; M. Verner, *Die Pyramiden* (Hamburg 1998); C. Berger et al., Reading a pyramid, in: *Hommages à Jean Leclant* I (Cairo 1994) 5–28.

Pyramid construction

The pyramids are situated on the West Bank of the Nile, the 'wrong' bank for the availability of good **limestone**. Due to the long distance that material had to be transported, only **casing** blocks were brought from the East Bank, while for **core masonry** the builders made do with the inferior-quality rock of the West Bank. Until the beginning of the 4th Dynasty, pyramids were constructed in 'steps' and erected using mantles which leaned inwards. From the reign of Sneferu, true pyramids were erected with horizontal courses of stone. It is not known whether the large 4th Dynasty pyramids contain internal structuring. The pyramids of **Menkaure**, **Userkaf**, **Neferirkare** and **Djedkare** had a stepped core, rising in six to eight steps. The core of the 4th Dynasty pyramids continued to consist of coarse block masonry, while that of the 5th and 6th Dynasty pyramids was made of rough fieldstones, and those of the 12th Dynasty (starting with Senwosret II) of **brick**. The core of the pyramids of **Senwosret I**, **Amenemhat II** and **Senwosret II** was additionally strengthened with a system of radial walls. The casing was generally made of limestone; only the pyramids listed below have **granite** casings:

Djedefre	probably the whole casing
Khafre	bottom course

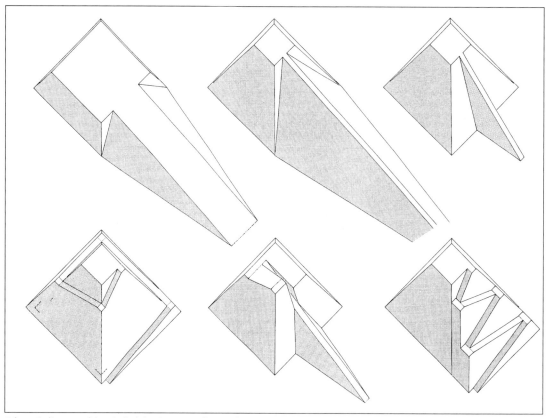

Schematic diagrams of the principal theories on use of pyramid ramp systems

Menkaure	16 lowest courses
Menkaure IIIa	bottom course
Shepseskaf	bottom course
Neferirkare	bottom course (or more?)

The bottom course of stones, 1–1.5 m high, exceeds the size of the following courses, which are only 0.6–0.8 m high. From the 12th Dynasty, all casing blocks were dowelled together (**cramps**). Rooms inside the pyramids of **Sneferu** and **Khufu**, that is, the burial chambers with an antechamber and a few side-chambers, were built high up in the core masonry and had to be protected against the pressure of the masonry above by complex **ceiling construction** techniques. In later pyramids these chambers were erected increasingly lower down in the rock. They were usually constructed in open pits, which were protected against vertical pressure by gigantic ceiling structures. Access to the construction pit was by a wide, sloping **building ramp**; after completion of the chambers, the sloping corridor was constructed inside the ramp, beginning from the bottom. The actual pyramid masonry was finally erected over it.

Planning, organisation, surveying (**measuring**) and the construction process are likely to have varied in individual cases, depending on the local conditions, and the size and type of building. The apparently all but impossible task was made easier by a corps of craftsmen, who had developed their skills since the Early Dynastic Period, as well as by a State-controlled system capable of raising and organising the necessary manpower (**architect**). Construction methods developed during the reign of Sneferu, from the pyramid of **Meidum** via the **Bent Pyramid** and the North Pyramid of **Dahshur** at such a rate that is was possible by the reign of **Khufu** to erect a pyramid which to this day amazes the beholder.

The **step mastabas** of the 3rd Dynasty have been shown to have had building ramps leading from all sides to the centre of the pyramid, enabling the tower-like nucleus to be built as high as possible. The outer mantles, sloping inwards, were placed around this core and then the construction ramp was dismantled back to the level of the bottom stage, as it had then become possible to erect smaller ramps on the individual steps already constructed; with the help of these the smoothed tip of the pyramid could be constructed. In the case of the later 'true' pyramids, blocks could be towed to a height of 30–50 m using many such ramps, with the help of **sledges** drawn by oxen, which meant that 50% of the total pyramid block material was able to be lifted that way. Core and casing blocks were fitted simultaneously in the same course and were locked together. How the upper parts of the pyramid were reached is unknown. Traces (**Meidum**) indicate that a steep ramp like a staircase was applied on the outside of the pyramid casing. The possibility of blocks having been lifted with the help of machine-like **lever** systems cannot be totally dismissed. although their nature remains a mystery, despite the description given by Herodotus and innumerable modern suggestions. A *shaduf*-like lever, like that which F.W. Hinkel assumes to have been employed in the erection of Meroitic pyramids, could not in practice have stood up to the demands on it. Neither would the 'rocker', a kind of rocking sledge, have been capable of such tasks, there being in any case no proof of its existence prior to the New Kingdom. Whether casing blocks were always finished after fitting, as in the case of Menkaure's pyramid, is not known.

Bibliography (selected): Choisy, *L'art de bâtir*, 106–113; Georges Goyon, *Le secret des bâtisseurs des grandes pyramides Khéops* (Paris 1977); D. Arnold, Pyramidenbau, in: Helck, *LÄ* V 1–4; R. Stadelmann, Snofru und die Pyramiden von Meidum und Dahschur, in: *MDAIK* 36 (1980) 437–449; D. Arnold, Überlegungen zum Problem des Pyramidenbaues, in: *MDAIK* 37 (1981) 15–28;

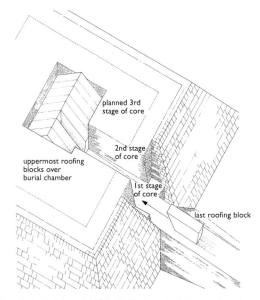

View of a typical pyramid of the 5–6th Dynasty during construction, showing ramps for positioning the roofing blocks of the burial chamber

F.W. Hinkel, Pyramide oder Pyramidenstumpf? In: *ZÄS* 109 (1982) 39–61; C. Rinaldi, *Le piramidi* (Milan 1983); Rosalie David, *The Pyramid Builders of Ancient Egypt. A Modern Investigation of Pharaoh's Workforce* (London-Boston-Henley 1986); M. Isler, On pyramid building, in: *JARCE* 22 (1985) 129–142 and 24 (1987) 95–112; Peter Hodges, *How the Pyramids were Built* (Longmead 1989); J.-Ph. Lauer, Le problème de la construction de la grande pyramide, in: *RdE* 40 (1989) 91–111; Arnold, *Building* 80ff., 98–101; Lehner, *Complete Pyramids* 202–227.

Pyramid temple

The pyramid temple of the Old Kingdom developed from a variety of architectural and religious roots to form a poorly understood multi-layered complex. Firstly, it was the stage on which were performed the practices of the royal statue and funerary cults, and of various associated divine cults, especially that of Re-Horakhty. Secondly, the decorative and statue programmes have symbolic aspects concerned with the establishment and maintenance of the king's rule, for example in the coronation, *sed*-festival or by the ritual destruction of enemies. And, finally, there are utilitarian aspects such as a landing stage and gate to the pyramid complex. Consequently, the architecture unites elements adopted from temple constructions with symbolic or representational aspects.

There is no evidence of any substantial cult installation associated with the **step mastabas** of the 3rd Dynasty. Modest offering places, in the form of a small courtyard with an offering table, appear in the time of Sneferu (**Meidum**) along the east side of pyramids. From **Khufu** onwards, the combination of a statue temple and a pillared court led to the creation of complexes on a monumental scale. Prior to **Shepseskaf** all cult structures stood isolated from the pyramid, and so had no **false door**. At the beginning of the 5th Dynasty, a group of rooms serving a funerary cult (including a false door) makes its appearance. The arrival of a combination of courtyard and statue temple with funerary cult rooms led to the development of a standardised type, which continued to be used into the 12th Dynasty. This type consisted of four distinct sections (see Fig. here for numbered elements, and Fig. under **Senwosret I**):

a) A narrow section at the front containing the **Per-weru** (5) and a pillared or columned court, dominated by **pylon**-like corner bastions in the north and south-east. Groups of magazines along the sides form part of the rear of the temple. Especially prominent in the decorative and statue programmes were elements connected with the establishment and maintenance of the king's power (destruction rituals); these were combined with the

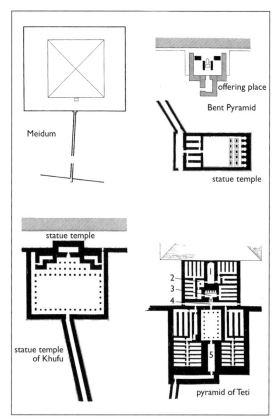

Development of the pyramid temple from Meidum to the 6th Dynasty. 1: chamber for funerary offerings; 2: chamber with single column; 3: statue temple; 4: door recess; 5: Per-weru

ancient motifs of the *sed*-festival, which also had the purpose of upholding the rule of the king.

The next two parts, b) and c), are separated from each other by a transverse corridor (4) contained within a wider section at the rear, on a raised level. The *sed*-festival motif is particularly emphasised in the decorative programme of the corridor.

b) Situated behind the **door recess** is the statue temple proper, which consists of a chapel with five shrines for the king's statues (3) and three to four magazines to the north.

c) Inserted between b) and d) are two rooms with two rows of five magazines in the south. The square-shaped room with a single pillar has a high ceiling and is a special feature (2). It is decorated with representations of destruction rituals and the assembly of the national gods at the *sed*-festival. Its particular function has not been determined.

d) Funerary offerings, from the time of Shepseskaf onwards, were placed in the **vaulted** funerary offering room (1), which is equipped with a false door, offering table and statue of the king, as well as a group of magazines in the north-west, consisting of a group of two rooms, followed by another group of five.

The complexes of **Senwosret I** and **Amenemhat II** were the last examples of this type of pyramid temple developed in the 5–6th Dynasty. **Senwosret II** shrunk the pyramid temple to a simple funerary cult place, and probably transferred the statue cult to the **valley temple**. **Senwosret III** also built a reduced pyramid temple but later added a vast temple to the south. At Hawara **Amenemhat III** developed the 'south temple' type, and united in the 'Labyrinth' a large number of cult buildings for the national gods.

Bibliography: Ricke, *Bemerkungen* II; D. Arnold, Rituale und Pyramidentempel, in: *MDAIK* 33 (1977) 1–14; Brinks, *Grabanlagen*; Stadelmann, Totentempel I, III, in: Helck, *LÄ* VI 694–699 and 706–711; Stadelmann, *Pyramiden*; D. Arnold, Totentempel II, in: Helck, *LÄ* VI 699–706; D. Arnold, Royal cult complexes of the Old and Middle Kingdoms, in: Byron Shafer, Ed., *Temples of Ancient Egypt* (Cornell 1997) 31–85; Rainer Stadelmann, *The Development of the Pyramid Temple in the Fourth Dynasty*; Quirke, *Temple* 1–16; David O'Connor, The interpretation of the Old Kingdom pyramid complex, in: *Stationen. Beiträge zur Kulturgeschichte Ägyptens* (Mainz 1998) 135–144.

Pyramid town

An official settlement for the priests, craftsmen and others associated with a royal mortuary foundation, attested to since the reign of Sneferu. It is usually situated in the immediate proximity of the **pyramid** or **valley temple** and surrounded by an **enclosure wall**. **Houses** and service facilities were erected to a uniform plan, the size of houses reflecting the position of their owner. Such settlements were often the starting point from which a **town** later developed. They should be distinguished from short-term workers' settlements intended only for the duration of **pyramid construction**. Despite their importance to the study of settlements, only the pyramid towns of **Khentkawes I** and **Senwosret II** (**Kahun**) have been excavated to date; the latter covered an area of 350 x 400 m = 140,000 sq m and had 5000–7000 inhabitants, which probably made it exceptionally large.

Bibliography: W.M. Flinders Petrie, *Kahun, Gurob and Hawara*, (London 1890) 21–32; W.M. Flinders Petrie, *Illahun, Kahun and Gurob* (London 1891) 5–8; Hassan, *Giza* IV 35–67; W. Helck, Bemerkungen zu den Pyramidenstädten im Alten Reich, in: *MDAIK* 15 (1957) 91–111; R. Stadelmann, La ville de pyramide à l'Ancien Empire, in: *RdE* 33 (1981) 67–77; R. Stadelmann, Pyramidenstadt, in: Helck, *LÄ* V 9–14.

Pyramidion

The final stone at the top of a **pyramid** and, less often, of an **obelisk**. The only example preserved from the Old Kingdom is the undecorated **limestone** pyramidion of the **Red Pyramid** of Sneferu. In the Middle Kingdom pyramidia were up to 1.30 m high, made of black **granite** and decorated with the eyes of the king, the barque of the sun and texts relating to heaven and the progress of the sun. Many examples from private **brick** pyramids of the New Kingdom (**Deir el-Medina**) and Late Period have been found which show the tomb owner greeting the sun. Fitting the pyramidion was technically simple if it had been raised, layer by layer, during construction.

Bibliography: G. Jéquier, *Deux pyramides du Moyen Empire* (Cairo 1933) 19–26, 58–60; A. Rammant-Peeters, *Les pyramidions égyptiens du Nouvel Empire* (Leiden 1983); K. Martin, Pyramidion, in: Helck, *LÄ* V 23–25; Arnold, *Amenemhet III* 14–16; Stadelmann, *Pyramiden*, Plate 29; H. de Meulenaere, Pyramidions d'Abydos, in: *JEOL* VII, 20 (1967–1968) 1–20; Zahi Hawass, The discovery of the pyramidion of the satellite pyramid of Khufu, in: *Iubilate Conlegae: Studies in Memory of Abd el Aziz Sadek*, Part I (San Antonio 1995) 105–121; Nabil Swelim, The Pyramidion of Khafra, in: *Iubilate Conlegae: Studies in Memory of Abd el Aziz Sadek*, Part II (San Antonio 1995) 57–62.

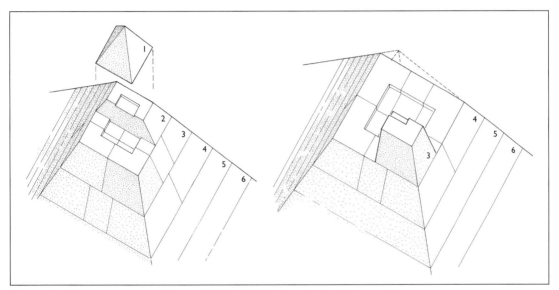

Construction of the uppermost courses of the pyramid of Khafre during the positioning of the pyramidion

Q

Qa'a, mastaba of

An archaic **brick** mastaba (3505) at Saqqara, 44 x 65.2 m, which has been dated to the 1st Dynasty (reign of Qa'a). It has colourful painted **niching**, in front of which is a brick bench with bulls' skulls. Attached to the north side is a large brick annexe with the remains of two wooden figures, like a mortuary temple. This would have been unusual for the Early Dynastic Period and it may be that it was usurped in the 3rd Dynasty and the temple added.

Bibliography: Walter B. Emery, *Great Tombs of the First Dynasty* (London 1958) 5–36.

(Qantir) *see* Per-Ramesses

Qasr 'Ain el-Zaijan

A temple in the Kharga Oasis measuring only 7.22 x 13.56 m, surrounded by a well-preserved **brick** enclosure of 26 x 68 m. Its façade formed a type of **pylon**. The Ptolemaic structure, dedicated to Amun of Hibis, was renewed in the rule of Antonius Pius. Instead of a **pronaos**, a brick-built fore-hall, 22 m long, was constructed in front of the main temple building (comparable to **El-Deir** and **Qasr Dush**). The main temple building comprises an antechamber and offering table room with a cult image recess. A precise assessment of this structure does not yet exist.

Bibliography: R. Naumann, Bauwerke der Oase Khargeh, in: *MDAIK* 8 (1939) 8–10; S. Sauneron, *Notes de Voyage* 290–291.

Qasr Dush

A Roman temple **fortress** set on an elevation at the southern end of the Kharga Oasis (Kysis). The interior is densely covered with barrack structures etc. Unlike all other oasis **temples**, this one is not dedicated to Amun but to Isis, Serapis and Horus. The main temple building measures 7.55 x 15.32 m and has a **pillared hall** with four slender columns, stairs to the roof, an offering table room and a sanctuary; the ceiling of the latter as well as that of two longish side-rooms is roofed with a barrel **vault**. The main temple building was later fronted with a taller **pronaos**. The **pylon** at the front of the temple has a monumental stone gate bearing a dedicatory inscription

dated AD 116 (Trajan). North of the gate lies a large forecourt with a pylon at its northern front. The temple was erected in the reign of Domitian inside an already existing fort and was completed in the reign of Hadrian with a forecourt added under Trajan. To the west and on the same elevation are the ruins of another temple, built completely of **brick**.

Bibliography: R. Naumann, Bauwerke der Oase Khargeh, in: *MDAIK* 8 (1939) 6–8; S. Sauneron, *Notes de Voyage* 291–294; S. Sauneron, Douch-Rapport préliminaire de la campagne de fouilles 1976, in: *BIFAO* 78 (1978) 5–10.

Qasr el-'Aguz

A small well-preserved temple dedicated to Thoth, built by Ptolemy VIII Euergetes II in front of **Medinet Habu**; probably a place of oracles or healing. The complex consists of a front structure like a **pronaos** and the main temple building, which has three consecutive transverse rooms.

Bibliography: *Description* II, Plate 18; Dominique Mallet, *Le Qasr el-Agouz* (Cairo 1909); J. Quaegebeur, Qasr el-Aguz, in: Helck, *LÄ* V 40–41.

Qasr el-Ghueda

A temple of Amun, measuring 10.40 x 23.53 m, in Kharga Oasis. The earliest part of the main temple building is surrounded by a fortification wall and dates from the reigns of Amasis and Darius I. It consists of a hall with four columns, an offering table room, stairs to the roof and three parallel sanctuaries for the Theban Triad. A **pronaos**

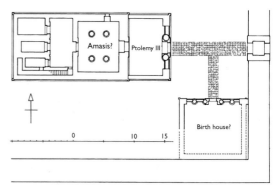

Plan of the temple of Amun at Qasr el-Ghueda

in front of the temple, with two columns between the **screen walls**, was probably erected in the reign of Ptolemy III. To the south of the main temple building is the façade of another structure, possibly a **birth house**. In front of the gate lies a processional **platform**.

Bibliography: Rudolf Naumann, Bauwerke der Oase Khargeh, in: *MDAIK* 8 (1939) 4–7; S. Sauneron, *Notes de Voyage* 286–289.

Qasr el-Megysbeh

The remains of a small temple of Alexander the Great dedicated to Amun-Re and Horus in **Bahariya Oasis**. A stone-built two-room shrine is surrounded by a temple precinct with densely arranged living accommodation and possible magazines.

Bibliography: A. Fakhry, *A Temple of Alexander the Great at Bahria Oasis*; A. Fakhry, *Bahria Oasis* (Cairo 1950) 41–47.

Qasr el-Sagha

A well-preserved small temple of the late 12th Dynasty, to the west of Lake Qarun, situated on an elevation on a former bank of the lake. Seven cult image shrines, aligned in parallel, open onto a shared offering table room (7.8 x 21 m). The anticipated front part of the temple, possibly a court and/or **pillared hall**, was never erected. The temple has no inscriptions, which means the names of the owner and the gods residing in the temple remain unknown; the

only name attested to is that of Sobek. The building is constructed of dark-brown calciferous **sandstone**, and is connected with the nearby Middle Kingdom settlement for troops or workmen and the transport facilities for the **basalt** mines at Gebel el-Qatrani. Three **brick**-paved streets divide the rectangular settlement, 80 x 114 m in size, into six rows of five houses each, themselves subdivided into five parallel units. The settlement must have accommodated 500–1000 inhabitants.

Bibliography: G. Schweinfurth, Ein altes Heiligtum an den Ufern des Möris, in: *Illustrierte Deutsche Monatshefte* (1895) 361–372; K. Bittel and O. Menghin, Kasr el Sagha, in: *MDAIK* 5 (1934) 1–10; M. Werbrouck, Le Temple de Qasr es-Sagha, in: *CdE* 25 (1950) 199–208; Dieter Arnold, *Der Tempel Qasr el-Sagha* (Mainz 1979). The settlement: J. Śliwa, Die Siedlung des Mittleren Reiches bei Qasr el-Sagha, in: *MDAIK* 42 (1986) 167–179; 48 (1993) 177–189; J. Śliwa, Qasr el-Sagha 1979–1988, in: *Meander* 47 (1992) 515–528.

Qasr Qarun

A temple of Sobek (19 x 28 m), dating from the Ptolemaic period and situated among the ruins of the Dionysias military settlement at the southern end of Lake Qarun. This **fortress**-like temple was constructed in the tradition of Late Period buildings, and surrounded by a high outer wall. It is preserved undamaged up to the **cavetto cornices**. The only portal is situated at the front. Three consecutive main halls inside are followed by the sanctuary. Lying along both sides are many side-rooms and stairs to the roof. The decoration in the temple is unfinished. In front of the façade are remains of a **kiosk** of columns. The ruins of a **barque station** lie 360 m in front of the temple, connected with it by a processional avenue.

Bibliography: *Description* IV, Plates 69–70; J. Schwartz and Henri Wild, *Qasr-Qarun/Dionysias 1948* (Cairo 1950); J. Schwartz, Alexandre Badawy and Henri Wild, *Qasr-Qarun/Dionysias 1948* (Cairo 1969).

View along the front of the seven naoi in the offering table room, 12th Dynasty temple of Qasr el-Sagha

Temple of Sobek at Qasr Qarun

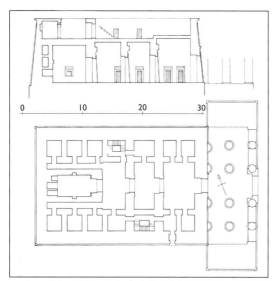

Section and plan of the temple of Sobek at Qasr Qarun

Qaw el-Kebir

The necropolis of **Antaeopolis**, lying on the East Bank of the Nile between Asyut and Akhmim, containing the **rock tombs** of the rulers of the 12th Upper Egyptian nome, Wahka I, Ibu and Wahka II (12th Dynasty). The tombs are extremely interesting architecturally: modelled on **pyramid temples**, they include a **valley temple**, **causeway** and mortuary temple, the latter consisting of a limestone **pylon** with a columned court beyond. Steep stairs across an arch lead to the next terrace with a **pillared hall** open at the front. Beyond this lies a longitudinal hall with rectangular pillars (corresponding to the **Per-weru**). From here stairs lead to the roof of the temple with a cult place. The walls of the antechambers were originally lined with slabs of **limestone** decorated with reliefs. Beyond the longitudinal hall lies another hall, 9.5 x 16.6 m, hewn out of the rock, its ceiling cut into a **vault** with a shallow curve. This room and the three statue chambers attached to the offering chamber are painted. The rock wall behind the longitudinal hall seems to have had a window allowing light into the rock-carved hall. Below the latter are the burial chambers containing the stone sarcophagi of the nomarchs and their families.

For the temple of Qaw el-Kebir, see **Antaeopolis**.

Bibliography: W.M.F. Petrie, *Antaeopolis* (London 1930); Hans Steckeweh, *Die Fürstengräber von Qaw* (Leipzig 1936).

Qertassi

A beautifully shaped early Roman **kiosk** which stood on a rocky elevation on the West Bank of the Nile 50 km south

of Aswan. Its 14 columns, made of brown **sandstone**, have **composite** and **Hathor capitals**. The building was probably a free-standing **barque station** for the goddess Isis of Philae, perhaps connected to a small temple on the East Bank which was still in existence in 1813. The kiosk has been re-erected next to the temple of **Kalabsha,** south of the high dam at Aswan (Sadd el-'Ali).

Bibliography: Gau, *Antiquités*, Plates 7–8; Günther Roeder, *Debod bis Bab Kalabsche* (Cairo 1911–12) 146–179; R. Bianchi, Qertassi, in: Helck, *LÄ* V 48–49.

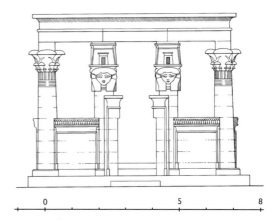

Elevation and view of early Roman kiosk at Qertassi

Quartzite

Granular silicified **sandstone**, consisting predominantly of quartz, its colour varying from yellowish grey to reddish. Its extreme hardness meant that it was used only occasionally in the 6th Dynasty, becoming more frequent from the 12th Dynasty for thresholds, pillars, sarcophagi, burial chambers and statues (**colossi of Memnon**). As one of its sources was the area of **Heliopolis**, it was seen as sacred to Re. The chief quarries are at **Gebel el-Ahmar** near Heliopolis as well as Gebel Tingar and Gebel Gulag near Aswan. The hardness of the material caused considerable problems in working. There is no information about how it was mined.

Bibliography: Lucas, *AEMI* 62–63, 418–419; R. and D. Klemm, Quarzit, in: Helck, *LÄ* V 50–53; De Putter, *Pierres* 95–99: Klemm, *Steine* 283–303.

Quay, *see* platform

Queens, tombs of

The burial places of queens in the 1st and 2nd Dynasties appear not to be differentiated, while in the reign of **Djoser** the queen's tomb took the form of a subsidiary burial in the **king's tomb**; later it was completely excluded from the

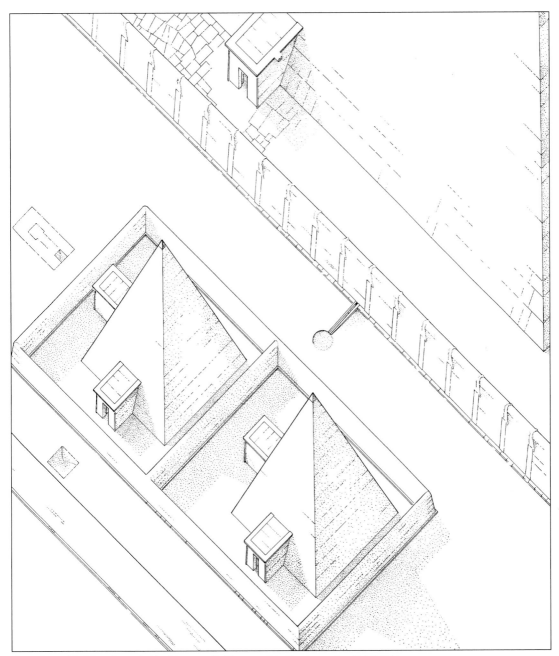

Queens' pyramids 6–7 on the north side of the pyramid of Senwosret I (with entrance chapel) at El-Lisht

precinct of the king's tomb. From the reign of **Khufu** to the 12th Dynasty, queens were provided with their own small pyramid complex near the king's pyramid. These cult sites largely follow the pattern of contemporary private **mastabas**, with neither a **valley temple** nor a causeway. Boat burials, on the other hand, were frequently added. At the same time, some queens were buried in mastabas. Very few queens received a burial chamber in the king's pyramid (exceptions are Weret in the pyramid of **Senwosret III**, two queens in that of **Amenemhat III**, and at an unknown king's tomb at South **Saqqara**).

A concentration of queens' tombs occurs in the New Kingdom at the Biban el-Harim (Ta-Set-Neferu) and its side-valleys. They have no attendant cult complexes, top structures or façades, consisting simply of two or three corridors or chambers in the rock, the last room forming the burial chamber. A few of these tombs have side-chambers for children. More elaborate complexes (Leblanc type No. II) developed under the influence of the tombs of the kings, with an antechamber with two pillars and a sarcophagus hall supported on four pillars. The most important tomb is that of **Nefertari**.

Bibliography: W. Helck, Königinnengräbertal, in: Helck, *LÄ* III 468–473; Mark Lehner, *The Pyramid Tomb of Hetep-heres and the Satellite Pyramid of Khufu* (Mainz 1985); R. Stadelmann, Königinnengrab und Pyramidenbezirk im Alten Reich, in: *ASAE* 71 (1987) 251–260; A.M. Dodson, The tombs of the queens of the Middle Kingdom, in: *ZÄS* 115 (1988) 123–136; Ch. Leblanc, Architecture et évolution chronologique des tombes de la Vallée des Reines, in: *BIFAO* 89 (1989) 227–247; Christian Leblanc, *Ta Set Neferou. Une necropole de Thebes-ouest et son histoire* I (Cairo 1989); Peter Munro. *Das Doppelgrab der Königinnen Nebet und Khenut. Der Unas-Friedhof Nord-West* I. (Mainz 1993); Jánosi, *Pyramidenanlagen*; Audran Labrousse, *Les pyramides des reines* (Milan 1999); N. and H. Strudwick, *Thebes in Egypt* (London 1999) 120–138.

Qurna

The modern settlement in the central part of the Theban necropolis between the Assasif valley, in the north, and **Deir el-Medina**, in the south, with **rock tombs** dating from the 11th to the 20th Dynasties. The place is named after the tomb of Sheikh Abd el-Qurna, which crowns the highest point. Nowadays the name 'Qurna' applies to the village which covers the necropolis as well as generally to the whole West Bank at **Thebes**. Included in this area is **Sety I**'s **'house of millions of years'**.

Qus

The remains of ancient Apollinopolis Parva, south of **Koptos**. All that has been found of the temple dedicated to Haroeris ('Horus the Elder') and Hekat are the remains of two huge gate structures situated 49 m apart, bearing inscriptions of Ptolemy XI Alexander II, and a **naos** of Ptolemy II. The main temple building probably lay to the east behind these ruins but it has disappeared below the modern settlement.

Bibliography: *Description* IV, Plate 1; A. Kamal, Le pylône de Qous, in: *ASAE* 3 (1902) 215–235.

R

Raising loads

Traditional methods of raising heavy loads consist of sloped areas or **building ramps**, a rope pulley and leverage. These still continued to be used in Egyptian construction long after other countries had adopted cranes, block and tackle, and the 'big wheel' (the treadmill principle).

Many examples of gently sloping construction **ramps** exist, which vary depending on the project, from piles of rubble to solidly constructed **brick** or stone ramps. The latter were not always practical in the construction of tall structures, such as **pyramids** and **pylons**, due to the quantities of material required to build them, lack of stability and enormous length. Large **temples**, on the other hand, may have been erected by the use of building ramps.

Little is known about the raising of loads using ropes, but stone grooves and pulleys, around which ropes would have passed, are preserved from the 4th Dynasty, and wooden wheels for simple rope pulleys existed from the Middle Kingdom onwards. The existence of crane-like hoists on two legs, reminiscent of the A-shaped collapsible ships' masts of the Old Kingdom, cannot be ruled out, and the *shaduf*, a water-raising device (attested to from the New Kingdom) may have had its counterpart in building technology. Two round bases, like columns, have been found on either side of a **building ramp** (Fig.) at **El-Lisht** and may have been part of some pulling or hoisting device.

The raising of heavy loads using wooden **levers** is attested to by lever sockets in building blocks. In modern times, G. Legrain needed 150 men using levers to lift the point of an obelisk which weighed 180 tons. Flinders Petrie calculated that 60–70 men could have raised the 50–60 tonne **granite** blocks which form the roof of the burial chamber of **Khufu** using levers and progressive underpinning. However, the fact that the **casing** blocks of several pyramids show lever holes only in their narrow sides indicates that they were used solely for lateral positioning and not for lifting. **Obelisks** were probably raised by the combined use of ramps, pulley ropes and levers.

Bibliography: Arnold, *Building* 66–72; F.W. Hinkel, Pyramide oder Pyramidenstumpf? in: *ZÄS* 108 (1981)105–124. General: J.J. Coulton, Lifting in early Greek architecture, in: *JHS* 94 (1974) 19.

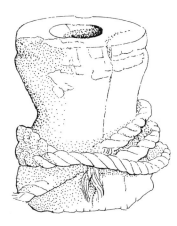

Pulley of New Kingdom date, from Deir el-Medina

Ramesses II, temple of (Abydos)

This king's **'house of millions of years'**, situated 270 m north-west of the temple of **Sety I**, is dedicated to the Abydene Triad (Osiris, Isis and Horus), some guest gods and the king's cult. The tightly sectioned plan of this structure is a 'model' for Egyptian **temples** of the New Kingdom. Thanks to its good state of preservation, the function and order of rooms is clear: the **pylon** is followed by a court with **statue pillars**; the hall on a raised level beyond with four barque rooms for the king's cult opening onto it; the hall of appearances and a large offering table hall, with three sanctuaries of the primary and some subordinate gods grouped around the latter. The reliefs executed in the tradition of the Sety temple are particularly fine. To the left of the offering table are a clothing room and the treasury. The suggestion that an unknown 'Osireion' of Ramesses II may be situated behind the temple is open to doubt.

Bibliography: M.A. Murray, The temple of Ramesses II at Abydos, in: *Ancient Egypt* (1916) 121–138; K.P. Kuhlmann, Der Tempel Ramses II. in Abydos, in: *MDAIK* 35 (1979) 189–193; 38 (1982) 355–362; Aufrère, *L'Égypte restituée*, 44–46.

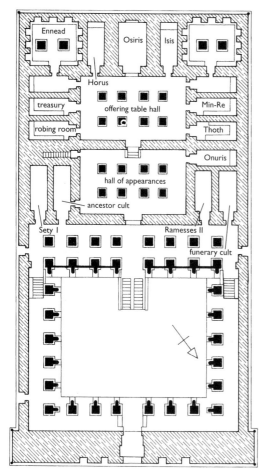

Plan of the 'house of millions of years' (temple) of Ramesses II at Abydos, showing room functions

View over the rear part of the temple of Ramesses II at Abydos

Ramesses III, barque station (Karnak)

An almost completely preserved **barque station** of this king stands in the first court of the Amun temple of **Karnak** (**Amun precinct**). The 24 x 62 m building contains all the essential elements of an independent temple: a **pylon** with two **colossal statues**, a court with two rows of eight **statue pillars**, and a **hypostyle hall**/offering chamber and the three sanctuaries of Amun, Mut and Khonsu. Restricted space prevented the introduction of more than the barque of Amun. The hall at the rear of the court stands on a raised level and has four statue pillars; its **screen walls**, at the front, are crowned with a **frieze of uraei**. The temple is similar to a severely damaged building of Ramesses II in the **Mut precinct**.

Bibliography: Georges Legrain, *Les temples de Karnak* (Brussels 1929) 85–123; Henri Chevrier, *Le temple reposoir de Ramsès III à Karnak* (Cairo 1933); University of Chicago, Oriental Institute Publications: *Reliefs and Inscriptions at Karnak, Vol.1: Ramses III's Temple within the Great Enclosure of Amun* (Chicago 1936).

Ramesseum

The largest of the many **'houses of millions of years'** on the West Bank at **Thebes** and one of the foremost preserved Egyptian temples built by Ramesses II. The complex, situated on the edge of the desert, rises in low terraces. The temple, which has a distinctly skewed plan, measures 58 x 183 m, and is surrounded by an **enclosure wall** of 180 x at least 257 m. The first **pylon** is 69 m wide and has partly collapsed. On the south side of the lower court is a **brick**-built cult palace. Opposite this are 11 colossal **statue pillars**. In front of the second pylon is the fallen seated statue of Ramesses II, 19 m high and weighing 1000 tonnes, made famous in Shelley's poem *Ozymandias*. In the upper court are two rows of eight statue pillars, 11 m high, facing each other, a monumental altar and at the rear two seated images of the king, 10 m high and carved of black **granite**. Beyond lies a **hypostyle hall** consisting of two rows of six central columns and six rows of smaller papyrus **columns** – a replica of the hypostyle hall at **Karnak**. Behind this are three smaller halls of columns, a barque sanctuary, the space for a **sun temple** and other structures. All rooms along the sides and at the rear of the temple have disappeared and their plan is not certain. Hekataios of Abdera described a gilded zodiac with golden images set into the temple roof. Attached to the temple on the north side is a smaller temple, its function the subject of conflicting opinions: it may perhaps have been a **birth house**. The **grain stores**, store houses and ancillary buildings are unusually well preserved. The enclosure was surrounded on all sides by **avenues of sphinxes** for barque processions around the walls. The Ramesseum was destroyed at an early date, possibly by an earthquake, and quantities of its building material were reused at **Medinet Habu**. A major programme of restoration is underway.

Bibliography: Extracts from the *Aegyptiaka* of Hekataios of Abdera, handed down by Diodoros, *Diodori* I/47–49, and Strabo, *Geographica* XVII/46, 810; *Description* II, Plates 27–37; James E. Quibell et al., *The Ramesseum* (London 1898); H. Carter, Report on the work done at the Ramesseum, in: *ASAE* 2 (1901) 193–195; E. Baraize, Deblaiement du Ramesseum, in: *ASAE* 8 (1907) 193–200; Hölscher, *Medinet Habu, Vol. 3*; G. Haeny, L'origine des traditions thébains concernant Memnon, in: *BIFAO* 64 (1966) 203–212; G. Goyon, Le grand cercle d'or du temple d'Osymandas, in: *BIFAO* 76 (1976) 289–300; *Jean-Claude Goyon and Hasan el-Ashiri, Le Ramesseum*, 12 Vols (Cairo 1973–79); R. Stadelmann, Ramesseum, in: Helck, *LÄ* V 91-98; Ch. Leblanc, Diodore, le tombeau d'Osymanyas et la statuaire du Ramesseum, in: *Mélanges Gamal Eddin Mokhtar* (Cairo 1985) 69–82; general, see *Memnonia* I onwards (Cairo from 1990–91); Aufrère, *L'Égypte restituée* 165–170; Jürgen Osing, Zur Funktion einiger Räume des Ramesseums, in: *Studies Simpson* II 635–646.

The Ramesseum from the northeast

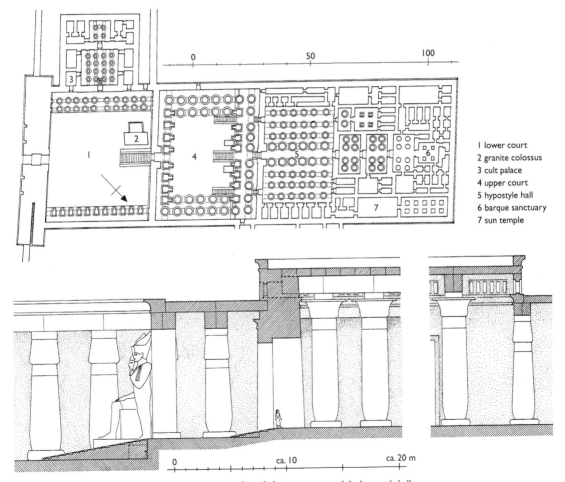

1 lower court
2 granite colossus
3 cult palace
4 upper court
5 hypostyle hall
6 barque sanctuary
7 sun temple

Plan of the Ramesseum and longitudinal and cross sections through the upper court and the hypostyle hall

Royal colossal statues in the north-east corner of the upper courtyard of the Ramesseum

Ramose, tomb of

The Theban tomb of the vizier Ramose (TT 55) belongs to the period of transition from the reign of Amenhotep III to that of Akhenaten. It is 68 m in length and so is a good example of the exaggerated monumental size of private tombs customary in that period, bearing comparison with the tomb of **Kheruef** and the slightly earlier tomb of **Amenemhat Surer**. Like a *saff* **tomb**, its forecourt is sunk deep below the ground level. The transverse hall beyond has four rows of eight short and squat papyrus **columns** and the room beyond has two rows of four columns of the same type. The last room leads into the cult chapel, which has statue recesses along three sides. As in the tomb of Kheruef and the tombs at **Amarna**, a winding corridor leads from the **pillared hall** to the burial complex.

Bibliography: N. de Garis Davies, *The Tomb of the Vizier Ramose* (London 1941); R. Stadelmann, Ramose, in: Helck, *LÄ* V 98–100.

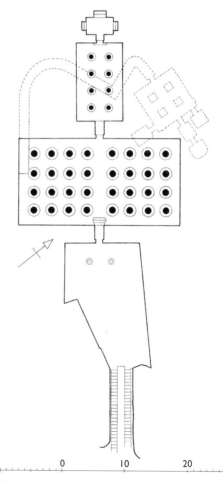

Plan of the tomb of Ramose (TT 55) at Thebes

View through the hypostyle hall into the interior of the temple

Ramp, *see also* building ramp, transport

There are many traces of transportation roads, dating from the Old Kingdom onwards, leading from **stone quarries** down to the Nile and from ports to building sites. In many cases they were formed by clearing away stones and piling these up along the sides. Where necessary they were supported on a bed of stones and, over depressions in the sand, they continued in the form of a bank: stone quarries at **Aswan**, **Gebel el-Qatrani** (10 km long), the road from Memphis, via Dahshur, to the Faiyum (50 km), **Hatnub** (17 km), the gneiss quarries at Toshka, west of Abu Simbel (80 km).

Building ramps leading from storage areas to the actual construction sites were shorter, on a slope of approximately 10–15° and 5 m wide. The core consisted of brick or rubble, with inserted beams, and with side-walls and a hard upper surface. Ramps were also used in burial rites performed on the roof of **mastabas** and, in burial chambers, for hoisting up the lid of a sarcophagus. There is evidence of their use in the construction of small **pyramids**. The nature of the ramps used in the construction of large pyramids is surrounded by controversy (**pyramid construction**).

Bibliography: Arnold, *Building* 79–101; I. Shaw, A survey at Hatnub, in: *Amarna Reports* III 189–212; I. Shaw, Pharaonic quarrying and mining: settlement and procurement in Egypt's marginal regions, in: *Antiquity* 68 (1994) 108–119.

Rawer, tomb of

An important tomb complex at **Giza**, occupied by many individual tombs of the Rawer family, some of them **mastabas** standing in front of the cliff, while others were no more than chambers carved out of the rock. A particularly interesting feature is the statue cult chamber, fronted by a cruciform corridor and an entrance recess with four *serdabs*.

Bibliography: Hassan, *Giza* I 1–61; George A. Reisner, *A History of the Giza Necropolis* I (Cambridge, Mass. 1942) 233–234.

Red Pyramid

The pyramid 'Appearance of Sneferu' at **Dahshur** was the last of three erected by this king from his 29th year onwards. The length of its base is 220 m, its height 105 m and its angle of slope 45° (like the upper section of the **Bent Pyramid**). The entrance is situated at a height of 28 m in the (now missing) **casing** on the north side. A steep corridor leads to the two antechambers lying at approximately ground level. Their ceilings are finished with impressive **corbelled vaults**. An opening 8 m up in the wall at the back of the rear chamber leads to the higher-level burial chamber, its ceiling forming a 14.67 m high corbelled vault. The **limestone pyramidion** is preserved and has a considerably steeper slope than the pyramid itself. On the east side of the pyramid is a temporary **brick**-built cult complex consisting of a central offering room and magazines along the sides, and in the north-east and south-east corners two largish unidentified monuments. These structures would have finally been built in stone. To the south-west are the **stone quarries** and a workmen's settlement. A stone building, 60 x 100 m, noted in the cultivation in 1904, may have been the **valley temple** (attested to in a protective decree of Pepy I) but it has since disappeared.

Bibliography: L. Borchardt, Ein Königserlaß aus Dahschur, in: *ZÄS* 42 (1905) 1–11; *MRA* III; Stadelmann, in: *MDAIK* 38 (1982) 109–123; 39 (1983) 207–223; Stadelmann, *Pyramiden* 100–105; R. Stadelmann et al., Pyramiden und Nekropole des Snofru in Dahschur, in: *MDAIK* 49 (1993) 259–267; Lehner, *Complete Pyramids* 104–105.

View over the ruins of the pyramid temple of Sneferu at the Red Pyramid, Dahshur

Reed buildings, *see* woven timber construction

Rehotep and Nefret, tomb of

An important **brick mastaba** of the early 4th Dynasty at **Meidum** (No. 6). Its cruciform cult chapel, lined with stone, was walled off when the mastaba underwent enlargement and was then used as a *serdab*, from which came the famous statue group of Rehotep and Nefret, now in the Egyptian Museum at Cairo (CG 3 and 4); the niche was later replaced with a cult place on the outside. (See also **Nefermaat and Atet**.)

Bibliography: W.M. Flinders Petrie, *Medum* (London 1892) 15–17; A.O. Bolshakov, Some observations on the early chronology of Meidum, in: *GM* 123 (1991) 11–20.

Rekhmire, tomb of

This **rock tomb** (TT 100) built by one of Thutmosis III's master-builders at Thebes for the vizier Rekhmire. The wall decoration make this tomb a monument of the first rank in terms of cultural history. The architecture is simple: a courtyard is situated in the gently sloping rock and the two interior rooms are T-shaped. The passage, 27 m long, is unusual in that its ceiling rises steeply towards the interior, reaching a height of 8 m. The rear wall accommodates a cult image niche 5 m above floor level. The wall decoration includes unique representations of construction work (see **brick**, **building ramp**, **scaffolding**, **stone working**, **transport**, Figs).

Bibliography: Norman de Garis Davies, *The Tomb of Rekh-mi-Re' at Thebes*, 2 Vols (New York 1944).

Relief pillar, *see also djed* **pillar**, **pillar**

Square **pillar**; many have symbolic decoration in raised relief. In the Old Kingdom they often represented lotus bundles; from the New Kingdom there are the **heraldic pillars** at **Karnak**, motifs from Hathor symbolism and, less often, *djed* **pillars**.

Bibliography: Borchardt, *Pflanzensäule* 10, 22; Jéquier, *Manuel* 158.

Re-use of blocks

When earlier buildings were replaced at the same site by new structures, the dismantled material was built into the foundations of the latter. In this way the property of the god concerned was preserved, while the new building stood on a pure and venerable base. Frequently older blocks were sent to a new site; for example, in Lower Egypt:

a) In the 18th Dynasty, **pyramid temples** were dismantled for re-use in temples in the Delta.

b) In the reign of Ramesses II, temples were dismantled for re-use at **Per-Ramesses**.

c) In the 21st Dynasty Per-Ramesses was dismantled for re-use at **Tanis**.

Other examples are:

d) Material from the pyramid temples of the 4–6th Dynasty was built into the pyramid of **Amenemhat I**.

e) Material (*talatat*) from the **sun temples** of Akhenaten was used in buildings of Horemheb and Ramesses II at **Karnak**, **Luxor** and **Hermopolis**.

The final phase was incorporation of these elements into Islamic buildings in Cairo, Mansura etc. To meet the strictures of Islam, inscriptions and depictions of living creatures were systematically 'killed' using chisels prior to their re-use.

It is unlikely that blocks for re-use in new buildings were selected on the basis of a symbolically significant system.

This type of building material re-use differs essentially from the later practice of removing complete monuments, such as **obelisks**, **sphinxes** and royal statuary, from pharaonic sites to embellish buildings in **Alexandria** or to display them as Egyptian spoils in Rome or Constantinople.

Bibliography: Alexandre Varille, *Quelques charactéristiques du temple Pharaonique* (Cairo 1946); R.A. Schwaller de Lubicz, *Le temple de l'homme: L'Apet sud à Louxor*, Vol. III (Paris 1957) 355–363; W. Helck, Wiederverwendung, in: Helck, *LÄ* VI 1264–1265.

Rock temple

A **temple** either carved out of the rock as a single hollow structure (= **speos**) or one having some additional free-standing structures at its front (= **hemispeos**). There was no recognisably distinct pattern to such temples, local conditions (width of the Nile, position in the desert) usually dictating the type of temple constructed. The plan corresponds to that of ordinary temples. Rock temple building followed the traditions of **rock tomb**

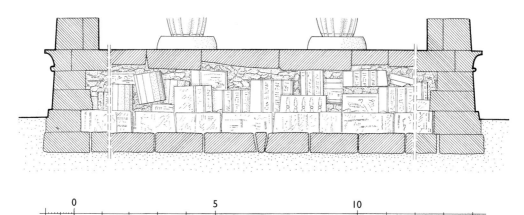

Foundations of the Luxor temple of Amenhotep III filled with re-used blocks (after Schwaler de Lubicz)

construction, and the open pillared façade, as well as transverse hall and ascent towards the sanctuary, indicate their relationship to rock tombs (**Speos Artemidos**, **Gebel el-Silsila**). Some rock temples may have had their origin in primitive cult caves. Six rock temples were established in **Nubia** in the reign of Ramesses II and they largely follow the common pattern of **pillared hall**, offering table room, sanctuary. They are apparently spaced a day's journey from one another. A noticeable number of rock temples are dedicated to Hathor, possibly connected with the concept of the Hathor cow emerging from the desert hills. Nubian rock temples were also associated with the idea that their caves were possibly the source of the Nile. G. Haeny stresses that rock temples were constructed in previously untouched regions and were thereby felt to penetrate into unearthly realms.

Larger rock temples (chronological list)

Rock temple	Dyn./reign	Dedication
Serabit el-Khadim	12th Dynasty	Hathor/deified kings
Speos Artemidos	Hatshepsut	Pakhet
Faras	Hatshepsut	Hathor of Ibshek
Salamuni	Thutmosis III	Hathor, Min
Ellesiya	Thutmosis III	Amun, king, Horus
Gebel Dosha	Thutmosis III	Hathor, king
Deir el-Bahari	Thutmosis III	Hathor
Wadi el-Sebu'a	Amenhotep III	Horus
Gebel el-Silsila	Horemheb	King, Amun, Mut, Khonsu, Sobek, Taweret, Thoth
Abahuda	Horemheb	Amun-Re, Thoth
Wadi Miya (Kanais)	Sety I	King, Amun-Re, Ennead, Re-Horakhty
El-Kab	Ramesses II	
Beit el-Wali	Ramesses II	King, Amun, Ptah
Gerf Hussein	Ramesses II	King, Ptah, Ptah-Tatenen, Hathor
Wadi el-Sebu'a	Ramesses II	King, Re-Horakhty
Derr	Ramesses II	King, Re-Horakhty, Amun-Re, Ptah
Abu Simbel	Ramesses II	King, Re-Horakhty, Amun-Re, Ptah
Abu Simbel	Ramesses II	Hathor, queen, king
El-Siririya	Merenptah	Hathor, queen
Gebel Barkal B 200	Taharqa	Amun
Gebel Barkal B 300	Taharqa	Amun
Speos Artemidos	Alexander IV	Hathor
Athribis	Graeco-Roman	Asklepios
Tehna	Nero	Hathor

Bibliography: J. Jacquet, Observations sur l'évolution architecturale des temples rupestres, in: *Cahiers d'Histoire Égyptienne (Cairo)* 10 (1966) 69–91; G. Haeny, Felstempel, in: Helck, *LÄ* II 161–169; D. Wildung, Höhlenheiligtum, in: Helck, *LÄ* II 1231–1232; Hein, *Ramessidische Bautätigkeit*; Irmgard Hein, Überlegungen zur Lage der Felstempel Ramses' II. in Nubien, in: Kurth, *Tempeltagung* 131–135.

Rock tomb

Following the traditional practices of **stone quarries**, these tombs are carved horizontally out of the rock, often having a structured façade. **Shaft tombs** do not belong to the category of rock tombs. *Saff* tombs, sunk in the desert plain, and the monumental Late Period tombs at **Thebes** represent transitional forms.

Bibliography (general): Vandier, *Manuel* II/1 293–386; Klaus Kuhlmann, *Materialien zur Archäologie und Geschichte des Raumes von Achmim* (Mainz 1983); Aidan Dodson, *Egyptian Rock-cut Tombs* (Princes Risborough 1991).

1. Old Kingdom

The deepening and enlargement of underground burial complexes during the 3rd Dynasty, as well as the realisation that rock tombs were proving to be more economical and more secure than the earlier **mastabas**, thus promising 'eternal' existence, were all factors underlying the development of rock tombs from the later 4th Dynasty onwards. This was true not only in the necropolis of the capital at **Giza**, but more especially in the necropoleis of officials in Upper Egypt. The steep desert escarpments and quarry walls there offered an ideal location. At first they followed the model of the mastaba (niched façade, corridor surrounding the rock interior – as at **Tehna**), but an independent type soon developed, with an entrance in the centre giving onto a transverse hall with a **false door** in the west wall. From the 6th Dynasty onwards this was enlarged into a **pillared hall**. The mouth of the burial shaft was originally located in a side-room behind the false door, but later was situated in the floor in front of it. The *serdab* was replaced by closeable statue recesses. There is a clear tendency from the 6th Dynasty onwards to intensify the monumental nature of the structure, by means of columns and emphasis on the central axis; this then slowed down, due to difficult economic conditions, until the 11th Dynasty.

Principal necropoleis: **Giza**, **Saqqara**, Deshasha, Sharuna (Kom el-Ahmar), **Tehna** el-Gebel, Gebel el-Teir, **Zawyet el-Mayitin**, Sheikh Sa'id, Quseir el-Amarna, **Meir**, Deir el-Gebrawi, El-Hawawish and **Salamuni**, Hagarsa, Qasr wa'l-Saiyad (First Intermediate Period),

Qurna, Gebelein (First Intermediate Period), Mo'alla (First Intermediate Period), Hierakonpolis and Aswan (Qubbet el-Hawa).

Bibliography: Vandier, *Manuel* I/1 293–322; H. Altenmüller, in: Schulz, *Egypt* 78–93.

2. Middle Kingdom

From the 11th Dynasty onwards, the rock tomb started to flourish as an Upper Egyptian architectural form with real monumental pretensions, attracting the admiration of passers-by, as suggested by façade inscriptions. Some rock tombs are accessed by a form of **valley temple** and a **causeway**. Following the concept of the tomb as the house of the deceased, it was provided with a monumental antechamber with polygonal **pillars** or plant **columns**; a roof at the front imitated the roof of a house. At the back there was an accessible cult area consisting of a hall orientated along the axis of the tomb, which emphasised the direction towards the statue niche (which now replaces the **false door**) at the centre of the rear wall (**cult target**). The ceiling is slightly arched, supported on pillars or plant columns, and is painted with splendid carpet patterns.

At **Thebes** rock tombs developed independently. During the First Intermediate Period and the 11th Dynasty *saff* **tombs** were built at El-Tarif. In the reign of Mentuhotep Nebhepetre several large tombs (Inyotef, Dagi and Meketre) were built to a type partly derived from the model of *saff* tombs. The interaction between the wide **pillared hall** and the short corridor leading to the cult chamber had already appeared in the **pyramid temple** of **Khafre**. This type was modified under Mentuhotep Nebhepetre, to become firstly a pillared tomb with a deep corridor and numerous burial chambers. Alongside it, probably in the later part of the king's reign, the precursor of the corridor tomb appeared, with a simple smooth façade and cult and burial complexes deep inside the hill, for example the tombs of Inyotef-iqer (TT 60), **Khety** (TT 311), Ipi (TT 315), Meru (TT 240), Harhotep (TT 314) and Queen Neferu (TT319). The corridor, cult chambers and burial chambers in these tombs were decorated and inscribed. The approach to the burial complexes of larger tombs occasionally took several changes or reverses of direction, intended to represent the paths of the underworld. This feature anticipates similar tendencies in the rock tombs of the New Kingdom.

The largest examples of Upper Egyptian rock tombs are those of the nomarchs of **Asyut** and **Qaw el-Kebir**, with their temple-like dimensions. They represent the end of the chain of development from the temple of **Mentuhotep** to the temple of **Hatshepsut**.

Other important necropoleis are those of **Beni Hasan**, **El-Bersha**, **Meir**, Durunka, **Deir Rifa**, **Qurna** and **Aswan**.

Bibliography: Helmut Brunner, *Die Anlage der ägyptischen Felsgräber bis zum Mittleren Reich* (Glückstadt 1936); Hans-Wolfgang Müller, *Die Felsengräber der Fürsten von Elephantine aus der Zeit des Mittleren Reiches* (Glückstadt 1940); Vandier, *Manuel* I/1 323–357; Dieter Arnold, Das Grab des Jnj.jtj.f. *Die Architektur* (Mainz 1971) 36–48; Dieter Arnold, *Die Gräber des Alten und Mitteren Reiches in El-Tarif* (Mainz 1976); Shedid, in: Schulz, *Egypt* 118–131.

3. New Kingdom

This period's most important necropolis of rock tombs is that on the West Bank at **Thebes** (Dra Abu el-Naga, Khokha, Sheikh Abd el-**Qurna** and Qurnet Murrai). The close proximity and occasional usurpation of Middle Kingdom tombs ensured contact with earlier examples. The clearest indication of this is the continuing strict adherence to the old T-shaped plan, with a transverse room and deep hall, finishing with a statue niche or separate statue chapel as the **cult target**. A **stela** and a **false door** are often found facing each other on the short walls at either end of the transverse hall. The tomb façade could be **niched** or have a **false door** (**Puyemre**, Amenuser) or, following the tradition of rock tombs of the Middle Kingdom, it might be broken up by a pillared portico, and have a row of frieze bricks (**funerary cone**) along the top. A frequent feature above the façade is a small **brick pyramid** (**Deir el-Medina**, **Nebwenenef**). From the reign of Amenhotep III onwards, high officials keenly imitated the size and furnishings of royal temples: transverse halls had up to four rows of eight, or three rows of fifteen, columns: the deep hall of the tomb of **Amenemhat Surer** was expanded into a veritable avenue of columns. Ideally, all available wall surfaces would have been covered with reliefs, paintings or inscriptions.

As the 18th Dynasty continued, the underground burial apartments became more important through the adoption of, or references to, architectural elements found in **kings' tombs** (bent axis, upper and lower tombs, sarcophagus hall with **pillars**, **Osiris tomb**). These enlarged burial apartments may have remained accessible after the burial for the observance of certain funerary rites. The frequently twisting descent to the subterranean burial systems may well represent the journey of the sun god in the underworld. From the post-Amarna and Ramesside periods, a type developed with an angled descent leading to the burial chamber, either at the end or in the middle. This trend particularly influenced the large Theban tombs of the Late Period and, together with a corresponding change in the decorative programme, removed the separation of the cult and burial parts of the tomb and the representation of 'this world' and the underworld, moving the emphasis to the admission of the deceased among the gods.

Of particular architectural interest are the tombs of **Tjay** (TT 23), **Puyemre** (TT 39), **Amenemopet** (TT 41), **Amenemhat Surer** (TT 48), **Ramose** (TT 55), User (TT 61), **Senenmut** (TT 71), **Ineni** (TT 81), Qenamun (TT 93), **Nebwenenef** (TT 157), **Parennefer** (TT 188) and **Kheruef** (TT 192). Other important necropoleis are at **Amarna**, **El-Kab** and **Hierakonpolis**.

Bibliography: C.S. Fisher, A group of Theban tombs, in: *University of Pennsylvania, The Museum Journal* 15 (1924) 28–49; M. Wegner, Stilentwicklung der thebanischen Beamtengräber, in: *MDAIK* 4 (1933) 38–164; Georg Steindorff and Walther Wolf, *Die thebanische Gräberwelt* (Glückstadt 1936); Charles F. Nims, *Thebes of the Pharaohs* (London 1965); D. Eigner, Das thebanische Grab des Amenhotep, Wesir von Unterägypten: die Architektur, in: *MDAIK* 39 (1983) 39–50; J. Assmann, Das Grab mit gewundenem Abstieg. Zum Typenwandel des Privat-Felsgrabes im Neuen Reich, in: *MDAIK* 40 (1984) 277–290; K.J. Seyfried, Bemerkungen zur Erweiterung der unterirdischen Anlagen einiger Gräber des Neuen Reiches in Theben, in: *ASAE* 71 (1987) 229–249; E. Dziobek, Eine Grabpyramide des frühen Neuen Reiches in Theben, in: *MDAIK* 45 (1989) 109–132; W. Schenkel, Zur Typologie des Felsgrabes, in: *Thebanische Beamtennekropolen,* Studien zur Archäologie und Geschichte Altägyptens 12 (Heidelberg 1995) 169–183; Friederike Kampp, *Die thebanische Nekropole* (Mainz 1996); Karl-Joachim Seyfried, Kammern, Nischen und Passagen in Felsgräbern des Neuen Reiches, *Stationen. Beiträge zur Kulturgeschichte Ägyptens* (Mainz 1998) 387–406; N. and H. Strudwick, *Thebes in Egypt* (London 1999) 139–173.

4. Late Period, *see also* **Thebes**

The Theban tombs of the 25th and 26th Dynasties are among the most important architectonic legacies of the Late Period, exceeding all the earlier Theban tombs in size and splendour of furnishings. They are no longer situated on the slope of the hill, but are set in the valleys of the northern and southern Assasif to allow space for their extensive superstructures. They are modelled on the royal mortuary temples and **Osiris tombs** of the New Kingdom. A **niched brick** wall, with an east-facing **pylon**, surrounds the courtyard, which is composed of three parts: a festival court, a court of offerings (with a **sun court** situated below) and the final section, below which is the dwelling of the deceased. Entrance stairs lead from the outside to an antechamber and the sun court with the **door recess**, leading into the monumental four-**pillared hall** and from there into the offering hall beyond. The burial apartments, situated at a lower level, have adopted features of the **kings' tombs** of the New

Kingdom, such as the bent axis, upper and lower tombs, and **vaulted** sarcophagus hall with astronomical depictions. They remained accessible for the performance of various rites during mortuary festivals. The elaborate decorative and textual programmes are developments of older models.

The most important examples are the tombs of **Harwa** (TT 37), **Karabasken and Karakhamun** (TT 391 and TT 223), **Montuemhat** (TT 34), **Pedamenophis** (TT 33), **Nespeqashuty** (TT 312), **Ibi** (TT 36), **Pabasa** (TT 279), **Padihorresnet** (TT 196), **Ankhhor** (TT 414), **Sheshonq** (TT 27) and **Padineith** (TT 197). Other important necropoleis are at **Giza** and **Saqqara**.

Bibliography: Dieter Eigner, *Grabbauten.*

5. Graeco-Roman Period

Rock tombs of this era are found at **Alexandria**, **Salamuni**, **Sawada**, **Taposiris Magna** and in the western oases.

Bibliography: H. Abou el-Atta, The relation between the Egyptian tombs and the Alexandrian hypogea, in: *ET* 16 (1972) 11–19.

Rock tomb construction

Rock tombs were created, like underground **stone quarries**, by removing the rock in stages. First, on the central axis below the intended ceiling level, a tunnel was driven into the rock along the axis of the tomb, as the basis for the rest of the layout. Side-tunnels were cut into the rock to either side of it and then backwards, in the direction of the entrance, deepening the structure by gradual removal of the rock. Where possible, excavated rock material was utilised for construction purposes. This situation is attested to in several unfinished tombs (**Beni Hasan**, **Amarna**). The initial stage of construction of **pillared halls** was the excavation of a central nave, followed by carving out recesses between the planned pillars, these spaces finally being joined at the rear of the pillars. The walls were prepared using coarse chisels or picks, final smoothing being provided by the use of a flat-bladed chisel. Before the final smoothing, any voids and gaps were filled with **gypsum**. Poor quality rock often required the walls to be faced with **limestone** or plastered with mud. Decorative designs were laid out in red paint, the details to be worked being outlined in black. Carving and painting often started before the rough work had been completed. Given uninterrupted progress, large tombs could be built and decorated within only a few years. Lack of lighting and fresh air and the problems of dragging the excavated rock to the surface imposed on shafts depth limits of 30–40 m and the extent of subterranean systems was limited to a depth of

150–200 m. Labourers in royal tombs formed two gangs said to have worked 'left and right'. Lighting, albeit only faint, was provided by oil lamps.

Bibliography: E. Mackay, The cutting and preparation of tomb-chapels in the Theban Necropolis, in: *JEA* 7 (1921) 154–168; F. Teichmann, in: Erik Hornung, Ed., *Das Grab des Haremhab im Tal der Könige* (Bern 1971) 32–37; Jaroslav Černý, *A Community of Workmen at Thebes in the Ramesside Period* (Cairo 1973); Jaroslav Černý, *The Valley of the Kings* (Cairo 1973); Eigner, *Grabbauten* 81–86; D. Arnold, Grabbau, in: Helck, *LÄ* II 847–851; Arnold, *Building* 211–218; M. Müller, Zum Werkverfahren an thebanischen Grabwänden des Neuen Reiches, in: *SAK* 13 (1986) 149–165; Eberhard Dziobek, *Das Grab des Ineni Theben Nr. 81* (Mainz 1992)18–28.

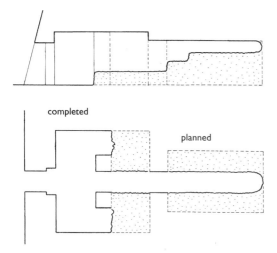

completed

planned

Method of constructing a rock tomb

Roof

In Egyptian architecture of historic times, roofs are almost without exception flat and usually surrounded by tall side-walls, in the case of houses allowing them to be used as living space, and in the case of temples to be used for cult practices (**roof chapel**). Hence, they were usually accessible by **stairs**. For roof construction see **ceiling construction**. In **brick** constructions, the upper surface was made watertight by a mud-plaster layer; in stone architecture this was often achieved by paving, using (irregular) slabs over the ceiling slabs. The surface was sometimes provided with complicated drainage systems (**roof drainage**). Joints were made watertight by the insertion of patching stones. Irregular ceiling height occasionally produced roofs with stepped levels connected by stairs (**Ramesses III temple**, Karnak) and was sometimes used to fit in **windows**. Depictions of early forms of roof are preserved in hieroglyphic signs and also in the shapes of shrines and sarcophagi. **Vaulted**

roofs were often used in domestic buildings from the Old Kingdom onwards and are found in some early **mastabas**, as well as in the tomb of **Shepseskaf** and related monuments. Intriguing, slightly arched wooden roofs were placed on **kiosks** (kiosk of **Augustus**).

Bibliography: Clark, *AEM* 154–161; G. Haeny, Dach, in: Helck, *LÄ* I 974–976. Good views of roofs in: Guido Alberto Rossi and Max Rodenbeck, *Egypt, Gift of the Nile. An Aerial Portrait* (New York 1992).

Roof chapel

A cult building found on the roofs of larger temples. Astronomical observation was carried out on the roofs of the **pyramid temples** of the Old Kingdom, and a zodiac circle in the ceiling of the **Ramesseum** served the same purpose. Structures associated with the sun cult were built on the roofs of New Kingdom temples (**Akhmenu**), and, similarly, on top of temples of the Ptolemaic period were erected **kiosks**, used in the ritual of the unification of divine images with the sun disc. The only roof chapel to have survived is the roofless kiosk on top of the temple of **Dendera**, which has 12 **Hathor-headed columns**, but the presence at many other temples of **stairs** for processions to the roof suggests the existence of chapels there too. Two Osiris chambers are built into the roof of the temple at Dendera.

Bibliography: Borchardt, *Tempel mit Umgang* 14–17; R. Stadelmann, Dachtempel, in: Helck, *LÄ* I 979; W. Helck, Tempeldach, in: Helck, *LÄ* VI 377.

Roof chapel of the temple of Hathor at Dendera

Roof drainage, *see also* drainage, water spouts

Despite sparse rainfall, Egyptian buildings are usually provided with elaborate drainage systems. These are particularly well preserved in the case of temple roofs, where rain water from the highest point of the roof is channelled downwards through sloping surfaces and gutters, before being finally released, as far as possible away from the building, through **water spouts**, which project from the top of the walls of the temple, usually

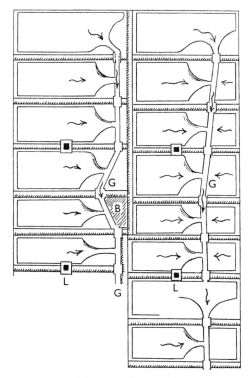

Water channels and light shafts on the roof of the temple of Sety I at Qurna

near the bottom edge of the **cavetto cornice** (**Iseum,** Fig.). Intricate guttering systems are preserved in the roofs of the temples of **Sety I** at Qurna and Abydos, and those of the Graeco-Roman period (**Philae**). From the Middle Kingdom, penetration of rain water is prevented by means of special covering of joints in the roof and raised edges around light holes. The temple of **Dakka** has a bridge-like aqueduct below the roofing slabs to carry rain water to the outside.

Bibliography: Clark, *AEM* 154–161; *Deir Chelouit*, Plates 41–42.

Rooms, function of

The function of nearly every room in a cult building is determined by a cultic or symbolic purpose. This was clearly indicated in terms of layout and form, and by means of **architectural decoration** and wall painting. The latter either depicts the procedures which took place in the room or refers to its function in some metaphoric way (**symbolism**). Thus, the cosmically 'correct' selection and arrangement of divine images was an important factor. The decorative and textual programmes in well-preserved temples enable one to reconstruct the functions of all the rooms (**Sety I**'s Abydos temple, **Edfu, Dendera**).

In secular buildings, too, the function of individual rooms, such as bedrooms, bathrooms (**bath**) or **grain stores**, can be determined from their particular form.

Bibliography: Arnold, *Wandrelief*; Richard H. Wilkinson, *Symbol and Magic in Egyptian Art* (London 1994) 60–81.

'Russian doll' technique

The practice of placing various structures one inside the other, with the intention of providing a protective or symbolic shell around the space, is a common feature of Egyptian architecture, the purpose being to provide protection or to express some symbolic meaning. There were artificial hills under the fill of the core of a **mastaba**; **niched** mastabas were cased with smooth walls (**Saqqara** S 3505); **step mastabas** formed the core of true pyramids; the Lower Egyptian **Per-nu** was placed inside niched **divine fortresses** (sarcophagi of the 12th Dynasty); and four different types of shrine were built one inside the other over the sarcophagus of Tutankhamun. A distinctive design element in the construction of step mastabas was the placing of sloping mantles of masonry against each side of the tower-like core.

Bibliography: Ricke, *Bemerkungen* I 10–11.

S

Sacred lake

Most Egyptian sanctuaries have an artificial body of water, such as a pond with rounded corners (**Maru temple**), a T-shaped pool in front of the façade, a horseshoe-shaped pond (at the temple of a lion god or goddess), a ring of water creating an artificial island or an actual sacred lake, in the form of a rectangular basin, surrounded by a wall, with (a late development) steps for access. The lake was surrounded by gardens of trees and served to beautify the house of the god(s), as well as being used for excursions of the cult barques and the performance of special rituals (such as cult plays about the birth of the god(s) and their victory over enemies). It also served to represent mythological areas of water.

Sacred lakes (preserved)

Site	Period/reign	Size (m)
Karnak	from Thutmosis III	77 x 120
Month precinct (Karnak)	Amenhotep III	16 x 18
Tanis	Nectanebo I	50 x 60
Armant	Ptolemaic (?)	26 x 30
Dendera	Roman	28 x 33
Medamud	Roman	15 x 17
El-Tod	Roman	11.5 x 16.2

Other sacred lakes are attested to in texts or visible in the landscape (**Sais**, **Bubastis**, **Heliopolis**, **Hermopolis**, **Abydos**, **Edfu** and others).

Ponds or basins of water surrounded by gardens near tombs, to provide for and offer cheer to the dead, were desirable but could only be achieved in practice in a few cases (**Khentkawes I**, **Amenhotep**, son of Hapu), and their place was usually taken by **models**, in the form of model basins of water or miniature gardens.

Bibliography: Bisson de la Roque, Le lac sacré de Tôd, in: *CdE* 24 (1937) 3-14; B. Gessler-Löhr, *Die heiligen Seen ägyptischer Tempel* (Hildesheim 1983); B. Gessler-Löhr, See, hlg., in: Helck, *LÄ* V 791–804; H.G. Fischer, An invocation offering basin of the Old Kingdom, in: *MDAIK* 47 (1991) 127-133.

Saff tomb

A form of **rock tomb** (Ar. *saff* = row) local to the area between Dendera and Gebelein, and particularly to the Theban site of El-Tarif. Earlier forms extend back as far as to the Old Kingdom, but they really flourished between the First Intermediate Period and the 11th Dynasty. The largest *saff* tombs at El-Tarif belong to Inyotef I–III (**kings' tombs** of the 11th Dynasty). Their forecourts, which were up to 300 m long and 75 m wide, were cut 4–5 m deep into the hard marl of the fore-desert. Along the side-walls there were entrances leading to the chambered tombs of the royal household. Standing along the rear face was a double row of 20–24 **pillars**. A corridor on the central axis (very occasionally decorated) led to a cult chamber supported by two pillars, with a further corridor from there leading to the burial chamber. Situated at the entrance to the court of the tomb of Wahankh Inyotef II was a **brick**-built cult chapel (perhaps representing a link between the **valley temple** of the Old Kingdom pyramid precincts and the valley temple of **'houses of millions of years'**). The kings' tombs at El-Tarif were surrounded by at least 250 private tombs, undecorated apart from white **plaster** and **stelae**, which were the precursors of the rock tombs of the 11th and 12th Dynasties at **Thebes**, which

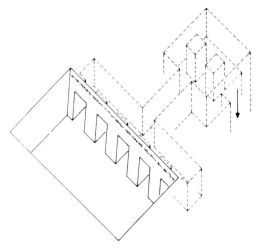

Schematic diagram of a *saff* tomb

had a pillared façade. The tomb of Iti at **Gebelein** has a façade of 14 pillars and, situated beyond the passages, brick-built chambers roofed with a barrel **vault**.

Bibliography: Dieter Arnold, Das Grab des Jnj.jtj.f. *Die Architektur* (Mainz 1971) 36–39; Dieter Arnold, *Gräber des Alten und Mittleren Reiches in El-Tarif* (Mainz 1976); Dieter Arnold, in: Helck, *LÄ* V 349–350; A.M. Donadoni Roveri el al., *Gebelein* (Turin 1994) 45–54; N. and H. Strudwick, *Thebes in Egypt* (London 1999) 92–95, 140, 146–148.

Sahure

This king's pyramid complex, 'The *Ba* of Sahure Appears', at **Abusir**, is the best preserved and researched example of its kind. The base length of the pyramid is 78.75 m, angle of slope 50°45', height 50 m. Its core is made up of five or six steps. The interior rooms are located above the bedrock and were built into an open trench purposely left in the **core masonry**. These rooms have partly collapsed as a result of the removal of the facing, and it has not yet been possible to excavate them. The pyramid precinct and **pyramid temple** are the first of a pattern which was to become typical of the 5th and 6th Dynasties. The **valley temple** stands on a quay complex and has an open entrance hall, with two rows of eight **columns**, which leads to a T-shaped inner room with a statue niche, continuing from there to the entrance into the **causeway**. To the south is a later annexe acting as the side-entrance with an entrance hall of four columns. The causeway, 235 m long, leads from the valley temple to the pyramid temple. It commences with a **Per-weru**, followed by an altar court surrounded by **granite** columns with palm capitals. To the west, on a levelled terrace, are a room with five statues, two anterooms and the funerary offering hall with a **false door**. There is a secondary pyramid (**cult pyramid**) on the south side of the temple.

Ruins of the pyramid temple of Sahure at Abusir following the excavations of 1907

Significant remains are preserved of the relief decoration which covered every one of the inner **limestone** walls of the valley and pyramid temples; the exterior walls were not decorated. The base of walls in important rooms was formed of black **basalt orthostats**. Door frames, columns and **architraves** were made of red granite, with green decoration and inscribed with sunken hieroglyphs.

Bibliography: Borchardt, *Sahu-Re*; Edwards, *Pyramids* 174–181; Stadelmann, *Pyramiden* 164–171; M. Verner, *Forgotten Pyramids, Lost Pharaohs, Abusir* (Prague 1994) 68–74; Lehner, *Complete Pyramids* 142–144.

Sais

The site of Sais, the capital of Egypt in the 26th Dynasty, and home of the temple of Neith (attested to from the 1st Dynasty onwards), which lay on the East Bank of the Rosetta branch of the Nile. However, it is so completely destroyed that now even its exact location is uncertain. In an area of ruins near Sa el-Hagar, Champollion and Lepsius observed the traces of a central temple building, 230 x 150 m in size, inside an enclosure measuring c. 675 x 675 m with 28 m thick walls.

Herodotus mentions large **obelisks**, a **sacred lake**, the tombs of kings Apries and Amasis in the court to the left, beside the main temple of Neith (which had large stone chapels with palm **columns**), and an **Osiris tomb** behind the main temple building; he also described a monolithic **granite naos** (10.5 m tall) of Amasis, brought to this site from Aswan by 2000 workers and then left at the entrance to the temple. This, together with the rest of the temple, was completely destroyed in the 14th century AD, and parts of it were taken to Cairo, Rosetta and other places. The family crypt of 'Psammitichos' is also mentioned by Strabo, and its existence was confirmed by the discovery nearby of the sarcophagus of Psamtek II.

Bibliography: Herodotos, Book II 169-70, 175, Book III 16; LD I 55, Texts 1–4; Strabo, *Geographica* 17 1 18; L. Habachi, Sais and its Monuments, in: *ASAE* 42 (1943) 369–376; J. Leclant, in: *Orientalia* 35 (1966) 132; J. Malek, Sais, in: *LÄ* V 355–357; R. el-Sayed, *Documents relatifs à Saïs et ses divinités* (Cairo 1975); R. el-Sayed, *La déesse Neith de Sais* (Cairo 1982); P. Wilson, Sais, surveying the Royal City, in: *Egyptian Archaeology* 12 (1998) 3–6.

Salamuni

High up on a slope, 9 km east of **Akhmim**, is the façade of a small **rock temple** of Thutmosis III, which was usurped and enlarged in the rule of Ay by the **architect** Nakhtmin. It may have been associated with the nearby **stone quarries**. The inner rooms of the temple underwent considerable alterations. Situated at the foot of the hill is a necropolis of **rock tombs** dating to the Old Kingdom, the Late Period and the Roman period.

Bibliography: K.P. Kuhlmann, Der Felstempel des Eje bei Akhmim, in: *MDAIK* 35 (1979) 165–188; K.P. Kuhlmann, *Materialien zur Archäologie und Geschichte des Raumes von Achmim* (Mainz 1983) 71–86.

Sanam (Abu Dom)

An important Napatan **palace** city on the West Bank of the Nile in the Sudan, opposite Napata, with a temple dedicated to Amun built by Taharqa consisting of a **pylon**, **pillared hall**, offering room, sanctuary and side-rooms, resembling the temples of **Kawa** and **Tabo**. To the north is a vast complex of store rooms (known as the 'treasury').

Bibliography: Griffith, in: Oxford Excavations in Nubia, in: Annals of Archaeology and Anthropology 9 (Liverpool 1921/22) 74-76; William Y. Adams, Nubia. Corridor to Africa (London 1977) 274-75.

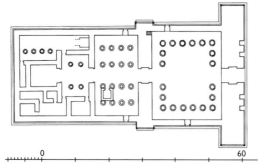

Plan of the Amun temple built by Taharqa at Sanam

Sandstone

Compacted sedimentary rock, made up of fine grains, mainly of quartz but also containing feldspar, splinters of rock and mica. It was favoured as a **building stone**. Its specific gravity is 2.0–2.65. This material was first used architecturally in the **'High Sand'** at **Hierakonpolis** (possibly in the early Old Kingdom), but it first came into more widespread use in the temple of **Mentuhotep** at Deir el-Bahari. From the middle of the 18th Dynasty, sandstone took over from **limestone**, which had previously been the norm, as the primary building material; for example, it was used in all the Theban temples (except that of **Hatshepsut**), every temple in **Nubia** and almost every Graeco-Roman temple. There are numerous **stone quarries** up-river from Esna to Nubia, particularly at **Gebel el-Silsila**.

Bibliography: Lucas, *AEMI* 55–57; R. Klemm, Sandstein, in: Helck, *LÄ* V 382–383; De Putter, *Pierres* 91–94; Klemm, *Steine* 225–281; Nicholson, *Materials* 54–56.

Sankhkare, temple of

Remains of a small temple on the northern hill towering over the Valley of the Kings (Thoth Hill). The complex consists of a **brick** enclosure (21 x 24 m) with one of the earliest known brick **pylons**. Within is a building measuring 8 x 10 m containing three chapels standing side-by-side with **limestone** shrines for the cult images. Dedicatory inscriptions are addressed to Horus. The brick temple was built on the ruins of an older (perhaps Early Dynastic) predecessor in stone.

Bibliography: G. Schweinfurth, Ein neu entdeckter Tempel in Theben, in: *ZÄS* 41 (1904) 22–25; W.M. Flinders Petrie, *Qurneh* (London 1909) 4–6; Hölscher, *Medinet Habu*, Vol. 2 4–5; G. Vörös, *Temple on the Pyramid of Thebes* (Budapest 1998); G. Vörös et al., Preliminary Report on the Excavations at Thoth Hill, Thebes, in: *MDAIK* 54 (1998) 335–340.

Saqqara

The central part of the Memphite necropolis between Abusir and Dahshur on a flat desert plateau which drops away sharply at the east. North Saqqara is occupied by the Early Dynastic **mastabas**. The mastabas of the Old Kingdom are in the central area, grouped around the precinct of **Djoser** and the pyramids of **Teti**, **Userkaf** and **Unas**. At South Saqqara are the pyramid precincts and necropoleis of **Pepy I**, **Merenre**, **Djedkare**, **Pepy II** and **Shepseskaf**. The area south of the Unas causeway is occupied by tombs of the New Kingdom and the Monastery of Apa Jeremias. North-west of the precinct of Djoser is the **Serapeum**. An **Anubieion**, a **Bubasteion** and an Asklepieion with extensive animal cemeteries were constructed during the Late Period inside large **brick** enclosures along the eastern edge of the desert at North Saqqara; cutting through the first of these is an avenue of **sphinxes** which leads from **Memphis** to the Serapeum.

Although many important monuments are known to exist here, considerable parts of the necropoleis remain completely unexplored.

Bibliography (general): J. de Morgan, *Carte de la nécropole memphite* (Cairo 1897); G. Goyon, Les ports des pyramides et le grand canal de Memphis, in: *RdE* 23 (1971) 137–163; Lauer, *Saqqara*; Jean-Philippe Lauer, *Cinquante années à Saqqara* (Cairo 1983); H.S. Smith, Saqqara, in: Helck, *LÄ* V 386–430; A.M. Roth, The organization of the royal cemeteries at Saqqara in the Old Kingdom, in: *JARCE* 25 (1988) 201–214; Saqqara, aux origines de l'Égypte pharaonique, in: *Les Dossiers d'Archéologie* 146/147 (1990); Jean-Philippe Lauer, *Les pyramides de Sakkara* (Cairo 1991); Bárta, *Abusir 2000*.

1. Large tombs of the 1st–3rd Dynasties

At the northern end of the necropolis, above the village of **Abusir**, are numerous monumental **brick** tombs of the

1st Dynasty onwards. Behind them, to the west, is a field of **mastabas** of the 3rd Dynasty (**Hesyre**). The question of whether or not the 1st Dynasty tombs, excavated in 1936–56 (partly by W.B. Emery), are royal or private tombs has been long disputed; they are more likely to be those of high officials, or at most royal **cenotaphs**. The most important tombs are (reign in parentheses):

S 2185 (Djer or later)
S 3035, belonging to Hemaka (Dewen): east stairs, large and deep burial chamber; important grave goods.
S 3036 (Dewen)
S 3038 belonging to Nebetka (possibly Anedjib), with a stepped superstructure; probably not originally a tomb.
S 3357 (Hor Aha): five sunken central chambers, boat burial and a **model** of an estate.
S 3471 (Djer): sunken main central chamber; mound of sand built in.
S 3500 (Qa'a)
S 3503 (Merineith)
S 3504 (Djet): surrounded by 350 bulls' heads.
S 3505 (Qa'a): **niched** mastaba with east stairs built into the masonry at a later date; a cult area to the north.
S 3506 (Dewen): with a boat burial.
S 3507 (Dewen): mound of sand built in.

Three royal tomb complexes (**gallery tomb**) are attested to from the second half of the 2nd Dynasty:

a) Hetepsekhemwy: a gallery below the pyramid temple of Unas, more than 120 m long, with a corridor blocked by four **limestone portcullises** and narrow magazines over 70 m long. There are impressions of the seals of Hetepsekhemwy and Reneb.

b) Ninetjer: a gallery in front of the south-east corner of the precinct of **Djoser**.

c) Reneb: the **stela** of 'Horus Reneb' from **Memphis**, now in the MMA, perhaps belonged to a gallery tomb below the west area of the precinct of Djoser.

Two vast precincts are visible on the surface of the desert to the west: the Gisr el-Mudir and the 'L-shaped enclosure'. It is not known whether they correspond to the fortresses of the royal tombs at **Abydos** or whether they are independent royal tomb complexes.

Bibliography: Barsanti, Rapports sur les déblaiements opérés autour de la pyramide d'Ounas, in: *ASAE* 2 (1901) 250–252; Barsanti, Fouilles autours de la pyramide d'Ounas, in: *ASAE* 3 (1902) 183–184; Walter B. Emery, *The Tomb of Hemaka* (Cairo 1938); Walter B. Emery, *The Tomb of Hor-aha* (Cairo 1939); Walter B. Emery, *Great Tombs of the First Dynasty*, 3 Vols (Cairo 1949, London 1954, 1958); Lauer, *Histoire monumentale* 16–62; H. Kees, Zur Problematik des archaischen Friedhofes bei Sakkara, in: *OLZ* 52 (1957) 12–20; H. Kees, Neues vom Archaischen Friedhof von Sakkara, *OLZ* 54 (1959)

565–570; H. Fischer, An Egyptian royal stela of the Second Dynasty, in: *Artibus Asiae* 24 (1962) 45–56; B.J. Kemp, The Egyptian 1st Dynasty royal cemetery, in: *Antiquity* 41 (1967) 22–32; P. Munro, Report on the work…of the 12th campaign, in: *Discussions in Egyptology* 26 (1993) 47–58; I. Mathieson et al., The National Museums of Scotland Saqqara Survey Project 1993–1995, in: *JEA* 83 (1997) 17–53.

2. Precinct of **Djoser**
3. Old Kingdom pyramids, *see* names of kings
4. Old Kingdom tombs, *see* **mastaba**

5. New Kingdom tombs
There are numerous examples of monumental mortuary temple-like tombs of New Kingdom date south of the **Unas** causeway. They are c. 15 x 50 m in area, usually consisting of up to three **pylons** and pillared courts, followed in many cases by a three-room cult complex, usually topped by a small pyramid. Superstructures are in many cases richly decorated with what are known as 'Memphite reliefs'. A shaft in the innermost courtyard leads to the underground complexes of rooms, which are often full of branching corridors, and in some cases decorated. Certain examples show architectural references to the **valley temples** and the **Per-weru** of the Old Kingdom. Tombs excavated up to the present are those of the group belonging to General (later King) **Horemheb**, Tia (sister of Ramesses II), **Ramose** (military official under Horemheb), Maya (Tutankhamun's treasurer) and Paser (master of construction to Ramesses II, **Temple tomb**, Fig.).

A cluster of New Kingdom **rock tombs** is located in the cliffs east of the pyramid of **Userkaf**. They date from the middle of the 18th Dynasty to the Ramesside period and are important for their well-preserved wall decoration. The most important are those of the vizier Aper-El and of the royal wet nurse Maïa.

Bibliography: Geoffrey T. Martin, *The Memphite Tomb of Horemheb* (London 1989); K. A. Kitchen, Memphite Tomb-Chapels in the New Kingdom and later, in: *Ägypten und altes Testament* (Wiesbaden 1989) 1, 272–284; Geoffrey T. Martin, *The Hidden Tombs of Memphis* (London 1991); S. Tawfiq, in: *MDAIK* 47 (1991) 403–409; A. Zivie, *Découverte à Saqqarah. Le vizir oublié* (Paris 1990). Good reconstructions: Aufrère, *L'Égypte restituée* III, 86–89.

6. Late Period complexes
In the area around the precinct of **Djoser** are numerous vast shafts, up to 25 m deep, which were constructed in the 25–30th Dynasties. At the bottom was a **crypt** roofed with a stone **vault** and containing an anthropoid sarcophagus. The shaft could be entered by a narrow

side-shaft with a connecting corridor. The lid of the sarcophagus was usually lowered on props which sank into shafts of sand (**lowering heavy loads**, Fig.); the pit was subsequently completely filled with loose sand as a protection against robbery. There are few remains of superstructures. Examples are Neferibre Sa-Neith, Wahibremen, Psamtek, Pentenisis and others. Similar complexes exist at **Giza** ('**Campbell's tomb**') and **Abusir** (**Wedjahorresnet**). The tomb of **Bakenrenef** differs from this form in that it has an extensive burial system.

Bibliography: Edda Bresciani et al., *La tomba di Ciennehebu, capo della flotta del re* (Pisa 1977); H.S. Smith and D.G. Jeffreys, The North-Saqqara temple-town survey, in: *JEA* 64 (1978) 10–21; H.S. Smith and D.G. Jeffreys, The Anubieion, North Saqqara, in: *JEA* 65 (1979) 17–29; Sue Davies and H.S. Smith, Sacred animal temples at Saqqara, in: Quirke, *Temple*, 112–131; D. Arnold, The Late Period tombs of Hor-Khebit, Wennefer and Wereshnefer at Saqqâra, in: *Études sur l'Ancien Empire et la nécropole de Saqqâra dédiées à Jean-Philippe Lauer* (Montpellier 1997) 31–54.

Saw

To date no saws of any significance have been found in Egypt, although their use by joiners, carpenters and boat builders is attested to in numerous depictions and by the discovery of **models**. Marks caused by sawing also testify to their use in cutting stone from the beginnings of **stone construction**: the precinct of **Djoser** (**limestone**), the pyramid of **Khufu** (**basalt paving**, **granite** sarcophagus, granite **portcullis**), and the **sun temple** of **Niuserre** (**alabaster**). Large blocks of granite, like sarcophagi and their lids, are likely to have been cut by free-swinging drag saws. Machine-like arrangements are conceivable. The front edge of two adjacent blocks was frequently adjusted by sawing in order to provide better fitting

Saw marks on the basalt paving of the pyramid temple of Khufu at Giza

joints (**casing** of **Unas** pyramid, **joint**). Quartz sand was used as an abrasive agent. Saw blades are likely to have worn out at a phenomenal rate.

Bibliography: Clark, *AEM* 203–204; R. Drenkhahn, Säge, in: Helck, *LÄ* V 33–34; Arnold, *Building* 266–277; R.G. Moores Jr., Evidence for use of a stone-cutting drag saw by the Fourth Dynasty Egyptians, in: *JARCE* 28 (1991) 139–148; E.-L. Schwandner, Der Schnitt im Stein, in: *Bautechnik der Antike. Beobachtungen zum Gebrauch der Steinsäge in der Antike* (Mainz 1991) 216–223.

Sawada

A drawing produced by the French expedition near 'Saouâdeh' in Middle Egypt (opposite Minya) depicts a beautiful underground **rock tomb**, Hellenistic in style, with Doric **columns** and an atrium-like **sun court**. The complex, comparable to the rock tombs at **Alexandria**, has completely vanished since that time.

Bibliography: *Description* IV, 68.

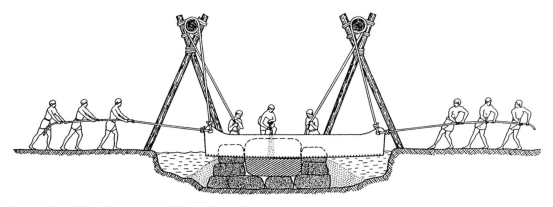

Reconstruction of a device for sawing stone (after R.G. Moores Jr)

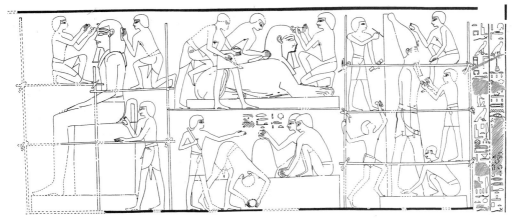

Scaffolding made from light poles used in producing statues, as depicted in the tomb of Rekhmire

Scaffolding

Light-pole scaffolding was used by stonemasons and sculptors, less for the raising of heavy loads than to enable the smoothing and decoration of wall areas and the construction of **columns** and **colossal statues**. The scaffolding was reinforced with ropes of twine and anchored deep into paving or rocky ground, holes being visible to this day (**pyramid temple** of **Khufu**, **Mentuhotep** temple, **hypostyle hall** of Ramesses III's temple at **Medinet Habu**, tomb of **Montuemhat**). The absence of scaffold holes (putlogs) in Egyptian masonry shows that suspended or bracketed scaffolding was not in use. Large areas of wall, like those of the pyramids, could not in any case have been covered with scaffolding.

Bibliography: Clark, *AEM* 194–195; Hölscher, *Medinet Habu* IV 32–33; Arnold, *Building* 231–236.

Screen wall

A type of screen, with its origins in reed **matting** suspended between wooden posts, which was represented in stone in the precinct of **Djoser**. Spaces between the pillars of **barque stations** from the Middle Kingdom and the New Kingdom were regularly filled in by a low parapet, with either a rounded or a square top. The screen walls between **statue pillars** or **columns** in temples and tombs of the New Kingdom are more sophisticated (Ramesses III's temples at **Medinet Habu** and **Karnak**, the tomb of Tutu at **Amarna**). In the Ethiopian period, screen walls in **kiosks** in front of **pylons** protected the interior from view: they are taller than a man's height, up to one half to two thirds the height of the column, topped with a **cavetto cornice** and **frieze of uraei**, with the shaft of the column protruding. There are beautiful screen walls of black **granite** in the 26th and 30th Dynasty temples of the Delta (**Philae**,

Fig.), and also those in Graeco-Roman **birth houses**, kiosks and **pronaoi**, some of monumental proportions, their passageways interestingly arranged. The surface area of screen walls provided plenty of space for decoration and inscriptions.

Bibliography: Many examples in: Jéquier, *Architecture*; D. Wildung, Schranken, in: Helck, *LÄ* 690–693.

Screen wall in the Roman birth house at Dendera, topped with a cornice and frieze of uraei

Sebennytos

Sebennytos (Samannud) is situated in the middle of the Delta. It was the home of the historian Manetho (around 290 BC) and the capital of Egypt during the reign of Nectanebo I. From here the rulers of the 30th Dynasty launched their 'Egyptian Revival' movement against the Persians, erecting of a chain of important temples throughout the country. The Phersos (Per-shu), the chief temple of Onuris-Shu, was a new building of Nectanebo I. Its decoration was begun in the reign of Nectanebo II, but was interrupted by the Persian invasion of 343 BC and was only completed under Philip Arrhidaeus and Ptolemy II. The Arab geographer and historian El-Maqrizi (AD 1364–1442) could still describe the Phersos as an Egyptian masterpiece, but it was dismantled soon afterwards. Until modern times about 40 decorated blocks, of **quartzite**, **basalt** and **granite**, were still to be seen, some of which have now made their way into foreign museums and the local store house at Samannud. The site itself, as well as the **kings' tombs** of the 30th Dynasty, which were probably situated within the temple precinct, have so far not undergone any archaeological investigation.

Bibliography: C.C. Edgar and G. Roeder, Der Isistempel von Behbêt, in: *Recueil de Travaux* 35 (1913) 89–116; A. Kamal, Sébennytos et son temple, in: *ASAE* 7 (1906) 87–94; A. Kamal, The Temple of Samanoud, in: *ASAE* 11 (1911) 90–96; G. Steindorff, Reliefs from the temples of Sebennytos and Iseion in American Collections, in: *Journal of the Walters Art Gallery* (1944–45) 39–59; N. Spencer, The temple of Onuris-Shu at Samanud, in: *Egyptian Archaeology* 14 (1999) 7–9; Arnold, *Temples* 127–128.

Sedeinga (Adaya)

An extensive archaeological site on the West Bank of the Nile between the Second and Third Cataracts, 5 km north of **Soleb**, with the now collapsed remains of a temple built by Amenhotep III for his spouse Tiye, identified with Isis-Hathor. There is a **kiosk** in front of the façade of the temple, a closed **pronaos** with two rows of four columns and a **hypostyle hall** beyond which has 16 **Hathor columns** with **channelled** shafts. The sanctuary area is lost. Excavations carried out in the 1960s have not been published.

Bibliography: *LD* I 114-15, III 82, Text V 228–30; J. Leclant, Sedeinga, in: Helck, *LÄ* V 780–781; M. Schiff-Giorgini, Première Campagne de Fouilles à Sedeinga, in: Kush 13 (1965) 112–115; M. Schiff-Giorgini 14 (1966) 244–261.

Seila

Remains of a small **step mastaba** of Sneferu, consisting of three steps, situated at Gebel el-Rus on the edge of the desert, at the south-east border of the Faiyum. The base measures 60 **cubits** (31.5 m) and the pyramid was originally 20.4 m in height with an angle of slope of 13–15°. There are the remains of two **stelae**, a naos and a seated figure of the king. No interior rooms have been found and there is no information concerning the function of the building.

Bibliography: L. Borchardt, Die Pyramide von Silah, in: *ASAE* 1 (1900) 211–214; *MRA* II 55–56; Lauer, *Histoire monumentale* 222–225; F. Gomaà, Gebel er-Rus, in: Helck, *LÄ* II 440; Dreyer, *Stufenpyramiden* 49–50; L.H. Lesko, Seila 1981, in: *JARCE* 25 (1988) 223–235.

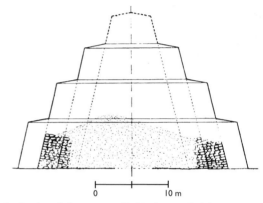

Section through the step pyramid of Sneferu at Seila (after J.-P. Lauer)

Sekhemkhet, funerary complex of

The unfinished funerary complex of king Djoser Sekhemkhet, the successor of Djoser, is situated to the south-west of the precinct of **Djoser**. It has a north–south orientation and originally covered an area of 185 x 262 m, later enlarged at the north and south to a total length of 545 m. The north (older) wall has beautiful **niched** decoration still in a good state of preservation. The (unfinished) **step mastaba** (122 x 122 m) is constructed in the form of 14 mantles, which are placed against the core at a slope of c. 15°. It was intended to consist of seven steps, reaching to a height of c. 70 m. The burial chamber, at a depth of 32 m, was not set into an open construction shaft, like that of Djoser, but was constructed by means of a sloping corridor. The chamber contains an undamaged and sealed, but empty, **alabaster** sarcophagus (perhaps for a queen). The burial chamber is surrounded on the west, north and east by a U-shaped set of corridors with a total of 136 magazines. Buried in the **South Tomb** is the body of a child. Dummy buildings, typical of the Djoser precinct, are absent here. The precinct still awaits complete investigation.

Bibliography: Zakaria Goneim, *The Buried Pyramid* (London 1956); Zakaria Goneim, *Horus Sekhem-khet, The Unfinished Step Pyramid at*

Sakkara I (Cairo 1957); Lauer, *Histoire monumentale* 179–206; J.P. Lauer, Au complexe funéraire de l'Horus Sekhem-khet, in: *Comptes rendus de l'Académie des Inscriptions et Belles-Lettres* (1967) 493–510; J.P. Lauer, Recherche et découverte du tombeau sud de l'Horus Sekhem-khet dans son complexe funéraire à Saqqarah, in: *RdE* 20 (1968) 97–107; *BIFAO* 36 (1955) 357–364, 48/49 (1969) 121–131; *MRA* II 13–19, Addenda I and II.

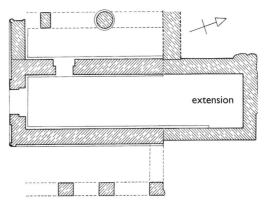

Plan of the chapel of Thutmosis III in the fortress of Semna

Remains of the northern enclosure wall of the funerary complex of Sekhemkhet at Saqqara

Semna

A border **fortress** of Amenemhat I and Senwosret III on the West Bank of the Nile, 60 km south of Wadi Halfa. It stands on a rock plateau, and has an L-shaped plan 135 m long. Towers jut out from the walls. Inside the fortress is a chapel originally dating from the Middle Kingdom, which was rebuilt, in stone, under Hatshepsut and Thutmosis III and dedicated to the deified Senwosret III and the god Dedun. It contains important wall decoration and inscriptions. The elongated **barque** sanctuary was extended at the rear and was probably intended to be surrounded by a portico, as at the temples of **Amada** and **Buhen**, but it remained unfinished. Next to this, and built over an earlier building of the 18th Dynasty, stands a **brick** temple of Taharqa. 110 m south-west of Semna is a rectangular fort-like structure with a keep and dry moat. The temple was moved to Khartoum in 1963–65; the opportunity to make a structural assessment was lost and the history of its construction thus remains unclear.

Bibliography: *LD* III 47–56; S. Clarke, Ancient Egyptian Frontier Fortresses, in: *JEA* 3 (1916) 169–172; Dows Dunham and Jozef Janssen, *Semna Kumma, Second Cataract Forts*, Vol.1 (Boston 1960) 5–73; K. Zibelius-Chen, Semna, in: Helck, *LÄ* V 843–844; Hein, *Ramessidische Bautätigkeit* 49–51; Ricardo A. Caminos, *Semna-Kumma*, 2 Vols (London 1998).

Senenmut, tombs of

Senenmut had two **rock tombs** built at **Thebes**, which act as a complement to each other as cult and burial complexes. The cult complex, TT 71, in Sheikh Abd el-**Qurna**, has a high terraced frontage beyond which is a **pylon**-like **niched** façade with a door in the centre and two sets of four **windows** in the recesses. This is followed by a transverse hall divided by two groups of four **pillars** into four halls, each with a different type of ceiling, probably representing different types of chapel (**Puyemre**). A high, narrow passage leads back to a statue niche set high up in the rear wall. The burial complex, TT 353, is situated in the Hatshepsut **stone quarry** and consists of a steep staircase and a total of four rock chambers. It is unfinished, with only the uppermost room decorated, with religious texts and an astronomical ceiling. However, the sarcophagus was not found in TT 353, but in TT 71.

Bibliography: Peter F. Dorman, *The Monuments of Senenmut: Problems in Historical Methodology* (London 1988); Peter F. Dorman, *The Tombs of Senenmut* (New York 1991).

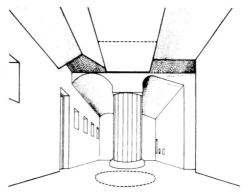

Reconstructed view through the transverse hall of the tomb of Senenmut (TT 71) at Thebes (after P. Dorman)

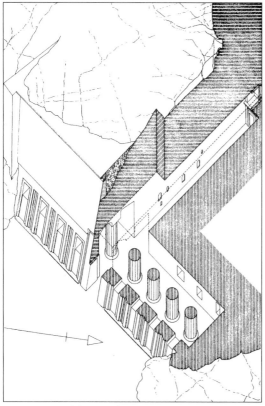

Reconstruction of the tomb of Senenmut (TT 71) at Thebes (after P. Dorman)

Senwosret I, pyramid of

The pyramid precinct 'United are the Places of Kheperkare' was erected by Senwosret I near the place now known as **El-Lisht**. It was conceived as a direct development of the complexes of the late Old Kingdom. The core of the pyramid 'Senwosret Surveys the Two Lands' (61.25 m high, with an area of 105 x 105 sq m), consists of rough stone masonry strengthened by radial support walls and encased with Tura **limestone**; the slope is 49°24'. The entrance corridor is built of **granite** but is only accessible as far as the level of the sub-soil water. The burial chamber has never been investigated. The **pyramid temple** differs from its Old Kingdom precursors in its lack of storage rooms. A new feature is the inner **enclosure wall** of limestone, which was decorated inside and outside, at intervals of 4.24 m, with 100 representations of the king's Horus name, each one 5 m high, above the **palace façade**. Within the outer enclosure wall are nine secondary pyramids, some of them added later for female members of the royal family, among them Queen Neferu and Princess Itakayet. A group of 10 seated limestone images of Senwosret I (now in the Egyptian Museum, Cairo) was found in the courtyard by J.E. Gautier in 1894/95. A **causeway** to the east leads to the **valley temple**, which has not yet been located. Some **statue pillars** in the causeway were added at a later stage to mark the precinct as a *sed*-festival complex.

Bibliography: J.E. Gautier and G. Jéquier, *Fouilles de Licht* (Cairo 1902); Edwards, *Pyramids* 218–225; Dieter Arnold, *The South*

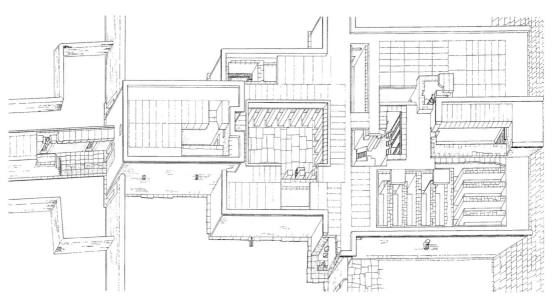

Reconstruction of the pyramid temple of Senwosret I at El-Lisht

Cemeteries of Lisht I: The Pyramid of Senwosret I (New York 1988); Felix Arnold, *The South Cemeteries of Lisht II: The Control Notes and Team Marks* (New York 1990); Dieter Arnold, *The South Cemeteries of Lisht III: The Pyramid Complex of Senwosret I* (New York 1991).

Senwosret II, pyramid of (Illahun, El-Lahun), see also Kahun

The pyramid precinct 'Senwosret is Mighty' was erected by Senwosret II at the entrance to the Faiyum. The **brick** masonry of the pyramid (area 107 x 107 m, height 48 m) was reinforced with radial support walls and stands on a mound of rock; the angle of the slope is calculated as 42°35'. The entrance to the pyramid is hidden in the floor of a **queen's tomb** and for the first time is not in what had been the traditional position: at the centre of the north side of the pyramid. The burial chamber contains a sarcophagus of exceptional technical perfection and is isolated from the surrounding rock by a corridor which runs around it and thereby represents an **Osiris tomb**. The inner **enclosure wall**, made of **limestone**, is niched (**niching**, Fig.). In the north-eastern corner of the outer courtyard there is a secondary pyramid, of which the interior rooms have yet to be located. The **pyramid temple**, which was an unusually small structure, is completely destroyed. The whole precinct was surrounded

by 42 trees, strengthening the association of the pyramid and its burial chamber with an **Osiris tomb**. The **valley temple**, in the associated **pyramid town** of **Kahun**, appears not to have been linked to the pyramid. The surrounding area contains a private necropolis, whose most important tomb is that of **Inpy**. Directly to the north of the pyramid is the royal tomb known as **El-Lahun tomb 621**.

Bibliography: W.M. Flinders Petrie, G. Brunton and M.A. Murray, *Lahun II* (London 1923); W.M. Flinders Petrie, *Illahun, Kahun and Gurob* (London 1891) 24ff.; D. Arnold, *El-Lahun*, in: Helck, *LÄ* III 909–911; Edwards, *Pyramids* 225–226.

Senwosret III, pyramid of

The large pyramid precinct of Senwosret III (area 192 x 299 m), stands on a plateau north-east of the **Red Pyramid** of Dahshur. It was originally surrounded by two rectangular **enclosure walls**, both **niched**. At the centre stands the pyramid, area 107 x 107 m, height 64.13 m, angle of slope c. 50°. The core consisted of **brick**, which was cased with **limestone**. The entrance to the pyramid was hidden in the west side, and led to the burial complex containing the king's chamber, with a **vaulted granite** ceiling, which still contains the magnificent niched granite sarcophagus. To the east is

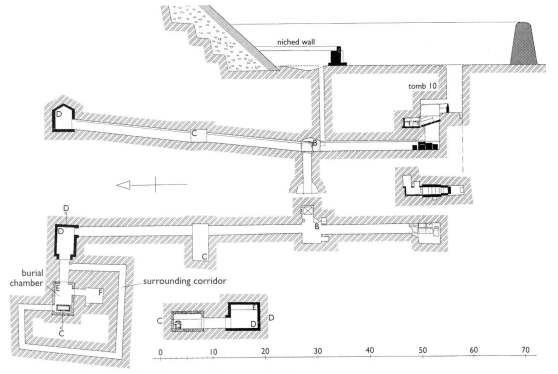

Plan and section of the inner chambers of the pyramid of Senwosret II at El-Lahun

View into the burial chamber of Senwosret III in his pyramid at Dahshur

the relatively small **pyramid temple**. A later enlargement of the precinct to the south gives the complex a north–south orientation. A large stone temple for the cult of the king stands in the new south court. It was accessed by a monumental **causeway** which entered the precinct at the south-east corner of the niched outer wall. To the south and north of the pyramid are seven pyramids of queens (No. 9, in the south-west corner, is that of Queen Weret II, find spot of some fine jewellery now in the Egyptian Museum, Cairo). North of the pyramid are two

long subterranean galleries containing the tomb chambers of 12 female members of the royal family and their sarcophagi; it was here, in 1895, that J. de Morgan found the jewellery of Princesses Merit and Sithathor (also in the Egyptian Museum, Cairo).

Bibliography: De Morgan, *Dahchour 1894* 47–85; De Morgan, *Dahchour 1894–1895* 87–97; D. Arnold, Das Labyrinth und seine Vorbilder, in: *MDAIK* 35 (1979) 2–5; Stadelmann, *Pyramiden* 238–240; Dieter Arnold, *The Pyramid Complex of Senwosret III at Dahschur. Architectural Studies* (New York 2001).

Senwosretankh, tomb of

A huge tomb complex, at **El-Lisht**, of a high official of the 12th Dynasty. The superstructure has a particularly splendid façade, now ruined, which puts this tomb on a par with a royal funerary **palace** of the Early Dynastic Period. The walls of the tomb chamber are perfectly preserved and inscribed with Pyramid Texts, as in the royal tombs of the Old Kingdom.

Bibliography: A. Lansing and W.C. Hayes, in: *BMMA* 28 II (Nov. 1933) 9–38

Serabit el-Khadim

An important sanctuary dedicated to Hathor in the south-western Sinai, on a mountain site, at the centre of Egyptian

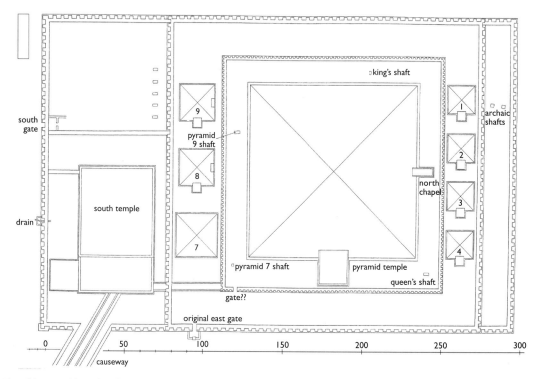

Plan of the pyramid complex of Senwosret III

View of the temple of Hathor at Serabit el-Khadim

turquoise mining. It was erected by workmen trained in Egypt. Due to the local terrain the temple is not symmetrical about its axis, but is rather an irregular rectangle, approximately 100 m long, surrounded by a wall of fieldstones. The main entrance (from a later period) in the short western side is flanked by **stelae** of Ramesses II and Sethnakht. Instead of open forecourts the visitor passes through a succession of 14 **pillared halls**, added in the 18–20th Dynasties, built of blocks cut to the required shape, finally reaching the actual inner court. The larger inner court with its rock shrines dates to the Middle Kingdom. The innermost corner contains the cult grottoes of Hathor and the god Sopdu, the earliest Egyptian **rock temples**. They were erected, side by side, in the south-eastern corner of the court by Amenemhat III and Amenemhat IV.

Numerous royal and private sculptures, **stelae** and offering stands have been found in the thick layers of waste containing broken **alabaster** and faience votive offerings. The water basins in the anterooms of the sanctuaries and evidence of intensive burning of incense are suggestive of cult practices from neighbouring Canaan. There are many stelae and inscriptions of importance for our knowledge of the expedition activities of the ancient Egyptians.

Bibliography: W. M. Flinders Petrie, *Researches in Sinai* (London 1906) 72–108, Plates 85–113; Alan H. Gardiner and T. Eric Peet, *The Inscriptions of Sinai* (London 1952), Plate 92 (plan); R. Gundlach, Serabit el-Chadim, in: Helck, *LÄ* V 866–868; D .Valbelle, Chapelle de Geb et temple de millions d'années dans le sanctuaire d'Hathor, maîtresse de la turquoise, in: *Genava* 44NS (1996) 61–70; D. Valbelle and Charles Bonnet, *Le sanctuaire d'Hathor maîtresse de la turquoise* (Paris 1996); D. Valbelle and Charles Bonnet, The Middle Kingdom temple of Hathor at Serabit el-Khadim, in: Quirke, *Temple* 82–89.

Serapeum (Alexandria)

Sanctuary of Serapis (Osiris-Hapy) erected by Ptolemy III on an artificial terrace in the south-west of the city. The rectangular temenos has a monumental approach and **gateway** structure with **obelisks** and many re-used Pharaonic monuments and statues, and is occupied not only by the Serapeum but a number of additional institutions (sanctuary of Anubis, Library and so on). The main temple contains the famous cult image of Serapis of Briaxis, which was destroyed under Theodosius in AD 391. Ancient sources and excavation

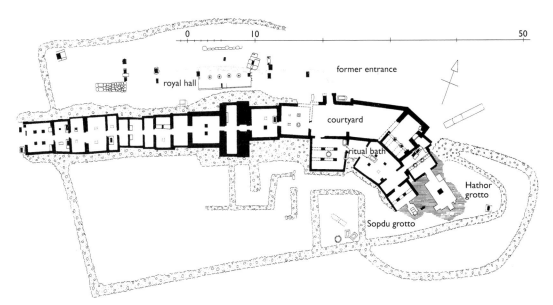

Plan of the temple of Hathor at Serabit el-Khadim

results permit only a partial reconstruction of the building. There is an extensive system of passages underground. Finds include many sculptures as well as blocks re-used from Pharaonic buildings.

'Pompey's Pillar', a Corinthian **column** 26.85 m high, stands in the grounds of the temple but does not belong to the latter, being rather a reminder of the merciful treatment of the city after its conquest by Diocletian in AD 297.

Bibliography: *Description* V, Plate 34; Alan Rowe, The Discovery of the Famous Temple and Enclosure of Serapis at Alexandria in: *AESE* 1946 Suppl. 2; Anne Roullet, The Egyptian and Egyptianizing monuments of imperial Rome, in: *EPRO* 20 (1972), Figs 349ff. Sanctuaries of Serapis outside Egypt: Jean-Claude Grenier, Décoration statuaire du 'Serapeum' de la ville Adriana, in: *MEFRA* 101 (1989).

Serapeum (Memphis)

Tomb precinct of the Apis bulls of **Memphis** at **Saqqara**. An avenue of **sphinxes** of Nectanebo I ran for c. 3 km from Memphis, through the **Anubieion**, and opened on to an important temenos which has only ever been briefly explored and is now again covered in sand. It is c. 300 x 320 m in size and contains, at the centre, the Osiris/Apis temple of Nectanebo I plus a number of secondary buildings.

Propylaea in the north wall give access to a processional way leading to the catacombs of the mothers of the Apis bulls in the north-east. The mortuary galleries below the Serapeum were excavated in 1850–54 by Mariette. A 'smaller' gallery, 68 m long, with wooden sarcophagi was started by Ramesses II. Lying at right angles to it is the later gallery, 198 m long, which contains the tombs of the bulls from the reign of Psamtek I to the end of the Ptolemaic period. The lower lying **vaulted crypts**, with **granite** sarcophagi weighing up to 65 tonnes, branch off this gallery. Inside the **enclosure wall** are some isolated Apis burials of the period from Amenhotep III to Sety I. Facing the Serapeum, to the east, there was a temple of Nectanebo II, which lay, until recently, under the modern rest-house, which has now been removed. Earlier buildings of Amenhotep III and Ramesses II are attested to by re-used blocks.

Bibliography: Auguste Mariette, *Le Sérapéum de Memphis* (Paris 1882); J.-P. Lauer, Mariette à Sakkarah, in: *Mélanges Mariette* (Cairo 1961) 3–55; M. Guilmot, Le Sarapieion de Memphis, in: *CdE* 37 (1962) 359–381; J. Vercoutter, Serapeum, in: Helck, *LÄ* V 868–870; Dorothy J. Thompson, *Memphis under the Ptolemies* (Princeton 1988) 212–265; Dieter Kessler, Die heiligen Tiere und der König, in: *Ägypten und Altes Testament*, Vol. 16 (Wiesbaden 1989) 57ff.

Serdab

In addition to the mortuary cult associated with a **false door**, the Egyptians sought to achieve the continued existence of non-royal persons by the maintenance of statues to act as substitutes for their bodies. Statue placement in private tombs (**mastaba**) varied according to local custom. Statues were first introduced in the late 3rd Dynasty or in the course of the 4th Dynasty. In 'old-fashioned' tombs, which had already been completed, they were put into a *serdab* (Ar. 'cellar'), which was specially added for this purpose. The *serdab* was hidden within the masonry of the superstructure, and connected by window slots to the rooms within the tomb, in most cases the entrance room, less often the cult chamber. Free-standing statue houses were erected in front of the façade of mastaba G 5230 (**Baefba**) at **Giza**, each with four *serdabs* containing 30–50 statues. The statue chambers in the statue house of Seshemnefer III at **Giza** have a **niched** façade and **false doors**. In the 6th Dynasty *serdabs* were also used to accommodate servant figures.

Kings did have funerary statues, but rather cult statues which needed to remain accessible to the cult and so could not be shut away in a *serdab*. The well-known statue of **Djoser** in a **serdab**-like shrine is exceptional.

Bibliography: Junker, Giza III, Fig. 33-34; E. Brovarski, Serdab, in: Helck, *LÄ* V 874-79.

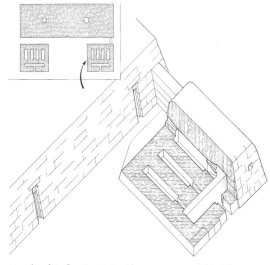

Mastaba of Baefba, Giza 5230, with two separate *serdab* buildings

'Serpent stone'

A **stela** with a round top, decreasing in width towards the bottom, which usually bears a depiction of a snake coiling its way upwards. They are found in pairs outside some temple entrances, especially at state sanctuaries. The earliest example comes from the precinct of **Djoser**; another, of Amenhotep III, is at **Athribis**. It is probably a relic, from the earliest religious ideas, for the protection of the house and for the rejuvenation of the king at his *sed*-festival. Some connection with similar monuments from early European cultures is not inconceivable.

Bibliography: *LD* II 9; Auguste Mariette, *Monuments divers recueillis en Égypte et en Nubie* (Paris 1889), Plate 63b; Naville, *Festival-Hall*, Plate 4b; H. Kees, Die Schlangensteine und ihre Beziehungen zu den Reichheiligtümern, in: *ZÄS* 57 (1922) 120–136; D. Wildung, Schlangensteine, in: Helck, *LÄ* V 655–656; Zahi Hawass, A fragmentary monument of Djoser, in: *JEA* 80 (1994) 45–56; Zahi Hawass, Doorjamb of King Djoser, in: *Egyptian Art in the Age of the Pyramids*, Exhibition Catalogue (New York 1999) 170–171.

Serra East

A Middle Kingdom **fortress** on the East Bank of the Nile at the Second Cataract, opposite **Aksha**. Its wall, 80 m long, is strengthened by towers and surrounded a harbour basin. It was still substantially intact until it was flooded by the waters of the reservoir.

Bibliography: *PM* VII 128; G.R. Hughes, Serra East, in: *Kush* 11 (1963) 124–129; J. Knudstad, Serra East and Dorginarti, *Kush* 14 (1966) 166–178; Hein, *Ramessidische Bautätigkeit* 40.

Sesebi

An important fortified **town** of the 18th Dynasty on the West Bank of the Upper Nile, between the Second and Third Cataracts. Its **enclosure wall**, measuring 200 x 270 m and laid out on a rectangular plan, is fortified with towers. The walls are 4.65 m thick and have four **gateways**. Inside are the remains of living quarters and large store houses for provisions. In the north-west is the once important triple temple of Amenhotep IV (51 x 61 m), now severely damaged, which was erected prior to year 6 of his reign and dedicated to Amun-Re, Mut and Khonsu. The front hall has two rows of four palm **columns**, three of which still stand. In the central

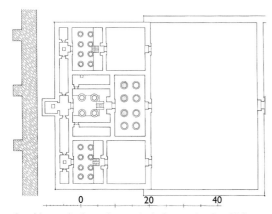

Plan of the temple of Amenhotep IV in the fortress city of Sesebi; fortress wall shown on left; surviving columns shaded

section, in front of the offering table room, is a chamber built on a raised **platform** with four columns, the **canopy** for a barque. In the northern side-room is a **crypt**. All three cult areas open onto a shared court.

Lying along the northern wall of the fortress is an open **sun temple** of Amenhotep IV, which consisted of an **altar** court, measuring 11.7 sq m, set on a terrace 2 m high and approached by stairs from the west. Sety I added a structure at the east. A publication of the excavations is awaited.

Bibliography: *LD* I, Plates 118–119; A.M. Blackman, Preliminary Report on the Excavations at Sesebi, in: *JEA* 23 (1937) 145–151; H.W. Fairman, Preliminary Report on the Excavations of Sesebi (Sudan) and 'Amarāh West, Anglo-Egyptian Sudan, 1937–38, in: *JEA* 24 (1938) 151–154; K. Zibelius-Chen, Sesebi, in: Helck, *LÄ* V 888–890; Hein, *Ramessidische Bautätigkeit* 61–62.

Sety I, temple at Abydos

1. Temple

The **'house of millions of years'** of Sety I is one of the most important preserved pharaonic temples for the history of Egyptian religion and art. The main building (56 x 157 m) is constructed mainly of **limestone** and stands inside a **brick** enclosure, measuring 220 x 273 m and protected with towers. The temple has seven parallel sanctuaries, and their approaches occupy the whole width of the temple, so that all ancillary rooms are displaced into a side-wing which protrudes to the south.

The temple rises in terraces along the slope of the desert. On the bottom terrace is a man-made lake with a quay, behind which stands the first **pylon** with royal **statue pillars** at its rear. Behind this, in the first court, is a **ramp** leading to the second pylon and the second court. Another ramp leads from there to the main temple building. The façade of the second pylon, as well as the façade of the temple proper, are in the form of open **pillared halls**. The temple originally had seven entrances, four of which were later walled up. Inside are two transverse pillared halls, connected to each other by seven doorways, corresponding to number of sanctuaries. Sanctuaries 1–4 contained the cult image and barque of the king, identified with Osiris, and the three state gods, Ptah, Re-Horakhty and Amun-Re. Sanctuaries 5–7 are dedicated to the Abydene Triad, Osiris, Isis and Horus. The rear walls of the sanctuaries are formed of double **false doors** (Fig.), through which the deity emerged in order to be united with the king's image. The ceilings are false stone **vaults**. The rear wall of the Osiris chapel is open to form the entrance to the transverse Osiris sanctuary. An annexe on the south side contains a chapel for Nefertum and Ptah-Sokar, a resting place for the divine barques, administrative rooms, magazines and stairs leading to the **Osiris tomb** situated behind the main temple building. The superb wall decoration is well preserved. The 'Abydos king list' is of immense importance to the reconstruction of Egyptian history: it contains the cartouches of the kings from Menes to Sety I. The work was finished in the early years of the reign of Ramesses II. The south-eastern corner of the precinct is occupied by a group of **grain stores** and there was probably a **sacred lake** to the north of the main temple building.

Bibliography: Algernon Caulfield, *The Temple of the Kings at Abydos (Sety I)* (London 1902); A.H. Gardiner, A.M. Calverley and M.F. Broome, *The Temple of King Sethos I at Abydos*, 4 Vols (London- Chicago, Vol. I

Forecourts and façade of the temple of Sety I at Abydos

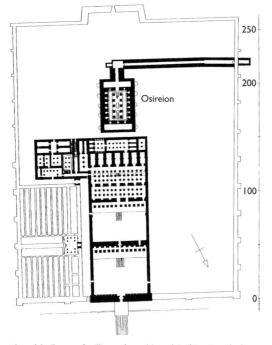

Plan of the 'house of millions of years' (temple) of Sety I at Abydos

1933, II 1935, III 1938, IV 1958); P. Barguet, Note sur le complexe architectural de Séti Ier à Abydos, in: *Kêmi* 16 (1962) 21–27; E.B. Ghazouli, The palace and magazines attached to the temple of Sety I at Abydos and the façade of this temple, in: *ASAE* 58 (1964) 99–186; A. Rosalie David, *Religious Ritual at Abydos (c.1300 BC)* (Warminster 1973); A. Rosalie David, *A Guide to Religious Ritual at Abydos* (Warminster 1981); Aufrère, *L'Égypte restituée* 41–44; J. Baines et al., Techniques of decoration in the hall of barques in the temple of Sethos I at Abydos, in: *JEA* 75 (1989) 13–30.

2. Osiris tomb, Osireion

This (**Osiris tomb**, Figs) is situated behind the west wall of the Osiris cult rooms. There was probably a mound over the tomb and the presence of tree pits has been demonstrated. The entrance to the underground complex lies to the north in front of the **enclosure wall**, consisting of a corridor 128 m long leading down to an antechamber which has a roof of relieving slabs. The structure of the main hall is fantastical and consists of an island surrounded by a deep moat upon which rested the (now lost) sarcophagus of Osiris-Sety. The ceiling of the room (spanning 7 m) was supported on two rows of five **granite pillars**, weighing 55 tonnes each. The water in the moat is fed by an underground canal which runs from the east underneath the temple. To the east is another transverse room with a ceiling of relieving slabs. The west side of the enclosure wall accommodates a brick pylon, 58 m wide, which connects the tomb of Osiris with the necropolis.

Bibliography: Margaret A. Murray, *The Osireion at Abydos* (London 1904); H. Frankfort, A. de Buck and B. Gunn, *The Cenotaph of Seti I at Abydos*, 2 Vols (London 1933); B.J. Kemp, Osireion, in: Helck, *LÄ* IV 622–623.

Sety I, temple at Qurna

The '**house of millions of years**' of Sety I and his father Ramesses I lies at the northern end of the Theban necropolis (**Qurna**). The core of the **sandstone** structure is preserved up to the roof. The **enclosure wall** (124 x 162 m) is fortified with towers and has a vast **pylon** at the east. Within is a forecourt with a cult **palace**, the second pylon, a **grain store** in the north, a well and a **sacred lake** to the south.

The main building (45 x 52 m) is fronted by 10 **columns**. There are three entrances leading to the interior, which is divided into three. The central part contains a hall with six columns, and side-chapels, of great importance in cult-historical terms, for the cult statue and barque of Sety I as well as the local form of Amun. Arranged along the rear wall are five chapels for the barques of Ptah-Sokar, Mut, Amun-Sety, Khonsu and

Nefertum-Osiris. To the west is the five-room cult complex dedicated to the deified Sety, equipped with a double **false door**. The northern area has a **sun court** and a high **altar**. The south part is the 'house of millions of years' for Osiris-Ramesses I, who was not able to erect his own 'house of millions of years' during his brief reign of less than two years. Behind this lay the slaughter yard. The decoration of the temple was completed under Ramesses II.

Bibliography: *Description* II, Plates 40–43; Prisse d'Avennes, *Histoire*, Plate 49; L.A. Christophe, La salle V du temple de Séthi Ier à Gournah, in: *BIFAO* 49 (1950) 117–180; Rainer Stadelmann, Der Tempel Sethos' I. in Qurna, in: *MDAIK* 28 (1972) 293–299; *MDAIK* 31 (1975) 353–356; *MDAIK* 33 (1977) 125–131; *MDAIK* 38 (1982) 395–405; Jürgen Osing, *Der Tempel Sethos I. in Gurna. Die Reliefs und Inschriften I* (Mainz 1977).

Shaft tomb

After the **rock tomb**, the most frequent form of tomb; also, often found inside a rock tomb. Superstructures in many cases consist of nothing more than a wall around a cult place. Variants run from relatively short shafts with a single chamber to large complexes for family or mass burials (a shaft tomb of the 13th Dynasty at **El-Lisht** consists of groups of up to 14 coffin chambers, spreading out like the fingers of a hand; a shaft tomb of the Roman period, 10–20 m deep, at **Hawawish** has up to seven layers of chambers). Shafts were usually no deeper than 10–15 m and only 1 x 2 m in size. The width increased up to 2 x 4 m where stone sarcophagi had to be lowered. A shaft of the Middle Kingdom at **El-Bersha** is 1.66 x 3.63 m in size with a depth of 35.55 m; the shaft in **Giza mastaba 2000** is 40 m deep. In the Late Period (**Saqqara**, **Abusir**, '**Campbell's tomb**') the shaft could measure up to 10 x 10 m, and the depth up to 30 m, accommodating a sarcophagus chamber, lined with masonry, at the bottom. Steps were inserted into the walls of shaft tombs for the workmen. Following the burial the shaft was blocked with rubble and boulders.

Shalfak

Relatively small Middle Kingdom rock-built fortification on the West Bank of the Nile (c. 60 km south of Wadi Halfa), in the form of an irregular rectangle. Its walls, 10 m thick, enclose an area of 47 x 95 m with rows of turrets close together. There is a large building in front of the **gateway**, the commander's house, some barracks and store houses.

Bibliography: G.A. Reisner, The Egyptian forts from Halfa to Semna, in: *Kush* 8 (1960) 16; Dows Dunham, *Uronarti Shalfak Mirgissa, Second Cataract Forts*, Vol.2 (Boston 1967) 115–137.

Shanhur

A relatively large but heavily damaged Roman temple 25 km north of Luxor, dedicated of Mut, Isis and other deities. Excavations and studies have been carried out since 1992. The rear part of the temple, containing a free-standing **naos** surrounded by the usual support rooms, was built under Augustus and is still preserved. A smaller shrine for the divine child Horudja, to the side of the front of the main temple, was decorated under Tiberius. Both buildings were later linked by a four-columned hall, and the resulting double temple was again enlarged, at an unknown date, by a **pronaos**, 29 m wide, with three rows of eight columns, which bracketed the two buildings but remained unfinished. All front parts of the temple are now flattened.

Bibliography: C. Traunecker, Schanhur, in: Helck, *LÄ* V 528–531; Jan Quaegebeur, Le temple romain de Chanhour, in: Kurth, *Tempeltagung* 199–226; Jan Quaegebeur, Excavating the forgotten temple of Shenhour (Upper Egypt), in: Quirke, *Temple* 159–167; Jan Quaegebeur, Le temple romain de Chenhour, in: Kurth, *Tempeltagung* 199–226; C. Traunecker et al., Chenhour: Rapport des travaux de 1996 et 1997, *Cahier de recherches de l'Institut de Papyrologie et Égyptologie de Lille* 19 (1998) 111–146.

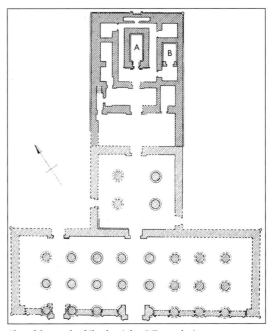

Plan of the temple of Shanhur (after C. Traunecker)

Sharuna

Ruins of Hut-nesut (Kom el-Ahmar el-Sawaris), a **town** north of Minya on the East Bank of the Nile. At this site in 1907 were found a large number of re-used blocks from a

limestone temple of Ptolemy I and Ptolemy II, dedicated to the local form of Horus and his parents Osiris and Hathor/Isis. Some particularly beautifully decorated blocks from here are now in Budapest, Vienna and Krakow. Although the find spot of these blocks has been identified, the location of the temple has not been found, despite intensive searching.

Bibliography: V. Wessetzky, Reliefs aus dem Tempel Ptolemaios' I. in Kom el-Ahmar-Sharuna in der Budapester und Wiener Ägyptischen Sammlung, in: *MDAIK* 33 (1977) 133–141; L. Gestermann et al., al-Kōm al-aḥmar /Sārūna, 1988, in: *GM* 104 (1988) 53–56, and 1989, in: *GM* 111 (1989) 10–12; L. Gestermann et al., Neue Spuren des ptolemäischen Tempels am Kom al-ahmar bei Saruna, in: *MDAIK* 48 (1992) 11–35.

Shena wab

An ancillary building within the temple precinct, used for the preparation and consecration of food offerings, common from the 25th Dynasty until the Ptolemaic period. From the original cult practice of consecrating offerings there developed an independent cult of offerings, which may have replaced the practice of making offerings within the temple.

The *shena wab* was a rectangular building of **brick** on a tall platform reached by a **ramp**. It was orientated at right angles to the axis of the main temple and had a central statue chapel for the temple's principal deity.

Main examples: the precincts of **Amun**, **Mut** and **Khonsu** at Karnak, **Medamud**, the Hibis temple at **El-Kharga** and **El-Kab**.

Bibliography: C. Traunecker, Les 'temples hauts' de Basse Époque: un aspect du fonctionnement économique des temples, in: *RdE* 38 (1987) 147–162.

Shepseskaf, tomb of (Mastabat el-Fara'un)

The otherworldly complex of king Shepseskaf at South **Saqqara**, constructed of vast **limestone** blocks, is known as 'The Cool Places of Shepseskaf'. It has a core built of

Core masonry and fallen casing blocks of the Mastabat el-Fara'un of Shepseskaf at Saqqara

stone and is shaped like a **mastaba**, measuring 74.40 x 99.60 m, and 18.7 m high. The **casing** is inclined at an angle of 61–69°, the lowest layer consisting of **granite**. The core was built in two steps and suggests that it had a casing in horizontal steps, inclined at a different angle. The lower part may have been decorated with **niching** and, like a **Butic** palace of the underworld, its shorter sides may have projected above the roof. The interior contains the king's tomb, with an antechamber, sarcophagus chamber and a group of six chapels to the east (see also **Menkaure**), constructed of granite blocks inside an open trench. The sarcophagus chamber is roofed with a ceiling of relieving slabs, 4.90 m high. The design of this room was the basis for the alignment of all the subsequent **kings' tombs** of the Old Kingdom. A new feature is the statue temple built against the east side of the core, which for the first time contained a **false door**. The forecourt was decorated with **niching**. The **brick**-built **causeway** had a barrel roof.

Bibliography: Gustave Jéquier, *Le Mastabat Faraoun* (Cairo 1928); *MRA* VI; W.K. Simpson, Mastabat el-Faraun, in: Helck, *LÄ* III 1231–1232: Müller, *Monumentalarchitektur* 151–155; Stadelmann, *Pyramiden* 151–155; Edwards, *Pyramids* 159–160; Lehner, *Complete Pyramids* (London 1997) 139.

Shepsesptah, *see* Ptahshepses

Sheshonq, tomb of

An important Theban tomb (TT 27) of the Late Period (c. 575 BC) in the lower Assasif with a tall superstructure of **brick**. The **enclosure wall** is divided by **pylons** into only two sections, compensating for the absence of an offering court, the traditional third part, by a bulge in the second pylon. The **niching** of the enclosure wall, which still survives, has recesses similar to **false doors**. The underground complex consists of a **sun court**, a **pillared hall**, a cult room and burial apartments.

Bibliography: S. Donadoni, Première campagne de Fouilles de l'Université de Rome à l'Asasif (1970), in: *ASAE* 61 (1973) 11–20; S. Donadoni, Relazione preliminare sulla II campagna di scavo nella tomba di Sesonq all'Asasif (1971), in: *Oriens Antiquus* 12 (1973) 19–22, 39–64; S. Donadoni, Première campagne de fouilles de l'Université de Roma à l'Asasif, in: *ASAE* 61 (1973) 11–20; Eigner, *Grabbauten* 55-56.

Sinki, *see also* step mastaba

The remains of a small, three-tiered **step mastaba** of the 3rd Dynasty, measuring c. 18.5 x 18.5 m, lie 8 km south of **Abydos**. No tomb chamber has been found.

Bibliography: Dreyer, *Stufenpyramiden* 47–48; G. Dreyer and N. Swelim, Die kleine Stufenpyramide von Abydos-Süd (Sinki), in: *MDAIK* 38 (1982) 83–95: W. Helck, Sinki, in: Helck, *LÄ* V 950.

Siwa Oasis

Siwa Oasis is 80 km long and lies 300 km south of the Mediterranean in the Libyan Desert. Within its principal town, El-Aghurmi, stands the **Ammoneion**. There are many ruins in the Oasis, mainly still awaiting study: the temple of Bilad el-Rum, the temples of Qasr el Ghashsham, Abu Shuruf and El-Zaytun. There are also numerous necropoleis of **rock tombs**.

Bibliography: H.M. von Minutoli, *Reise zum Tempel des Jupiter Ammon* (Berlin 1820); G. Steindorff, *Eine archäologische Reise durch die lybische Wüste zur Amonsoase Siwe* (Gotha 1904); G. Steindorff, *Durch die lybische Wüste zur Amonsoase* (Bielefeld 1904); J.E. Quibell, A visit to Siwa, in: *ASAE* 18 (1918) 78–112; Ahmed Fakhry, *Siwa Oasis. Its History and Antiquities* (Cairo 1944); Ahmen Fakhry, *The Oases of Egypt I. Siwa Oasis* (Cairo 1973); J. Osing, Siwa, in: Helck, *LÄ* V 965–968; K.P. Kuhlmann, The Preservation of the Temple of the Oracle, in: *ASAE* 75 (1999–2000) 63–89; K.P. Kuhlmann, *Das Ammoneion* (Mainz 1988).

Sledge

In comparison to rollers and the very infrequent **wheel**, sledges were the principal means of transporting heavy loads in Egypt. Only a few genuine wooden sledges have been found: a 4.2 m long working sledge was discovered at the pyramid precinct of **Senwosret III**, while a ceremonial cedarwood sledge, 1.73 m long, came from the pyramid of **Senwosret I**, and a sledge with a gilded **naos** was found among grave goods in the tomb of Tutankhamun. Wall reliefs depict granite columns and **architraves** for the **Unas** pyramid temple lying on sledges, similarly **obelisks** of Hatshepsut (for which the length of the sledge must have exceeded 30 m), and the transport of an **alabaster colossus** at **El-Bersha**

weighing c. 58 tonnes. A relief at the **stone quarry** of Ma'asara shows the transport of a large **limestone** block on a sledge drawn by oxen. It is not known what these sledges, used to transport the 1000 tonne colossi of Amenhotep III and Ramesses II, looked like.

Bibliography: Choisy, *L'art de bâtir* 117–120; Clark, *AEM* 88ff.; Arnold, *Building* 276–280; R. Partridge, *Transport in Ancient Egypt* (London 1996) 131–139.

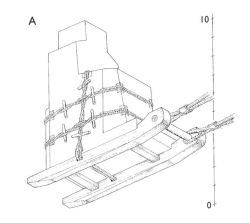

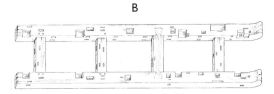

A: reconstruction of the sledge depicted in the tomb of Djehutihotep at El-Bersha (after A. Choisy); B: sledge in the pyramid complex of Senwosret III at Dahshur

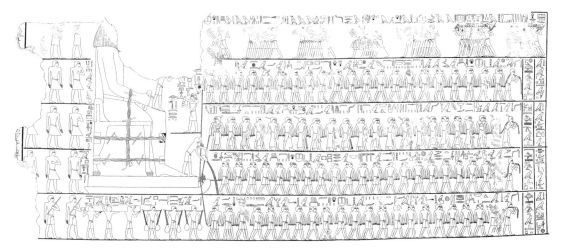

Transport by sledge of a colossal statue, as depicted in the tomb of Djehutihotep (No. 2) at El-Bersha

Sliding blocks

Slabs or blocks used to block the entrance to a tomb, which were levered or rolled out of recesses in the wall, replacing the more lightweight **portcullises** in pyramids and large private tombs of the 12th and 13th Dynasty (**Amenemhat II, Khendjer**). Occasionally they were moved on wooden rails (north **mastaba** at **El-Lisht**) or on a sloping surface (unknown king of the 13th Dynasty at **Saqqara**). This usage culminated in the reign of **Amenemhat III** at **Hawara**, where **quartzite** blocks weighing up to 18 tonnes were (not all of which could, however, be slid into place). In rare examples blocks are encountered which could be moved directly over the stone or by means of bronze wheels on rails, in order to close off secret doors etc. It is unlikely that pyramids were closed temporarily using moveable slabs of stone, as related in the fantastical accounts of Strabo, 17.1.33.

Bibliography: Herodotus, *History* II 121; Strabo, *Geographica* 17 1 33. L. Borchardt, Zur Geschichte der Pyramiden VIII, in: *ZÄS* 35 (1897) 87–89; Borchardt, *Entstehung der Pyramide* 12; Louis A. Christophe, *Karnak-Nord III* (Cairo 1951) 16, Plate 42; H.S.K. Bakry, The discovery of a temple of Sobk in upper Egypt, in: *MDAIK* 27 (1971) 139–140; Arnold, *Building* 226–229, Fig. 6.28.

Sment el-Kharab (Isment, Dakhla Oasis)

Significant remains of the **town** of Kellis, the ancient capital of the **Dakhla Oasis**, including a small three-room temple, built of stone, dedicated to Tutu, Neith and Tapshai. In front of it are four painted **brick** shrines and a Roman **birth house** with a painted **vaulted** brick ceiling.

Bibliography: Accounts of excavations: *Bulletin of the Australian Centre for Egyptology* 2 (1991) 43–50; 3 (1992) 42–46; 4 (1993) 17–25; 5 (1994) 37–42; 6 (1995) 51–58; *Bulletin of the Society for the Study of Egyptian Antiquities* 19 (1989) 6–16.

Sneferu, Snofru, *see* Bent Pyramid, Red Pyramid

Soleb temple

Monumental temple for the cult of Amenhotep III identified with Amun, on the West Bank of the Nile, 500 km south of Aswan. The temple was originally small, and was enlarged in stages, eventually becoming a tripartite structure 130 m long. From a **terraced temple** on the bank of the Nile, a processional way led up to the first **pylon**, standing within the **enclosure wall** (210 x 240 m), fortified with bastions. In front of as well as behind the pylon were two pairs of **obelisks**. An avenue of ram-headed **sphinxes** led from there to the second

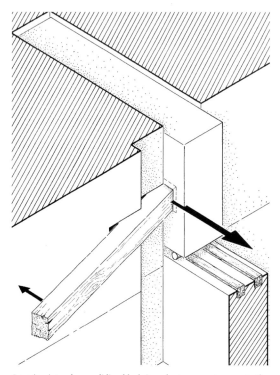

Levering into place a sliding block in order to prevent access to the northern mastaba at El-Lisht

Pillars in the temple of Amenhotep III at Soleb

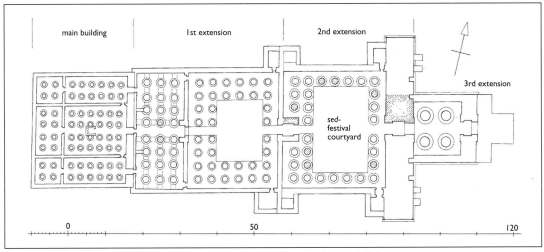

Plan of the temple of Soleb showing construction phases; parts of the temple still standing are shaded

pylon, in front of which were two obelisks and six **colossal statues**. These structures were later removed to make room for a massive **kiosk** with four palm **columns** (Fig.), c. 14 m high. Behind lay two colonnaded courts with particularly well-proportioned papyrus columns. The main temple building had three axes with numerous **hypostyle halls** and three sanctuaries. The transverse hall at the back is reminiscent of that at **Luxor** temple.

Part of the wall around the second court still bears the remains of a depiction of a *sed*-festival, which originally probably continued all the way around the wall (as in the mortuary temple of the king). Sculptures from the temple were transported to **Gebel Barkal** by the Ethiopian king Amanislo. Publication is forthcoming of the results of an examination of the temple's structure carried out in the 1960s.

Bibliography: *LD* I, Plates 116–117; M. Schiff-Giorgini and J. Janssen, Preliminary Excavation Reports, in: *Kush* 6 (1958) 84–86; 7 (1959) 154–157, 166–169; 9 (1961) 185–209; 10 (1962) 152–161; 12 (1964) 87–95; Michaela Schiff-Giorgini, *Soleb* I (Florence 1965); J. Leclant, Soleb, in: Hleck, *LÄ* V 1076–1080.

South Tomb

Along the south wall of the precinct of **Djoser** lies the monumental secondary burial place of the king, in the form of a **step mastaba**, orientated east–west, with a

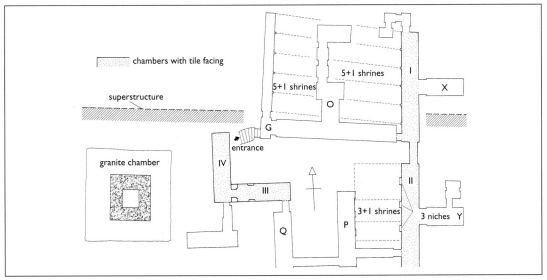

Schematic plan of the South Tomb in the Djoser precinct at Saqqara (the four corridors decorated with tiles shown stippled)

vaulted ceiling. A structure like a **palace**, which stands in front of it, is crowned with a **frieze of uraei**. Below the ground is an extensive system of corridors arranged like a massive **model building**, some of them faced with bluish green tiles, the whole intended to represent a funerary palace; these rooms are sometimes called 'blue chambers' (**architectural ceramics**). Parts of the walls are now kept in Berlin, the MMA and the Egyptian Museum, Cairo. The **granite** burial chamber, added later, does not seem suitable for a real burial and may have been used for a statue burial. Under the step mastaba is an unfinished tomb complex corresponding to that of the South Tomb. A simplified form of South Tomb is found for **Sekhemkhet** and later kings.

Bibliography: Cecil M. Firth and J.E Quibell, *The Step Pyramid* (Cairo 1935) 54–64, Plates 35–49; Jean-Philippe Lauer, *La pyramide à degrés* I (Cairo 1936) 94–112, Plates 31–37.

Speos

A temple completely cut out of the rock, for example **Speos Artemidos** and **Abu Simbel**, differing from a **hemispeos**, the front parts of which are free-standing constructions. In some cases, the speos may have originally been a **stone quarry**.

Bibliography: R. Klemm, Vom Steinbruch zum Tempel, in: *ZÄS* 115 (1988) 41–51.

Speos Artemidos (Istabl Antar)

The **speos** of the lion goddess Pakhet, situated south of the tombs at **Beni Hasan** in a lonely desert valley, possibly associated with the nearby quarries. Its origins probably go back to the Middle Kingdom, but it was first decorated in the reign of Hatshepsut. The temple follows the **rock tomb** type and has a four-pillar façade 15 m wide, leading to a transverse hall, its ceiling supported on four pillars, and a sanctuary. The sanctuary was not decorated until the reign of Sety I; the decoration is incomplete.

Bibliography: *LD* Text II 108–112; H. Goedicke, Speos Artemidos, in: Helck, *LÄ* V 1138–1139; R. Klemm, Vom Steinbruch zum Tempel, in: *ZÄS* 115 (1988) 45–46; S. Bickel and J.-L. Chappaz, Missions épigraphiques du Fonds de l'Égyptologie de Genève au Speos Artémidos, in: *BSEG* 12 (1988) 9–24; J.L. Chappaz, Recherches au Spéos Artémidos, in: Kurth, *Tempeltagung* 23–31.

Sphinx (Giza)

The largest sculpture in Egypt (length c. 73.5 m, height c. 20 m), carved out of the local **limestone** in the shape of a reclining lion with the head of a king, wearing a headcloth, uraeus and beard. It was originally completed with masonry, painted and surrounded by a courtyard. In the New Kingdom a small cult place was set up between the paws. An open stairway and **altars** were erected in front of it in the Roman period. The monument should be attributed to **Khafre** rather than **Khufu**. Its association with the **Harmakhis temple** in front of it is not certain. To the north are further cult buildings, like the temple of Amenhotep II.

The intention may have been to represent the king as an earthly manifestation of the Horus god Hauron (Horemakhet) in the form of a sphinx, and thereby as the sun god, who appears in three main forms (Khepri, Re and Atum).

The current attempt to ascribe the Sphinx to an unknown, pre-Egyptian culture has no serious foundation.

Monumental sphinxes are also known elsewhere: at **Tanis** the **granite** sphinxes, 4.79 m long, of Amenemhat II (now in the Egyptian Museum, Cairo and the Louvre), the temple of **Hatshepsut**, 3.5 m long (now in the Egyptian Museum, Cairo, and the MMA), the **Memnoneion**, and a large limestone sphinx at Mitrahina.

Bibliography: Hassan, *Giza* VIII (Cairo 1953); Ricke, *Harmachistempel*; R. Anthes, Was veranlaßte Chefren zum Bau des Tempels vor der Sphinx?, in: *Festschrift Ricke* 47–58; J. Assmann, Harmachis, in: Helck, *LÄ* II 992–996; C. Coche-Zivie, Sphinx, in: Helck, *LÄ* V

The Great Sphinx at Giza with its paws clad in limestone and the cult area between them

1139–1147; M. Lehner, Reconstructing the Sphinx, in: *Cambridge Archaeological Journal* 2 (1992) 1–26; Stadelmann, *Pyramiden von Giza* 172–174; Z. Hawass and M. Lehner, The passage under the Sphinx, in: *Hommages à Jean Leclant, BdE* 160/1 (1994) 201–216; Z. Hawass and M. Lehner, The Sphinx, who built it, and why?, in: *Archaeology* 47 (1994) 30–47; Lehner, *Complete Pyramids* 127–133.

Sphinxes, avenue of

Processional routes and approaches to temples (and less commonly to the space in front of temples) were frequently flanked by recumbent figures of animals or combinations of creatures, generally known as 'sphinxes', with walls at the side. The avenue of sphinxes in front of the temple of **Khonsu** at **Karnak** was 20–21 m wide from wall to wall and the avenue itself between the sphinxes was 12–13 m wide. The total number of sphinxes in the Karnak-**Luxor** area was 1292.

Sphinxes combine an archaic form of the king with the animal sacred to the lord of the particular temple, serving as a powerful and frightening being, which indicated and protected the approach to sacred places. The following combinations are known:

a) A lion with the head of the king wearing the headcloth and in some cases also the double crown (androsphinx). This is the most frequent and only real form of the sphinx, examples being the two rows of 365 sphinxes in the avenue between Karnak and Luxor, and the avenues of sphinxes north of the precinct of **Mut** and in front of the precinct of **Month** at Karnak.

b) A ram's head on the body of a lion (criosphinx), usually with a small figure of a king in front of its chest. This form is always linked with the cult of Amun, to whom the ram was sacred. Examples are found in the avenue in front of the temple of **Khonsu** (Amenhotep III's early structure), in front of the first **pylon** and first court at Karnak (Ramesses II, usurped by Panedjem I), or from the **Soleb** temple, now in Berlin. An exceptional form is the unmodified figure of a recumbent ram, as in the temple of **Khonsu** avenue and the precinct of **Mut**.

c) The head of a falcon on the body of a lion (falcon lion, hierakosphinx). This is probably not a true griffin, since it has neither wings nor a griffin's claws, and it is likely that it represents the king in the form of the Horus falcon. This form is very rare: **Abu Simbel** and **Wadi el-Sebu'a**.

d) Sphinxes with the head of a jackal, crocodile or snake are extremely rare. Examples are known from the mortuary temple of **Amenhotep III** at **Thebes**.

Bibliography: Ursula Schweitzer, Löwe und Sphinx im Alten Ägypten, *Ägyptolog. Forschungen* 15 (1948); A.M. Badawy, The approach to the

Avenue of sphinxes in front of the temple of Luxor

Egyptian temple, in: *ZÄS* 102 (1975) 79–90; C. Traunecker, in: *Karnak en Égypte*, Dossiers histoire et archéologie 61 (1982) 34–42; F. Laroche-Traunecker, Données nouvelles sur ler abords du temple de Khonsou, in: *Karnak* VII 313–334; M. El-Molla et al., L'allée sacrée du temple de Khonsou, in: *Karnak* IX 239–262.

Stairs, stepped ramp

Stairs built of **brick** were already used in the **mastabas** of the 1st Dynasty (Hemaka). A staircase 18.5 m high, with a 63° slope, was intended to lead from the antechamber to the burial chamber of the **Bent Pyramid**; otherwise, from **Amenemhat III** onwards the entrances to pyramids are in the form of stairs. In stone buildings several steps were carved from one block placed on a slope. New Kingdom **pylons** have narrow staircases with a straight flight. Large free-standing flights of stairs exist at the New Kingdom palace of **Ballas** and a Roman example stands at the front of the temple of **Tehna**, at **Zawyet el-Mayitin** and in front of the **Sphinx** at **Giza**. Winding stairs occur frequently, such as in the temple of **Deir el-Medina**, the pylon at **Edfu** and in **houses**.

Stepped ramps with low, slightly sloping steps and slides at the sides or in the centre are found in monumental structures; in temples they were used for the transport of barques and are flanked by **balustrades**; they were also used in tombs for the lowering of sarcophagi.

Stairs in houses were often laid on obliquely ascending beams (**Amarna**), or else the individual steps were erected on wooden beams across the direction of the flight. From the Middle Kingdom, stairs were in some cases supported on brick barrel **vaults**. The surface of construction stairs was reinforced with timber (pyramid of **Senwosret I**).

The average rise per step in Egypt, according to Eigner, was 20–32 cm; 7 of the 20 cm height per step is lost by the considerable forward slope of the step area.

Bibliography: Jéquier, *Manuel* 141–146; Clark, *AEM* 178–180; Eigner, *Grabbauten* 86–87. For the importance of stairs in religion: W. Helck, Treppe, in: Helck, *LÄ* VI 757–758.

Statue pillar, *see also* pillar

Standing figure of a king or a god, with the back leaning against a pillar or wall (**pillar**, **Ramesseum**, Figs). It was probably derived from royal seated figures set up in front of walls, such as in the court of the pyramid temple of **Khafre**. Unlike the caryatids and Atlantes of Greek art, such figures do not carry any load: they are merely joined to the background by being carved out of the same blocks. Statue pillars of the king (incorrectly termed 'Osirides') are found from the precinct of **Djoser** onwards as essential components of *sed*-festival architecture and hence are characteristic elements of the façades and forecourts of '**houses of millions of years**': **Hatshepsut**, **Memnoneion**, **Ramesseum**, **Ramesses II** (Abydos, **rock temples** in Nubia), **Sety I** (Abydos), **Medinet Habu**. The earliest true statue pillars occur in the **causeway** of **Senwosret I**. Those in the courtyard of Akhenaten's precinct of the **Aten** at **Karnak** represent the king as a hermaphrodite (?) primeval god. The mummiform figure used in statue pillars is probably a bodyless abstraction of divine kingship. A statue pillar with an attached Bes figure, from temple B 300 at **Gebel Barkal**, time of Taharqa, is an unusual form.

Bibliography: D. Lambrechts, Les colosses osiriaques et dérivés, in: *Revue des Arch. et Historiens de l'Art de Louvain* 11 (1978) 187–188; C. Leblanc, Piliers et colosses de type 'osiriaque' dans le contexte des temples de culte royal, in: *BIFAO* 80 (1980) 69–89; C. Leblanc, Le culte rendu aux colosses 'Osiriaques' durant le Nouvel Empire, in: *BIFAO* 82 (1982) 295–311; D. Arnold, Osirispfeiler, in: Helck, *LÄ* IV 633–634.

Stela

An upright stone monument, usually inscribed or decorated. Stelae have been found throughout the world since pre-history. In Egypt, the term is also used to refer to such monuments leaning against a wall or set into one. Stelae must, in principle, be distinguished from **false doors** and decorated slab stelae. They first appear in both royal and private tombs of the 1st and occasionally the 2nd Dynasty, bearing the name of the deceased, in pairs in royal tombs and with a rounded top. Nothing is known about where they were erected. Subsequently, in private tombs stelae gave way to false doors and, from the 2nd to the 4th Dynasty, to slab stelae, while they disappeared completely in royal tombs. The pairs of stelae of Sneferu, at the pyramid of **Meidum**, the **Bent Pyramid** and its secondary pyramid, as well as in the statue temple, are an exception and probably served to mark these complexes as cenotaphs. As the forms of stelae grew unchecked during the First Intermediate Period, the traditional false door in private tombs gave way first to a mixture of false doors and stelae and then, from the 11th Dynasty onwards, to inscribed and decorated stelae, which were rounded at the top but set into the wall. Subsequently, some stelae were also decorated with a **cavetto cornice** at the top.

Bibliography: Vandier, *Manuel* I/2 724–774, II/1 386–522; K. Martin, Stele, in: Helck, *LÄ* VI 1–6; R. Stadelmann, Scheintür oder Stelen im Totentempel des AR, in: *MDAIK* 39 (1983) 237–241.

The following stela-like monuments are also found, outside the funerary context:

a) '**Serpent stone**'

b) *Benben* **stone**: A primeval stone fetish in the form of a stela or pyramid, which had its own shrine at **Heliopolis** (the *benben* house) and so was part of the symbolism of the sun and the **primeval mound** there. It was transplanted by Akhenaten to the Aten temples, where it appeared in the form of a stela with a rounded top. No archaeological remains have survived.

Bibliography: Bonnet, *Reallexikon der ägyptischen Religionsgeschichte* (Berlin 1952) 100–101, 684–685; E. Otto, Benben, in: Helck, *LÄ* I 694–695.

c) In the 6th Dynasty, a mixed form of **obelisk** and stela was placed in pairs at the entrance of private and queens' tombs at **Saqqara** and **Aswan**.

Bibliography: Jánosi, *Pyramidenanlagen* 265.

d) Boundary stela (**Amarna**): a total of 14 rock-cut stelae, up to 7.5 m high, dating from years 4–8 of the reign of Akhenaten, marked the boundaries of Amarna and contained a government proclamation. They were flanked by rock-cut statues of the royal family worshipping the sun.

Bibliography: Norman de Garis Davies, *The Rock Tombs of El Amarna* V (London 1908) 19–34, Plates 25–44; W.J. Murnane and C.C. Van Siclen III, *The Boundary Stelae of Akhenaten* (London-New York 1993).

e) The stela at **Abgig**.

Step mastaba

The superstructure of the **kings' tombs** of the 3rd Dynasty, which consists of several mantles sloping in towards the tower-like core, their height increasing in steps towards the middle. The **core masonry** consists of rough stones, and they usually had a smooth outer **casing**. The **joints** of the individual layers slope sharply inwards. The first step mastaba, in the precinct of **Djoser**, came about by the increase, in stages, of the height of an original flat **mastaba** on a rectangular ground plan. This demonstrates clearly that the concept of a stepped royal tomb did not exist at the time that the precinct of Djoser was being planned. (The heaped mounds seen in the cores of mastabas of the 1st Dynasty, and the stepped sections of **Saqqara** tomb 3038 do not represent forerunners of step mastabas; they have a completely different origin and meaning.) The introduction of stepped structures was probably an expression of a new and 'increased claim to monumentality' (German *Monumentalanspruch*, H. Ricke) associated with kingship at that time. The monument of Djoser was followed by the construction of a step mastaba on a square ground plan by **Sekhemkhet** and that of an unknown ruler at

Zawyet el-Aryan. There are seven small step mastabas of the late 3rd Dynasty in Middle and Upper Egypt, but they have no burial chamber and no precinct around them, and so are not really considered royal tombs. For technical or symbolic reasons, the stepped inner core continued in use in some pyramids of the 4–6th Dynasties. In Upper Nubia step mastabas continued to be built over private tombs during the New Kingdom.

Step mastabas

	Steps	Mantles	Base length (cubits)
Djoser	6	12	240
Sekhemkhet	7	14	232 (?)
Zawyet el-Aryan	5 (?)	13–14	150
Elephantine	3	?	35
South **Edfu**	3	?	35–36
El-Kula	3–4	3	35
Nubt (Ombos)	3?	?	35
Sinki	3	3	35
Zawyet el-Mayitin	3–4	4	43
Seila	4	3 + x	48
Meidum E1	7	8	210
Meidum E2	8	9	230

Bibliography: Lauer, *Histoire monumentale*; J.-P. Lauer, Les petites pyramides a degrés de la IIIe dynastie, in: *Rev. arch.* (1961) 5–15, 290–310; J.-P. Lauer, Nouvelles remarques sur les pyramides à degrés de la IIIe dynastie, in: *Orientalia* 35 (1966) 440–448; G. Dreyer and W. Kaiser, Zu den kleinen Stufenpyramiden Ober- und Mittelägyptens, in: *MDAIK* 36 (1980) 43–59; G. Dreyer, Nordweststadt: Stufenpyramide, in: *MDAIK* 36 (1980) 276–280; Arnold, *Building* 176–179.

Step pyramid, *see also* step mastaba

In this book all stepped structures are called for preference step mastabas, firstly because the term step pyramid reflects a contortion of the geometrical definition of a pyramid and secondly because stepped structures and pyramids represent two functionally distinct building forms which should not be united under the term 'pyramid'.

Stone construction

The most important building material in Egypt until the Graeco-Roman period was unfired mud **brick**. At all times, stone construction was considered a luxury, its use restricted to buildings erected for eternity. The intention was to ensure the continuance of divine kingship and powers, which required the occasional use of stone elements in the 1st Dynasty: **Saqqara** tomb 2185 (reign of Djer), Saqqara tomb 3506 (reign of Den). From the 2nd Dynasty onwards this led to the introduction of complete stone structures:

a) Archaic temple (1st Dynasty?) at **Gebelein** with **limestone** reliefs.

b) In the 13th year of the reign of Peribsen, the annals of the Old Kingdom (the Palermo stone) record the construction of a stone temple.

c) In the tomb of Peribsen's successor, Khasekhemwy, at **Abydos** the burial chamber was paved with limestone slabs and its walls were faced with block masonry.

d) **Granite** door frames of Khasekhemwy from **Hierakonpolis** (Cairo JdE 33895/CG 57107).

e) Nuclei of 2nd Dynasty tombs at **Helwan** were cased with limestone.

f) Vast stone **funerary enclosures** and tomb structures of the 2nd Dynasty kings at Saqqara.

The culmination of early stone construction is to be found in the 3rd Dynasty precinct of **Djoser**. All subsequent royal funerary structures were executed in stone, the temples of the gods only exceptionally. 4th Dynasty examples are known: granite blocks of Khufu from Tida in the Delta, of Khufu and Khafre from **Bubastis**, the temple of **Harmakhis** built by Khafre, and the granite pillars of Userkaf from El-Tod. From the end of the 3rd Dynasty onwards, limestone became increasingly frequent in private **mastabas**, initially as the facing of cult chapels and subsequently also in the mastaba core (**Nefermaat**, unnamed mastaba in front of the Teti pyramid at Saqqara). From the 3rd to the 12th Dynasty, granite is the regular material in royal burial chambers and associated corridors, as well as for the casing of **pyramids** and temple walls.

From the Middle Kingdom onwards, the temples of the gods began to be predominantly stone buildings, or were faced with stone. In the reign of Mentuhotep Nebhepetre, the more robust material **sandstone** was introduced which gave more scope to the architect. Improved masonry techniques from the reign of Amenemhat III onwards enabled the use of **quartzite** in special architectural projects. From Thutmosis III onwards, **sandstone** gradually displaced limestone except at **Abydos** and at other building sites in Middle Egypt where limestone quarries were close by. **Granite** was employed in the New Kingdom predominantly for **obelisks, colossal statues**, thresholds, with the exception of the Osireion of **Sety I** at Abydos which was mainly built of granite. An archaising tendency in the Late Period onwards led to the reintroduction of hard stone (**granite, basalt**) in temple construction

(**Bubastis, Sebennytos, Iseum, Tanis**). Temples in the Ptolemaic and Roman periods were exclusively of **sandstone**.

Bibliography: Lucas, *Materials* 48–79; W. Wood, The archaic stone tombs at Helwan, in: *JEA* 73 (1987) 59–70.

Stone quarry

The Nile valley is bordered on both sides by **limestone** and **sandstone** cliffs (the latter extending from above Esna to Nubia), while at Aswan the famous rose **granite** (**syenite**) appears. As a result, the Egyptian builders could quite easily transport their construction materials by boat. The **alabaster** quarries at **Hatnub** (17 km east of Amarna), the **basalt** quarries at Gebel el-Qatrani (10 km west of Lake Faiyum), as well as the hard stone quarries at Wadi Hammamat (nearly 100 km east of Qena) and the gneiss quarries at Toshka (80 km from the Nile), on the contrary, could be reached only by expeditions using quarry roads (**ramp**), which required certain infrastructure to provide wells, accommodation and supplies. Important limestone quarries, especially during the Pyramid Age, were at Tura and Ma'sara, to the south-east of Cairo and in Middle Egypt, while the large sandstone quarries of the New Kingdom were located at **Gebel el-Silsila**, north of Aswan. All over the country, stone quarries were of local significance. It is assumed that most of the building material for the pyramids was quarried immediately beside the building site.

Limestone and sandstone were in many cases mined in gallery quarries, with the ceilings of their vast interiors supported on pillars left by earlier work. Many such **pillared halls** may have been converted into **rock temples** at a later date. Quarries are also sources for the study of half-finished monuments, such as the **obelisk** at **Aswan**, and offer insights into the settlements of quarry workers. Throughout Egyptian history, stones from earlier buildings served as building material (**re-use of blocks**). Pharaonic stone quarries not only provide important technical information, but also contain many historical inscriptions, such as reports of expeditions or the opening up of new galleries and walls for particular building projects. Ancient quarries are under threat from modern mining.

Bibliography: Clark, *AEM* 12–33; H. Goedicke, Some remarks on stone quarrying in the Egyptian Middle Kingdom, in: *JARCE* 3 (1964) 43–50; R. Klemm, Steinbruch, in: Helck, *LÄ* V 1276–1283; I. Shaw, A survey at Hatnub, in: B. Kemp, Ed., *Amarna Reports* III (London 1986) 189–212; I. Shaw, The 1986 Survey of Hatnub, in: B. Kemp, Ed., *Amarna Reports* IV (London 1987) 160–167; J.A. Harrel, *Newsletter of the American Research Center in Egypt* 146 (1989) 3–5; Arnold, *Building* 27–41; Golvin, *Karnak* 96–98; Rosemarie and Dietrich

Quarries. Left: unfinished obelisk in the granite quarry at Aswan; right: limestone quarries at Zawyet el-Mayitin (Zawyet Sultan) with blocks which have been almost completely hewn out but not removed (photographs Martin Isler)

Klemm, *Die Steine der Pharaonen* (Munich 1981); Klemm, *Steine*; I. Shaw, Pharaonic quarrying and mining, in: *Antiquity* 68 (1994) 108–119. Ancient quarries: Angelina Dworakowska, *Quarries in Ancient Greece* (Wroclaw 1975); Angelina Dworakowska, *Quarries in Roman Provinces* (Wroclaw 1983); Angelina Dworakowska, *Die Steinbrüche von Selinunt* (Mainz 1990); Manolis Korres, *Vom Penteli zum Parthenon* (Munich 1992) 6–31; *Ancient Stones: Quarrying, Trade and Provenance*, Acta Archaeologica Lovaniensia 4 (Louvain 1993); Angelina Dworakowska, Steinbruch und Tempel, in: *Antike Welt* 25 (1994) 122–139.

Stone quarrying techniques

The procedure by which both hard and soft stone was quarried was the same, in that the blocks were completely isolated from the surrounding rock by trenching, after which they were split off the surface below and pulled forwards out of their rock-bed.

Both **limestone** and **sandstone** were initially mined open-cast until the material there was exhausted and it was necessary to pursue the better rock below ground. In this way were formed the stone quarry frontages, several kilometres long, in the quarrying areas of Tura, Middle Egypt and **Gebel el-Silsila**, with large entrances leading to huge underground halls, their ceilings borne on huge

pillars. Underground mining required at the outset a low corridor to be chiselled out below the quarry ceiling. Passing along this, masons had access to the other side of the stone in order to separate it from the rear wall. In order to facilitate access to and removal of the blocks, they were quarried out in steps. In its final state, the wall of a quarry is almost vertical with slightly projecting steps. In the Early Dynastic Period and the Old Kingdom, hard stone was predominantly obtained by collecting blocks lying loose on the surface. True open-cast mining did not start until the New Kingdom.

For tools used on softer rock, see **stone working**. The only way hard stone could be quarried in pharaonic times was using stone tools (dolerite balls). Work in the **granite** quarries was used as a punishment for convicts. The method of quarrying for **quartzite** is still unclear. Wedges seem not to have been used until the arrival of iron in the Roman period. The theory that the Egyptians wetted the wooden wedges, causing them to swell, is purely hypothetical, and the effectiveness is disputed.

Bibliography: Clark, *AEM* 12–22; Engelbach, *Obelisk*; J. Roeder, Zur Steinbruchsgeschichte des Rosengranits von Aswan, in: *Archäologischer Anzeiger* 3 (1965) 467– 552; Arnold, *Building* 31–41; Goyon, *Karnak* 96–98; Klemm, *Steine* 320–324.

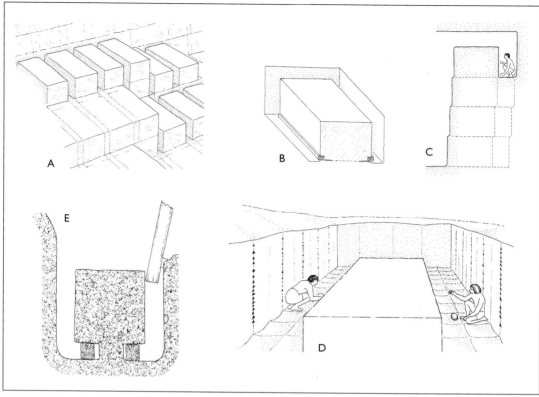

Quarrying techniques: A: cutting out blocks in steps with quarry trenches in the open; B: separating a limestone block using a long wooden wedge soaked with water; C: cutting the first block below the ceiling in a covered quarry; D: cutting a granite block by abrading the stone with dolorite balls; E: separating a granite block using levers

Stone working

Despite the relatively ready availability of stone for building purposes, the Egyptians were extremely economical in its use, preferring to fit together complicated angled **joints** and to add material by patching, using time-consuming labour, rather than smoothing off protrusions to produce a rectangular block. Each block was cut to the individual shape required by its position; isodomic ashlar masonry, consisting of regular-sized, pre-shaped stone blocks, did not appear until the Graeco-Roman period (**masonry**), with a few exceptions (*talatat*). The processing of 'soft' **limestone** and **sandstone** was very similar to wood carving methods, being carried out using copper or bronze chisels. Hard stone (**granite, quartzite, diorite, basalt**) was worked using the methods of stone vessel production (**drilling, sawing,** rubbing, percussion). Our understanding of the processing of some forms of hard limestone and sandstone remains uncertain; traces on unfinished blocks and rock walls indicate the employment of picks and flat-bladed chisels. The copper

and bronze chisels which survive from pharaonic times would have been unsuitable because of the severe wear they would have suffered, even after tempering. Tools much used on both soft and hard stone were the **saw** and grinding stone.

Blocks were usually delivered from the quarry in rough condition. Of the six faces of a rectangular block,

Checking and smoothing off a limestone block, as depicted in the tomb of Rekhmire

only the sides which would come into contact with already existing masonry (the underside and one of the narrow ends), would initially be dressed. The second narrow face was dressed only when the next block was being fitted; the front edge was frequently sawn (**saw, anathyrosis**). The top surface was also left undressed until the following layer was put in place. Frequently, that surface would be stepped to enable fitting of blocks of a particular size. The rear side of blocks was usually left completely undressed, while the front was not dressed until the building was complete (**bosses**). Straightness of a wall was maintained by measuring the upper edge of the front of each block and working it to the required level. The flatness of the surface was checked with the help of the frequently attested to 'boning rods' (a rope extended between two wooden posts of equal length, checks being carried out with the help of a third post).

Particular care was needed with corner blocks from which other blocks were to be measured. The corners of the unfinished first **pylon** of **Karnak** display the manner in which the sloping and tapering corner **torus moulding** was fitted there. In **column manufacture**, **capitals** were handled, in the same way as statues, by projection of their proportions on the six sides of the block to be worked on. Preliminary drawings of **columns**, capitals and statues, as well as sculptors' **models** of capitals, have survived.

Blocks made of hard stone, **architraves**, **obelisks**, and so on, were produced in their final state at the stone quarry, where specialists in hard stone techniques were immediately to hand. Processing of hard stone was avoided at the building site, softer stones being worked on there for preference. This method of working relies on precise planning and specification at the time of ordering.

Bibliography: Clark, *AEM* 12–33; Lucas, *AEMI* 65–74; L. Störk, Steinbearbeitung, in: Helck, *LÄ* V 1274–1276; Jaritz, *Terrassen* 33–36; Arnold, *Building* 41–48; Golvin, *Karnak* 96–98, 108ff.; S. Donadoni, Le pietre di Madinet Madi, in: *Pyramid Studies and Other Essays Presented to I.E.S. Edwards* (London 1988) 61–67; Klemm, *Steine* 94–97, 320–324; Nicholson, *Materials* 63–69.

Structure, *see also* style

Generally, this is the static part of the structural development of Egyptian architecture, which, independent of the changeable nature of **style** at all periods, shaped its inner structure. Its main characteristic is its dominance of canonical principles, such as frontality, **symmetry**, parallelism, **orientation** and the contrasting interplay of crystalline and strictly geometrical forms with plant/organic forms (**columns**). Students of structuralism understand the composition of a building, or the combination of its elements, by reference to its architectonic structure (as compared to function).

Bibliography: H. Ricke, *Bemerkungen* I 5–11; W. Schenkel, Architektonische Struktur versus Funktion: Zur Analyse altägyptischer Architektur, in: *GM* 39 (1980) 89–103.

Style, *see also* structure

According to Ricke, style formed part of the structural development of Egyptian architecture; it was the variable component which stretched beyond the unchangeable nature of the **structure**. Due to the extent of damage which Egyptian monuments have suffered, their style is difficult to understand, attracting little attention, and is moreover not accepted as a means of expression for individual **architects**. During the planning stage of a project, the architect had only limited stylistic freedom due to purely functional constraints: a dominating tradition and the necessity of including elements from earlier examples. Despite this, the architect did have some scope in the selection, arrangement, dimensioning and ordering of these elements (compare, for example, the huge variety in form of Theban **rock tombs** of the New Kingdom and the Late Period). Highly varied effects could be achieved by the arrangement of elements such as **columns**; for instance, columns of the same type and diameter may differ in height, have variable spacing or be differently painted (for example, the difference between the **hypostyle halls** at **Karnak** and at the **Ramesseum**). Steckeweh has drawn attention to an 'Upper Egyptian building style' in the Middle Kingdom and the Thutmoside period: an architecture with an external effect and linked to its landscape, with huge courts, and walls broken up by **pillared halls** and surrounding passageways.

Noticeable stylistic differences can also be observed in the development of later Egyptian temple buildings distinguishing such periods as the Ramesside Era, the 25th Dynasty, the 29–30th Dynasties, the Ptolemaic period and the Roman age.

Bibliography: Ricke, *Bemerkungen* I, 11–14; H. Steckeweh, Oberägyptische Architektur zu Beginn des Mittleren und des Neuen Reiches, in: *VI. Internationaler Kongreß für Archäologie 1939* (Berlin 1940) 261–263; Arnold, *Temples* 26–27, 44, 95–96, 144–150, 226.

Stylobate, *see also* plinth

The essential base on which **columns** stand. Many stone-built structures in Egypt were constructed on a raised base as a protection against the water of the inundation, for aesthetic reasons or, in the case of a cult building, to symbolise a **primeval mound**, as well as to mark a particular spot as the place of the 'first time' (an Egyptian term for creation). **Barque stations, kiosks** and similar have very distinct stylobates crowned with a **cavetto cornice**. Likewise the rear section of the temple at **Luxor** (**re-use of blocks**, Fig.), the **Month** and **Opet** temples and those of **Ramesses III** at **Karnak** and at **Medinet Habu** are raised. Similarly, the shrines for the cult image at **pyramid temples** and at the temples of **Qasr el-Sagha** and **Medinet Madi**, as well as the row of shrines in the upper terrace's rear wall in the **Hatshepsut** temple, all stand on a tall stylobate. In the Ptolemaic period, all walls, **screen walls**, door frames, even **column bases**, are separated from the floor by a pedestal.

Bibliography: Jéquier, *Manuel* 39–45.

Sun court

An important structural feature of Late Period Theban tombs, this is a court situated deep in the rock within the second courtyard of a tomb complex, usually having **pillared halls** either along one side or completely surrounding it. Provided with an offering table and plant basin, this feature developed out of the tradition of New Kingdom tombs (**Kheruef, Amenemopet**) and formed a symbolic junction between the spheres of light (Re) and darkness (Osiris). A **door recess** in the rear wall leads into the inner tomb.

Bibliography: Jan Assmann, *Das Grab des Basa (Nr.389) in der thebanischen Nekropole* (Mainz 1973) 45–46; Eigner, *Grabbauten* 118–120.

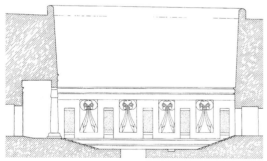

Reconstructed longitudinal section of the sun court of the tomb of Montuemhat at Thebes (see under Montuemhat for plan)

Sun temple

Cult complexes for deities who represent aspects of the sun, including the Aten, Atum, Khepri, Harmakhis, Re, Re-Horakhty and others, are attested to from the 2nd and 3rd Dynasties and widespread in Egypt:

a) The **Harmakhis** temple of Khafre at Giza.

b) **Userkaf** and five subsequent kings of the 5th Dynasty erected sun temples which were perhaps close to their **pyramid** precincts at **Abusir**. Only those of Userkaf and **Niuserre** have been found and excavated. These, presumably like all the others, consisted of an open cult court with a central **obelisk** or monument to the sun. It appears that they were originally built of mud **brick**, gradually being recast in stone and, during that process, modified or enlarged. These sanctuaries were dedicated not only to the sun god but also to the 'Son of Re', i.e. the king, united with his father after his death, thereby bringing about a close connection with the pyramid precinct nearby. No sun temples are attested to after Menkauhor.

The names of the sun temples of the following 5th Dynasty kings are known:

Userkaf: Nekhen-Re (at Abu Gurob, excavated)
Sahure: Sekhet-Re (position unknown)
Neferirkare: Set-ib-Re (position unknown)
Neferefre: Hetep-Re (position unknown, possibly usurped by Niuserre)
Niuserre: Shesep-ib-Re (Abu Gurob, excavated)
Menkauhor: Akhet-Re (position unknown).

c) From the early 18th Dynasty, sun temples became closely connected with the cult of the king, the 'shades of Re' or 'mirrors of the sun' (*shut-Re*), in the form of unpretentious structures, usually subordinate to, or economically tied to, a major temple. 'Sun shades' for Tiye, Nefertiti, Meritaten and Ankhesenpaaten are attested to at **Amarna**, and were perhaps places for the transference and regeneration of divine creative power and fertility. They may have had a function similar to:

d) sun cult places inside '**houses of millions of years**', on the roof of the **Akhmenu** and next to the Great Temple of **Abu Simbel**, this last decorated with a decorative programme and emblems based on solar symbolism (**pylon**, obelisks, high **altar** and baboons adoring the sun). These places were probably the prototypes of the *wabet* in later temples.

d) Akhenaten's temples to the **Aten** at **Karnak** and **Amarna** consisted of pylons as gates of the sun, courtyards containing numerous individual, small altars overlooked by a monumental and accessible high altar.

The form of the sun temple at **Heliopolis** is not known. The building of **Taharqa** at **Karnak** also has solar aspects and is of an exceptional form.

Bibliography: Peet, *City of Akhenaten* III; W. Kaiser, Zu den Sonnenheiligtümern der 5. Dynastie, in: *MDAIK* 14 (1956) 104–116; E. Winter, Zur Deutung der Sonnenheiligtümer der 5. Dynastie, in: *Wiener Zeitschrift für die Kunde des Morgenlandes* 54 (1957) 222–233; R. Stadelmann, swt-Rc als Kultstätte des Sonnengottes im Neuen

Reich, in: *MDAIK* 25 (1969) 159–178; P. Barguet, Note sur le grand temple d'Aton à el-Amarna, in: *Revue d'Égyptologie* 28 (1976) 148–151; E. Uphill, The Per-Aten at Amarna, in: *JNES* 29 (1970) 151–166; R. Stadelmann, Sonnenheiligtum, in: Helck, *LÄ* V 1094–1099; R. Stadelmann, Sonnenschatten, in: Helck, *LÄ* V 1103–1104; J. Assmann, Das Dekorationsprogramm der königlichen Sonnenheiligtümer des Neuen Reiches nach der Fassung der Spätzeit, in: *ZÄS* 110 (1983) 91–98; Dietrich Wildung, *Sonnenkönig, Sonnengott* (Munich 1985); M. Verner, Remarques sur le temple solaire Htp-R', in: *BIFAO* 87 (1987) 293–297; R. Stadelmann, Userkaf in Saqqara und Abusir, in: Bárta, *Abusir 2000* 529–542.

Syenite, *see also* granite

The incorrect name given to the dark granite from **Aswan** (= Syene). True syenite is not used in Egyptian architecture.

Bibliography: R. Klemm, Syenit, in: Helck, *LÄ* VI 112–113.

Symbolism

Egyptian architecture uses a 'language' of typical symbols ('*pars pro toto*') to invoke historical, mythological and religious facts and events from the primeval origins of the Egyptian cosmos, thereby preserving, in an effective state, the resulting 'petrified' world order. In extreme cases it replicates, in stone, more abstractly than realistically, true or imagined earlier structures that were imbued with power. The symbolic content of Egyptian architecture is therefore not confined to quotations in the form of wall paintings or other decorative elements; rather, it actually determines itself the form of structures. Some concepts can be represented by a large number of symbols, which unite architectural forms and wall decoration. The following are a selection:

a) *The sun and its journey*: pairs of **pylons**, pairs of **obelisks**, *benben* stone, barque of the sun, open capitals on **columns**, **pyramidion** and its decoration, use of **quartzite**, **orientation** on an east–west axis, conducting light into buildings, open courtyards, position on the roof, wall decoration with 'seasons' theme, books of the afterlife.

b) *Osiris and the underworld*: the **king's tomb** (representing the underworld), **false door**, books of the afterlife, wall decoration with 'resurrection' theme.

c) *Creation*: **pyramid**, **primeval mound**, *benben* **stone**, **terraced temple**, primeval ocean and island symbolism.

d) *Cosmos*: starry sky, **vaulted** ceiling, forest of plant **columns**, black floors and black wall bases, light-coloured walls, **orientation** of a building's axis, this world and the underworld indicated by spatial positioning 'above' or 'below' (building of **Taharqa** at **Karnak**), wall decoration with human figures and 'four parts of the world' and 'Two Lands' motifs, the **king's tomb** as the underworld, books of the afterlife.

e) *Victory and rule of Ma'at over (and protection from) chaos*: **sphinxes** and lions in sculpture and in wall decoration, symbolism of **palaces** (**niching**), royal statues, statues of enemies, depictions of the hunt and warfare (destruction rituals), scenes of tribute in wall decoration.

f) *Unification of the land*: bundles of lilies and papyrus, the double crown in depictions of the king, coronation of the king shown in wall decoration.

g) *The 'Two Lands'*: state sanctuaries in architecture and wall decoration, heraldic plants (**heraldic pillar**), red and white crown in depictions of the king, state gods and crown deities, processions of the nomes and deities.

h) *Endurance of kingship*: *sed*-festival symbolism (rows of chapels, *sed*-festival throne, **Per-wer** and **Per-nu** chapels with corresponding roof shapes, royal statues, *sed*-festival theme in wall decoration), lion bed, reception of the king among the gods, 'offering of millions of years', wall decoration with theme of king participating in the journey of the sun.

i) *Palace*: façade with **niching**, **palace-façade false door**.

These symbols, once created, retained their significance in Egyptian architecture for an extensive period, only rarely become ornamental elements with no meaning.

Numerical symbolism has some role in architecture (especially the numbers 2, 3, 4, 7, 8, 10), and similarly symbolism associated with materials and colours.

Bibliography (select): S. Giedion, *The Beginnings of Architecture* (London 1964); Adolf Reinle, *Zeichensprache der Architektur* (Zurich/Munich 1976, 2nd Ed., 1984); A. Varille, Quelques caractéristiques du temple pharaonique, in: *Le Musée vivant* 18 (1954) 20–24; *Schwaller de Lubicz, Le temple dans l'homme. L'Apet du Sud à Louxor*, 3 Vols (Paris 1957); A. Badawy, The architectural symbolism of the mammisi-chapels in Egypt, in: *CdE* 38 (1963) 78–90; A. Badawy, The symbolism of the temples at Amarna, in: *ZÄS* 87 (1962) 79–95; A. Saleh, The so-called 'primeval hill' and other related elevations in ancient Egypt, in: *MDAIK* 25 (1969) 110–120; H. Brunner, Die Sonnenbahn in ägyptischen Tempeln, in: *Archäologie und Altes Testament (Festschrift Kurt Galling)* (1970) 27–34; A.J. Spencer, The brick foundations of Late Period peripteral temples and their mythological origin, in: *Studies Fairman* (Warminster 1979) 132–137; Günter Bandmann, *Mittelalterliche Architektur als Bedeutungsträger* (Berlin 1979); W. Westendorf, Maat, die Führerin des Sonnenlichtes in der Architektur, in: *ZÄS* 97 (1971) 143–146; E. Graefe, Der Sonnenaufgang zwischen den

Pylontürmen, in: *Orientalia Lovaniensia Periodica* 14 (1983) 55–79; R.B. Finnestad, *Image of the World and Symbol of the Creator* (Wiesbaden 1985); P. Kaplony, Wappenpflanze(n), in: Helck, *LÄ* VI 1146–1152; E. Hornung, Symbol, Symbolik, in: Helck, *LÄ* VI 122–132; E. Hornung, Der Tempel als Kosmos, in: *Geist der Pharaonenzeit* (Basle 1992) 108–122; D.M. Mostafa, Reflexions sur la fonction cosmographique du temple égyptien, in: *Varia Aegyptiaca* 5 (1989) 103–118; Richard H. Wilkinson, *Symbol and Magic in Egyptian Art* (London, 1994); J. Baines, 'Temple Symbolism', in: *Royal Anthropological Institute News* 15:3 (1976) 10–15.

Symmetry

The Egyptian image of the world was shaped by dualistic ideas, and their constant striving after order and balance demanded that their architecture was planned and structured on an axially symmetrical basis. In sacred buildings symmetry is consciously broken up for cultic reasons or in order to avoid total symmetry.

Bibliography: Henry G. Fischer, *The Orientation of Hieroglyphs* (New York 1977) 13–15, 41–45; E. Hornung, Zur Symmetrie in Kunst und Denken der Ägypter, in: *Ägypten Dauer und Wandel* (SDAIK 18, 1985) 71–77.

T

Tabo (Tebo, Argoa)

The remains of a temple (possibly dedicated to Amun) of the 25th Dynasty, perhaps dating from the reign of Taharqa. South of Kerma near the Third Cataract, it is constructed of re-used material of Middle Kingdom and New Kingdom date. In front of the first **pylon** are two **colossal statues** made of **granite** of the Meroitic king Natakamani (12 BC–AD 12), now in the Khartoum Museum). Behind is a courtyard, surrounded on four sides by a colonnade, the second **pylon** and a hall with four rows of five columns. The temple is similar to those of **Kawa** and **Sanam**. It was probably erected on top of an earlier building which was destroyed during the Amarna period and restored under Ramesses II.

Bibliography: *LD* I 120, Text V 247–248; Ch. Maystre, Excavations at Tabo, in: *Kush* 15 (1967/68) 193–199; H. Jacquet-Gordon, in: *JEA* 55 (1969) 103–111; Hein, *Ramessidische Bautätigkeit* 63.

Taffa (Tafa)

Two small temples of the time of Augustus on the West Bank of the Nile, 45 km south of Aswan, to the north of **Kalabsha**. The smaller, rectangular north temple is unfinished and has an open front with two columns *in antis* (**anta**). The temple was transferred to the Netherlands and re-erected in 1978 in the Rijksmuseum van Oudheden at Leiden. The remains of the larger temple to the south were destroyed in the 19th century. Some remains were re-discovered during the UNESCO campaign. This temple had a rectangular sanctuary surrounded by a **pronaos** with six columns and an open front. The complex was surround by an **enclosure wall** with a small **pylon**.

Bibliography: Gau, *Antiquités*, Plates 10–11; Hans D. Schneider, *Taffeh. Rond de wederopbouw van een Nubische tempel* (Gravenhage 1979); M.J. Raven, The Temple of Taffeh, in: *Oudheidkundige Mededelingen uit het Rijksmuseum van Oudheden te Leiden* 76 (1996) 41–52.

Taharqa, colonnade of

The monumental **barque station** of Taharqa in the first (Bubastite) courtyard at **Karnak** (**Khonsu** temple). Between two rows of five (one still standing) papyrus **columns** (**column production**, Fig.), linked by **screen walls**, is a high base for the divine barque. The structure was 19.73 m high, and 16.25 m in width, too wide to support a roof.

Bibliography: J. Lauffray, La colonnade-propylée occidentale de Karnak, dite 'Kiosque de Taharqa', in: *Karnak* III 111–164.

Taharqa, pyramid of

This king's pyramid stands in the necropolis of Nuri, on the Upper Nile above Kareima. It is an example of the Ethiopian-period **pyramid**, which was a new development of traditional Egyptian structures. It was originally a smaller pyramid made of **sandstone** which was enlarged to 51.75 x 51.75 m (angle of slope 69°); its height is 60 m. The usual cult chapel is absent. The burial

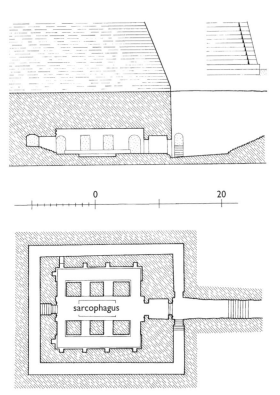

Plan and section of the inner chambers of the pyramid of Taharqa at Nuri; above right, corner construction of a Meroitic pyramid

chambers, which are not decorated, take the form of an **Osiris tomb**.

Bibliography: Dows Dunham, *The Royal Cemeteries of Kush, Vol. 2 Nuri* (Boston 1955) 6–9.

Talatat

Small stone blocks, measuring c. 27 x 27 x 54 cm (corresponding to 0.5 x 0.5 x 1 **cubit**) which were used in the constructions of Akhenaten in the precinct of the **Aten** at Karnak (**sandstone**) and in **Amarna** (**limestone**). Their brick-like uniformity, coupled with their lightness, allowed building projects to progress speedily. Blocks were used in exceptionally thin walls and laid in alternate rows of headers and stretchers; the arrangement is known from the impressions left in the **mortar** in foundation ditches. After Akhenaten's temples were abandoned, in the reign of Tutankhamun, they were completely dismantled under Horemheb and Ramesses II, their construction materials being re-used at **Karnak**, **Medamud**, **Hermopolis** and **Antinopolis**. Several thousand decorated *talatat* have been found at these sites. A scene, 12 m long, has been reassembled in the Luxor Museum by Philippe Marle.

Bibliography: Rainer Hanke, *Amarna-Reliefs aus Hermopolis* Hildesheimer Ägyptologische Beiträge 2 (Hildesheim 1991); J. Lauffrey, Les 'telatat' du IXe pylone et le Teny-menou, in: *Karnak* VI 67–89; J.-L. Chappaz, Un nouvelle assemblage de telâtât; une paroi du rwd-mnw d'Aton, in: *Karnak* VIII 81–119.

Tanis

The remains of biblical Zoan (Numbers 13, 22) lie at the north-eastern edge of the Delta, covering an area of 1200 x 1600 m, in the form of a mound of rubble (*kom*) 35 m high. This was the capital city of the 21st Dynasty, replacing **Per-Ramesses**, 22 km to the south-west, which had probably been abandoned due to the branch of the Nile silting up. The city contained enormous temple structures built using material brought from the old capital, which had itself been constructed from re-used blocks of the Old, Middle and New Kingdoms by the Ramesside kings. Only the temple precincts of Amun and Anta have been excavated to date, which occupy approximately one tenth of the *kom*.

The main temple was dedicated to Amun of Thebes. A processional way led to the **enclosure wall** (370 x 430 m and 15 m thick), built by successive kings from Nectanebo II to Ptolemy II, replacing a smaller enclosure of Psusennes I. Entrance was through a monumental **gateway** of Sheshonq III built of **granite** blocks from earlier buildings (which have now been partially reconstructed). Parts of a **colossal statue** of Ramesses II,

21–30 m high, of granite and weighing c. 1000 tonnes, which originated in Per-Ramesses, were found here. Inside the forecourt, behind the gateway, is a hall with four monolithic palm **columns**, more than 11 m tall (possibly usurped from a temple of the Middle Kingdom). They were surrounded by smaller papyrus columns. From here, a processional way led to the first **pylon**, no longer in existence, built of **limestone** by Osorkon III, which formed the entrance to the temple building proper. Behind the first pylon was an enclosed courtyard with an **obelisk** of Ramesses II, 17 m high, standing at the rear in front of the second pylon. Behind the latter was the second courtyard, in which were found two colossal **sphinxes** of Amenemhat II, the 'Hyksos sphinxes' of Amenemhat III and numerous monuments of the Middle and New Kingdoms. The third pylon, built by Osorkon III, was apparently constructed of granite, with four obelisks and four **sandstone** statues of Ramesses II. This formed the façade of the main temple building of Psusennes I and Siamun. On the two long sides and at the rear it was enclosed by a system of limestone and **brick** walls. From the evidence of blocks scattered in the area it is apparent that the core of this building was made of granite. The front section consisted of a **pillared hall** formed of monolithic granite **columns** with closed papyrus capitals (possibly of Middle Kingdom origin). Two columns of this type may have stood directly in front of the sanctuary. Relief blocks belonging to the sanctuary and other temple

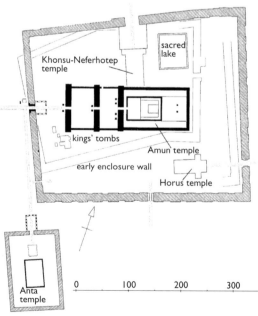

Plan of the temple precinct of Tanis

View from the east over the ruins of the Amun temple at Tanis

rooms which must have stood here have survived, but it is not possible to suggest how they might be reconstructed. There are also four small obelisks here, but their context is unclear. From the first pylon to the outside of the wall the temple measured 234 m in length. Attached to the back of the main temple building was an **addorsed temple** with 10 palm columns of Old Kingdom date and two obelisks. In total 23 obelisks have been found at Tanis.

On the north side, a smaller temple dedicated by Nectanebo I to Khonsu-Neferhotep is built against the side of the main building. It consists of a wide colonnaded forecourt, a pylon (measuring 8 x 45 m) and a second court inside. Nothing is known about this main temple building. To the east is a **sacred lake** measuring 62 x 73 m. To the south is a temple to Horus built by Nectanebo II and Ptolemy II.

The important sanctuary of the Syrian goddess Anta (equivalent to the Egyptian Mut) and Khonsu lies to the south-west outside the great enclosure wall. It originally dated to the time of Siamun and Apries, but was rebuilt in the reign of Ptolemy IV. All that is left, apart from its foundations, are the remains of the granite palm capital columns. The building, measuring 41 x 64 m, was constructed of limestone with its own entrance **kiosk**.

See also **kings' tombs** (2a.).

Bibliography: A. Mariette, Fragments et documents relatifs aux fouilles de Sân, in: *RT* 9 (1887) 1–20; Maspero, *ASAE* 5 (1905) 203–214; W.M. Flinders Petrie, *Tanis I 1883–1884* (London 1885), *II* (London 1888); Excavation reports of P. Montet et al., in: *Kêmi* 5 (1935), 11 (1950), 12 (1952) and *ASAE* 39 (1939) 529–539, 46 (1946) 311–322; P. Montet et al., *Les nouvelles fouilles de Tanis* (1929–1932) (Paris 1933); P. Montet et al., *Les constructions et le tombeau d'Osorkon II à Tanis* (Paris 1957); P. Montet et al., *Le lac sacré de Tanis* (Paris 1966); J. Yoyotte, Quatre années de recherches sur Tanis (1966–1969), in: *BSFE* 57 (1970) 19–30; R. Stadelmann, Das Grab im Tempelhof, in: *MDAIK* 27 (1971) 111–123; P. Brissaud and J. Yoyotte, Mission française des fouilles de Tanis, in: *BIFAO* 78 (1978) 130–140; P. Brissaud and J. Yoyotte, *Fouilles à Tanis. Résultats et problèmes. L'Égyptologie en 1879*, Vol. 1 (CRNS Paris 1982) 195–201; M. Römer, Tanis, in: Helck, *LÄ* VI 194–209; P. Brissaud et al., *Cahiers de Tanis* I (Paris 1987); Henri Stierlin, *Tanis, Vergessene Schätze der Pharaonen* (Hirmer Verlag 1987); Henri Stierlin and Christiane Ziegler, *Tanis, trésor des Pharaons* (Fribourg 1987).

Taposiris Magna (Abusir)

Important ruins of a **town** 45 km to the west of **Alexandria** on the coast, with a lighthouse, 17 m high, and a well-preserved Osiris sanctuary dating from the Ptolemaic period. A stone **pylon** with a staircase is built into the east wall of the stone **enclosure wall**, 84 x 84 m, with protruding and recessed sections. The temple building was destroyed when a church was built in its place. There are some well-preserved tombs and dwelling houses decorated with **plaster** and mosaics.

Bibliography: E Breccia, *Alexandrea ad Aegyptum* (Bergamo 1914) 123–130; J.Y. Brinton, Restoration of the temple of Abusir, in: *Archeology* 1 (1948) 186-87.

Tarkhan

An important necropolis between **El-Lisht** and **Meidum**, with large **mastabas** of the 1st Dynasty. Tombs No. 1060 (a single mastaba 16.6 x 36 m), No. 2038 (13.3 x 32.7 m) and No. 2050 (15.6 x 36 m) are elaborately **niched**, the recesses being lined with wood.

Bibliography: W.M. Flinders Petrie et al., *Tarkhan I and Memphis V* (London 1913), W.M. Flinders Petrie, *Tarkhan* II (London 1914); D. Wildung, Tarchan, in: HElck, *LÄ* VI 233.

Tehna (Tehneh, Akoris)

On the East Bank of the Nile to the north of Minya, a vast archaeological site including the ruins of the ancient **town** of Akoris, with the remains of several temples. A Hathor temple is attested to here from the 5th Dynasty onwards. Remains have been found of a temple of the Roman period, designated A, high up in the rock, consisting of a single room rock-cut chapel with a statue niche; temple B is a four-room **rock temple** of Ramesses II, with a **pronaos** of two rows of four columns and an approach ramp added in the Roman period; temple C is a small Roman rock-cut chapel.

Bibliography: *LD* Text II 50–54; Ahmed Bey Kamal, Fouilles à Tehneh, in: *ASAE* 4 (1903) 232–241; G. Lefebvre, Rapport sur les fouilles exécutées à Tehnéh…, in: *ASAE* 6 (1905) 141–158; R. Gundlach, Tehne (Akoris), in: Helck, *LÄ* VI 304–305.

Tell el-Amarna, *see* Amarna

Tell el-Balamun

An extensive *tell* (mound of ruins), 8 km north-west of Shirbin (Delta), with the remains of a completely destroyed Ptolemaic temple. In the southern corner of a mud brick enclosure, measuring 350 x 360 m, is a **brick** platform, erected using **cellular construction**, for a **fortress** of Psamtek I, 54 x 61 m in size. The enclosure was enlarged under Nectanebo I to an area of 410 x 420 m and accommodates a temple to Amun (70 x 150 m) and possibly a **birth house**; remains include a **granite naos**, basalt blocks and fragments of statues. There was probably an earlier Ramesside structure here.

Bibliography: *Orientalia* 61 (1992) 231–232; A.J. Spencer, Work of the British Museum at Tell el-Balamun, in: *Egyptian Archaeology* 7 (1995) 9–11; A.J. Spencer, *Excavations at Tell el-Balamun 1991–1994* (London 1996); *A.J. Spencer, Excavations at Tell el-Balamun 1995–1998* (London 1999); A.J. Spencer, British Museum expedition to Tell el-Balamun, in: *ASAE* 75 (1999/2000) 1–9.

Tell el-Dab'a (Avaris)

Important remains of an extensive city on the Pelusian branch of the Nile in the north-east Delta, situated around a lake south-west of **Per-Ramesses**, which has been identified as Avaris, the capital city of the Hyksos. The earliest settlement, laid out on an orthogonal plan, was Egyptian and dates from the First Intermediate Period/12th Dynasty. A large settlement was formed by the Canaanites during the 13th Dynasty (= Middle Bronze Age II A–C, Hyksos) consisting of extensive farmsteads with smaller dwellings arranged like the coils of snail shells. There are **brick** tombs containing foreign burials, some of them underneath the **houses**, which consist of chambers roofed with a single or double **vault**. From the same period are some mortuary temples, which have a **pylon**, transverse hall, sanctuary with two parallel side-rooms, and several platforms of a Canaanite type. At the western edge of the remains (Ezbet Helmi, Tell el-Qirqafa) is an underground structure, 47 x 71 m, built by **cellular construction**, which would have been below a **palace** of the late Hyksos period. Next to it, some extremely important fragments of Minoan wall paintings were found in 1991/92 which must have originated in the palace. On the northern edge of the remains is the Middle Kingdom temple of **Ezbet Rushdi**.

Bibliography: M. Bietak, *Tell ed-Dab'a* II (Vienna 1975); M. Bietak, *Avaris and Piramesse* (London 1981); M. Bietak, Tell ed-Dab'a, in: Helck, *LÄ* VI 321–323; M. Bietak., Eine Palastanlage aus der Zeit des späten Mittleren Reiches, in: *Anzeiger der phil.-hist. Kl. der Österr. Akad. d. Wiss.* (184) 121; M. Bietak, Der Friedhof in einem Palastgarten, in: *Levante* 2 (1992) 47–75; M. Bietak, Kleine ägyptische Tempel und Wohnhäuser des späten Mittleren Reiches, in: *Hommages à Jean Leclant*, BdE 106 (1993) 1–23; E. Czerny, *Tell el-Dab'a IX. Eine Plansiedlung des frühere Mittleren Reiches* (Vienna 1999); M. Bietak, The Center of Hyksos Rule: Avaris, in: E. Oren, Ed., *The Hyksos. New Historical and Archaeological Perspectives* (Philadelphia 1997) 87–128.

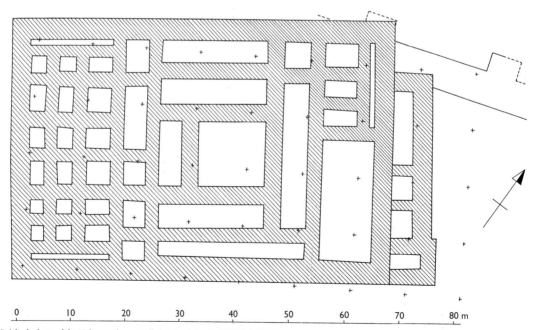

Brick platform of the Hyksos palace at Tell el-Dab'a (plan by M. Bietak, 1997)

Tell el-Kedua (Migdol)

An extensive area of ruins north-east of El-Qantara, surrounding the important border **fortress** at the start of the 'Ways of Horus', the desert road to Palestine (**Pelusium**). The location of the New Kingdom Migdol has not yet been identified. A 200 x 200 m fortress was built by Psamtek I at Tell el-Kedua with a wall over 10 m in thickness and equipped with 15 towers. Although it withstood Nebuchadnezzar in 601 BC, it was taken by Cambyses in 525 BC. To the south is Tell el-Herr, an area covered with several fortresses one upon another, the last of them being a late Roman-Byzantine fortification (88 x 89 m) with fired **brick** walls.

Bibliography: E. Louis and D. Valebelle, Les trois dernières fortresses de Tell el-Herr, in: *Sociétés urbaines en Égypte et le Soudan* (Lille 1988) 61–71.

Tell el-Moqdam (Leontopolis)

A once important *kom* (mound of ruins) in the eastern Delta, 10 km south-east of Mit Ghamr, with the remains of the temple of Miysis and Bastet built by Osorkon II (**'house of millions of years'**) and monuments of the Middle and New Kingdoms.

Bibliography: Edouard Naville, *Ahnas el-Medineh* (London 1894) 29–31; F. Gomaà, Tell el-Moqdam, in: Helck, *LÄ* VI 351–352; C.A. Redmount and R. Friedman, The 1993 Field Season of the Berkeley Tell el-Muqdam Project, in: *Newsletter of the American Research Center in Egypt, New York* 164 (Winter 1994) 1–10.

Tell el-Retaba (Tell el-Retabeh)

A fortified temple **town** at Wadi Tumilat, principally Ramesside but dating from the Middle Kingdom. It is surrounded by an enclosure measuring 200 x 480 m. There are the remains of a vast **high gate** (covering an area of 23 x 34 m) and a temple of Ramesses II (possibly dedicated to Atum and Seth) with a decorated façade.

Bibliography: W.M. Flinders Petrie, *Hyksos and Israelite Cities* (London 1906) 28–34.

Tell el-Yahudiya

Extensive mound 20 km north-east of **Heliopolis**, with a brick **enclosure wall**, 60 m thick, at least 11 m high and with rounded corners and an area of 450–470 sq m. Its interior was filled up with sand and was probably a huge **primeval mound** on which stood a sanctuary. The complex possibly dates to the Middle Kingdom or an earlier period. The surface of the mound was levelled in the reign of Ramesses II, who erected a new sanctuary over it, of which only a few remains are preserved. Lying to the west of the 'primeval mound' are the ruins of a **palace** of Ramesses III, findspot of a large quantity of faience tiles (**architectural decoration**).

Directly beside the **brick** enclosure lies a fortified **town** with a fort-like centre, erected by the exiled Jewish High Priest Onias with the permission of Ptolemy VI and provided with a temple.

Bibliography: E. Naville, Les fouilles du Delta pendant l'hiver de 1887, in: *RT* 10 (1888) 50–56; W.M. Flinders Petrie, *Hyksos and Israelite Cities* (London 1906); H. Ricke, Der Hohe Sand von Heliopolis, in: *ZÄS* 71 (1935) 108–109; A.-P. Zivie, Tell el-Jahudija, in: Helck, *LÄ* VI 331–335; J.M. Modrzejewski, *The Jews of Egypt* (Princeton 1995) 124–129.

Tell Ibrahim Awad

Remains of a mud **brick** temple of the early Middle Kingdom. Excavations are underway.

Bibliography: D. Eigner, A temple of the early Middle Kingdom at Tell Ibrahim Awad, in: *The Nile Delta in Transition: 4th–3rd Millennium B.C.* (Tel Aviv 1992) 69–77; W.M. Van Haarlem, Temple deposits at Tell Ibrahim Awad II – an update, in: *GM* 154 (1996) 31–34.

Temple, *see also* addorsed chapel, altar, ambulatory temple, barque station, birth house, 'High Sand', 'house of millions of years', kiosk, Maru temple, Meret, multiple shrine, naos, north chapel, platform, pronaos, pylon, pyramid temple, rock temple, roof chapel, sun temple, valley temple

Already in the Early Dynastic Period, monumental areas, closely linked to the **palace**, had developed which entirely served the cult of the king (*hut*), distinguished by Horus-kingship. Shrines of perishable material (*per*) were built for the divine powers of the Pre-dynastic and Early Dynastic Periods. Forms were very varied and no

The Early Dynastic Period temple of Satet at Elephantine

unifying scheme indicating a centralised administration can be discerned. Despite a lack of finds, it has recently been suggested that monumental temples built of **brick** began to exist as early as the time of the Unification. Evidence available to date is as follows:

a) Late Pre-historic sanctuary of Min at **Koptos**, with **colossal statues** of Min (now in Oxford).

b) Early Dynastic sanctuary of Satet at **Elephantine**, built over in the Old Kingdom.

c) Early Dynastic sanctuary of Khentyimentyu at **Abydos**, replaced by a brick temple of the Old Kingdom.

d) **Primeval mound** at **Hierakonpolis** between the Late Pre-dynastic period and 2nd/3rd Dynasty, with decorated **granite** blocks of Khasekhemwy (now in the Egyptian Museum Cairo). Above it a **multiple shrine** (Fig.) of brick (Old or Middle Kingdom).

e) **Limestone** fragments of a shrine of the 2nd or 3rd Dynasty from **Gebelein** (now in Turin).

f) Limestone fragments of a shrine of Djoser from **Heliopolis** (now in Turin).

g) The almost completely preserved temple of **Harmakhis** at Giza (uninscribed). Other stone temples from the 4th Dynasty onwards are attested to by individual finds.

h) The sun sanctuary of **Niuserre** at Abu Ghurob.

From the Middle Kingdom onwards, coinciding with the reduction in the divine standing of the king and the growing importance of the gods themselves, the gods' primitive brick shrines were replaced by stone structures (**multiple shrine**). The growing independence of cult structures led to the development of particular features: separation of sacred and secular architecture, together with a reduction in the concept of the temple as a house; axial construction; emphasis on **gateways**; the sanctuary (**naos**) often enlarged into a multiple shrine. From the Thutmoside period onwards, the increasing importance of processions of the gods (**Hatshepsut**, **Karnak**) promoted the creation of the New Kingdom processional temples with processional ways, series of **pylons** and **barque stations**. The impulse of the Upper Egyptian building traditions (**Mentuhotep** Nebhepetre) led to the opening up of the temple front with monumental **hypostyle halls**. **Ambulatory temples** start to appear. Within the temple, halls of **columns** take on great significance. At the same time, the thickness of walls is reduced, allowing rooms to be widened and enabling the interior of the temple to be largely taken up by columned halls. There was a preference for transverse halls. Very large buildings were erected for the cult of the king in the reign of Amenhotep III (**Luxor**, **Memnoneion**, **Soleb**). The development of the temples of the **Aten**, during the **Amarna** period, interrupted the

tradition for a few years. Ramesside programmes of temple construction, from Nubia all the way to the Mediterranean coast, continued the older style. The main temple building formed a stretched out unit, divided into sections by a succession of pylons and courtyards. Squat columns produced a feeling of closeness.

The 26–30th Dynasties experienced a renaissance of ancient Egyptian traditions: the main buildings of temples had a completely closed façade, and were preferably built of hard stone. **Hypaetral** sanctuaries and the first columns with **composite capitals** started to appear. State building programmes under the Ptolemies and Romans gave a fresh impetus to temple construction, and the development of **pronaoi** and composite capitals for columns reached a new high point. Hellenistic building concepts can be discerned in the slender proportions, greater sense of space and more flexible arrangement of individual elements. In spite of this, traditional forms dominated, and show flexibility by the creation of the barque sanctuary as a dominant structure encircled by chapels, as well as a new type of **birth house** surrounded by a colonnade with **screen walls**. This development was frozen in the Roman period with a standardised plan for all divine temples.

Bibliography (select): Perrot, *L'Égypte* 323–450; E. Baldwin Smith, *Egyptian Architecture as Cultural Expression* (New York and London 1938); P. Gilbert, Éléments hellénistiques de l'architecture de Philae, in: *CdE* 36 (1961) 196–208; Frank Teichmann, *Der Mensch und sein Tempel. Ägypten* (Stuttgart 1978); J. Monnet Saleh, Les représentations de temples sur plates-formes à pieux, de la poterie gerzéenne d'Égypte, in: *BIFAO* 83 (1983) 263–296; Patricia Spencer, *The Egyptian Temple. A Lexicographical Study* (London, Boston, etc. 1984); R. Stadelmann, Tempel, in: Helck, *LÄ* VI 355–357; R.B. Finnestad, *Image of the World and Symbol of the Creator* (Wiesbaden, 1985); D. Arnold, Tempelarchitektur, in: Helck, *LÄ* VI 359–363; D. Arnold, Die Tempel Ägyptens (Zurich 1992) 14–28; Aufrère, *L'Égypte restituée*; David O'Connor, The status of early Egyptian temples: an alternative theory, in: *The Followers of Horus: Studies dedicated to Michael Allen Hoffman*, Oxbow Monograph 20 (1992) 83–98; M. Bietak, 'Götterwohnung und Menschenwohnung'. Die Entstehung eines Tempeltyps des Mittleren Reiches aus der zeitgenössischen Wohnarchitektur, in: Kurth, *Tempeltagung* 13–22; D. van der Plas, Tempel in Ägypten, in: Kurth, *Tempeltagung* 239–254; Stefan Wimmer, Egyptian temples in Canaan and Sinai, in: *Studies in Egyptology Presented to Miriam Lichtheim, II, Jerusalem 1990*, 1065–1106; Dieter Kurth, in: Schulz-Seidel, *Egypt* 296–311; R. Wilkinson, *The Complete Temples of Ancient Egypt* (London, 2000).

Temple tomb

The concept of the **mastaba** became distorted as early as the Old Kingdom by the incorporation of increasing numbers of rooms in the interior core of the mastaba; this expanded in the 6th Dynasty, resulting in monumental temple tombs. In the Middle Kingdom the concept of the mastaba became an archaising trend, the cult complex being changed by the adoption of elements from **pyramid temples** and *ka*-houses to become a new form of temple tomb (**Ihy and Hetep, Inpy**, Mentuhotep (vizier) and **Senwosretankh**). The influence of royal tomb complexes and temples dedicated to gods is apparent in the large tombs erected at **Asyut** and **Qaw el-Kebir**.

The concept of a temple of the gods is adopted in temple tombs of the New Kingdom, where it appears in the form of the **multiple shrine** with a forecourt and an **enclosure wall** fronted by a **pylon**. The central room is usually the principal cult centre, occasionally topped with a small **pyramid**; side-rooms serve to accommodate statues (**Amenhotep** – son of Hapu, officials' tombs at **Saqqara**). The burial complexes were accessible via a shaft. Examples of this type in the 22nd– 26th Dynasties are found to the west of the temple of **Medinet Habu**. In the monumental Theban tombs of the Late Period, all the structures except the pylon and enclosure walls have moved underground. Graeco-Roman examples exist in the necropoleis of **Alexandria**.

Bibliography: Eigner, *Gräbbauten*; Geoffrey T. Martin, *The Hidden Tombs of Memphis* (London 1991); Karl J. Seyfried, Entwicklung in der Grabarchitektur des Neuen Reiches, in: *Problems and Priorities in Egyptian Archaeology* 219–253.

Terraced temple

Following the principle that, in theory, all Egyptian temples stand on a **primeval mound** and that building sites lie on ground which naturally rose towards the desert, the sanctuary area of every Egyptian temple is raised above the level of the front parts by at least one step. In some cases there was a succession of terraces connected by ramps, rising to a height of up to 20 m, the result being a true **terraced temple**, such as the temples of **Mentuhotep** Nebhepetre, **Hatshepsut** and **Thutmosis III** at Deir el-Bahari, **Sety I** at Abydos and the **Ramesseum**. Temples standing on a flat surface are also frequently distinguished by a high platform, e.g. the temple of **Opet** at Karnak, the temple of **Luxor**, the **birth house** of **Kom Ombo** and others.

Bibliography: D. Arnold, Terrassentempel, in: Helck, *LÄ* VI 456–457.

Teti, pyramid of

The severely ruined pyramid complex of Teti, 'The Places of Teti Endure', stands on the northern plateau at **Saqqara**. The base length of the pyramid was 78.75 m (150 **cubits**) and it reached a height of 52.5 m. The core was erected in five steps. The rooms inside were constructed inside an open trench in the rock, 10 m deep. The sarcophagus chamber is roofed with three layers of relieving slabs; like the antechamber, it is inscribed with Pyramid Texts. The **pyramid temple** (Fig.) follows a 6th

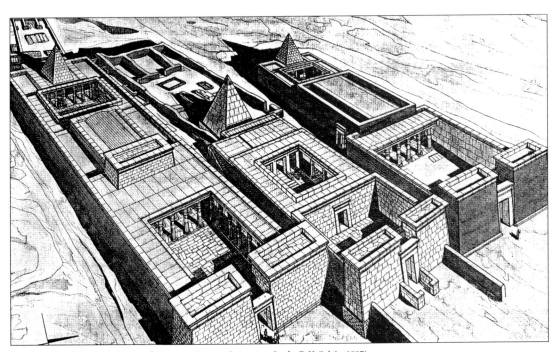

Temple tombs of Horemheb, Maya and Ramose at Saqqara (reconstruction by F.-U. Golvin, 1997)

Dynasty plan. The **causeway** and **valley temple** have not yet been discovered.

Bibliography: Vito Maragioglio and Celeste Rinaldi, *Notizie sulle Piramidi di Zedefrâ, Zedkarâ Isesi, Teti* (Turin 1962), Plate 9; J.-Ph. Lauer and J. Leclant, *Le temple haut du complex funéraire du roi Téti* (Cairo 1972); Stadelmann, *Pyramiden* 188–191; A. Labrousse, L'architecture des pyramides à textes (Cairo 1996) 43–68, 132, 140, 158, 161, 172; Lehner, *Complete Pyramids* 156–157.

Thebes

The site of Thebes developed relatively late, in the 11th Dynasty, from modest beginnings to become one of the largest temple cities of the Old World, called 'hundred-gated Thebes' by Homer. Dozens of sanctuaries are still spread over a trapezoidal area of land covering c. 5 x 7 km, divided diagonally or bounded on its eastern side by the Nile, here c. 1 km wide (its course in antiquity is not known). The temple landscape on the East Bank is formed of large temple precincts, the central **Amun** precinct with the **Month** precinct on its north side, the **Mut** precinct in the south, Akhenaten's temple to the **Aten** to the east and, 2.5 km to the south, beside the Nile, the **Luxor** temple. On the West Bank, thousands of **rock tombs** are dispersed along the base of the hills. The religious significance of Thebes was enhanced by the presence of more than 50 **kings' tombs** of the 11–17th and 18–20th Dynasties, the latter in the Valley of the Kings (Biban el-Muluk) and the West Valley, as well as the tombs of queens and royal children in the Valley of the Queens (Biban el-Melikat). Lying along the edge of the cultivation are the associated cult complexes, **'houses of millions of years'**.

'Houses of millions of years' at Thebes (north to south)
Sety I
Amenhotep I and Ahmose-Nefertari
Hatshepsut
Thutmosis III (at Deir el-Bahari)
Mentuhotep Nebhepetre
Ramesses IV
Thutmosis III
Siptah
Amenhotep II
Ramesses II (**Ramesseum**)
Thutmosis IV
Tawosret
Merenptah
Amenhotep III
Ramesses IV
Thutmosis II
Ay and **Horemheb**
Ramesses III (Medinet Habu)

In addition, there are further private mortuary temples and other cult areas on the West Bank. Amenhotep III's **palace town** at **Malqata** lies at the southern end of the West Bank complexes.

The density of these religious institutions made Thebes into the religious capital of the country as early as in the 18th Dynasty, while the administrative capital moved to **Memphis**, and later to the eastern Delta. Despite this, Thebes remained the religious centre and the true home of the essence of traditional Egypt, making it a powerful force not to be underestimated by those ruling in Memphis and **Alexandria**. Clusters of habitations so far excavated are at Malqata, **Medinet Habu** and **Deir el-Medina**, besides the Month precinct, and near Abu el-Gud (200 m north of the Amun precinct).

In 661 BC Thebes was badly damaged by the Assyrians, and probably again during the anti-Ptolemaic Upper Egyptian uprising from 207–06 to 187–86 BC, events that initiated the gradual decay of the Theban monuments.

Despite all damage these ruins have suffered, they form one of the most impressive areas of tombs and temples in the world. There have been numerous scientific attempts since the Napoleonic Expedition of 1799 to document the buildings, and their reliefs and inscriptions. which are a unique source for understanding pharaonic religion, history and art.

Bibliography (selected): Charles F. Nims, *Thebes of the Pharaohs* (London 1965); Eberhard Otto, *Osiris und Amun: Kult und heilige Stätten* (Munich 1968). R. Stadelmann, Theben, in: Helck, *LÄ* VI 465–473; Auffrère, *L'Égypte restitué* I 53–214; Friederike Kampp, *Die thebanische Nekropole* (Mainz 1996); N. and H. Strudwick, *Thebes in Egypt* (London 1999).

Thoth Hill, *see* Sankhkare

Thutmosis III, temple of (Deir el-Bahari)

Thutmosis III's **'house of millions of years'**, known as Djeser-akhet, was constructed at **Deir el-Bahari** on a high platform, so that it rises above the level of the temples of **Mentuhotep** and **Hatshepsut**. Its remains were discovered in 1962 by J. Lipińska. The complex included a **valley temple** (yet to be discovered) and a processional way, the lower part of which was planted with two rows of trees. Halfway towards the temple stood a **barque station**. An enormous ramp led up to the temple, set 20 m above the ground. The front of the temple seems to have consisted of a pillared **pronaos**-like structure. This was followed by a large **hypostyle hall** with eight taller **columns** which raised the centre basilica-style, surrounded by columns of lesser height. Behind this part was the central sanctuary with cult image chambers and other groups of rooms along both sides. Thousands of fragments of shattered wall decoration have been found, some of them beautifully painted, emphasising the *ka* aspect of the king's cult.

At the same height as the Mentuhotep temple was the cave shrine of the Hathor cow, belonging to the Thutmosis temple. In 1906, the cult image, made of **limestone** was found completely undamaged inside the completely preserved sanctuary (now in the Egyptian Museum, Cairo).

To the north of the **Ramesseum** are the remains of another 'house of millions of years' of Thutmosis III, called Henket-ankh. This sanctuary, erected on two terraces, had a façade with 10 **statue pillars** and was surrounded by an **brick** enclosure, measuring 85 x 148 m, with a **pylon**. A **sun temple** and a Hathor cult area are also attested to.

Bibliography: Herbert Ricke, *Der Totentempel Thutmoses' III.* (Cairo 1939); Jadwiga Lipińska, The architectural design of the temple of Thutmosis III at Deir el-Bahari, in: *MDAIK* 25 (1969) 85–89; Jadwiga Lipińska, *Deir-el-Bahari II. The Temple of Thutmosis III. Architecture* (Warsaw 1977); P. Gilbert, Le temple de Thoutmosis III à Deir el-Bahari, in: *CdE* 104 (1977) 252–259; M. Dolinska, Some remarks about the function of the Thutmosis III temple at Deir el-Bahari, in: Kurth, *Tempeltagung* 33–45; J. Wiercinska, La procession d'Amon dans la décoration du temple de Thoutmosis III à Deir el-Bahari, in: *ET* 14 (1990) 61–90; J. Wiercinska, Les dimensions de la barque d'Amon suivant les données du temple de Thoutmosis III à Deir el-Bahari, in: *ET* 16 (1992) 263–269; J. Lipińska, Deir el-Bahari, Temple of Thutmosis III 1978–1980, in: *ET* 14 (1990) 365–367; N. Beaux, La chapelle d'Hathor de Thoutmosis III, in: *Iubilate Conlegae: Studies in Memory of Abedl Aziz Sadek* (San Antonio 1995) 59–66.

Tiled casing, *see* **architectural ceramics**

Timber, *see also* timber construction

Native timber species attested to in Egyptian architecture are acacia (*Acacia nilotica*), crown of thorns (*Zizyphus spina Christi*), date palm (*Phoenix dactylifera*), dom palm (*Hyphaene thebaica*), sycamore (*Ficus sycomorus*), tamarisk (*Tamarix nilotica, T. articulata*).

Foreign species – fir (*Abies cicilica*), juniper (*Juniperus phoenicea*), cedar (*Cedrus libani*) and cypress (*Cupressus sempervirens*) – were imported by state-controlled shipping companies from Palestinian, Syrian and Anatolian sites, and from Crete and Cyprus. The requirement for timber was already considerable during the 1st Dynasty for **ceiling construction** in **mastabas**. An import of 40 shiploads is recorded in the reign of Sneferu. Timber-felling is illustrated on the outside wall of the **hypostyle hall** at **Karnak** (19th Dynasty). The probably fictional character, Wenamun (20th Dynasty), travelled to Lebanon to purchase timber.

Bibliography: V. Loret, Quelques notes sur l'arbre âch, in: *ASAE* 16 (1916) 33–51; Jéquier, *Manuel* 5–9; Lucas, *AEMI* 429–456; C. Müller, Holz, in: Helck, *LÄ* II 1264–1269; Russell Meiggs, *Trees and Timber in the Ancient Mediterranean World* (Oxford–New York 1982); Nicholson, *Materials* 334–371.

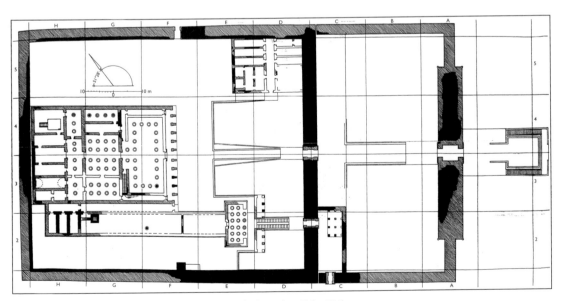

Mortuary temple of Thutmosis III north of the Ramesseum (plan by Herbert Ricke, 1939)

Timber construction

The shortage of native-grown timber in Egypt did not facilitate the erection of separate timber structures; possible exceptions may have been **naoi**, barque shrines, throne **kiosks** and catafalques. Timber was used in association with **brick**, mainly in **house** building, to construct **door** frames, thresholds, wall recesses and window lintels, and also the shafts of **columns**. In houses of the Ptolemaic period to late antiquity (**Medinet Madi**, **Dima**, **Karanis**, Abu Mena), the corners of walls, wall foundations and, from the Old Kingdom onwards, door frames were reinforced with intricate timberwork. Instances of timber panelling are found at **Dima**. Flat ceilings in tombs (**mastabas of Abydos** and **Saqqara** 3505, 3504 and 3036) and houses from the early dynastic period onwards were in principle constructed of timber beams, although expensive timber ceilings were if possible replaced with a brick **vault**. **Stairs** were sometimes surfaced with timber as a protection against wear. **Building ramps**, brick **pillars** and large **enclosure walls** were regularly reinforced with timber beams fitted into the brick masonry (in walls, either horizontally or at an angle to their course). Exceptional uses were as props to provide protection in chambers threatened with collapse: in the **Bent Pyramid** and the pyramid of **Amenemhat III** at Dahshur, and in the construction of a bridge across the King's Road at **Amarna**, where the beams were 5 m long and 60 cm in diameter. Timber combined with stone was used in only a few rare cases in sacred buildings: in **flagpoles**, more than 30 m high, along the façades of **pylons** or in association with doors. Timber ceilings do not appear in temple buildings until the Late Period, in exceptionally wide kiosks, entrance halls and similar, for example the **Augustus** kiosk at Philae (11.5 m wide). Demand in the building industry was extensive for ships, **sledges** and **scaffolding**.

Bibliography: Borchardt, *Nefer-ir-ke-Re* 19–22; Arthur E.R. Boak, *Soknopaiou Nesos* (Michigan 1935); D. Arnold, Holzbau, in: Helck, *LÄ* II 1269–1270; P. Grossmann, Holzbewehrung im römischen und spätantiken Mauerwerk in Ägypten, in: Bautechnik der Antike (Mainz 1991) 56–62; Dieter Arnold, Holzdächer spätzeitlicher ägyptischer Tempel, in: M. Bietak, Ed., *Archäische Griechische Tempel und Altägypten* (Vienna 2001) 107–115.

Tjary (Try, Thery), tomb of

Monumental **rock tomb** of the Late Period at **Giza**. The cult complex consists of an entrance hall and three chapels in a cruciform arrangement.

Bibliography: William M. Flinders Petrie, *Gizeh and Rifeh* (London 1907) 28–29; Wafaa El-Sadeek, *Twenty-Sixth Dynasty Necropolis at Gizeh: An Analysis of the Tomb of Thery*, Publications of the Institute für Afrikanistik und Ägyptologie No. 29 (Vienna 1984).

Tjay, tomb of

A monumental **rock tomb** (TT 23), dating from the reign of Merenptah, with a **pylon**, pillared forecourt and, cut at an angle in the rock, a broad hall with two chapels and a deep hall aligned on the axis. Behind this lies a rock chamber, containing a **granite** sarcophagus, and a cult chapel surrounded on three sides by rock statues.

Bibliography: *LD* Text III 252–253; Plan, PM I 1 30; F. Kampp, *Die thebanische Nekropole* (Mainz 1996) 206–209.

Tomb, *see* cenotaph, kings' tombs, mastaba, queens' tombs, *saff* tomb

Bibliography (general): D. Arnold, Grab, in: Helck, *LÄ* II 826–837; J. Assmann et al., Ed., *Thebanische Beamtennekropolen*, Studien zur Archäologie und Geschichte Altägyptens 12 (Heidelberg 1995); Friederike Kampp, *Die thebanische Nekropole* (Mainz 1996); Karl J. Seyfried, Entwicklung in der Grabarchitektur des Neuen Reiches, in: *Problems and Priorities in Egyptian Archaeology*, 219–253; Barbara Engelmann-von Carnap, *Die Struktur des thebanischen Beamten-friedhofs in der ersten Hälfte des 18. Dynastie* (Berlin 1999).

Tombs of 2nd Dynasty kings at Saqqara, *see* gallery tomb

Torus moulding, *see* cavetto cornice, torus moulding

Town, *see also* pyramid town

Concentrations of dwellings housing several thousand inhabitants, similar to towns, had already come into

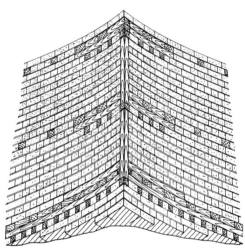

Corner of house II 201 at Dima, reinforced with timber beams (after A.E.R. Boak)

existence between 4800 and 3600 BC (Merimde, 240,000 sq m; **El-Ma'adi**, 180,000 sq m; El-Omari). Planned settlements from the period of the Unification led to the formation of fortified settlements built on a round or oval plan (**Elephantine**, **El-Kab**) with their principal streets intersecting to form a cross. The embryos from which towns developed were the royal residences and **fortresses**, pyramid foundations (**pyramid town**) and divine temples which developed from the Middle Kingdom onwards.

Excavations afford us a glimpse into small- to medium-sized new towns, in some cases founded by the state: **Abydos, Amarna, Aniba, Buhen, Deir el-Medina, Edfu, Elephantine, El-Lisht** North, **Kahun, Medinet Habu, Sesebi, Tell el-Dab'a**.

The habitation areas of the largest towns (**Alexandria, Buto, Sais, Mendes, Tanis, Bubastis, Heliopolis, Memphis, Herakleopolis, Hermopolis, Thebes**) remain largely unexplored; excavation of town sites is hindered by groundwater and modern structures erected over them. The governing focus was the temple precinct in the centre, occupying up to one quarter of the total area, with its processional ways which, with their high **enclosure walls** were not accessible to general traffic, but instead divided the town into distinct quarters. The continual growth of the temple precincts, together with the subsequent erection of enclosure walls, caused the loss of large areas of the towns. Dwelling **houses** several storeys high were frequent even in smaller settlements, reflecting a shortage of space. Other determining factors in town development were alignment relating to the Nile and canals, **orientation** according to the points of the compass, strict division of the quarters according to social status and, in the later cities (**Alexandria, Memphis**), according to nationality. There is no surviving evidence of public spaces, market places, warehouses and the like in pharaonic towns (although, if they did exist, they were perhaps beside a canal or river bank).

The 'governor's' residence was often given special emphasis. Streets were occasionally paved with **bricks** and provided with gutters. Ptolemaic-Roman examples are found at **Karanis, Dima** and **Medinet Madi**.

Workmen's settlements with accommodation for several hundred workers, dating from the Old Kingdom to the New Kingdom, are preserved near the work area: **Deir el-Medina**, Gebel el-Zet (a **gypsum** quarry in the Faiyum), Wadi el-Hudi (a fortified settlement of the Old Kingdom at the amethyst mines to the south-east of Aswan), Wadi el-Garawi (an Old Kingdom settlement, 30 km south of Cairo). These settlements consist mostly of basic accommodation made out of rough stones and occasionally have a small shrine. They were often protected against attack by an enclosure wall.

About any other sites, such as the capitals of nomes, we can only make guesses, supported by the position of temples, form and extent of rubble heaps, former branches of the Nile, and so on. When attempting to calculate the size of Egyptian towns and their population size we must take into account the fact that the main focus tended to change frequently, so that parts of towns would fall into disuse and remain uninhabited, and that the temple precincts covered a large portion of the total area. Population density is calculated to have been 500 heads per hectare (10,000 sq m), so that a town of 1 million sq m would have had a maximum population of 50,000.

Major towns/cities: areas and maximum populations (approx.)

Town/city	Dimensions (m)	Area (mn m^2)	Max. pop.
Alexandria	2000 x 1600	3.2	160,000
Tanis	1200 x 1600	2	100,000
Piramesse	1500 x 2500	3.75	187,500
Mendes/ Thmuis	1600 x 600	1	50,000
Bubastis	900 x 2100	1.89	94,500
Heliopolis	900 x 1800	1.6	80,000
Memphis	1300 x 2000	2.6	130,000
Kahun	400 x 350	1.4	7000
Antinopolis	500 x 540	0.27	13,500
Amarna	1000 x 2000	2.0	100,000
Karnak-Luxor	1000 x 2000		
	500 x 1000	2.5	125,000
Deir el-Medina	50 x 132	0.0066	330
Koptos	1800 x 1500	2.5	135,000
Elephantine	200 x 225	0.045	2250
Old Kingdom	90 x 180	0.016	800
Aniba			
New Kingdom	200 x 400	0.08	4000
Buhen			
New Kingdom	200 x 500	0.1	5000
Sesebi	200 x 270	0.054	2700

Bibliography (select; see further under place names): H.W. Fairman, *Town Planning in Pharaonic Egypt* (Liverpool 1949) (not seen); A. Badawy, Orthogonal and Axial Town Planning in Egypt, in: *ZÄS* 85 (1960) 1–12; P.J. Ucko, Ed., *Man, Settlement and Urbanism* (London 1972); B.J. Kemp, The early development of towns in Egypt, in: *Antiquity* 5 (1977) 185–200; B. Kemp, The city of el-Amarna as a source for the study of urban society in ancient Egypt, in: *World*

Archaeology 9 (1977–78) 123–139; M. Bietak, Stadtanlage, in: Helck, *LÄ* V 1233–1249; Eric P. Uphill, *Egyptian Towns and Cities* (Aylesbury 1988); Dominique Valbelle, L'Égypte pharaonique, in: Jean-Louis Huat et al., *Naissance des Cités* (Paris 1990) 255–322; Diana Craig Patch, *The Origin and Development of Urbanism in Ancient Egypt*, dissertation (Philadelphia 1991); Martin Ziermann, *Befestigungsanlagen und Stadtentwicklung in der Frühzeit und im Alten Reich* (Mainz 1993); Christian Tietze, Amarna, Wohn- und Lebensverhältnisse in einer ägyptischen Stadt, in: Bietak, *House and Palace* 231–237.

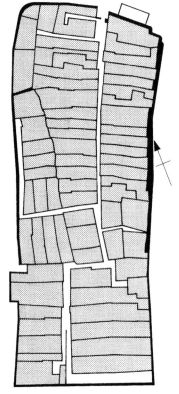

Schematic plan of the New Kingdom workmen's village at Deir el-Medina, showing houses and streets

Trajan, kiosk of (Philae), *see* Augustus, kiosk of (Philae)

Transport, *see also* wheeled transport

Weight bearers and donkeys were a natural means of transport; unwieldy or heavy loads were carried using yokes carried on the shoulder or on stretchers, some examples of which have been found. Divine barques were carried on stretchers, in the case of the barque of Amun at **Karnak** on the shoulders of 40 men. Wherever possible, overland distance was minimised by transport on boats.

An inscription at the **stone quarries** at **Gebel el-Silsila** records that 3000 men transported the construction materials for Ramesses III's temple at **Medinet Habu** on 40 ships. Some ostraka record the quantities of stone material transported to the **Ramesseum**. 2.5 million blocks each weighing 1 tonne were brought from local quarries for the pyramid of **Khufu**. The weight of a single load moved in the Old and Middle Kingdoms did not exceed 60–120 tonnes. In the New Kingdom, statues and **obelisks** weighing 300–500 tonnes were transported from the quarries at **Aswan**. **Colossi** weighing up to 1000 tonnes were successfully transported in the reigns of Amenhotep III and Ramesses II.

The only means of transport for construction materials attested to archaeologically are rollers, ropes and **sledges**, the latter towed by men or oxen and requiring solid roads and **ramps**. Modern experience and experiments indicate that towing required three men per tonne, provided that friction was reduced by wetting the surface of the road. It is calculated that the colossus of Ramesses II could have been towed by either 1000 men or 200 oxen.

Bibliography: Arnold, *Building* 57–66, 281–282; R. Partridge, *Transport in Ancient Egypt* (London 1996).

Carrying bricks on yokes, as depicted in the tomb of Rekhmire

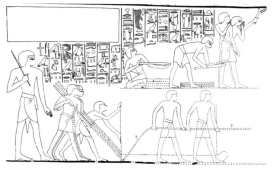

Pushing and pulling a sledge loaded with a block of stone, as depicted in the tomb of Rekhmire

Transport road, *see* **ramp**

Try, tomb of, *see* **Tjary, tomb of**

Tukh el-Qaramus

A once vast *kom* (mound of ruins) between Abukir and
Hehia (in the Delta) containing a temple **enclosure wall**,
16 m thick, measuring 454 x 514 m. The interior is divided
in two, with a **limestone** temple, c. 136 m long, at the rear
within its own enclosure. Foundation deposits indicate
that it was built by Philip Arrhidaeus (323–316 BC).

Bibliography: Edouard Naville, *The Mound of the Jew and the City of
Onias* (London 1890) 28; C.C. Edgar, Report on the Excavations at
Toukh el-Qaramous, in: *ASAE* 7 (1906) 205–212.

Tuna el-Gebel

Extensive necropoleis at **Hermopolis**, west of Deirut.
Important features are the Ptolemaic animal cemeteries
in the south (El-Fasagi) provided with cult structures
above ground (Ibiotapheion) and extensive subterranean
catacombs.

Behind the Ibiotapheion, underneath the dunes, are a
number of almost completely preserved house- and
temple-like tomb structures in a wealth of forms, dating
from the Ptolemaic and Roman periods. Free-standing
stairs lead in many cases to a high podium, on which
stands a **temple tomb**. Built in a mixed Egyptian-Greek
style, many of them have a **pronaos**, behind which is the
actual cult chapel with wall recesses, apses and wall
paintings. The burial chambers are cut in the rock
below. The most important complex is the temple tomb
of Petosiris, the deified high priest of Hermopolis
(c. 300–285 BC). It is built in pure Egyptian style and has a
pronaos at ground level, with four columns at the front,
joined to a hall containing four pillars. The motifs of the
wall decoration are Egyptian (hieroglyphs), while the style
and clothing of the people depicted are Greek. There are
the remains of two chapels dedicated by Ptolemy I to the
cult of the sacred baboons of Thoth (parts of them now
reconstructed in the Pelizaeus Museum at Hildesheim).

Bibliography: Gustave Lefebvre, *Le tombeau de Petosiris* (Cairo 1924);
Sami Gabra and Paul Perdrizet, *Rapport sur les fouilles d'Hermoupolis
ouest (Touna el-Gebel)* (Cairo 1941); Philippe Derchain, Zwei Kapellen
des Ptolemäus I. Soter in Hildesheim, in: *Zeitschrift des Museums zu
Hildesheim, NF* (1961); S. Nakaten, Petosiris, in: Helck, *LÄ* IV
995–998; D. Keßler, Tuna el-Gebel, in: Helck, *LÄ* VI 797–804.

Ty, tomb of

This 5th Dynasty **mastaba** at **Saqqara** (D 22), of the
reign of Niuserre, is notable for its unique relief
decoration. The rooms inside the mastaba take up only
one half of the interior of the L-shaped core. The **door
recess**, which has a **serdab**, is followed by a monumental
pillared courtyard. The offering chamber, containing a
false door and a large serdab, is reached by a corridor.
Like the mastaba of **Mereruka**, that of Ty has an
unusually large burial chamber with a sarcophagus niche
and an enormous sarcophagus.

Bibliography: Georg Steindorff, *Das Grab des Ti* (Leipzig 1913);
L. Epron and H. Wild, *Le tombeau de Ti*, 3 Pts (Cairo 1933–1966).

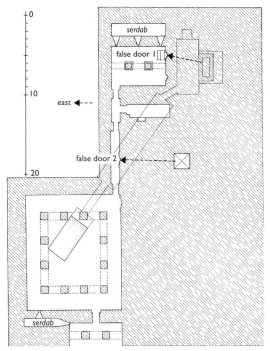

Plan of the mastaba of Ty at Saqqara, showing the false doors
orientated to the east and aligned with the tomb chambers

Temple tomb of Ptolemais in the necropolis of Tuna el-Gebel

U

Unas, pyramid of

The pyramid of Unas, called 'The Places of Unas are Complete', lies south of the precinct of **Djoser** at **Saqqara**. It measured 57.75 sq m (110 **cubits**), with a slope of 53°, and its original height was 43 m. The importance of this pyramid is that it was the first to contain Pyramid Texts, both in the antechamber and in the sarcophagus chamber. This chamber has a ceiling of relieving slabs; the black **basalt** sarcophagus of the king stands in a recess decorated with a **palace façade**. The **pyramid temple** follows the plan typical of the 5th and 6th Dynasties; **granite** palm **columns** from its courtyard are now in the Egyptian Museum in Cairo, the Louvre, the British Museum and the MMA. Considerable parts of the **causeway**, which is 666 m long, and changes direction several times, and of its relief decoration are either preserved or have been reconstructed (showing column

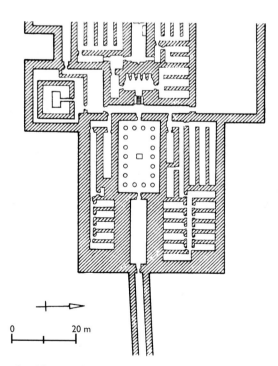

0   20 m

Plan of the pyramid temple of Unas at Saqqara (after R. Stadelmann)

transport on ships, market scenes, starving Bedouin, battle scenes). Remains of the **valley temple** are situated on a broad terrace above the harbour basin, with approach ways leading to it from both sides. This temple fits, in development terms, between those of **Niuserre** and **Pepy II**.

Bibliography: *MRA* VIII 98ff.; A. Labrousse, J.-Ph. Lauer and J. Leclant, *Le temple haut du complexe funéraire du roi Ounas* (Cairo 1977); A.M. Moussa, Excavations in the valley temple of King Unas at Saqqara, in: *ASAE* 70 (1984–85) 33–34; Stadelmann, *Pyramiden* 184–188; Peter Munro, *Der Unas-Friedhof Nord-West* I (Mainz 1993); A. Labrousse, *L'architecture des pyramides à textes* (Cairo 1996) 15–41, 98, 114, 116, 131, 139, 158, 161, 172.

Uronarti

A triangular **fortress** of Senwosret III at the Second Cataract, south of Wadi Halfa, named Khesef-Iunu, measuring 57 x 114 x 126 m, with strong bastions and closely positioned turrets on the walls. There are remains of a commander's residence and a temple dedicated to Senwosret III, Month and Re-Horakhty, which was rebuilt in stone in the 18th Dynasty.

Bibliography: G.A. Reisner, The Egyptian forts from Halfa to Semna, in: *Kush* 8 (1960) 13–16; Dows Dunham, *Uronarti Shalfak Mirgissa, Second Cataract Forts*, Vol. II (Boston 1967) 3–112; C. van Siclen III, *The Chapel of Sesostris III at Uronarti* (San Antonio 1982); K. Zibelius-Chen, Uronarti, in: Helck, *LÄ* VI 893–894.

Userkaf, pyramid of

The pyramid precinct 'Pure are the Places of Userkaf' at **Saqqara** is partially orientated towards the nearby precinct of **Djoser**. Like the latter, it has a north–south alignment, with the entrance in the south-eastern corner. The mortuary cult and the **cult temple** are separated: on the east side of the pyramid is a small three-roomed mortuary cult area with a **false door**, while the cult temple is to the south of the pyramid, having a wide courtyard surrounded by **granite** pillars, as well as royal statues of granite and **dolerite** (the head of a more than life-size statue of the deified king is now in the Egyptian Museum, Cairo). The three or five niches in the southern part of the building probably contained further statues of the king. In the south-western corner was a secondary pyramid. The remains of some of the outstanding reliefs were probably re-used in the pyramid of **Amenemhat I** at **El-Lisht**. The pyramid, which was 73.30 x 73.30 m, 49 m high, and had an angle of slope of 53°, is evidence of the decline, at the start of the 5th Dynasty, in the importance of pyramids in the concept of the deification of the king. The rooms inside the pyramid were faced with **limestone**; the saddle roof of the sarcophagus chamber was built of blocks of limestone.

Bibliography: J.-P. Lauer, Le temple haut de la pyramid du roi Ouserkaf à Saqqarah, in: *ASAE* 53 (1955) 119–133; A. El-Khouly, Excavations at the Pyramid of Userkaf, in: *JSSEA* 15 (1985) 86–87; J.-Ph. Lauer, publication in process; Stadelmann, *Pyramiden* 159–163; Edwards, *Pyramids of Egypt* 171–174; Lehner, *Complete Pyramids* 140–141.

Userkaf, sun temple of

The badly damaged sun temple of Userkaf lies 400 m north-west of the pyramids at **Abusir**. Originally it contained an **obelisk** erected on a elevated **base** within a rectangular cult courtyard (61 x 61 m) with rounded corners, later enlarged to 49 x 86 m. In front of the east side of the base of the obelisk, measuring 21 x 21 m, are two chapels each with a statue shrine, a **brick altar** standing between them. Several buildings are built into the front of the approach to the obelisk from the south. In the valley, connected to the sun temple by a **causeway**, are the remains of an important stone temple, measuring 34.7 x 52.5 m, with a pillared courtyard and five to seven statue shrines, similar to the **valley temple** at the **Bent Pyramid**.

Bibliography: Ricke, *Userkaf*.

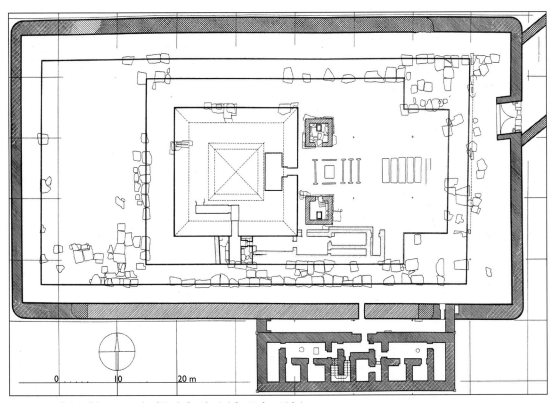

Reconstructed plan of the sun temple of Userkaf at Abusir (after Herbert Ricke)

V

Valley temple

From the reign of Sneferu until the end of the 12th Dynasty, valley temples were constructed along edge of the cultivation and on the banks of canals, being linked by a **causeway** to the associated **pyramid temple**. In the Middle Kingdom, similar complexes were also constructed at private tombs at **Qaw el-Kebir**, **Thebes** and **Aswan**. The last known example is found at the temple of **Hatshepsut** at **Deir el-Bahari**.

The earliest completely preserved valley temple is that of **Khafre**. Those of **Menkaure**, **Sahure**, **Niuserre**, **Unas**, **Pepy II**, **Senwosret II** and **Amenemhat III** at Dahshur have been excavated. There are numerous other valley temples in the cultivation which have not been investigated.

Valley temples were built at the edge of a canal on a terrace, with a monumental quay as a landing place for large boats, and had chapels for statues of the founder of the temple and possibly cult places on the roof which were accessible via stairs. During the reign of Sneferu a new type of pyramid complex was introduced from which was removed the old elements connected with the interaction between the king and the gods (as represented in the **Djoser** complex), which were displaced to the valley. Consequently, the valley temples may in effect have continued the traditions of the **divine fortresses** and **funerary enclosures** of the early dynasties. The Abusir papyri (5/6th Dynasty) and festival calendars record that Sokar, Hathor, the divine standards (in other words, the old Followers of Horus) and other gods visited the pyramid complex with their barques, and were probably received at the valley temple by images representing the king. The survival of the concept of the contact between the Horus king and the state gods is also manifested in the statue groups of the king with various gods from the valley temples of Menkaure and others.

Certain features of the valley temple continued in cult terraces, which were built from the New Kingdom onwards opposite the **pylon** at the edge of the canal or river, at the point where the cult image awaited the arrival of the barques of other deities. The old interpretation of valley temples as embalming houses is no longer tenable.

Bibliography: Bernhard Grdseloff, *Das ägyptische Reinigungszelt* (Cairo 1941), discussed by E. Drioton, in: *ASAE* 40 (1941) 1007–1014; Ricke, *Bemerkungen* 86–114; Paule Posener-Kriéger, *Les archives du temple funéraire de Néferirkarê-Kakaï* II (Cairo 1976) 549–563; V.A. Donohue, Pr-nfr, in: *JEA* 64 (1978) 143–148; Edwards, *Pyramids* 136–138; Stadelmann, Taltempel, in: Helck, *LÄ* VI 189–193; Arnold, *Temples* 288–292.

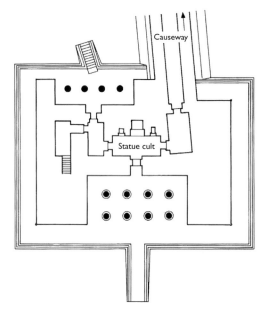

Plan of the valley temple of Sahure at Abusir

Vault, *see also* ceiling construction, cupola

Simple arches and vaults were developed soon after the introduction of **brick construction** (tomb 3500 at **Saqqara**, reign of Qa'a). They were erected in **houses** and storage buildings and in underground corridors of tombs to roof over large gates, long narrow rooms, corridors and staircases. Ring or barrel vaults, used widely in the Orient, were used, formed of layers of horizontal or upright bricks which leant against a wall and could therefore be erected without a supporting framework or centring. In the case of larger vaults, ring vaults may have

Brick vaults in the grain stores of the Ramesseum

served as a supporting framework during the construction of the actual overlying vault made of vertical bricks to form a barrel vault. Smaller cap vaults and complicated arched belt structures started to appear in the Old Kingdom at **Giza**, where the body of the vault consisted of rounded red painted ribs, in this case resting on protruding ledges (**bricks, moulded**), which give the appearance of a roof of reed **matting**.

Starting as early as the Old Kingdom, particularly thin and slightly curved vaulting bricks were used in places, with lengthwise grooves for improved adhesion of the **mortar** (**bricks, moulded**, Fig.). Less frequent are vaults of non-inclined arches; i.e. they utilised layers of straight bricks which were unable to be erected without centring, in which case the hollow space below would presumably have been filled with earth. Smaller vaults were formed by a single ring in the barrel vault, with broken pieces of brick or small stones being used to fill the wedge-shaped gaps. Examples of long barrel vaults exist in the boat pit of the pyramid of **Senwosret III** (spanning 4.10 m with an apex height of 2.43 m) and in the magazine buildings of the **Ramesseum** (with a span of up to 3.70 m and an apex height of 2.43 m). The destroyed magazines at the temple of **Sety I** at Abydos were 39 m long and up to 6.8 m wide, the vault constructed of bricks of dimensions 7.5 x 22 x 60 cm, the edges along their lower surface being trimmed. Particularly impressive are the vaults above the throne hall of Ramesses III at **Medinet Habu**, resting on the **architraves**, which are supported on **columns**. The largest span which can be proven to have existed is 7.7 m, in the mortuary temple of **Amenhotep** (son of Hapu), and 8.6 m in the stables at Medinet Habu (18th and 20th Dynasties). The largest vaults, albeit not free-standing, with a span of up to 12 m, exist above the pressure-relieving slabs in the pyramids of the late 12th and 13th Dynasties.

Cross-vaults being unknown, the junction between two barrels had to be overlaid with beams. A vault found in 1992 at **Dahshur**, the earliest so far discovered in a stone building, forms the ceiling of the burial chamber of a 4th Dynasty **mastaba**, having a 2.62 m span. Some weight-relieving vaults have been found dating back to the 4th Dynasty (also at Dahshur). Genuine vaults up to 2.80 m wide, made of wedge-shaped voussoirs, which date to around 760 BC, are found in the burial chapels of the 'divine consorts' at Medinet Habu and in tomb vaults at **Giza** ('Campbell's tomb'), **Abusir** (Wedjahorresnet) and **Saqqara** (Neferibre Sa-Neith, Wahibre-men, Hor). The **Per-weru** and mortuary offering halls of **pyramid temples** from the 5th Dynasty onwards had ceilings constructed of upright slabs, the underside of which was carved out to give a curved appearance (5.25 m span, 6–7 m high). **Corbelled vaults** were also hollowed out underneath to achieve a vaulted effect (such as the room of the sanctuary of **Hatshepsut's** temple and the temple of **Sety I** at Abydos). From the 4th to the 12th Dynasty the underside of relieving slabs was also carved out. The largest true stone vaults known in Egypt are only 2.8 m wide, as compared with 6.48 m in Greece and 24.5 m in the Bridge of Fabricius at Rome.

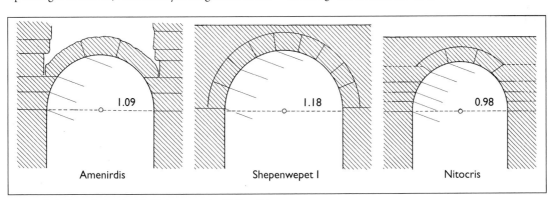

Stone vaults in the tomb chapels of the 'divine consorts' at Medinet Habu

Bibliography: Choisy, *L'art de bâtir* 42–51; Jéquier, *Manuel* 303–314; Clark, *AEM* 181–191; Junker, *Giza* V 156–159; H. Fathy, La vôute dans l'architecture égyptienne, in: *La Revue du Caire* 27, No. 137 (1951) 14–20; A. Badawy, Brick vaults and domes in the Giza necropolis, in: *Abdel-Moneim Abu-Bakr, Excavations at Giza, 1949–1950* (Cairo 1953) 129–143; G. Thorel, in: *Le Ramesseum. Les annexes nord-ouest* (Centre for Documentation, Cairo 1976) 29–51; P. Gilbert, Voûtes et arceaux les plus anciens en Egypte et en Mesopotamie, in: *Bull. de l'Academie Royale de Belgique* 60 (1978) 116–127; J. Brinks, Gewölbe, in: Helck, *LÄ* II 589–594; Spencer, *Brick Architecture* 123–127; Eigner, *Grabbauten* 78–79; M. Verner, La tombe d'Oudjahorresnet, in: *BIFAO* 89 (1989) 283–290; Arnold, *Building* 200–201; Nicholson, *Materials* .93–96. General: P.J. Neve, Hethitischer Gewölbebau, in: *Bautechnik der Antike* (Mainz 1991) 161–165; B. Wesenberg, Zur Entstehung des griechischen Keilsteingewölbes, in: *Bautechnik der Antike* (Mainz 1991) 252–258; Klaus Dornisch, *Die griechischen Bogentore. Zur Entstehung und Verbreitung des griechisehen Keilsteingewölbes,* Europäische Hochschulschriften (Frankfurt 1992) 225–228; Salah el-Naggat, *Les voûtes dans l'architecture de l'Égypte ancienne* (Cairo 1999).

W

Wabet

The Egyptian word *wabet* means 'the pure (place)' and is used, in later temples, of a small group of rooms near the stairs which lead to the roof, consisting of an unroofed **sun court** behind which was a raised cult room. The latter is separated from the courtyard by a **screen wall** with two columns. The *wabet* was used in New Year festivities for celebrating the union of the cult images with the sun disc. Its forerunners were probably the **sun temples** attached to the New Kingdom 'houses of millions of years'. Examples are found at **Dendera**, **Shanhur**, **El-Qal'a**, **Edfu**, **Kom Ombo** and **Kalabsha**.

Bibliography: Maurice Alliot, *Le culte d'Horus à Edfou* (Cairo 1954) 309–374; F. Daumas, Neujahr, in: Helck, *LÄ* V 466–472.

The *wabet* of the Hathor temple at Dendera, with Hathor columns and a frieze of uraei

Wadi el-Sebu'a

Site of a small rock chapel of Amenhotep III dedicated to the Nubian Horus, on the West Bank of the Nile 165 km south of Aswan. Ramesses II constructed a larger **rock temple** (109 m in length) nearby, dedicated to himself, Re-Horakhty and, principally, Amun-Re. A processional way led from a **platform** on the river bank, through two **brick pylons** to the third pylon, made of **sandstone**, and from there to the rock sanctuary proper (**hemispeos**). A richly varied array of statues lines the approach (**sphinxes, avenue of**).

Half of the **pillared hall** stood in the open air, while the offering room, together with three cult image rooms, were carved completely out of the rock. The execution is rough and provincial. In 1964 the temple was moved 4 km to the west.

Bibliography: Gau, *Antiquités*, Plates 42–47; Prisse d'Avennes, *Histoire*, Plate 48; Henry Gauthier, *Le temple de Ouadi es'Sebouâ* (Cairo 1912); R. Gundlach, Sebua, in: Helck, *LÄ* V 768–769; Hein, *Ramessidische Bautätigkeit* 17–20.

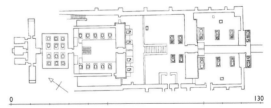

Plan of the temple of Ramesses II at Wadi el-Sebu'a

Wadi Miya (Kanais, Redesiah, Wadi Abbad)

A well-preserved **rock temple** of Sety I at a watering place on the road to the gold mines in the Eastern Desert, 55 km from **Edfu**. It is dedicated to Amun-Re and his Ennead. The **hemispeos** has a **pronaos** 8.46 m wide, with four columns and two rock-cut statues of the king by the entrance. Within the rock is a four-pillared hall, with two side-recesses and three chapels in the rear wall. The central chapel contains seated statues of Sety I, Amun-Re and Re-Horakhty.

Bibliography: *LD* Text IV 75–83; H. Gauthier, Le temple de l'Ouâdi Mîyah (el-Knais), in: *BIFAO* 17 (1920) 1–38; S. Schott, Der Tempel

Sethos I. im Wâdi Mia, in: *Nachrichten d. Akademie d. Wissenschaften Göttingen* 6 (1961) 123–189.

Wall, *see also* curved wall, wavy wall

a) Brick walls. In Egyptian brick and stone structures, vertical walls are found next to walls with a **batter** (approximately 83° slope, or 2–3 fingers per **cubit**) and with a rounded top. The batter was not only to improve stability, because walls only 1–2 m high were sloped. The batter in brickwork was produced by replacing, from the bottom upwards, headers with layers of stretchers or by laying the bricks at the necessary angle to produce a herringbone bond. The inside or rear face of brick or stone walls often has less of a slope or may be vertical. Brick structures are often depicted with rounded crenellations on top. The height of the wall is between two and a half and three times its thickness.

b) Stone walls. Free-standing and outer walls made of stone were also battered. Their inner surface, however, was always vertical. The upper edge had a rounded or irregular profile. The core of the wall was often filled with rough stones and the like, and only the outer casing was made of smoothed blocks joined together by pegs.

c) Large **enclosure walls**. In the Graeco-Roman period the lower portion of enclosure walls was often built of **sandstone**, the upper part of brick (**Armant, Philae, Kalabsha**). The corners of brick walls at this period were often reinforced with stones (**Luxor, El-Tod, Edfu**).

Bibliography: Jéquier, *Manuel* 77–109; Hölscher, *Chefren* 554; Borchardt, *Sahu-Re* 68; Borchardt, *Ne-user-Re* 97; Eigner, *Grabbauten* 70–75.

Wall pillar, *see* pilaster

Water spout, *see also* drainage, roof drainage

The **pyramid temples** of the Old and Middle Kingdoms were provided with water spouts to provide drainage, consisting of long stone gutters, with a U-shaped cross-section, open at the top. From the reign of Niuserre onwards, the gutter fed out between the paws (rather than the mouth) of the front parts of lions (pyramid and sun temple of **Niuserre**, pyramid temple of **Senwosret I**, **Chapelle Blanche, Medinet Habu, Khonsu** temple). In Ptolemaic temples these water spouts rested on huge corbels with apotropaic inscriptions and representations for the protection of the opening in the wall of the temple (**Edfu, Dendera**).

Bibliography: Jéquier, *Manuel* 55–56; H. Chevrier, in: *ASAE* 29 (1929) 137: Arnold, Wasserspeier, in: Helck, *LÄ* VI 1155–1156; Serge Sauneron and Henri Stierlin, *Die letzten Tempel Ägyptens* (Zurich 1978) 52, 55; Zivie, *Deir Chelouit*, Plate 41–42.

Wavy wall, pan bedding

From the 13th Dynasty onwards the **walls** of **houses**, and from the reign of Nectanebo I onwards the **enclosure walls** of temples, were constructed with undulating courses of **bricks**. The walls were divided into sections with either concave or convex courses (pan bedding) which, when viewed from the front, had a wavy appearance. The danger of bricks cracking was prevented by their being laid dry (**brick construction**). The side pressure produced by this undulating construction ensured that the bricks were kept in close bond. The interior strength of walls was increased by beams or reed **matting**, inserted lengthwise or across the direction of the wall. The lower sections of a wall sometimes consisted of undulating **sandstone** masonry (for example at **Armant, Kalabsha, Philae, Taffa**). Corners were strengthened by the courses of bricks being laid so that they sloped towards the inside, thus increasing the effect of bonded quoining. The outer casing of walls sometimes consisted of fired bricks. A secondary interpretation of the 'wave' effect could be as a representation of the primeval ocean. In the Roman period wavy walls were sometimes imitated in **stone** without any technical need (such as at **Dendera, Philae, Kalabsha**). At **Taposiris Magna** 'waves' were painted on to a horizontal course of stone.

Bibliography: Choisy, *L'art de bâtir* 21–42; Clark, *AEM* 210–211; G. Haeny, A short architectural history of Philae, in: *JEA* 85 (1985) 215 A.1; J.-C. Golvin et al., Essay d'explication des murs 'à assis courbes', in: *Comptes rendues de l'Académie des Inscriptions* 58 (1990) 905–946; Nicholson, *Materials* 91.

Undulating enclosure wall of the Amun precinct at Karnak, in parts laid dry

Way station, *see* barque station

Wedjahorresnet, tomb of

A monumental shaft tomb of the end of the 26th Dynasty, south-west of the pyramids at **Abusir**. The main shaft, 23 m deep, with the sarcophagus chamber at the bottom, communicates directly with the secondary shafts surrounding it on all sides; the latter were filled with sand in order to hinder tomb robbers. Other Late Period tombs in the area have not been examined.

Bibliography: Miroslav Verner, *Forgotten Pharaohs, Lost Pyramids, Abusir* (Prague 1994) 195–208.

Wheeled transport, *see also* transport

The use of wheels for military and hunting chariots, and carriages for the transport of funerary barques and cult images is well documented from the Hyksos period (1630–1520 BC) onwards. Vehicles with four wheels appear from the 18th Dynasty onwards. Less well known is the existence of sturdy transport carriages (drawn by up to 12 oxen) in the New Kingdom. (Much earlier forerunners are shown in tomb paintings of the late Old Kingdom and the 11th Dynasty showing siege towers with wheels; depictions of movable siege towers exist from the 6th Dynasty onwards.) This indicates that the wheel was used in the transport of heavy loads more frequently than is generally assumed. Transport of stone (such as **granite** columns weighing 48 tonnes for the Pantheon in Rome) from Mons Claudianus and Porphyrites to the Nile valley, carried out using wheeled vehicles in the Roman period, may have had forerunners in Pharaonic times.

The use of wheeled equipment in building is not yet attested to but may have been fairly common. The soft surface of the desert sand and the mud of the cultivation may have been a serious obstacle for heavy carriages but not so much for **sledges**.

Bibliography: J.J. Coulton, *Greek Architects at Work* (Ithaca, NY 1977) 141–144; Manolis Korres, *Vom Penteli zum Parthenon* (Munich 1992) 32–38; Arnold, *Building* 281–282; R. Partridge, *Transport in Ancient Egypt* (London 1996).

Window

Despite the climatic conditions of Egypt, windows play a major role in Egyptian architecture. Larger window apertures have vertical or horizontal grilles or wooden shutters. Varieties of window grille range from a simple branch to vertical bars or carved ornaments (attested to by finds and from representations). The masonry of brick **mastabas** of the Old Kingdom also has vertical window slots or clusters of drill holes. Window sills and window lintels are kept apart by a number of vertical bars. Window lintels are often simply boards supporting the masonry or the **roof**.

Temple buildings of **stone** tend to have interesting apertures for admitting light (**Mentuhotep** and **Opet** temples, Figs). The slots (so-called 'windows of Shu'),

Sandstone window grille from the throne room of the palace of Ramesses III at Medinet Habu

which usually arc obliquely, widen towards the inside, ending if possible at an angle between the ceiling and the wall of the structure. The opening is protected against rain on the outside by a surrounding ledge. Stone grilles in the form of lavish ornaments or simple vertical slits are found in stone or **brick** buildings. The earliest examples with grilles in the shape of *djed* pillars are found in the **Djoser** precinct, while monumental ones (so-called 'claustra') are found in the **hypostyle hall** at Karnak (8–12 slits, 5.20 m high, per window; **ceiling construction**, Fig.) and in the palace of Ramesses III at **Medinet Habu**. Some windows at **Dendera** and **Deir el-Medina** have stone grilles in the form of small temple façades or in the shape of ranges of columns with **Hathor capitals**.

Window grilles of the Ptolemaic extension to the 18th Dynasty temple at Medinet Habu

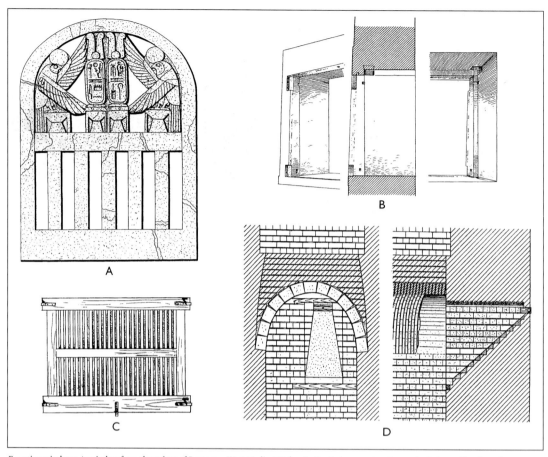

Egyptian windows. A: window from the palace of Ramesses III at Medinet Habu; B–C: window construction and window grilles from the east gate of Ramesses III at Medinet Habu; D: cellar window from Roman house II 201 at Dima

Special forms of window are found above door openings, often of richly ornamented wooden lattice work; highly detailed imitations in stone are found as supra-portals above **false doors** in temples and tombs (**Puyemre**). In cultic structures, slits or drill holes provide a link between the *serdab* and the offering room.

Bibliography: Perrot, *L'Égypte* 614–621; Edouard Naville, *The XIth Dynasty Temple at Deir el-Bahari* (London 1910) Plates 14–19; Jéquier, *Manuel* 129–135; Clark, *AEM* 170–177; Junker, *Giza* III, Fig. 34; Boak, *Karanis* I–II; Junker, *Soknopaiou Nesos* (Ann Arbor 1935); G. Haeny, Fenster, in: Helck, *LÄ* II 168–169; P. Kaplony, Fenster des Schu, in: Helck, *LÄ* II 169–170.

'Window of appearances'

Depictions in private tombs of the 18th Dynasty show that royal residences had 'windows (or balconies) of appearances', where the king showed himself to his subjects or presented gifts. The balconies had upholstered **balustrades** and a **canopy** providing shade. Severe damage suffered by the **palaces** has so far prevented the existence of this feature being proved archaeologically. In Theban **'houses of millions of years'**, the 'window of appearances' gives out from the cult palace into the forecourt of the temple lying in front of it. A staircase, on the palace side, leads to a magnificent window, which is decorated with royal emblems on the side of the court. It probably had a purely cultic function, as the 'heavens' from which the king 'shines', 'so as to make his father Amun-Re appear at his valley festival'.

Bibliography: N. de G. Davies, The place of audience in the palace, in: *ZÄS* 60 (1925) 50–56; U. Hölscher, Erscheinungsfenster und Erscheinungsbalkon im königlichen Palast, in: *ZÄS* 67 (1939) 43–51; R. Stadelmann, Tempelpalast und Erscheinungsfenster, in: *Dessin architectural* 29 (1973) 221–242; B.J. Kemp, The window of appearance at El-Amarna, in: *JEA* 62 (1976) 81–99; D. Arnold, Erscheinungsfenster, in: Helck, *LÄ* II 14; B.J. Kemp, Discovery and renewal at Amarna, *Egyptian Archaeology* 1 (1991) 19–22.

Woven timber construction, reed buildings

A pre-historic method of making fragile structures prior to the erection of buildings of **brick** and **stone** but which continued (and continue) to be used alongside the latter in the provision of temporary accommodation, animal shelters, arbours and protective roofs (examples at Merimde-Benisalame, El-Omari, Hammamiya, **El-Ma'adi** and El-Tarif). Frames were built of native species of timber and palm stems, and clothed in reeds and papyrus mats, in some cases covered with mud, i.e. 'wattle and daub' covering. Representations in hieroglyphs dating from the 1st Dynasty (on cylinder seals) indicate the presence at that time of monumental examples used as residences of chiefs or kings (**Per-nu, Per-wer**). Forms developed on such prototypes were used in stone structures from the time of Djoser onwards. This type of 'palace of mats' is represented in the tiled decorations lining the Main and South Tombs of **Djoser**. Individual architectural elements, such as the **drum**, **cavetto cornice** and torus moulding, *kheker frieze*, rounded beam ceiling, as well as some forms of plant **columns**, have their origin in woven timber buildings.

Modern hut made of palm stems and sugar cane

Bibliography: I.E.S. Edwards, Some early dynastic contributions to Egyptian architecture, in: *MDAIK* 35 (1949) 123–128; A. Badawy, La première architecture en Égypte, in: *ASAE* 51 (1951) 1–23; Ricke, *Bemerkungen* I 25–38; K. Kuhlmann, Rohrbau, in: Helck, *LÄ* V 288–294; Labelle Prussin, *African Nomadic Architecture* (Washington-London 1995).

Z

Zawyet el-Aryan

Remains of two royal tombs south of **Giza**, both inadequately examined and now built over with a military camp.

a) An incomplete 3rd Dynasty **step mastaba**, erected on the desert plateau, 84 m in size, constructed in 14 courses of masonry. 24 m below the centre is the burial chamber, surrounded on the east, north and west sides by

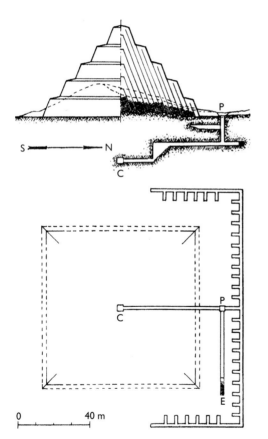

Plan and section of the step mastaba at Zawyet el-Aryan (after J.-P. Lauer)

corridors in a U-shaped arrangement, with a total of 32 magazines. Its ascription to King Khaba is hypothetical.

Bibliography: Reisner, *Development* 151–153; *MRA* II 41–49, Lauer, *Histoire monumentale* 206–211; Stadelmann, *Pyramiden* 77; Stadelmann, Saujet el-Arjan, in: Helck, *LÄ* V 495–497; Mark Lehner, Z 500 and the layer pyramid of Zawiyet el-Aryan, in: *Studies Simpson* II, 507–522.

b) An abandoned 4th Dynasty pyramid building project in the fore-desert, ascribed to the kings following Djedefre (Baka/Nebka, Hordjedef or Bauefre). The completed parts were an open shaft, 21 m deep, for construction of the burial chamber, and the **building ramp** sloping down in two steps from the north. At the bottom of the shaft is a deep stone foundation with an unused oval **granite** sarcophagus, around which the chamber was to have been constructed. The pyramid was planned to measure 210 x 210 m, with a precinct of 420 x 465 m.

Bibliography: A. Barsanti, Ouverture de la pyramide de Zaouiét el-Aryàn, in: *ASAE* 2 (1901) 92–94; A. Barsanti, Zaouiét el-Aryân, in: *ASAE* 7 (1906) 226–281; J.-Ph. Lauer, Sur l'age et l'attribution possible de l'excavation monumentale de Zaouiet el-Aryàn, in: *RdE* 14 (1962) 21–36; *MRA* VI 16–29; Stadelmann, *Pyramiden* 140–141.

Zawyet el-Mayitin (Zawyet el-Amwat, Zawyet Sultan

The important remains of a city, 7 km upstream of el-Minya, with an enormous necropolis dating from pre-dynastic to Ptolemaic times, containing numerous **rock tombs** of the Old and New Kingdoms. In the northern area is a small **step mastaba** of the 3rd Dynasty, constructed in four steps, measuring 22.5 x 22.5 m, and originally approximately 17 m high. There are some remains of its **casing**. No burial chamber has been found.

Bibliography: R. Weill, Fouilles à Tounah et à Zaouiêt el-Maiétin, in: *CRAIBL* (1912) 484–490; Lauer, *Histoire monumentale* 225–227; Dreyer and Kaiser, *Stufenpyramiden* 48–49; J. Osing, *Das Grab des Nefersecheru in Zawyet Sulṭan* (Mainz 1992).

Maps

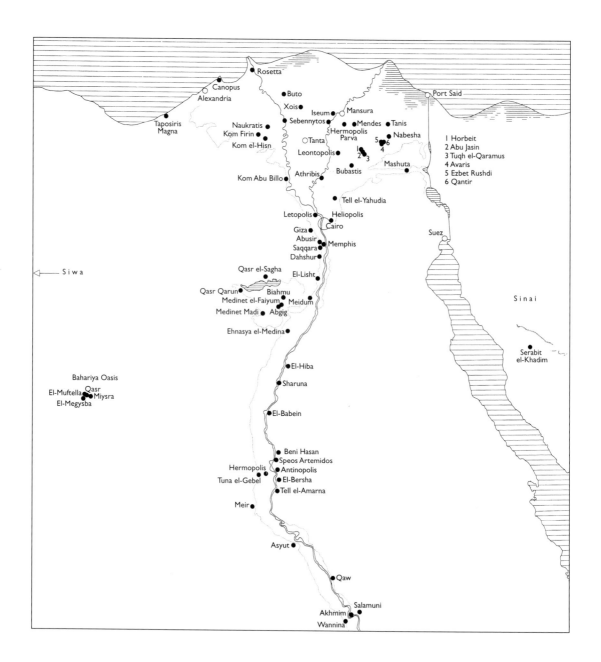

Rosetta
Canopus
Alexandria
Taposiris
Magna
Buto
Xois
Iseum
Mansura
Naukratis
Sebennytos
Mendes
Tanis
Kom Firin
Hermopolis
Parva
Nabesha
Kom el-Hisn
Tanta
5 6
Leontopolis
1
2
3
4
Bubastis
Mashuta
Athribis
Kom Abu Billo
Tell el-Yahudia
Letopolis
Heliopolis
Cairo
Giza
Abusir
Memphis
Saqqara
Dahshur
Qasr el-Sagha
El-Lisht
Qasr Qarun
Biahmu
Medinet el-Faiyum
Meidum
Medinet Madi
Abgig
Ehnasya el-Medina
Siwa
Port Said
Suez
Sinai
1 Horbeit
2 Abu Jasin
3 Tuqh el-Qaramus
4 Avaris
5 Ezbet Rushdi
6 Qantir

El-Hiba
Sharuna
Serabit
el-Khadim
Bahariya Oasis
El-Muftella
Qasr
Miysra
El-Megysba
El-Babein
Beni Hasan
Speos Artemidos
Hermopolis
Antinopolis
Tuna el-Gebel
El-Bersha
Tell el-Amarna
Meir
Asyut
Qaw
Salamuni
Akhmim
Wannina

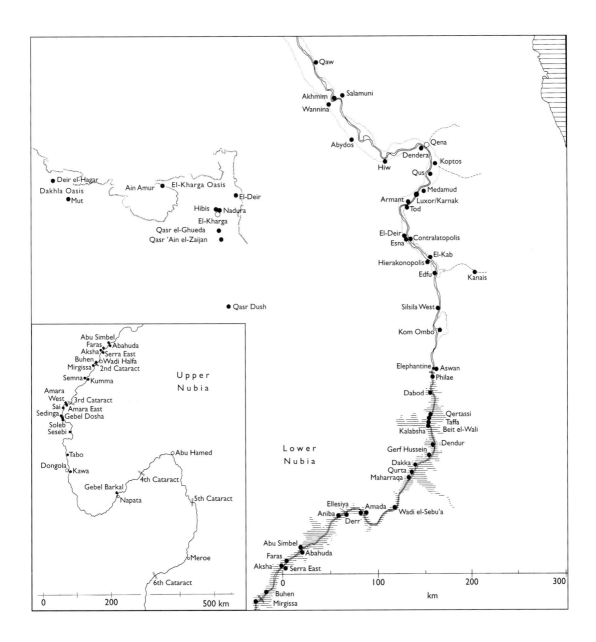

Glossary

Ba: Aspect of the individual similar to personality. It was frequently represented as a bird with the head and arms of a human.

Canopic (jars): Containers for the viscera separated from the corpse during mummification. Ideally they took the form of four alabaster jars with human and animal heads, placed in a sarcophagus-like stone box.

Cartouche: In hieroglyphs, an enclosure containing the throne or birth name of the ruler. It was perhaps originally derived from the *shen* ring, a knotted ship's rope, which was a symbol of eternity and which was extended from a circle to an oval shape to accommodate the kings name.

Cataract: Rapids on the upper part of the Nile, formed from hard layers of rock which hindered river traffic. The first cataract is at Aswan, the second at Wadi Halfa, the third at Kerma, and the fourth upstream from Gebel Barkal.

Ennead: Group of nine (three times three, meaning 'many') divinities at principal cult centres, for example Heliopolis.

Gebel: Mountain, hill (Ar.).

Intercolumnium: Space between two pillars or columns.

Ka: Highly important aspect of the individual, for gods and humans, but very difficult for modern thinking to grasp. It is associated with, among other things, the dignity and life force of a person. Born as a form of double, the *ka* survived bodily death. It was represented by two bent arms reaching upwards with open hands.

Kom: As *tell* (below), a mound of ruins (Ar.).

Sed-festival: Festival, incorporating elaborate ritual dramas, for the renewal of the ruling power of the king. Ideally it took place 30 years after his accession or his designation as next in line to the throne.

Tell: As *kom* (above), a mound of ruins (Ar.).

Triad: Group of three gods – usually a divine family – worshipped at a cult centre.

Wadi: Dry desert valley (Ar.).

Chronological Table

Egyptian chronology was for many years considered 'secure'. More recently, the chronological foundations of the 1st and 12th Dynasties, as well as of the whole Second Intermediate Period, have been called into question, and doubt has been cast on the length of the Third Intermediate Period.

Late Pre-historic Period   **3200–3100**
(Naqada IIIb, protodynastic)
Dynasty 0

    3200–3100
    Ni-Hor
    Hat-Hor
    Iri-Hor
    Ka/Sekhen
    Horus Narmer
    Scorpion

Early Dynastic Period (Thinite period)   **3100–2600**
1st Dynasty

    3100–2885
    Horus Aha (Menes)
    Athothis I
    Horus Djer
    Meryneith
    Horus Wadj (Djet)
    Horus Dewen (Den, Udimu)
    Horus 'Adjib
    Horus Semerkhet
    Horus Qa'a

2nd Dynasty

    2885–2700
    Horus Hetepsekhemwy (Netjenbau)
    Horus Raneb (Nebre, Kau?)
    Horus Ninetjer
    Seth Peribsen (Sekhemib?)
    Horus-Seth Khasekhem(wy)
    and perhaps other ephemeral rulers

3rd Dynasty

    2700–2600
    Horus Zanakht (Nebka)
    Horus Netjerykhet (Djoser)
    Horus Sekhemkhet (Djoserti)
    Nebkare(?) Khaba(?)
    Horus Kahedjet (Huni?)
    and perhaps other ephemeral rulers

Old Kingdom	**2600–2137**	
4th Dynasty	2600–2450	
	Sneferu	2600–2555
	Khufu (Cheops)	2555–2520
	Djedefre (Radjedef)	2520–2512
	Khafre (Chephren)	2512–2477
	Baka(?)	2477–2472
	Menkaure (Mykerinos)	2472–2454
	Shepseskaf	2454–2450
	and perhaps other ephemeral rulers	
5th Dynasty	2450–2325	
	Userkaf	
	Sahure	
	Neferirkare-Kakai	
	Shepseskare	
	Neferefre-Isi (Raneferef)	
	Niuserre-Ini	
	Menkauhor	
	Djedkare-Isesi	
	Unas	
6th Dynasty	2325–2137	
	Teti	
	Pepi I Merire	
	Merenre	
	Pepi II Neferkare	
	and three ephemeral rulers	
First Intermediate Period	**2137–2040**	
7–8th Dynasties	2150–2134	
	numerous ephemeral rulers	
9-10th Dynasties (in Herakleopolis)	2134–2040	
	local rulers	
11th Dynasty before the Unification (2040)	2134–2040	
	local rulers in Thebes, the last of which were Inyotef I–III and Mentuhotep Nebhepetre	
Middle Kingdom	**2040–1650**	
11th Dynasty after the Unification (2040)	2040–1991	
	Mentuhotep Nebhepetre	
	Mentuhotep Sankhkare	
	Mentuhotep Nebtawyre	
12th Dynasty	1991–1783	
	Amenemhat I Sehetepibre	1991–1962
	Senwosret I Kheperkare	1971–1926
	Amenemhat II Nubkaure	1929–1892

	Senwosret II Khakheperre	1897–1878
	Senwosret III Khakaure	1878–1841
	Amenemhat III Nimaatre	1844–1797
	Amenemhat IV Maatkherure	1799–1787
	Sobeknofru (Nofru-Sobek)	1787–1783

13th Dynasty

1783 –1650
numerous mostly ephemeral rulers,
partly in Memphis

Second Intermediate Period **1650–1550**
14th Dynasty

1710–1650
numerous ephemeral rulers in the Delta,
contemporary with the 13th and 15th
Dynasties

15th Dynasty

'Great' Hyksos rulers   1650–1550
Salitis
Sheshi
Iaqobher
Khyan
Apophis
Khamudi

16th Dynasty

1650–1550
numerous ephemeral Hyksos rulers and
their Lower Egyptian vassals

17th Dynasty

1650–1550
approximately 15 Theban rulers
contemporary with the 15th and 16th
Dynasties, the last of which were
Seqenenre Ta'o und Kamose

New Kingdom **1550–1070**
18th Dynasty

1550–1308

Ahmose	1550–1525
Amenhotep I	1525–1504
Thutmosis I	1504–1492
Thutmosis II	1492–1479
Thutmosis III	1479–1425
Hatshepsut	1473–1458
Amenhotep II	1427–1401
Thutmosis IV	1401–1391
Amenhotep III	1391–1353
Amenhotep IV/Akhenaten	1364–1348
Tutankhamun	1348–1338
Ay	1338–1335
Horemheb	1335–1308

19th Dynasty	1307–1196	
	Ramesses I	1307–1306
	Sety I	1306–1290
	Ramesses II	1290–1224
	Merenptah	1224–1214
	Sety II	1214–1204
	Siptah	1204–1198
	Tawosret	1198–1196
20th Dynasty	1196–1070	
	Sethnakht	1196–1194
	Ramesses III	1194–1163
	Ramesses IV	1163–1156
	Ramesses V	1156–1151
	Ramesses VI	1151–1143
	Ramesses VII	1143–1136
	Ramesses VIII	1136–1131
	Ramesses IX	1131–1112
	Ramesses X	1112–1100
	Ramesses XI	1100–1070

Third Intermediate Period   **1070–712**

21st Dynasty (in Tanis)	1069–945	
	Smendes	1069–1043
	Psusennes I	1039–991
	Amenemope	993–984
	Siamun	978–959
	Psusennes II	959–945

further ephemeral rulers in Tanis, and at the same time eight high priests of Amun ruling from Thebes

22nd Dynasty (in Bubastis)	945–715	
	Sheshonq I	945–924
	Osorkon I	924– 889
	Sheshonq II	c. 890
	Takeloth I	889–874
	Osorkon II	874–850
	Takeloth II	850–825
	Sheshonq III	825–773
	Pimai	773–767
	Sheshonq V	767–730
	Osorkon IV	730–715

23rd Dynasty (in Leontopolis)   820–718

approximately seven rulers contemporary with the 22nd, 24th and 25th Dynasties

24th Dynasty (in Sais)	730–712 ephemeral; two rulers, Tefnakht and Bakenrenef, contemporary with the 23rd and 25th dynasties	
Late Period		
25th Dynasty (Ethiopian)	760–656	
	Kashta	760–747
	Piankhi	747–716
	Shabaka	716–702
	Shebitku	702–690
	Taharqa	690–664
	Tantamani	664–656
26th Dynasty	664–525	
	Psamtek I	664–610
	Necho II	610–595
	Psamtek II	595–589
	Apries	589–570
	Amasis	570–526
	Psamtek III	526–525
27th Dynasty (First Persian Period)	525–404	
28–29th Dynasty	404–380 ephemeral Egyptian rulers in Mendes	
30th Dynasty	380–343	
	Nectanebo I Nakhtnebef	379/380–361/360
	Teos	361/360–359/358
	Nectanebo II Nakhtherhebef	359/358–342/341
31st Dynasty (Second Persian Period)		342–332
Macedonian Dynasty	332–310	
	Alexander the Great	332–323
	Philip Arrhidaeus	323–317
	Alexander II	316–305
Ptolemaic Dynasty	304–30	
	Ptolemy I Soter	304–285
	Ptolemy II Philadelphus	284–247
	Ptolemy III Euergetes I	246–222
	Ptolemy IV Philopator	221–205
	Ptolemy V Epiphanes	205–180
	Ptolemy VI Philometor	180–145
	Ptolemy VII Neos Philopator	145
	Ptolemy VIII Euergetes II	164–163, 145–116
	Cleopatra III	116–101
	Ptolemy IX Soter II	116–107, 88–80
	Ptolemy X Alexander I	101–88

Ptolemy XI Alexander II	80
Ptolemy XII Neos Dionysos (Auletes)	80–51
Cleopatra VII Philopator with	
Ptolemy XIII, XIV and XV (Caesarion)	51–30

Roman rule

(Roman and Western Roman emperors appearing on Egyptian monuments)

30 BC to AD 642

Augustus	30 BC to AD 14
Tiberius	14–37
Gaius (Caligula)	37–41
Claudius	41–54
Nero	54–68
Galba	68–69
Otho	69
Vespasian	69–79
Titus	79–81
Domitian	81–96
Nerva	96–98
Trajan	98–117
Hadrian	117–138
Antoninus Pius	138–161
Lucius Verus	161–169
Marcus Aurelius	161–180
Commodus	180–192
Septimus Severus	193–211
Caracalla	198–217
Geta	209–212
Macrinus	217–218
Marcus Julius Philippus	244–249
Decius	249–251

In September, AD 642 the Byzantine Emperor Constantine II surrendered Egypt to the Arabs

Select Bibliography

Books (titles abbreviated in text indicated in bold)

Arnold, *Amenemhet III:* Dieter Arnold, *Der Pyramidenbezirk des Königs Amenemhet III. in Dahschur* (Mainz 1987)

Arnold, *Building:* Dieter Arnold, *Building in Egypt. Pharaonic Stone Masonry* (New York 1991)

Arnold, *Temples:* Dieter Arnold, *Temples of the Last Pharaohs* (New York 1999)

Arnold, *Wandrelief:* Dieter Arnold, *Wandrelief und Raumfunktion in ägyptischen Tempeln des Neuen Reiches* (Berlin 1962)

Dieter Arnold, *Die Tempel Ägyptens. Götterwohnungen, Kultstätten, Baudenkmäler* (Zurich 1992)

Aufrère, *L'Égypte restituée:* S. Aufrère, J.-Cl. Golvin and J.-Cl. Goyon, *L'Égypte restituée. Sites et temples de Haute Égypte* (Paris 1991)

Olivier Aurenche, *Dictionnaire illustrée multilingue de l'architecture du proche orient ancien* (Lyons-Paris 1977)

Badawy, *Architecture:* Alexander Badawy, *A History of Egyptian Architecture*, 3 Vols (Berkeley-Los Angeles 1954, 1966, 1968)

Badawy, *Dessin architectural:* Alexandre Badawy, *Le dessin architectural chez les anciens égyptiens* (Cairo 1948)

Earl Baldwin Smith, Egyptian Architecture as Cultural Expression (New York 1938, reprinted Watkins Glen, NY 1968)

Bárta, *Abusir 2000:* M. Bárta and J. Krejcí, Eds, *Abusir and Saqqara in the Year 2000* (Prague 2000)

Bietak, *Haus und Palast:* see *House and Palace* in B)

Bietak, *House and Palace:* M. Bietak, *House and Palace in Ancient Egypt* (Vienna 1996)

Boak, *Karanis H:* Arthur E.R. Boak, Ed., *Karanis, The Temples, Coin Hoards, Botanical and Zoological Reports, Seasons 1924–31* (Ann Arbor 1933)

Boak, *Karanis I:* Arthur E.R. Boak and Enoch Peterson, *Karanis. Topographical and Architectural Report of Excavations during the Seasons 1924–28* (Ann Arbor 1931)

Borchardt, *Tell el-Amarna:* Ludwig Borchardt and Herbert Ricke, *Die Wohnhäuser in Tell el-Amarna* (Berlin 1980)

Borchardt, *Chephren:* Ludwig Borchardt, *Das Grabdenkmal des Königs Chephren* (Leipzig 1912)

Borchardt, *Entstehung der Pyramide:* Ludwig Borchardt, *Die Entstehung der Pyramide an der Baugeschichte der Pyramide von Mejdum nachgewiesen* (Berlin 1928)

Borchardt, *Nefer-ir-ke-Re:* Ludwig Borchardt, *Das Grabdenkmal des Königs Nefer-ir-ke-Re* (Leipzig 1909)

Borchardt, *Ne-user-Re:* Ludwig Borchardt, *Das Grabdenkmal des Königs Ne-user-Re* (Leipzig 1907)

Borchardt, *Pflanzensäule:* Ludwig Borchardt, *Die agyptischen Pflanzensäule* (Berlin 1897)

Borchardt, *Re-Heiligtum:* Ludwig Borchardt, *Das Re-Heiligtum des Königs Ne-woser-Re (Rathures)* (Berlin 1905)

Borchardt, *Sahu-Re:* Ludwig Borchardt, *Das Grabdenkmal des Königs Sahu-Re* (Leipzig 1910)

Borchardt, *Tempel mit Umgang:* Ludwig Borchardt, *Ägyptische Tempel mit Umgang* (Cairo 1938)

Brinks, *Grabanlagen:* Jurgen Brinks, *Die Entwicklung der königlichen Grabanlagen des Alten Reiches*, Hildesheimer Ägyptologische Beiträge 10 (Hildesheim 1979)

Clark, *AEM:* Somers Clark and R. Engelbach, *Ancient Egyptian Masonry. The Building Craft* (London 1930)

Choisy, *L'art de bâtir:* Auguste Choisy, *L'art de bâtir chez les égyptiens* (Paris 1904, reprinted Sala Bolognese 1977)

Jean-Louis de Cenival, Henri Stierlin and Marcel Breuer, *Ägypten. Das Zeitalter der Pharaonen* (Lausanne n.d.)

De Morgan, *Dahchour I–II:* Jacques de Morgan, *Fouilles à Dahchour mars-juin 1894* (Vienna 1895); *Fouilles à Dahchour en 1894–95* (Vienna 1903)

De Putter, *Pierres:* Thierry de Putter and Christina Karishausen, *Les pierres utilisées dans la sculpture et l 'architecture de l'Égypte pharaonique* (Brussels 1992)

Description: *Description de l'Égypte, contenant plusieurs remarques curieuses sur la Geographie ancienne et moderne de ce Païs, sur ses Monuments anciens*, etc., 10 Vols (Paris 1809–1828)

Diodoros, *Diodori:* Diodoros of Sicily, the Loeb Classical Library (Cambridge, MA 1995)

Dreyer, *Stufenpyramiden:* G. Dreyer and W. Kaiser, Zu den kleinen Stufenpyramiden Ober- und Mittelägyptens. in: *MDAIK* 36 (1980) 43–59

Edwards, *Pyramids:* I.E.S. Edwards, *The Pyramids of Egypt* (London reprinted 1985)

Eigner, *Grabbauten:* Diethelm Eigner, *Die monumentalen Grabbauten der Spätzeit in der thebanischen Nekropole* (Vienna 1984)

Engelbach, *Obelisks:* Reginald Engelbach, *The Aswân Obelisk* (Cairo 1922)

Festschrift Ricke: *Aufsätze zum 70. Geburtstag von Herbert Ricke*, BeiträgeBf 12 (Wiesbaden 1971)

Gau, *Antiquités:* François Chrétien Gau, *Antiquités de la Nubie* (Stuttgart–Paris 1822)

Siegfried Giedion, T*he Eternal Present. The Beginnings of Architecture*, 2 Vols (London 1957)

Golvin, *Karnak:* Jean-Claude Golvin and Jean-Claude Goyon, *Les bâtisseurs de Karnak* (Paris 1987)

Haeny, *Basilikale Anlagen:* Gerhard Haeny, *Basilikale Anlagen in der ägyptischen Baukunst des Neuen Reiches* (Wiesbaden 1970)

Hassan, *Giza, I–X:* Selim Hassan, *Excavations at Giza*, 10 Vols (Cairo 1932–1960)

Heck, *LÄ:* Wolfang Helck and Eberhard Otto, Eds, *Lexikon der Ägyptologie*, 6 Vols, (Wiesbaden 1975–1986)

Hein, *Ramessidische Bautätigkeit:* Irmgard Hein, *Die Ramessidische Bautätigkeit in Nubien*, Göttinger Orientforschungen 22 (Wiesbaden 1991)

Herodotus, *History:* Herodotus, *History* (The Loeb Classical Library, Cambridge, MA 1996)

Hölscher, *Chephren:* Uvo Hölscher, *Das Grabdenkmal des Königs Chephren* (Leipzig 1912)

Hölscher, *Medinet Habu, I–IV:* Uvo Hölscher, *The Excavations of Medinet Habu*, Vols I and III,*The Mortuary Temple of Ramses III*, Part 1–2 (Chicago 1941, 1951); Vol. II, *The Temples of the Eighteenth Dynasty* (Chicago 1939); Vol. V, *The Post-Ramesside Remains* (Chicago 1954)

Jánosi, *Pyramidenanlagen:* Peter Jánosi, *Die Pyramidenanlagen der Königinnen des Alten und Mittleren Reiches*, Dissertation (Vienna 1988)

Jaritz, *Terrassen:* Horst Jaritz, *Die Terrassen vor den Tempeln des Chnum und der Satet*, Elephantine Vol. 3 (Mainz 1980)

Jéquier, *Architecture:* Gustave Jéquier, *L'architecture et la decoration dans l'ancienne Égypte*, 3 Vols (Paris 1911, 1920, 1924)

Jéquier, *Manuel:* Gustave Jéquier, *Manuel d'archéologie égyptienne. Les éléments de l'architecture* (Paris 1924)

Junker, *Giza, I–XII:* Hermann Junker, *Giza*, 12 Vols (Vienna 1929–1955)

***Karnak* I–IX:** *Cahiers de Karnak*, 8 Vols, Cairo, *Karnak* I = *Kêmi* 18, 1968; II = 19, 1969; III = 20, 1970; IV = 21, 1971; V = 1975; VI = 1980; VII = 1982; VIII = 1987; IX = 1993.

Klemm, *Steine:* Rosemarie and Dietrich D. Klemm, *Steine und Steinbrüche im Alten Ägypten* (Berlin etc .1993)

Koenigsberger, *Tür:* Otto Koenigsberger, *Die Konstruktion der ägyptischen Tür* (Ägyptolog. Forschungen 2 (Glückstadt 1936)

Lauer, *Histoire monumentale:* Jean-Philippe Lauer, *Histoire monumentale des pyramides d'Égypte* (Cairo 1962)

Lauer, *Mystère:* Jean-Philippe Lauer, *Le mystère des pyramides* (Paris 1974)

Lauer, *Saqqara:* Jean-Philippe Lauer, *Saqqara. The Royal Cemetery of Memphis* (London 1976)

Lepsius, *Denkmaeler:* Carl Richard Lepsius, *Denkmaeler aus Aegypten and Aethiopien*, VI Parts in 12 Vols (Berlin 1849–1859)

Lehner, *Complete Pyramids:* Mark Lehner, *The Complete Pyramids* (London 1997)

Lucas, *AEMI:* A. Lucas and J.R. Harris, *Ancient Egyptian Materials and Industries*, 4th Ed. (London 1962)

Maragioglio, *L'architecttura II–VIII:* Vito Maragioglio and Celeste Ambrogio Rinaldi, *L'architettura della piramidi menfite*, 7 text and 6 plate vols (Rapallo 1963–1977)

Müller, *Monumentalarchitektur:* Hans Wolfgang Müller, Gedanken zur Entstehung, Interpretation und Rekonstruktion ältester ägyptischer Monumentalarchitektur, in: *Ägypten – Dauer und Wandel* (Mainz 1985) 7–33

Naville, *Festival-Hall:* Edouard Naville, *The Festival-Hall of Osorkon II. in the Great Temple of Bubastis (1887-1889)* (London 1892)

Nicholson, *Materials:* Paul Nicholson and Ian Shaw et al., *Ancient Egyptian Materials and Technology* (Cambridge 2000)

Perrot, *L'Égypte*: Georges Perrot and Charles Chipiez, *Histoire de l'art dans l'antiquité*, Vol. I. *L'Égypte* (Paris 1882)

Peet, *City of Akhenaten I–III*: T.E. Peet and C.L. Woolley, *The City of Akhenaten* I (London 1923); H. Frankfort and J.D.S. Pendlebury, *The City of Akhenaten* II (London 1933); J.D.S. Pendlebury, *The City of Akhenaten* III: text and plate vols (London 1951)

Petrie, *Pyramids*: William M. Flinders Petrie, *The Pyramids and Temples of Gizeh* (London 1883)

Pliny, *Naturalis Historia*: C. Plinius Secundus the Elder (23/24 BC to AD 79), *Naturalis Historia*, Joyce Irene Whalley, (London 1982)

Porter, *Bibliography I–VII*: Bertha Porter and Rosalind Moss, *Topographical Bibliography of Ancient Egyptian Hieroglyphic Texts, Reliefs, and Paintings*, 7 Vols, some 2nd Eds by Jaromir Malek (Oxford 1927–1981)

Prisse d'Avennes, *Histoire*: Emile Prisse d'Avennes, *Histoire de l'art égyptien d'après les monuments, Atlas* Vol. 1. *Architecture* (Paris 1878)

Quirke, *Temple*: Stephen Quirke, *The Temple in Ancient Egypt* (London 1997)

Reisner, *Giza*: George Andrew Reisner, *A History of the Giza Necropolis I* (Cambridge, Mass. 1942)

Reisner, *Development*: George A. Reisner, *The Development of the Egyptian Tomb down to the Accession of Cheops* (Cambridge 1963)

Ricke, *Bemerkungen I–II*: Herbert Ricke, *Bemerkungen zur ägyptischen Baukunst des Alten Reiches*, Vol. I (Zürich 1944), Vol. II (Cairo 1950)

Ricke, *Harmachistempel*: Herbert Ricke and Sigfried Schott, *Der Harmachistempel des Chefren in Giseh*, BeitrageBf 10 (Wiesbaden 1970)

Ricke, *Kamutef*: Herbert Ricke, *Das Kamutef-Heiligtum Hatschepsuts und Thutmosis III . in Kornak* (Cairo 1954)

Ricke, *Userkaf I*: Herbert Ricke, *Das Sonnenheiligtum des Konigs Userkaf*, 2 Vols (Wiesbaden 1965, 1969)

Ricke, *Wohnhäuser*: Ludwig Borchardt and Herbert Ricke, *Die Wohnhäuser in Tell el-Amarna* (Berlin 1980)

Schulz, *Egypt*: Regine Schulz, *Ägypten: die Welt der Pharaonen* (Cologne 1997)

Spencer, *Brick Architecture*: A.J. Spencer, *Brick Architecture in Ancient Egypt* (Warminster 1979)

Stadelmann, *Pyramiden von Giza*: Rainer Stadelmann, *Die großen Pyramiden von Giza* (Graz 1990)

Stadelmann, *Pyramiden*: Rainer Stadelmann, *Die Ägyptischen Pyramiden*, 2nd Ed. (Darmstadt 1991)

Stevenson Smith, *Art*: W. Stevenson Smith, *The Art and Architecture of Ancient Egypt* (London 1958, 1981)

Strabo, *Geographica*: *The Geography of Strabo*, Vol. VIII (Cambridge, MA 1982)

***Studies Simpson*:** Peter Der Manuelian (Ed.), *Studies in Honor of William Kelly Simpson*, 2 Vols (Boston, MA 1996)

***Tempeltagung*:** Rolf Gundlach and Matthias Rochholz (Eds), *Ägyptologische Tempeltagung* (Wiesbaden 1995)

Vandier, *Manuel*: J. Vandier, *Manuel d'archéologie égyptienne*, Vols I/2, II/1–2 (Paris 1952, 1954, 1955)

***VI. Congresso*:** *VI. Congresso internationale di Egittologia*, 2 Vols (Turin 1992–1993)

Vitruvius, *Architecture*: Marcus Vitruvius Pollio (time of Caesar and Augustus), *The Ten Books on Architecture*, Ingrid D. Rowland and Thomas Noble Howe (Eds) (Cambridge 2001)

R. Wilkinson, *The Complete Temples of Ancient Egypt* (London 2001)

Zivie, *Deir Chelouit*: Christiane M. Zivie et al., *Le temple de Deir Chelouit*, Vol. IV, *Etude Architecturale* (Cairo 1992)

Journals and Book Series (with abbreviated titles)

ÄA	*Archäologischer Anzeiger des Deutschen Archäologischen Institutes (Berlin)*
ASAE	*Annales du Service des Antiquités de l'Égypte (Cairo)*
BASOR	*Bulletin of the American Schools of Oriental Research*
BdE	Bibliothèque d'étude (Cairo)
BeiträgeBf	Beiträge zur Ägyptischen Bauforschung und Altertumskunde (Wiesbaden)
BIE	*Bulletin de l'institut d'Égypte (Cairo)*
BIFAO	*Bulletin de 1' Institut français d'Archéologie orientale (Cairo)*
BMMA	*Bulletin of the Metropolitan Museum of Art, New York*
BSEG	*Bulletin de la Société d'Égyptologie de Genève*
BSFE	*Bulletin de la Société française d'Égyptologie (Paris)*
CdE	*Chronique d'Égypte (Brussels)*

CNRS	Centre national de la recherche scientifique (Paris)
CRAIBL	Comptes rendus des séances de l'Academie des inscriptions et belle lettres (Paris)
DAI	Deutsches Archäologisches Institut (German Archaeological Institute)
EPRO	Études préliminaires aux religions orientales dans l'émpire romain (Leiden)
ET	Études et Travaux (Warsaw)
FIFAO	Fouilles de l'Institut français d'archéologie orientale du Caire (Cairo)
GM	Göttinger Miszellen (Göttingen)
JARCE	Journal of the American Research Center in Cairo
JDAI	Jahres
JEA	Journal of Egyptian Archaeology (London)
JEOL	Jaarbericht van het Vooraziatisch–Egyptischen Genootschap 'Ex oriente lux' (Leiden)
JHS	Journal of Hellenic Studies (Athens)
JNES	Journal of Near Eastern Studies (Chicago)
JSSEA	Journal of the Society for the Study of Egyptian Antiquities (Toronto)
KMT	K.M.T., A Modern Journal of Ancient Egypt (San Fransisco)
MÄS	Münchner ägyptologische studien (Munich)
MDAIK	Mitteilungen des Deutschen Archäologischen Instituts, Abteilung Kairo (Cairo)
MIFAO	Mémoires de l'Institut Français d'Archéologie Oriental (Cairo)
MIO	Mitteilungen des Instituts für Orientforschung (Berlin)
OIP	Oriental Institute Publications (Chicago)
OLZ	Orientalistische Literaturzeitung (Berlin)
Orientalia	Orientalia (Rome)
RdE	Revue d'Égyptologie (Paris)
RT	Recueil de Travaux rélatifs á la philogie et à l'archéologie égyptiennes et assyriennes (Paris)
SAK	Studien zur Altägyptischen Kultur (Hamburg)
SDAIK	Sonderhette des Deutschen Archäologischen Instituts Kairo (Cairo)
SSEA Journal	Society of the Studies of Egyptian Antiquities (Toronto)
WZKM	Wiener Zeitschrift für die Kunde des Morgenlandes (Vienna)
ZÄS	Zeitschrift für ägyptische Sprache und Altertumskunde (Berlin)